Imagining Ireland's Pasts

Imagining Ireland's Pasts

Early Modern Ireland through the Centuries

NICHOLAS CANNY

Great Clarendon Street, Oxford, OX2 6DP,
United Kingdom

Oxford University Press is a department of the University of Oxford.
It furthers the University's objective of excellence in research, scholarship,
and education by publishing worldwide. Oxford is a registered trade mark of
Oxford University Press in the UK and in certain other countries

© Nicholas Canny 2021

The moral rights of the author have been asserted

First published 2021
First published in paperback 2024

All rights reserved. No part of this publication may be reproduced, stored in
a retrieval system, or transmitted, in any form or by any means, without the
prior permission in writing of Oxford University Press, or as expressly permitted
by law, by licence or under terms agreed with the appropriate reprographics
rights organization. Enquiries concerning reproduction outside the scope of the
above should be sent to the Rights Department, Oxford University Press, at the
address above

You must not circulate this work in any other form
and you must impose this same condition on any acquirer

Published in the United States of America by Oxford University Press
198 Madison Avenue, New York, NY 10016, United States of America

British Library Cataloguing in Publication Data
Data available

Library of Congress Cataloging in Publication Data
Data available

ISBN 978–0–19–880896–1 (Hbk.)
ISBN 978–0–19–891142–5 (Pbk.)

DOI: 10.1093/oso/9780198808961.001.0001

Links to third party websites are provided by Oxford in good faith and
for information only. Oxford disclaims any responsibility for the materials
contained in any third party website referenced in this work.

To all who have studied and debated history with me over the years: undergraduates, postgraduates, early stage researchers, colleagues, audiences, family, and friends

Preface

I came to write this book by accident rather than design. When, in 2001, *Making Ireland British* appeared in print, I resolved it would be my last major statement on Irish history. I also decided, given the time it had taken to complete that book, that it would be my last to be anchored in manuscript sources. The first resolution stemmed from my concern to avoid being repetitious, and the second because I could not contemplate spending another quarter century in the archives squinting at manuscripts in the hope of finding something fresh to say. Moreover, I was secretly envious of the comparative ease with which scholars who worked with printed sources seemed able to produce books. At the same time, I had, through my interest in Atlantic History, that I sustained by being joint editor with Philip Morgan of the *Oxford Handbook of the Atlantic World, 1450–1850* (2011), decided that my next book would be on that subject, and I used the material I had assembled after an initial foray in research libraries to prepare the Raleigh Lecture in History for 2011 that I presented to the British Academy. This was later published as 'A Protestant or Catholic Atlantic World? Confessional Divisions and the Writing of Natural History', *Proceedings of the British Academy*, vol. 181 (2012), 83–121.

However, by 2011, and some years before then, I had become painfully aware that my cherished research plan was being set awry because I had become involved with a sequence of fresh responsibilities (Vice President for Research at University of Galway, 2005–08, President of the Royal Irish Academy, 2008–11, and Member of the Scientific Council of the European Research Council, 2011–16) that gave me but limited opportunity for research and writing. One happy occurrence that helped to keep my academic research interests alive at the outset of this 'second career' was an invitation to become Parnell Research Fellow at Magdalene College, Cambridge for 2005–06. The principal requirement for the fellowship, besides partaking of the hospitality of the College, was to present a formal lecture on a subject relating to Ireland's history in the nineteenth century. This inadvertently brought me back to Irish history, but I abided by my resolution to limit my investigations to printed sources since, for the lecture, I addressed why, in the nineteenth century, so many historians of different religious and political allegiances had become involved with the study of Ireland's history during the sixteenth and seventeenth centuries.

This brief foray, as well as my marginal involvement with a research project entitled *Writing the Nation* led by Stefan Berger, Christoph Conrad, and Guy

Marchal and funded by the European Science Foundation between 2003 and 2008, whetted my interest in historiography. However, I was not at liberty to develop that interest until I had fulfilled the various administrative obligations I had undertaken. Then in 2015, as the end of my administrative undertakings was in sight, I had the good fortune to be approached by Stephanie Ireland, then a new commissioning editor for history, to enquire if I had anything in mind for another book for Oxford University Press. Having reflected on her query, I expressed a willingness to write a short book on how Ireland's history during the early modern centuries had been approached by different authors over time. She responded with a request that I put my thoughts on paper in the form of a book proposal that she could have appraised by external readers. All three of the readers appointed by the Press were enthusiastic and this encouraged me to proceed. However, the book that has resulted has shaped out differently from what I proposed in 2015.

What has materialized is the product of several years of reading, reflection, and writing and is much different from the snappy book that I had initially intended. The book that is before you is much longer than what I had first envisaged. Its greater length is due in part to a recommendation by one of the readers that I devote an extra chapter to county, rather than country, history, with a view to explaining how, in Ireland, the two literatures intersected with each other. More generally the book grew longer because the more I looked into the subject the more authors I identified in every century who had written interestingly, and sometimes provocatively, on Ireland's history during the early modern era. The book that has emerged is also different (in this case truncated) from what I had initially in mind because I have allowed my narrative to taper off in the middle of the twentieth century, and have fallen short of bringing the subject down to the present. This omission, as I explain in Chapter 12, is justified because, after an extraordinary burst of enthusiasm, interest in events in Ireland during the sixteenth and seventeenth century fizzled out towards the close of the nineteenth century and did not catch fire again, and then for different reasons, until the second half of the twentieth century. A detailed consideration of what has been published on the subject since this revival would, I believe, require a volume of its own.

It will become clear to readers as the book unfolds that attempting to identify trends or patterns in historical writing on early modern Ireland over the centuries has proven problematic for several reasons. The first, which was not unique to Ireland, was that at any given moment there were disputed versions of what had happened in past centuries. The more glaring differences in interpretation usually broke down along denominational lines. However, clear divisions between Protestant and Catholic interpretations such as emerged with history writing in several other countries were, in the case of Ireland, made more complex by ethnic, cultural, and political factors.

On the Catholic side differences in interpretation of Ireland's history emerged between people who were of Gaelic ancestry and those who were of Anglo-Norman descent, while among Protestants differences in opinion became discernible at an early stage between authors, usually of English or Scottish ancestry, who were products of the plantations of the sixteenth and seventeenth centuries, and those who considered themselves to be indigenous Irish Protestants. Essentially each set of authors extolled the merits of their own ancestors and of the communal group with which they identified. They were writing also to give hope and guidance to the people they were addressing in their own generation in what always were uncertain times.

It may have been the widespread acceptance in succeeding generations that the future for those in Ireland for whom they wrote would always be in doubt, which attracted authors to the traumatic events of the early modern centuries that seemed even more troubled than the epoch through which they themselves were living. All authors were therefore usually studying the early modern past either to identify how stability had been secured after a period of chaos, or to establish how redress might be secured for those who had experienced setbacks. Disentangling the story in the nineteenth century became even more complex because some Protestant authors adopted a nationalist stance that was not always welcomed by Catholic associates or by the Catholic Church.

History writing on the Catholic and nationalist sides was also rendered more complex because in each passing century some authors came from the Irish communities that had been forced by circumstances to seek refuge abroad. As a consequence differences in interpreting Ireland's past became apparent between authors who wrote to uphold the interests of those resident in Ireland who were reconciled to establishing a working relationship with a government that was not necessarily well disposed towards them, and those who were resigned to being permanent exiles unless some dramatic turn of events, which they encouraged, would provide those for whom they wrote with the opportunity to recover what they considered their birthright. The matter was further complicated because histories by figures in exile, whether Philip O'Sullivan Beare in the seventeenth century, or Mathew Carey and John Mitchel in the nineteenth century, attracted audiences in Ireland as well as among communities in exile and thus rendered it more difficult to arrive at an agreed version of the past on which all Catholics might agree.

We noted that different Protestant understandings about the past sometimes also broke down along ancestral lines. However the most striking difference between Protestant authors that emerged concerned their various views on whether former governments had been serious about reforming, and thus stabilizing, the country, and whether the means they had employed to promote reform had been appropriate. Conflicting opinions between Protestants on how to interpret the past became more complex when those of their number who saw merit in establishing political links with Catholics constructed a historical narrative to justify such an amalgamation in the present and into the future.

Unravelling the strands of Irish historiography proved even more difficult because what might be considered reasoned historical narratives co-existed with what Guy Beiner would call vernacular histories of the past that were cultivated in Protestant as well as in Catholic communities. It will be explained, following the example of Beiner, that vernacular histories were not necessarily oral histories and that oral renditions of the past, where they existed, were intertwined with written accounts. Such interconnections meant that in Ireland, unlike in most other countries, historians in succeeding centuries experienced greater difficulty in establishing a distance between themselves and the events of previous centuries on which they commented. Thus, for example, as we shall learn in Chapter 7, the depictions given by Canon Patrick White of the depredations attributed in Irish Catholic folk memory to Morrogh O'Brien, baron (later earl) of Inchiquin, at the sack of Cashel in 1647, were as vivid as if they had just happened. This was as White would have wanted it, both because he placed more trust in folk memory than in documentary sources, and because he wished to evoke a revulsion among his audience against the act of persecution that he described in lurid detail, hoping that this would make his readers, whether at home or in exile, ever more steadfast in the faith of their ancestors. Similarly, as we see in Chapter 12, when Mary Hickson, aided by James Anthony Froude, discussed in 1884 the sufferings endured by Protestants in Ulster in the rebellion of 1641, she wrote as if she had been a witness to what had occurred. This is not surprising since Hickson's narrative was based largely on what had been written on the subject in 1646 by John Temple, which, because of its immediacy to the events, might be considered part of the episode itself. Also, because of the frequency with which reference had been made to Temple's text in Protestant sermons in the intervening centuries, this had become part of Irish Protestant vernacular history. This remembered history was now considered relevant by Hickson and Froude because they believed, and wanted their readers to believe, that the rebellion of 1641 was but a rehearsal for the Land War of 1879–81.

This book proceeds chronologically but, as will be clear from what has been said, it does not, as is the case with the historiographies of most countries, trace a linear development from narratives written by historians who had a close personal involvement with happenings in the sixteenth and seventeenth centuries to accounts composed by authors who, because of distance in time and place, proved themselves capable both of taking a neutral stance in commenting on emotive events and of reflecting on their tragedy. The book will draw attention to some authors who at different times did prove themselves capable of offering a sympathetic interpretation of the events they described. However, it will refer more frequently to historians who permitted events from the early modern past to flow into the present and who used the recollection of those events to serve present purposes. The pursuit of such polemics through history, it will be argued, persisted until the late nineteenth century, by which time it had become clear that other pasts, besides that for the early modern centuries, were better suited to serve present needs.

It is my hope that readers will read the entire book to get a sense of how the subject developed over time. However, I am also aware that many people will not persevere to the end of what is a long book, and that many students of history, or of literature for that matter, will be interested only in sections since many university courses deal with particular topics or with narrowly circumscribed historical episodes. To assist those who may wish to dip into the book rather than read the whole I have devised a simple architectural structure that will become clear from the chapter titles and subtitles. By following these, readers may navigate themselves more readily to particular episodes or authors. In saying this, I can also advise that readers who are interested primarily in, for example, the opinions of Young Ireland authors on early modern topics, will find most of what they want to know in Chapter 8. However, they will also need to make use of the index to see how the views of individuals from the 1840s generation who lived longer lives (here John Mitchel, C.P. Meehan, and Charles Gavan Duffy come to mind) changed over time. Similarly, readers who are interested primarily in the historical writings of particular individuals will again need to use the index because an appraisal of all of the writings of any one individual is not necessarily conducted in one chapter. Readers, for example, who want to learn of the writings of M.F. Cusack, 'The Nun of Kenmare', will find a good deal about her in Chapter 9 but her story spills over into Chapter 10. Similarly, readers will learn much in Chapter 10 of the historical endeavours of Mary Hickson at the point when she saw herself as a rival to Cusack, but they will gain a full understanding of Hickson's achievements only when they pursue her story into Chapters 11 and 12.

This book is original to the extent that it is the first study of how a sequence of historians from the sixteenth to the twentieth centuries, and from different backgrounds and allegiances, have interpreted the principal events that occurred in early modern Ireland. I consider it also to be the first book that demonstrates the extent to which writing on Ireland's history bulked large within the literary output in Ireland in each succeeding century including the nineteenth which witnessed what is frequently referred to as Ireland's literary renaissance. My endeavour in tracking what was said over time of the early modern centuries will, I hope, inspire other authors to investigate how subjects such as the history of Ireland in pre-Norman times, or the twelfth-century conquest, or the impact of the Penal Laws have been interpreted by a range of authors in succeeding generations. Studies of this kind would, I believe, break new ground because previous publications on Irish historiography have been principally concerned with the totality of the historical writings on Ireland by particular authors. In saying this I do not seek to devalue these studies since they have provided

xii PREFACE

foundations on which this edifice has been constructed. The authors to whom I am most indebted will become evident from the text, the bibliography, and the footnote references.

More particularly I would like to acknowledge the assistance of those who have had a direct input to this text by reading and advising on particular chapters or sections of the book. Alan Ford gave generously of his time and expertise when commenting on drafts of Chapters 3 and 4 and corrected several errors that I had made. John Cunningham also provided helpful advice on queries I put to him concerning Cromwellian Ireland and furnished me with advance copies of papers he had written and that were then still in press. Bernadette Cunningham also offered criticism of a talk she heard me give, and supplied me with an advance copy of a paper that has since been published and that proved helpful on several points. Clare O'Halloran graciously answered a few queries concerning matter I have covered in Chapter 6, and Maurice Bric read and commented on what I had to say of Mathew Carey. I wish to thank Tom Bartlett for a critique of two versions of Chapter 7 and for correcting me on some critical points, and Claire Connolly who commented on an early version of Chapter 8. However, I regret that I was prevented by the onset of COVID-19, and the sudden and prolonged closure of research libraries, from following up on Claire Connolly's suggestion that I investigate the interplay between history writing and the novel in the nineteenth century. I am grateful to Pádraig Lenihan for an informed critique of what appears in Chapter 8 on the Young Irelanders as historians. My thanks go also to Marc Caball and Maurice Bric for advice on Mary Hickson, and Maurice Bric read and commented on what I have written on both Hickson and M.F. Cusack. When it came to local history, Ciarán Ó Murchadha was a ready and reliable guide. I am also grateful to Ciaran Brady for letting me have a copy of an unpublished paper on John Prendergast that I had heard him deliver at a seminar at Sidney Sussex College, Cambridge. Needless to say while I am grateful to all of these scholars for their advice and encouragement, none of them is responsible for any errors that persist in this book.

Since this, unlike all previous books I have written, is based on printed sources my principal thanks go to the librarian and staff of all institutions I visited but especially the two libraries where I was able to consult most of the material: the James Hardiman Library at the University of Galway and the Library of the Royal Irish Academy. Among these, my usual helpers were Geraldine Curtin in the special collections room in the James Hardiman Library and Sophie Evans in the Library of the Royal Irish Academy.

As I have already indicated, my research was curtailed and I was left with no choice but to take to writing because of the shutdown occasioned by COVID-19. The composition was completed in my home study and I am grateful to my wife, Morwena Denis, for making my life as trouble-free as possible during what nationally and internationally was a traumatic time. The research office at the

University of Galway provided a subvention to cover the cost of making an index and procuring a cover illustration and I am particularly appreciative that the University recognizes that retired staff members can be 'research active' and deserve support. At the Press, I am grateful to Stephanie Ireland for encouraging me to undertake the book, to Cathryn Steele for offering technical advice and discussing progress, and to Katie Bishop for being generous and reasonable about time extensions as time for the delivery of text approached.

N.C.

University of Galway

Contents

1. The Renaissance, the Reformation, and the Writing of Ireland's History in the Sixteenth Century   1
   - 1.1   Introduction   1
   - 1.2   The Humanist Turn   4
   - 1.3   Apocalyptic Histories of Ireland   14
   - 1.4   Conclusion   24

2. Composing Counter-Narratives in the Sixteenth and Seventeenth Centuries   29
   - 2.1   Introduction   29
   - 2.2   Initial Reactions from Gaelic Ireland   30
   - 2.3   Preparing the Way for Counter-Narratives   35
   - 2.4   David Rothe's *Analecta Sacra*: A Revised Old English Perspective on the Past   38
   - 2.5   Philip O'Sullivan Beare's *Historia Catholicae Iberniae Compendium*: A History for the Dispossessed   45
   - 2.6   Geoffrey Keating's, *Foras Feasa ar Éirinn*: A History for the Catholic Community in Ireland   51
   - 2.7   Conclusion   56

3. New Histories for a New Ireland   60
   - 3.1   Introduction   60
   - 3.2   Stafford and Gainsford: Memorialists of War   61
   - 3.3   Sir John Davies: Applied History in the Civil Domain   66
   - 3.4   Ussher and Ware: Applied History in the Spiritual Domain   74
   - 3.5   Conclusion   84

4. The 1641 Rebellion and Ireland's Contested Pasts   89
   - 4.1   Introduction   89
   - 4.2   After 1641: Protestant Re-Considerations of Ireland's Pasts   90
   - 4.3   Catholic Responses to the Revised Protestant Narrative   104
   - 4.4   A History for the Dispossessed   111
   - 4.5   Conclusion   121

5. Eighteenth-Century Aristocratic Histories of Ireland during the Sixteenth and Seventeenth Centuries   125
   - 5.1   Introduction   125
   - 5.2   Histories of the Clanricard Burkes   125
   - 5.3   Carte's Life of Ormond   133
   - 5.4   New Histories for New Nobles   148
   - 5.5   Charles Smith's Critique of the New Nobles   153
   - 5.6   Conclusion   161

xvi CONTENTS

6. Enlightenment Historians of Ireland and their Critics   165
   6.1 Introduction   165
   6.2 David Hume's Concern with Early Modern Ireland   167
   6.3 An Irish Contribution to Philosophical History?   172
   6.4 Popular Challenges to Philosophical History   187
   6.5 Conclusion   196

7. The Vernacular Alternatives Composed during the
   Age of Revolutions   199
   7.1 Introduction   199
   7.2 Catholic Vernacular Histories of Ireland   200
   7.3 Protestant Vernacular Histories of Ireland   212
   7.4 Conclusion   219

8. Re-Imagining Ireland's Early Modern Past: The Young Ireland
   Agenda, Dissident Views, and the Catholic Alternative   221
   8.1 Introduction   221
   8.2 The Historians of Young Ireland and the Early Modern Past   221
   8.3 Revived Catholicism and the Early Modern Past   243
   8.4 Conclusion   253

9. Re-Imagining Ireland's Early Modern Past during the Later
   Nineteenth Century   257
   9.1 Introduction   257
   9.2 Refining Catholic Interpretations in a Time of Uncertainty:
        The Writings of Margaret Anna Cusack   258
   9.3 Rethinking Inclusivity in an Era of Conflict: The Trajectory
        of John Mitchel   264
   9.4 Landowners in Ireland's History: The Musings
        of John P. Prendergast   271
   9.5 One Unionist's Re-Interpretation of Ireland's Early Modern
        Past: The Contribution of J.A. Froude   280
   9.6 Conclusion   289

10. Fresh Unionist Re-Appraisals of the History of Early
    Modern Ireland   291
    10.1 Introduction   291
    10.2 County History or Country History   292
    10.3 County Kerry as a Test Case: The Early Writings
          of Mary Agnes Hickson   294
    10.4 A Unionist Historian of County Sligo: W.G. Wood-Martin   301
    10.5 James Frost: An Elite Historian of County Clare   308
    10.6 An Ulster Perspective on Ireland's Past: The Writings
          of the Reverend George Hill   315
    10.7 Conclusion   324

CONTENTS xvii

11. The Birth and Early Demise of a Liberal Interpretation of
    Ireland's Early Modern Past — 326
    11.1 Introduction — 326
    11.2 W.E.H. Lecky: The Doyen of Liberal History — 327
    11.3 Archdeacon Terence O'Rorke and a Catholic History for
         County Sligo — 333
    11.4 Canon Patrick White: A Catholic-Nationalist Historian
         of County Clare — 338
    11.5 Hickson's Response to the Exclusivist Turn — 350
    11.6 Conclusion — 354

12. The Failure of the Imagination Concerning Ireland's Pasts — 356
    12.1 Introduction — 356
    12.2 Hickson's Last Stand — 359
    12.3 Unionist Reactions to Hickson's Challenge — 366
    12.4 Conclusion and Epilogue — 373

References — 383
Index — 401

1

The Renaissance, the Reformation, and the Writing of Ireland's History in the Sixteenth Century

1.1 Introduction

Renaissance humanists are usually credited with having made the writing of histories a reputable intellectual pursuit as they drew a distinction between history writing, which by their standards necessitated critical thinking, and antiquarianism, which for them involved no more than the transmission of received wisdom from generation to generation. Humanists demonstrated how historians might deploy linguistic and archaeological skills to authenticate documents and monuments from past centuries, and to discredit those they considered fabrications. To this end some historians proved their credentials by challenging the origin myths that had traced the founders of communities back in secular time to some fabled ancestor, or back in biblical time to one of the three sons of Noah; usually on the grounds that such claims could not be authenticated from classical sources. They also scorned the knowledge that was customarily transmitted in annals because it was frequently fatalistic and took insufficient account of complexity. For example, humanists criticized annalists for attributing the occasional prosperity of communities to the sagacity of exceptional rulers, and the long interludes of dearth and confusion, which was the normal human condition, to the death or overthrow of good rulers. Humanists also considered the compilers of annals to be ill equipped to trace communal ancestry, because unlike historians they were not acquainted with classical authors such as Herodotus and Livy whose texts were now recommended as models to show how classical sources could be used to trace the origins of communities.[1]

The cultivation of historical knowledge as it had been traditionally practised in Ireland, as in other European countries, certainly fell short of the standards favoured by humanists. However, the Irish tradition was unusual in that it was sustained by two memory traditions, which frequently came into conflict. The

---

[1] The literature on this subject is vast and for reliable guidance see Donald R. Kelley, *Foundations of Modern Historical Scholarship: Language, Law and History in the French Renaissance* (New York, 1970) and Anthony Grafton, *Forgers and Critics: Creativity and Duplicity in Western Scholarship* (Princeton, N.J., 1990).

Imagining Ireland's Pasts: Early Modern Ireland through the Centuries. Nicholas Canny, Oxford University Press (2021).
© Nicholas Canny. DOI: 10.1093/oso/9780198808961.003.0001

2 IMAGINING IRELAND'S PASTS

first was associated with those learned Gaelic families whose function was to laud whichever ruling family had provided patronage to them and their ancestors down the centuries. These encomiastic effusions dwelt on the military successes of past or present members of the ruling family, usually against neighbouring lords. Besides praising the deeds and achievements of individual lords or dynasties, the learned classes sometimes identified themselves collectively with a wider Gaelic cultural community with which former high kings of Ireland and several provincial kings had been associated. And, as they did so, they frequently exulted in how, after a prolonged struggle, the ancestors of those who patronized them (the *Gaedhel*) had, in the eleventh century, succeeded in recovering their patrimonies from the Norse foreign invaders (the *Gallaibh*), who had sacrilegiously destroyed everything the Gaelic Irish held dear.[2]

The second memory tradition in Ireland was associated with members of the community of English ancestry who traced their arrival on the island to the twelfth-century invaders from England and Wales during the reign of King Henry II.[3] That king had visited Ireland only after the more gruesome fighting had ended, but he had then accepted submission from several Gaelic Irish lords, and had also initiated procedures to reform the Christian church in Ireland and bring it into compliance with Roman norms. This latter was in fulfilment of an injunction issued to King Henry in 1154 by the Pope.[4]

This invasion of Ireland had been further justified by Gerald of Wales [Giraldus Cambrensis] in two texts, one, *Expugnatio Hibernica*, lauding the feats of the invading knights during the course of the conquest of Ireland, and the other, *Historia et Topographia*, denouncing the Gaelic population for their barbaric practices which Gerald had condemned as inimical to Christian and civil living.[5] The population of English descent in Ireland had always cherished these texts because the deeds of their ancestors justified their presence in the country. These texts also served to dissuade those of their community who lived in close proximity to Gaelic lordships from compromising their civility either by intermarrying with the Gaelic Irish or adopting their language and customs. Those who cultivated the memory of Gerald also hoped that his texts would remind the English crown of its responsibility to assist its loyal Irish subjects in

---

[2] J.H. Todd, ed., *Cogadh Gaedhel re Gallaibh: The War of the Gaedhil with the Gaill, or The Invasions of Ireland by the Danes and other Norsemen* (London, 1867).

[3] The best recent depiction of this English Irish community, albeit for the later decades of the sixteenth century, is that in Ruth Canning, *The Old English in Early Modern Ireland: The Palesmen and the Nine Year's War, 1594–1603* (Woodbridge, 2019), 1–6.

[4] Art Cosgrove, ed., *A New History of Ireland*, vol. 2, *Medieval Ireland, 1169–1534* (Oxford, 1987), 43–155, esp. 57–60; for a general narrative of the Norman conquest, Colin Veach, 'Conquest and Conquerors', Brendan Smith, ed., *The Cambridge History of Ireland*, vol. 1, *600–1550* (Cambridge, 2018), 157–84.

[5] *Giraldus Cambrensis [Gerald of Wales], Expugnatio Hibernica: The Conquest of Ireland by Giraldus Cambrensis*, ed., A.B. Scott and F.X. Martin (Dublin, 1978); *Giraldus Cambrensis [Gerald of Wales] The History and Topography of Ireland* trans. and ed., John J. O'Meara (revised edition, Mountrath, 1982).

their ongoing struggle to uphold their position against their Gaelic adversaries. The arguments of Gerald of Wales had also, through the centuries, been underpinned by various enactments of the medieval Irish parliament—a body representing the English community in Ireland—that had been designed to halt the 'degeneration' of that population from the civility of their ancestors to the barbarity of their Gaelic neighbours.[6]

The learned classes of Gaelic Ireland seem to have had some understanding of the hostility towards them that was being cultivated by the literate members of the English community in Ireland but there had never been any meaningful dialogue between the two. Rather, their annalists and poets sometimes encouraged their patrons to make good for the failings of their ancestors by reversing the conquest. To this end the English in Ireland, like the Norse before them, were frequently referred to by the annalists as Gall [foreigners], thus implying that these too might be expelled from the country by the Gael as the Norse, the earlier Gall, had been expelled in the eleventh century. It is unsurprising therefore that when the compilers of the work known popularly as the 'Annals of the Four Masters' (a composite work gleaned from several earlier annals and brought to completion in 1616[7]) recorded the death in 1554 of Cahir Mac Murrogh, 'a warlike man', they mentioned that he might have become lord of the province of Leinster had it not been for 'the invasion of the English'. Here the invasion (*gabhaltas gall*) to which the annalists referred was that of the twelfth century, which they now called to mind because it had been instigated by Dermot Mac Morrogh, King of Leinster, and ancestor of the Cahir who had died in 1554.[8]

That the term *gall* continued to be used by the Gaelic learned classes to describe all people of English descent in Ireland, including those who had intermarried with Gaelic families and had adopted some of their customs, suggested that the Gaelic authors, no less than the descendants of the conquerors, accepted that the conflict between Gael and Gall would persist indefinitely. However, as they reported on developments of the sixteenth century, especially after King Henry VIII of England had severed the connection between his kingdom and the Papacy, the Gaelic annalists began to distinguish between their traditional English adversaries who had been born in Ireland, who they continued to refer to as Gall, and recent arrivals from England, who they began to describe fairly consistently as Saxons. Thus, for example, it was reported in the Annals of Ulster for 1533 that 'the king of the Saxons' (*rígh Saxan*) had 'gone against the church' and had done

---

[6] Cosgrove, ed., *A New History of Ireland*, vol. 2, 386–90.

[7] Bernadette Cunningham, *The Annals of the Four Masters: Irish History, Kingship and Society in the Early Seventeenth Century* (Dublin, 2010); Gearóid Mac Niocaill, 'The Medieval Irish Annals', published O Donnell lecture (Dublin, 1975).

[8] John O'Donovan, ed., Annála *Ríoghachta Éireann, Annals of the Kingdom of Ireland*, vol. 5 (Dublin, 1851), 1528–9; this will be referred to hereafter as Annals of the Four Masters with an abbreviation, *AFM*.

4 IMAGINING IRELAND'S PASTS

'many foolish things'. When the same annalists reported smugly of the beheading in 1536 of Anne Boleyn on a charge of adultery, they expressed disappointment that King Henry VIII had not, at the same time, relented on his straying from the faith (*o n-a sheachran creidim*).[9]

1.2 The Humanist Turn

The above citation, which is not unusual, shows that Irish annalists of the sixteenth century were more politically astute than their humanist critics (and some recent scholars) acknowledged, and were certainly aware that fresh plans for extending crown authority in Ireland were being considered in London. It is unlikely, however, that the Gaelic learned classes would, at this juncture, have had any knowledge of the new humanist historiography, and credit for introducing that to Ireland rests with Richard Stanihurst, a Dublin student at University College, Oxford, who invited Edmund Campion, one of his teachers—a distinguished humanist and fellow of St John's College, Oxford—to accompany him to Dublin. Stanihurst seems to have hoped that Campion would write a history of Ireland that would comply with humanist standards. The invitation to Campion is likely to have been previously approved by Stanihurst's family, and perhaps by a wider circle within the English community in Ireland, since Campion acknowledged that he was treated hospitably during his stay in Dublin. It is also probable that Sir Henry Sidney, who had been governor of Ireland since 1565, was aware of Campion's plans for a history of Ireland since Campion enjoyed the patronage of the earl of Leicester with whom Sidney was in regular contact and to whose sister Sidney was married. We can be more certain that Sidney was acquainted with Richard Stanihurst who had dedicated his first book, *Harmonia*, to Sidney, and was the son of James Stanihurst, recorder of Dublin, who had been elected speaker in the lower house of the Irish parliament of 1569–71.[10] Given that Sidney considered himself a patron of humanist scholarship, and was always concerned to find precedents for whatever policies he favoured for Ireland, we can take it that he too would have welcomed a humanist history of Ireland.[11]

Sidney does not seem to have realized that Campion, an ordained deacon in the Church of England, was on the brink of converting to Catholicism and was

---

[9] B. Mc Carthy, ed., *The Annals of Ulster*, vol. 3, *1379–1541* (Dublin, 1895), 592–3, 608–9.

[10] John Barry and Hiram Morgan, eds., *Great Deeds in Ireland: Richard Stanihurst's* De Rebus in Hibernia Gestis (Cork, 2013), 1–12; Colm Lennon, *Richard Stanihurst, the Dubliner, 1547–1618* (Dublin, 1981), 1–67.

[11] The best proof of Sidney's interest in having a usable past available to him is that he had Bermingham tower in Dublin Castle refurbished for the storage of government records, and commissioned the printing of all the statutes passed by successive Irish parliaments; Ciaran Brady, ed., *A Viceroy's Vindication? Sir Henry Sidney's Memoir of Service in Ireland, 1556–78* (Cork, 2002).

THE WRITING OF IRELAND'S HISTORY   5

probably influencing Richard Stanihurst in that direction. However, in 1571 when Campion's religious inclinations were brought to Sidney's attention by some of the governor's more strident English-born Protestant colleagues, he secretly warned Campion that he was about to be arrested, thus making it possible for him to escape imprisonment and complete his writing on Ireland's history in the Barnwall household in north County Dublin. From there, after a ten-week seclusion, Campion returned to England through the nearby port of Drogheda.[12]

These developments meant that Campion's stay in Ireland (from the summer of 1570 to the spring of 1571) was less than a year in duration and his research for his history of Ireland seems to have been conducted, for the most part, in the home of James Stanihurst whose books and records, as well the personal recollection of James Stanihurst and other Pale associates, were the principal sources on which Campion based his *Two Bokes of the Histories of Ireland*. Campion claimed apologetically, if improbably, that he had been able to devote no more than ten weeks to the task. His text, which he had hoped to see into print, was available only in manuscript copies until 1633.[13] One such manuscript copy became available to Raphael Holinshed when he was preparing some notes on Ireland's history for inclusion in the first edition of his *Chronicle* published in 1577. This, or another copy, was also available to Richard Stanihurst when he wrote a text on contemporary conditions in Ireland that appeared in print in the first edition of Holinshed's *Chronicle*. This meant that although Campion's text remained unprinted in his lifetime, many of his opinions were circulated to an extensive sixteenth-century English-reading public through these two elements of the Irish section to Holinshed's *Chronicle*.

The circumstances under which Campion visited Ireland, the short duration of his stay, and the limited range of sources available to him, all combined to ensure that his *Two Bokes of the Histories of Ireland* were little more than a modification upon, and a chronological extension of, what Gerald of Wales had written in the twelfth century. One of Campion's objectives was to revise the texts of Gerald of Wales to make them comply with humanist standards. Campion thought it worthwhile to rehabilitate them because he considered Gerald the only person in medieval times who had brought 'some indifferent furniture' to the 'chronicle' of Ireland. However, as a humanist, Campion saw the need to revise what Gerald had written in the light of what some 'foreign writers' had had to say 'incidentally' of Ireland's history. Then when he moved forward in time from where the account

---

[12] Soon after his arrival in England Campion left there for Continental Europe where he studied to become a Jesuit priest before returning as a missionary to England where he was arrested and executed, thus becoming a martyr for the Catholic faith; see Gerard Kilroy, *Edmund Campion: A Scholarly Life* (London, 2015).

[13] Campion's text was then published, together with other histories of Ireland, by the Protestant antiquarian in James Ware, *A Historie of Ireland, collected by three learned authors, viz., Meredith Hanmer...Edmund Campion...and Edmund Spenser* (Dublin, 1633).

6 IMAGINING IRELAND'S PASTS

of Gerald of Wales had tapered off, Campion gleaned information from 'a number of brief extracts of rolls and records and scattered papers' that had been put at his disposal in Dublin.[14] Finally, when composing an account of what had happened in Ireland since the death of King Henry VIII, Campion took his 'instructions by mouth' presumably from the 'friendly gentlemen' in Dublin who had helped him 'to frame a story'. He dismissed, with the contemptuous tone typical of humanists, the 'Irish chronicles' that he understood, presumably from these same gentlemen in Dublin, were 'full...of lewd examples, idle tales and genealogies'.[15]

Campion praised Gerald of Wales for having learned 'to mistrust' all 'Irish antiquities', and he explained apologetically that he had been misled by the 'fable' that the first inhabitants of Ireland were descended from a niece of Noah, only because no countervailing authority had been available to him at the time.[16] Campion now corrected this error because Livy had instructed historians to pay special attention to the tracing of 'first foundations'. Otherwise, Campion adopted the account of events given by Gerald of Wales after he had purged it of those 'vain and frivolous' opinions that had crept into his narrative. On the question of origin, Campion suggested subtly that Ireland had been subjected to rule from England on several occasions in the antique past which, he contended, gave 'the Britaines an elder right to the realm of Ireland than by the conquest of Henry the Second'.[17] Similarly, when he explained, at considerable length, how Christianity had been brought to Ireland by St Patrick, he contended that the saint had been born 'in the marches of England and Scotland', thus underlining his all-embracing theme that everything meritorious in Irish society had been brought there from England.[18] His discourse on Patrick provided Campion with the opportunity to discuss the lives of other saints associated with Ireland. He identified but a few of these whose lives could be authenticated by 'authors of good credit'.[19] This, in turn, led to his discussion of the Viking invasion of Ireland, and while Campion mentioned that the Vikings had suffered an ultimate defeat in 1014 at the battle of Clontarf, he credited them with the establishment of several of Ireland's port towns, including Dublin, and also with being the progenitors of some of Dublin's leading families that had resulted from some marriages contracted between Viking traders and Irish women. Campion also emphasized that the Vikings, or Norsemen, were the ancestors of the Normans who had accompanied William the Conqueror in the invasion of England, and whose descendants had conquered Ireland on behalf of King Henry II, a century later. All such conquering people were, according to Campion, more civilized than the Gaelic Irish who, after they had been 'delivered of slavery' following the defeat of the Vikings, again 'fell to

---

[14] A.F. Vossen, ed., *Two Bokes of the Histories of Ireland compiled by Edmunde Campion* (Assen, The Netherlands, 1963), text, 2.

[15] Vossen, ed., *Two Bokes,* text, 5.   [16] Vossen, ed., *Two Bokes,* text, 26.

[17] Vossen, ed., *Two Bokes,* text, 34.   [18] Vossen, ed., *Two Bokes,* text, 44.

[19] Vossen, ed., *Two Bokes,* text, 50.

their own vomit in persecuting one another'.[20] Besides his praise of the towns founded by the Vikings, Campion had little positive to say of Ireland's pre-conquest population other than of a few clergy who had subordinated themselves to the Archbishop of Canterbury, until such time as Lawrence O'Toole, once Abbot of Glendalough, was 'installed at home [as Archbishop of Dublin] by Gelasius primate of Armagh'.[21]

What Campion wrote on the earlier history of Ireland was as a preliminary to his consideration of the twelfth-century conquest of Ireland, which deviated little from the account written by Gerald of Wales. Here, Campion explained that the Irish bishops had convened a synod at Cashel, at the insistence of King Henry, where, having 'perused' the Papal bull of 1154 that had authorized the conquest of Ireland, they 'commandeth allegiance' to the king 'under straight pains' and thus 'repressed the fury of their countrymen'.[22] Then, as Campion brought his narration forward from where Gerald of Wales had ended, he made frequent reference to the claims made by several English monarchs to rule over Ireland either by right of conquest or by virtue of the submissions made to successive English rulers by Irish princes.[23]

Campion proceeded quickly through the reigns of those medieval English rulers who involved themselves in Irish affairs, and paused only to identify precedents for events that had troubled the country during his own lifetime. The most troubling of these contemporary events related to the action of the brothers of the earl of Ormond and others of English ancestry who had taken arms against the crown's representative in the years 1569–71. The precedent he identified for this eruption had occurred during the reign of Edward III when 'the English of birth and the English of blood' fell to 'words' and 'divided in factions' because the governor of that time had revoked certain franchises and liberties that had been granted by the crown to some lords of English ancestry. Such ill-advised actions, he contended, made it possible for the Gaelic Irish to recover ground from a divided English community, as he feared was about to happen again.[24] In similar vein, Campion narrated how, in the 1530s, the government of Sir William Skeffington had encountered an 'uproar among the merchants and their apprentices in Dublin' which the governor and mayor had been able to 'appease' with difficulty, and which Campion considered an evil precedent for the popular disturbance that had arisen within the Pale to counter the efforts of Sidney to introduce a land tax, known as cess, to help defray the cost of defending the Pale.[25]

---

[20] Vossen, ed., *Two Bokes,* text, 59. [21] Vossen, ed., *Two Bokes,* text, 62.
[22] Vossen, ed., *Two Bokes,* text, 73. [23] Vossen, ed., *Two Bokes,* text, 79–81.
[24] Vossen, ed., *Two Bokes,* text, 98.
[25] Campion offered details on the opposition to Sidney in Vossen, ed., *Two Bokes,* text, 142; Nicholas Canny, 'The Formation of the Old English Elite in Ireland' (Dublin, published O'Donnell lecture, 1975); Ciaran Brady, *The Chief Governors: The Rise and Fall of Reform Government in Tudor Ireland, 1536–88* (Cambridge, 1964), 88–91, 46–9, 153–4; the word cess possibly derived from the Irish word *cíos* meaning rent.

8 IMAGINING IRELAND'S PASTS

When he discussed more recent events, and particularly the Fitzgerald rebellion of the 1530s that had brought about the downfall of the house of Kildare until it was restored in the reign of Queen Mary, Campion bewailed what he considered the unnecessary jealousy that had been allowed to develop between the Butler and Fitzgerald houses. This, he asserted, had even been encouraged by Cardinal Wolsey whose arrogance, in Campion's eyes, had been ultimately responsible for the Kildare rebellion. Then, as he proceeded forward to his own time, Campion offered pen pictures and appraisals of all English governors who had served in Ireland since the 1530s. Most of these accounts were positive, and became lyrical when Campion spoke of the recent governorships of Sussex and of Sidney. Indeed, of all the governors who had held office since the 1530s, Campion had reservation only with Sir Anthony St Leger who he 'counted forward and pliable to the taste of King Edward VI's reign', and, to this end, had 'rimed against the real presence for his pastime'.[26] Campion also seemed unimpressed by the legislative programme enacted by the Irish parliament of 1541–42 'wherein the Geraldines were attainted, abbeys suppressed, the King named Supreme Head and King of Ireland, because he recognized no longer to hold it of the Pope'.[27] He thought it important that many Gaelic lords had 'appeared' before this parliament and submitted themselves to the governor, and subsequently to the king in England, in transactions known to historians as the Policy of Surrender and Regrant.[28] On this subject, Campion hinted that St Leger had judged badly in permitting Con O'Neill, who became earl of Tyrone, to declare 'his base son Matthew' to be heir to his earldom instead of Shane O'Neill, who was 'the only son of his body nulier begotten' but was passed over because he was then 'little esteemed'.[29]

Campion's account of the calamities that, he believed, had stemmed from the slighting of Shane O'Neill in 1542 gave him an opportunity to detail how Sussex and then Sidney had 'vanquished' Shane O'Neill after he had dared to challenge the authority of Queen Elizabeth. This served as a preliminary to Campion's discussion of 'the Butler rebellion' of 1569–71 led by the brothers of the earl of Ormond and their associates. On this, he credited the earl of Ormond with having quietened these 'broyles', thus performing 'a right good piece of service worthy to be remembered'.[30]

---

[26] Vossen, ed., *Two Bokes*, text, 135; here Campion was referring to the Catholic doctrine of the Real Presence in the Eucharist which was emphatically denied by Protestants.

[27] Vossen, ed., *Two Bokes*, text, 134; this appraisal of that parliament is very much at odds with the account in Brendan Bradshaw, *The Irish Constitutional Revolution of the Sixteenth Century* (Cambridge, 1979).

[28] Christopher Maginn, '"Surrender and Regrant" in the Historiography of Sixteenth-Century Ireland', *Sixteenth Century Journal*, 38 (2007), 955–74; the subject also features prominently in Bradshaw, *The Irish Constitutional Revolution*. Campion and Bale, unlike Bradshaw, considered St Leger and Cusack to be committed Protestants.

[29] Vossen, ed., *Two Bokes*, text, 134.   [30] Vossen, ed., *Two Bokes*, text, 142.

Having brought his narrative of political events in Ireland down to his own time, Campion concluded it with a detailed account of the closing ceremony at the Irish parliament of 1569–71. He claimed to have attended this parliament as an observer and taken 'notes' of the concluding speeches given by the Speaker James Stanihurst (father to Richard Stanihurst) and by the Governor Sir Henry Sidney. Campion celebrated how the two orators had agreed on the role that education might play in reforming a commonwealth, and he explained that while each had regretted the failure of parliament to reach agreement on the establishment of a university in Dublin, they remained optimistic that this project would soon proceed. Campion also narrated how James Stanihurst had expressed enthusiasm for a statute that made it mandatory to have a grammar school established in each diocese, believing that the 'young fry [would then be] likely to prove good members of this commonwealth' equipped 'with a pure English tongue, habit, fashion, discipline' and be thus prepared utterly to 'forget the affinity of their unbroken borderers, who possibly might be won by this example, or at the least wise lose the opportunity … to infect other[s]'.[31]

Campion claimed that Sidney had concurred with this optimistic message, but had then raised the question of the costs associated with the maintenance of an English garrison to defend the civil community in Ireland from attacks by these same borderers. Here, according to Campion, Sidney rounded upon those opposed to the collection of the cess that he considered necessary to supplement the revenue being provided by the crown to maintain the garrison. At the same time, as Campion reported, Sidney had discredited the arguments that had been voiced by those opposed to the payment of this land tax on the grounds that, in England, the crown enjoyed no such prerogative power. Sidney, according to Campion, had pointed to the fundamental difference between the circumstances under which crown subjects lived in England and in Ireland, arguing that England was 'quiet within itself, thoroughly peopled … walled [from foreign invasion] with the wide ocean', and requiring to be 'guarded with an army' only on the border with Scotland. He had then, claimed Campion, contrasted this situation with Ireland where the crown subjects had 'foes' within the 'bosom' of their 'countries', who were 'more in number [and] richer of ground' than themselves. Thus, according to Campion, Sidney had concluded his speech by emphasizing how subjects in Ireland required the 'help of the crown soldiers' as well as their 'own valiantnes' to provide for their security. Thus, said Campion, the governor had returned to the particular Irish issue of how provision might be made for the maintenance of the garrison.

The tone of Sidney's oration, as reported by Campion, seemed less optimistic than that of James Stanihurst, and Campion suggested that each seemed to

---

[31] Vossen, ed., *Two Bokes,* text, 144.

10 IMAGINING IRELAND'S PASTS

concede that tension would persist between the English community of the Pale and their Gaelic neighbours. This meant that the 'reform' that each envisaged concerned the recall to civility of those people of English blood who had succumbed to the barbarism of their Gaelic neighbours, rather than bringing the Gaelic Irish to civility. It was logical therefore, as Campion explained, that Sidney should have concluded his address to parliament with the assurance that, for Ireland, the government was primarily concerned with 'the preservation of a nation derived from our ancestors, engrafted and incorporate into one body with us' who were being constantly 'disturbed by a sort of barbarous [barbarism] odious to God and man'.[32]

If we accept Campion's rendition of Sidney's speech to parliament it indicates that the governor was, at that juncture, in agreement with the interpretation of Ireland's history that had been first formulated in the twelfth century by Gerald of Wales, and that Campion had just recast in humanist guise. This effectively credited the population of English descent in Ireland with having upheld their position and that of English civility in Ireland with some support from the crown. Therefore Sidney's only criticism of the English community in Ireland was directed against those outside the Pale who had become degenerate, and those within the Pale who had objected to taxes being raised to contribute towards the cost of defending the crown's loyal community in Ireland.

This same interpretation of Ireland's past and recent history reached a much wider audience, at least in the English-reading world, with the publication in 1577 of the first edition of Raphael Holinshed's *Chronicles*.[33] Here again the contributors made a deliberate effort to associate Sir Henry Sidney, who served as governor of the country for a second term, 1575–78, with this interpretation of Ireland's history, and to this end Holinshed dedicated the entire section on Ireland to Sidney. Then Richard Stanihurst introduced his own text, 'A Treatise containing a Plain and Perfect Description of Ireland' (better known as the 'Description of Ireland'), with an epistle addressed to Sidney.[34] In this, Stanihurst explained that he had written so that readers would have a 'better understanding of the histories appertaining to that land' as these had been compiled by Holinshed from the beginning of time to the close of the reign of Henry VII and by Stanihurst himself

---

[32] Vossen, ed., *Two Bokes*, text, 148–9.

[33] The Irish section to the first Holinshed edition is entitled *The Historie of Ireland from the first inhabitation...1509, collected by Raphaell Holinshed, and continued...1547 by Richard Stanyhurst* (London, 1577); that to the second edition is entitled *The Second Volume of Chronicles containing the Description, Conquest, Inhabitation and Troublesome Estate of Ireland first collected by Raphael Holinshed and...continued...until this present time of Sir John Perrot...by John Hooker, alias Vowell* (London, 1587). Most citations are from the second edition. For a comparative study of the organization of the two editions see Stephen Booth, *The Book Called Holinshed's Chronicles* (Book Club of California, Los Angeles, 1968).

[34] Stanihurst's epistle to Sidney stands alone as an 'Epistle Dedicatory' in Holinshed, 1587, where it had been an integral part of the treatise in the first edition.

THE WRITING OF IRELAND'S HISTORY   11

for the reign of Henry VIII.[35] The longer of these two historical sections, compiled by Holinshed, proved to be little more than a rendition of what Gerald of Wales had had to say on the subject as this had been corrected, interpreted, and expanded upon by Campion. In acknowledging his source, Holinshed explained that 'a copy' of Campion's *Two Bokes of the Histories of Ireland* had come into the hands of Reginald Wolf, who had been planning to write the narration on Ireland. When he died in 1573 it fell to Holinshed to complete the task. The Holinshed text led logically to the contribution by Richard Stanihurst on the 'History of the Reign of Henry VIII', where he reminded 'good governors' of 'diverse events worthy to be remembered, and sundry sound examples daily to be followed'.[36] The prime example (or lesson) that he conveyed to governors was that the rebellion of the Fitzgerald's of Kildare in the 1530s, that had led to the overthrow of their house (until it was restored by Queen Mary), had been entirely avoidable.[37] The rebellion, he claimed, had had the disastrous consequence of removing trammels from the Gaelic enemies of the community of the Pale who previously had been held in check by the Fitzgeralds at their own cost.

This message emerged all the more clearly in Stanihurst's 'Description of Ireland' which he obviously wrote to counter those English detractors of Ireland who, when castigating the inhabitants of Ireland for their depravity, failed to recognize that the country was divided between 'the English Pale and the Irishry'.[38] He complained that those who scoffed at Ireland and its inhabitants frequently used the story that St Patrick had banished snakes from Ireland to mock the people of the country by asserting that, after Patrick's intervention, there was 'no poisoned or venomous thing in Ireland, but only the people'.[39] This suggestion that 'the place [was] better than the inhabitants'[40] was, averred Stanihurst, ignoring the fact that, following the conquest of the country in the twelfth century, parts of Ireland had been populated by '*collonnes*, of the Latin word *coloni*', brought there by the conquering knights from England and Wales who had made the areas they inhabited 'mere English'.[41] Moreover the descendants of these colonists had, through the centuries, upheld English practice in law, apparel, and language to the point where, in places, the language spoken by the inhabitants still contained 'the dregs of the old ancient Chaucer English', and where 'Dublin, the beauty and eye of Ireland' was 'commonly called the Irish or young London'.[42] And as Stanihurst listed the notable scholars that Ireland had

[35] 'Treatise', 1, Holinshed, 1587.   [36] Stanihurst's 'Epistle Dedicatory', Holinshed, 1587.
[37] Vincent P. Carey, *Surviving the Tudors: The 'Wizard' Earl of Kildare and English Rule in Ireland, 1537–1586* (Dublin, 2002).
[38] 'Treatise', 3, Holinshed, 1587. Stanihurst there defined the Pale as stretching from Dundalk to Carlow or Kilkenny.
[39] Treatise', 11, Holinshed, 1587; Willy Maley, *Nation, State and Empire in English Renaissance Literature* (Basingstoke, 2003), esp. 59–61.
[40] 'Treatise', 15, Holinshed, 1587.   [41] 'Treatise', 3–4, Holinshed, 1587.
[42] 'Treatise', 4–5, 21, Holinshed, 1587.

12 IMAGINING IRELAND'S PASTS

produced through the centuries he mentioned that 'no grammar school in Ireland [was] as good; none in England better' than that maintained by Peter White at Kilkenny where Stanihurst himself had attended before proceeding to University College, Oxford.[43]

Stanihurst's 'Description of Ireland' detailed the barbaric practices of the Gaelic Irish in more graphic terms than Campion had employed, and suggested that their condition was in no way different from what had been written of their ancestors by Gerald of Wales.[44] In saying so, he explained that they were not incorrigible, and insisted that if 'sound preachers and sincere livers' were provided by the government to 'convert' them, they 'would be reckoned as civil' in 'two or three ages'.[45] However, rather than await such a distant and uncertain outcome, Stanihurst, like Campion, concluded that the reform of Ireland would best be commenced by consolidating the position of the English population of Ireland whose civility was exemplary. This, he claimed, would prepare the way for reforming those 'English by birth' who had 'become degenerate and...quite altered' as if they 'had tasted of Circe's poisoned cup' because they had been 'conversant with the savage sort'.[46]

Advocating this message seemed more urgent in 1577 than when Campion had written in 1571, because it had become evident in the intervening years that the English governors in Ireland, and the political community in England, were no longer convinced that the English population in Ireland was suited, or equipped, to uphold, much less extend, crown influence in Ireland. It was already apparent in 1577, when the Irish contributions to Holinshed's *Chronicle* appeared in print, that Sir Henry Sidney, whose service was lauded repeatedly in the text, was at loggerheads on political and on religious matters with the English community in Ireland, who would soon become known as the Old English. The political issues came to the fore because, as has been explained by Ciaran Brady, the only hope that Sidney had of pursuing an ambitious policy for Ireland after 1575, when he had agreed to serve as governor of Ireland for a second time, was by expanding upon his earlier stratagem of using prerogative powers to compel the crown's subjects in Ireland to contribute to the cost of governance through the payment of a land tax.[47] Where his previous revenue-raising stratagem had raised principled objections only from a dissident group associated with a handwritten pamphlet circulated under the name of Tom Truth, his second intervention aroused open objection from a broad spread of the community within the Pale during Sidney's second term as governor. Opposition became more widespread as it became clear that Sidney's financial demands would be more onerous, and more enduring, than what he had demanded previously, and opposition mounted

---

[43] 'Treatise', 34, Holinshed, 1587.
[44] 'Treatise', 67–9, Holinshed, 1587.   [45] 'Treatise', 14, Holinshed, 1587.
[46] 'Treatise', 6, Holinshed, 1587.   [47] Brady, *The Chief Governors*, 136–58.

THE WRITING OF IRELAND'S HISTORY   13

also because Sidney, with the agreement of officials in London, had begun to appoint English-born officials rather than Irish-born lawyers as posts fell vacant in the Dublin administration. An added grievance was that with the appointment of more English-born people, not only to senior administrative posts but also to bishoprics and as officers in the army, the composition of the council that advised the governor was dramatically changed, with the majority of members having become English and Protestant rather than Irish-born people of English descent.[48]

Sidney's changed attitude towards the Pale community may explain why those there who previously had been willing to embrace Protestantism, or to conform outwardly with the official religion of the state, now began to withdraw from involvement with the Protestant church and even to identify themselves openly as Catholics. A prime example was Richard Stanihurst, whose father James was possibly a Protestant, and who himself had used a vocabulary in his 'Description of Ireland' that suggested a commitment to Protestant reform. If his compliance had been simulated, it had become clear to him in 1573, when he failed to secure any official appointment on the death of his father, that no material benefit was to be gained from outward conformity. When he was denied the posting he may have considered his birthright, Stanihurst eked out a living as tutor to the children of Gerald, earl of Kildare, until 1579, when, after the death of his first wife, he put his inheritance into the hands of feofees of trust.[49] Then, following the example of Campion, he went into exile in Continental Europe where he became a Spanish pensioner, married an English Catholic wife, and became involved with diplomatic as well as scholarly activity. Later, after the death of his second wife, he joined a seminary where he was ordained as a Catholic priest.[50]

The reason most frequently cited by Sidney and his associates in government for favouring English-born people for administrative posts in Dublin was because the English community there was too closed in upon itself and that Irish-born lawyers and administrators were unable to act impartially, especially when the interests of English-born subjects, or those of the crown, were in contention. Such arguments concerning 'kindred and affinity between judge and party' had been voiced on Sidney's behalf by his secretary Edmund Tremayne as early as 1571, and had become commonplace among English-born commentators on Ireland by 1575 when Sidney returned there as governor.[51] However, another issue that had changed Sidney's attitude towards appointing Irish-born people to official positions was that during the years he had spent in England and in Wales (1571–75) he had become identified more firmly with the political grouping

---

[48] Canny, 'The Formation of the Old English Elite in Ireland'; Canning, *The Old English in Early Modern Ireland*.

[49] Colm Lennon, *Richard Stanihurst, the Dubliner*, 35–40.

[50] Lennon, *Richard Stanihurst, the Dubliner*, 41–67.

[51] Edmund Tremayne, 'Notes for the Reformation of Ireland, 1571', *Reform Treatises on Tudor Ireland, 1537–1599*, ed., David Heffernan (Dublin, 2016), 72–83; quotation, 74.

14 IMAGINING IRELAND'S PASTS

formed around the earl of Leicester that favoured a rigid Protestant line in state affairs following the excommunication of Queen Elizabeth by the papacy in 1570. This meant that the governor who resumed office in Ireland in 1575 was no longer willing to turn a blind eye to recusancy, as he had done in 1571 when he enabled Edmund Campion to evade arrest.[52] This change in attitude meant that Sidney had begun to require that all nominees for office in Ireland take the oath of supremacy, but it meant also that he could no longer accept as valid humanist histories of Ireland composed by Catholics such as Campion and Stanihurst, even when they were dedicated to Leicester, as Campion's history had been, or addressed to Sidney himself, as was the case with Stanihurst's contribution to Holinshed's *Chronicle*. These were now found wanting because they were, in the words of Hiram Morgan, 'making the past authorise the present'.[53] The 'present' being authorized was one in which the English community of the Pale would continue to determine the country's destiny. Since Sidney could no longer countenance that, he solicited a new history for Ireland that would be every bit as flattering to himself as the humanist histories had been, but that would also demonstrate the need for a Protestant future to which the population of Ireland might be led by English-born godly actors.

1.3 Apocalyptic Histories of Ireland

One model of how such a revised history might be structured was already to hand in the shape of *The Vocacyon of John Bale*, published in 1553, that had been cited by Stanihurst as one of the works he had consulted.[54] Bale, an Englishman, had been a Cistercian monk before converting to Protestantism, and had served briefly as bishop of Ossory just before Queen Mary's accession to the throne. His purposes in writing were to explain what trials a true believer might have to endure when giving witness to the Gospel, and to assure 'the followers of Christ's Gospel', to whom his text was addressed, that prayer and fasting were the best means of securing deliverance from danger by a merciful God. Bale intended especially that his narrative should identify the responsibilities attached to the

---

[52] It is worth noting that Mark A. Hutchison represents Sidney as a hardline Protestant from the outset of his career in Ireland in Hutchison, *Calvinism, Reform and the Absolutist State in Elizabethan Ireland* (London, 2015).

[53] Barry and Morgan, eds., *Great Deeds in Ireland*, 31.

[54] All citations from Bale's text are from *The Vocacyon of John Bale* in *The Harleian Miscellany*, vol. 6 (London 1810), 437–64; on the text see Steven Ellis, 'John Bale, bishop of Ossory, 1552–3', *Journal of the Butler Society*, vol. 2, 1984, 283–93; and J.A. George, 'The vocacyon of Johan Bale, 1553: a retrospective sermon from Ireland', in Alan Fletcher and Raymond Gillespie, eds., *Irish Preaching, 700–1700* (Dublin, 2001), 94–107; the most sympathetic account of the Bale episode is in John Seaton Reid, *History of the Presbyterian Church in Ireland, edited with additional notes* by W.D. Killen, 3 vols., (Belfast, 1867), vol. 1, 35–41; there, 40–1, Reid described Bale as 'the only sincere reformer that the Church in Ireland enjoyed at this critical period of her history'.

'office of a Christian bishop'[55] What he had to say of Ireland was incidental to his greater purpose as he narrated how he, who was 'but a clod of corruption' who had recently been brought to death's door by ill health, had been identified by King Edward VI himself as the person who should serve as bishop of Ossory. His selection was all the more dramatic because King Edward had been led to believe that Bale was dead and buried until he espied him on a street in Southampton on 15 August 1552. Bale did not explain why the king chose to appoint him to Ossory rather than in any other vacant Irish bishopric but it was probably because Thomas Butler, the young earl of Ormond, and Barnaby Fitzpatrick, the future baron of Upper Ossory, whose patrimonies lay within the Ossory diocese, were companions of the boy king at court.

As Bale detailed the journey of himself, his wife, and a servant from Bristol to Waterford and thence to Dublin, where he was to be invested as bishop, he expressed abhorrence at the 'abominable idolatries' he witnessed being upheld by the clergy in Ireland who still conducted the communion service like the popish Mass, neglected preaching, refused to abandon their mistresses and get married, and favoured 'chanting, piping and singing [in Latin]' rather than expounding psalms in English.[56] While he complained of the clergy and members of the political establishment who obstructed his efforts to have himself made a bishop as the king had prescribed, he credited the Lord Chancellor, Thomas Cusack, with having been a 'special good lord and earnest aider' while 'much of the people' in Dublin 'did greatly rejoice of our coming thither, thinking [that] by our preaching the Pope's superstition would diminish and the true Christian religion increase'. Similarly he reported how, when he reached his diocese at Kilkenny, where he 'preached every Sunday and holy days in Lent', he experienced continuous obstruction from the serving clergy who wanted to know nothing of the Book of Common Prayer, or of reforming their personal lives. Despite their opposition he continued to preach to 'the people' who he 'established...in the doctrine of repentance'.[57] Bale insisted that 'the people' who had been attending his sermons continued to support him after it became known that King Edward had died and would likely be succeeded by Mary, his Catholic half-sister, and after the local noblemen, Lord Mountgarret and the baron of Upper Ossory (the father of Barnaby Fitzpatrick who had been the king's whipping boy at court), had joined with the clergy to restore the Catholic Mass. At this juncture, according to his narrative, Bale took 'Christ's testament' in his hand and went to Market Cross in Kilkenny, 'the people in great number following' where he preached. There also, 'the young men' of Kilkenny performed two plays on religious themes, 'with organ, plainges and songs', that he himself had written. He also recounted how he and his household had been physically attacked and robbed at his residence some

---

[55] Bale, *Vocaycon*, 437.   [56] Bale, *Vocaycon*, 448–9.   [57] Bale, *Vocaycon*, 449.

16   IMAGINING IRELAND'S PASTS

miles from Kilkenny, but that most had escaped thanks to Robert Shea [probably Shee], the mayor of Kilkenny, who Bale found 'a man sober, wise and godly...a rare thing in that land'.[58] Then he narrated how when the survivors returned to Kilkenny 'the young men [sang] psalms and other godly songs all the way in rejoice of [his] deliverance' and 'the people, in great number, with candles in their hands' praised God that he was safe.[59] This final act led to Bale's retreat from his diocese and his return to England from where, as a committed Protestant, he had later to flee from the persecutions of Queen Mary and find refuge in Protestant Europe.

When he published his text in 1553, Bale, as mentioned, had intended it as an inspiration for Protestants (particularly English Protestants) who suffered from persecution wherever they might be. However, he also considered his text to be a history of one single experience that provided evidence of God's solicitude for his true followers and 'the long continuance of the Christian church from his time to this our time'. In the course of doing so, he paused 'to say somewhat of the Christian church of our realm in those days called Britain, and now called England' with a view to demonstrating how it had subsequently been made 'the filthy synagogue of Satan' by 'the school doctors' until King Henry VIII, and then Edward VI, had sought to restore it to the pristine condition of 'the primitive church'.[60] Bale, unlike the humanist authors, expressed no reverence for classical sources, but he was every bit as concerned as the humanists to authenticate his pronouncements by citation from reputable authorities—this time the scriptures and the works of such as the Venerable Bede, Matthew Paris, and John Wycliffe.

We noted that Bale wrote his text to encourage English Protestants who were suffering religious persecution during the reign of Queen Mary. However, its Irish dimension would have been of interest to Lord Deputy Sidney and those associated with him in Ireland in the 1570s because it presented evidence that the 'people' in the Anglicized areas of Ireland, and especially the young men, had been then eager to hear the Gospel preached to them in the 1550s but had been discouraged, or prevented, from doing so by the elite members of that same community. Bale had identified a few exceptions to this blank condemnation of the elite, particularly Sir Thomas Cusack, a close associate of Sir Anthony St Leger, who Campion had also identified as a zealous Protestant. However, what Bale had to say more generally of his experience would have served in the mid-1570s to cast doubt on the political as well as the religious loyalty of the leaders of the Old English community in Ireland. His narrative would also have made it clear to English readers in the 1570s that the revolt of the brothers of the earl of Ormond in 1569–71 was not without precedent, because Bale had explained that when rumours reached Ireland of the death of King Edward 'the

---

[58] Bale, *Vocaycon*, 450–51.   [59] Bale, *Vocaycon*, 453.   [60] Bale, *Vocaycon*, 438, 443.

THE WRITING OF IRELAND'S HISTORY   17

ruffians of that wild nation' had rebelled against 'the English captains' as had always been their 'lewd custom' whenever a change of monarch was in prospect. Another contention of Bale that would have interested Sidney and his associates was that the malcontents of 1553 had also 'conspired into the very deaths of so many English [born] men and women as were therein alive', and had threatened 'to have set up a king of their own' and circulated the false report 'that the young earl of Ormond, and Barnaby, the Baron of Upper Ossory's son, were both slain in the court of London'.[61]

The narrative of Bale would have been considered especially pertinent by government officials in the mid 1570s because it supplied independent evidence for the contention of English observers that those parts of Ireland dominated by 'the English by blood' were far from civil, and that the leaders in these areas were generally opposed to their society being reformed in either its secular or spiritual aspects. At the same time it would also have confirmed their wishful thinking that the population at large in the English-speaking parts of Ireland were open to reform but were being prevented by their betters from engaging with it.

Bale's text was not as useful as it might have been for Sidney because it related to a particular episode that had occurred some years before he had taken up his first posting to Ireland. It was seemingly to compensate for this deficiency that he commissioned an illustrated history in verse that was published in 1581 by one John Derricke under the title *The Image of Ireland, with a Discoverie of Woodkarne*.[62] This text, with a striking set of woodcuts, was produced by John Day, who had been Master of the Stationers Company since 1580, and is best known as the publisher of the first and second editions of John Foxe's *Actes and Monuments of the Church* (1563), known popularly as *Foxe's Book of Martyrs*.[63] The use of woodcuts by Derricke suggests a Bale as well as a Foxe influence since Bale had garnished his text with a single woodcut juxtaposing an 'English Christian' with an 'Irish Papist' which, in the words of J.A George, might be considered 'a visual sermon'.[64] A more certain indication of Bale's influence was Derricke's focus on woodkerne [*ceithirne choille*], which followed logically from Bale's condemnation of the oppressive and illegal practice of coigne and livery which, he had asserted, was being 'countenanced' by 'Irish lords and their under captains' in the name of defending the Pale. This passage, that Bale had inserted almost as an afterthought, justified his concluding pronouncement that there were three categories of people in Ireland, 'priests, lawyers and kearnes which will

---

[61]   Bale, *Vocaycon*, 450.

[62]   John Derricke *The Image of Ireland, with a Discoverie of Woodkarne* (London, 1581); the edition cited here is the facsimile edition ed., D.B. Quinn (Belfast, 1985); Vincent P. Carey, John Derricke's *Image of Ireland*, Sir Henry Sidney and the Massacre at Mullaghmast, 1578', *Irish Historical Studies*, 31 (1999), 305–27.

[63]   Preface by Liam Miller to Derricke, *Image*, ix–xv.

[64]   George, 'The vocaycon of Johan Bale, 1553', 96.

18   IMAGING IRELAND'S PASTS

not suffer faith, truth and honesty to dwell there'. Derricke obviously agreed with this proposition and took it as a convenient point of departure for his own text.[65]

Because *The Image of Ireland* was written in verse, scholars tend to consider Derricke as a versifier who was also a skilled draftsman who had made drawings on location. However, he was also a gifted propagandist who used his text to contextualize the well-chosen woodcuts that had been made from his own drawings, probably by John Day, or an employee in Day's workshop.[66] In sharp contrast to the boasting of the humanists, Derricke explained that he had come 'to write some pleasant history', not by virtue of special training but because the 'holy and immortal God' had directed him to do so, and had equipped him with the 'three principal things' required by 'every chronicler and writer of histories, that is to say, Invention, Memory and pleasant Conveyance'. He suggested that it was God also who had decreed that he should use these talents to write about Ireland rather than any other topic.[67] Having thus identified himself as an apocalyptic historian after the manner of Bale and John Foxe, whose works he cited, Derricke quickly addressed the supposed expulsion by St Patrick of all venomous creatures from Ireland and wondered why, when doing so, the 'holy saint' had not also sought to 'convert' the kern, who, in Derricke's experience, were the obstacle to Ireland becoming a 'fertile land'.[68] Then, as he deplored the incessant raids of Irish kern on the settled population he pondered 'why men of th'English Pale' should 'in such a crew delight'. Thus, in one line, he rejected the fundamental premise of Campion and Stanihurst, which held that the population in Ireland of English descent had always been the upholders of civility there, and were therefore best placed to promote the reform of the country. Instead he despaired of the civility of their own communities, and concluded the first section of his text on the pessimistic note that the kern in Ireland had become so perverse that only an intervention by God would 'turn them to a better life' because, if mortals had had the power to do so, 'then Sidney [would have]...long since achieved the same'.[69]

In the second section of *The Image*, Derricke explained that his primary purpose was to inform 'the world' of the 'inclination' and 'gestures' and 'wicked life of the kern 'through pictures and protractors made/by painter's cunning skill'.[70] In practice, however, only four of the eleven woodcuts that accompanied his text described the raiding and feasting of the kern, while a fifth multi-sequence plate depicted a troop of English soldiers returning victorious after they had wreaked vengeance on a band of kern. The remainder of Derricke's portfolio of woodcuts served rather as a homage to Sir Henry Sidney. Five of them illustrated

---

[65] Bale, *Vocaycon*, 463; the word kearne, or more frequently kerne, was an Anglicized version of the Irish word *ceithearn* meaning foot soldier; wood kearnes or *ceithirne choille* signified outlaws.
[66] Introduction by D.B. Quinn to Derricke, xvii–xxx.   [67] Derricke, 181–2.
[68] Derricke, 187–8.   [69] Derricke, 188.   [70] Derricke, 189.

THE WRITING OF IRELAND'S HISTORY   19

Sidney's state progress through Ireland, beginning with his departure from Dublin castle and concluding with his return to the city. A further woodcut depicted the miserable condition to which Rory Oge O'Moore has been reduced through the endeavours of Sidney, and the final plate showed Turlough Luineach O'Neill, 'the Great O'Neill', being received by Sidney to the queen's mercy. The text accompanying the first four woodcuts left no doubt that the actions of the kern proved them to be 'mortal foes unto the commonwealth'. Text and illustrations detailed also how these kern had been spurred to their nefarious actions first by their bards, who narrated how their fathers had won 'great renown' by similar 'noble conquests done', and then also by their friars, who affirmed 'that it is/an alms deed to God/to make the English subjects taste/the Irish rebels' rod'.[71] Such assertions authenticated Derricke's general contention that the kern acted perversely because they were in thrall to the agents of Satan and the Pope.

The other set of woodcuts, treating of Sidney's actions during his second period as governor of Ireland, belie Derricke's previous fatalistic pronouncement because they demonstrate that even if Sidney has not succeeded in reforming the kern he had proven that it was possible to defeat them and restore order for the benefit of the settled community. These woodcuts also made it clear that Derricke, or perhaps Sidney, recognized that the political culture in the country was 'performative' as Barbara Stollberg-Riliger has observed of European political culture more generally during the early modern era.[72] Thus Sidney was invariably portrayed in the woodcuts as a man of action demonstrating how 'worthy' he was 'to represent the person of a queen'.[73] In so doing, Sidney, with his officers and the English soldiers at their command, were seen to be acting alone without assistance from Ireland's population of English descent, whose only appearance in the woodcuts was that of robed members of Dublin corporation obsequiously welcoming Sidney back to their city where he was being 'received with joy on every part', after he had completed a triumphant state progress on which he had brought to heel those who had previously threatened their prosperity.[74]

Derricke, unlike Bale and the humanist historians, did not bolster his arguments with reference to either classical or biblical sources, since to have done so would have been implausible for somebody who had no pretensions to being considered a scholar. However, he made good for this shortcoming by presenting himself as an eye witness who, through his use of woodcuts and his word pictures, was sharing with those 'whose minds [were]...virtuously occupied...in laudable exercises' what he himself had witnessed.[75] Derricke also broke new ground by

---

[71] Derricke, 192–3.
[72] On this see Barbara Stollberg-Rilinger, 'La communication symbolique à l'époque pré-moderne. Concepts, thèses, perspectives de recherche', *Trivium*, vol. 2 (2008), https://dol.org/10.4000/trivium.1152.
[73] Derricke, introduction to plate xii.   [74] Derricke, plate x.
[75] Derricke, introduction to his text.

20 IMAGINING IRELAND'S PASTS

representing the kern as exotic, and by hinting that all Irish lords, regardless of ancestry, were tolerant of the kern and even employed them surreptitiously. In so doing, Derricke was making the case that while Ireland may have been designated a kingdom in 1541, even those parts of the country that were dominated by people of English descent were socially inferior to England, and might be brought to the good order that prevailed in the more settled parts of England by the forceful actions of an English governor backed by English captains. However, despite the pessimism with which he commenced his text, Derricke concluded that a committed and able governor, such as Sidney, could achieve positive outcomes in the most unlikely places. As proof of this he recounted, and illustrated, how Turlough Luineach O'Neill had been persuaded by Sidney to become a subject of the crown, after which he, with a 'heart...set as 'twere in flames of fire', became determined to 'scourge...evil livers and disturbers of her majesty's people' and become a defender 'of her good subjects'.[76]

When Derricke was publishing his *Image of Ireland* another English author and associate of Sidney, John Hooker, alias Vowell, was engaged on a substantially revised Irish section to Holinshed's *Chronicle* that appeared in the second edition of that compilation published in 1587. Hooker was an established historian and antiquarian from Exeter who had been in Ireland since 1567 when he had quickly become infamous in the eyes of the Old English community in Ireland because he had put his talents as an antiquarian at the disposal of his patron Sir Peter Carew, also from Devon. His work for Carew was to establish title for him to extensive properties in Ireland that were, for the most part, in the possession of Irish proprietors of English descent. We noted how these intrusions by Carew had contributed to the outbreak of rebellion in 1569–71. However, Hooker's association with Carew also provided him with the opportunity to acquire a first-hand knowledge of Irish records, which, when added to his established reputation as a historian, made him the ideal person to redesign and re-interpret the entire Irish section of Holinshed's *Chronicle*. As well as editing and re-ordering the text, Hooker also wrote a fresh chapter on the 'History of Ireland 1546–1586', to bring the narrative down to the year in which the second edition of Holinshed's *Chronicle* went to press. Hooker also added to the contemporary look of the compilation by juxtaposing his rendition of what had transpired in Ireland in the recent past with a reprint of the 'Description of Ireland' by Richard Stanihurst that had already appeared in the 1577 edition of the *Chronicle*. Reprinting the Stanihurst text served Hooker's purpose because, as noted, it had portrayed the Gaelic inhabitants of Ireland in the same negative terms in which Gerald of Wales had described their ancestors four centuries previously. To make sure that no

---

[76] Derricke, 210–11.

reader of the re-edited Irish section of Holinshed's *Chronicle* would fail to comprehend his contention that the barbarism of the Gaelic Irish had remained constant over time, Hooker also included an English translation that he himself had made of the *Historia et Topographia* of Ireland. This was the text by Gerald of Wales that provided graphic negative depictions of the Gaelic Irish. Hooker substituted this for the summary of the *Expugnatio Hibernica*. This latter was the text, also by Gerald of Wales, that provided the narration of the conquest of Ireland, which Raphael Holinshed had included in the first edition of the *Chronicle*.

This rearrangement by Hooker lent the authority of Gerald of Wales who, by the 1570s, was respected by humanists as well as by members the Old English community, to Stanihurst's disparagement of the Gaelic population of his own generation. However, by demonstrating that the Gaelic population in Ireland in the sixteenth century were no closer to being civil than their ancestors had been in the twelfth century, Hooker discredited the claims made by Campion and Stanihurst that the people of English descent in Ireland had been, and still were, those most committed to, and capable of, completing the civilizing mission initiated by King Henry II.

Hooker further eroded the credibility of the English community in Ireland in the eyes of the audience in England to which Holinshed's *Chronicle* was principally addressed, when he discoursed on the 'Troublesome Estate of Ireland' in the course of writing the history of Ireland from the reign of Henry VIII forward to 1586. He placed this section on Ireland's very recent history immediately after Richard Stanihurst's discourse on the Kildare rebellion of the 1530s that Hooker reprinted from the 1577 edition of Holinshed's *Chronicle*. Stanihurst, as we will recall, had there upheld Campion's argument that the Kildare rebellion had been an avoidable tragedy in which members of the Fitzgerald family had become ensnared because of the machinations of Cardinal Wolsey and his clients. Hooker now made it clear in his own historical narrative that he considered Stanihurst's pronouncement as no more than special pleading. Instead, he represented the Kildare rebellion as a pre-meditated rejection of the authority of King Henry VIII by a lord of English blood. Such behaviour, he contended, was consistent with the actions of Irish lords of English descent both in the centuries that had preceded the rebellion of the 1530s, and in subsequent decades. In his discussion of recent events, Hooker dwelt first on the rebellion of 1569–71, led by three brothers of the earl of Ormond and a cousin of the earl of Desmond, that had been directed particularly against Sir Peter Carew who, as noted, had brought Hooker to Ireland. Hooker could speak with seeming authority on this rebellion both because he had been an eyewitness to what had happened and, as the agent of Sir Peter Carew, had become a target of attack. Its occurrence, he pronounced, cast doubt on the loyalty of the Butlers of Ormond, one of the two most influential

22 IMAGINING IRELAND'S PASTS

dynasties of English descent in Ireland, the other being the Fitzgeralds, earls of Kildare and of Desmond.

After his discussion of the Butler revolt, Hooker proceeded to consider the even more recent rebellion, where he had again been a participant/witness, that of Gerald, sixteenth earl of Desmond, and his kindred 'against her sacred Majesty'. This, he asserted, was the 'most unnatural' of the rebellions he discussed because a family of English descent had entered into an alliance with foreign intruders to oppose a legitimate English monarch. In detailing the suppression of that revolt, Hooker gave special attention to the part played by himself and his Devonian patrons, who now included Walter Raleigh and Humphrey Gilbert as well as Sir Peter Carew, in crushing the revolt. Hooker seemed to derive particular satisfaction from describing how the English forces had annihilated the invading Italian/Iberian force at Smerwick, how Nicholas Sander, an English seminary priest, had suffered an ignominious death, and how Sir John of Desmond, brother to the earl of Desmond, and then the earl himself, had been tracked down and killed, after which their mutilated corpses and heads had been put on public display to deter others who might have had rebellion in mind.

Hooker obviously intended that his citation of evidence concerning all these recent revolts in Ireland would expose the falsity of the contention of both Stanihurst and Campion that members of the Old English community in Ireland had always been exemplary upholders of English civility. To clinch his case, Hooker, following the example of Edmund Tremayne, also from the English West Country, expounded on the disordered condition of Ireland, including within the English Pale, at the time that Sidney had first arrived as governor. This had brought Tremayne to the same conclusion as Derricke that the English governor, backed by English troops, was the only reliable upholder of the crown's interest in Ireland. It thus became possible for Hooker to argue that an English governor was the only person who might be entrusted with responsibility to complete the unfinished conquest. This led to Hooker's overall conclusion that over the forty-year span, 1546–86, in Ireland 'most part of all the actions in that age consisted...in continual wars, rebellions and hostility, either against their most sacred kings and queens or amongst themselves'. All of the actions that Hooker had detailed had been perpetrated by people of English descent. This gave him all the more reason to condemn them as 'a Pharoical and stiff necked people' that had experienced 'a heavy but just judgement of God' who had permitted desolation and famine to descend on the province of Munster. Hooker considered this outcome, which he described in graphic detail, as a just punishment, not only because it would not have been appropriate for him to question divine intervention but also because those who had defied the authority of the queen were people of English blood who had consorted with 'foreign princes' and with 'traitorous Jesuits', the instruments of Satan and of 'that great city upon seven hills that mighty Babylon, the mother of all wickedness and abominations upon the

THE WRITING OF IRELAND'S HISTORY 23

earth'.[77] Hooker was also satisfied that what had transpired in Munster had had a positive outcome because it had provided both a manifestation of God's 'severe judgement against traitors, rebels and disobedient', and also 'of his mercy and loving kindness upon the obedient and dutiful'. These latter were obviously the people in Ireland, whether of English or Irish birth, or of English or Gaelic ancestry, who had supported the governor and the policies he pursued, including, as could be inferred from the Protestant eschatology that Hooker invoked, the promotion of the Protestant reformation.[78]

These outpourings demonstrate the extent to which Hooker, who took pride in his humanist credentials, had come to be influenced also by Protestant apocalyptic historians, including John Foxe and Philip Melanchton, whose works he considered exemplary, and by Bale and Derricke, who had been the first in Ireland to publish texts is this mode. While all apocalyptic authors dwelt on the tribulations that true believers encountered as a test of their faith, they (even Bale who had written at an especially dark moment for Protestants) remained confident that their cause would eventually prevail. Hooker had more reason than most to be optimistic because he wrote in 1586 when those most opposed to reform in Munster and in Ireland had been comprehensively defeated, and when the government was proceeding with a plantation programme designed to reform all of Munster politically, socially, and religiously.

Later, after it had transpired that the God-given opportunity to reform the province had been let slip, Protestant authors began to predict that those who had not met their responsibility to promote reform would suffer dire punishment if they did not act immediately to remedy their failings. The most influential of the authors who warned that divine retribution was about to beset England as well as Ireland because of English neglect of Irish disorder was the poet Edmund Spenser in his prose dialogue *A View of the Present State of Ireland*, that he had completed by 1596 when the plantation settlement, from which he had personally benefited, seemed in danger of overthrow. This text can hardly be considered a history in the conventional sense, but James Ware described it as such in 1633 when he published a bowdlerized version of Spenser's *View* along with other sixteenth-century histories of Ireland, including that by Campion.[79] This categorization was perhaps justified because, while Spenser eschewed the narrative structure that we associate with conventional histories, it shared the historical assumptions, concerns, interests, and even the vocabulary of the apocalyptic historians whose works we have been discussing. Thus Spenser, like the historians who wrote in the apocalyptic style, strove to use his knowledge of the past, and of the scriptures, to divine the circumstances under which God would permit punishment to fall on those who had failed to complete the reform of Ireland. Then when tragedy did

[77] Holinshed, 1587, 458–60.   [78] Holinshed, 1587, 103.
[79] Ware, *A Historie of Ireland, … Hanmer … Campion … and Spenser.*

24 IMAGINING IRELAND'S PASTS

strike in Munster in 1598, and the settlement in which Spenser had been involved was overthrown by bloody insurrectionists, it encouraged another outpouring of Protestant apocalyptic writings, demanding that vengeance be taken upon the perpetrators of the attack, while, at the same time, it identified as Protestant martyrs those who had been killed in the onslaught.[80]

Recent scholars have given considerable attention to such manuscript texts and have even suggested that Spenser was their author because some of the themes and vocabulary he had used in the *View* recurred in these later texts. It will be evident from what has been discussed in this chapter that the master text that influenced all such apocalyptic compositions, including Spenser's *View*, was John Hooker's contribution to the second edition of Holinshed's *Chronicle* because this had a circulation advantage over all competitors given that it had been printed in one of the best-known compilations in the English language of the sixteenth century.[81]

In the light of this it seems that one significance of these later texts, including Spenser's *View*, is that they elaborated the predictive dimension to most apocalyptic writing. This was absent from the Hooker master text because Hooker was writing at the moment when it seemed that the final victory of the godly had been achieved. Therefore when we consider all of these apocalyptic texts together it becomes clear that authors were more concerned with the history of their own time than that of any previous century because this provided them with a unique sense of purpose in the country whose destiny they were striving to shape after the manner that God, who controlled all destinies, considered appropriate. The preoccupation of these authors with recent history did not mean that they ignored what had occurred in previous centuries but they tended increasingly to use the past as a storehouse of knowledge to demonstrate that anything good that had ever come to Ireland had derived from England. In this way they were refuting the contention of the Old English that had been articulated in the humanist historical texts of Campion and Stanihurst that it had been the Old English and their ancestors who had upheld civility in Ireland ever since the twelfth century.

1.4 Conclusion

This chapter will have explained how the decade of the 1570s proved an especially fertile one for the writing of histories of Ireland in the English language. It will have shown also that most of the histories that had appeared in print had been

---

[80] Willy Maley, ed., 'The Supplication of the Blood of the English...Cryeng out of the Yearth for Revenge', Analecta *Hibernica*, 36 (1995), 3–77; Hiram Morgan, '"Tempt not God too long, O Queen": Elizabeth and the Irish Crisis of the 1590s', Brendan Kane and Valerie McGowan-Doyle, eds., Elizabeth*I and Ireland* (Cambridge, 2014), 209–38.

[81] Nicholas Canny, 'Irish Sources for Spenser's View', *Spenser Studies*, 31, 32 (2017/2018), 495–510.

THE WRITING OF IRELAND'S HISTORY   25

either encouraged or sponsored by Sir Henry Sidney, who served intermittently as governor of Ireland from 1565 to 1578. Authors sought to associate Sidney with such writing because he was a recognized patron of learning. For his part, Sidney seemed to welcome such flattery because history writing gave a sense of purpose to the policies he wished to pursue and because the several authors paused to laud what they identified as his achievements. The earlier histories with which Sidney was linked and that concerned his first period as governor, 1565–71, can be described as humanist histories while the later set, associated with his second period as governor, 1575–78, were conceived in the Protestant apocalyptic tradition. This later preference of Sidney for apocalyptic over humanist writing can be attributed both to the fact that the humanist interpretation of Ireland's history continued to be favoured by the Old English community with which he had an increasingly strained relationship, and to Sidney's own gravitation towards a more rigid Protestant position as Queen Elizabeth's reign progressed.

Much attention has been given to the differences that can be identified between these two historical interpretations and the polemics to which these differences gave rise. However, it may be appropriate also to allude to what they shared in common. They were united in respecting the proposition that had been articulated by Gerald of Wales in the twelfth century that the Gaelic population of the country lacked civility, and, because of this, also lacked a history. There was agreement therefore that the Gaelic Irish had been brought into historic time only through their associations with England, and particularly with the English conquest of Ireland in the twelfth century. Their agreement over this, as mentioned, did not prevent our several authors from speculating over such matters as the origins of Ireland's first inhabitants, or if St Patrick had really evangelized the country. However, these were diversionary debates that should not distract from the agreement among authors that, following the twelfth-century conquest of Ireland, the history of that country had become intertwined with that of England because the two jurisdictions were, thereafter, ruled by a shared monarch.

This issue on which the two groups of historians could agree led, however, to a fundamental disagreement. The humanist historians contended that the success of the conquest had brought colonies of civil people into Ireland who had set about absorbing the barbaric Gaelic population into a civil polity through a mixture of force and persuasion. In opposition to this, the apocalyptic historians argued that the twelfth century conquest had done no more than provide residents in Ireland, whether pre- or post-conquest, with the possibility of becoming civil people. This possibility had arisen, they claimed, because people resident in Ireland, like the population of England itself, had enjoyed the good fortune to be governed by a monarchical dynasty that produced a few rulers who had striven to rescue the population of England, and the population also of its dependency in Ireland, from the corruption that had contaminated all aspects of life once the

26 IMAGINING IRELAND'S PASTS

church had abandoned the simplicity of its founders and become enthralled by a corrupt papacy. Thus, when John Derricke identified the English rulers who were worthy of commendation, he commenced with King Arthur as the first to establish the 'British' monarchy on secure foundations. Then, on the authority of John Foxe's *Acts and Monuments*, he identified King Henry II as the ruler who had increased 'in honour and in fame' 'the sceptre of the noble realm of England' by extending its authority in several directions, including into Ireland. The status of the English monarchy was further enhanced, according to Derricke, by King Edward III, who among his many valiant actions had challenged the Pope to fight him in single combat, which challenge, when declined, forced 'the beast' to cease interfering in politics. No other English ruler matched this achievement, claimed Derricke, until Henry VIII released his 'people and kingdom' from being 'subject unto the Pope of Rome, that presumptuous prelate'. This work of liberation had been resumed, he asserted, by Queen Elizabeth, who had not only brought peace and prosperity to her subjects but had also 'continued in the course of her father by suppressing the Pope, and, with more severity' had 'wounded so the Pope/that to recover his former strength,/he liveth void of hope'.[82]

Other apocalyptic historians might have included further godly rulers, notably King Edward VI, on the list of memorable monarchs. However, they would have agreed with the essential proposition that the promotion of reform was a process that would likely take several centuries to complete and would necessarily include the reform of religion. For such authors, the argument of the humanist historians that parts of Ireland had been made civil at one moment in time by its twelfth-century conquerors was implausible, especially since the apocalyptic historians contended that the twelfth-century conquerors, and the colonists they had introduced to Ireland, had not been fully civil themselves. This was put most emphatically in Spenser's *View* where Eudoxus, the lead interlocutor in the dialogue, pronounced that 'it was even the other day' (i.e. at the time of the Protestant Reformation) 'that England grew civil' and that 'in the reign of Henry II when Ireland was first planted with English', England itself had been 'very rude and barbarous'.[83] The contention of the humanists was further challenged by the assertion that the conquerors and settlers of the twelfth century, and their descendants, had fallen even further from civility because of their close association with their Gaelic neighbours. From there it became possible to conclude, as happened in Spenser's *View*, that the descendants of the twelfth-century conquerors had, through the process of degeneration, become even less civil than the Gaelic population they had always decried as barbarians.[84] In order to give substance to such propositions these apocalyptic historians, all of them

---

[82] Derricke, 177–80.
[83] W.L. Renwick, ed., Edmund Spenser, *A View of the Present State of Ireland* (Oxford, 1970), 67.
[84] Renwick, ed., Spenser, *View*, 48.

English-born Protestants, deliberated particularly on the significance of the history of their own times. This entitles them to be considered the first historians of what today has come to be known as early modern Ireland.

Much of what was written in these histories was polemical. However, some Irish historians of recent years have suggested that after Richard Stanihurst had left Ireland and settled in Continental Europe, he abandoned his customary polemics to write more positively of the Gaelic Irish, and to respond to the taunts and provocations of authors such as John Hooker. The publication to which these authors refer was another history of Ireland, *De rebus in Hibernia gestis*, that Stanihurst wrote in Latin, presumably for the benefit of continental audiences, and published in 1584 at Leiden. In this text, Stanihurst, when enumerating people of Irish birth who had earned an international reputation for scholarship, certainly gave greater recognition to the cultural contribution of people of Gaelic lineage than he had done seven years previously in his 'Description of Ireland'. However, even when he praised individuals, notably Columbanus and Gall, who had been recognized as saints in the Continental locations in which they had ministered because they had conducted their lives 'according to the true precepts of religion', he remarked condescendingly that this was noteworthy because in Gaelic society 'religion had no power against looting, plunder and murder'. The best that Stanihurst could say more generally of the Gaelic Irish in 1584 was that they were 'not devoid of all civilization'. Therefore his primary purpose in 1584, as in 1577, was to extol the merits and achievements of people in Ireland of English ancestry, presumably in the hope that these would yet be entrusted by the crown with completing the conquest and reform of Ireland that had been launched in the twelfth century. In his anxiety to press home his argument Stanihurst continued to denigrate Gaelic society as a preliminary to lauding the twelfth-century conquerors and their descendants whose ambition had always been to bring the Gaelic order to an end.[85]

Stanihurst's plaintiff effort to persuade himself, his readers, and possibly the English crown and government, that the Old English were still best equipped to complete the conquest of Ireland was not unlike the position adopted by Christopher St Lawrence, seventh baron of Howth, when he assembled material for a history of Ireland that he hoped would serve as a response to the actions and assertions of Sir Henry Sidney, particularly during his second period as governor of Ireland. In her analysis of this material, Valerie McGowan-Doyle has demonstrated that while Howth acknowledged some failures on the part of the medieval ancestors of the Old English, he argued steadfastly that they had generally been a loyal people, and clearly more loyal than the crown's subjects in England who, he calculated, had proven themselves more prone to treason than

---

[85] Barry and Morgan, eds., *Great Deeds in Ireland*, 133, 111.

the English community in Ireland.[86] It may have been as well for Baron Howth that he never completed his projected history because whatever chance there had been in the late 1570s of persuading the crown to retain confidence in its Old English subjects because of services rendered by their ancestors, this was no longer a realistic prospect in the 1580s. This situation had become altogether different both because the apocalyptic authors had cited evidence to challenge this version of Ireland's history, and because, by dwelling on the rebelliousness of the Old English in present times, they discredited the claims being made by the Old English apologists that they should be considered the crown's most loyal subjects. Thus as humanist historiography was subsumed into that favoured by the apocalyptic authors, the Old English authors can be seen to have failed to meet the challenge of writing a history of their own time that would counter that being published by those who had become bent upon their destruction.

[86] Valerie McGowan Doyle, *The Book of Howth: The Elizabethan Re-conquest of Ireland and the Old English* (Cork, 2011), esp. 77.

2

Composing Counter-Narratives in the Sixteenth and Seventeenth Centuries

2.1 Introduction

In the first chapter we noted how sixteenth-century historians of Ireland who wrote in the English language all endorsed the condemnation of Gaelic Irish society that had been formulated in the twelfth century by Gerald of Wales. It was explained how authors fell into this mould whether they were Catholic or Protestant, or born in Ireland or in England, or identified with the humanist or with the Protestant providential strands of historical scholarship. Moreover authors vied with each other to denigrate Gaelic society of their own time just as Gerald of Wales had castigated the Gaelic world of the twelfth century.

It is impossible to know who in Ireland, beyond the seemingly small community of people who were literate in the English language, were acquainted with what was written by these historians. However, the arguments of the Gaelic detractors are likely to have reached a wider audience in England, as well as in the English-speaking community in Ireland, both because they featured in the 1587 edition of Holinshed's *Chronicle* and because popularized renditions of their arguments were regurgitated in scores of unflattering English-language pamphlets on Irish subjects that became a staple of English publishing from the sixteenth century forward.[1]

The better-educated people within the English Pale in Ireland are likely to have been startled by several of these English-language polemics, and would have been especially distressed by those compositions by Protestant authors that criticized the Old English community in much the same terms that authors from the Pale had been using to disparage Ireland's Gaelic population. This turn made it necessary for representatives of the Old English community to plead plaintively, as Richard Stanihurst had done as early as 1577, that people of English descent in Ireland were as civil as any other subjects of the Crown, and perhaps more loyal to the English monarchy.

This Old English line of defence became ever more difficult to sustain once Protestant authors began to cite apparently irrefutable evidence that the leaders of the English community in Ireland had always been truculent and, in recent years,

---

[1] D.B. Quinn, *The Elizabethans and the Irish* (Ithaca, N.Y., 1966).

Imagining Ireland's Pasts: Early Modern Ireland through the Centuries. Nicholas Canny, Oxford University Press (2021).
© Nicholas Canny. DOI: 10.1093/oso/9780198808961.003.0002

more rebellious than the Gaelic Irish lords who had been criticized so insistently by authors from the Pale. The credibility of the Old English was further compromised as they clung ever more doggedly to Catholicism when it was becoming widely accepted in England that the ultimate proof of loyalty to the Crown was the willingness of subjects to embrace Protestantism. These developments made it difficult for Old English authors, or at least those of them who remained in Ireland, to mount a counter-narrative to the historical orthodoxy being expounded by Protestant zealots such as John Hooker. We noted how Hooker was able to make his case more credible by republishing those writings of Richard Stanihurst that seemed to corroborate his own arguments. This made it all the more urgent that authors from Gaelic Ireland should mount a response of some kind even if this was more to boost morale within their own community than to persuade people beyond its confines, most of whom, like Stanihurst, had no knowledge of Irish.

2.2 Initial Reactions from Gaelic Ireland

If members of the literate learned classes in Gaelic Ireland were but dimly aware of the negative depictions of their society being communicated in the English language by authors from both England and the English Pale, they were keenly conscious of the aggressive and insensitive manner in which members of their community were being treated by English officials and adventurers, and their Irish collaborators. This awareness was reflected in the manner in which annalists reported the events of their own time even when they employed traditional formats for the circulation of their opinions. The narrative mode of the annals composed in the late sixteenth century was consistent with those of earlier centuries, with authors, for example, continuing to dedicate as much attention to obituaries as to other subjects. However, the authors now paused more frequently to identify innovations that had been introduced by the government or its agents, and to offer condemnatory comments on particular atrocities regardless of whether these had been perpetrated by people of English or of Irish birth.

In addressing novelty, the compliers of the *Annals of the Four Masters* noted, for example, that Teig O'Brien was, in 1570, the first person to be appointed as sheriff of Thomond [*céd shirriam Tuadhmumhan*], and then for 1571 they mentioned the arrival in Munster of Sir John Perrot as its first provincial president. Their reference to Perrot as the first '*President Saxanach*', suggests that they were reconciled to the office of president of Munster, and presumably also that of Connacht, being always held by an Englishman.[2] The annalists also

---

[2] *A.F.M.*, vol. 6, 1653–5.

SIXTEENTH AND SEVENTEENTH CENTURIES   31

deemed novel and reprehensible the action of Conor O'Brien, earl of Thomond (a noted supporter of government) in hanging Owen Roe Mac a Bháird and Muiris Ó Cléirigh, each a member of a distinguished learned family and each skilled in antiquities and literature [*seanchus agus i ndán*]. It was with some satisfaction therefore that the annalists noted that Thomond had become the subject of satirical verses because of this treacherous act [*fellghníomh*].[3]

The same compilers mentioned with apparent approval the return of Sir Henry Sidney as governor of Ireland in 1575 and of his subsequent efforts to promote order and justice in his perambulations throughout the country. However, they were horror-stricken by what they described as the ugly and abominable act [*feall urghranna adhuathmhar*] committed by the English in Leinster and Meath when, in 1578, they massacred at Mullaghmast those from the Gaelic community who had previously lived under the protection of the Crown.[4] Similarly, the action of the president of Munster (in this instance Sir William Drury) in asserting his authority over the lordship of Thomond by using martial law was also considered innovatory and therefore condemned as inconsiderate [*miothuiccsigh*].[5]

The annalists seem to have detected a general coarsening of life in Ireland and acknowledged that it was not only the English who were casting aside previous moral restraints, as when they condemned Sir John of Desmond (brother to the earl of Desmond) for the murder of Henry Davells and his companion whom they had 'beheaded... while they were asleep in their beds and couches'.[6] While the annalists could thus identify breaches of a moral economy, they were guarded in apportioning blame for the outbreak of the hostilities that led to major military conflicts and they even continued to discern noble qualities in some Crown officials. Thus, when they noted, with a hint of resentment, that Sir Nicholas Malby had been rewarded with grants of land in perpetuity for his seven years' service as president of Connacht, they saluted him as 'a man learned in the languages and tongues of the islands of the west of Europe, a brave and victorious man in battles fought throughout Ireland, Scotland and France in the service of his sovereign'.[7]

The annalists also recorded the influence that confessional difference was beginning to exercise on events in Ireland as when they remarked that James Eustace had entered into rebellion in 1579 after he had 'embraced the Catholic faith and renounced his sovereign'. Similarly, when they commented on the arrival in Dingle in 1580 of the small force that had been funded by the Papacy to support the rebellion of James Fitzmaurice Fitzgerald, the annalists remarked that it would have proven more challenging for the government had the invading force

---

[3] *A.F.M.*, vol. 6, 1656–7.
[4] *A.F.M.*, vol. 6, 1695–7; on this incident see Vincent Carey, 'John Derricke's *Image of Ireland, Sir Henry Sidney, and the massacre at Mullaghmast, 1578*'.
[5] *A.F.M.*, vol. 6, 1697–9.   [6] *A.F.M.*, vol. 6, 1714–5.   [7] *A.F.M.*, vol. 6, 1793–6.

32   IMAGINING IRELAND'S PASTS

come ashore in Limerick, Cork, or Galway, in which towns, they believed, many people would have renounced their allegiance to the Crown because of their commitment to Catholicism.[8] However they continued to recognize that people on the Irish side had conflicting loyalties, and it was not until the very end of the conflict, when the annalists were recording the deaths respectively of Red Hugh O'Donnell and of Hugh O'Neill, earl of Tyrone, that they suggested that these had always been guided by religious considerations. Thus they mentioned how, after the military defeat at Kinsale, O'Donnell had travelled to Spain in the hope of procuring further military support from King Philip III who, they contended, was sympathetic to the Gaelic Irish both because they were of Milesian ancestry and because he was a monarch 'most willing to assist those who always fought in defence of the Roman Catholic religion'.[9] Then, in 1616, when recording the death in Rome of Hugh O'Neill, earl of Tyrone, the annalists commended him for having been warlike 'in defending his religion and patrimony against his enemies' and for having been 'a pious and charitable lord [*tighearna diadha, dércach*].[10]

If the annalists identified what was novel among the events they recorded, they, for the most part, stuck to their primary task of composing a narrative of the more important events that had influenced their lives, and refrained from framing judgements as the Renaissance and Protestant providential authors had been trained to do. The annalists understood that Nicholas Sander, the English seminary priest who died in Munster in 1581, had been 'the supporting pillar of the Catholic faith and the chief counsellor of the Geraldines during the course of the war in Munster' but, otherwise, they did not discern any shape or purpose to the conflict in that province, or in Ireland more generally, during the 1580s. On the contrary, when they noted the death in prison in Dublin of Barnaby Fitzpatrick, Baron of Upper Ossory, they reflected that it was a cause of 'wonder to the Irish' that Fitzpatrick should have been detained in prison by the government given that 'he was a man who had been brought up in England in his youth' and was 'acquainted with the manners and customs of the court'.[11] Similarly, when announcing the arrival as governor in Ireland of Arthur Lord Grey de Wilton, who would soon be excoriated by Old English commentators for his severe handling of the rebellion in Munster, the annalists welcomed one who had come 'with higher titles and honours' than Sir William Pelham, his immediate predecessor.[12]

Lughaidh Ó Cléirigh, a member of an illustrious annalistic family, made a valiant effort to make good for the narrative element that was missing from the annals when he expanded upon the conventional obituary element of the annals to compose a biography of Aodh Rua Ó Domhnaill (or Red Hugh O'Donnell).

---

[8] *A.F.M.*, vol. 6, 1737, 1739.   [9] *A.F.M.*, vol. 6, 2290–1.   [10] *A.F.M.*, vol. 6, 2372–5.
[11] *A.F.M.*, vol. 6, 1753.   [12] *A.F.M.*, vol. 6, 1735–7.

SIXTEENTH AND SEVENTEENTH CENTURIES   33

This man, together with his confederate and brother-in-law, Hugh O'Neill, earl of Tyrone, had led a formidable challenge that almost brought an end to English dominance in Ireland during the closing years of Queen Elizabeth's reign. Ó Cléirigh commenced his text with a summary of the family background and early childhood of O'Donnell previous to 1587 when, as Ó Cléirigh represented it, Red Hugh had been deceitfully captured by agents of the Crown and held in Dublin Castle as a hostage for his father's good behaviour. He then detailed two failed efforts by O'Donnell to elude captivity before he made his final escape and returned to Ulster. There, after some months' convalescence from frostbite, he was inaugurated as head of the O'Donnell lordship in place of his father who resigned in his favour. When Red Hugh was thus elevated, he was, according to Ó Cléirigh, fulfilling an ancient prophecy that such a godly ruler would become king of the lordship and rule for nine years. Then, with the benefit of hindsight, Ó Cléirigh narrated the achievements of O'Donnell in each of nine consecutive years until 1602 when he died in Simancas in Spain as he was attempting to secure a royal audience with King Philip III (then at Valladolid). His mission, according to Ó Cléirigh, was to persuade that monarch to provide further military aid to enable him, and his Irish confederates, to renew the war against Queen Elizabeth's government.

Ó Cléirigh's account traced how O'Donnell, working in conjunction with O'Neill, had year by year sought to motivate the lords of Ulster to oppose English incursions in the province by reminding them how they, the Gaelic Irish [*siol Ghaeidil Glais*], had long suffered injustices at the hands of the English [*Gallaibh*] who had robbed them of their inheritances, incarcerated them without cause, and executed them without trial.[13] The narrative explained further that it was O'Donnell, working in conjunction with the Catholic bishops of Ulster, who had made the first overtures to the king of Spain for financial and military assistance, and Ó Cléirigh's narrative gave O'Donnell, rather than O'Neill, credit for having maintained this contact with Spain for the duration of the war.[14] O'Donnell remained in focus as Ó Cléirigh detailed how O'Donnell had extended the confederation beyond Ulster by assisting several of the lords of the province of Connacht to overthrow their rivals. Ó Cléirigh explained that O'Donnell's most effective means of building a confederacy was by seizing the moveable property of those who seemed reluctant to join his cause. He also described how O'Donnell's every success was a provocation to the provincial president in Connacht and therefore to the government in Dublin. Therefore, he lauded the success of O'Donnell, usually acting alone but sometimes in conjunction with O'Neill, in

---

[13] Lughaidh Ó Cléirigh, *Beatha Aodha Ruaidh Uí Dhomhnaill by Lughaidh Ó Cléirigh*, ed., Paul Walsh (London, 1948), 58–9.

[14] Ó Cléirigh, *Beatha...Uí Dhomhnaill*, 60–1, 140–1, 190–1, 210–11, 280–5, 310–11.

34 IMAGINING IRELAND'S PASTS

defeating successive efforts by the government to recover its authority in Connacht and in Ulster.

Ó Cléirigh described, and exulted in, each successive victory by O'Donnell (or O'Donnell in alliance with O'Neill) over English commanders. These, with the exception of Richard Bingham, he saluted as brave and honourable, However Ó Cléirigh regretted the occasional defection of members of the confederacy—including some of O'Donnell's own kin—and also the insufficiency of the aid that had been sent to them by the king of Spain. These factors, added to what he considered the bungled tactics employed by O'Neill's army on the battlefield of Kinsale, explained for Ó Cléirigh why the Gaelic forces with their Spanish allies had been defeated on the field of Kinsale. Thereafter, as he represented it, they had been unable to defend their patrimonies [*a athardha*] from incursions by Crown forces.[15]

There was nothing in Ó Cléirigh's narrative to suggest that he was writing to counter English language histories of Ireland, or that he was even aware of their existence. However, it appears that as a history of its own time, Ó Cléirigh's *Beatha Aodha Ruaidh Uí Dhomhnaill* displayed a keener understanding of the wider issues than any previous prose or poetic work composed in Gaelic Ireland. It was novel, in asserting that the English government, aided by its Irish allies, was bent on dispossessing those in the country (or at least those in the Gaelic areas) who resisted Crown intrusions into their localities. The text was original also in explaining how O'Donnell, aided by O'Neill, framed a confederacy to enable those wishing to defend their patrimonies from outside interference to do so collectively. Ó Cléirigh explained also that not all lords of Gaelic ancestry belonged to this confederacy, and he came close to admitting that for each lord who joined the confederacy, a rival claimant to power within that particular lordship solicited support from the government.

Ó Cléirigh's account was concerned essentially with Gaelic Ireland but in discussing O'Donnell's relationships with the Burke dynasties in Mayo and Galway (whose ancestors had established themselves in Connacht following the twelfth-century conquest) he made it clear that O'Donnell welcomed such lords as members of the confederacy, presumably because they had adopted several Gaelic practices and had remained loyal to Catholicism. Ó Cléirigh also detailed how it was O'Donnell's association with Catholic bishops that had enabled him to solicit financial and military support from Spain, but he insisted that the war being fought was to achieve fairness and justice in relation to political power and the ownership of land. In so doing he refrained from describing the war as a

---

[15] Ó Cléirigh, *Beatha... Uí Dhomhnaill*, 286–7; the term *athardha* corresponded to *patria* as it was then used in Catholic Europe to invoke provincial, local, or civic loyalties; I.A.A. Thompson, 'Castile, Spain and the monarchy: the political community from *patria natural* to *patria nacional*', Richard Kagan and Geoffrey Parker, eds., *Spain, Europe and the Atlantic World: Essays in Honour of John H. Elliott* (Cambridge, 1995), 125–59.

struggle for religious freedom, even when it was being described as such both by Hugh O'Neill, earl of Tyrone, and by some of the Catholic clergy who were acting as conduits to the papacy and the Spanish monarchy.[16]

2.3 Preparing the Way for Counter-Narratives

Catholic bishops would have agreed with Lughaidh Ó Cléirigh that the expansion and consolidation of Crown influence in Ireland threatened the security of all lords who, previously, had been relatively free from sustained government control. The bishops would have differed from Ó Cléirigh only in identifying religious persecution as the principal hardship being experienced by Irish lords during the later decades of the sixteenth century. They, or their representatives, were therefore quick to designate the Desmond insurrection in Munster, the revolt in Leinster led by James Eustace, Viscount Baltinglass, and the war emanating from Ulster, led by O'Neill and O'Donnell, as wars which were fought for the defence of Catholicism. They considered themselves free to do so because the Pope had excommunicated Queen Elizabeth in 1570, and because the senior clergy who had spent time on the Continent would have been aware of the religious dimension to the conflicts then being fought out in France, the Low Countries, and elsewhere. More pragmatically, they recognized that the only possible means of persuading the lords in Ireland, who they knew to be divided culturally, ethnically, and by faction, to abandon their differences, was by alluding to the common Catholicism that was shared by most of them and which was under assault.[17]

The bishops became more entrenched in their views because of the persecution that clerics had witnessed or experienced during the closing decades of the sixteenth century. Details of all persecutions that had been endured were recorded by the Catholic clergy who were thus equipped to highlight episodes such as the death of Dermot O'Hurley, Archbishop of Cashel, who, soon after his return from the Continent, had been arrested, tortured and, in 1584, hanged by the state authorities in Dublin. The Irish lords emphasized the religious dimension to their grievances also because it was only by proclaiming that they were in arms to secure freedom to practise Catholicism that they stood any chance of persuading the papacy or the Spanish monarchy to provide them with financial or military support.

Some Irish lords, or the clergy who wrote on their behalves, followed this advice when soliciting support from Catholic Europe. The prime example of this

---

[16] See the 1598 text Peter Lombard, *De Regno Hiberniae, insulsa sanctorum, commentarius*, ed., P.F. Moran (Dublin, 1868).

[17] Henry Jefferies, *The Irish Church and the Tudor Reformations* (Dublin, 2010).

36 IMAGINING IRELAND'S PASTS

is the overture made by Peter Lombard, a priest from Waterford resident on the Continent, who addressed Pope Clement giving him reason why he should declare the Ulster revolt of the 1590s a religious war. Had the Pope been agreeable to do so it would have placed all Catholics in Ireland under a moral obligation to support the cause.[18]

More relevant to our present concerns is that those Irish Catholic authors who had found refuge in Catholic Europe after the failure of their various challenges to government authority also emphasized in the histories they wrote that all conflict with Crown forces in sixteenth-century Ireland had been motivated primarily by the desire to achieve religious freedom. Most such histories were composed by clerics who had travelled to the Continent either to secure an education or to escape persecution. This left Philip O'Sullivan Beare as exceptional in being a lay historian of high social standing whose family had lost their lands and status as a consequence of defeat in battle. This new generation of historians included individuals from both Old English and Gaelic lineages. The latter were obviously familiar with the annalistic and biographical accounts that had been composed in Ireland, while Old English authors, and soon also those of Gaelic lineage, knew of the histories of Ireland that had been published in the English language in the recent past. These were all therefore concerned to counter that which they considered untrue or inappropriate by citing from what they had witnessed or experienced.

All historians of Ireland who had spent time on the Continent would have become acquainted with the many Catholic confessional histories of other European communities that had been written in recent years, some with the purpose of countering the historical arguments being advanced by Protestant historians to justify their rejection of what, for centuries, had been the established religious order within their respective communities. Such histories would have reminded Irish Catholic scholars of the need to write similar histories for Ireland in the hope that this would encourage those in the country who had remained loyal to the faith. These Continental publications would also have introduced Irish authors to the methods and standards of proof expected of contemporary historical scholarship, as well as to the polemical and confessional nature of historical discourse as it had developed in Europe over the course of the sixteenth century.[19]

---

[18] Lombard, *De Regno Hiberniae*.

[19] For those who studied in Spanish seminaries the prime exemplar of Catholic history writing would have been Juan de Mariana, *Historiae de rebus Hispaniae* (Madrid, 1592). De Mariana expanded upon and translated from the original Latin into a Castilian edition *Historia general de España* (Madrid, 1601). Professor Alison Forrestal advises me that Irish emigrants exposed to French Catholic writing of the time would have become acquainted with polemical and stridently anti-Protestant histories of France, on which see Thierry Wanegffelen, *Une difficile Fidélité. Catholiques malgré le concile en France XVIe–XVIIe siècles* (Paris, 1999), 52–5. Irish students, especially those from the Pale, would have taken a special interest in English Catholic historical disputation being engaged upon

These Irish authors were, to some extent, catching up on lost time since they had enjoyed little opportunity in war-torn Ireland of the late sixteenth century to write considered accounts of these conflicts as they were happening. Some Catholic clerics on the Continent analysed the data on persecution that had been transmitted to them from Ireland as conflict was still under way, and these had begun to append the names of those who had been killed to the list of Irish saints from earlier centuries and to describe as martyrs all Catholics, especially all Catholic clergy, who had been killed or executed during the course of the recent conflict.[20]

Once they set about composing retrospective accounts, either in secure Continental locations or sometimes after they had returned to Ireland, Irish scholars drew upon these hagiographical compilations to sustain Catholic interpretations of Ireland's ancient and recent histories, aimed particularly at countering what they considered unacceptable in the accounts of Ireland's past written by Protestants. For them, as for their Protestant counterparts, defeat was success postponed, and they sought to defend Ireland's Catholic population, in the past as in the present, from the calumnies of their opponents, and to guide them for future actions that would enable them to maintain or recover the land and positions they had lost and to practise their faith.

If Catholic historians of Ireland were agreed on objectives, they experienced difficulty in deciding upon a common narrative. They were united in asserting that English Protestant soldiers had, over the course of the sixteenth century, behaved treacherously, destroyed property and desecrated revered places and objects. They were ready also, in true providential style, to identify these calamities as a divine punishment for the spiritual failings of Irish people and as a spur to amendment. After that, glaring interpretative differences emerged between various authors, and these were determined by factors as varied as whether they came from Gaelic or Old English backgrounds, or whether their original patrons had endured in Ireland or had lost their status and estates (if not their lives) in the recent conflict. Such differences could, in the case of clerics, be exaggerated by their affiliation with a particular religious order since seminarians from the Gaelic parts of Ireland were drawn disproportionately to the Franciscan order and those from Old English backgrounds were represented disproportionately in Jesuit houses.

---

from Continental bases; on this see Felicity Heal, 'Appropriating History: Catholic and Protestant Polemics and the National Past', Paulina Kewes, ed., *The Uses of History in Early Modern England* (San Marino, Ca., 2006), 105–28. Irish authors would have been especially interested in the posthumous history of the English reformation by Nicholas Sander who had travelled to Ireland where he lost his life in the Desmond rebellion; Nicholas Sander, *De Origine ac Progressu Schismatis Anglicani* [1586], ed. and trans., D. Lewis (London, 1877).

[20] For an early published example of Irish hagiography see Thomas Messingham, *Florilegium insulae sanctorum* (Paris, 1624).

38 IMAGINING IRELAND'S PASTS

Differences of opinion between authors became more pronounced once the British and Spanish monarchies agreed to live in peace with one another following the Treaty of London of 1604. Thereafter, accounts written by authors from Old English backgrounds tended to look positively at the treaty in the hope that their patrons in Ireland, where these had retained their property, would succeed in negotiating greater tolerance for the practice of Catholicism. On the other hand, authors from Gaelic backgrounds tended to believe that the dispossessed Irish and the Catholic Church would recover the positions they had lost in Ireland only after England had been defeated by Spain in battle. Those who held this view expected that the Irish soldiers who had enlisted with Spain in the aftermath of defeat at home would play a decisive role in extending to Ireland the conflict that would be fought between England and Spain at sea and on the Continent. To further complicate matters some authors changed their positions to coincide with changes in political circumstances. Thus, as was demonstrated long since by J.J. Silke, Peter Lombard who had been intransigent in his outlook while the Spanish monarchy was supporting military action in Ireland, became an advocate of conciliation from the moment Spain had signed a treaty with England. Thereafter, he encouraged the papacy to appoint clergy to vacant senior positions in the Irish church who would adhere to this moderate stance.[21]

2.4 David Rothe's *Analecta Sacra*: A Revised Old English Perspective on the Past

The negotiation of peace between England and Spain could not have come at a better time for those Old English exiles attending seminaries in Spanish territories. Previous to this they had been compromised in their dealings with the Spanish authorities because many of their kin in Ireland had remained neutral, or had even fought for the English Crown, throughout the Nine Years War (1594–1603)—a conflict that the Spanish monarchy, like the Irish bishops, had considered a Catholic cause.[22] Moreover, while Old English seminarians had chosen to study on the Continent because the training of priests was prohibited in Ireland, they continued to represent themselves as loyal subjects of the English Crown. Doing so was reasonable because many of their kin had fought for the queen during the Nine Years War, and most of their patrons, who usually enjoyed a relatively secure position in Ireland, continued to negotiate some religious and political tolerance for Catholics as a reward for their proven loyalty.[23]

---

[21] J.J. Silke, 'Later relations between Primate Peter Lombard and Hugh O'Neill', *Irish Theological Quarterly*, vol. 22 (1955), 15–30; Silke, 'Primate Lombard and James I', *Irish Theological Quarterly*, vol. 22 (1955), 124–50.

[22] Canning, *The Old English in Early Modern Ireland*.

[23] Aidan Clarke, *The Old English in Ireland, 1625–42* (London, 1966).

SIXTEENTH AND SEVENTEENTH CENTURIES   39

Once political circumstances changed after the signing of the Treaty of London, the Spanish monarchy began to look more favourably on the position that most Old English exiles had adopted. Now the Spanish authorities satisfied themselves that they would be meeting their obligations towards their former Catholic allies in Ireland, as well as to their supporters in England and Scotland, by encouraging the government of King James to be more benevolent towards Catholics and accept them as true subjects.[24]

This encouraged Old English authors to write a narrative of Ireland's past that would be consistent with their present ambitions. The most comprehensive of such histories was the *Analecta Sacra* composed during the early decades of the seventeenth century by David Rothe (1573–1650) and published in various editions in Paris and Cologne between 1616 and 1619.[25] Rothe, who had been born in Kilkenny and schooled in that town, spent an extended interlude on the Continent at Douai, Salamanca, and Rome. After this experience he returned to Ireland in 1609, initially as vicar apostolic in his native diocese of Ossory, and later as bishop of the diocese, a position to which he was nominated by the Pope in 1618 and held until his death in 1650.[26] This senior cleric was well placed to write a history that would be compatible with Old English interests and sensibilities, both because he was familiar with Catholic histories of several European countries that might serve as models for him, and because he had first-hand experience of the rapidly changing political and diplomatic contexts within which Catholics in Ireland were seeking to negotiate an improvement in their position as subjects of the British monarchy.

The final published version of Rothe's text was complex because its several elements had been written at different times in response to particular problems, and because different segments had been addressed to different audiences. These dedicatees included King James VI & I[27] and his heir, Charles, Prince of Wales,[28] some secular and spiritual rulers on the European Continent,[29] and Irish Catholic clergy and laity.[30] The fact that the text was published in Latin, particularly since some of it may have been drafted originally in English, suggests that Rothe was providing a narrative that he hoped would prove beneficial to priests and seminarians for future pastoral work in Ireland, and would satisfy the curiosity

---

[24] For a general but insightful consideration of Old English history writing over time see David Finnegan, 'Old English views of Gaelic Irish History and the emergence of an Irish Catholic nation, c. 1569–1640', Brian Mac Cuarta, S.J., ed., *Reshaping Ireland, 1550–1700: Colonization and its Consequences; essays presented to Nicholas Canny* (Dublin, 2011), 187–213.

[25] David Rothe, *Analecta Sacra Nova et Mira de Rebus Catholicorum in Hibernia Pro fide & Religione gestis, divisa in tres partes*, ed., P. F. Moran (Dublin, 1884). This edition includes all the editions with appended supplements published by Rothe during the interlude 1616–19.

[26] For a biographical note on Rothe see that by Thomas O'Connor, *Dictionary of Irish Biography*, vol. 8, 621–3; O'Connor points out that, although Rothe was nominated as bishop in 1618, he was not actually consecrated until 1620 when he had to travel from Ireland to Paris for that purpose.

[27] Rothe, *Analecta*, 169–73.   [28] Rothe, *Analecta*, 9–14.   [29] Rothe, *Analecta*, 3–8.

[30] Rothe, *Analecta*, 179–88.

40   IMAGINING IRELAND'S PASTS

about Ireland of better-educated Catholic elite readers on the Continent. His central argument was that the Irish were a cultured people who had been ardent Catholics ever since they had first received the faith from St Patrick. This was in sharp contradiction to what had been said of them by Gerald of Wales whose writings on Ireland had not only inspired Stanihurst but were still being consulted on the Continent.[31]

To support his rehabilitation of the reputation of Ireland's population previous to the Norman Conquest, Rothe identified the many Irish saints whose spiritual endeavours had earned them respect throughout Europe.[32] To his list, Rothe appended the names of several individuals who had suffered martyrdom in the recent past at the hands of English officials. In doing so, Rothe emphasized that the officials acted on the authority of legislation passed by the Irish parliament during the reign of Queen Elizabeth, and that of fresh enactments of the parliament of 1613–15 that had been approved by King James VI & I.

Individual elements of Rothe's *Analecta* might be described variously as political discourse,[33] theological polemic, and Catholic martyrology,[34] but a historical narrative underpinned the entire text. With this, Rothe sought deliberately to displace the interpretations of Ireland's history that he believed to be fixed in the minds of the various audiences he was addressing. Rothe's narrative proceeded from very different assumptions from those held by the historians whose interpretations he was seeking to refute. His first assumption, at which his Protestant rivals would have looked askance, held that Catholicism, which he considered the only orthodox Christian religion, had been largely responsible for the amelioration of society throughout Europe, and therefore also in Ireland, from its first institution by Christ. Catholicism, he asserted, had fostered honour, virtue, and humane interaction between individuals, and he credited those Catholics whose characters had been moulded by this religion with having promoted urbanization, industry, and equitable laws and institutions.[35] Because of its progressive character, claimed Rothe, Catholicism had necessarily come into conflict with tyrannical pagans and heretics.[36] Rothe substantiated this by reference to the sufferings endured by the martyrs of the early church at the hands of Roman tyrants, and he dovetailed this narrative with an account of the

---

[31] The best recent appraisal of the text is that by Colm Lennon, 'Political thought of Irish Counter-Reformation churchmen; the testimony of the "Analecta" of Bishop David Rothe', Hiram Morgan, ed., *Political Ideology in Ireland, 1541–1641* (Dublin, 1999), 181–202. In this Lennon posits the idea that the English manuscript text N.L.I., Ms. 643, was the original from which the later Latin versions were developed; Anthony Pagden, *The Fall of Natural Man: The American Indian and the Origins of Comparative Ethnology* (Cambridge, 1982), 70–1.

[32] Rothe, *Analecta*, 90–1; in an effort to maximize the number of Irish saints, Rothe published a later book challenging the claim for his country that Thomas Dempster, a Scottish Catholic polemicist, had made for several saints that Rothe had considered indubitably Irish; David Rothe, *Hibernia resurgens* (Paris, 1621).

[33] Rothe, *Analecta*, 229–30.   [34] Rothe, *Analecta*, 355–94, esp., 382–94.

[35] Rothe, *Analecta*, 100.   [36] Rothe, *Analecta*, 85–6.

injustices inflicted by the governments of Queen Elizabeth and King James upon Catholics in Ireland.

As he thus moved from his general pronouncements to speak more particularly of Ireland, Rothe explained how the Christian message that had been introduced there by St Patrick had made it possible for Irish people to assist in the re-Christianization of Europe in the aftermath of the barbaric invasions, and to resist, and eventually overcome, the Viking invaders who had striven to quench spirituality throughout Ireland.[37] Rothe claimed that the success of the Irish in thus overcoming adversity meant that the condition of Catholicism in Ireland had been robust when the English Crown had first become involved there in the twelfth century. He therefore insisted that Irish Catholicism had already been re-invigorated and brought into conformity with Roman best practice by reforms introduced by St Malachy and St Laurence O'Toole.[38] Then, citing Gerald of Wales, Rothe asserted that when King Henry II of England had been designated Lord of Ireland by Pope Adrian IV in 1154, that king and his successors had been given responsibility, under the terms of the bull *Laudabiliter* to uphold and further the reform of the church in Ireland, even though, as Rothe represented it, it was scarcely in need of reform.[39] In so far as Henry's endeavour was placed in jeopardy, according to Rothe, it was due first to the dubious character of some of those who had settled in Ireland following the twelfth-century conquest, and then to the tense relations that developed between Crown officials and the king's new Irish subjects. To support this allegation, Rothe cited the intervention by Pope John XXII into Irish affairs in 1317 when that Pope had reminded King Edward II that he, as successor to King Henry II, had been bound by what that king had agreed with Pope Adrian IV in 1154.[40]

Even as he took account of such lapses, Rothe declared himself satisfied that the English monarchs had, in general, enabled the Irish Nation (*Nationis Hibernorum*)[41] to remain constant in its loyalty to the Catholic faith[42] until King Henry VIII took it upon himself, for purely carnal reasons, to declare himself head of the church. This departure from Christian culture (*contra Orthodoxos Christi cultores*), according to Rothe, proved a 'catastrophe' because it had breached the division between spiritual and secular powers that had been decreed by Christ himself and that, according to Rothe, had been preserved throughout the Christian world for centuries.[43]

The consequences of this rash action by a headstrong monarch were, according to Rothe, entirely predictable as the church in England lapsed from being merely schismatic to becoming heretical, and therefore also tyrannical. It was with sadness therefore that Rothe chronicled the deterioration in the relationship

---

[37] Rothe, *Analecta*, 90–1.   [38] Rothe, *Analecta*, 102, 111, 348.   [39] Rothe, *Analecta*, 116.
[40] Rothe, *Analecta*, 119.   [41] Rothe, *Analecta*, 23.   [42] Rothe, *Analecta*, 26, 281, 322.
[43] Rothe, *Analecta*, 80, 59.

42 IMAGINING IRELAND'S PASTS

between the Crown and its loyal subjects in Ireland over the course of the sixteenth century, and the enactment of legislation that had resulted in the persecution of Irish people who had sought valiantly to remain loyal to their faith while also being true to their monarch.

To substantiate such charges, Rothe detailed the legislation that had been enacted by Irish parliaments during Queen Elizabeth's reign to compel Catholics to comply with the Crown's wishes in matters of religion. Then he bewailed the further penalties that had been enforced by proclamation in the reign of James VI and I, and those that had been proposed, against strident opposition, to the Irish parliament of 1613–15.[44] Following this, he further explained that, whenever legislation had proven insufficient to meet the purposes of Crown officials, they had resorted to martial law and other extra-legal procedures to persecute those who had remained Catholic while continuing to be demonstrably loyal to the Crown.

Rothe likened the sufferings endured by Irish Catholics in Elizabethan and Jacobean times to those of the early Christians at the hands of Nero. In so doing he elaborated upon the martyrs' deaths that had been inflicted upon three of Ireland's bishops: Dermot O'Hurley, Archbishop of Cashel, put to death after torture in Dublin in 1584; Richard Creagh, Archbishop of Armagh, who had died in the Tower of London in 1588; and Cornelius O'Devany, Bishop of Down and Connor, who had been hanged, drawn, and quartered in Dublin in 1612.[45] Rothe thought it appropriate to highlight the sufferings endured by these bishops because of their role as spiritual leaders of their communities, but he took account also of the sufferings of others in Ireland, clerical and lay, male and female, who had been denied the right to owe allegiance to their faith as well as to their monarch.[46] To substantiate his case that the government's efforts had been counter-productive, Rothe cited the acknowledgement by William Cecil, Lord Burghley, that the attempt to promote Protestantism by force in sixteenth-century Ireland had proven futile. Rothe corroborated this judgement by alluding to what he claimed were death-bed reconversions to Catholicism by some of the few prominent Irish people who had represented themselves as converts to Protestantism, and had even become persecutors of Catholics during their working lives. Among these he included the lawyers Nicholas Walsh and Gerald Comerford and the statesman Thomas Butler, earl of Ormond.[47]

The prime reasons why Protestantism failed to take root in Ireland, according to Rothe, were that Irish people had proven themselves committed to Catholicism from the moment of their first conversion, and because those Protestant clergy who had been given responsibility for diverting them to Protestant beliefs had

---

[44] Rothe, *Analecta*, 238–64, 282–6.   [45] Rothe, *Analecta*, 368, 381, 423–9; 395–422; 290, 386.
[46] Rothe, *Analecta*, 355–94, esp., 382–94.   [47] Rothe, *Analecta*, 124, 43–4.

been worldly people who led scandalous lives and lacked spiritual conviction.[48] Under these circumstances, he claimed, persecution had strengthened the Irish people in their religious resolve just as early Christians had become more committed to their faith because of the persecution that had been meted out to them by the Ancient Romans.[49] Then, as he detailed the hardships that had been imposed on Catholics first by Sir Arthur Chichester[50] and then by Oliver St John[51] (each a governor appointed by King James), he likened these governors to tyrannical Roman emperors. He also expressed the disappointment of the Irish Catholic community that King James, in whom they had pinned hope of deliverance both because he was of Gaelic lineage and son of the martyred Mary Queen of Scots, had proven himself as intolerant of Catholicism as Queen Elizabeth had been.[52] It was for this reason that Rothe dedicated the first of his published volumes to Charles, Prince of Wales, in the hope that when Charles succeeded to the throne he would discard the evil counsellors who had persuaded his father that Catholics in Ireland were but half subjects notwithstanding their proven loyalty to him.

Rothe obviously intended that his narrative would displace those promoted in the prevailing English language histories with which he would have disagreed on several points and with which some of his intended readers would have been familiar. However, for the most part, he chose to ignore these texts rather than argue against them point by point. Thus, of the authors whose histories we discussed in the first chapter, Rothe made reference only to Gerald of Wales and Richard Stanihurst and then only when he needed to cite them to sustain his own arguments.[53] Instead of engaging in debate with authors with whom he would necessarily disagree, Rothe composed a fresh narrative that he hoped would prove more persuasive than those of his adversaries for his intended audiences. In doing so he was careful to authenticate whatever propositions he put forward by citing both English official sources and the records compiled by individuals who had been witnesses to the persecutions suffered by Irish Catholics as these became martyrs for the faith. By thus combining documentary evidence with eyewitness accounts Rothe was meeting the standards of proof expected from historians of his day, whether Catholic or Protestant. However, his citation of authorities from the past showed that he was continuing to write in the tradition of the scholastics.

Some Irish scholars believe that Rothe should be considered a humanist scholar because of his interest in the Roman past and his occasional citation from classical authors. However, he, like John Hooker, had no pretensions to join such

---

[48] Rothe, *Analecta*, 130–5.   [49] Rothe, *Analecta*, 299.
[50] Rothe, *Analecta*, 72, 125–30, 145, 165, 187.   [51] Rothe, *Analecta*, 212–18.
[52] Rothe, *Analecta*, 135, 139.
[53] Rothe, *Analecta*, 40, 93, 102, 111, 112, 141, 433; Rothe on several occasions cited from Camden's *Brittania* but again to substantiate arguments of his own rather than to state his disagreement with Camden over particular issues.

company. Each had had a classical training, and each could, when it suited his purpose, cite classical texts to sustain an argument. However, neither one considered the Ancient World a place worthy of emulation in the way that humanists invariably did. Rothe, as was noted, considered Ancient Rome to have been an imperfect tyrannical society, and for Hooker, no less than for Rothe, the lost golden age was not when Ancient Rome had dominated much of Europe but rather when the power of Rome was in eclipse and Christianity had first begun to prevail over barbarism.

When he set about proving this in the case of Ireland, Rothe, as already mentioned, looked to the scholarly endeavours of Irish saints who had won respect on the Continent. His fundamental difference with respect to Protestant authors such as Bale and Hooker was that, where they contended that the purity of the early Christian Church had been lost through corruption by the papacy, before it had been partially revived with the onset of the Protestant Reformation, Rothe credited Irish people with having struggled at all times to maintain the purity of their church even when confronted by the tyrannical actions of King Henry VIII and his Protestant successors. This meant that Rothe, no less than Hooker, could end his narrative on a positive note because, where Hooker had anticipated a fresh efflorescence of Christianity in Ireland as the Protestant Reformation gained ground, Rothe was satisfied that 'the Irish nation' had become ever more committed to Catholicism, as individuals suffered persecution at the hands of the officials of Queen Elizabeth and King James. He also believed that Irish people were about to be rewarded for such suffering by a relaxation of the laws under which they were being penalized for practising their faith.

Rothe's work is therefore best described as Catholic history analogous to the Catholic narratives being composed in other European countries at that time to displace, or pre-empt, Protestant histories of those same communities. His history parted company with all previous accounts of Ireland's past, whether these had been written in Irish or English, in presuming that all customary residents in the country, irrespective of lineage, belonged to an Irish nation that was defined by allegiance to Catholicism and, presumably, by place of birth. By so doing he was jettisoning both the notion fostered by Old English authors that genetic descent from English ancestry was a prerequisite to being civil, and the view fostered by the Gaelic learned classes that it was necessary to have embraced the language, customs, attire, and inheritance practices of the Gaels as well as Catholicism before being considered a fully fledged member of their community.

Rothe's history also ran counter to histories that had been written by recent authors, whether English or Irish, Protestant or Catholic, by emphasizing the inherent loyalty to the English monarchy of people resident in Ireland regardless of lineage, rank, or cultural preferences. It was presumably in an effort to preserve this illusion that he made but brief mention of the various insurrections (*insurrectionem*) that had occurred in Ireland over the course of the sixteenth century, and then only to say that those who had become involved with such disturbances had been driven from their loyalty by religious persecutions inflicted upon them by unscrupulous minor Crown officials.[54] One proof of the loyalty of Irish people to the Crown, according to Rothe, was that they had been generally opposed to the rise to power of Shane O'Neill during the 1560s. Here Rothe pointed to the way in which Archbishop Richard Creagh had been a consistent critic of O'Neill. Despite this, as Rothe ruefully explained, state officials had punished Creagh because he had remained loyal to his faith as well as to the Crown.[55]

The most original aspect of Rothe's text was his countering the view that the English conquest of the twelfth century had marked a major disjunction in Ireland's history. His fundamental proposition was that conquerors and conquered had each been a civil and Christian people. This, as he saw it, meant that there was no obstacle in the way of people of Irish birth of both Gaelic and English lineages owing allegiance to Stuart monarchs, since these were kings who had had Gaelic progenitors and were also lineal successors to King Henry II who had been designated by the Pope as the legitimate ruler of Ireland.

2.5 Philip O'Sullivan Beare's *Historia Catholicae Iberniae Compendium*: A History for the Dispossessed

The interpretation of Ireland's past elaborated in David Rothe's *Analecta* represented a fresh departure but there was no disguising that he was using history to give solace to those Catholic elite families in Ireland (whether of English or Gaelic lineage) who still enjoyed what seemed to be secure positions in the country. Thus, while he acknowledged that the plantations implemented in Munster, Ulster, and elsewhere had been morally unjust, Rothe suggested no remedy for those who had been deprived of their patrimonies.[56] Neither did the *Analecta* offer much consolation to those exiled Catholic clergy who had come from parts of Ireland that appeared under such firm Protestant control that it seemed unlikely they would ever have the opportunity to return to pursue pastoral duties. The *Analecta* rather seems to have been intended by Rothe as a pragmatic guide for Catholic clerics in Ireland and for those Catholic elite families who had retained their positions in the country and were involved in negotiating greater freedom for the practice of Catholicism from a Protestant monarch.

The *Analecta* would therefore have held little appeal for those Irish exiles, both clerical and lay, who were beginning to despair of any future for them in the country of their birth. These exiles, as noted, tended to come more from Gaelic

[54] Rothe, *Analecta*, 275–6.   [55] Rothe, *Analecta*, 275.
[56] Rothe, *Analecta*, 218–20, 127, 135, 147.

46 IMAGINING IRELAND'S PASTS

than Old English backgrounds, were associated more often with the Franciscan order than with the Jesuits, and, when in Spain, cultivated those courtiers who had never become reconciled to being at peace with England. These courtiers were constantly alert for pretexts that would give Spain a reason to renew the hostilities that had been abandoned in 1604. The Irish dissidents encouraged these courtiers that in any future conflict between the Spanish and British monarchies Spain should open hostilities by invading Ireland. As they offered this advice, the Irish dissidents assured their Spanish audience that the Irish population had become so alienated by harsh usage at the hands of the officials of the British monarch that they could be counted on to give much more fulsome support to any Spanish invading force than had been the case in 1601 when the earlier Spanish expedition had disembarked at Kinsale.[57]

This was certainly the view of Philip O'Sullivan Beare (1590–1636). His family had suffered the loss of their lands in west Munster and had been forced in 1602 to seek refuge in Spain, because of the support they had provided to the Spanish expedition to Kinsale and because they had persisted in arms in west Munster after the Spaniards had withdrawn from the town of Kinsale. The head of the dynasty, Donal O'Sullivan Beare, was considered by the Spanish monarchy to be so worthy of special recognition that, exceptionally among this first wave of Irish emigrants, he was granted a noble title, that of Conde de Berehaven. It is unsurprising that Berehaven's cousin Philip, who was but twelve in 1602, was admitted for schooling to a college at the University of Santiago de Compostela, then managed by Franciscans who had been given special responsibility for the education of the younger members of destitute Irish noble houses.[58]

The original expectation of the O'Sullivan Beare family was that Philip would become a priest. However, having decided against ordination, he established contact with Berehaven, his ennobled cousin, and with Florence Conry (Flaithrí Ó Maolchonaire), titular Archbishop of Tuam. These, as early as 1610, had been lobbying both to have another Spanish military force sent to Ireland and to prevent the Irish college at Compostela from being transferred from Franciscan to Jesuit control. The lobbyists failed to achieve either objective, and Philip O'Sullivan Beare's credibility in Spain was further weakened when, in 1618, he was one of several people who had been involved in a skirmish in which Berehaven was killed.[59]

---

[57] Ciaran O'Scea, *Surviving Kinsale: Irish Emigration and Identity Formation in Early Modern Spain, 1601–40* (Manchester, 2015), 161–87; Benjamin Hazard, *Faith and Patronage: The Political Career of Flaithrí Ó Maolchonaire, C.1560–1629* (Dublin, 2010); Igor Pérez Tostado, *Irish Influence at the Court of Spain in the Seventeenth Century* (Dublin, 2008); Óscar Recio Morales, *Ireland and the Spanish Empire, 1600–1825* (Dublin, 2010), 48–101.

[58] O'Scea, *Surviving Kinsale*, 153.

[59] See a biographical note on Philip O'Sullivan Beare by Hiram Morgan, *Dictionary of Irish Biography*, 7, 986–8; Clare Carroll, 'From Defeat to Defiance; O'Sullivan Beare's account of the battle

SIXTEENTH AND SEVENTEENTH CENTURIES 47

O'Sullivan Beare had apparently been working on his *Compendium* despite such distractions but his text that he had brought to completion in 1618 was not published until 1621.[60] At this juncture Philip IV had succeeded his father on the throne, and Spain was about to renew conflict with the United Provinces, thus ending a military cessation that had obtained since 1608. In 1618 also, Ferdinand, a cousin to Philip IV who sat on the Austrian throne, had decided to recover the Crown of Bohemia from the Protestant Frederick, Elector of the Palatinate, who had defied Habsburg wishes by accepting an invitation from the nobility of Bohemia to become their king. It may have been the renewal of conflict on several fronts (a conflict that would become the Thirty Years War, 1618–48) that suggested to Philip O'Sullivan Beare that this was an opportune moment to publish his *Compendium*. He dedicated the work to Philip IV, asserting that Catholicism could survive in Ireland only if Spain resumed conflict with the British monarchy and encouraged an Irish insurrection against English rule. He expected this overture to prove tempting for Philip IV because Prince Frederick of the Palatinate, who had insulted the Habsburgs by accepting the Crown of Bohemia, was married to Elizabeth, daughter of King James of England. Moreover, there was a strong war faction at the English court seeking to have King James provide military support for his dispossessed son-in-law who was being hailed as a Protestant hero standing boldly against Habsburg aggression.

What O'Sullivan Beare and his associates had not anticipated was that, far from engaging in a continental war, King James had decided to seek a Spanish bride for his son and heir, Charles, Prince of Wales. Moreover, while the prolonged negotiations were under way, King James expressed himself willing to relax the legal disabilities under which his Catholic subjects had previously suffered. This meant that the purpose behind publishing the *Compendium* in 1621 was defeated by circumstances. Therefore it was not until 1625, when talks for a Spanish match with Charles, Prince of Wales, had broken down, that it became possible to again imagine that Spain would contemplate providing military support to Catholics in Ireland.[61]

If O'Sullivan Beare's text did not serve the immediate political purpose its author had intended, it provides a valuable insight into the narrative of Ireland's past that its author, and the particular cohort of Irish exiles with whom O'Sullivan Beare was associated, believed would best meet their present and future ambitions. The text itself, and also the unpublished writings composed by, or

---

of Kinsale, the campaign in west Cork, and the Great March', Hiram Morgan, ed., *The Battle of Kinsale* (Bray, 2004), 217–28; O'Scea, *Surviving Kinsale*, 44–5, 174–81.

[60] Philip O'Sullivan Beare, *Historiae Catholicae Iberniae Compendium* (Lisbon, 1621); *Ireland under Elizabeth*, ed. and trans., Matthew J. Byrne (Dublin, 1903); *Selections from the Zoilomastix of Philip O'Sullivan Beare*, ed., Thomas J. O'Donnell (Dublin, 1960).

[61] Alexander Salmon, ed., *The Spanish Match: Prince Charles's Journey to Madrid, 1623* (Aldershot, 2006); Glyn Redworth, 'Perfidious Hispania? Ireland and the Spanish Match, 1603–23', Hiram Morgan, ed., *The Battle of Kinsale*, 255–64.

48 IMAGINING IRELAND'S PASTS

attributed to, Philip O'Sullivan Beare, have been expertly and independently analysed by Clare Carroll, Hiram Morgan, and Ian Campbell, which makes it possible for me, on the basis of their work, to summarize the principal arguments of the *Compendium,* and to identify the issues over which O'Sullivan Beare and David Rothe differed.[62]

O'Sullivan Beare placed even more emphasis than had Rothe on the civility of Ireland's population before St Patrick had introduced them to Christianity, and on the Hispanic origins of the Milesians from whom, both agreed, Ireland's Gaelic population had sprung.[63] The supposed civility and nobility of Ireland's population explained for O'Sullivan Beare the ease with which the Irish had been converted to Christianity, and he was at one with Rothe concerning the vital role that Irish missionaries had played in re-Christianizing Europe, including Britain, in the aftermath of the barbaric invasions. This brought him quickly to what Gerald of Wales had had to say of the twelfth-century intervention by King Henry II in Ireland and of the role of the bull *Laudibiliter* in justifying that action. Here O'Sullivan Beare parted company with Rothe, first in questioning the integrity of Gerald of Wales (which meant challenging also the integrity of Richard Stanihurst who had written in that same tradition), and second in asserting that this twelfth-century English intervention in Ireland, like all subsequent involvement by English monarchs in Irish affairs, lacked legitimacy. Because of this, he argued that the Norman Invasion had introduced chaos to a previously ordered and reformed commonwealth and church. His essential propositions were that the Irish were more civil than the intruders and that English people had always been inclined towards heresy. O'Sullivan Bear's account of the injustices suffered by Irish people, especially those of Gaelic ancestry, who, he insisted, had never been conceded full legal rights under English law, served as a preliminary to his denigration of English rule after King Henry VIII had broken with the papacy. After this, he claimed, unjust rule had given way to tyrannical deeds by people who quickly lapsed into heresy.

This brief summary will make it clear that O'Sullivan Beare was at one with authors associated with the annalistic tradition in depicting those in the country of Gaelic ancestry as culturally superior to all newcomers from England, regardless of the century in which they had arrived. This brought him into immediate conflict with authors from the community of English descent in

---

[62] Clare Carroll, 'Irish and Spanish cultural and political relations in the work of O'Sullivan Beare', in Hiram Morgan, ed., *Political Ideology in Ireland, 1541–1641* (Dublin, 1999), 229–53; Clare Carroll, *Circe's Cup; Cultural Transformations in Early Modern Ireland* (Cork, 2001), esp. 104–34; Hiram Morgan, 'Un pueblo unido...: the politics of Philip O'Sullivan Beare', in Enrique García Hernán, Miguel Ángel de Bunes, Óscar Recio Morales, and Bernardo J. García García, eds., *Irlanda y la monarquía Hispánica, Kinsale, 1601–2001: Guerra, política, exilio y religión* (Madrid, 2002), 265–82; Ian Campbell, *Renaissance Humanism and Ethnicity before Race: The Irish and the English in the Seventeenth Century* (Manchester, 2013), esp. 87–96.

[63] For Rothe on the Milesian origin of the Irish see *Analecta*, 88.

Ireland who, proceeding from the assertion of Gerald of Wales that civilization had only come to Ireland with the Norman conquest, explained in their narratives how some of those people of English ancestry had 'degenerated' to the condition of their barbaric Gaelic neighbours. Instead, O'Sullivan Beare insisted that those people of English ancestry who had adopted the language, culture, and modes of succession of the Gaelic Irish, or who had intermarried with Gaelic families, had been or were in the process of becoming, elevated to the level of their Gaelic associates who were more honourable than they. This trans valuation of values, as it would have appeared to anybody who identified with the tradition of Gerald of Wales, meant that, where Rothe had spoken of an Irish nation being defined by the Catholicism of its members, O'Sullivan Beare drew a distinction between those in Ireland of Gaelic ancestry, whom he referred to as *veterens Iberni*, and those of English descent, whom he called *novi Iberni*. These latter, even when they adopted the language and customs of the Gaelic Irish, were necessarily less honourable than the Gaels because they were not of Milesian ancestry. O'Sullivan Beare conceded that some of the *novi Iberni* had been gradually melded into Gaelic society so as to be almost indistinguishable from their Gaelic mentors. However, he still insisted that those resident within the English Pale and in the principal towns who clung to English ways left themselves exposed to contamination from English malign influences and were therefore neither true Catholics nor true Irish even when they made claims to being both. The further evidence that O'Sullivan Beare cited to justify his compartmentalization of Ireland's Catholic population into two, or several, segments, was the behaviour of the different groups during the wars of the sixteenth century. He conceded that at that time many of the *novi Iberni* who had assimilated to Gaelic manners had joined with the '*veterens Iberni*' to establish a common front against the heretical English forces. However, he found that those of the *novi Iberni* who had remained Anglicized had stood aloof from the conflict or had supported the forces of the Crown.

O'Sullivan Beare's analysis of political and cultural divisions in Ireland served as a preliminary to his detailed narration of the succession of conflicts that had occurred in Ireland during the sixteenth century. He considered that each such insurrection had been part of a continuous effort by Irish lords, some of Gaelic descent and some of English ancestry, sometimes with assistance from the papacy and from Spain and sometimes fighting on their own, to defend Catholicism and their patrimonies from the heretical English who had been aided by pernicious allies of Irish birth. Because of the importance he attached to continuity and to Continental connections, O'Sullivan Beare termed the conflict the Fifteen Years' War, and he gave particular attention to the fighting and the destruction of property and society that had been perpetrated by the forces of the Crown in the province of Munster both in the 1580s and in the years leading up to the final expulsion of his own family and their dependants from Ireland in 1602. His

50 IMAGINING IRELAND'S PASTS

narrative drew variously on the recollections of soldiers who had fought in the final phase of the conflict, and on the records of the sufferings of Catholics that had been recorded by those clergy who had found refuge on the Continent. The result was a graphic depiction of the sufferings endured by those (including his own family) who, as he represented it, had fought for their faith as well as their patrimonies. Even as O'Sullivan Beare deplored that some in Ireland who professed Catholicism had failed to rally to the cause, he was writing essentially to solicit further military support from Spain to support renewed conflict in Ireland. O'Sullivan Beare continued to argue therefore that the Spanish monarchy should consider itself obliged to support such an initiative. He believed that the monarch had such a responsibility, first because those Irish who had lost their inheritances and were living in exile had been encouraged by Spain to confront the English heretics who lorded over them, and second because Irish nobles who had suffered during the course of the conflict belonged to the same Milesian genetic stock as Spain's own nobility.

When we consider together the histories composed by Rothe and by O'Sullivan Beare, it becomes clear that they were both seeking to imagine a past that would prove useful to the community that each was addressing, and provide that same community with guidance on how they might best navigate their way in an uncertain future. The two authors were in general agreement over the facts concerning the sufferings that Irish people had endured at the hands of unthinking Crown officials in the recent past, and they were of one mind also that religious persecution, leading even to martyrdom, had been a fundamental aspect of what the Irish had suffered during those decades. However, Rothe seemed to accept that what had been lost could never be recovered. This led to his pragmatic recommendation that those Irish Catholics who had survived the cataclysm should—regardless of ancestry—work co-operatively both to avert possible future reverses and to negotiate an improvement upon their present condition.

This conciliatory approach obviously held no appeal for O'Sullivan Beare and other exiles whose only hope of recovering their lost status and patrimonies rested with future military action aided by Spain. To this end, O'Sullivan Beare constructed a version of Ireland's past to match his ambitions for its future. The past he imagined was very much in the Gaelic tradition that identified Irish people, usually claiming Milesian ancestry, who had, in every generation since the Norman Conquest, presented forceful resistance to a corrupting English presence in the country. This resistance, as he represented it, had become more strident in recent decades when English influence had become especially malignant following the onset of the Protestant Reformation. Then, as O'Sullivan Beare detailed the course of these insurrections, which became part of continuous war, he glorified the actions of the leaders on the Irish side. In the course of doing so he also identified those individuals and groups in Ireland who had taken the side of the Crown against their countrymen and co-religionists. The narrative that he unfolded made it apparent that it was these latter, for the most part, who had retained control of their patrimonies in Ireland, while those who had challenged the English presence had either lost their lives or been forced into exile after they had been deprived of their estates and social positions. Therefore the *Nationis Hibernorum* of Rothe's imagination held little meaning or appeal for O'Sullivan Beare. This was so because it provided no place for the exiled community to which he belonged. The only hope that this community would recover the status and property of which it had been unjustly deprived relied upon further Spanish invasion of Ireland that O'Sullivan Beare's *Historia Catholicae Iberniae* was written to justify.

2.6 Geoffrey Keating's, *Foras Feasa ar Éirinn*: A History for the Catholic Community in Ireland

The fact that David Rothe and Philip O'Sullivan Beare each chose to publish in Latin suggests that they wrote primarily with Continental audiences and elite (largely clerical) Irish audiences in mind. Geoffrey Keating, on the other hand, opted to write in Irish obviously with the intention of directing his material, much of it only in manuscript copy, towards those Catholic audiences in Ireland where Irish was the vernacular. The readers he would have had in mind are likely to have been members of the learned elite (or what survived of them) in Gaelic Ireland, and the many priests serving in the country who had not had the benefit of seminary training. What he communicated was therefore probably designed to further the education of priests and literate laity, and it certainly provided clergy with material to incorporate into their sermons, and Irish language poets with themes they were to repeat and develop in their compositions.

Geoffrey Keating (*c*.1580–1644), like Rothe, was of English lineage and, again like Rothe, came from a fairly comfortable family background—in his case from a farming community in south Tipperary. He appears to have grown up there before proceeding to the Continent for the formal education he received at Douai and Rheims (where he appears to have been awarded the degree of Doctor of Divinity). Then he seems to have taught for a time at the Irish college that had been established at Bordeaux in 1603. He became well known for his publication of two theological works in the Irish language that would certainly have assisted priests in Ireland in the preparation of sermons. After an extensive sojourn on the Continent, Keating became involved with pastoral work in his own native diocese of Lismore from the beginning of the 1620s until his death, no later than 1644. It is likely that he was compiling evidence for his *Foras Feasa* from the moment of his return to Ireland, or even before then, since his text was ready for circulation

52 IMAGINING IRELAND'S PASTS

in Irish language manuscript formats from the close of 1634 onward. An English translation of the work, again in manuscript form, was available by 1635, and a Latin manuscript translation was made on the Continent during the 1650s.[64]

Bernadette Cunningham has established all of these details in her definitive study of Keating and his *Foras Feasa*. She has also established that Keating's *Foras Feasa* became the most influential interpretation of Ireland's past available to the Catholic community in Ireland whose first language was Irish during the seventeenth century. To support her case she has calculated the frequency with which reference was made to the *Foras Feasa* in other seventeenth-century texts, and she has demonstrated how several of the themes developed by Keating were duplicated in demotic Gaelic verse narrations of Ireland's history composed over the course of the later seventeenth century and into the eighteenth century.[65]

Despite its proven popularity in the seventeenth century, Keating's *Foras Feasa* may not seem especially relevant to this present study given that, unlike Rothe or O'Sullivan Beare, Keating said nothing directly of events in Ireland during the sixteenth and seventeenth centuries in a work that was principally concerned with the history of Ireland from the time of Adam to the English conquest of the twelfth century. However, the work warrants attention here because Keating, like all historians, intended the past of which he wrote to be usable for people of his own time, and he developed many of his arguments about Ireland's ancient past to assist the interpretation of more recent events. His purpose, as he made clear in his polemical preface (*díonbhrollach*), was to counter the renditions of Ireland's past that had been communicated by a named list of authors who, he insisted, had all been inspired by the negative portrayal of Ireland's Gaelic population presented in the twelfth century by Gerald of Wales. His list of offenders included Edmund Spenser, Richard Stanihurst, Meredith Hanmer, William Camden, John Barclay, Fynes Moryson, Sir John Davies, and Edmund Campion. Of these only Hanmer and Barclay had written specifically about the earlier centuries to which Keating gave prime attention.[66]

As he proceeded, Keating cast doubt on the integrity or credibility of each of the adversaries he identified by pointing to particular erroneous assertions that each had made. He also dismissed them collectively because they had followed slavishly in the wake of Gerald of Wales [*ar lorg Chambrens*].[67] This indebtedness,

---

[64] Bernadette Cunningham, *The World of Geoffrey Keating: History, Myth and Religion in Seventeenth-Century Ireland* (Dublin, 2000), 173, 176, 187; biographical entry by Bernadette Cunningham, *Dictionary of Irish Biography*, vol. 5, 42–4; Pádraig Ó Riain, ed., *Geoffrey Keating's Foras Feasa ar Éirinn: Reassessments* (London, 2008).

[65] Cunningham, *The World of Geoffrey Keating*.

[66] Another of his contemporaries who Keating upbraided for having written negatively was Samuel Daniel who in 1612, and again in 1617, had published a history of England from earliest times to the reign of Edward III.

[67] Keating, *Foras Feasa ar Éirinn le Seathrún Céitinn D.D.: The History of Ireland by Geoffrey Keating D.D.*, vol. 1, 12.

he asserted, was exposed by the tendency of all authors to introduce their various works by praising the natural resources of Ireland as a preliminary to debasing its population in the past and degrading it in the present. Keating likened all such authors to beetles who, when fluttering about in summertime, passed over sweet-smelling flowers before alighting and wallowing in animal dung. All his named rivals had, according to this analogy, offended both by ignoring the virtuous, spiritual, and hospitable actions of Irish nobles of Gaelic and of English ancestry, and by mocking these same lords and their descendants for their supposed cultural deficits. As he warmed to this theme in his preface, Keating asserted that nobles in Ireland had been such generous patrons of scholarship that Ireland had come to possess one of the most extensive literary archives of any European country.

One purpose behind Keating's decision to dwell on Ireland's earlier history was to demonstrate both the variety and richness of that archive and his own ability to study and appreciate it.[68] The emphasis he thus placed on sources and skills made it possible for him to dismiss the history of Ireland in earlier times that had been published as recently as 1633 by Meredith Hanmer, an English Protestant divine. Hanmer had written with distinction about the early history of England but he was, in Keating's opinion, unqualified to write of Ireland's history because he was neither familiar with the pertinent archive nor with the language with which to unlock its secrets.[69] Keating found that Richard Stanihurst also fell short of these standards even as he acknowledged that Stanihurst was of the same genetic stock as himself, who also, like Keating, had become a priest.[70] The ultimate transgression of Stanihurst, according to Keating, was that he had made a virtue of being ignorant of the Irish language lest any association with it should diminish his own cultural standing. An outraged Keating pronounced that Stanihurst was unfit to be considered a historian on three grounds. First, he had begun to write on Ireland's history at such an early age that he could not possibly have mastered the knowledge and skills that the task demanded; second, Stanihurst had continued to be blindly ignorant [*dall aineolach*] of the Irish language and therefore also of the sources appertaining to Ireland's pre-conquest past; and third, he was ambitious [*uaillmhianach*], by which Keating meant that Stanihurst

---

[68] Keating, *Foras Feasa ar Éirinn*, vol. 1, 4–5, 80–3.

[69] Meredith Hanmer, Chronicle of Ireland, James Ware, ed., *A Historie of Ireland,...Hanmer...Ca mpion...and Spenser* (Dublin, 1633); For a biographical note on Hanmer see that by Judy Barry, *Dictionary of Irish Biography*, vol. 4, 437–8.

[70] Keating, *Foras Feasa ar Éirinn*, vol. 1, 42–3, contended that Stanihurst in his later years, following his ordination, had 'promised to recall most part of the contemptuous things he had written concerning Ireland' and that his revised opinion was 'now in print, to be exhibited in Ireland'. This passage seems to satisfy some recent scholars that Stanihurst, in *De Rebus in Hibernia Gestis*, looked more generously on the Gaelic Irish than he had done in his earlier work. Any such amelioration in attitude was, as I have argued in Chapter 1, never more than modest.

54 IMAGINING IRELAND'S PASTS

had written negatively of his country and its people in the hope of receiving pre-ferment in return.[71]

The tone of Keating's onslaught upon those from Britain and the English Pale, who had presented as received wisdom what he represented as ill-informed accounts of Ireland's pre-conquest past, indicates how committed he was to circulating a counter-narrative to discredit their contention that without the twelfth-century English conquest of Ireland the Gaelic Irish would never have been rescued from incivility and obscurity. He challenged this assumption first by detailing the richness of the literary archive that the Gaelic Irish had been assembling from a remarkably early date and the noble actions that had stemmed from that commitment to learning. This was a prelude to his questioning the veracity of the account of the twelfth-century conquest that had been provided by Gerald of Wales.

Keating's exposition on the cultural richness of life in pre-Christian Ireland explained the facility with which the Gaelic Irish had been converted to Christianity. Then, following the example of Rothe, Keating detailed how Christianity had quickly flourished in Ireland and become internationally famous. This Christian fervour had persisted, he contended, until some of Ireland's leaders had succumbed to the sin of pride, after which God had permitted the Vikings to assail them and deprive them of wealth, power, and territory. The humiliation and persecution that then descended on the country had endured, according to Keating, until a penitent Brian Bóroimhe, Ireland's High King, was given divine assistance to defeat the Vikings at the battle of Clontarf in 1014. Even then the price of victory was high because Brian was assassinated by one of the vanquished even as he was offering thanks to God for his success.

Keating, like Rothe, accepted that the interlude following the death of Brian Bóroimhe was one of political uncertainty in Ireland but one in which the Irish Church had, nonetheless, succeeded in re-structuring itself along diocesan lines, and one when Ireland's true nobles [*fíoruaisle Éireann*] ceded the High Kinship of Ireland to Pope Urban II in 1092 because they had been unable to agree among themselves on a political succession. Thereafter, according to Keating, 'the Pope of Rome had possession of, and authority and sovereignty over Ireland' until 1154 when Pope Adrian IV granted the lordship of Ireland to Henry II, and in doing so had bound that king and his successors to the terms of the bull *Laudibiliter*.[72]

This sometimes fanciful construction of events by Keating made it possible for him to suggest that Pope Adrian, an Englishman, had been mistaken or misled into thinking that the Irish Church was in need of reform. He then asserted that the Church had fallen into the dilapidated condition in which Gerald of Wales

---

[71] Keating, *Foras Feasa ar Éirinn*, vol. 1, 40–3.
[72] Keating, *Foras Feasa ar Éirinn*, vol. 3, 346–7; Keating seems to have taken liberty with known facts in making this claim for the surrender of Ireland to Pope Urban in 1092.

had found it only because five knights from England and Wales, who had preceded Henry II to Ireland, had undone much of the good work that had been promoted by Irish lords over the previous century. These five—Strongbow [Richard de Clare Earl of Pembroke] (whom Keating referred to as Stranguell [*iarla o' Stranguell*]), Robert Fitz Stephen, Hugo de Lacy, John de Courcy, and William Fitz Aldemel—with some unnamed accomplices, had, according to Keating, 'through the plundering of churches and clerics, bloody deeds of treachery and violent tyranny' effected 'more evil deeds than all the Gaels that lived from the time of Brian to the Norman invasion'. Then, as Keating detailed the tyrannical acts of these five offenders, he explained how, due to their own misdeeds [*trén-a n-olcaibh féin*], the majority [*urmhór*] of them, together with some unnamed followers, had not been blessed by sons to inherit what they had seized.[73] This hint at further divine intervention enabled Keating to conclude that the population of English descent, who constituted a significant element of Ireland's population in his own time, were not the seed of conquerors, as Gerald of Wales and Stanihurst had insisted. Rather, he contended, these were the descendants of other lords [*taoisigh oile*] who had been invited to Ireland by King Henry II after he had accepted submissions from most existing Gaelic lords in Ireland who had recognized him as their sovereign ruler as they had been enjoined to do by papal decree.[74]

These actions by King Henry had, in the eyes of Keating, legitimized him and his successors as the rightful rulers of Ireland. Similarly, the cohort of lords and their descendants, who had been introduced to Ireland by King Henry II, had become legitimate rulers because they had done 'much good through building churches and abbeys and giving church lands to clerics for their support'. As a consequence, God had blessed them with plentiful progeny that included such prominent noble dynasties as the Fitzgeralds, the Burkes, the Butlers, and the Barrys. Then, having identified these senior houses, Keating listed a string of lesser lineages, including his own family, who, by their actions, had, regardless of rank, proven themselves noble.[75]

As he rewrote the history of Ireland's ancient past and of the conquest of the twelfth century, Keating was discarding the contention that had preoccupied most previous authors, whether of Gaelic or English ancestry, over which ruling group should be entrusted with Ireland's destiny. Then, out of desire to end the traditional animosity that had vexed relations between lords of Gaelic and English descent, Keating proposed that respect should be shown to all lords whose ancestors had behaved nobly.[76] To facilitate this, Keating encouraged his readers

---

[73] Keating, *Foras Feasa ar Éirinn*, vol. 3, 358–69; quotation 358.

[74] Keating, *Foras Feasa ar Éirinn*, vol. 3, 368–9.

[75] Keating, *Foras Feasa ar Éirinn*, vol. 3, 368–9.

[76] On changing and conflicting concepts of honour in early modern Ireland see Brendan Kane, *The Politics and Culture of Honour in Britain and Ireland, 1541–1641* (Cambridge, 2010).

56 IMAGINING IRELAND'S PASTS

to engage in what might best be described as a Freudian exercise in active forgetfulness, which he sustained through the full course of *Foras Feasa ar Éirinn* by disregarding the internecine conflict that previous authors, in every tradition, had considered the most striking feature of Ireland's history in earlier centuries. Had Keating taken account of this, his narrative would likely have been overwhelmed by evidence of disunity between Irish lords, and of occasional warfare between one or more of Ireland's noble houses and representatives of the Crown. The pursuit of any such narrative would have brought him inevitably to the field of Kinsale where representatives of Irish noble families, and even members of the same Irish noble house, had fought on opposing sides. By ignoring such realities, and by refusing to follow Stanihurst and O'Sullivan Beare in decreeing whether it was families of Gaelic or of English ancestry (*Gael nó Gall*) that were best equipped to uphold civility in Ireland, Keating was able to salute as *Éireannaigh* [Irish people] all those whose behaviour showed them to be worthy members of the community. Keating seems to have considered this nomenclature an Irish-language equivalent of Rothe's *Nationis Hibernorum*, since each presumed that all people who had been born in Ireland who were Catholic and who (and whose ancestors) had behaved honourably were a singular people. These too were of one mind that they should respect the suzerainty of England's monarchs over Ireland because the papacy had decreed that King Henry II and his descendants should rule there.[77] Thus the conclusion and the guiding principle that Keating had divined from ancient history were reasonably consonant with those at which David Rothe had arrived by using evidence relating to more recent happenings. Also, like Rothe, Keating was writing about people resident in Ireland and *Foras Feasa* offered scant consolation to those Irish forced to live in exile.

2.7 Conclusion

This chapter will have shown that all literate elements in what was still a complex Irish society registered some response in historical format to what they would have seen as the traumatic events that had beset their country during the sixteenth and seventeenth centuries. The annalists among them could do little more than

---

[77] Cunningham, *The World of Geoffrey Keating*, 109–11, 131. I would suggest that Keating did not always employ the word *Éireannaigh* as a generic substitute for *Gael* and *Gall*. From my reading of the text I find that Keating first used the term in *Foras Feasa ar Éirinn* (vol. 1, 8) to designate the pre-Christian inhabitants of the island. Later he employed the word (Keating, *Foras Feasa ar Éirinn*, vol. 1, 58) to describe the inhabitants of Ireland as a human collectivity regardless of rank. Then, in the course of translating a passage from Sir John Davies where that author had referred to the Catholic Irish of his own time as a single people regardless of lineage, Keating then followed the example of Davies and used the word *Éireannaigh* (Keating, *Foras Feasa ar Éirinn*, vol. 3, 368) to describe Catholics in Ireland as a single people.

record their despair at the coarsening of daily life, and explain how difficult it was to envision what future they, and the communities they served, might expect. We have learned also how those literate people who had escaped the maelstrom at home by establishing contact with educational institutions in Catholic Europe recognized the need to write histories for Ireland offering some rational explanation of what had happened in the recent past that would provide guidance for the future.

One stimulus to write histories of Ireland came from the realization that scholars in their host countries had been devoting considerable attention to revisiting the past glories of their ancestors and claiming a place for their particular polities, and for Catholicism, in a European political environment that was undergoing rapid change. Such official histories always had some polemical aspect, which became strident, when, as happened in France and the Low Countries, it proved necessary to discredit alternative views of the past that had been put forward by Protestant dissidents within their own communities. These various histories provided models for Irish authors in exile—as they did for Catholic exiles from other European countries (including England and Scotland)—and encouraged them to write histories to counter what were becoming official Protestant narratives. In the case of Irish authors in exile, their concern was to defend the standing and reputation of Ireland and its people from its detractors, and to explain why the exiles, and their kin at home, should be given foreign assistance to uphold the position of Catholicism in the land of their birth.

It was especially important for those who went to Spain that they should write histories of Ireland that would clear the Irish population, and especially the Gaelic Irish population, of the disparagement that had been cast upon their ancestors by Gerald of Wales, whose compositions continued to be known and respected on the Continent. This was all the more pertinent because Gerald of Wales had been used by Richard Stanihurst to denigrate the current generation of Irish people of Gaelic descent. Ciaran O'Scea has explained that apologetic histories of Ireland suited to countering the views of Gerald of Wales and his recent imitators were urgently required because exiles from Ireland were disembarking in large numbers in La Coruña and its hinterland at the precise moment when thousands of Moriscos and Jewish *conversos* were being expelled from Spain on the grounds that they did not meet with Castilian or Christian standards of civility.[78] Under these circumstances, histories were needed to demonstrate how Irish people had contributed to the enhancement of civil and Christian living both at home and abroad, in the past and in the present. Irish Catholic history writing of these decades was understandably polemical, and even occasionally providential, given

[78] O'Scea, *Surviving Kinsale*, 153–5.

58 IMAGINING IRELAND'S PASTS

the recent experience that had forced the authors into exile. However, its unique feature was that authors devoted particular attention to proving through history the civility of all of Ireland's populations including those of Gaelic ancestry who had been subjected to particular criticism by Gerald of Wales and those who wrote in that tradition.

We have detailed in this chapter how several authors met this requirement, and how the differences in interpretation that emerged in this fresh body of writing were influenced principally by whether the authors believed that they, and the Irish communities they served, could look forward to a secure future in Ireland or that, short of some unexpected turn of fortune's wheel, they would likely live permanently in exile. Rothe, writing in Latin, and Keating, writing in Irish, were the representatives of the first historical stream, while O'Sullivan Beare, writing in Latin, made the case for the dispossessed. In doing so he held out the hope that these would one day recover through military means the status and property of which they had been unjustly deprived.

Authors may have differed about future prospects, but what they all wrote was polemical to the extent that they represented the recent struggle that had taken place in Ireland as primarily religious in character. Therefore, through the citation of historical examples, they were setting out to prove that loyalty to Catholicism was a prerequisite to being considered Irish. This meant that, in their view, members of Irish families, such as the O'Briens of Thomond and the Butlers of Ormond who had converted to Protestantism, were no more entitled to be considered Irish than were Protestant planters and officials from England and Scotland who had settled in the country in the recent past.

Marc Caball does not consider this an especially original insight since he has been able to demonstrate, from an analysis of Gaelic verse composed during those same decades, that what he refers to as the 'collocation' of Gaelic culture and Catholicism had become a commonplace in Irish language poetry, especially that composed in exile. In support of this he has drawn attention to a well-known poem composed by Keating himself in 1606, where that author gave voice to these sentiments long before he returned to Ireland to compose his *Foras Feasa*.[79] This observation, I would suggest, is both original and correct and explains that what often have been treated as two distinct literary elements should be considered separate seams in a single body of knowledge. However, I would suggest that the formal histories, published or in manuscript, served as repositories of knowledge that poets could draw upon selectively to serve whatever political position or stratagem was favoured by the patrons or the communities they served at particular moments.

---

[79] Marc Caball, *Poets and Politics: Reaction and Continuity in Irish Poetry, 1558–1625* (Cork, 1998), see esp. 130–1.

SIXTEENTH AND SEVENTEENTH CENTURIES   59

Thus we find that poets who wrote from exile tended to replicate the ideas that had been put forward by O'Sullivan Beare, whereas poets patronized by families with an apparently secure position in Ireland favoured the more conciliatory narrative of Ireland's history delineated by each of Rothe and Keating. Such tendencies would explain the optimistic poems that favoured the stance taken by Catholic political actors in Ireland in their dealings with the government of King Charles I when negotiating an improvement in their condition. Such optimism, and poems to sustain it, persisted into the early 1640s when the Confederation of Kilkenny was in its infancy. Its motto, pro *Deo, pro Rege, et pro Patria*, reads like a summation of what Rothe and Keating had written. However, when the Confederacy broke into factions along the traditional Old English/Gaelic Irish fault lines, and when Archbishop Rinuccini, the papal nuncio to Ireland, was denied support from the more conservative members of the Confederacy, Gaelic poets looked more to the arguments articulated by O'Sullivan Beare. These arguments, with which Rinuccini was in full agreement, held that it was only those Irish of Gaelic ancestry who had adhered rigidly to the dictates of the papacy who could be regarded as truly Irish. This meant that, for the nuncio, those of Irish birth who had consorted closely with the English government and its laws were necessarily tainted by heresy even when they were professed Catholics.[80]

---

[80] Tadhg Ó hAnnracháin, *Catholic Reformation in Ireland: The Mission of Rinuccini, 1645–1649* (Oxford, 2002), 212–23.

3
New Histories for a New Ireland

3.1 Introduction

Most of the histories we have been considering in the first two chapters were written either because their authors wished to defend the English interest in Ireland when it seemed in doubt, or because various Irish authors wished to reclaim some respect for Ireland's Gaelic and/or Catholic pasts that were being disparaged by critics. One purpose behind the disparagement was to justify a conquest of Ireland, and commentators were divided over whether this was a fresh re-conquest or the completion of a process that had been under way since the twelfth century. There was no doubt however that a conquest had been accomplished, after which a fresh cohort of authors who had supported that effort dedicated themselves to writing new histories for Ireland to celebrate, or even to take credit for, its achievement. More particularly, authors ransacked the past for lessons that would help them delineate possible futures for a country over which the authority of a British monarch had been established for the first time. These same authors considered their responsibility all the greater because the monarch was a Protestant.

One of the concerns of all authors was that those who had been vanquished were numerically the dominant element in the country's population, and remained in possession of the principal resources of the country. This was compounded by the fact that they continued to be attached to the old religion. On the positive side our authors all believed that the legitimacy of the British monarch's claim to rule over Ireland could no longer be questioned since it had just been reasserted by conquest.

Some of those who had been closely associated with the fighting came forward to describe and celebrate what they had witnessed or experienced. Their discussion of military matters left civilian and clerical authors free to reflect on the past, including the recent past, as they pondered how they might shape a state and/or church that would accommodate natives as well as newcomers within a framework of governance pleasing both to their peers and the monarchy in London. From the first category of authors we will consider histories written by Thomas Stafford and Thomas Gainsford, and from the many authors who discussed civil and church matters in historical context we will consider works by John Davies, James Ussher, and James Ware.

Imagining Ireland's Pasts: Early Modern Ireland through the Centuries. Nicholas Canny, Oxford University Press (2021). © Nicholas Canny. DOI: 10.1093/oso/9780198808961.003.0003

3.2 Stafford and Gainsford: Memorialists of War

Thomas Stafford (1576?–1655) was the natural born son of Sir George Carew (later earl of Totnes) by an Irish mother who had been married to a Captain Stafford having served in Ireland under Carew's command.[1] Carew himself had had a long and varied military experience in Ireland, commencing in 1569–70 when he had supported his cousin Sir Peter Carew during that adventurer's tempestuous involvement with the Butler Revolt. The pinnacle of George Carew's Irish career was the interlude, 1600–03, when he served as Lord President of Munster. During those years, Stafford was employed by his father in a secretarial capacity, but was released intermittently from his duties to engage with military and naval activity in the later stages of the war in Munster.[2] Although not published until 1633, *Pacata Hibernia* had been 'composed', according to Stafford, 'by the direction and appointment' of Carew 'while the actions were fresh in the memories of men'. Given this commission, Stafford expounded upon the virtues and achievements of Carew in Munster both in the years preceding the Spanish invasion of that province in September 1601 and during the course of the ensuing conflict that included not only the battle of Kinsale on 24 December 1601 but the mopping-up operation that persisted in west Munster until the taking of Dunboy Castle. This episode, as noted in Chapter 2, was also of particular interest to Philip O'Sullivan Beare because it was then that the last of the Spanish contingent surrendered and returned to Spain. It was then also that those of the Irish, including the O'Sullivan Beare family, who had remained attached to the Spanish to the end, were forced to abandon their lands and find refuge on the Continent.[3]

Stafford detailed how Carew had taken steps to ensure the loyalty of most Irish lords in Munster in the years preceding the Spanish invasion. These actions, he insisted, had left the Spaniards without significant allies in Munster until Red Hugh O'Donnell and Hugh O'Neill, earl of Tyrone, marched from Ulster with their respective armies to join forces with the Spaniards who had been pinned within the town of Kinsale by the royal army. Stafford gave particular attention to Carew's service, together with that of his Irish allies, in forcing the Spanish invading force to withdraw from all the positions they had occupied in Munster.

The purpose of *Pacata Hibernia*, according to Stafford, was to celebrate the 'great actions of worthy and eminent persons', and particularly those of his own

---

[1] On Stafford see the biographical note by Terry Clavin and Darren McGettigan in the *Dictionary of Irish Biography*, vol. 8, 1112–4.

[2] On Carew see the biographical note by Terry Clavin in the *Dictionary of Irish Biography*, vol. 2, 326–33.

[3] Thomas Stafford, *Pacata Hibernia, Ireland Appeased and Reduced: or A History of the Late Warres of Ireland, Especially within the Province of Mounster*...(London, 1633) reprinted under the title *Pacata Hibernia; or a History of the Wars in Ireland, during the Reign of Queen Elizabeth* (2 vols., Dublin, 1810); quotation from the 1810 edition, vol. 1, 'Dedication to the reader'; Clare Carroll, 'From Defeat to Defiance', Hiram Morgan, ed., *The Battle of Kinsale*, 217–28.

62 IMAGINING IRELAND'S PASTS

natural father whose property and papers he had inherited in 1629 on the death of Carew, by then earl of Totnes. Stafford's complaint was that Carew's contribution to the war had not been adequately recognized. To rectify this, Stafford insinuated repeatedly that it was Carew's far-sighted actions in asserting Crown authority over Munster rather than the much-vaunted strategic vision of Mountjoy that explained why English arms had prevailed not only on the battlefield at Kinsale but also in the later tortuous fighting in west Munster for which Carew had been solely responsible.[4] Stafford's *Pacata Hibernia* may therefore be considered a counterbalance to Fynes Moryson's *Itinerary* where that author, who had been Mountjoy's secretary, credited his master with every military success in Ireland from 1599 until the final submission of Hugh O'Neill, earl of Tyrone, in March 1603.[5] Moreover where Moryson limited himself to describing what he had witnessed and to praising Mountjoy for his patience and far-sightedness, Stafford identified his own work as a 'History' to serve multiple purposes since history was 'a powerful suggester and Recorder of God's providence in public Blessings and Judgements, the Mother of Experience, the Nurse of Truth [and] the common bond and ligature, which unites present times with all ages past, and makes them one'.[6]

The 'subject matter' of his history was, in Stafford's words 'the final Dispersion of that cloud of rebellion, which hath so long hung over that Kingdom of Ireland...performed by the prudent fortitude of the English Nation', and more particularly by the 'Actions' of George Carew previous to, at, and subsequent to the battle of Kinsale, 'the last and greatest Scene of that Tragedie'. He was confident that his narrative would give his English readers reason to exult in 'the puissant valour of [their] victorious Countrymen', because, as well as suppressing rebels in Ireland, they had confronted 'a powerful Invasion of a brave and warlike Nation [the Spanish]' who they had 'sent home to their Native Land'. However, Stafford was satisfied that his history also included 'much matter of contentment' for Irish readers because they could there 'observe the loyal fidelity of the greater part [of the Irish Nation] to their lawful Prince, though animated to disloyalty by the strongest persuasions of their Spiritual Pastor, with promises of heavenly reward'.[7]

This criticism of the papacy, and several other anti-Catholic outbursts in the text, suggest that with *Pacata Hibernia* Stafford was continuing the Protestant apocalyptic narrative of Ireland's past from where John Hooker had left off. Such influences are not surprising since Hooker, as mentioned in Chapter 1, had first come to Ireland as a client of Sir Peter Carew, and some of Hooker's unpublished

---

[4] Stafford, *Pacata Hibernia*, vol. 1, 'Dedication to the king'.
[5] Fynes Moryson, *An Itinerary*...(London, 1617), 4 vols., Glasgow, 1907–08); Graham Kew, ed., 'The Irish Sections of Fynes Moryson's Unpublished Itinerary', *Analecta Hibernica*, 37 (1998), 79–132.
[6] Stafford, *Pacata Hibernia*, vol. 1, 'Dedication to the king'.
[7] Stafford, *Pacata Hibernia*, vol. 1, 'Dedication to the reader'.

writings were retained among the papers of George Carew. Moreover, part of Stafford's text was, by his own admission, drawn from 'a General History of that Kingdom of Ireland' that he had found unfinished among Carew's papers.[8] Such accidents, I would suggest, explain the occasional intrusion of Hooker-like anti-Catholic invective into Stafford's text.[9] However, by 1633, when Stafford's text was published, his outlook would have differed considerably from that of Hooker because, following his service in Ireland, Stafford had attended first at the court of Queen Anne, the Danish wife of King James VI and I who had Catholic leanings, and subsequently at the court of Queen Henrietta Maria, a committed Catholic whose court served as a haven for English, Irish, and foreign Catholics.

Where we can isolate Stafford's personal opinion within a text that was composed of different elements, we find that he had reached the conclusion that neither the papacy nor the Spanish monarchy had ever had any real interest in Ireland in itself but had considered the country rather as a 'bridge' over which Spanish troops might have 'invaded England, the conquest and ruin whereof was the main mark whereat they aimed'.[10] When it came to discussing events in Ireland, Stafford considered that the service of George Carew had demonstrated how Irish lords, including those who professed Catholicism, might be induced, or persuaded, to become reliable supporters of the Crown when handled firmly. Thus he described how when Carew had taken up his duties as president of Munster he had found 'all the inhabitants...in open and actual rebellion, except some few of the better sort' and the cities and walled town particularly 'besotted and bewitched with the Popish priests, Jesuits and seminaries [seminary priests]'.[11] It was to Carew's credit, claimed Stafford, that he had retained the allegiance of these 'few' loyal supporters of the Crown who might otherwise have joined with the lords of the other provinces in 'a strict combination...to make themselves absolute commanders of all Ireland' and to have the English 'banished'.[12] Carew's strategy, according to Stafford, was to work closely with those who remained loyal with the purpose of winning or compelling the loyalty of others. The result was that, when the Spaniards had first disembarked at Kinsale and points further west, they attracted few significant local supporters.

When he conceded that some lords who had been won over by Carew had subsequently defected to the invaders, Stafford considered this 'little wonder' 'considering what power religion and gold hath in the hearts of men, both which

---

[8] Stafford, *Pacata Hibernia*, vol. 1, 'Dedication to the king'.

[9] Stafford's outburst concerning the Pope's excommunication of Queen Elizabeth in 1570, for example (Stafford, *Pacata Hibernia*, vol. 2, 678–9), used much the same terminology as had Hooker in his bombastic denunciation of 'the antichristian lowing of this prophane bull [that did] lively delineate and plainly demonstrate that purple harlot, which had made all nations drunk with the dregs of her fornication, having seated herself upon the seven hills of Rome'.

[10] Stafford, *Pacata Hibernia*, vol. 2, 350–1; this assertion chimes with the interpretation outlined in Glyn Redworth, 'Perfidious Hispania?', Hiram Morgan, ed., *The Battle of Kinsale*, 255–64.

[11] Stafford, *Pacata Hibernia*, vol. 1, 5–6.   [12] Stafford, *Pacata Hibernia*, vol. 1, 2.

the Spanish brought with them into Ireland'.[13] However, despite such defections, Strafford was satisfied that sufficient of 'the well affected Irish' remained steadfast, and he considered this the factor that had made victory possible.[14] Among the loyal ones, Stafford instanced Richard Burke, fourth earl of Clanricard, compared with whom 'no man did bloody his sword more than his Lordship did' on the field of battle, and who permitted his men to take no prisoners, despite their opponents being their fellow countrymen and co-religionists. Stafford therefore considered it appropriate that Lord Mountjoy had knighted Clanricard on the field of battle, and that Clanricard had received a special letter of commendation from Queen Elizabeth. To make it clear that Clanricard was not the only one in his family who had remained loyal, Stafford also detailed the military services of Sir Thomas Burke, the earl's brother.[15]

Where Stafford isolated for special commendation the Catholic earl of Clanricard, with whom he had probably become acquainted at the court of Henrietta Maria, his praise for the Protestant Donogh O'Brien, fourth earl of Thomond, was even more fulsome.[16] Here, he detailed the role Thomond had played at the siege of Dunboy Castle and later in bringing recalcitrant lords in County Kerry to heel. Stafford declared himself particularly impressed because Thomond had severed all connections with his sister Honora, the wife of Thomas Fitzmaurice, baron Lixnaw, once he suspected that she and her husband had behaved treacherously in dealing with the Crown.[17] Thomond, he believed, not only exemplified how loyally an Irish lord could behave but had proven himself effective in negotiating with his fellow countrymen, probably because he could communicate with them in their own language. Even the notorious rebel Captain Richard Tyrell, according to Stafford, would have 'negotiated with Thomond but the Jesuit Archer, Fitz Morris and Donell Osulevan would not permit him'.[18] Thomond, he claimed, had gone into battle confident of success because he had learnt from a prophecy that Kinsale was 'a place ordained wherein the honour and safety of the queen of England, the reputation of the English nation, the cause of religion, and the crown of Ireland must be by arms disputed'.[19]

While Stafford praised the proven loyalty of these two Irish lords (one Catholic and one Protestant), he wrote also of the 'false hearts of the superstitious Irish', as exemplified by John Burke of County Limerick who, despite having assumed the appearance of being loyal after he had 'married a daughter of Sir George Thornton and settled well on his estate', later abandoned his family and his responsibilities

---

[13] Stafford, *Pacata Hibernia*, vol. 2, 400.   [14] Stafford, *Pacata Hibernia*, vol. 2, 525.

[15] For a biographical note on Clanricard see that by Robert Armstrong, *Dictionary of Irish Biography*, vol. 2, 55–6; Stafford, *Pacata Hibernia*, vol. 2, 658–9, 683.

[16] For a biographical note on Thomond see that by Bernadette Cunningham, *Dictionary of Irish Biography*, vol. 7, 28–30.

[17] Stafford, *Pacata Hibernia*, vol. 2, 516–21.   [18] Stafford, *Pacata Hibernia*, vol. 2, 543–4.

[19] Stafford, *Pacata Hibernia*, vol. 2, 350–1.

NEW HISTORIES FOR A NEW IRELAND   65

to gain military experience with the king of Spain.[20] However, notwithstanding such betrayals, Stafford remained convinced in 1633 that the way forward for the Crown in Ireland was to work in co-operation with those Irish lords who showed themselves willing to become Crown subjects. In support of his own opinion, he published a copy of an advisory letter that had been written by George Carew in 1603 when he was about to resign his service as president of Munster. In this, Carew had advised against 'the Irish [being] utterly rooted out' now that military victory had been achieved. Instead, Carew had counselled the government to 'deal liberally with the Irish lords...or such as are now of great reputation amongst them in the distribution of such lands as they have formerly possessed' with a view to achieving 'the speedy settling' of the country. Carew was of the opinion in 1603, as was Stafford thirty years later, that if those favoured by the government were subsequently to defect, as John Burke from Limerick had done, the authorities would be fully entitled to confiscate their lands on which they 'may plant English or other Irish'.[21]

The issue of whether or not it was appropriate for the Crown to place trust in Irish lords had been a core issue also in 1619 for Thomas Gainsford (1566–1624) when he had published on the recent war in Ireland. Gainsford was an English pamphleteer who had served as an officer during the later stages of the Nine Years' War, including service under the command of Richard Burke, earl of Clanricard. Since his principal income now seems to have derived from his publications, Gainsford, in 1619, took advantage of the popular curiosity that had been reawakened in England when news filtered through of the death in exile in Rome in 1616 of Hugh O'Neill, earl of Tyrone, who had been Queen Elizabeth's most formidable Irish adversary.[22] Gainsford, like Stafford, intended his work to be 'exemplary' to illustrate the ignominious fate that awaited those who were lured by the empty seductions of foreign rulers to abandon the loyalty due to their legitimate monarchs. Tyrone, as he was represented by Gainsford, owed everything that he had ever held in Ireland to the queen because she had conceded to him the inheritance, and ultimately the title, that had been held by his imputed grandfather, Con O'Neill, earl of Tyrone, thus defying his dynastic rivals who 'imputed [him to be] the son of a smith of Dundalk'. Gainsford acknowledged that Tyrone had reciprocated the trust placed in him by Elizabeth until 1588 when some of the survivors of the Spanish Armada who had gone ashore in Ulster 'choked his loyalty and cast dust in the eyes of his faithfulness', thus leading him into a rebellion. Tyrone's defection, said Gainsford, became serious following his 'notorious victory' at the Yellow Ford, after which, for a time, he came close to destroying England's interest in Ireland and was 'proclaimed the deliverer of his

---

[20] Stafford, *Pacata Hibernia*, vol. 2, 685.   [21] Stafford, *Pacata Hibernia*, vol. 2, 703.
[22] Thomas Gainsford, *The True, Exemplary and Remarkable History of the Earl of Tyrone* (London, 1619).

66 IMAGINING IRELAND'S PASTS

country and protector of the Catholic cause'.[23] Over time, as Gainsford explained, the Crown forces commanded by Lord Mountjoy snuffed out this rebellion, supported by Spain, and Tyrone was ultimately forced to seek refuge abroad. Then, according to Gainsford, Tyrone was left until his death in 1616 to eke out a pitiable existence in Rome as 'the subject of charity' enjoying 'only a supplement from some special Cardinals'.[24]

Gainsford's graphic depiction 'of [Tyrone's] fearful wretchedness and final extirpation' was designed to deter other Irish lords from forsaking their loyalty to their rightful monarch. However, in pointing to this example, Gainsford also explained how Tyrone's career might have turned out differently had he followed the course set by Richard Burke, earl of Clanricard, who, as was mentioned, had been Gainsford's senior officer on the field of Kinsale.[25] Gainsford considered a comparison between Tyrone and Clanricard apposite because each was a grandson of an Irish lord who, in 1542, had agreed to owe fealty to an English monarch under the so-called surrender and re-grant negotiations promoted by the government of King Henry VIII.[26] Clanricard, as Gainsford described it, had lived up to the pledge made by his grandfather in 1542 by fighting for his monarch on the field of Kinsale, after which he had flourished as a major landowner in both Ireland and England, and as a courtier in England. Tyrone, on the other hand, had broken his pledge to his legitimate monarch and suffered the consequences. In making this point, Gainsford, like Stafford, was acknowledging that the service of loyal Irish lords—including Irish Catholic lords—had been crucial to the military victory achieved by the army of Mountjoy. Thus logically, according to Gainsford, and here he was again of one mind with Stafford, the Crown should continue to cherish those in Ireland who were truly noble and honourable since its authority rested on slim foundations.[27]

3.3 Sir John Davies: Applied History in the Civil Domain

Neither Thomas Stafford nor Thomas Gainsford can be considered a profound thinker, which places them at odds with Sir John Davies (1569–1626) who,

---

[23] Gainsford, *Tyrone*, 1, 9, 15; in attributing Tyrone's paternity to a blacksmith in Dundalk Gainsford was misremembering the charge that Tyrone's father, Matthew or Feardorcha O'Neill, was the son of a Dundalk blacksmith named Kelly by one of Con O'Neill's mistresses.

[24] Gainsford, *Tyrone*, 24, 25.   [25] Gainsford, *Tyrone*, 'Title page'.

[26] Maginn, '"Surrender and Regrant" in the historiography of sixteenth-century Ireland'; W.F. Butler, 'The Policy of Surrender and Re-grant', in *Royal Society of Antiquaries of Ireland Jrl.*, 43 (1912/13), 47–65, and 99–127; the steps involved in a surrender are described in Steven G. Ellis, *Tudor Ireland; Crown, Community and Conflicts of Cultures, 1470–1603* (London, 1985), 137–8; details on the sequence of surrenders are supplied in S.J. Connolly, *Contested Island: Ireland, 1460–1630* (Oxford, 2007), 106–9.

[27] Thomas Gainsford had offered an appraisal of the weakness of the Crown's position in Ireland in Chapter 17, entitled 'The Description of Ireland', of his longer work *The Glory of England* (London, 1618).

during his years as Solicitor General for Ireland (1603–06) and then as Attorney General (1606–19), used his sharp intelligence to devise legal means by which the indigenous population might be absorbed into a polity that would be dominated by upholders of the English interest in the country.[28] In thus placing confidence in the common law as an instrument to promote reform, Davies was acting in the fashion that one would expect of a product of the English Inns of Court, where, in the words of Lauren Working, members 'emphasized the transformative, reforming power of the law in creating civil subjects'.[29]

As he pondered the task that confronted him in Ireland, Davies invoked the previous attempts that had been made—especially in the recent past—to employ the law to assimilate the Irish—and particularly the Gaelic Irish—into a civil polity. Since Davies had a high opinion of his own capabilities, he expected to improve significantly upon previous efforts at assimilation. As he contemplated precedents from which he might proceed he engaged in correspondence with superiors prior to pleading a sequence of legal cases before the courts in Dublin that he expected would enable his programme of regeneration of Irish society through the law, backed, in the short term, by the military arm of the state. Having put his procedures in place, Davies, in 1612, published a carefully argued text, popularly referred to as Davies' *Discovery*, addressed to King James VI and I, which quickly became one of the most frequently-cited historical works of the seventeenth century. The *Discovery* is especially pertinent to the present chapter both because of the selective attention it gave to events in Ireland over the sixty years previous to its publication and because it proceeded from the assumption that the legal, social, and political restructuring that Davies was in the process of implementing were certain, within a generation, to render society in Ireland indistinguishable from that in England.[30]

Davies, like Stafford and Gainsford, attached importance to the experiment of 1542, by which the government of King Henry VIII sought to transform lords and chieftains who had come to power after the Gaelic manner into Irish nobles whose authority derived from the Crown. Again, like the other two authors, Davies considered that the initiative had produced positive outcomes in the cases of the lordships of Thomond and Clanricard, but not so in the case of the Tyrone lordship. However, where Stafford and Gainsford had attributed the contrast in outcomes to personality differences between the inheritors of the lordships in the

---

[28] For a biographical note on Davies see that by Robert Armstrong, *Dictionary of Irish Biography* vol. 3, 70–4; Hans Pawlisch, *Sir John Davies and the Conquest of Ireland* (Cambridge, 1985).

[29] Lauren Working, 'Locating Colonization at the Jacobean Inns of Court', *Historical Journal*, vol. 61 (2018), 29–51; quotation 32.

[30] John Davies, *A Discovery of the True Causes why Ireland was never entirely subdued, and brought under Obedience of the Crowne of England, until the beginning of his Majesties happy raigne* (London, 1612).

68 IMAGINING IRELAND'S PASTS

third generation, Davies considered that the different results were principally as a consequence of misjudgement and neglect by the state.

The biggest misjudgement of all, in Davies's opinion, was that in 1603 Tyrone had been pardoned by King James VI and I for his past offences and restored to the same title and lordship that had been conceded to his grandfather in 1542, with but some minor exclusions. This meant that he had been given the entire lordship of Tyrone in demesne including, as it had been put by Tyrone himself when his entitlement was being challenged by Davies, 'all and singular the castles, lordships, manors, lands, tenements, rents, reversions, services, advowsons, knights fees and other hereditaments whatever he [his grandfather] lately [previous to 1542] had in Tyrone'.[31] While Davies did not dispute that these were the words used in the patent issued to the first earl of Tyrone in 1542, and renewed to Tyrone in 1603, he was aware that some of the Crown officials who had negotiated the terms of the grant in 1542 had fostered doubts concerning the merits of the award. He had it in mind that one critic had pronounced in 1542 that what was being transacted was tantamount to permitting one lord to enjoy 'a country under his rule no less...than the shire of Kent'.[32] Moreover, Davies, who had worked diligently to comprehend what had been tenurial practice under Gaelic law, contended that what had been granted to the first earl of Tyrone in 1542, and perpetuated in 1603, had inflicted a serious injustice upon the collateral members of the O'Neill dynasty and on the heads of the principal kinship groups who had traditionally resided within the Tyrone lordship. All such, he insisted, had previously enjoyed positions under Gaelic law that approximated to that of tenants-in-chief under English common law because, under Gaelic law, a lord enjoyed but a 'seignory' of certain rents and duties from the principal kinship groups resident within his lordships together with 'some special demesnes'.[33]

Davies further believed that when subsequent governments in Ireland had become aware of the injustice that had been consequential upon all the grants of 1542, they had sought to remedy the inequity by bringing a bill before the Irish parliament of 1569/71 that had given the government authority to assign property within Gaelic lordships to 'gentlemen and freeholders' as well as to 'lords'.[34] Davies argued further that the Dublin government had acted upon this fresh

---

[31] 'To the King's Most Excellent Majesty: The Humble petition of Hugh, earl of Tyrone', no date but filed under December 1606; Kew, N.A, S.P. 63, vol. 219, nos. 153, 154, f. 230.

[32] Lord Deputy and Council to King Henry VIII, 24 Oct. 1541 in *State Papers during the reign of Henry VIII* (11 vols., London, 1830–52), vol. III, contd., 339–44; for a more succinct version see Steven G. Ellis and James Murray, eds., *Calendar of State Papers Ireland: Tudor Period, 1509–1547* (Dublin, 2017), 325–6.

[33] Davies to Salisbury, 12 Nov. 1606, Kew, N.A, S.P. 63, vol. 219, no. 132, ff. 168–75.

[34] The legislation to which Davies was likely making reference was 'An Act Authorising the Governor...by advice of the more part of the Privy Council...to grant letters patent to the Irishry and degenerate men of English name of their lands', *The Statutes at Large passed in the parliaments held in Ireland...1310–1786* (20 vols., Dublin, 1786–1801), vol. 1, 367–8.

legislation whenever it had the opportunity to do so. Thus, in the cases of the lordships of Thomond and Clanricard, it had compelled the descendants of the first grantees to acknowledge the existence of freeholders within their respective lordships, and to recognize them as proprietors of lands within the lordship that would be free from interference by the ruling lord. Davies acknowledged that no similar modification had been introduced in the case of the Tyrone grant because in that same parliament the grant made in 1542 to Con O'Neill had been effectively revoked and the entire Tyrone lordship had been designated Crown property following the Act of Attainder of Shane O'Neill. The benefit to the Crown from this act, which might have been transmitted ultimately to the lesser proprietors, had been lost in 1585, according to Davies, when Hugh O'Neill had been restored to the title and estates that had been conceded to his grandfather in 1542. Tyrone later forfeited what he had then received when he had committed treason by entering upon rebellion, and the Crown again secured title to the lordship under the terms of the act of attainder of Shane O'Neill. However, according to Davies, all the inequities had been reinstituted in 1603 when King James had pardoned Tyrone for all past offences and conceded to him an even more specific grant than he had received in 1585 and again on the same terms as that given to his grandfather in 1542. In order to illustrate the anomaly that had been thus created, Davies asked people to imagine if Donogh O'Brien, fourth earl of Thomond—a proprietor, we may recall, who was considered exemplary by both Stafford and Gainsford—considered himself entitled to reduce all occupiers of land within his lordship to the status of tenants at will, 'his revenue would be increased sevenfold... a thing with which this earl [Thomond] would not let pass, if it stood with the law and his duty to bring it to pass'.[35]

In this case, and in all his other pleading concerning the reform of Ireland, Davies purported that the moral justification for English reform efforts in Ireland had always been to defend the weak and defenceless against the tyrannical ambitions of great lords regardless of ancestry. On this ground he was willing to see merit in the patents granted to some Irish lords in 1542 only to the extent that these transactions had commenced a process whereby Irish lords had been gradually persuaded to accept English legal practices relating to property management and inheritance instead of what had been practised under the Gaelic 'brehon' law which, as we shall see, he considered especially repulsive.[36] Moreover, as noted, Davies was further encouraged when he looked forward from 1542 to some modified surrenders that had been enforced by later governors because these had given legal recognition to freeholders and tenants-in-chief, as well as to head landlords. Davies also looked positively on the compositions that had been

---

[35] Davies to Salisbury, 1 July 1607, Kew, N.A., S.P. 63, vol. 222, no. 95, ff. 6–9.
[36] Davies used the term 'brehon' law to describe Gaelic land law where disputes were resolved by a judge or *breitheamh* (hence brehon) who was a client of the lord.

introduced, or attempted, by provincial presidents in the provinces of Connacht and Munster because, under these arrangements, freeholders as well as lords made a direct contribution to the Crown towards the cost of government. He held that all such initiatives had collectively opened 'a passage' through which the agents of the Crown might, in his generation, proceed to 'the unreformed parts of this kingdom' with a view to promoting 'civil government' in those areas. By this he meant compelling those lords whom the king was prepared to recognize as proprietors 'to settle their seignories & possessions in a course of inheritance according to the course of the common law'.[37]

Davies, like the politicians of 1542, always gave priority to having proprietors in Ireland hold their land from the Crown by English tenure because this provided the best assurance that, on the death of the proprietor, title would transfer to the designated heir who was usually the eldest son. Such a predictable arrangement was considered vital by Davies because he considered the ownership of property by individuals to be the essential guarantor of individual liberty. He asserted that wherever there was no certain ownership of property (as he contended had obtained under 'brehon' law) and where succession to property by primogeniture did not prevail (as he contended had been inhibited by the Gaelic custom of 'tanistry') the inevitable consequence was a regime of terror where the powerful would seize control of property from all rivals.[38] Wherever and whenever this occurred, claimed Davies, those who had acquired property by force lacked the incentive to improve what they had seized because they lacked the certainty that they could transmit it to a designated heir. Under these circumstances, those who had come into the possession of property by the sword exploited it ruthlessly to the detriment of the poor when the quality of the land, on which the livelihoods of cultivators depended, was exhausted by overuse.

One purpose behind Davies's exposition on the merits of possessive individualism was to denigrate Gaelic practices that, he asserted, discouraged both individual ownership and the regulated transmission of property to heirs. He sought to universalize his conclusions by inviting his audience to imagine that 'if we [the English] were a poor and naked people, as many nations in America be, we would easily agree to be judged by the next man we meet and so make short end of every controversy'.[39] Therefore, for Davies, the introduction to Ireland both of individual ownership of land and succession to property by primogeniture were the first benefits that had accrued from the extension of English common law to a barbaric people because 'a commonwealth cannot subsist without a certain

---

[37] Davies, *Discovery*, sig. Li 2, r and v; Li 4, r.

[38] Davies' expression 'tanistry' derived from the Irish word *tánaise* designating the person chosen from within a four-generation kinship group to succeed the ruling Gaelic lord while that lord was still in power.

[39] *Le Premier Report des Cases et Matters en Ley…John Davys* (Dublin, 1615) 'Introduction to Lord Ellesmere', 6v; C.B. Macpherson, *The Political Theory of Possessive Individualism* (Oxford, 1962).

NEW HISTORIES FOR A NEW IRELAND   71

ownership, or if the right of inheritance of land doth not rest in some person'.[40] Therefore to speed up the process by which proprietors were being conceded titles to land that would hold good in English common law, Davies, in 1608, pleaded a case before the court of King's Bench in Ireland that led to that court handing down the judgement that the Gaelic practice of inheritance—which the court dubbed the 'law of tanistry'—was but 'a custom which is contrary to the public good...and is repugnant to the law of reason'. Proceeding from there, the court further ruled that the 'said custom of tanistry' was void in itself and abolished when the common law of England was established'.[41]

Even as Davies looked positively at the procedures that had been put in place in 1542 as these had been subsequently modified by legislation in the parliament of 1569–71, he averred that what had been thus provided for in 1542 alone was 'but a ceremony prescribed by the act to be done by the Irishry, to the end that they may be estop't afterwards to claim their Irish chiefrys and exactions or other title except under the letters patent'. Therefore, since 'the final purpose of the makers of the act [of 1569–71] was to settle all the possession of this kingdom in the course of common law', he believed that all titles to property throughout the kingdom would have to be further scrutinized, and all proprietors in the country should be given the opportunity to establish title to their property that would hold good in English common law. This, according to his reasoning, would become the first pillar to uphold a civil society.[42]

As Davies thus outlined an agenda for future action based on the experience of the recent past he also made it clear that a second requirement of any civil society was that all people who committed an offence should, regardless of rank, be liable to trial before the courts of common law. This, he contended, had been understood also by those who had promoted the reforms of the 1540s, and he argued that it was with the purpose of extending English law into the previously Gaelic lordships that the members of the Irish parliament of 1541–42 had enacted the kingship act of 1541 which had declared King Henry VIII and his successors to be kings of Ireland, rather than as previously lords of that country. This act, he pronounced in 1608, had a potentially revolutionary import because 'after the making of this act all the mere Irish were from henceforth accepted and reputed subjects and liege men to the kings and queens of England and had the benefit and protection of the law of England, when they would use or demand it'.[43]

---

[40] *A Report of Cases and Matters in Law Resolved in the King's Courts in Ireland Collected and Digested by Sir John Davies* (Dublin, 1762), 89.

[41] 'The Case of Tanistry', in *A Report...by Sir John Davies*, 86; for a detailed study of the case see Pawlisch, *Davies*, 55–83.

[42] *A Report...by Sir John Davies*, 86; I wish to thank Dr Padraig Lenihan for explaining that *estop't* was a legal term meaning prevented.

[43] *A Report...by Sir John Davies*, 107; this same interpretation of the kingship act underpins Brendan Bradshaw, *The Irish Constitutional Revolution*, even though that author did not seem to appreciate that he had been anticipated by Davies.

72 IMAGINING IRELAND'S PASTS

As Davies stated his enthusiasm for the theory that justified the 1541 act, he concluded that it had proven impossible during subsequent decades of the sixteenth century to extend English law into Gaelic areas because the 'king's writ cannot run but where there is a county and a sheriff'. Therefore, while he saluted Sussex, Sidney and Perrot as three governors who had delineated boundaries for some new counties, he concluded that common-law procedures had been unable to function because most parts of the country had been disturbed either by war or preparations for war in almost every decade. Indeed, he found that some of the measures taken by reformers in parliament to promote the extension of common law into the provinces were contradicted by other acts designed to regulate rather than eliminate the private armies customarily maintained by Irish lords. Here he would have had in mind acts concerning the practice of 'booking' whereby every lord who retained 'horsemen or footmen called kerne' would be held responsible for their behaviour and would present in writing to the authorities a list of all such servants for whose behaviour he would be answerable.[44] As he studied the statutes enacted in the sixteenth century, Davies could see how legislation of this kind, designed to prevent the armed followers of lords from trespassing upon the civilian population, particularly within the Pale, had the unintended consequence of increasing the dependency of followers upon the lords who employed them. The rights of individuals, and therefore their ability to act as independent jurors, were even further diminished, according to Davies, when English captains were appointed as seneschals over Gaelic lordships with authority to maintain order by martial law. This led to his conclusion that such sixteenth-century developments made it impossible to operate a court system satisfactorily, and not so at all in extensive tracts of the country, especially in Ulster, that had not been designated shire ground until he himself had put procedures in place for doing so. Therefore, Davies could pronounce that it was not until 1603 that, for the first time, 'the common law' could be 'communicated to all persons' throughout the country. In order to facilitate this, Davies considered it necessary to have King James issue a proclamation in 1606 clarifying the benefits of the 1541 act by stating that all denizens in Ireland, regardless of social position or ethnic background, were equal before the law in the eyes of the Crown.[45]

Davies was concerned in his diverse writings to convey the impression that the Crown, and the succession of governors who had represented it in Ireland over the course of the sixteenth century, had always sought to absorb the two elements

---

[44] 'Reformation of Ireland: Ordinances and Provisions made in Parliament 12 July 33 Henry VIII', *Cal. Carew Ms.* vol. 1, doc. 157, 180–2; similar legislation 'An act that Five Persons of the best and eldest of every nation amongst the Irishry, shall bring in all the idle persons of their surname', was passed in the Irish parliament of 1569, *Statutes at Large... 1310–1786*, vol. 1, 319; on the further development of booking see Ciaran Brady, 'Tudor Reform Strategies in Sixteenth-Century Ireland', Brian Mac Cuarta, ed., *Reshaping Ireland, 1550–1700*, 21–42, esp. 36–7.

[45] *A Report... by Sir John Davies*, 102, 107.

of the population into a single Anglicized polity. His purpose in writing *The Discovery*, he pronounced in self-serving fashion, was to identify the reasons why that ambition had not been realized until King James had come to the throne. Even as he took credit for creating the conditions under which the law could become the instrument of absorbing all people in Ireland into a single exemplary polity, Davies complained that, in some instances, 'the multitude' remained content 'to be followers of such as could master and defend them', even though their former lords had been defeated in battle by 'the Crown of England' whose authority was 'brai'd (as it were) in a mortar with the Sword, Famine & Pestilence'. Thus even though the *Discovery* provided no account of the fighting that had taken place, Davies, no less that Stafford and Gainsford, celebrated the 'entire, perfect and final conquest of Ireland', after which the people 'altogether submitted themselves to the English government, received the laws and magistrates, and most gladly embraced the King's pardon and peace in all parts of the realm, with demonstrations of joy and comfort'.[46]

Even as Davies acknowledged that the reforms had been enabled by a conquest, he emphasized the clemency with which King James had proceeded. This became apparent, claimed Davies (and here he invoked civil rather than common law) when one allowed that, in the aftermath of a 'new conquest', the monarch enjoyed 'the lordship paramount of all the lands in the realm' which, as had been the practice in Ancient Rome, entitled him to dispose of land to servants and warriors 'or to such colonies as he will plant immediately upon the conquest'. Instead of acting as a 'conqueror', King James, according to Davies, had decided to forego his entitlement, and had, instead, received some of the previously rebellious 'natives or ancient inhabitants...into his protection and avoweth them for his subjects' and permitted them to 'continue their possessions...by good title...according to the rules of the law which the conqueror hath allowed or established if they will submit themselves to it'.[47] Moreover, claimed Davies, it was only when some of these lords had spurned this generosity and solicited support from the King of Spain that King James had decided to act upon his entitlement and introduce a comprehensive plantation over much of the province of Ulster.[48]

Davies, as we recall from Chapter 2, was one of the many authors denounced by Geoffrey Keating as malignant opponents of Catholic and Gaelic interests and institutions in Ireland. Keating's identification of Davies as an opponent is unsurprising, since besides being a fluent writer and prying lawyer, Davies was also one of the prime architects of the Ulster plantation, and the leading civilian

---

[46] Davies, *Discovery*, sig. k4 r.

[47] 'The Case of Tanistry', in *A Report...by Sir John Davies*, 111; Pawlisch, *Davies*, 161–75.

[48] Davies was here referring to the so-called 'Flight of the Earls' in September 1607 when the earls of Tyrone and Tyrconnell and Cúconnacht McGuire fled Ulster for the Continent. It was presumed by the government that their sudden departure was an acknowledgement by them that they had committed treason by continuing to conspire with the king of Spain.

74 IMAGINING IRELAND'S PASTS

intelligence behind the so-called Mandates controversy of 1605 when the authorities required some of Dublin's leading Catholic citizens to attend at designated Protestant services under threat of severe financial penalties. Davies, as Keating well knew, had also been responsible for manipulating representation in the Irish parliament of 1613–15 to ensure it would have a Protestant majority.[49] While Keating was fully justified in representing Davies as an opponent of the interests of elite Catholics in Ireland, Davies was also one of the more prominent and articulate of the English settlers of his generation in Ireland who believed that the country could look forward to a harmonious and prosperous future because he, and the government he served, had established a social, legal, and political framework suited to accommodating natives as well as newcomers as equal subjects of a common monarch. Davies remained optimistic that this could be achieved because he was convinced that Ireland's populations, when ruled by a benevolent monarch, were as amenable to reform as those of any other country. This confidence, as we have seen from the evidence presented in this chapter, stemmed from his belief that English common law and the possessive individualism it fostered were effective instruments of reform.

These ideas may have been already fixed in Davies's mind when he arrived in Ireland, but he received further confirmation of his opinions from his study of the country's history, both over the long term, since the Norman Conquest, and in the shorter term, since 1542. Each exercise satisfied him that all previous efforts at assimilating Ireland's diverse population into a single civil polity had failed because successive governments had denied the benefits of English common law to the entire population. The opportunity to remedy this deficit had, he argued, been made possible by the recent conquest following which 'the Law' had begun to 'make her progress & circuit about the realm, under the protection of the sword (as Virgo, the figure of Justice, is by Leo in the Zodiac) until the people have perfectly learned the lesson of obedience, & the conquest be established in the hearts of all men'. This, together with 'mixt plantation of British & Irish' was, he contended, making it possible for the populations of Britain and Ireland to 'grow up together in one nation', leading to his expectation that, in the next generation, the populations of Ireland would 'in tongue & heart, and every way else become English so as there [would] be no difference or distinction but the Irish sea betwixt us'.[50]

3.4 Ussher and Ware: Applied History in the Spiritual Domain

Davies in his *Discovery* made it clear that he spoke only of 'civil', including 'martial', affairs, and, following the example of Spenser in 1596, he refused 'to speak of

---

[49] Pawlisch, *Davies*, 3–33, 103–21, 161–75.
[50] Davies, *Discovery*, sigs, N, N3, K3, v, and Mm 2, r and v.

the State Ecclesiastical.[51] This reticence is probably explained by the recognition by both authors that Protestant opinion in England and Ireland was still divided on what character a truly reformed church should assume, and by their awareness that bishops of the established church held a proprietorial view of their responsibility in this domain. Moreover, at the time that Davies published his *Discovery* in 1612, James Ussher (1581–1656), who was well on the way to becoming Ireland's most famous Protestant theological scholar and controversialist, was already applying history to the task of identifying a place for a Protestant church in Irish society.[52]

Ussher seemed the ideal person to undertake this exercise because his family on his father's side came from a Dublin merchant lineage who had become early converts to Protestantism, while his mother was Margaret Stanihurst, sister to the scholar/historian Richard Stanihurst, whose publications on Ireland were discussed in Chapter 1. From the moment he was ordained a minister in 1601, Ussher dedicated himself to winning the allegiance of the Dublin merchant community, including many of his own kin, to the Protestant faith. His personal contribution to the reform effort was through preaching and public disputation with Catholic priests, including a Jesuit cousin, over contested theological issues. At the same time he was one of those who encouraged the government to pressurize merchants and landowners in the Pale into religious compliance by enforcing the laws against recusancy. One outcome of this pressure was the 1605 stratagem of mandating named wealthy individuals to present for service on specified dates, with which, as noted, John Davies was also associated.[53] Ussher, like his ancestors on both sides, considered it a matter of civic pride that Dublin and Ireland should have its own university, but, unlike his Catholic cousins, he considered the primary purpose of that university—Trinity College, Dublin—to be the promotion of Protestantism. This was his opinion when he enrolled in its first class in 1594, and when he graduated with a bachelor's degree in 1598 and a master's degree in 1601.

Once James Ussher had completed his formal education and been ordained a minister by his uncle Henry Ussher, Archbishop of Armagh, he commenced study of the history of the universal Christian church since its first foundations, and of the controversies and practices that, over time, had led to a once true Christian religion becoming corrupted by false doctrine and malpractice. Like all Protestants, Ussher believed that this corrupt state of the church had persisted

---

[51] Davies, *Discovery*, sig. O, v; Spenser, *View*, 161.
[52] For a biographical note on Ussher see that by John McCafferty, *Dictionary of Irish Biography* vol. 9, 621–9, and for a detailed study of his career, Alan Ford, *James Ussher: Theology, History, and Politics in Early-Modern Ireland and England* (Oxford, 2007); see also Ford, 'The Irish historical renaissance and the shaping of Protestant history', Alan Ford and John McCafferty, eds., *The Origins of Sectarianism in Early Modern Ireland* (Cambridge, 2005), 127–57.
[53] Ford, *James Ussher*, 30–1.

until Protestant reformers had begun the work of restoring it to first principles. Ussher considered it vital that he, and all Protestant divines who passed through Trinity College, Dublin, should be equipped to speak authoritatively on these matters, and be thus in a position to convince Catholics of the errors of their ways. It was to this end that in 1607 he accepted to become Professor of Theological Controversies at Trinity College, Dublin, and began to assemble a library that would contain the evidence that would sustain the various controversies in which he engaged, initially in sermons and disputations with adversaries, and later in print.

Ussher's bibliographic efforts and his interest in manuscript sources gave him cause to establish and maintain contact with the leading Protestant historical and antiquarian scholars of his generation, initially in England, and then throughout Protestant Europe. Ussher's international reputation stemmed both from his deployment of his linguistic skills in Latin, Greek, Hebrew, and some oriental languages, to establish the character of the early Christian church, and from his calculation from biblical chronology that the world had been created on the evening before 23 October 4004 B C.[54] At the same time, Ussher pondered how Christianity had first come to Ireland, and also to Britain, and how the churches established in both countries related to the primitive Christian church.[55]

As Ussher developed this interest in the origins of Irish Christianity, he established links, sometimes directly and at other times through intermediaries, with Irish Catholic scholars, some based in Catholic countries on the Continent and some in Ireland. These included the Irish Franciscan, John Colgan, who worked for many years, principally from Louvain, on a collective project on the lives of Irish saints that did not come to fruition until 1645.[56] Ussher considered it necessary to make such contacts because Irish Catholic students on the Continent had access to archival sources relating to Irish church history that were beyond his reach.[57] At the same time Ussher corresponded with Catholic scholars based in Ireland who were grappling with the same historical problems that concerned him, including scholars who had ready access to manuscript sources in the Irish language.

This latter correspondence included some exchanges on scholarly questions with David Rothe who, as a Catholic bishop, would have been regarded by Ussher

---

[54] Dáibhí Ó Cróinín, 'Archbishop James Ussher (1581–1656) and the history of the Easter', *Studia Traditionis Theologiae*, vol. 26 (2018), 309–51.

[55] Alan Ford, 'Shaping History: James Ussher and the Church of Ireland', Mark Empey, Alan Ford, and Miriam Moffitt, eds., *The Church of Ireland and its Past: History, Interpretation and Identity* (Dublin, 2017), 19–35.

[56] John Colgan, *Acta sanctorum veteris et maiores Scotiae, seu, Hiberniae sanctorum insulae* (Louvain, 1645); for a biographical note on Colgan see that by Colmán N. Ó Clabaigh, *Dictionary of Irish Biography*, vol. 2, 658–60.

[57] Brendan Connor to Ussher, 10 July 1641, Elizabethanne Boran, ed., *The Correspondence of James Ussher, 1600–1656* (3 vols., Dublin, 2015), vol. 3, doc. 490, 859–61.

as a competitor for souls and whose *Analecta Sacra*, discussed in Chapter 2, had come to the attention of the authorities because of the 'many foul implications' it had cast on the government and because it even 'toucheth the title of the crown itself'.[58] Such factors did not deter Ussher from opening an indirect, and later a direct and polite, correspondence with Rothe who shared his interest in the life of St Patrick and was, like him, seeking to identify who had been the immediate successors to St Patrick as Archbishops of Armagh.[59]

Such interests and such contacts meant that Ussher became respectful of Irish culture, including the Irish language, in a way that his maternal uncle, the culture-bound Richard Stanihurst, was not. Even before he assumed episcopal responsibility, first as Bishop of Meath, 1621–25, and then as Archbishop of Armagh, 1625–56, Ussher seems to have become more hopeful of winning converts among the Gaelic population of Ireland through evangelical efforts than in forcing the English-speaking community of the Pale to comply, because he had found that these latter had been drilled in Catholic apologetics by priests, including some of his own Jesuit cousins. Ussher's generous attitude to Gaelic culture is perhaps best exemplified in a letter he wrote to the Huguenot scholar Louis le Dieu, based in Leiden, in which he explained that no dictionary of the Irish language was available in print despite the language itself being 'particularly elegant and rich'. The deficiency existed, he said, because there had 'not yet been anyone who [had] put his mind to cultivating it in that way as we see almost [all] other vernacular languages of Europe [had] been cultivated in this age'.[60]

Ussher, and also his cousin Robert Ussher, who in 1630 was elected Provost of Trinity College, Dublin, considered that all candidates for the ministry in that college should have some formal training in the Irish language, and Ussher was also anxious to have more religious literature available in print in Irish. Up to this time the only Irish language printed books suited to Protestant evangelization were a simple catechism, the New Testament, and the Book of Common Prayer. He considered his own particular contribution to rendering Protestantism more appealing to Irish people to be his documentary demonstration that St Patrick had been a real historical person who, as he put it to Rothe, 'did exercise a kind of apostleship here, though not so much as St Peter's was, yet as large every whit as that of St Augustine'.[61] What he did not mention to Rothe, but which he confided to William Camden, the English antiquarian, was that while he was

---

[58] Thomas Ryves to Camden [1618], Boran, ed., *Ussher Correspondence*, vol. 1, doc. 67(i), 153.

[59] William Malone, S.J. to Ussher, 5 Apr. 1619. Boran, ed., *Ussher Correspondence*, vol. 1, doc. 75, 162–3; Rothe (on behalf of Ussher) to William Malone, 5 Apr. 1619, Boran, ed., *Ussher Correspondence*, vol. 1, doc. 76, 163–4; Ussher to Rothe [Apr–June] 1619, Boran, ed., *Ussher Correspondence*, vol. 1, doc. 79, 167–70; a sequence of letters and enclosures Rothe to Ussher [1619], Boran, ed., *Ussher Correspondence*, vol. 1, docs. 80, 80 (i) 80 (ii), 81, 82, 85, 86, 171–206.

[60] Ussher to Louis le Dieu, January 1637, Boran, ed., *Ussher Correspondence*, vol. 2, doc. 429, 716–7.

[61] Ussher to Rothe [1619], Boran, ed., *Ussher Correspondence*, vol. 1, doc. 81, 186; the St Augustine to whom he referred was Augustine of Canterbury, the apostle to England.

78 IMAGINING IRELAND'S PASTS

authenticating the existence of St Patrick he was discrediting 'that pack of ridiculous miracles, which later writers had fastened upon St Patrick'.[62]

After he had completed these exercises in authentication and purification, Ussher pronounced in 1622, and at further length in 1631, that the Protestant religion being promoted by what he took to describing as 'our Church of Ireland'—in contradistinction to the Church of England—was that which had been first introduced to the country by St Patrick. This, like all Christian churches, had, he contended, become corrupt over the course of the centuries, and had only recently been restored by reformers (including himself) at a sequence of church synods to its original pristine purity.[63] Then, once Ussher had established to his satisfaction that this original Patrician church had been truly Protestant, he took to tracing a line of episcopal succession from St Patrick to demonstrate how the bishops of his own generation in Ireland could trace a spiritual lineage back to St Patrick and from thence to St Peter.

We noted how Ussher had sought in his correspondence with Rothe to reach a consensus on who had been the likely immediate successors to St Patrick. However, he left it to James Ware (1594–1666), a former pupil and very much the disciple of Ussher, to trace how the spiritual line had been transmitted forward to their own time.[64] Ware engaged with this project even though he pursued an administrative career rather than one in the church. It was probably at Ussher's urging that Ware, who graduated in 1611 from Trinity College, Dublin, learned to read texts, including medieval texts, in the Irish language, and to understand spoken Irish even when he could not converse in the language. His understanding of Irish enabled him to interact more closely with Gaelic scholars of his own generation than Ussher had been able to do. Such connections helped him with his investigation into the succession of bishops that he brought to partial fruition in the 1620s, and also with his identification of Ireland's scholars and their achievements through the centuries that he published in the 1630s.[65] As he proceeded with these undertakings, Ware continued to seek the approval of Ussher.[66]

---

[62] Ussher to Camden, 8 June 1618, Boran, ed., *Ussher Correspondence,* vol. 1.doc. 67, 151–2.

[63] James Ussher, *An Epistle Concerning the Religion of the Ancient Irish* (Dublin, 1622); Ussher, *A Discourse of the Religion Anciently Professed by the Irish and British* (London, 1631); for an example of his use of the phrase 'our Church of Ireland' see Ussher to Luke Challoner, 9 Apr. 1613, Boran, ed., *Ussher Correspondence,* vol. 1, doc. 29, 92–3; Ford, *James Ussher,* 118–32.

[64] For a biographical note on James Ware see that by William O'Sullivan, *Dictionary of Irish Biography,* vol. 9, 798–9, Mark Empey, 'Creating a Usable Past: James and Robert Ware', Empey, Ford, and Moffitt, eds., *The Church of Ireland and its Past,* 36–56.

[65] The entire task of listing ecclesiastics was not completed by Ware until 1665 when he published a composite work with some new material, James Ware, *De praesulibus Hiberniae* (Dublin, 1665). However, he made good progress with his work on ecclesiastics during the 1620s when he published books on succession in the archbishoprics of Cashel and Tuam and on episcopal succession in all the dioceses in the province of Leinster; James Ware, *Archiepiscoporum Casseliensium et Tuamensium vitae* (Dublin, 1626), James Ware, *De praesulibus Lageniae sive provinciae Dubliniensis* (Dublin, 1628). These were followed by James Ware, *De scriptoribus Hiberniae* (Dublin, 1639).

[66] Ware to Ussher, 21 September 1627, Boran, ed., *Ussher Correspondence,* vol. 2, doc. 240, 402.

The fact that Ware's compilations dealt with years that extended to the close of the sixteenth century meant that it was he who isolated many of the controversies that would preoccupy historians of early modern Ireland for centuries to come. Prime among these was his contention that most of the Protestant bishops appointed to the various dioceses in Ireland from the 1530s to his own day had maintained a traceable link to the past even when he showed how several of them navigated their way through the religious changes associated with the reigns of King Henry VIII, Edward VI, Mary, and Elizabeth.

Mark Empey, in his study of the publications of James Ware, has been impressed by their 'impartiality' and their freedom from 'polemic'. This is justified to the extent that Ware sought always to anchor his conclusions in verifiable fact, and to avoid the anti-Catholic invective that we noted in the publications of Hooker and that had been repeated in the writings of many Protestant controversialists.[67] However, these virtues were lost on his Catholic contemporaries who were necessarily offended by Ware's refusal to recognize as bishops those Catholics who had been appointed by the Pope to Irish diocese after Henry VIII had broken with Rome. Their objection was that Ware was giving the Protestant bishops of his own generation the exclusive claim to being the legitimate successors to St Patrick and successors also to the Irish saints and scholars who had evangelized much of Europe, including Britain, after the barbaric invasions. Catholics would also have disagreed with Ware's argument (which supported Ussher's opinion on the same subject) that bishops in Ireland (with the exception of the Dublin archdiocese which had been sometimes subject to Canterbury) had been traditionally chosen locally rather than appointed by the Pope.[68]

There was no way that any Protestant author who touched on such matters could have avoided discommoding Catholic opinion. However, Ware, like Ussher, was careful to avoid causing unnecessary offence to Ireland's Catholic population, not least because in the 1620s it seemed that Protestants were destined to be sharing the resources of the country with Catholics into the foreseeable future unless Catholics could be persuaded to convert to the state church. On this latter prospect, Ussher and presumably Ware still fostered hopes, however forlorn, that their Catholic neighbours would be persuaded to embrace 'true religion' and become members of the only church that was authentically Irish. This may explain why, when Ware identified those scholars who down the centuries had contributed to Ireland's reputation as a land where learning was cherished, he took care to acknowledge those of Gaelic ancestry as well as those of English and Welsh descent. Also in his discussion of authors of more recent times he acknowledged the accomplishments of those who were Catholic as well as those of the Protestant faith. Ware may have seen himself with his *De scriptoribus Hiberniae* to be

---

[67] Alan Ford, The*Protestant Reformation in Ireland, 1590–1641* (Frankfurt am Main, 1985), 202–21.
[68] Empey, 'Creating a Usable Past', 37.

80 IMAGINING IRELAND'S PASTS

resuming the task of rehabilitating Ireland's international scholarly reputation that had been attempted more selectively by Richard Stanihurst, whose publications were discussed in Chapter 1. Such a rehabilitation was all the more necessary both because the works of Gerald of Wales, which had blackened the reputation of all residents in Ireland, continued to be respected on the Continent as well as in Britain, and because Irish people, especially those of Gaelic ancestry, continued to be subjected to a barrage of abuse from English-language pamphleteers writing from both Ireland and Britain. Ware was, of course, better equipped than Stanihurst to rehabilitate Ireland's reputation for scholarship because he could appraise what had been written in Irish as well as that which had been communicated in Latin or English. He could also speak with some authority on authors who had been active previous to the twelfth-century conquest, a subject that was of little concern to Stanihurst.

Given Ware's concern to be conciliatory towards Irish Catholics, it is less easy to explain why, in 1633, he also published a compilation entitled *A Historie of Ireland* to which we have already had occasion to refer in Chapters 1 and 2. This, as noted, comprised works by Edmund Campion, Edmund Spenser, and Meredith Hanmer, each of whom had written of Ireland in the tradition of Gerald of Wales.[69] Ware appears to have undertaken this task because when Thomas, Viscount Wentworth, had been nominated in 1632 to serve as governor in Ireland and set about briefing himself for his new responsibility, he had enquired after histories of Ireland, especially since the reign of King Henry VIII, that corresponded with histories of England written by such authors as Francis Bacon, William Camden, and Francis Godwin. Since no such work existed in print, Ware edited three unpublished texts that would meet the deficit of writing on Ireland until 'some' person would 'hereafter...do the like for Ireland' as Bacon and the others had done for England.[70] Then, as Ware took account of the inadequacy of the texts he was editing for his newly appointed governor, and of the controversial opinions that had been put forward in 1596 by Edmund Spenser in *A View of the Present State of Ireland* that had previously been available only in manuscript, he argued that its belated publication served to illustrate how 'the happy peace' that had come to prevail in Ireland in 1633 contrasted with 'former turbulent tempestuous times'. Moreover, Ware took it upon himself to have 'some passages' of the Spenser text 'tempered with more moderation' given 'the good effects which the last thirty years peace have produced in this land, both in obedience to the laws as also in traffic, husbandry, civility and learning' as compared with 'the troubles and miseries of the time when [Spenser] wrote it'. In thus justifying his

---

[69] James Ware, *A Historie of Ireland, collected by three learned authors viz. Meredith Hanmer...Edmund Campion...and Edmund Spenser*; Alan Ford sees Hanmer, a Welshman, as less strident than the others; Ford, 'The Irish historical renaissance', 142–3.

[70] Ware, *A Historie of Ireland*, 'Preface by Ware'.

NEW HISTORIES FOR A NEW IRELAND   81

bowdlerization of the text, Ware expressed himself satisfied that Spenser would 'surely' have 'omitted' these same 'passages' lest they 'may seem to lay either a particular aspersion upon some families or general upon the nation'. Ware may also have been taking Irish sensibilities into account by omitting some of Spenser's more disdainful remarks on Irish culture.[71]

It appears therefore that, at this juncture, Ware was seeking to reconcile Wentworth's appetite for information on Ireland with his own concern to remain on good terms with the Catholic community who he had supplied with an honourable past in the hope that this would further his ambition, and that of Ussher, to convert them to Protestantism. These two were similarly hopeful that the appointment of Wentworth, who in his previous role as Lord President of the North in England had established a reputation for ruthless efficiency in the service of King Charles, would further this cause. Ussher, as was noted, believed that the key to conversion rested with the word being preached in the appropriate language by a properly educated clergy to a populace who would be compelled to attend church. There he hoped they would be convinced to return to the faith preached by St Patrick and professed by their forebears in ancient times, which, according to Ussher, had been restored by the Church of Ireland.[72]

Ussher was satisfied that he had played his part in furthering his objective by seeing to it that an appropriate education for the training of clergy was provided at Trinity College, Dublin, and by working alone, and with Ware, in providing the historical rationale for his reform ambitions. He believed, however, that these ambitions had been frustrated by a variety of factors, which he hoped the new governor would remedy. The first was the appropriation by lay people—Protestant as well as Catholic—of lands that properly belonged to the church for the maintenance of parish clergy, which these lay proprietors had diverted to secular purposes. One consequence of such trespass on church lands was that, where clergy were appointed to parishes that had been thus denuded of resources, they did not enjoy adequate livings and were more beholden to the lords who had chosen them for parish duty than to their bishops who were their spiritual superiors. Since Wentworth was also concerned about this issue, Ussher saluted his new governor as 'a new Zerubbabel raised by God, for the making up of the ruins of this decayed Church' by opposing 'the greatest' who had 'made the Patrimony of the Church the Inheritance of their Sons and Daughters'.[73]

---

[71] Ware, *A Historie of Ireland*, 'Preface by Ware'. The edition of Spenser's *View* most readily available today is this bowdlerized version, Andrew Hadfield and Willy Maley, eds., *Edmund Spenser, A View of the State of Ireland, from the first printed edition (1633)* (Oxford, 1997); the Renwick edition, cited in the present volume, was based on the manuscript copy in the Bodleian library, and is certainly closer to what Spenser composed; on Ware's emendations to the original, Ford, 'The Irish historical renaissance', 154–5.

[72] Ford, *James Ussher*, 85–103 and 119–32.

[73] Ussher to Laud, 13 Feb. 1634, Boran, ed., *Ussher Correspondence*, vol. 2, doc. 375, 627–8; the biblical reference is to the rebuilding of the Temple. Ussher was here likely referring to the notorious

82 IMAGINING IRELAND'S PASTS

The second issue that Ussher believed had frustrated his plan was that successive governors had lost their nerve when it came to imposing financial penalties upon propertied Catholics who refused to attend at Protestant service. Wentworth's predecessors had justified their failure in this matter on the grounds that doing so would have driven Catholics into rebellion when the strength of the government was still fragile. More recently, Catholics had begun to make overtures to King Charles and offered to pay money to the government in return for a variety of privileges, known as the Graces that included the de facto freedom from such penalties. What Ussher described as the 'toleration for that religion in consideration of the payment of a great sum' was, in his opinion, a scandal, which, he expected, Wentworth would no longer tolerate.[74]

Ussher was correct in believing that Wentworth would look dimly on the Graces, even when the governor's principal concern was because they were depriving the Crown of the possibility of proceeding with further plantations rather than because they promised to permit Catholics to practise their religion without fear of the law. Because of these priorities Wentworth refrained from penalizing Catholics for non-conformity, but this did not mean, as Ussher and his associates feared, and as Wentworth wanted Catholics to believe, that the new governor was reconciled to an indefinite toleration of Catholicism in Ireland. Rather his view, which differed somewhat from that of Ussher, was that the best means of promoting Protestantism in Ireland was by sponsoring further plantations that would result in an increase in the Protestant population (and particularly Protestant proprietorship) in those parts of the country that had previously been dominated by Catholic lords. By doing so, he contended, he would strengthen the supports available to bishops and ministers, and ensure that all lands that belonged rightfully to the church would be released from lay control.[75]

Ussher might have taken some solace from this had he known what Wentworth had in mind, but he would then also have been brought to recognize that Wentworth intended to defer Ussher's entire strategy for reforming Ireland in religion, and was rejecting the history of Ireland that made sense of that strategy. This was made clear to Ussher when Wentworth publicly rejected the concept of an indigenous Church of Ireland that enjoyed independent authority to define its unique confession of faith in line with the origin myth devised or imagined by Ussher. Instead, Wentworth insisted that the doctrine, discipline, and liturgy of the church in Ireland should be identical with that being decided upon by

---

absorption of church lands into his patrimony by Richard Boyle, earl of Cork, that Wentworth was seeking to redress; on Boyle see Nicholas Canny, *The Upstart Earl: A Study of the Social and Mental World of Richard Boyle, First Earl of Cork, 1566–1643* (Cambridge, 1982), 9–18; David Edwards and Colin Rynne, eds., *The Colonial World of Richard Boyle, First Earl of Cork* (Dublin, 2018).

[74] Cited Nicholas Canny, *Making Ireland British, 1580–1650* (Oxford, 2001), 267; on the Graces see Aidan Clarke, *The Old English in Ireland*, esp. 28–59.

[75] Canny, *Making Ireland British*, 275–97.

Archbishop Laud for the Church of England. Therefore, when Wentworth convened a fresh convention of the church in Ireland in 1634–35, it was primarily to have it abandon the Irish Articles defined in 1615 with scholarly advice from Ussher. Wentworth pursued this policy forcefully, against the wishes of Ussher and many of the existing clergy, but with the assistance of John Bramhall who had arrived in Ireland as chaplain to Wentworth and was appointed Bishop of Derry in 1634. By such means, in this convocation of 1634–35, the Church of Ireland was, as Alan Ford has phrased it, brought into 'congruity' with the Church of England.[76]

Ussher, and we may presume Ware, was each disappointed by this turn of events, not least because it made nonsense of what they had invested in imagining a history for Ireland that both provided all the inhabitants of the country with reason why they should take pride in indigenous Irish language and written culture, and made the case that the reformed religion of their generation was one of the notable products of that culture. Instead, their government, which Ussher as a bishop and Ware as an official were required to obey, insisted, as the earlier apocalyptic historians had argued, that Ireland had become a barbaric place, and that Christianity, no less than civility, had been first introduced into Ireland from England by St Patrick and had to be repeatedly reinforced from there, especially during the reigns of Henry II, Henry VIII, Edward VI, Queen Elizabeth, King James VI and I, and latterly King Charles. They were further required to accept that, when it came to the definition of doctrine and liturgical practice, the church in Ireland had no choice but to fall into line with what was decreed in England for the English church. The official position following Wentworth's rule in Ireland, and even more so following the events that would beset the country in the 1640s and the 1650s, was that true religion, like good government, was to be promoted primarily in the English language and by force should persuasion prove ineffective. We can take it that Ware, who was trusted by Wentworth to the end, became reconciled to this position.[77] The fact that Ussher offered spiritual consolation to his governor on the scaffold in 1640 suggests that he also came to accept that Wentworth's strategy of building up the position of the church in Ireland as a prelude to using the full rigour of the law to compel Catholics to attend Protestant service was the only means of reaping the fruits of the conquest that had been

---

[76] Ford, *James Ussher*, 178–207, quotation 194; John McCafferty, 'John Bramhall and the Church of Ireland in the 1630s', A. Ford, J. McGuire, and K. Milne, eds., *'As by law established': The Church of Ireland since the Reformation* (Dublin, 1995), 100–11; for a biographical note on John Bramhall see that by John McCafferty, *Dictionary of Irish Biography* vol. 1, 777–80, and for the definitive work John McCafferty, *The Reconstruction of the Church of Ireland: Bishop Bramhall and the Laudian Reforms, 1633-1641* (Cambridge, 2007).

[77] On Ussher's attendance upon Strafford on the scaffold, Nicholas Canny, 'The Haliday Collection: a printed source for the seventeenth century', *Proceedings of the Royal Irish Academy*, vol. 113 (2013), 279–307, esp., 295–6, 306.

84   IMAGINING IRELAND'S PASTS

achieved four decades previously. This, in spiritual terms, meant bringing the population of the country to conform to the religion of their prince in defiance of the objection to that policy which, as we saw in Chapter 2, had been voiced so stridently by Rothe in *Analecta Sacra*.

3.5 Conclusion

The authors whose works we have been considering may seem a motley collection, but, for all their differences, the historical works they produced shared several features. The first is that all accepted that human affairs were controlled ultimately by Providence to whom they gave full credit for the conquest of Ireland that had been brought to completion by the close of the reign of Queen Elizabeth. Acceptance of this meant that, as godly people, they considered themselves morally obliged to bring the country into conformity with divine expectations in spiritual as well as in civil matters. Within this paradigm our authors recognized that the Protestant population of the country, which was principally of British extraction, would for a time at least have to live side by side with the majority Catholic population who, up to this point, had remained aloof from the civil and religious order that the government, and Providence, desired. As they looked to what had happened in the sixteenth century, they attributed much of the blame for the continued attachment to Catholicism of the majority of Ireland's population to deficient English strategies. Once the authors whose works we considered took account of this they seemed satisfied that the Irish, like any other people, would, in the aftermath of a comprehensive conquest, acquiesce in the reform being promoted by the government. Therefore the question that all our authors asked from history, including the history of the recent past, was how they, unlike their predecessors, might secure the goodwill of the diverse populations of the country to bring Ireland to the reformed condition that they all desired.

There the commonality ends, as individual historians drew different lessons from the same past. Stafford and Gainsford, each a historian of the recent war, were generous in praising the English commanders who had achieved victory, but each contended that the commanders in question could not have succeeded without significant assistance from Irish lords. Both authors made special mention of the earls of Clanricard and Thomond, who they also praised for having proven themselves exemplary rulers of their respective lordships. Stafford's and Gainsford's histories were therefore optimistic in that their reading of the recent past suggested to them that a better future for Ireland could be achieved most readily through co-operation between a reform-minded government and such elite figures who would bring the message of reform to those beneath them on the social scale.

NEW HISTORIES FOR A NEW IRELAND   85

This proposition, which was consistent with the thinking behind the surrender and re-grant arrangement of 1542, was very much at variance with the views of the lawyer Sir John Davies. His reading of Ireland's past convinced him that the established elites in Ireland had always treated their social inferiors tyrannically and had induced them frequently to conspire against the Crown. Therefore, as a legal officer of the government, he employed English common law to liberate those being held in thrall by their oppressors. There was, he suggested, ample proof that these were ready to grasp at the prospect of being set free and even reformed. Thus, according to Davies, when Edmund Pelham, the Chief Baron of the Exchequer, had accompanied him in 1603 on the first ever circuit of assize conducted in the province of Ulster, the 'multitude...did reverence him as if he had been an angel sent from heaven'.[78] Davies further explained that he and Pelham experienced no difficulty in identifying people in Ulster who were willing to act as sub-sheriffs and jurors, and Davies also secured the co-operation of some members of Gaelic learned families to supply him with whatever information he required on Gaelic institutional life to assist him in making the case that any claims to position or property being justified under Gaelic law should not be recognized by common-law courts.

As Davies reached out to those who might assist him in his various ventures, he found it necessary to employ interpreters who knew both English and Irish, since Fynes Moryson, who had observed the unfolding of the reform process, had noted that 'in Ulster...all the gentlemen and common people (excepting only the judges' train) and the very jurymen put upon life and death and all trials of law, commonly sp[o]ke Irish, many Spanish, and few or none could or would speak English'.[79] Such reliance on interpreters, as Patricia Palmer has observed, would have placed all the Gaelic Irish at a disadvantage relative to English speakers or government officials, which was acknowledged by Davies when he remarked that the Irish suffered 'great inconvenience in moving their suits by an interpreter'. However, his reading of Ireland's history, as outlined in his *Discovery*, suggested to him that it would be inappropriate for him or other officials to learn to conduct business in the Irish language, lest they, like previous waves of English settlers in Ireland, would be thought to be degenerating to the uncivil condition of their Irish neighbours. Instead, said Davies, the Irish should send 'their children to schools, especially to learn the English language', since this was the proven method of bringing 'a disorderly people...to obedience by the wisdom and

---

[78] Davies to Cecil, 1 December 1603, N.A., S.P. 63 vol. 215, no. 114, f. 261.
[79] Fynes Moryson, 'Of the Commonwealth of Ireland', C. Litton Falkiner, ed., *Illustrations of Irish history and Topography* (London, 1904), 262.

86 IMAGINING IRELAND'S PASTS

discretion of the magistrates' so that within two or three years Ireland would 'grow rich and happy and, in good faith, I think, loyal'.[80]

These remarks by Davies related to his dealings with Gaelic Ulster, but it is clear from what he had to say in the *Discovery* of Ireland's recent history that his attitude towards the more Anglicized lords in the country was hardly more positive than what he thought of Gaelic lords. He insisted in the *Discovery* that the historical record had shown how lords of English extraction could be as tyrannical towards their tenants as any Gaelic lord. Furthermore, he demonstrated how the ancestors of these lords of English lineage had rebelled frequently against Crown government, had perversely brought several governors into disgrace, and were obdurate opponents of religious reform. On a personal level, Davies faulted the Lords of the Pale because whenever he had pleaded legal cases before the courts in Dublin in the interest of advancing the reform of the country, his opponents had invariably been lawyers from those elite families who had taken up practice in Ireland after they had spent time at the Inns of Court in London. For all these reasons, Davies was also determined to make Irish lords of English descent amenable to the law, and he attempted to discipline them in 1605 by mandating them to attend at Protestant service, and later by rearranging constituencies to reduce their representation at the same time that he increased Protestant representation in the 1613–15 parliament. Davies's purpose in dealing with the Lords of the Pale was no different from that governing his relationship with the Gaelic lords in Ulster, which was to undermine their authority, thus making it possible for the government's reform efforts to reach their dependants without hindrance.

It seems that James Ussher, and those associated with his endeavour to achieve the spiritual regeneration of Ireland, were, or became, as doubtful as Davies about the possibility of mediating reform through the existing elites. Ussher, as noted, concerned himself initially with seeking to persuade the elite in the Pale, including his own kin, to conform in religion. Had they responded favourably it is likely that he, as had been intended also of the reformers of 1542, would have then attempted to spread reform outwards from the Pale into other parts of the country. However, when the elite within the Pale spurned his overtures, Ussher did not contemplate proceeding with religious reform from the bottom up but rather employed every device at his disposal to force their compliance. In this respect, like Stafford and Gainsford, he could not imagine reform proceeding without the co-operation of elites.

This, on first appearance, seems at variance with Ussher's concern to have clergy trained so they could conduct their spiritual duties among the Irish-speaking

---

[80] Patricia Palmer, *Language and Conquest in Early Modern Ireland: English Renaissance Literature and Elizabethan Imperial Expansion* (Cambridge, 2001); Davies, *Discovery*, sig. Mm 2 r and v; Davies to Cecil, N.A., S.P. 63, vol. 216, no. 15, ff. 44–7.

communities of the country. What he had in mind there was possibly the conversion of natives in the planted counties of Ulster where the surviving native population would have been both Irish-speaking and usually tenants on lands assigned to the church or on the estates of Protestant servitors. Anybody wishing to engage in missionary work among the native population in such areas would obviously have done so in co-operation with the proprietors of the land they farmed, in which case religious conversion would have become a step towards civil conversion. Even if this was the case, Ussher's enthusiasm for the Irish language was limited. Thus, while he celebrated the success of ministers who had won converts by preaching the word, he himself made no attempt to learn Irish despite his proven aptitude as a linguist. When we take such considerations into account, it seems that Ussher's hope of securing Irish support for the reformed message was not so much by using the Irish language as a medium for communicating the word—we can associate this rather with a few isolated individuals, notably the Irishman William Daniel and the Englishman William Bedell—as by tracing Irish roots for an indigenous Protestant church. This discovery, which Ussher was able to justify by reference to Ireland's ancient past, was obviously designed by him more with the elite than the multitude in mind. Alan Ford has referred to this concern of Ussher, which he shared with Ware, as an expression of a patriotic Protestant interpretation of Ireland's history, with each using the phrase *Hibernia nostra*. He contends that by such means they hoped to win the goodwill of the Irish elite for a Protestant church from which they had become alienated by the persistent debasement of their culture both by the church's ministers and by admirers of the writings of Gerald of Wales.[81]

This would suggest that the views of Davies and Ussher were not as far from each other as may seem from an initial reading. Each, as was the case also with Stafford and Gainsford, drew principles from the past that they hoped would have application in the future. However, in the cases of Davies and Ussher each looked forward also to a return to a lost golden age rather than a mere renovation of existing society. For Davies, whose principal concern was civil matters, this meant a return to a time when Ireland had provided significant support to the English monarchy by supplying financial or military backing for the pursuit of foreign wars. His task, he asserted, was that of transforming a land, which 'like the lean cow of Egypt, in Pharaohs dream, [had been] devouring the fat of England' to 'becoming as fruitful as the land of Canaan'.[82] For Ussher, and also for Ware, the return in question was to a time when the spirit of Christianity in Ireland had been the envy of Europe, which, he insisted, it had been until it had been overcome by the corrupting influence of the papacy.

Wentworth shared Davies's vision of the past when he assumed office as governor of Ireland in 1633. In spiritual matters, however, Wentworth did not

---

[81] Ford, 'The Irish historical renaissance', 153–5.   [82] Davies, *Discovery*, sig. Oo.

88 IMAGINING IRELAND'S PASTS

envisage any return to a lost Irish golden age but an acceptance rather that what was required was to promote in Ireland what John McCafferty has termed 'Ireland's English Reformation'.[83] Perhaps most galling for Ussher and Ware, who were asked to participate what for them was a volte-face, was that Wentworth's preferred path to reform was consistent with what had been recommended a half-century earlier by Spenser whose *View of the State of Ireland* had been one of the histories that Ware had edited for the edification of his new governor.

---

[83] McCafferty, *The Reconstruction of the Church of Ireland*, title of chapter 1.

4

The 1641 Rebellion and Ireland's Contested Pasts

4.1 Introduction

Most readers will have some understanding of how the policies pursued by Wentworth alienated the several interest groups in Ireland, most of whom, for different reasons, arrived at the conclusion that their governor was a tyrant. However, while all groups were aggrieved over the authoritarian behaviour of Wentworth, this was not sufficient to persuade them to disregard past animosities and present a united front against a common oppressor. They were especially reluctant to appear truculent so long as King Charles supported Wentworth. However, once the authority of the monarch was challenged, first by his Protestant subjects in Scotland and then by some strident members of the English parliament, most political figures in Ireland abandoned Wentworth (by now earl of Strafford) to his fate or even contributed to his destruction. At this point the politically active in Ireland strove also to extract concessions from whichever competing groups in Britain they happened to have associations.

It was against this background that those segments of the discontented Catholic gentry, principally from Gaelic families who had no such contacts, conspired to better their position by forceful means. Since the rebels proceeded secretly, historians have been unable to unravel the full scope of the conspiracy. What materialized was a seizure by them of several castles in the planted areas of Ulster, and an alleged plan, which, if it existed, proved a dramatic failure, to seize the arms stored by the government in Dublin Castle.[1] These events triggered a major conflagration in Ireland that was, with but occasional intermission, destined to persist for eleven years. When the fighting had come to an end, all Catholic and all Royalist forces in Ireland had been suppressed by the forces of the English parliament commanded by Oliver Cromwell, with assistance from some Irish Protestants.[2] This conflict and its final outcome gave rise to a fresh outpouring of literature where a sequence of authors, frequently writing in historical format, justified the actions taken by whichever group they championed by reference to the past.

---

[1] Michael Perceval-Maxwell, *The Outbreak of the Irish Rebellion of 1641* (Dublin, 1994).
[2] Micheál Ó Siochrú, *Confederate Ireland, 1642–49: A Constitutional and Political Analysis* (Dublin, 1999); Pádraig Lenihan, *Confederate Catholics at War, 1641–49* (Cork, 2001).

Imagining Ireland's Pasts: Early Modern Ireland through the Centuries. Nicholas Canny, Oxford University Press (2021).
© Nicholas Canny. DOI: 10.1093/oso/9780198808961.003.0004

4.2 After 1641: Protestant Re-Considerations of Ireland's Pasts

The eleven-year interlude of conflict and uncertainty between 1641 and 1652 was obviously not a propitious time for people to engage in historical reflection. Nonetheless, the sudden and unexpected turn of events triggered an immediate and enduring outpouring of pamphlet literature from the Protestant community in Ireland. This had a historical dimension to the extent that several authors saw the need to detail events from the recent past. This was to explain to the authorities, and also to the wider public in England and in Scotland, why the Protestant community that, until 1641, had boasted of the grip it had established over the Catholic population, had succumbed so readily to an attack from people they had previously represented as supine. As they sought to explain this apparent anomaly, authors detailed the tribulations that supposedly peace-loving Protestant settlers had endured after 1641 at the hands of allegedly bloodthirsty assailants. Such narrations were as a preliminary to soliciting military support from all possible sources in England and Scotland with a view to recovering what they had lost and to taking revenge upon the Catholics who, they contended, had, without provocation, attacked, robbed, and killed their Protestant neighbours.[3]

The authors of these early pamphlets were also at pains to authenticate the benevolent attitude of government officials towards all elements of Ireland's population by providing details on the actions of the government in Dublin both in the weeks and months leading to the insurrection of the Catholics on the eve of 23 October 1641 (the precise date, we may recall, to which Ussher had traced the creation), and again in the months immediately following that episode.[4] This citation of detail was thought necessary to counter the arguments being addressed to the king by the Catholic community of the Pale that the Ulster Catholic lords had been provoked into rebellion by harsh actions of government officials. Authors also considered it important to counter the further suggestion that it was the refusal of the government to place trust in the members of the Pale community, when they had offered to assist the government in bringing the Ulster rebels to book, that had left these leaders of the Old English community with no option in 1642 but to join the aggrieved Ulster Catholic insurgents in a Confederacy. Another argument that had to be challenged was that those who had joined this Confederacy were claiming they had done so to counter the

---

[3] Aidan Clarke, 'The 1641 rebellion and anti-popery in Ireland', in Brian Mac Cuarta, ed., *Ulster 1641: Aspects of the Rising* (Belfast, 1993), 139–57; for an examination of much of this pamphlet literature see Mairéad O'Keefe, 'The Politics of Irish Protestants, 1641–1660' (M.A. thesis, NUI Galway, 1991).

[4] On Ussher's date for the creation see Chapter 3 ; Nicholas Bernard, who wrote the first biography of Ussher cited a sermon given by Ussher in 1601 where he supposedly predicted the occurrence of the 1641 rebellion, Ford, *Ussher*, 30–1.

THE 1641 REBELLION AND IRELAND'S CONTESTED PASTS   91

ambitions of some Dublin officials, and some radical members of the Westminster parliament, to deprive them of their estates.[5]

The counter-argument of the Protestant authors to such suggestions held that a universal 'treason and rebellion' had been long plotted 'by the disloyal and perfidious Romanists, the incendiaries of all Christendom' at several 'conventicles and meetings', particularly at an alleged convocation convened in May 1641 at a friary in Multifarnham in County Westmeath. The 'plot' then agreed upon, according to the author of one such pamphlet, was to have 'select men' invite 'themselves to breakfast or dinner' to 'most of the king's forts and castles throughout the realm' on 23 October 1641 with a view to taking these defensible positions by surprise. It was further stated that the next step in their plan had been to unleash 'a multitude of desperate, savage barbarous fellows' to slaughter and terrorize the Protestant population of the country, proclaiming 'now are ye wild Irish as well as we'. This outcome had been thwarted, according to this reporter, by 'the providence of God' acting through 'the honest man Owen O'Connolly, being an Irish man but a Protestant' who had divulged to the authorities that a plot was afoot to take Dublin Castle. Once the universal attack had been thus pre-empted, our author claimed that the Old English of the Pale had for one month continued to insist that it was only 'some malcontented Old Irish' who had entered upon a revolt. This, according to the anonymous author, was refuted by the fact that the Old English had later joined with the Ulster insurgents. Their doing so satisfied the author that, from the outset, the rebellion had been 'Universal, Romish and devilish even for a kingdom'. The author further argued that the Irish Catholics had settled on this stratagem only because an earlier plot had not proceeded as well as had been intended. This earlier plot, 'practiced by the lurking Jesuits, and their adherents the Romanists in general', had been designed, it was asserted, to provoke a civil war between King Charles I and his subjects in Scotland.[6]

The initial spurt of Protestant pamphlet literature concerning the outbreak of hostilities in 1641 thus represents one side of what was to become a contentious debate between Protestants and Anglophone Catholics in Ireland over who was responsible for the breakdown of order that led to the prolonged warfare of the mid-seventeenth century. In order to satisfy authorities in England that officials in Dublin were in no way culpable for the dual Catholic resort to arms, Protestant pamphleteers detailed the actions of the government in Dublin about this time, even to the extent of reproducing copies of official documents to demonstrate that officials in Dublin had always acted with probity and impartiality. The hope

---

[5] Eamon Darcy, *The Irish Rebellion of 1641 and the Wars of the Three Kingdoms* (Woodbridge, 2013), 153–7.

[6] *A perfect relation of the beginning and continuation of the Irish rebellion from May last [May 1641] to this present 12 January 1641* [1641/2] (London, 1641/2), sigs. A3r, A3v, Br, Bv, A3r.

92   IMAGINING IRELAND'S PASTS

of the pamphleteers and the officials who inspired them was that their candour concerning the actions and discussions that had been taking place within the inner circles of government would make it clear that officials in Dublin bore no responsibility for the outbreak of disturbances.[7]

While the pamphleteers may have satisfied the authorities in London (but not Catholics in Ireland) on this score, it still did not explain why the Protestant community in Ireland had succumbed so easily to an attack by those they had always represented as weak and unthreatening. The emphasis placed by all pamphleteers on the brutal nature of the attacks made upon particular families or individuals (particularly upon clergy and their womenfolk) offered an oblique answer to this conundrum in that it implied that the Irish who had attacked the innocent Protestant community had, by their actions, proven themselves to be barbarians who, by their very nature, were opponents of everything that symbolized civility.

If this explained for some why the Irish acted as they did in 1641, the question remained why those who were now being represented as inherently barbaric had been quiescent for so long and lived in apparent amity with their Protestant neighbours. The pamphleteers addressed this issue in a manner designed to convince militant Protestants in England by invoking the supposed clandestine activities against the Protestant Reformation and the British state that had been under way everywhere since the commencement of the Reformation. Such actions, they insisted, were being constantly plotted by the papacy in conjunction with the major Catholic monarchies in Europe, and also with the Catholic clergy and their patrons in Ireland and Britain, who were now identified as the local agents of these foreign powers. Pointing to such connections made it possible for pamphleteers to suggest that the apparent contentedness of Irish Catholics in the months and years previous to the uprising in 1641 had been but simulated at the suggestion of the Catholic clergy with the purpose of putting the government and the Protestant settler community off their guard. All, as Henry Jones put it, had taken place 'at the instigation of the Popish priests, friars and Jesuits with other firebrands and incendiaries of the State...out of that ancient and known hatred the Church of Rome beareth to the reformed religion'. What had happened, insisted Jones, was that the gullible and barbaric population of Ireland had been used by the Catholic clergy to execute 'their long laid conspiracy' which they had deferred until they were confident they could effect a 'combination from parts foreign with those at home' by bringing in soldiers from Flanders and France

---

[7] To this end the authorities in Dublin commissioned the clergyman Henry Jones, Dean of Kilmore, to print *A Remonstrance of divers remarkable passages concerning the church and kingdom of Ireland* (London 1642) that Jones was authorized to present before the English House of Commons; Toby Barnard, '1641; a bibliographical essay', Brian Mac Cuarta, ed., *Ulster 1641*, 173–86.

THE 1641 REBELLION AND IRELAND'S CONTESTED PASTS   93

after the manner of what had happened during the Wars of Religion in France, as was proven by the 'allusion' made by the conspirators 'to that League in France'.[8]

These various arguments, which were adumbrated and asserted in the pamphlets issued in the months and years immediately following the rising in 1641, were elaborated upon by individual Protestants when, from the early months of 1642 onward, they gave sworn public testimony before a series of government-appointed commissioners, of which Henry Jones was the convenor, concerning what they had experienced or witnessed during the rebellion.[9] Some of the assertions made in this testimony, now known as the 1641 depositions, were possibly inspired by the early pamphlets, while extracts from particular depositions were cited as evidence in pamphlets published subsequent to the collection of the depositions. This indicates how pamphlet publication and deposition collecting became mutually supporting. We find, for example, that Thomas Waring who had been involved with Henry Jones in the collection of the depositions, published a pamphlet, which John Cunningham has demonstrated was the composite work of Waring and John Hall, an English propagandist and close associate of Milton, that was intended to bring readers up to date with their thinking until such time as Waring would get about to printing 'a large volume of depositions'.[10] Pamphlets and depositions were sometimes dedicated to describing particular incidents that had happened during the course of the insurrection, but some also situated the insurrection in a broader context. Each individual pamphlet, like each particular deposition, was represented as a history, and collectively they contributed to the creation of a Protestant memory of Ireland's history that was very different from that which had been cultivated by Ussher and Ware.

The Protestant authors of this new generation looked back to the apocalyptic writers of the sixteenth century, and, like them, they denied Ireland's Catholics any history worthy of recall. As it was put in 1650 by John Hall in his section of *A brief narration*, anybody who would take a 'right view' of the Irish would find them to be 'incapable of any impressions of virtue or honour' since they were 'a root of such a profound sloth, and lethargic supinitie that they will say they are merely a kind of reptile, things creeping on their bellies and feeding on the dirt of the earth'. Moreover, when the condition of the Irish was considered historically,

---

[8] Henry Jones *A Remonstrance of divers remarkable passages*, sigs. Bv, Br, B2v.

[9] Aidan Clarke, 'The commission for the despoiled subject, 1641-7', Brian Mac Cuarta, ed., *Reshaping Ireland*, 241-60; for a discussion of how the depositions came into being see Clarke, 'The 1641 depositions', P. Fox, ed., *Treasures of the Library, Trinity College, Dublin* (Dublin, 1984), 111-22.

[10] The depositions, housed in the Library of Trinity College, Dublin Mss. 809-841, can be accessed online at http://1641.tcd.ie.; John Cunningham, 'Milton, John Hall and Thomas Waring's *Brief Narration of the Rebellion in Ireland*', *Milton Quarterly*, 53 (2019), 69-85; T[homas]W[aring] with J[ohn] H[all], *A brief narration of the plotting, beginning and carrying of that execrable rebellion and butchery in Ireland* (London, 1650); the interconnection between the manuscript depositions and pamphleteering is discussed in Eamon Darcy, *The Irish Rebellion*, 141-3.

94 IMAGINING IRELAND'S PASTS

there was ample proof, claimed Hall, that they could not 'by the conversation and culture of the more polite English...be shap't into any adumbration of Civility and tersnesse, but still remain a people so exquisitely savage, so barbarously lothsom, so monstrously enclyn'd, that they were as uncapable of any impressions of virtue and honour, as they have shewed themselves susceptible of the most bestial lewdnesse, and consumate impiety'.[11]

Again, like the earlier apocalyptic authors, the Protestant reporters on the real or imagined events of 1641 looked with confidence to the future because they took survival of their community from the universal slaughter that had been intended by their assailants to mean that the assault had been part of a providential plan to test the faith of true believers. There was no longer any suggestion, as there had been in the writings of Ussher and Ware, that God tended to permit people (or at least godly people) some latitude in the management of secular affairs. Instead authors proceeded from the assumption that providential oversight of humans was constant, and that providential intervention occurred frequently to test, reward, and punish mere mortals. The ultimate victory of the community of true believers in Ireland was the proof that they had been sufficiently punished for past failings, the chief of which had been their tolerance of Catholicism. What they had endured was being re-enacted in their publications to remind their readers and future generations of Protestants that they must never again fail to suppress ungodly living when it was within their power to do so.[12]

These several themes, which were touched upon sometimes individually and sometimes in clusters by particular authors, were all brought together in 1646 by Sir John Temple, who had been Master of the Rolls in Dublin at the time of the insurrection of 1641. The resulting book published in London was entitled *The Irish Rebellion: or an History of the Attempts of the Irish Papists to extirpate the Protestants in the Kingdom of Ireland*. This proved the most successful and most enduring of the many Protestant publications dedicated to describing, explaining, and contextualizing what supposedly had happened in Ireland in 1641–42.[13]

Temple's book, which exerted an early and continuing influence on Irish Protestant opinion, was a history not only, as its subtitle suggests, of the events

---

[11] T[homas]W[aring] with J[ohn] H[all], *A brief narration*, 41–2; Cunningham, 'Milton, John Hall and Thomas Waring's *Brief Narration*'.

[12] See, for example, Henry Jones as cited in Clarke, 'The commission for the despoiled subject', 254.

[13] John Temple, *The Irish Rebellion: or an History of the Attempts of the Irish Papists to extirpate the Protestants in the Kingdom of Ireland; together with the Barbarous Cruelties and Bloody Massacres which ensued thereupon* (London, 1646); the edition cited here is the anniversary edition published in 1746. For suggestions on of how this text was read by some Protestants in the seventeenth century, and for indications on how it was assembled, see Raymond Gillespie, 'Temple's Fate; reading *The Irish Rebellion* in late seventeenth-century Ireland', Ciaran Brady and Jane Ohlmeyer, eds., *British Interventions in Early Modern Ireland* (Cambridge, 2005), 315–33; for twenty-first century readings of the text see Nicholas Canny, '1641 in a colonial context', Micheál Ó Siochrú and Jane Ohlmeyer, eds., *Ireland 1641: Contexts and Reactions* (Manchester, 2013), 52–70; Eamon Darcy, *The Irish Rebellion*, 96–101.

THE 1641 REBELLION AND IRELAND'S CONTESTED PASTS   95

leading up to the insurrection of 1641 but a reinterpretation of the history of Ireland from the time of the first English conquest of the twelfth century to Temple's own time. Temple encouraged his readers to think expansively by likening his task of explaining and describing what had happened in Ireland in 1641 to that undertaken, but never completed, by Monsieur du Plessis, a minister of state to King Henry IV of France, 'to write a History of those times wherein he lived', when the notorious St Bartholomew's Day Massacre, had been enacted.[14] Temple, like du Plessis when writing of massacre in France, wished posterity to know 'of the first beginnings and fatal progress of this rebellion, together with the horrid cruelties most unmercifully exercised by the Irish Rebels, upon the British and Protestants within this Kingdom of Ireland'.[15]

In his effort to explain what, he claimed, was the barbaric behaviour of the Irish in 1641, Temple reverted to Gerald of Wales to sustain his assertion that, while missionaries from Britain had done everything possible to effect 'the conversion of a barbarous people' in Ireland, the Irish had persisted with their 'depraved and barbarous manners' until 1172, when King Henry II of England undertook 'to conquer Ireland and reduce those beastly men unto the way of truth'.[16] This condition of the people, averred Temple, left King Henry with no option but to seize 'by the sword...all the lands of the whole kingdom', which, claimed Temple, had been further justified because the fertile land and rich resources in the country lay neglected because of the retarded condition of the people.[17]

Temple continued throughout his narrative to juxtapose the supposed barbarism of the people with the fertility of the land, and he used this trope to explain why, over the centuries, several English monarchs had persisted with the effort to introduce civil institutions and enterprising colonies to Ireland. Their purpose in doing so, he claimed, was to ensure that the resources with which God had endowed the country would be made available for the benefit of all humanity. Despite their benevolence, he claimed, monarchs had found repeatedly that whenever the hand of friendship had been extended to the Irish they had spurned it with brutal attacks so that 'Ireland hath long remained a true Aceldama, a Field of Blood, an unsatiated sepulchre of the English nation'.[18] Temple professed, after the manner of Sir John Davies, that this cycle of violence appeared to have been brought to an end once the army of Queen Elizabeth had secured a comprehensive military victory over all opponents and after a sequence of plantations had introduced some Protestant newcomers. These, he claimed, had brought such 'civility' to the country that 'the whole Kingdom began exceedingly to flourish...the

---

[14] Temple, *The Irish Rebellion*, preface, v.   [15] Temple, *The Irish Rebellion*, preface, vii.
[16] Temple, *The Irish Rebellion*, 6–7.   [17] Temple, *The Irish Rebellion*, 5–6.
[18] Temple, *The Irish Rebellion*, 13; Aceldama was the place in Jerusalem where Judas had purchased the potter's field with the blood money he had received for betraying Christ.

96 IMAGINING IRELAND'S PASTS

people to multiply and increase, and the very Irish seemed to be much satisfied with the benefits of that peaceable government, and general tranquillity, which they so happily enjoyed.[19]

Temple then asserted that during the reign of King Charles I, Irish Catholics had been ruled by a government that was so 'sweet tempered, and carried on with great lenity and moderation' that it had permitted them to enjoy 'the private exercise of all their religious rites and ceremonies...without any manner of disturbance'.[20] Indeed, claimed Temple, the country became so placid that it seemed that the optimistic outcome predicted in 1612 by Sir John Davies had been achieved, and Temple detailed how the 'two nations', having 'lived together 40 years in peace, with great security and comfort', appeared 'consolidated...into one body, knit and compacted together' to the extent that their interactions suggested they 'might make up a constant and perpetual Union betwixt them'.[21]

The sudden resort to rebellion by the Irish on 23 October 1641, asserted Temple, established that this apparent contentment of the Irish had been simulated so they would be given the opportunity to insinuate themselves into the homes, communities, and affections of the settlers until they could 'seize most treacherously' the fortified positions held by the English, and surprise, rob, and murder all British Protestants in Ireland. This stratagem, claimed Temple, meant that the 'English were...easily over-run...and so suddenly swallowed up before they could make any manner of resistance in the very beginnings of the rebellion'.[22] In detailing how this had occurred, Temple provided graphic descriptions of how previous obligations had been suddenly cast aside by the Irish as they indulged with barbaric abandon in the slaughter of their former neighbours.[23]

Therefore, for Temple, as for many of the pamphleteers who had preceded him in print, the tranquillity of the country previous to the insurrection, the suddenness and universality of the outbreak, and the uniform character of the assault launched against Protestant settlers in all parts of the country, combined to make it clear that the insurrection was the outcome of a long-prepared conspiracy. Temple then mentioned the intelligence provided to the government in Dublin by Owen O'Connolly on the evening of 22 October 1641 to the effect that some Irish Catholic noblemen intended to seize the arms stored in Dublin Castle as a preliminary to slaughtering all Protestants within the city. O'Connolly's testimony satisfied Temple, as it had the earlier pamphleteers, that the insurrection that actually did take place in Ulster the following day was part of a universal plot that would have been enacted also in Dublin but for the warning given by O'Connolly who, averred Temple, was 'a gentleman of a mere Irish family, but one

---

[19] Temple, *The Irish Rebellion*, 20–1.   [20] Temple, *The Irish Rebellion*, 23–4.
[21] Temple, *The Irish Rebellion*, 25.   [22] Temple, *The Irish Rebellion*, 60, 68.
[23] Temple, *The Irish Rebellion*, 61–2.

THE 1641 REBELLION AND IRELAND'S CONTESTED PASTS   97

that had long lived among the English, and had been trained up in the true Protestant religion'. While the information supplied by O'Connolly had saved the castle and the city, it came too late, according to Temple, to save the Protestant population of Ulster.[24] His testimony on what had occurred in that province came from the depositions, 'taken upon oath', from the Protestant survivors of the insurrection, which satisfied him that the rebels intended a 'universal destruction of all the British and Protestants there planted'.[25]

Given the low regard that Temple and his colleagues in the Dublin government had of the capability of Irish Catholic lords, he denied them credit for devising such a devious scheme. The organizers, he pronounced, were the Continentally trained priests, who had, as if by witchcraft, 'charmed the Irish, and laid such bloody impressions upon them, as it was held, according to the Maxims they had received, a mortal sin to give any relief or protection to the English'.[26]

It was not difficult for the priests to thus gull the Irish lords into rebellion, claimed Temple, because, notwithstanding the English-style attire in which the leaders of the Irish were depicted in contemporary woodcuts, they remained as barbaric as those of their ancestors who had submitted to King Henry II, and those who had turned their backs on the benevolent rule of Queen Elizabeth. Indeed, their actions of 1641, according to Temple, proved that they were more proficient at killing than any of their progenitors because they had been permitted to live 'promiscuously among the British in all parts'.[27] The lesson to be learned from this manifestation of duplicity and barbarity by the Irish lords and their subordinates, claimed Temple, was that the British should abandon the repeated efforts that had been made over several centuries to draw the Irish to civility and should instead have 'such a wall of separation set up betwixt the Irish and British as it shall not be in their [the Irish] power to rise up (as now and in all former ages they have done) to destroy and root them [the British] out in a moment'.[28]

Thus, notwithstanding his assertion that Owen O'Connolly was a true convert whose action had saved the Protestant community in Dublin from being obliterated, Temple was as insistent as any of the apocalyptic historians from the sixteenth century that Irish people could never become the cultural and legal equals of English people because of their inherent barbarism. In doing this he was turning his back not only on the conciliatory attitude of Ussher and Ware who had conceded a civil pedigree to the Irish but he was also disregarding the arguments of Spenser and Davies that barbaric Irish people (or at least those of them who survived the military defeats inflicted upon them) could be made indistinguishable from civil English people by being subjected to a comprehensive conquest followed by a rigidly enforced reform programme.

---

[24] Temple, *The Irish Rebellion*, 30.   [25] Temple, *The Irish Rebellion*, 215–6.
[26] Temple, *The Irish Rebellion*, 61.   [27] Temple, *The Irish Rebellion*, 61.
[28] Temple, *The Irish Rebellion*, preface, viii.

98 IMAGINING IRELAND'S PASTS

Temple justified this apparent volte-face both by reference to Irish and European precedent, and by liberal citation from the anti-Irish invective of Gerald of Wales. Far more convincing for Temple was his belief that the assault endured by Protestants in Ireland in 1641 had been intended by God as a test of their faith. This was the aspect of his argument that made his *History of the Irish Rebellion* a text that would be accorded the same reverence by future generations of Irish Protestants as was given by English Protestants to John Foxe's *Book of Martyrs* or by French Huguenots to Jean Crespin's *Actes des martyrs*.[29] Acceptance of this belief meant that they could read their deliverance as proof that they had been received back into divine favour and that, in time, God would have Ireland 'to be re-planted with British and settled in peace again'.[30] However, for Temple, what had occurred made it clear also that divine favour could be as easily withdrawn if the true believers failed to remedy their past failures. For him as for the many authors who followed in his tradition, the most heinous of these failures had been their readiness to turn a blind eye to Catholic religious practice when it was in their power to banish such 'idolatry' from their midst.

Many Irish Protestants of the later seventeenth and eighteenth century believed that Temple's injunction to separate Irish Catholics from true believers had been fulfilled by the enactment of laws against popery, but others asserted that God would be placated only if the Protestants wreaked vengeance upon the entire Catholic population once they had achieved military dominance over them. This, according to John Hall in that same pamphlet usually attributed solely to Thomas Waring, had been partly accomplished by Cromwell's slaughter of Catholics at Drogheda and Wexford in 1649. However, Hall still believed that 'we', by whom he meant Protestant Parliamentarians, 'may warrantably and righteously endeavour the extirpation of them who by their hellish designs and accomplished patricides [had] endeavoured and highly attempted to make us to be no more a people'.[31] This assertion by Hall in the aftermath of the Cromwellian conquest was only marginally more extreme that the sentiments expressed by Temple in 1646, and both were in sharp contrast to the hope expressed by Davies in 1612 that the Irish and British settler populations would become a single loyal population under the British monarchy. It stood in contrast also to the self-satisfied remark made by James Ware in 1633 to which Alan Ford has drawn our attention. In that, Ware, citing the Roman poet Claudian, pronounced approvingly that, after close

---

[29] John Foxe, *Acts and Monuments of these latter and perilous days* (London, 1563); soon known popularly as *Foxe's Book of Martyrs*; Jean Crespin, *Actes des martyrs deduits en sept livres...Hus* (Geneva, 1564); on the importance attached by future generations of Protestants to Temple see Toby Barnard, '1641; a bibliographic essay', and Gillespie, 'Temple's Fate'; see also Sarah Covington, '"Those Savage Days of Memory": John Temple and his Narrative of the 1641 Rebellion', Fionnuala Dillane, Naomi McAreavey, and Emilie Pine, eds., *The Body in Pain in Irish Literature and Culture* (London, 2016), 57–76.

[30] Temple, *The Irish Rebellion*, preface, vii.

[31] T[homas]W[aring] with J[ohn] H[all], *A brief narration*, 58.

THE 1641 REBELLION AND IRELAND'S CONTESTED PASTS   99

on thirty years of peace, the diverse populations in Ireland had become 'united as one people' as had happened similarly when traditional divisions between peoples had been overcome in Ancient Rome.[32]

If Hall offered a more extreme solution than Temple for averting God's wrath, he agreed with him that Irish people, by which was meant Irish Catholics, had no history besides that which showed them to have been perverse opponents of every attempt that had been made to reform them. This view became entrenched in the minds of many Protestant authors and we find, for example, that Edmund Borlase, a Protestant historian of the next generation and a son of Sir John Borlase who had been one of Ireland's joint governors in 1641, stated baldly in 1675 that Ireland's history was no more than a record of the efforts of successive English rulers since 1172 to introduce 'good' things to the country and of the endeavours of the Irish to counter this benevolence through rebellion.[33] In this, Borlase was endorsing for his generation what had been stated some thirty years previously by such as Temple, Waring, and Hall. Militant Protestants thought it important that this narrative of what had happened in Ireland in 1641, and the inferences that could be drawn from it, should be rehearsed regularly because, as Hall pronounced, it would put Protestants on their guard by reminding them that rebellion was 'natural and necessary' to the Irish who 'even in the flourishing times of Queen Elizabeth they nine times forsook their obedience'.[34]

Thus for Protestants of the seventeenth and the eighteenth centuries, the history of what happened in Ireland from the reign of Queen Elizabeth to 1641 was a time of especial importance in the overall history of the country, as events in the reigns of Henry VIII and Edward VI were now treated summarily, despite these being the reigns in which religious reform had been introduced to Ireland, as had been made clear in previous Protestant accounts. Greater attention was now given to what had happened in the reign of Queen Elizabeth because this could be used to illustrate how the Irish—and Temple exemplified this by reference to Hugh O'Neill, earl of Tyrone—had persistently rejected the peace overtures that had been extended to them. From there, authors proceeded to speak favourably of the endeavours made to bring further civility in Ireland through the instrument of plantation during the reign of King James VI and I. Then, when it came to the reign of Charles I, they explained that Catholics had then been treated leniently, which, as Thomas Waring put it, had given 'the Romish clergy' the opportunity to plot the destruction of Protestantism 'first within England, Ireland and Scotland and afterwards in what ends of the world soever it...should be taught and professed'.[35] Then also, according to Hall, who

---

[32] Ford, 'The Irish Historical Renaissance', 155.
[33] Edmund Borlase, *The Reduction of Ireland to the Crown of England* (London, 1675).
[34] T[homas]W[aring] with J[ohn] H[all], *A brief narration*, 58.
[35] T[homas]W[aring] with J[ohn] H[all], *A brief narration*, 2.

became a dedicated supporter of Oliver Cromwell and an apologist for the regicide, Irish Catholics had found in Wentworth 'a Lord Lieutenant according to their own hearts' who, by his treatment of the London Companies in the Ulster Plantation, had proven himself to be more hostile to Protestants than to Catholics as he sought on behalf of 'a Protestant king' to indulge 'traitorous Papists' and 'to lull and stupefy his own subjects'.[36]

This interpretation of what had transpired in Ireland during the early modern centuries had to be revised following the Restoration of 1660 to render it palatable to a Protestant community that now wished to represent itself as Royalist even when many of its prominent members were known to have served the Parliamentary cause.[37] This imperative explains why it was Temple's narration of events, rather than the Waring/Hall anti-monarchical tirade, that retained wide acceptance within Ireland's Protestant community after 1660, even when, as Eamon Darcy has explained, Temple's interpretation was now mediated through Samuel Clarke, *A general martyrologie*.[38]

It is clear that pronouncements such as these represented a rejection of the attitudes towards the indigenous populations of Ireland that had been expressed by such as Ussher and Ware in the 1630s, and an abandonment of the prospect that the diverse populations of the country might, one day, become united as a single, loyal, Anglicized, Protestant population. This is not to suggest that Ussher or Temple would have thought differently from Temple on the extent to which the 1641 rebellion represented a fundamental breach of trust that should be dealt with severely. Rather what was being denied, and this represented a return to the apocalyptic Protestant views that had won favour in the sixteenth century and to the opinions expressed by Gerald of Wales in the twelfth century, was that any civilization had ever existed in Ireland previous to the English conquests of the country, and that any Irish people were amenable to being reformed.

We do not know if the events of 1641, and what ensued thereafter, gave James Ussher any reason to depart from the culturally conciliatory views he had expressed in the 1630s given that he spent the last two decades of his life in England where he concentrated on biblical scholarship prior to his death in 1656. However, we have solid reason to believe that James Ware stood firmly by his cultural views even though the rebels had killed a brother of his. Ware, who, as noted, had been a staunch supporter of Wentworth, remained a firm Royalist and bitter opponent of the Cromwellian regime and had spent most of the years of conflict and the Interregnum in exile from Ireland, first in England and later in France. Then, soon after Charles II had recovered his throne in 1660, Ware

---

[36] T[homas]W[aring] with J[ohn] H[all], *A brief narration*, 58.

[37] Aidan Clarke, *Prelude to Restoration in Ireland: The End of the Commonwealth, 1659–1660* (Cambridge, 1999).

[38] Eamon Darcy, *The Irish Rebellion*, 144–6; Samuel Clarke, *A Generall Martyrologie* (London, 1651).

THE 1641 REBELLION AND IRELAND'S CONTESTED PASTS   101

resumed his post as auditor general in Ireland, and resumed also his scholarly activity in which he had maintained an interest during his years in exile. Soon after his return to Ireland he became aware of two Gaelic scholars, Dubhaltach Mac Fhirbhisigh (c.1600–71), a Connacht genealogist, and Roderic O'Flaherty (1629–1718), an antiquary from County Galway, who had each been engaged upon Ireland's history during his absence from the country. Therefore Ware, like Ussher in his dealings with Irish scholars a generation previously, sought to learn of the findings of these two later Catholic scholars. He did so both through correspondence and by inviting them to Dublin in the years prior to his death in 1666. Such contacts, added to his own family links with the McRagnalls, may explain how Ware became acquainted also with the publications of John Lynch (c.1599–1677), a Catholic scholar-priest from Galway, who had taken up residence in France, and continued to publish from there.[39]

Ware's continued interaction with Irish Catholic scholars and his persistent interest in, and respect for, Irish culture of earlier centuries did nothing to diminish his reputation as a scholar even when his writings had lost their persuasive powers for Irish Protestants who had endured the trauma of 1641. It was probably because of the scholarly reputation that James Ware had enjoyed in earlier years, and because of his known association with Ussher, whose name continued to be revered by the Protestant international, that his son Robert Ware, who inherited his father's papers, and later again Walter Harris, who had married Ware's great-granddaughter, each took steps to adapt the published work of James Ware to serve the needs and interests of the Irish Protestants of their respective generations. Robert Ware took the first step to co-opt his father's reputation to serve this greater cause when preparing an English translation of his father's writings. Two English-language editions of the complete works of James Ware, published respectively by Robert Ware in 1705 and by Walter Harris in 1764, were based on Robert Ware's translation from the original Latin.[40] These editions were 'revised and improved' in two ways. First, Robert Ware purported that his father had left in his 'custody' a corrected version of the printed Latin edition of his works, which before his death he had 'interleaved' with 'many corrections and additions in his own hand', with the intention 'had he lived...to have published a new edition of his writings which he had enlarged and corrected'. Robert Ware used this fiction to modify his father's work in translation with a view to making these publications more useful for present political purposes, always insisting that

[39] Nollaig Ó Muraíle, *The Celebrated Antiquary Dubhaltach Mac Fhirbhisighh (c. 1600–71): His Lineage, Life and Learning* (Maynooth, 1996), 99–101, 194–5, 219, 246–63; Richard Sharpe, ed., *Roderick O'Flaherty's Letters...1696–1709* (Dublin, 2013), 1, 32, 36–7; on Lynch see Campbell, *Renaissance Humanism*, esp. 113–23.

[40] Robert Ware, *The Antiquities and History of Ireland by...Sir James Ware* (Dublin, 1705); Walter Harris, *The Whole Works of Sir James Ware concerning Ireland revised and improved* (Dublin, 1764); D. Mc Culloch, 'Foxes, firebrands and forgery; Robert Ware's pollution of reformation history', *Historical Journal*, 54 (2011), 307–46.

his translation was of 'this corrected and interleaved book'.[41] The second way in which Robert Ware, and later Walter Harris, adapted the writings of James Ware was by updating them by adding fresh biographical sketches of Irish authors and actors who had lived and worked throughout the full course of the seventeenth century.[42]

These revised English language editions of the works of James Ware were less laudatory of Irish culture than the original Latin texts of James Ware. Then, for the sixteenth and seventeenth centuries, the English language editions included more critical political comment on passing events than James Ware had ever composed. The translator/editors were especially concerned to introduce 'many particulars relating to the rebellion of 1641 which do not occur in the histories of those times'. On the positive side these particulars included entries on many Protestant personalities who had been involved with the suppression of that rebellion, especially as in the cases of James Butler, first duke of Ormond, and Roger Boyle, first earl of Orrery, where the individuals held positions of influence in the Restoration period. Then, when it came to considering the scholarly achievements of Irish Catholic clergy of the seventeenth century, the editors of the English text continued to acknowledge and summarize the publications of the individuals much as James Ware would have done. However, they alluded also to the links these clergy had had with 'the Pope, Cardinals and other Ecclesiastics whose main endeavour was to destroy the religion of peace preached by Christ and his apostles'. Thus, for example, Robert Ware devoted nine pages in the English-language text to describing the scholarly publications of the Franciscan, Luke Wadding, in laudatory fashion. Having done so, he included the assertion that it had been his father's wish, given the quality of Wadding's scholarship, that he 'could excuse him from the hand he had in fomenting and aiding the Irish rebellion which broke out in 1641; the only action of his life that hath tarnished his great virtues'.[43]

It is likely that Sir James Ware would have been at one with his son and with Walter Harris in condemning all people associated with the 1641 rebellion, and that he too would have seen it as a defining moment in Ireland's history. However, by a clever sleight of hand Ware's family successors were co-opting him posthumously into the ranks of those historians who condemned all of Ireland's population as barbaric and incapable of being reformed. As they did so they were suggesting that the only matters in Ireland's history worthy of recall were episodes, such as the 1641 rebellion, that provided evidence of the perfidy of Irish papists.

---

[41] Walter Harris, *The Whole Works of Sir James Ware*, 149.
[42] Walter Harris, *The Whole Works of Sir James Ware*, 150.
[43] Walter Harris, *The Whole Works of Sir James Ware*, 130–9; for a recent appraisal on Wadding see Matteo Binasco, ed., *Luke Wadding, the Irish Franciscans and Global Catholicism* (N.Y. and Abington, 2020).

THE 1641 REBELLION AND IRELAND'S CONTESTED PASTS   103

While the writings of James Ware were thus modified to serve the needs of a Protestant interpretation of Ireland's history, especially that concerning the seventeenth century, new Protestant authors came forward to add to the narrative particularly following the scare associated with the fabricated Popish Plot of 1678–79,[44] and again after 1688 when Irish Catholics continued to support the Catholic King James II after he had been ousted from his throne by his Protestant daughter Mary with her husband William of Orange. On both occasions it was broadcast widely that the extermination by Catholics of all Protestants in the country had been intended, and that the events of 1641 would have been re-enacted were it not that the plans of the Catholics had been frustrated by accidental occurrences and by the vigilance of a Protestant community. Even then, after Protestants had emerged victorious from the Jacobite/Williamite conflict of 1688–91, authors complained of how they had been compelled by the government of King James II, when he technically had still been their legitimate monarch, to contribute towards the maintenance of Catholic regiments that, as they saw it, had been raised to oppress Protestants.

In this context Archbishop William King detailed how many Protestants, particularly Protestant clergy, had thought it better to flee for security to England after 1688 in the knowledge that 'every forty years we constantly have had a rebellion' of Catholics bent on 'the utter extirpation' of Protestantism. This had been prevented in the 1690s, according to King, only because Protestants in Ireland had defended themselves with support from King William of Orange who 'was raised up by God to be a deliverer to us and the Protestant cause'. While Archbishop King celebrated this deliverance, he still pointed to the need for further curtailing the power of Catholics in Ireland because, even when they had lacked the opportunity to destroy the Protestants, as he insisted Catholics had attempted to do in 1641, 'they had devoured us in their imagination'. The curtailment of the power of Catholics favoured by Archbishop King took the form of yet another confiscation of property and the enactment through the parliaments in Dublin and Westminster of a suite of laws against the 'growth of Popery', which, in Catholic parlance, would become known as the Penal Laws.[45]

Historians of recent years who have tracked the dates when *The Irish Rebellion* by Sir John Temple was reprinted, and when analogous texts were published, have found that this unadulterated Protestant interpretation of Ireland's history for the early modern centuries was refreshed in people's minds whenever external factors

---

[44] John Gibney, *Ireland and the Popish Plot* (Basingstoke, 2009).

[45] William King, *The State of the Protestants of Ireland under the Late King James's Government* (London, 1691), 147–8, 288–9; J.G. Simms, *The Williamite Confiscation in Ireland, 1690–1703* (London, 1956); on the background to the enactment of the Penal Laws see Ian McBride, *Eighteenth-Century Ireland: The Isle of Slaves* (Dublin, 2009), Sean Connolly, *Divided Kingdom, Ireland 1630–1800* (Oxford, 2008), esp. 197–207; and Thomas O'Connor, 'The Catholic Church and Catholics in an Era of Sanctions and Restraints', in James Kelly, ed., *The Cambridge History of Ireland*, vol. III (Cambridge, 2018), 257–79.

104   IMAGINING IRELAND'S PASTS

raised the possibility that foreign aid would tempt Catholics to resort once more to arms to recover what they had lost because of their involvement with successive rebellions of the sixteenth and seventeenth centuries.[46] This interpretation, which was extended to a wider Protestant audience by the preaching (and sometimes printing) of sermons in Protestant (including Presbyterian) churches throughout Ireland each year on the anniversary date of 23 October, frequently included a backwards glance to the reign of Queen Elizabeth to find evidence of the propensity of Irish Catholics to rebel. Protestant authors, clergy, and officials remained attached to this account throughout the eighteenth century and into the nineteenth century, both because it fostered unity within a community that was divided along denominational and social lines, and because it helped them justify their opposition to any relaxation of a politico/religious code that was being described as anomalous in more enlightened times, especially when viewed in an international context. However, it was also convenient that at more relaxed moments, those Protestants, and particularly elite Protestants of Irish ancestry whose families had only conformed to Protestantism at the outset of the eighteenth century, who wished to know something about Ireland's more distant past and the place of their progenitors within it could consult the antiquarian works of Sir James Ware, as these had been sanitized by his son and the husband of his great-granddaughter without compromising the apocalyptic narrative that had been pursued so grippingly by Sir John Temple.

4.3 Catholic Responses to the Revised Protestant Narrative

The repeated recitation of this revised Protestant narrative meant that Catholics who retained some property and position in Ireland considered it essential to contest this rendition of events lest it be thought that they were abandoning their claim to being loyal subjects of the Crown. As they constructed a response to the arguments of the Protestant historians, they too dwelt on the wars of the mid seventeenth century, if only to argue that they and their ancestors, most of them of Old English descent, had always conducted themselves loyally. As they did so they could not but notice the providential tenor of the histories being written by their adversaries. However, they refrained from responding in kind, preferring to counter the charges being made against them by challenging the integrity of the evidence being cited, and by asserting that they were innocent of any involvement in planning, or participating in, the 1641 rebellion. They succeeded in infuriating Temple in what he described as a 'most infamous pamphlet', known as the '*Remonstrance*' issued by the Old English landowners of the Pale at Trim in 1642.

---

[46] Toby Barnard, '1641: a Bibliographic Essay'; John Gibney, *The Shadow of a Year: The 1641 Rebellion in Irish History and Memory* (Madison, Wi., 2013).

THE 1641 REBELLION AND IRELAND'S CONTESTED PASTS   105

This, claimed Temple, had been composed by those who previously had represented themselves as supporters of the government to justify their making common cause with the Ulster rebels in the Catholic Confederacy, established in 1642. Temple's principal objection to the 'Remonstrance' was that it had asserted that the government in Dublin had been 'tyrannical' in its dealing with the Old English, and he absolutely refuted the further allegation of the Old English that they had been left with no choice but to arm themselves to protect their property from a likely invasion from Ulster because the government had declined their offer to assist it in defending the Pale from incursion. Temple also dismissed as hyperbolic the catalogue of injustices that the Old English claimed they had been forced to endure since Wentworth had become governor of Ireland 'as if their oppressions might be paralleled with the Israelitish vassalage in the Land of Egypt and their persecutors for religion equalled to those of the primitive times'.[47]

What Temple had to say in this critique of the Catholic 'Remonstrance' gave a reasonable summary of its arguments. Authors representing the interests of Old English Catholics for several decades thereafter persisted with the arguments then outlined. Their essential proposition was that, in the decades before 1641, Catholic landowners in Ireland other than those in Ulster had never deviated in thought or action from being loyal subjects of the Crown. In stating this they conceded that the Old English had joined the insurgents in 1642 but only because they had been left with no other means to defend themselves from grasping Dublin officials seeking to profit from their destruction. Moreover, they insisted that in the years subsequent to 1642 when they had joined the Confederacy, they had continued to be loyal subjects, citing their readiness to enter negotiations with the government in 1643, 1646, and 1648. As the apologists for the Old English alluded to these ceasefires in what became an Eleven Years War (1641–52), they emphasized that those of their Catholic colleagues who took their lead from Archbishop Rinuccini, papal nuncio to the Confederacy 1645–49, no less than Protestant zealots such as Temple, had been bitterly opposed to any cessations that might lead to a compromise settlement with the Crown. This led to further arguments by authors who continued to write on behalf of the Old English interest in the later seventeenth and into the eighteenth centuries. The most important of these arguments was that those who had been consistent in their loyalty to the Crown throughout the full course of the conflict in Ireland, and particularly those, regardless of religion, who had followed King Charles II into exile after his father had been executed, should, following the Restoration of 1660, have been reinstated to everything of which they had been deprived under

---

[47] Temple, *The Irish Rebellion*, preface, xiii–xiv; by primitive times Temple would have meant when Christians had been persecuted by Roman rulers; citations from 'The Remonstrance of The Catholics of Ireland, given at Trim, 17 March, 1642' come from a copy printed in John Curry, *Historical Memoirs of the Irish Rebellion in the year 1641, Extracted from Parliamentary Journals, State Acts and the most eminent Protestant Historians* (London, 1758), 226–47.

the Cromwellian settlement. Eighteenth-century apologists for those Catholic landowners who remained in possession of some property in Ireland, notwithstanding the rigours of the Penal Laws, continued to lobby for a recovery of some of the social and political power of which their ancestors had been deprived on the grounds that they and their ancestors had been consistent in their loyalty to the Crown.

The Catholic authors associated with such literature advanced a counter-argument to each Protestant pronouncement concerning the inherent untrustworthiness of all Catholics. However, they seem to have decided at the outset that a more effective means of discrediting the arguments of their opponents was by questioning the authenticity of the evidence being cited by Protestant authors to sustain the various charges that were levelling against Catholics. Roderic O'Flaherty, the Gaelic Irish antiquarian, when commenting in 1682 upon *The Reduction of Ireland to the Crown of England* by Edmund Borlase that had been published in London six years previously, demonstrated this method effectively. Although of Gaelic ancestry, O'Flaherty seems to have been drawn to scholarship through his association both with the Galway lawyers, patronized by the earl of Clanricard, who had come to political prominence during the proceedings of the Catholic Confederation, and also through his links with John Lynch, a scion of one of those families, who had served as Catholic Archdeacon of Tuam while the Confederacy was in the ascendant and had continued to write on Ireland's past from the security of exile in France during Cromwellian and Restoration times.[48]

In his review of the Borlase text, O'Flaherty pronounced it to be no more than a recasting of the arguments advanced in Temple *A History of the Irish Rebellion* where he claimed that Temple (like Henry Jones, Thomas Waring, and John Hall) had based his appraisal of what had happened in 1641 on the authority of sworn depositions collected from Protestants in the aftermath of the 1641 insurrection. By doing so, averred O'Flaherty, Borlase was relying on the false assumption made by Temple that '140,000 souls' had been murdered in Ireland 'in a few weeks' following the initial uprising. This, O'Flaherty pronounced, was implausible because 'there were not [then] so many thousands of Protestants living in Ireland, much less in Ulster, where most of the murders were said to have been committed'. Rather, he insisted, if murders had taken place in Ireland about this time Irish Catholics had been the victims of 'the first massacres' perpetrated by English and Scottish people 'in cold blood'. It was such injustice, he argued, that had spurred Irish Catholics to take retaliatory action in 1641. Here, O'Flaherty, like other Catholic authors, was referring first to so-called atrocities

---

[48] Donald Cregan, 'Catholic Admissions to the English Inns of Court', *Irish Jurist*, 5 (1970), 95–114; Cregan, 'Irish Recusant Lawyers in Politics in the Reign of James 1', *Irish Jurist*, 5 (1970), 306–20; Campbell, *Renaissance Humanism*, 41–4, 85–6, 113–23, 171–2.

THE 1641 REBELLION AND IRELAND'S CONTESTED PASTS   107

committed by English soldiers and adventurers in Ireland in Elizabethan times, then to the execution of Catholics by martial law in the seventeenth century, and finally to an alleged 'massacre' of Irish Catholic refugees by Protestant forces said to have taken place in November 1641 at Islandmagee in County Antrim.[49] The Catholic authors contended that it was this last incident that had precipitated Catholic attacks upon Protestant settlers in Ulster in the weeks and months thereafter.

As Catholic authors, including O'Flaherty, acknowledged that attacks upon Protestants had taken place, they insisted that these 'revenge killings' were nothing like the premeditated massacre of the entire Protestant population that Protestant authors alleged had been planned and attempted. Then to further discredit those who were accusing Catholics of having been the initiators of bloody actions, O'Flaherty looked to their subsequent behaviour. In doing so, he pronounced it to be 'a strange paradox that such as...continually professed their due allegiance to his majesty', by which he meant Irish Catholic landowners associated with the Confederacy, were those who had been declared by their Protestant opponents to be 'the only rebels, and not those who openly professed by word and deed to deface all marks of sovereignty and plucketh up by the root monarchy'.[50] Here, O'Flaherty was alluding to the fact that in Ireland, unlike in Britain, those Protestants who had supported and benefited from the Cromwellian regime had, with few exceptions, been permitted to retain their property and power following the Restoration, while most of those Catholics who had remained loyal to the Crown, and even gone into exile with Charles II and his brother James, had received but scant compensation.[51]

This intervention by Roderic O'Flaherty seemed apposite first because it demonstrated how, speaking on behalf of the remnants of a Catholic elite, he extended the historical enquiry that had been encouraged by the Protestant authors backwards to the reign of Queen Elizabeth. Then, as we look forward in time, his investigations provided a link with the eighteenth-century Catholic antiquary, Charles O'Conor of Belangare, who was one of the most consistent advocates of the rehabilitation of Irish Catholics. Given that O'Conor's own historical interest related more to earlier centuries, from which he was able to cite evidence concerning the cultural attainments of Irish people, he left it to his

---

[49] Kenneth Nicholls, 'The Other Massacre: English Killing of Irish, 1641–2', D. Edwards, P. Lenihan, and C Tait, eds., *Age of Atrocity: Violence and Political Conflict in Early Modern Ireland* (Dublin, 2007), 176–91; see also R.S., *A Collection of some of the Murthers and Massacres committed on the Irish in Ireland since 23rdOctober 1641* (London, 1662); Roderic O'Flaherty to Mr Downing, 17 Jan. 1681/2, *A Chorographical Description of West or Iar Connacht, 1684 by Roderic O'Flaherty*, ed., James Hardiman (Dublin, 1846), 431–3.

[50] O'Flaherty to Downing, 17 Jan. 1681/2, Hardiman, ed., *A Chorographical Description*, 431–3.

[51] Ted Mc Cormick, 'Restoration Politics, 1660–1691', Jane Ohlmeyer, ed., *The Cambridge History of Ireland*, vol. 2, *1550–1730* (Cambridge, 2018), 96–119.

108 IMAGINING IRELAND'S PASTS

associate John Curry, an Irish Catholic physician, to write a fresh account of what had transpired in Ireland during the sixteenth and seventeenth centuries.

Curry's interventions were to counter fresh Protestant renditions of those events that, as noted, continued to be published over the course of the eighteenth century. His initial foray was to challenge what Walter Harris had had to say on the events of 1641 when he had issued a warning to Ireland's Protestant population of the possibility that Catholics in Ireland might associate themselves with the attempt being made in 1745–46 by the exiled Stuart pretender to wrest the British Crown from the Hanovarian dynasty that had occupied the British throne since 1714. Curry, like O'Flaherty and many other Catholic authors, challenged what had been said concerning the number of Protestants who had been killed by Catholic rebels in 1641 by 'the first writers of this rebellion', among whom he mentioned Temple, Roger Boyle, first earl of Orrery, and Borlase.[52] This was as a preliminary to his looking back in time to offer some long-term explanations of why some Irish had rebelled in the first instance. His arguments were bolstered by his inclusion in his text of a full reprint of the 'Remonstrance of the Catholics of Ireland', issued in 1642, where they had identified as their adversaries the two Lords Justice of that time 'and other Ministers of State' who with 'the assistance of the malignant party in England', by which they had meant radicals in the English parliament, had planned the 'extirpation' of the 'religion and nation' of Irish Catholics. The 'Remonstrance', on which Curry's argument was heavily reliant, had shown also that the Palesmen of 1642 had complained because as Catholics they and their ancestors had been rendered 'incapable of places of honour and trust' by the reformation legislation enacted in Ireland in the second year of Queen Elizabeth's reign. This, they contended, had resulted in 'men of mean condition and quality' being appointed to rule over them. This statement of Catholic grievance of 1642, which Curry was endorsing in 1758, had proceeded thereafter to complain how, in the reigns of James 1 and Charles I, some of these people of lowly origin had made fortunes 'built...on the ruins of the Catholique natives'.[53]

Curry left no doubt in his introduction to his *Historical Memoirs* that he, like the authors of the 'Remonstrance' of 1642, was convinced that the rebellion of 1641 could be attributed to 'the cruelties and wrongs which the Irish suffered in Queen Elizabeth's reign'. His later historical work, entitled *An Historical and Critical Review of the Civil Wars in Ireland from the reigns of Queen Elizabeth to the Settlement under King William*, elaborated upon this point in considerable detail.[54] There he credited Queen Elizabeth with having 'had admirable talents for government', but he railed at 'the well attested acts of cruelty and perfidy'

---

[52] Curry, *Historical Memoirs*, ix.   [53] Curry, *Historical Memoirs*, 227–8.
[54] John Curry, *An Historical and Critical Review of the Civil Wars in Ireland from the reigns of Queen Elizabeth to the Settlement under King William* (Dublin, 1775).

perpetrated by her representatives upon the 'natives'. Prime among the atrocities he mentioned were the murder by Walter, earl of Essex, of some of the O'Neills of Clandeboy at a feast to which Essex had invited them, the killing, after they had surrendered to government forces, of the expeditionary force that had come ashore at Smerwick, and the sequence of injustices that had led to the earl of Desmond and then the earl of Tyrone entering sequentially into rebellion.[55] Curry's discourse on the acts of cruelty committed by the English army in Ireland during the course of the Elizabethan wars culminated in his reference to 'a dreadful famine' caused by deliberate crop destruction on which he cited Fynes Moryson. These injustices were even more flagrant, averred Curry, because (and here he took up a core argument in the histories by Stafford and Gainsford) 'the greater part of the Irish in this war had fought for the queen against their countrymen'.[56] Following this, he expounded upon the even greater injustices inflicted upon the Irish during the reign of King James VI and I, who he described as 'a great and determined enemy to his Popish subjects', who had been succeeded by King Charles I who had 'trod (and trod ruinously) in his father's steps'.[57]

Curry conceded that it was the 'Ulster Irish' who had suffered most at this juncture, and he believed that it was 'the memory of past grievances' added to 'the dread of present destruction' that had 'made the Northern men, already ruined' grow 'desperate' and to follow the example of 'the Scottish Covenanters' by resorting to arms as the only means of securing their 'property and spiritual liberty'.[58] Then, in the later and longer section of his *Historical and Critical Review*, Curry detailed the unfair way in which Catholic landowners in the other provinces had been subsequently treated despite the fact that they had been the people in Ireland most consistently loyal to the monarch from the reign of Elizabeth to that of King William. These, he contended, had been treated as Gaelic Irish lords had been dealt with in past centuries. This, for Curry, who was writing to uphold Old English interests, proved that 'the perverseness so long imputed to the Irish as a people was no longer charged on their nature but on their religion'.[59]

Curry's *Historical and Critical Review*, like his other historical writings, added depth and breadth to the study of early modern Ireland and moved the subject away from the arid polemics over whether or not a massacre of Protestants had occurred in 1641 and how many Protestants could possibly have been killed in any such massacre. In the course of doing so, he produced credible evidence that not only Cromwell but most British rulers and their representatives in Ireland had been guilty of flagrant injustices against Catholic proprietors, and especially those of Old English lineage. This led to his conclusion that the government of his

---

[55] Curry, *An Historical and Critical Review*, vii, 4–7, 9–11, 14–18.
[56] Curry, *An Historical and Critical Review*, 28.
[57] Curry, *An Historical and Critical Review*, x, 33 ff.
[58] Curry, *An Historical and Critical Review*, x, xi, xii.
[59] Curry, *An Historical and Critical Review*, vii.

110   IMAGINING IRELAND'S PASTS

own day could, even at that late stage, offer some compensation to those loyal Catholic proprietors who, having survived the cataclysm, were still suffering from unjustified penalties. The quickest remedy, he contended, would be to revoke some of the laws that had been enacted against Catholics as part of the Williamite settlement of Ireland.

Curry's compositions, like all history writing of the time, was written with a purpose in view, this being the preservation, and hopefully the improvement, of the position of those Catholics who still enjoyed some property and social respect in Ireland. As he argued that these survivors and their ancestors had been consistently loyal to the British monarchy, whether Stuart or Hanovarian, he seemed to concede that there was no hope of making a similar argument in favour of those Irish Catholics who had lost everything in the Cromwellian and Williamite confiscations. In thus abandoning them to their fate, Curry was following in the tradition of an earlier generation of Irish Catholic historians, notably Rothe and Keating, who in the years before 1641 had conceded tacitly that those who had lost their estates during the course of the first wave of plantations would have to become reconciled to living in exile. Thus Curry's pleas, like the arguments of those who had written in the sixteenth, seventeenth, and eighteenth centuries to uphold the interests of Old English Catholics, were concerned primarily to represent in a positive light those Catholics and their ancestors who still retained control of some property and political influence in Ireland. Therefore, as a historian, Curry was asking his readers to imagine a past that would justify such a partial compensation for the losses suffered by Catholics.

Authors, like Curry, writing on behalf of Catholics who still enjoyed some property and status in Ireland, invariably expressed sympathy for the Gaelic Irish who had lost everything in plantations. However he sometimes conceded that it was the rash actions of the Ulster lords in 1641 that had brought ruin upon their co-religionists who, up to that point, had enjoyed a secure position. Thus in the course of making his plea for the rehabilitation of the survivors, Curry pronounced in 1758 that 'the rebellion [of 1641] was so far from being universal in the beginning, as is pretended, that it was confined to the remains of the ancient Irish rebels in the north and some in the planted county of Leitrim'.[60] This sentiment, which had been but thinly concealed by the more cautious members of the Catholic Confederacy during the seventeenth century, made it clear to yet another generation of dispossessed Irish that, if they were to occupy any place in the historical memory of their country, they, like those who had been forced into exile by the initial wave of plantations, would have to compose a narrative of their own that would give hope for the future as well as a place in the past to those families who had been deprived entirely of their

---

[60] John Curry, *Historical Memoirs*, x.

property and position. Some of those who had lost everything by the close of the seventeenth century, as had been the case with the victims of earlier plantations, had become permanent exiles. However, as Kevin Whelan has documented in the case of County Wexford, others persisted in Ireland in a reduced status, usually by paying rent to Protestant proprietors for the use of farms on property that had once been theirs. These, according to Whelan, cherished memories of past losses, believing that they might recover them at some future time.[61]

4.4 A History for the Dispossessed

It was mentioned in Chapter 2 that those from among the vanquished who were best equipped to write reflectively on what they were witnessing during the course of the wars in Ireland of the late sixteenth century could do little more than record data on the sufferings of Irish Catholics, or exult in the few victories they achieved. This information, as mentioned, was used to authenticate the histories that these authors composed after they had settled in secure scholarly environments in Continental Europe. Most such authors, with the notable exception of Philip O'Sullivan Beare, were clerics, and even he, we may recall, had spent some time in a seminary.

Circumstances must have been more favourable for the writing of historical narrations during the course of the Eleven Years War, 1641–52, if we are to judge by the stream of contemporary comment offered mostly, but not exclusively, by priests in Latin, Irish, and English as events unfolded in Ireland. Part of the explanation for this relatively greater output was that there were many more Continentally-trained clergy, and also more English-trained Irish lawyers, present in the country by the mid-seventeenth century than had been the case fifty years earlier. On the other hand, the number of professional Irish-language authors in Ireland had probably been reduced considerably by then. However, this loss in numbers was compensated for by those authors, many of them priests, who had broken with the rigid conventions associated with scholarship in the Irish language and had begun to contribute to the discourse on current events, and those of the recent past, in less formal modes.[62] The possibility of composing reflective historical writing, in whatever language, remained possible during the years 1642–46 in those parts of the country controlled by the armies of the Catholic Confederacy. Also, even more so than in the sixteenth century, the more militant Catholic clergy believed they had an obligation to influence contemporary

---

[61] Kevin Whelan, 'The regional impact of Irish Catholicism, 1700–1850', W. Smyth and K. Whelan, eds., *Common Ground: Essays on the Historical Geography of Ireland* (Cork, 1988), 253–77.
[62] Mícheál Mac Craith, 'The political and religious thought of Florence Conry and Hugh McCaughwell', Ford and McCafferty, eds., *The Origins of Sectarianism*, 183–202, esp. 193.

112   IMAGINING IRELAND'S PASTS

politics by offering comment on recent and current events. This became even truer after 1643 when Pier Francesco Scarampi arrived in Ireland as papal agent to the Confederacy, and during the years 1645–49 when Archbishop Gian Battista Rinuccini served in Ireland as papal nuncio to the Confederacy. These emissaries of the Pope and their committed followers in Ireland considered themselves to be engaged upon a holy war to reinstate Catholicism to the position it had enjoyed before the Reformation.[63] The authors of the more unambiguous Catholic commentaries made it plain that they understood the motto of the Confederacy— *pro Deo, pro rege et pro patria*—to mean that the prime purpose of the war was to further Catholicism. This for them meant that upholding the authority of King Charles I, and enabling existing Catholic landowners to retain their patrimonies were secondary to this objective.[64]

These, and other authors who wrote in a similar vein, were obviously acquainted with the writings of Philip O'Sullivan Beare, since they regularly endorsed his message that the only people in Ireland who might be considered truly Irish were those who followed Catholic directives to the letter.[65] Such assumptions explain why, when they wrote of the seventeenth century, these same authors identified the military leader Owen Roe O'Neill, and the soldiers who had accompanied him to Ireland from Continental service, as the Catholic combatants most deserving of the financial support that the papacy had offered to the cause.[66]

All commentators of the mid-seventeenth century regardless of lineage believed Ireland to be a kingdom on a par with Scotland and England and presumably on a par also with monarchies on the European Continent. Recent scholars of the Irish literature composed at this time have demonstrated that the learned orders in Gaelic Ireland were as much attached to this idea, as were authors of English ancestry. This explains why, after 1603, some Gaelic authors welcomed King James VI of Scotland as king of Ireland, alluding both to King James's Gaelic pedigree and to the expectation that, as a son of Mary Queen of

---

[63] Tadhg Ó hAnnracháin, *Catholic Reformation in Ireland: The Mission of Rinnuccini* (Oxford, 2002); this contrasts with the sixteenth century where, as Marc Caball has stated, 'there is no significant evidence extant to suggest that the poets [writing within the Gaelic tradition] were conscious of a transcendent loyalty to Tridentine Catholicism', Caball, 'Religion, culture and the bardic elite in early modern Ireland', Ford and McCafferty, eds., *The Origins of Sectarianism*, 158–82, quotation 179.

[64] The most comprehensive was the unpublished *Commentarius Rinuccianus* drafted in Ireland by Richard O'Ferrall and Robert O'Connell, two Capuchin friars, as the events they discussed were happening. They completed the text in Florence in the early 1660s; *Commentarius Rinuccianus, de sedis apostolicae legatione ad foederatos Hiberniae catholicos per annos 1645–9*, ed., Stanilaus Kavanagh (6 vols., Dublin, 1932–49); Jason Mc Hugh, ' "Soldier of Christ"; the political and ecclesiastical career of Nicholas French, Catholic bishop of Ferns (1603–1678)' (Ph.D. thesis, NUI Galway, 2005).

[65] Declan Downey, 'Purity of blood and purity of faith in early modern Ireland', Ford and McCafferty, eds., *The Origins of Sectarianism*, 216–28, esp., 221–3.

[66] Ó hAnnracháin, *Catholic Reformation in Ireland*, 154–8; Jerrold I. Casway, *Owen Roe O'Neill and the Struggle for Catholic Ireland* (Philadelphia, 1984).

THE 1641 REBELLION AND IRELAND'S CONTESTED PASTS   113

Scots, he would be more sympathetic towards Irish Catholics than any conceivable English monarch.[67] However, despite such early enthusiasm, Gaelic poets soon began to register their disenchantment with their new king both because he failed to meet their expectations in relation to Catholicism and because he supported the policy of plantation for Ulster.[68] Thus while Irish Catholic commentators who wrote in the English common-law tradition persisted in professing loyalty to King James and, more enthusiastically (with the notable exception of John Curry), to his successor King Charles I, Gaelic authors became increasingly disenchanted with King James and were decidedly unimpressed by his successor.[69] Indeed, some Irish exiles on the Continent became so alienated from the British monarchy that they entertained the idea, which had been canvassed also during the Nine Years War, that a Continental Catholic monarch or an Irish lord might become king in Ireland. Some of the more radical exiles even favoured Ireland becoming a republic (presumably a Catholic equivalent of the United Provinces) that would be independent of the British state.[70] Thus, while most articulate people in the Gaelic Catholic community of this time, like their counterparts in the Old English areas, may be considered monarchists, this did not necessarily mean that they all recognized the Stuarts as their legitimate rulers.

Another theme that emerged in the writings of Gaelic authors of the first half of the seventeenth century, and that would persist thereafter, concerned the social cleavage they believed to be developing between Ireland's peasant population and their traditional overlords who the authors identified as the natural leaders of their communities. This can be sustained by reference to three compositions: that written soon after 1613 by the anonymous author of the first element of the prose text *Pairlement Chloinne Tomáis*; the unidentified person who wrote the sequel to that text composed after 1662; and the Munster poet Dáibhí Ó Bruadair in the verses composed by him in the 1650s and 1660s. The authors of all three texts voiced contempt for people of low degree who they considered were subverting the social order by imitating, and co-operating with, newly designated British proprietors who had been granted ownership of land that had traditionally belonged to Irish Catholic nobles.[71] For example, the opening passage to the 1662

---

[67] Breandán Ó Buachalla, *Aisling Ghéar: na Stíobhartaigh agus an tAos Léinn* (Dublin, 1996), 3–66; Marc Caball, *Poets and Politics*, 85–93; Mac Craith, 'The political and religious thought', esp., 183–4, 198–9.

[68] Gerard Farrell, *The 'Mere Irish' and the Colonisation of Ulster, 1570–1641* (Cham, Switzerland, 2017), 85, 106, 108; for an example of hostility to plantation expressed in verse, Canny, *Making Ireland British*, 427.

[69] Geoffrey Keating, on whom see Chapter 2, may be considered a possible exception in that he welcomed the coronation of both James and Charles; but then Keating was of Old English ancestry; Keating, *Foras Feasa ar Éirinn*, 1, 208.

[70] Tomás Ó Fiaich, 'Republicanism and Separatism in the Seventeenth Century', *Léachtaí Cholm Cille*, 2 (1971), 74–87.

[71] *Pairlement Chloinne Tomáis*, ed., N.J.A. Williams (Dublin, 1981); *Duanaire Dháibhidh Uí Bhruadair*, ed., J.C. Mac Erlean, (3 vols., London, 1910, 1913, 1917), 'Créacht do dháil mé', part 1,

114 IMAGINING IRELAND'S PASTS

sequel to *Pairlement Chloinne Tomáis* mockingly identified Domhnall Ó Pluburnáin [Donal, descendant of the blabbering one], the supposed convener of that *Pairlement*, as a person who had been recently designated a magistrate and a knight, who recognized *Oiliféir Cromuil* [Oliver Cromwell] as his Protector ['*na phrotector aige*], and who boasted how Cromwell had been designated *rígh* [king]. Ó Pluburnáin, we are told, had been given credit in a chronicle compiled by the peasants because he had brought them '*suaimhnios, mil, uachtar agas onóir*' [contentment, honey, cream, and honour], in exchange for which they were to abandon their faith. He and the peasants are portrayed as having considered this a fair bargain because peasants were being permitted to cultivate barley, which had previously been denied to them. The author expanded his mockery of the insubordinate peasants when he described how they had welcomed Ó Pluburnáin's overture to Cromwell to remain permanently in command as a means of ensuring that none of the Kavanaghs or Byrnes or Nolans or Kinsellas or Rices or Roches would ever again recover their ancestral lands. Thus Ó Pluburnáin was being represented as somebody who venerated Cromwell because he had effected a social revolution that had made it possible for the man of the flail to become prosperous while leaving the man of property with nothing ['*is d'fhág fear na dúithche ar nothing*'].[72] In their mocking disparagement of peasants who had taken advantage of political circumstances to move above what was considered their natural station, these same Gaelic authors explained that the peasants had been able readily to established an affinity with British planters since these too were people who lacked culture and honour.

Such wry commentary on how the social worlds with which they had been familiar had been turned upside down by Cromwell's intervention opened the way for some poets to posit an explanation for why the military forces of the Confederacy had failed generally to match those of their opponents. This issue was addressed by Toirdhealbach Ó Conchubhair, a Donegal versifier, when criticizing the Irish leaders for permitting those who previously had been cowherds to rise to become junior officers. This, he contended, had led to the unsurprising outcome that the Irish soldiers had proven themselves more interested in robbing English settlers than in confronting their opponents in the field.[73] In the course of his narration this author implied that some Irish nobles had behaved as cowardly as the upstart peasants, and in a second poem, where he occasionally abandoned verse to express himself in enraged prose, Ó Conchubhair voiced his contempt for the nobles of Old English lineage who, in a Royalist army

---

26–50, see esp. verses 7, 23–6; 'Do shaoilios dá ríribh', Duanaire *Dháibhidh Uí Bhruadair*, part 2, 14–15.

[72] *Pairlement Chloinne Tomáis*, 42–3.

[73] 'A óga do ghlach na hairm' [You youths who have taken up arms] by Toirdhealbach Ó Conchubhair, ed., Cuthbert Mhágh Craith, O.F.M., 'The Franciscan Fathers', ed., *Father Luke Wadding: Commemorative Volume* (Dublin, 1957), 422–9.

THE 1641 REBELLION AND IRELAND'S CONTESTED PASTS   115

commanded by James Butler, marquess of Ormond, had failed at the battle of Rathmines in August 1649 to present any significant resistance to the Parliamentary army commanded by Colonel Michael Jones. They had been more interested, he exclaimed, in protecting their baggage train than in defeating their opponents, and he laughed with scorn at the great cavalier with his scarf and buff coat fleeing from the field without a feather in his cap.[74]

In thus criticizing the Catholic nobility, commanded by the Protestant Ormond to whom many of the landed Catholic nobles were related in blood or by marriage, Ó Conchubhair was harking back to the proposition advanced by Philip O'Sullivan Beare that Irish nobles of English ancestry were neither truly Irish nor truly Catholic. This suggestion, which had been disregarded by Gaelic authors in Ireland during the earlier part of the seventeenth century, was voiced more regularly when Irish forces began to suffer reverses in the field. We find for example that Pádraigín Haicéad, a Dominican priest/poet from County Tipperary, and himself of Old English lineage, exhorted all Irishmen collectively and individually [*'fir Éireann uile ó aicme go h-aonduine'*] in his poem *Éirigh mo dhúiche le Dia* [Arise my locality with God!] to make common cause with those who had risen in 1641 to defend their religion and reputation [*a gcreideamh a gclú 's a gcáil*].[75] However, by 1646 he was expressing doubt over the steadfastness of the more prosperous Catholic lords in Ireland, most of them Old English, in his equally famous, '*Músgail do mhisneach, a Banbha*' [Arouse your courage, Ireland!]. There, he decried the 'Faction' within the Confederation who had secretly negotiated a peace settlement with heretics [*le heiricidhibh*]. This settlement with the Protestant marquess of Ormond was all the more reprehensible in the mind of Haicéad because those Catholics who had entered upon it had justified their action by citing reasons of state [*réasún sdáit*] to explain why they had acted against the directive of the papal nuncio and contrary to the Confederate oath that bound them to persist with the struggle until the true faith had been restored in Ireland. Their breach of their pledge, as Haicéad explained, had resulted in the members of this Faction, and their subordinates, being excommunicated by the papacy. It was this expulsion of some Irish people from the Christian community, he believed, that accounted for the recent reverses suffered by all Catholics, and he believed that worse would follow if they did not collectively repent for this transgression by the few. However, rather than succumb to despair, Haicéad pronounced in the apocalyptic words that Temple had attributed to the Old English historians, that redemption would be as

---

[74] 'Ar gcúla tú cúrsa Corinél Seónsa? '[Have you heard of the doings of Colonel Jones?] by Toirdhealbach Ó Conchubhair, ed., Cuthbert Mhágh Craith, O.F.M., *Father Luke Wadding: Commemorative Volume*, 428–33; on the battle of Rathmines see James Scott Wheeler, *Cromwell in Ireland* (Dublin, 1999), 75–9.

[75] '*Éirigh mo dhúiche le Dia*', *Filíocht Phádraigín Haicéad*, ed., Máire Ní Cheallacháin (Dublin, 1962), 33–7, esp. lines 53–4 and 71.

116 IMAGINING IRELAND'S PASTS

available to the repentant people of Catholic Ireland as it had been for the Israelites when they had been enslaved in Egypt.[76] Under these circumstances, Haicéad, like the nuncio, came to pin all his hopes on the Ulster army led by Owen Roe O'Neill. It is unsurprising therefore when, after the death of O'Neill, and after this force too had been destroyed at the battle of Scarrifhollis, 1650, an anonymous, probably priestly, author lamented in *Do chuala scéal do chéas gach ló mé* [I heard a story that afflicts me daily] the loss of property by Ireland's nobility, the cancellation of whatever rights that Irish people had previously enjoyed, and the expulsion from the country of the Catholic clergy. This author considered the onslaught on the clergy as the heaviest of these afflictions because it meant that Mass could no longer be said, infants would no longer be christened, and the community would be deprived of the means to secure salvation. The ultimate tragedy, according to this author, was that the outcome was the product not of the strength of their foes [*neart naimhead*] but of divine vengeance [*díoltas Dé*] that had fallen upon the Irish for the litany of sins they had committed when victory had been within their grasp. Therefore the only consolation offered by this author was that the state of dejection to which the Irish had been reduced might be suddenly reversed once God was satisfied they had become penitent and had been sufficiently punished for their transgressions.[77]

These various themes, which had been touched upon by individual authors as the events they dwelt upon were still fresh in people's minds, were absorbed into the more reflective verse histories of Ireland composed soon after the Cromwellian conquest of Ireland. These come within the purview of this study because they may have reached wider audiences than any printed texts. Furthermore, the many manuscript copies of the original texts, as well as later expansions and imitations of them that were made over the course of the seventeenth, eighteenth, and even into the nineteenth centuries, show how quickly the interpretation of Ireland's history, particularly during the early modern centuries, became remembered history in Irish-speaking Ireland.[78]

Most of these verse commentaries on events of the recent past touched upon the history of Ireland, and the succession of people who had been dominant there since the time of the flood. This was elaborated upon in *Tuireamh na hÉireann* [Ireland's Lamentation], composed by an author from west Munster, that took the form of a history of Ireland concerned particularly with events in the sixteenth

---

[76] 'Músgail do mhisneach, a Banbha', *Filíocht Phádraigín Haicéad*, 38–43, esp. prose introduction, 38 and lines 29–40, 91, and 113–20.

[77] 'Do chuala scéal do chéas gach ló mé', *Nua-Dhunaire*, vol. 1, ed., Pádraig de Brún, Breandán Ó Buachalla and Tomás Ó Concheanainn (Dublin, 1971), 31–4, esp. lines 11–20 and 76–88.

[78] Vincent Morley, *Ó Chéitinn go Raiftearaí* (Dublin, 2011); Morley, *The Popular Mind in Eighteenth-Century Ireland* (Cork, 2017); Joep Leerssen, *Mere Irish and Fíor-Ghael: Studies in the Ida of Irish Nationality, its Development and Literary Expression prior to the Nineteenth Century* (Cork, 1996); T.J. Dunne, 'The Gaelic Response to conquest and colonization: the evidence of the poetry', *Studia Hibernica*, vol. 20 (1980), 7–30.

THE 1641 REBELLION AND IRELAND'S CONTESTED PASTS   117

and seventeenth centuries.[79] After a quick survey of Ireland's earlier history, the author slowed his pace at the point when King Henry VIII broke with Rome, and then proceeded through the reigns of Elizabeth, James I, and Charles I to show how each successive ruler brought novel injustices and disappointments upon a people who were well disposed to being ruled by them.[80] This brought the author to Oliver Cromwell and his closest associates, who were named individually. The poet seemed awestruck by the discipline and sense of purpose of the Cromwellian forces as he described how they set about bringing the conquest of Ireland to completion ['s iad so do chríochnaigh conquest Éireann].[81]

By employing the English word 'conquest' to describe the task completed by Cromwell and his henchmen, the author was suggesting that their achievement was novel while being also the culmination of a process that had been under way since the reign of Henry VIII. Previous Irish-language authors who had spoken judgmentally of English actions in Ireland had likened them to those of the Vikings, but the Vikings were denounced by the writer of Tuireamh na hÉireann only because they had secured temporary dominance over Ireland [do bhuaig tamall ceannas na hÉireann], which had been terminated by Brian Boru [Brian Bóraimhe] in a single battle.[82] The Viking onslaught therefore had resulted in no conquest, and when it came to the Normans, whose twelfth-century invasion of Ireland had been customarily referred to in English and Latin narratives as a conquest, the author of Tuireamh na hÉireann said only that they had seized the country [do ghabhadar Éire], and he then stated that the seizure was partly justified because King Henry II had been authorized by a papal bull to secure justice and faith in Ireland [ceart is creidimh do sheasamh i n-Éirinn].[83] The author also looked benignly on the Norman invasion because it had brought a cultured, Christian people to the country who, over the course of time, had intermingled with the Irish nobility to the point where the Irish had become foreign and the foreigners Irish [do bhí an Gaeul Gallda 's an Gall Gaeulach].[84]

This appraisal was consistent with what Geoffrey Keating had had to say on the subject some twenty years previously, and left our author free to pronounce that it was only the followers of promiscuous Calvin and voracious Luther [Cailbhin coitcheann is Lútar craosach] who had developed ambitions to conquer the country.[85] Then, as he detailed the chaos and devastation that had accompanied

---

[79] 'Tuireamh na hÉireann', Five Seventeenth-Century Political Poems, ed., Cecile O'Rahilly (Dublin, 1977), 50–82.

[80] 'Tuireamh na hÉireann', 72–4.   [81] 'Tuireamh na hÉireann', 76, quotation, line 376.

[82] 'Tuireamh na hÉireann', 70, quotation, line 244.

[83] 'Tuireamh na hÉireann', 71, quotation, line 267.

[84] 'Tuireamh na hÉireann', 71–2, quotation, line 280.

[85] 'Tuireamh na hÉireann', 72, quotation, line 282; on the importation of such sectarian vocabulary of abuse from Continental texts into Irish language literature, Mac Craith, 'The political and religious thought', 197.

118 IMAGINING IRELAND'S PASTS

this conquest, the author concluded that these signified that the end of the world was nigh ['s iad so comharthaí dheire an tsaogail].[86]

The author of Tuireamh na hÉireann thus made his case for the uniqueness of the Cromwellian conquest. Then, as he mentioned the military reverses and the dispossessions that had been experienced by the various noble lineages of Gaelic ancestry, whom he named individually, and also by many Irish Catholic families of English descent, whom he also identified by name, the author was suggesting that if the two peoples had remained united they could have held their position against any adversary.[87] Thus, as in Do chuala scéal do chéas gach ló mé, the author of Tuireamh na hÉireann also attributed the destruction of Ireland's noble families not to the strength of their enemy [neart námhad] but to their own disunity.[88] Then, as with Pádraigín Haicéad, the author identified the differences that had emerged among the Confederates over their interaction with the papal nuncio as the fundamental one. This for him was confirmed by the fact that the joint spread of plague and famine throughout Ireland coincided with the moment when the blessed nuncio [an Nuntius naofa] had been left with no choice but to abandon the country because Irish leaders had failed to unite under his leadership.[89]

This author, like others before him, was suggesting that the unity between the Gaelic Irish and the Old English that had been encouraged by such as Geoffrey Keating and David Rothe had not endured when their separate interests had been subjected to external pressure. However, it was not a simple matter of the Old English refusing to be supportive of the Gaelic Irish since he pointed to more complex divisions within the Irish community, as when he remarked on the oddity of a foreign general (by which he can only have meant the English-born marquess of Ormond) having command of an Irish army, and an Irish general (by which he can only have meant Morrogh O'Brien, baron of Inchiquin) fighting at the head of a foreign army. All such divisions, he contended, had enabled the Cromwellians to prevail because they, unlike the Irish, had remained united to attain clearly defined objectives.[90] As he neared his conclusion, this author, like many of his Irish language counterparts of the time, isolated symbols of the humiliation of Irish Catholics, such as transplantation to Connacht and transportation to Jamaica, to which he, like others who composed macaronic verse, employed English words to describe.[91] At this point, the author's concern became that of exhorting his audience not to succumb to the sin of despair, and to accept with forbearance the evils that had befallen them because of their own failings [sinn féin do thuill gach ní tá déanta], and to petition God, the Virgin Mary, and a long list of saints to grant them absolution for past transgressions as a

---

[86] 'Tuireamh na hÉireann', 72, quotation, line 295.
[87] 'Tuireamh na hÉireann', 74, 76–8.
[88] 'Tuireamh na hÉireann', 75, quotation, line 359.
[89] 'Tuireamh na hÉireann', 75, quotation, line 355.
[90] 'Tuireamh na hÉireann', 75, quotation, lines 362–3.
[91] 'Tuireamh na hÉireann', 79, quotation, line 429.

THE 1641 REBELLION AND IRELAND'S CONTESTED PASTS 119

preliminary to being liberated from the thralldom under which God was permitting they to suffer.[92]

This fatalistic acceptance that any improvement in the condition of the Irish required divine intervention was shared by many Irish language authors of the time. Some, however, qualified this with the hope that sudden change in political or military circumstances (a turn of Fortune's wheel) might bring relief to them. Thus, for example, Éamonn an Dúna, another Munster poet, looked forward to the early return to Ireland of those Irish who had followed Charles II into exile on the Continent and had entered into military service with his brother James, Duke of York. That author expected that once Charles II, whom he saluted as his *'léader'*, was restored to power, those who had fought for his cause would soon be granted title to the property and social positions that had been taken from them to reward the supporters of Cromwell.[93]

This too was the expectation of Dáibhí Ó Bruadair, the well-known Munster poet, in the verses he composed in the years immediately following the Restoration. However, when the issue of establishing a fresh land settlement in Ireland to replace that implemented under Cromwell was frustrated by delays and half-promises, Ó Bruadair's early optimism gave way to disenchantment as he witnessed those who had been supporters of Cromwell remaining in possession of their ill-gotten gains and those who had forfeited these estates because they had supported their king receiving scant compensation.[94] During these years, Ó Bruadair also complained repeatedly of his own loss in status as a poet in what, he believed, had become a more material world.[95] Then, at the time of the Popish Plot of 1679–82, he concluded that whatever limited advances Catholics had made since 1660 were about to be reversed.[96] Once James, duke of York, who had converted to Catholicism, succeeded his brother on the throne as King James 11, and after James had appointed Richard Talbot, earl of Tyrconnell, as governor of Ireland, this gloom of the author suddenly gave way to renewed optimism.[97] At this juncture, Ó Bruadair exulted over how the political and social order in Ireland was being suddenly reversed. However, his enthusiasm again turned to despair as the military support provided to Tyrconnell by Ireland's Catholic proprietors proved insufficient to maintain King James on his throne against the challenge presented by Prince William of Orange. This defeat initially struck

---

[92] 'Tuireamh na hÉireann', 79–82; quotation 80, line 456.

[93] Éamon an Dúna, 'Mo lá leóin go n-éagad', *Five Seventeenth-Century Political Poems*, 83–100; quotation 100, line 414.

[94] 'Suim Purgadóra bhfear nÉireann', *Duanaire Dháibhidh Uí Bhruadair*, part 3, 12–23; Leerssen, *Mere Irish and Fíor-Gheal*, 220–8.

[95] 'Is mairg nár chrean re maitheas saoghalta', Duanaire *Dháibhidh Uí Bhruadair*, part 2, 24–33.

[96] Dá bhfaice mo phrionnsa', *Duanaire Dháibhidh Uí Bhruadair*, part 2, 218–9; 'Searc na suadh an chrobhaing chumhra', *Duanaire Dháibhidh Uí Bhruadair*, part 2, 264–88.

[97] This turn of events is followed in a sequence of poems published in *Duanaire Dháibhidh Uí Bhruadair*, part 3, 64–125.

120 IMAGINING IRELAND'S PASTS

Ó Bruadair as final as he witnessed the exile from Ireland of most Catholic officers and men who had survived to the end of the conflict. Therefore in *An Longbhriseadh* [The Shipwreck], following the example of the Irish poets who had chronicled the Irish defeat of the 1650s, he sought to divine why Ireland's leaders had again failed to hold their own against their adversaries in the field when victory seemed attainable. Like the authors of the 1650s, Ó Bruadair attributed the failure of this more recent generation to their lack of unity, to the disrespect shown by the peasantry towards their social betters, and to the sins of the Irish for which they had lost divine favour that they could never hope to recover until they had become duly repentant.[98] While he was thus leaving the fate of the Irish in the hands of Providence, Ó Bruadair offered a glimmer of hope when he addressed the Irish officers who, after their defeat in Ireland, pursued military careers on the Continent, usually now in the service France. His hope was that if they achieved victory over their English opponents in foreign conflicts it would make it possible for them to recover their lost positions in Ireland by force.[99] To this extent these later poems of Dáibhí Ó Bruadair served as an entrée to the *Aisling*, or allegorical vision poetry of eighteenth-century Ireland, much of it promoting the Jacobite cause.

This poetry, which was not presented in historical mode, has been the subject of recent scholarly analyses by Breandán Ó Buachalla, Éamonn Ó Ciardha, and Vincent Morley.[100] The *Aisling* poetry is relevant to our present purposes principally because it bears witness to a consonance of opinion between Irish-language authors of the seventeenth and eighteenth centuries concerning the contours of Ireland's history, especially for the early modern centuries. Vincent Morley has confirmed this in his study of the Irish-language literature from the eighteenth century that was presented in historical format.[101] In doing so he has demonstrated that several later verse histories of Ireland were little more than updatings of *Tuaireamh na hÉireann* with every fresh hardship experienced by Irish Catholics being presented as a prolongation of the trauma associated with Cromwell and his followers. These later travails included the Williamite War and confiscation, the enactment of the so-called penal laws against Catholics, and the execution of individual priests at moments of political or social tension. All such were considered to be in breach of an unwritten moral code, and they were all subsumed into a narrative of Ireland's history for the early modern centuries. This commenced with an account of how Henry VIII and later Queen Elizabeth had become corrupted by the doctrines of Luther and Calvin, after which they and

---

[98] 'An Longbhriseadh', *Duanaire Dháibhidh Uí Bhruadair*, part 3, 164–81.

[99] 'Is liachtain leasuighthe ar chiach do charadsa', Duanaire *Dháibhidh Uí Bhruadair*, part 3, 222–5.

[100] Ó Buachalla, *Aisling Ghéar*; Éamonn Ó Ciardha, *Ireland and the Jacobite Cause, 1685–1766: A Fatal Attraction* (Dublin, 2002); Vincent Morley, 'Irish Jacobitism, 1691–1790', Kelly, ed., *The Cambridge History of Ireland*, vol. 3, 23–47.

[101] Morley, *The Popular Mind in Eighteenth-Century Ireland*, 242–77.

THE 1641 REBELLION AND IRELAND'S CONTESTED PASTS   121

their adherents sought to impose these doctrines upon an unwilling Irish population whose wealth they also coveted. Such covetousness explained why English, and later Scots, adventurers were unleashed to seize Ireland's resources at the expense of the traditional elites. The various verse histories named the rulers to whom they attributed each successive injustice, but their complaints over these individuals were dwarfed by what they had to say of the iniquities perpetrated by Cromwell. Of all of Ireland's leaders, Owen Roe O'Neill, the victor over the Scots at the Battle of Benburb in 1646, was identified as the only one who might have defeated Cromwell had not death intervened to deprive Ireland's Catholic population, and the church, of their stoutest defender.[102]

The rendition of Ireland's history during the early modern centuries that was recorded in Irish-language verse histories of the seventeenth and eighteenth centuries was thus very much the history of those of the Irish elite who had been dispossessed. As such, it was perpetuating for a new generation what Philip O'Sullivan Beare had had to say at the outset of the seventeenth century on behalf of those who had become the victims of English conquest up to that time. Following the example of O'Sullivan Beare this new narrative suggested that the only people who might be considered truly Irish were those whose steadfastness had been tested to the extreme and those who had adhered to the strictest papal definition of what it was to be Catholic. By these standards it was excluding both those families (mostly of Old English ancestry) that had been enriched at the expense of the church when they had accepted gifts of the monastic property from King Henry VIII, and those individuals (again mostly of Old English ancestry) who had engaged in peace negotiations with King Charles I and his Protestant representatives in Ireland against the express wishes of the papal nuncio. On the positive side this narrative also shared the belief that those who had been dispossessed would ultimately recover everything they had lost. Even this prospect faded as the eighteenth century proceeded. Therefore Vincent Morley's finding that Jacobite sentiment continued to be fostered at a popular level supports the suggestion of Kevin Whelan that the cultivation of the notion that the condition of the dispossessed would one day be improved began to present more of a social than a political threat to the established order.[103]

4.5 Conclusion

It will have become evident that at least three different narratives of Ireland's past were formulated in the years and decades following the Irish rebellion of 1641.

---

[102] Vincent Morley, *An Crann as Coill: Aodh Buí Mac Cruitín, c. 1680–1755* (Dublin, 1995); Morley, *Ó Chéitinn go Raiftearaí.*
[103] Morley, 'Irish Jacobitism'.

All three proceeded from the assumption that developments in Ireland from the 1560s to the 1690s constituted a single continuum, but agreement ceased at this point. Their fundamental disagreement concerned the intentions and actions of successive governments during this period. Protestant authors insisted that authorities in London and their agents in Ireland had been engaged upon a programme of reform designed to benefit all people in the country regardless of ethnic origin or nationality. They were particularly concerned to illustrate how successive ameliorative interventions had been spurned by the Irish, who had thus proven themselves to be as attached to barbaric living as to debased religion. Catholic authors accepted the chronology put forward by their Protestant counterparts, but they asserted that those of their ancestors who had resorted to arms, including in 1641, had done so because they had been left with no alternative since government agents seemed intent on robbing them under the cloak of reform.

Protestant authors in Ireland and Britain chose a historical format when pursuing their side of the polemic, expecting that their narrative would restore their reputations and policies in the eyes of senior officials in Britain and of the wider Protestant community in Ireland and Britain. It was possibly with a view to retaining the support of this wider public that authors regularly invoked Providence to explain unexpected outcomes. However, while a few of this new generation of providential historians, after the manner of John Derricke in the sixteenth century, made a virtue of their lack of learning, the more sophisticated ones were unabashed at putting their erudition on display. Also, once they had shown appropriate deference to Providence, they sustained their arguments by citing evidence from official sources that they considered incontrovertible.

This new generation of Protestant historians had not only to defend themselves from criticism by Catholic authors who had access to patronage in Royalist circles but they also considered it necessary to construct a version of Ireland's past that would be different from what had been written by their immediate predecessors. These, we may recall, had written positively of Ireland's cultural achievements in previous centuries, presumably in the expectation that they would continue to live in close co-operation with Catholic neighbours who still commanded much of the country's resources and who were, for the moment, enjoying an unofficial toleration of Catholicism.

The new authors envisaged no such compromise for the future and distanced themselves from what they now considered a mistaken view of the past. Instead, they reverted to the arguments expounded by Gerald of Wales in the twelfth century and his admirers in subsequent centuries. Then, depending on the date of composition, they cited the various sixteenth-century Irish rebellions, or the 1641 rebellion, or Irish Jacobite opposition to William of Orange, or all three, as evidence that the barbarism of all of Ireland's Catholics, and not only those of Gaelic descent, was innate and persistent. Then, by corrupting what James Ware had written of Ireland's past, these Protestant authors co-opted him as one of their own, thus suggesting that Irish Protestant interpretations of the country's history had after all been consistent over time.

We noted that it was Catholics of Old English lineage who considered themselves most threatened by this revised Protestant interpretation of Ireland's past. Their Protestant critics, according to these Catholic authors, were thus able to malign most Irish people because they were just so many papists. Old English authors also considered that their interests were being threatened by this new historiography because they continued to believe that they still had a moral claim to recover from the Crown the property of which they had been unjustly deprived by Cromwell and his accomplices. The target audience for the authors of these Old English versions of the past were senior officials and politicians in London. They therefore assigned no role to Providence in their rendition of Ireland's past, but rather emphasized how they and their ancestors had been consistent upholders of the English interest in the country for which they had received scant recognition or recompense. This led to their further argument that they had been deprived of property and power both because of the unjustified malignancy of Protestant officials and the injudicious actions of their co-religionists of Gaelic ancestry.

This jettisoning by Old English authors of their Gaelic co-religionists who had been their allies in the Confederation of Kilkenny left our third group of historians with no hope that the Gaelic Irish, whose cause they had championed, stood any chance of recovering the power and estates they had lost through conventional channels. The audience that these authors had in mind were those who had been dispossessed of their property and positions and who were either in exile or suffering in reduced circumstances in Ireland. The purposes behind the historical narratives elaborated in this vernacular historiography were therefore to promote group solidarity not only among the dispossessed but also among the Irish poor who, they feared, might be seduced by the material benefits they were being offered by the planter elite. Since the history they wrote was one of repeated defeat and humiliation, the only explanation they could offer for the degradation of those whose cause they championed was that they had incurred divine displeasure because of their own human weakness. Then, in almost all these narrations, this apparent surrender to providential fatalism was offset by expressions of hope, or even the certitude, that an apocalyptic reversal of fortunes would inevitably occur when they would become dominant over their satanic foes who had lorded it over them for so long.

While it is possible to disentangle three distinct narrative threads of Ireland's history that were composed in the years following the 1641 rebellion it is less easy to establish what the authors of each knew of the alternative versions of the past with which they were competing. The Protestant authors and the historians representing Old English interests were, as noted, engaged on a polemical

124 IMAGINING IRELAND'S PASTS

discourse, and they therefore tracked the arguments of their rivals with a view to refuting them. This leaves us to wonder what each knew of the arguments being put forward in the Irish-language vernacular history.

The Old English authors who wished to distance themselves from the actions taken by their Gaelic co-religionists in 1641 would have had even stronger reasons to remain aloof from the compositions of those who had become apologists for those actions. This did not mean that they were ignorant of what was being expressed even when they were not conversant in the Irish language. Bernadette Cunningham has shown that an English-language manuscript edition of Geoffrey Keating's *Foras Feasa* circulated widely within the English-speaking community in Ireland, and an English-language summation of what was being communicated in the Irish-language verse histories of the 1650s was replicated in considerable detail in an anonymous manuscript text entitled 'An Aphorismical Discovery of Treasonable Faction' that was circulated within the Anglophone community.[104] That members of the Protestant community had knowledge of the subversive ideas being circulated is suggested by the fact that at least one copy of the manuscript that has survived was preserved in Protestant custody. That Protestants had some knowledge of the versions of Ireland's history that were being cherished by their more extreme opponents is supported by the fact that English-language verses such as the infamous 'Lilliburlero', probably written in 1687, and the *Irish Hudibras*, published in 1689, are essentially line by line refutations of the hopes being expressed in Irish-language verse at precisely the same time.[105]

This all points to the likelihood that historians within each of the interlinked communities that developed in Ireland as the eighteenth century proceeded had a good understanding of the pasts for Ireland that were being imagined by those they recognized as rivals in a contest to have their interpretation accepted as the only true version of the country's history.

---

[104] Cunningham, *The World of Geoffrey Keating*, 175–7; Anonymous, 'An Aphorismical Discovery of Treasonable Faction', J.T. Gilbert, *A Contemporary History of Affairs in Ireland, from 1641–1652*, 3 vols. (Dublin, 1879); the text is threaded through the three volumes.

[105] *Verse in English from Tudor and Stuart Ireland*, ed., Andrew Carpenter (Cork, 2003), 504–8, 518–23.

5

Eighteenth-Century Aristocratic Histories of Ireland during the Sixteenth and Seventeenth Centuries

5.1 Introduction

It may seem from Chapter 4, and from recent publications on Irish historiography, that historians in eighteenth-century Ireland took an interest in events of the sixteenth and seventeenth centuries only when they wished to explain why the country had been persistently disturbed politically at that time, and to engage in polemics concerning the 1641 rebellion and what followed in its wake. Chapter 4 may also have suggested that historians, Protestant and Catholic alike, continued to believe that the course of human affairs was controlled ultimately by Providence, even though they lived through an age that considered itself enlightened.

By way of corrective Chapters 5 and 6 will look at the work of some eighteenth-century authors who explained historical change in secular terms. These proceeded from the assumption that humans controlled, and were therefore responsible for, their political destinies, even as they allowed for plans being set awry by contingencies such as natural disasters or unexpected military outcomes. Among those who subscribed to this secular view of history were those who presumed that those best placed to influence the course of events were those who occupied prominent positions in society. This in the case of Ireland led to the writing of history that was patronized by or even written by nobles. Those associated with aristocratic history wrote almost invariably to extol the virtues and achievements of distinguished ancestors or to remove any blemishes that may have been cast on the reputations of these progenitors.

5.2 Histories of the Clanricard Burkes

The writing of history had in every century been encouraged and sustained by elites who hoped that their standing in the present would be enhanced by the rehearsal of the actions of their ancestors. This stimulus was as potent in the eighteenth as in any previous century, but investigation into the past could occasion difficulty when political choices made by progenitors during periods of

Imagining Ireland's Pasts: Early Modern Ireland through the Centuries. Nicholas Canny, Oxford University Press (2021).
© Nicholas Canny. DOI: 10.1093/oso/9780198808961.003.0005

126   IMAGINING IRELAND'S PASTS

civil conflict in the sixteenth and seventeenth centuries compromised their eighteenth-century successors. Members of aristocratic houses, who found themselves embarrassed or even handicapped by what, with the benefit of hindsight, could be seen to have been the political misjudgements of ancestors, looked to history to demonstrate that the contribution made by their family to the betterment of society over the long term far outweighed any momentary lapses made by some of its members at a moment of civil conflict.

The first Irish aristocratic house in the eighteenth century that saw the need to explain as well as glorify the actions of ancestors in previous centuries was that of the Burkes, earls of Clanricard. To this end Michael, 10th earl of Clanricard (in 1722), and his son John, 11th earl of Clanricard (in 1757), each commissioned the publication of some of the memoirs and letters of Ulick Burke, 5th earl and 1st marquess of Clanricard (and 2nd earl of St Albans in the English peerage). These editions provided a pretext for offering general appraisals of the positive role played by their family in Ireland's history since medieval times but most especially since the mid-sixteenth century.[1] The two earls were of one mind that the marquess had been the most distinguished of their many illustrious ancestors, but they considered it necessary to rehabilitate memories of his achievements—in one case because his reputation had been tarnished by what others had said of him, and in the second because his successors to the title had not behaved with the same sagacity as their most distinguished ancestor.

Ulick Burke (1604–58), 5th earl of Clanricard (marquess in 1645), was known to have been a consistent supporter of King Charles I in Ireland from the outbreak of the 1641 rebellion to the execution of that monarch, after which he served as titular Lord Deputy of Ireland (in place of the marquess of Ormond who had left for France) in the name of King Charles II from 1650 until August 1653. After this he abandoned Ireland to the supporters of the English parliament and retired to London for the remainder of the Civil War in England. Although born in Ireland, Ulick Burke had spent most of his childhood in England where his father Richard Burke, 4th earl of Clanricard, built a residence named Sommerhill overlooking the town of Tonbridge in Kent, where he lived with his wife Frances, the daughter of Sir Francis Walsingham (widow successively of Sir Philip Sidney and the disgraced 2nd earl of Essex) with their own two children and occasionally some of the Essex step children.[2]

The documents included in the slim 1722 text, of which but 250 copies were printed, were concerned primarily with the interlude when the marquess had

---

[1] The provenance of these two letter-books are discussed by John Lowe is his introduction to an edition of a third *Letter-Book of the Earl of Clanricarde, 1643–47*, ed., John Lowe (Dublin, 1983), Introduction, ix–xi.

[2] For a biographical note on Ulick Burke see that by Aoife Duignan, *Dictionary of Irish Biography*, vol. 2, 69–73; I have chosen to spell the title name as Clanricard, rather than Clanricarde as some holders preferred, and the family name as Burke rather that Burgh or de Burgh or de Burgo.

been titular Lord Deputy of Ireland on behalf of the uncrowned Charles II. They were presented as evidence that when Clanricard had served as governor he had behaved honourably when he, and the more conciliatory members of the Confederation of Kilkenny, had negotiated with the cash-rich but landless duke of Lorraine. The purpose of the negotiation was to secure financial and military support from Lorraine that would enable the Confederates to continue the fight against the English parliamentary armies in Ireland at a time when 'only a little nook of the country consisting of some small tracts of land within Connacht and Munster' was 'left to the King'.[3] The merit of the edition, according to its editor, was that it was not in any way 'forged or spurious' but rather 'had the distinguishing marks of a true original' that demonstrated how, in his discussions with Lorraine, the marquess had been guided by 'his own generosity and a friendly regard to the singular misfortunes of the royal family of England' and that Lorraine had become interested in Ireland only out of a concern for 'the royal family then nearly stripped of three kingdoms, as also for a nation of his own religion, now upon the brink of ruin'.[4] The 10th earl considered it necessary to put these documents into the public domain because the motivation of each party to the Lorraine negotiations had been called into question by Richard Cox, in his stridently anti-Catholic text *Hibernia Anglicana*. There, Cox had invoked the authority of Clarendon's *History of Great Britain* to support his allegation that Lorraine had entered upon negotiations concerning the possibility of his providing military and financial support to those in Ireland who were still resisting the forces of the English parliament in Ireland only because these resisters would countenance having Lorraine, rather than Charles II, as their king in Ireland.[5]

Michael, 10th earl of Clanricard, obviously considered it essential that he establish that the man he considered his most distinguished ancestor had never flinched in his loyalty to the British monarchy. This explains his sponsoring this brief collection of documents that were introduced by an anonymous editor who added a lengthy and inchoate introduction that the editor described as a 'Dissertation'. One Thomas O'Sullevane, a Gaelic scholar and lawyer then based in London at the Middle Temple, has since been identified as the probable author of

---

[3] *Memoirs of the Right Honourable Marquis of Clanricarde, Lord Deputy General of Ireland* (London, 1722), liv; the most detailed account of the negotiations conducted by the ambassador sent by Lorraine to Ireland was that re-constructed by Clarendon in the mid 1650s; on this see Edward Hyde, Earl of Clarendon, *A Short View of the State and Condition of the Kingdom of Ireland*, Jane Ohlmeyer (Oxford, 2020), 101–19; I am grateful to Professor Ohlmeyer for allowing me to consult her edition at the proof stage.

[4] *Memoirs of... Clanricarde*, 1722, lii, lv.

[5] *Memoirs of... Clanricarde*, 1722, xi, xxxvi; Richard Cox, *Hibernia Anglicana, or, The History of Ireland, from the Conquest thereof by the English to this present time* (London, 1689–90); we learn from Clarendon, *A Short View of the State... of Ireland*, 112, that while this was the opinion of Clarendon concerning the motivation both of Lorraine's ambassador to Ireland and of Ireland's Catholic bishops, he exempted Clanricard from the charge. Clarendon, in fact, praised 'this eminent Catholic lord' who was consistently loyal to his monarch.

128 IMAGINING IRELAND'S PASTS

this 'Dissertation'.[6] O'Sullevane, presumably at the instigation of his patron, emphasized (as was borne out by the documents) that there never had been any doubt concerning Clanricard's loyalty to Charles II when the Lorraine negotiations were underway. Furthermore, he asserted that Ulick Burke had been a steadfast supporter of King Charles I and his government in Ireland in 1641 when rebellion had first broken in Ulster even though, as had been the case with the Lords of the Pale, the officials in government had refused to place trust in Clanricard because he was a Catholic peer. The documents put forward in 1722 did not shed any light on this second matter, but O' Sullevane addressed it and, in the course of doing so, invoked the arguments concerning the origins of the 1641 rebellion articulated by Roderic O'Flaherty, which we discussed in Chapter 4. Following this, O'Sullevane queried the supposed 'spontaneity and universality' of the rebellion, and contended that it was the 'rigour and severity' of Parsons and Borlase, the two Lords Justices, that explained why a rebellion that was originally confined to Ulster spread subsequently to other parts of the country, including into Connacht. Then, still following O'Flaherty, O'Sullevane pointed to the implausibility of several of the estimates of the number of Protestants supposedly 'murdered' in the rebellion, which, he decreed, were further exaggerated 'from the pulpit itself every year' with 'hideous relations' of how Protestants had been maltreated. O'Sullevane, and presumably his patron, was alarmed that such reports were being 'taken for fact and truth... with the vulgar at least', and appealed to 'men of impartial good sense' to take notice of what Sir William Petty had had to say on the subject. This too, he hoped, would dispel the suggestion that Clanricard had been slack in quelling the rebellion in Connacht since, claimed O'Sullevane, the disturbances had been confined to Ulster for some considerable time after the initial outbreak.[7]

The successor of the 10th earl of Clanricard, who styled himself John Smyth de Burgh, 11th earl of Clanricarde and 'a true Englishman', seems to have been personally responsible for the 1757 edition of the *Memoirs and Letters* of that same ancestor.[8] Unlike its predecessor, the collection of 1757 included documents that demonstrated how Ulick Burke 'a nobleman of singular merit and unblemished loyalty to King Charles the first' had proven himself 'very useful on the breaking out of the rebellion' because 'as soon as he had certain intelligence of

---

[6] Robin Flower and Myles Dillon, eds., *Catalogue of Irish Manuscripts in the British Museum*, vol. 3 (London, 1953); Introduction by Robin Flower, esp. 15–17; I am grateful to Bernadette Cunningham for drawing my attention to this publication and also for a pre-publication copy of Bernadette Cunningham, 'Myths and Memoirs of Ulick Burke, Marquess of Clanricarde (1604–1658)', *Journal of Galway Archaeological and Historical Society,* vol. 71 (2019), 7–18. John Lowe took it as given that O'Sullevane was the editor, *Letter-Book*, ed., Lowe, Introduction, vi.

[7] *Memoirs of...Clanricarde*, 1722, xxiv–xxvi.

[8] He used this style because his mother Anne was the daughter and co-heir of John Smyth, one of the governors of the bank of England, and the earl had his family name changed to de Burgh by act of parliament.

the rising in the North' he supplied eight companies out of his own store and without the least assistance from the state. By so doing, it was stated, he 'preserved his own country in peace longer than any other in the kingdom'.[9] As further proof of the loyalty of the marquess, the 11th earl emphasized how his ancestor had, in 1648, 'warmly espoused...the cessation between the Lord Inchiquin and the Irish', which peace, he pointed out, had brought 'the Nuncio's decree of excommunication upon those Catholics in the Confederacy who supported it'. The 11th earl emphasized that Ulick, although a Catholic, was unmoved by this papal interference, and put all religious consideration aside when he compelled the town of 'Galway...to proclaim the cessation, renounce the nuncio, and pay a considerable sum of money'. This action, according to the 11th earl, reduced the ability of the marquess to serve the titular King Charles II as governor of Ireland because 'the intrigues of the clergy' fomented the 'disaffection of his officers', with the result that he as governor was left with no option but, with royal consent, to resign his position and retire to England.[10]

Bernadette Cunningham has explained how the 11th earl made much of the English as well as the royalist credentials of the marquess, even to the extent of claiming London as his birthplace when, in fact, he had been born in Athlone. She has also detailed how the 11th earl also fabricated a close affinity between Ulick Burke and James Butler, marquess (later duke) of Ormond, by inventing a fictive daughter of Clanricard and an imaginary son of Ormond to 'authenticate' a supposed marriage alliance between children of the two marquesses.[11] The 11th earl also contended that Ulick Burke and James Butler had shared a political ideology, as proof of which he included in his introduction a copy of 'a short comparative character of the two greatest Irishmen of that age, the marquesses of Ormond and Clanricard'. This text, supposedly authored by one Mr Justice Lindsay, which may also be fictional, purported that 'these two illustrious persons...who lived in those times of confusion and misery' were 'of equal magnanimity, but of different persuasions in religion'. More particularly, the document showed how, during their service in Ireland, each had displayed a consistent 'loyalty to their prince and an abstracted love for the true interest of their country'. This, it was stated, reflected particularly well on Clanricard because unlike Ormond he had been raised in 'an erroneous religion' but had nonetheless always managed to confine his spiritual allegiance 'to the religion of the church, not of the court of Rome'.[12]

The desire of the 11th earl of Clanricard to link Ulick Burke with James Butler was probably encouraged by the publication in 1735–36 of Thomas Carte's

---

[9] *The Memoirs and Letters of Ulick, Marquis of Clanricarde and Earl of St Albans...Lord Lieutenant of Ireland...now first published by the present earl of Clanricarde* (London, 1757), xiv.

[10] *The Memoirs and Letters of Clanricarde*, 1757, xv.

[11] Cunningham, 'Myths and Memoirs', 8, 10–11, 12–13.

[12] *The Memoirs and Letters of Clanricarde*, 1757, xix–xx.

130   IMAGINING IRELAND'S PASTS

three-volume biographical study of James Butler, duke of Ormond, that was authenticated by a substantial body of documents, drawn mostly from the Butler family archive. In this Carte had composed a narrative of Ireland's history for the sixteenth and seventeenth centuries through the life stories of Thomas Butler, 10th earl of Ormond (1531–1614) and of James Butler (1610–88) 12th earl, 1st marquess (1642), and 1st duke (1661) of Ormond.[13] The 11th earl of Clanricard could not equal this study with one on his own family, both because the surviving Clanricard family papers could not compare with the archive that had been assembled by the Butlers of Ormond down the centuries and because the earl lacked Carte's ability as a historian.[14] However, the eleventh earl made most of what he had available to him when in 1757 he published a single volume that was almost identical in appearance to the three-volume folio compilation by Carte. This was altogether more impressive than the shabby volume that his father had commissioned, and that he chose to ignore. Despite its elegant appearance, the Clanricarde *Memoir* of 1757 was vacuous when compared with Carte's volumes. However, the earl seems to have seen benefit in imitating what Carte had done, not least because all references made by Carte to the marquess of Clanricard had been positive and suggested that the two nobles had indeed worked closely together to support their king. Carte had also demonstrated how history could be used to salvage the reputation of a family that had become tarnished because of disastrous political miscalculation by some of its members. One means that Carte had done so was by including in his introduction a sketch of the Butler family involvement with the British monarchy and with Ireland since medieval times. This obviously served as a template for a similar rendition of the history of the Burke/Bourke/de Burgo/de Burgh family that the 11th earl of Clanricard furnished in his introduction to the 1757 edition.

In this, the earl traced the family of de Burgh, as he now called them, to the time of Charlemagne, and then followed their movement from Normandy to England with William the Conqueror and, a century later, from England into Ireland with Hugh de Lacy. The ancestors of the Clanricard Burkes, like those of the Butlers of Ormond, were therefore represented as having been long associated with the onward march of civilization. Having made this point, the editor slackened his pace in the sixteenth century to explain how an ancestor named Ulick had married Margaret Butler, daughter of Piers, earl of Ormond, who bore him a son, also named Ulick but 'called by the Irish ne gan' [*na gceann*], signifying the beheader'.[15] He then explained how in 1543, this latter Ulick had surrendered

---

[13] Thomas Carte, *The Life of James, duke of Ormond*, 3 vols. (London, 1735, 1736).

[14] Even as matters stood, the correspondence of Ulick Burke that was edited and published by the 11th earl came from copies of letters by the marquess in the possession of Lord Chancellor Jocelyn in Ireland. These appear to have been acquired from the Donnellan family whose ancestor had been legal advisors to the marquess.

[15] *The Memoirs and Letters of Clanricarde*, 1757, x–xi.

EIGHTEENTH-CENTURY ARISTOCRATIC HISTORIES OF IRELAND 131

his 'vast territories', consisting of six baronies, to King Henry VIII who 're-granted' them to him with the title earl of Clanricard. From there the editor detailed, with some embellishment, how the 2nd earl, named Richard, 'called by the Irish Sassanagh the Englishman' and the 3rd earl, again Ulick, had assisted government officials in suppressing rebellion in the province of Connacht.[16] In doing so he elided matters that would have cast a shadow on the family's reputation as Carte had done when he glided past the occasion in 1569–71when the three brothers of Thomas Butler, the 10th earl of Ormond, had entered into open rebellion. Instead of dwelling on blemishes, Clanricard hasted to explain how Richard, the son of the third earl, who would become 4th earl on his father's death in 1601, had so distinguished himself fighting for Queen Elizabeth at the battle of Kinsale that he became known as 'Richard of Kinsale'. Here, the editor cited Fynes Moryson as witness to the bravery of Richard on the field of battle, but his account of the later deeds of Richard, and his brother Sir Thomas de Burgh, in the continuing conflict in Munster was obviously taken directly, but unacknowledged, from Thomas Stafford *Pacata Hibernia*, as we discussed in Chapter 3. The 'great reputation' that the fourth earl had then earned, as well as his marriage to Frances the daughter to Sir Francis Walsingham, enabled the editor to expound on Clanricard's accession to wealth and favour not only in Ireland but also in England where he was granted the English title of earl of St Albans.[17]

The editor's fulsome praise of this ancestor opened the way for even greater effusion on the merits and loyal service of the 4th earl's son Ulick, who came into his estates and titles on his father's death in 1635. This praise was understandable since the ostensible purpose of the volume was to bring one of the letter-books of Ulick, 5th earl and first Marquess of Clanricard to public attention.[18] The letter-book itself sustained the commentary on the loyalty of the marquess to both Charles I and Charles II, but the 11th earl was again economical with the truth when this suited the past he wished to portray. Thus he ignored the manner in which both Ulick and his father had opposed Wentworth's efforts to introduce a plantation to Connacht, and he also disregarded how Ulick had interacted with his stepbrother, the 3rd earl of Essex, a leading Parliamentarian, to avoid having his estates in England sequestered during the English Civil War.

It was important to the 11th earl that the marquess, whom he was presenting as a role model, should appear to have an unblemished record of loyalty to the Crown because as he expanded his family history he acknowledged that the immediate successors to the marquess had not been as judicious as their ancestor

[16] *The Memoirs and Letters of Clanricarde*, 1757, xi–xii.
[17] *The Memoirs and Letters of Clanricarde*, 1757, xii; for what Stafford had to say of the third earl and his brother see Chapter 3, p. 64.
[18] *The Memoirs and Letters of Clanricarde*, 1757, xii–xiii.

132   IMAGINING IRELAND'S PASTS

had been. The cousins who inherited the estates of the marquess remained loyal to the Stuart monarchs, and the only concern of the 11th earl was that his own more immediate predecessors Richard, the 8th earl and John the 9th earl, and their closest male relatives, had exceeded their brief by continuing to support King James II after he had been ousted from the British throne in 1688, and by fighting for him in Ireland against the army of King William. As a consequence several of the family had been forced into exile where, as the 11th earl recorded with apparent pride, they had distinguished themselves in Spanish and in French military service for which they had been decorated and rewarded by the monarchs of their adopted countries. However, of those who had remained at home John, the 9th earl, had been taken prisoner at the battle of Aughrim by the victorious Williamite army, after which he was stripped of his titles and forfeited his estate 'for his adherence to the said unfortunate king'. The family, according to the 11th earl, was partially rehabilitated in 1702 after Queen Anne, a Protestant daughter to King James II, had ascended the throne. At that time, following protracted negotiations, provision was made to have the 'next Protestant relatives' of the Clanricard family become 'guardians' to those sons of the 8th and the 9th earls, who would be educated 'in the Protestant religion', in return for which the family was 'acquitted of all treasons and attainders'.[19]

After this, the narrator's father Michael, after an education at Eton and Christ Church, Oxford, became 10th earl of Clanricard in 1712. It was he, as mentioned, who had sponsored the 1722 edition of one letter book of his ancestor, hoping thereby to cleanse the reputation of the marquess from any taint associated with his dealings with the duke of Lorraine. Then, when John Smyth de Burgh, 11th earl of Clanricard, edited another letter book in 1757, he praised the endeavours of all of his ancestors as well as the marquess. The total record, he claimed in his dedication to King George II, provided evidence of the 'unsullied loyalty of his family [and]...the loss of honours, life and fortune in the royal cause'. Then, in reflecting on the 'mistaken ill-placed zeal' of those who had fought for James II, 'the Prince then on the throne', he did not either 'blame their conduct' or vindicate it, but rather balanced what the family had 'suffered' for 'a wrong placed...adherence to an unfortunate prince' against the long record of family service to a succession of monarchs. He thus argued that his family, which, he contended, had 'received fewer favours from the Crown' than any other of similar rank, should no longer be shunned by those in power since they were as ready to serve the Hanoverians as the marquess and his immediate predecessors had served the Tudor and Stuart monarchs.[20]

---

[19] *The Memoirs and Letters of Clanricarde*, 1757, xvi–xviii.
[20] *The Memoirs and Letters of Clanricarde*, 1757, dedication 'To the King'.

5.3 Carte's Life of Ormond

Clanricard's use of history to rehabilitate a family's standing, was, I have suggested, inspired by the effort of Thomas Carte (1686–1754), a High Anglican minister and an accomplished historian, to restore the reputation of the family of the Butlers of Ormond through history.[21] Carte, who had spent time as a Jacobite exile on the Continent, undertook to write a history of James Butler, 12th earl, 1st marquess, and 1st duke of Ormond (1610–88) at the request of Charles Butler, 2nd earl of Arran, and grandson of the 1st duke of Ormond. Arran himself and his older brother James, who had succeeded their grandfather as 2nd duke of Ormond in 1688, had been closely associated with, and had been favoured by, King James II, but as Protestants they, unlike the Clanricard Burkes, had taken the side of William of Orange after 1688.[22] King William rewarded both James Butler, the 2nd duke, and his brother Charles for this strategic switch of sides by appointing them to significant military posts. In an effort to ensure that they would remain in favour into the future these two maintained contact with the exiled Stuart court in France, thinking that one of their number might succeed to the throne following the death of William and Mary, who had no legitimate heirs. The Butler brothers were, as it transpired, entirely happy when the succession fell to Queen Anne in 1702, a Protestant daughter of James II, who reigned until 1714. Still trying to secure a future for the family among the service nobility, the 2nd duke, who was mired in debt, supported the claim of the exiled descendants of James II in France to succeed Queen Anne, who also lacked a direct descendant. The Whig nobility, who considered that all Catholic descendants of James II should be debarred from the throne on religious grounds, countered this claim in England. Therefore, when the Whig nobility recovered power following the death of Queen Anne in 1714, they offered the throne to George elector of Hanover (whose ancestral claim traced back to James VI and I), who was duly crowned as King George I in 1714. This left Ormond and his brother politically marginalized. Recognizing this the 2nd duke fled to France in June 1715 where he remained, until his death in 1745, as a soldier and courtier to the Old Pretender. Ormond considered this preferable to facing his creditors and a likely impeachment by the Whig- dominated Westminster parliament.

The immediate consequence for the Butler family was that the duke's titles were revoked and the Butler English estates were sequestered. In Ireland the estates of the Butlers of Ormond fell into the hands of creditors and government officials, and Charles, earl of Arran, continued to live under a cloud because of his past

---

[21] For a biographical note on Thomas Carte see that by Éamonn Ó Ciardha, *Dictionary of Irish Biography*, vol. 2, 390–1.

[22] For a biographical note on James Butler, 2nd duke of Ormond, see that by David Hayton, *Dictionary of Irish Biography*, vol. 2, 145–50.

134 IMAGING IRELAND'S PASTS

conduct and his known contacts with his exiled brother. In order to recover some standing for the family in Ireland, Arran in 1721 secured a loan to purchase back the Butler Irish estates, including Kilkenny Castle. However, he had to remain content with the junior Butler title of earl of Arran.[23]

It was against this background that Arran invited Thomas Carte to undertake a biographical study of the 1st duke, whose dedicated service to both King Charles I and King Charles II was legendary. Carte and his patron believed that one means of restoring the reputation of the Butlers as loyal servants of the Crown was by reviving memories of the services both of the 1st duke and also of Thomas Butler, 10th earl of Ormond. This nobleman had been grandfather to the wife of the 1st duke, and a known favourite of Queen Elizabeth. To facilitate the history, Arran gave Carte access to the family archives in Kilkenny Castle where, as Carte put it, the 1st duke had 'preserved his papers with...care and method from the time of his first entry upon public business, when it was perhaps dangerous as well as difficult to keep them', and had continued to do so in the 'more settled times' of his later years.[24]

After a perusal of the entire archive, Carte returned to England with bundles of these papers, which he augmented from other sources concerning developments in Britain and Ireland during the sixteenth and the seventeenth centuries. Among the papers he consulted were the Clarendon papers, some records left by Archbishop Rinuccini of his time as papal nuncio in Ireland, the memoirs of the marquess of Clanricard for the years 1641–43, and the anonymous unpublished 'Aphorismical Discovery' that Carte found among papers held by John Stearne, Bishop of Clogher.[25]

Carte explained that Arran had commissioned him to do two things. His first responsibility was to explain how that earl's 'noble ancestors had in a course of some hundreds of years set...a constant example of hereditary loyalty', and his second was to detail how the 1st duke of Ormond had overcome 'such eminent trials, temptations and difficulties as very rarely happen and to which few minds are equal'. Arran also commissioned Carte to narrate how this 'truly great and good man' had provided 'an example of heroic virtue, loyalty and honour as is fit for the imitation of latest posterity'.[26] As he proceeded with his commission, Carte insisted that he was relating 'things as [he] found them', seeking always to be 'impartial', knowing that any historian who wrote 'history with views of serving a party may perhaps do a present job for them' but would not 'please their successors' and would do 'a lasting disservice to his country'.[27] To prove his good

[23] For a biographical note on Charles, 2nd earl of Arran, see that by Éamonn Ó Ciardha, *Dictionary of Irish Biography*, vol. 2, 100–1.
[24] Carte, *The Life...of Ormond*, vol. 1, Preface, i–ii.
[25] Carte, *The Life...of Ormond*, vol. 1, Preface, iii–vi.
[26] Carte, *Life...of Ormond*, vol. 1, Carte to the earl of Arran.
[27] Carte, *The Life...of Ormond*, vol. 1, Preface, xii.

EIGHTEENTH-CENTURY ARISTOCRATIC HISTORIES OF IRELAND 135

faith, and to allow the evidence speak for itself, Carte, in 1735, published his third volume containing a selection of the documents that related to his subject down to the year 1649, before he published volumes 1 and 2 in 1736 where he presented his interpretation of the documentary evidence.[28]

For the first of his tasks, Carte established a template, which, as I have suggested, was that followed by the 11th earl of Clanricard when tracing his family background. Here, Carte discussed the origin of the Butler name and the role played by the de Botillers, in extending English Crown authority over a recalcitrant Irish population.[29] The first whose actions he detailed was 'Edmond le Botiller', who had upheld English influence in Ireland 'in very unquiet times when the Irish were continually breaking out into rebellion and the Scots, under command of Robert de Bruce's brother infested the kingdom'.[30] Carte accorded considerable attention also to Piers Butler, better known to historians as Piers Ruadh [Red Piers] (*c*.1467–1539), who, he averred, 'had greatly distinguished himself on many occasions in the service of the Crown, and been successful in suppressing the insurrection of the Irish'.[31] Here, Carte turned a blind eye to the well-known fact that Piers Butler had, in the words of David Edwards, been a 'murderer and a usurper' who had overcome rival claims to the Butler lands and titles from the English Boleyn and St Leger families by demonstrating his own indispensability to upholding the Crown's interest in Ireland.[32] Carte was, however, correct in identifying Piers as an effective ruler who had promoted English influence in the lordship and in the country, and who had been eventually rewarded by the Crown by being recognized as the 8th earl of Ormond. The next person to receive close attention was Piers's grandson, Thomas Butler (1531–1614) who held title as the 10th earl of Ormond, 1546–1614, the first five years of them spent as a ward of court.[33] Lauding the achievements of the 10th earl was made easy for Carte because that earl had left occasional autobiographical notes among his papers, and had commissioned more elaborate encomia of his career in Irish and in Latin.[34]

---

[28] Carte, *The Life...of Ormond*, vol. 3, Preface.
[29] Carte, *The Life...of Ormond*, vol. 1, Introduction, ii.
[30] Carte, *The Life...of Ormond*, vol. 1, Introduction, xxx; for a biographical note on Edmund Butler (le Botiller) d.1321, 'justiciar of Ireland and magnate', see that by Ronan McKay in *Dictionary of Irish Biography*, vol. 2, 103–4.
[31] Carte, *The Life...of Ormond*, vol. 1, Introduction, xlv; for a biographical note on Piers Ruadh Butler (*c*.1467–1539) 8th earl of Ormond and 1st earl of Ossory, see that by David Beresford, *Dictionary of Irish Biography*, vol. 2, 164–5; see also David Edwards, *The Ormond Lordship in County Kilkenny, 1515–1642: The Rise and Fall of Butler Feudal Power* (Dublin, 2003), esp., 81–90.
[32] Edwards, *The Ormond Lordship*, 83.
[33] For a biographical note on Thomas Butler (1531–1614), 10th earl of Ormond, see that by David Edwards, *Dictionary of Irish Biography*, vol. 2, 183–6; see also David Edwards, *The Ormond Lordship in County Kilkenny*.
[34] *Poems of the Butlers*, ed., James Carney (Dublin, 1945); *The Tipperary Hero: Dermot O'Meara's Ormonious (1615)*, ed. and trans., David Edwards and Keith Sidwell (Turnhout, Belgium, 2011).

136   IMAGINING IRELAND'S PASTS

Carte therefore did no more that endorse how the 10th earl wanted his service to the Crown to be remembered. Besides his boyhood years spent at court 'where he was instructed in learning and other accomplishments' along with King Edward VI, 'who took great delight in his company', the services he engaged upon were: assisting the duke of Somerset against the Scots at the battle of Musselburgh (1547); his military support for Queen Mary in 1554 at the time of Wyatt's rebellion; his high standing with Queen Elizabeth who 'considered him her relation'; his conflict with the earl of Desmond at the battle of Affane in 1564–65; his return from the English court in 1569 to recall to obedience his brothers who had entered into revolt; his involvement with the suppression of the Desmond rebellion in the 1570s and the 1580s; his continuing engagement with military affairs for the duration of Tyrone's rebellion, including his being taken prisoner; and finally his retirement from public affairs at the end of the reign of Queen Elizabeth when he 'was then seventy years old', after which 'the earl had nothing to do but to spend the remainder of his days in quiet and provide for the succession of his family'.[35] Besides offering detail on each of these episodes, Carte offered his own appraisal of Ormond, whom he considered 'a man of great parts, admirable judgment, great experience and a prodigious memory'. He was, moreover, 'a Protestant and frequently recommended to the queen his own chaplains and other men of merit to vacant bishoprics'. Indeed, in Carte's judgement, Ormond's only weakness was his 'too great a passion for the fair sex', which Carte considered a 'great vice', but one outweighed by 'his outstanding virtue', which was that 'he perfectly from his heart abhorred rebellion and detested all rebels'.[36]

It will be clear from these examples how the approach to history writing adopted by those eighteenth-century authors of aristocratic history differed from that of the providential historians, whose works they occasionally cited and sometimes challenged. They distinguished between 'profane' and 'sacred' history, and presumed that in the secular domain people were, for the most part, the shapers of their own destinies. This left the historian with the function of appraising 'truth, explanation and judgment' in seeking to establish why people acted as they did.[37] They did not deny that society frequently lapsed into chaos, as had happened in the mid-seventeenth century, but they did not concede that this had been inevitable, and believed that in the past, as in the present and into the future, good order could be achieved when people of high social standing and forceful character worked in conjunction with, and on behalf of, legitimate monarchs. Such leaders would necessarily be of ancient lineage and draw

---

[35] Carte, *The Life...of Ormond*, vol. 1, Introduction, lii–liii.

[36] Carte, *The Life...of Ormond*, vol. 1, Introduction, lxv.

[37] *Memoirs of...Clanricarde*, 1722, ix; the distinction between profane and sacred was made by the editor, Thomas O' Sullevane.

EIGHTEENTH-CENTURY ARISTOCRATIC HISTORIES OF IRELAND 137

inspiration from the example of their predecessors, and would ideally have had the benefit of a formal education that would equip them to behave with decorum, to master the skills necessary to being effective on the field of battle and in the council chamber, and to be acquainted with the languages, especially Latin, that would enable them to become involved with events in foreign countries and courts while also being servants of Britain's monarchs. Those who would fulfil their leadership role effectively would also have attended occasionally at court and be known and trusted by the ruling monarch.

We have seen how those who wrote of Ulick Burke, marquess of Clanricard, represented him as such an exemplary nobleman, and Carte endorsed this finding when he declared Clanricard to have been 'truly wise, truly good, and truly honourable'. Carte made it clear that this was as he expected, since Clanricard was 'descended of a very noble and ancient family of English race which came over into Ireland at the time of the conquest, in which they had a considerable hand'.[38] What held true of the Clanricard Burkes was even truer of the Butlers of Ormond, since 'the chief branch of the Ormond family had ever continued loyal to the crown, and had never been concerned in any rebellion against it from the time of the first settlement in Ireland, for the space of five hundred years'.[39] Then, as Carte discussed those who had been heads of the Butler house during the sixteenth and seventeenth century, he considered the efforts of Thomas Butler, the 10th earl of Ormond, and of James Butler, the 12th earl (and later 1st marquess and 1st duke of Ormond), especially commendable because each had promoted peace and prosperity in their country according to the wishes of the monarchs they had served.

Forcefulness of character was considered by these authors to be particularly important for noblemen in Ireland because, unlike their counterparts in England, they had been engaged upon a continuing effort to maintain order over a 'conquered' native population.[40] These, in Carte's opinion, were being constantly stirred up by two disruptive elements; the 'Romish clergy' and 'the old Irish septs', by which he meant 'the descendants of the old captains and chiefs' who were 'still at large' despite having forfeited their property following their involvement with previous rebellions.[41] While Carte thus acknowledged that the seventeenth century had not been entirely settled, he believed that those who threatened good order had been losing their potency because, as he put it, the various plantations and compositions that had been implemented during the reign of King James I enjoyed the support of the 'middle Irish [who] being made freeholders in great numbers were so pleased at getting rid of the tyranny and exactions of their old lords' and, with them, 'the miseries they had lately endured in Tyrone's rebellion'.[42]

---

[38] Carte, *Life...of Ormond*, vol. 1, 212–13.   [39] Carte, *Life...of Ormond*, 3.
[40] Carte, *Life...of Ormond*, 67.   [41] Carte, *Life...of Ormond*, 154.
[42] Carte, *Life...of Ormond*, vol. 1, 44–5.

138 IMAGINING IRELAND'S PASTS

Carte could thus speak positively of the steps taken by the monarchs, with advice from noble families such as the Clanricard Burkes and the Butlers of Ormond, to bring permanent peace to Ireland and to have the Irish accept the British monarchs as their legitimate rulers. Moreover, like some of the Gaelic authors cited in Chapter 3, he considered that King James 1 'might probably have ruled in their hearts' because they had looked with favour at 'his extraction from the Old Kings of Ireland'.[43] This possibility had been hindered, according to Carte, by two elements in Ireland. The first was 'the swarms of Jesuits and Priests educated in the seminaries' and the second was 'the recusant lawyers, a powerful body of men'. Together, according to Carte, these had diverted people from the path of reform and from allegiance to their king.[44]

Another, and for Carte a more pernicious factor that had alienated people from the government was that those people from England who had been attracted to service in Ireland had been driven by the desire to promote their material interests over encouraging the civil and spiritual reform of the Irish population. The problem, as Carte put it bluntly, was that in 'an age of adventurers and projectors; the general taste of the world ran in favour of new discoveries and planting of countries; and such as were not hardy enough to venture into the remote parts of the earth fancied they might make a fortune nearer home by settling and planting in Ireland'.[45] Thus, while Carte would have been aware that the reputation of his chosen hero, the 1st duke of Ormond, had been vilified by Catholic historians, notably Bishop Nicholas French, he chose to ignore this lest it should distract from his attack on English-born Crown servants in Ireland who, he believed, had been most responsible for frustrating the reform efforts of two heads of the Butler dynasty.[46]

From this, Carte concluded, and the editors of the two Clanricard volumes took the same position, that loyal Irish-born nobles might have persuaded the Irish population to respect the British monarchy over the course of the sixteenth and seventeenth centuries had they not had to deal with the problem of keeping in check the blatant self-interest of these English adventurers who had made their way to Ireland. Carte illustrated this most effectively by constructing counterfactuals to posit how tragedies might have been averted if successive monarchs had acted prudently, or had taken advice from the small number of honourable nobles who had always put the public good, and loyalty to the monarch above private interest. These, according to Carte, included Thomas Butler and James Butler of Ormond; Thomas, Viscount Wentworth (later earl of Strafford); and Ulick Burke, marquess of Clanricard.

---

[43] Carte, *Life... of Ormond*, vol. 1, 33. [44] Carte, *Life... of Ormond*, vol. 1, 33.

[45] Carte, *Life... of Ormond*, vol. 1, 27.

[46] On French and his unrelenting attacks upon the duke of Ormond see Jason McHugh, "'Soldier of Christ'".

EIGHTEENTH-CENTURY ARISTOCRATIC HISTORIES OF IRELAND   139

On the monarchs themselves Carte praised the Tudor rulers collectively for having upheld the mystique of monarchy. He spoke highly also of King Charles II of whom James, duke of Ormond, had thought so highly that he 'always wore his hat as that king did...and imitated him constantly in his habit as well as behaviour'.[47] However, Carte was not impressed by King James VI and I who, he alleged, had during his years as king in Scotland (1567–1603) been obliged to consort almost as an equal with his nobles there, and then, after 1603, when he succeeded to the English throne, had behaved familiarly also with subjects in England. This laxity, according to Carte, left it to King Charles I to restore some 'decorum' at court, and his efforts to do so had resulted in difficult relationships with some powerful subjects who began to conspire against him. Thus Carte posited that 'had King Charles immediately succeeded Queen Elizabeth, his reign had been more happy to the nation' since he proved himself 'not fit to struggle with the difficulties in which his father left him involved'.[48]

Carte also employed counterfactuals in his discussion of the service rendered by Thomas, earl of Ormond, to Queen Elizabeth. He asserted that, when Ormond had been put in charge of the military effort to bring the Desmond rebellion to a conclusion, 'all would have been ended, if he had continued a little longer in power, but another had been put in his stead to reap the advantage, and have the honour of his labours'.[49] The other, whom Carte did not name, was Arthur Lord Grey de Wilton, a client of the earl of Leicester. Carte insisted that Leicester had not only been a persistent opponent of Ormond at court but also the person responsible for placing English Protestants of Puritan inclination in Ireland. The immediate consequence of the unnecessary change of management in Munster, according to Carte, was that the advice offered to the queen by Ormond on how to bring permanent tranquility to Munster had been ignored. His advice, according to Carte, was that the property that had come into Crown possession due to Desmond's rebellion should have been 'given to noblemen and gentlemen of Munster', who had supported Ormond in suppressing the rebellion, 'who had followers to inhabit them, and who were ready at hand to defend them themselves'. Instead, he said, the fruits of victory had gone to English Protestants, many associates of Leicester, which deprived the Crown of the opportunity to consolidate the goodwill of Irish subjects who had proven themselves loyal. The alternative chosen, according to Carte, had led to future tragedy because 'all the undertakers in that province, who had come out of England', like the English who had been involved in the Leix-Offaly plantation thirty years previously, 'were unequal to the work of a plantation'. The final outcome was that when a further

---

[47] Carte, *Life...of Ormond*, vol. 2, 551.   [48] Carte, *Life...of Ormond*, vol. 1, 354–5.
[49] Carte, *Life...of Ormond*, vol. 1, Introduction, lvi.

140   IMAGINING IRELAND'S PASTS

insurrection happened in 1590s the planters 'forsook their castles and dwellings before they were so much as attacked, or had a sight of the rebels'.[50]

Another malconsequence of the path chosen, according to Carte, was that 'the Protestants in Ireland were generally of the Puritanical stamp, furious in their opposition to the Papists, and (like their brethren in England) jealous of the prerogative, desirous to cramp the power, and indisposed to supply the necessities, of the crown'.[51] The descendants of such zealots in the seventeenth century, with Archbishop Ussher as their spiritual leader, had, according to Carte, promoted a Calvinist liturgy in the Irish church that had been consolidated by 'a shoal of factions and irregular Puritans, brought by Hugh Montgomery and other planters out of Scotland'. Carte credited Wentworth with having curbed these excesses and brought the liturgy of the Irish Church into conformity with that in England. However, he believed the corrective had come too late because 'several' of the Calvinist pronouncements had already given 'great offence to the Roman Catholics, and hindered their conversion'.[52]

Carte was convinced that the well-intended actions of James Butler, who would become 1st duke of Ormond, had been similarly stymied by the same type of people as those who had dogged the path of the 10th earl in promoting reform in Ireland. This English-born earl had been first brought to his inheritance in Ireland in 1633 when Thomas, Viscount Wentworth, went there to assume duties as governor. The young earl could have had no better tutor, claimed Carte, since Wentworth, was 'a statesman of as great abilities as any age hath produced' and one moreover who 'had very little of self interest in him' and was 'an excellent judge of men as well as business'.[53] The first major responsibility to which Wentworth assigned Ormond, according to Carte, was to command the Irish army (for the most part Catholic soldiers under Protestant officers) that Wentworth had intended him to transport into western Scotland in 1638 with a view to diverting the Covenanter army from invading England. This initiative, claimed Carte, was aborted because the king was persuaded against it by Scots and by those in England and Ireland who soon proved themselves to be the king's enemies. Nonetheless, Carte remained convinced that if the campaign had proceeded 'the king [would have] retrieved his affairs and prevented the calamities

---

[50] Carte, *Life... of Ormond*, vol. 1, Introduction, lix; there appears to be no substance to the suggestion of Carte that a disproportionate number of those chosen to become proprietors in the Munster plantation were associated with Leicester's circle, on which subject see Michael MacCarthy-Morrogh, *The Munster Plantation: English Migration to Southern Ireland, 1583–1641* (Oxford, 1986), 46–69.

[51] Carte, *Life... of Ormond*, vol. 1, 61.

[52] Carte, *Life... of Ormond*, vol. 1, 68, 77; on Wentworth's role in this matter see Alan Ford, *James Ussher: Theology, History and Politics*, esp. 174–207; John McCafferty, *The Reconstruction of the Church of Ireland*.

[53] Carte, *Life... of Ormond*, vol. 1, 54, 56, 61; for a different view of Wentworth and self-interest see Hugh Kearney, *Strafford in Ireland, 1633–41* (Manchester, 1959), esp. 171–85.

EIGHTEENTH-CENTURY ARISTOCRATIC HISTORIES OF IRELAND 141

which afterwards befell him and his family'.[54] Then, as Carte traced the downfall and eventual execution of Wentworth (earl of Strafford from 1640) that he attributed to the king's enemies in England and Ireland, he claimed that, before his death, Strafford had recommended that Ormond be appointed as governor of Ireland. If the king had followed this advice, said Carte, it 'would in all probability have prevented the rebellion in Ireland or crushed it at its birth'.[55] Then, if no rebellion had happened in Ireland, 'the faction in England' would not have dared take up arms against their king.

In order to sustain such pronouncement Carte enquired 'what were the true causes and motives to the Irish rebellion, who had the greatest hand in kindling, spreading and continuing the flame, and who were the most concerned in the iniquity of that affair'?[56] On this, Carte accepted John Temple's assertion that the government in Ireland had been taken by surprise by the rebellion because the country seemed prosperous after forty years of peace, and because Catholics were being permitted the 'quiet exercise of their religion in a private way' and were pleased that the 'Graces', for which they had advanced money more than a decade previously, would finally 'be established by law'.[57] This happy prognostication, Carte conceded, did not dissuade some priests and dispossessed Gaelic lords from plotting an 'insurrection' as the only means to dislodge the plantations that had been in place for thirty years, and to resolve the financial difficulties in which some lords had fallen due to 'licentious living'.[58] However, Carte remained convinced that 'the design indeed of an insurrection was confined only to the Old Irish' and would therefore have been easily contained.[59] More accusingly, he pronounced that the disturbance had spread beyond Ulster because, instead of following Strafford's advice to have Ormond as governor, the king had been persuaded in June 1641 to nominate Robert Sidney, earl of Leicester, as Lord Lieutenant. Since Leicester did not travel to Ireland, Sir William Parsons and Sir John Borlase were left to execute power as joint lords justices. Carte insisted repeatedly that these two had behaved rashly from the moment they had become aware that a rebellion had broken out in Ulster.

The actions and inaction of the two lords justices, according to Carte, had exacerbated an already difficult situation by provoking a spread of the rebellion throughout the country. This, he believed, was entirely predictable since, in his view, each of the two lords justices lacked both the pedigree and education to be governor. Borlase, according to Carte, was a 'quiet and easy man', who had become 'a good soldier' in the Low Countries, but 'understood nothing else' and was further unsuitable because 'in Holland [he had] entertained the principles of the

---

[54] Carte, *Life...of Ormond*, vol. 1, 103, 104, 132.   [55] Carte, *Life...of Ormond*, vol. 1, 116.
[56] Carte, *Life...of Ormond*, Preface, xii.
[57] On 'The Graces' see Aidan Clarke, *The Old English in Ireland*; Carte, *Life...of Ormond*, 153.
[58] Carte, *Life...of Ormond*, vol. 1, 153–6.   [59] Carte, *Life...of Ormond*, vol. 1, 156–7, 165.

142 IMAGINING IRELAND'S PASTS

Calvinists'.[60] Parsons, according to Carte, was 'a person of mean extract, bred up to read and write, which faculty…was all his learning'. He was even further unsuited, according to Carte, because he had been a client of Leicester in Elizabethan England and had imbibed 'early Puritanical sentiments' and, following the death of Leicester, had decamped in Ireland with but £40 to his name after which he rose to considerable wealth first through corrupt dealings in the office of the escheator general, and later as master of the Court of Wards. There, according to Carte, he had engrossed several manors throughout Ireland, most notoriously (on which Carte provided details) in his 'scandalous prosecution' of Phelim Byrne in Wicklow, with the result that Parsons became 'the most obnoxious person that could have been found out to be made a Lord Justice'.[61]

Carte was suggesting therefore that events in Ireland in the seventeenth century followed the course set in the reign of Queen Elizabeth with potentially loyal subjects being given good reason to suspect that unfit officers of the Crown were bent on profiting from their destruction. Moreover, Ormond, who was still head of the army, had pronounced 'that the rebels [in Ulster] ought to be immediately attacked', but, instead of enabling this action, Parsons and Borlase 'showed an aversion to his [Ormond's] person and did all they could to make his command of the army disagreeable and shackled him in the exercise of it'.[62] The same, in Carte's opinion, had happened in Munster, where the provincial president, Sir William St Leger, was 'a good old soldier, of good experience and great activity', and the settlers under his command would have been able to defend themselves if the Lords Justices had given them military resources.[63] Then, in Connacht where few Protestants resided, Carte explained how Clanricard, although a Catholic, remained 'strongly attached to the crown' and, through his actions demonstrated that 'no man loved his country more or his friend better'. Nonetheless, the Justices, as they had done in Munster, refused support to those who were committed to maintaining order in Connacht. Such failures, according to Carte, were compounded by the proroguing of parliament by the Lords Justices against the specific advice of Ormond and Viscount Dillon, and by their issuing a proclamation which Carte believed had 'terrified' all Catholics into believing they were all being identified as rebels. It was this mismanagement by Parsons and Borlase, according to Carte, that had led to 'the general defection of the kingdom'.[64]

Carte was satisfied that Ormond alone, or Ormond aided by Viscount Dillon and Clanricard and Sir William St Leger, might have quelled the rebellion from the outset, and would certainly have prevented it from spreading from Ulster to the other provinces. They would have succeeded, he believed, because they all

---

[60] Carte, *Life…of Ormond*, vol. 1, 191.

[61] Carte, *Life…of Ormond*, vol. 1, 191; on the controversy concerning the Byrne land see Hugh Kearney, *Strafford in Ireland*, 174–6.

[62] Carte, *Life…of Ormond*, vol. 1, 195.   [63] Carte, *Life…of Ormond*, vol. 1, 211.

[64] Carte, *Life…of Ormond*, vol. 1, 212–16.

EIGHTEENTH-CENTURY ARISTOCRATIC HISTORIES OF IRELAND 143

belonged to ancient lineages with proud records of loyalty to the English Crown and could therefore be counted on to put public service above their private interests. Instead, a group of Puritan English people who had come to Ireland during the Nine Year's War had, by the mid-seventeenth century, gained control over government in Dublin. Then he explained how Sir John Clotworthy, an English Presbyterian who held a seat in the Westminster parliament as well as land in County Antrim, became a link between the Dublin officials and 'the faction in England' who then made 'use of the Irish rebellion' to bring about the destruction of the monarchy. For all these parties, he claimed, 'it served much better to make a bluster and noise about the rebellion of Ireland than to take any effective means to suppress it'. Therefore, Carte asserted, the 'cunning' Sir William Parsons was an early 'favourer' of the English parliament, and from the outset, 'the great hopes of the Lords Justices in Ireland lay in the Parliament of England'.[65]

The Justices, claimed Carte, had continued to deny supplies to Ormond as head of the army because a successful military campaign would have deprived them of the 'gains' they hoped to make 'by the forfeiture of the rebels'.[66] Instead, according to Carte, they maintained a secret correspondence with their superior, Robert Sidney, earl of Leicester, whose allegiance was by then shifting from king to parliament, while in Ireland they granted free rein to Sir Charles Coote. Carte depicted Coote as an English soldier/adventurer who had arrived in Ireland during the Elizabethan wars and had enriched himself by corrupt means. Then Carte contended that Coote in his haste to add to his already considerable estate 'was not very scrupulous in distinguishing between the innocent and the guilty' and became infamous in the eyes of all Irish Catholics for 'his inhuman executions and promiscuous murders of people'. His actions, claimed Carte, made Catholics suspect that a decision had been taken to destroy them all, and their worst fears seemed confirmed by the treatment doled out by the Lords Justices to a sequence of Catholics of high social standing, including the English Catholic James Touchet, earl of Castlehaven.[67]

Carte identified what he saw as the deliberate alienation of potential allies by the Lords Justices as part of their 'designs...for the extirpation of the Old English, the perpetuating of the war, and the desolation of the realm by which whoever was a gainer his Majesty was sure to be a loser'.[68] Carte asserted that the trauma that beset England as well as Ireland could have been avoided had Ormond been in charge, and he argued that Ireland in general would have returned to its traditional loyalty had the king been permitted to travel there when he had wished to do so. Carte believed that this journey did not take place because,

---

[65] Carte, *Life...of Ormond*, vol. 1, 195; for a biographical note on Clotworthy see that by Raymond Gillespie, *Dictionary of Irish Biography*, vol. 2, 601–2.

[66] Carte, *Life...of Ormond*, vol. 1, 227. [67] Carte, *Life...of Ormond*, vol. 1, 291, 298.

[68] Carte, *Life...of Ormond*, vol. 1, 303, 368.

following the passage of the Adventurers' Act of 1642, members of the English parliament had as much interest as the Lords Justices in seeing that further Irish proprietors would be provoked into rebellion because the £400,000 that had been furnished by the 'adventurers' to enable a military conquest of Ireland was secured by Irish land that had not yet been declared confiscate to the Crown.[69]

Given these developments, Carte considered that by 21 January 1644, when Ormond was finally appointed by Charles I as Lord Lieutenant of Ireland, the 'time was elapsed when he could have done good'.[70] Under the circumstances, according to Carte, Ormond could do no more between then and 1650, when he joined the royal court in exile on the Continent, than attempt 'uniting all Ireland under his obedience' with the intention of preventing the forces of the English parliament from gaining control of Ireland. This, Carte believed, was 'the only visible means of saving His Majesty's life, and retrieving his affairs'.[71] However, on this occasion, claimed Carte, Ormond faced opposition not only from the usual source of corrupt officials but also from Ireland's Catholic bishops who had become increasingly intransigent due to the 'intrigues of the Nuncio' who, Carte believed, was anxious to 'cast off the authority of the Crown of England' and to have Ireland placed under the jurisdiction of a Catholic prince. The bishops' candidate for this role was Charles, duke of Lorraine, who, in Carte's words, was 'an artful designing man, covetous, rapacious, saving of his money' with an aspiration to become king of Ireland 'in the name of Spain'.[72]

The Lorraine intervention happened after Ormond had left the country following his defeat by a Parliamentary army led by Michael Jones at the battle of Rathmines, August 1649. Carte, in a passage that contrasted sharply with the explanation offered for this same defeat by Gaelic authors discussed in Chapter 4, absolved Ormond from any responsibility, saying it 'was owing chiefly to the inexperience of a great many of the Irish officers...and the rawness of their soldiers'.[73] When he could do no more for the royalist cause in Ireland, said Carte, Ormond 'delivered up the government to the Commissioners of the Parliament', and retired to the Continent to join the court of the heir to Charles I whom Ormond had already 'caused...to be proclaimed king as Charles II' following the 'murder of the king' on 30 January 1649.[74]

---

[69] Carte, Life...of Ormond, vol. 1, 307, 308, 463; on the 'Adventurers' Act' see Karl Bottigheimer, English Money and Irish Land: The 'Adventurers' in the Cromwellian Settlement of Ireland (Oxford, 1971); David Brown, Empire and Enterprise: Money, Power and the Adventurers for Irish Land during the British Civil Wars (Manchester, 2020).

[70] Carte, Life...of Ormond, vol. 1, 475. [71] Carte, Life...of Ormond, vol. 2, 41.

[72] Carte, Life...of Ormond, vol. 2, 150–1.

[73] Carte, Life...of Ormond, vol. 2, 257; for the contrasting Gaelic account of the defeat see Chapter 4, p. 115.

[74] Carte, Life...of Ormond, vol. 2, 52, 55, 78–81.

Carte did not considered it necessary to furnish any documentary material for his reconstruction of the later phases of the career of James Butler because he believed that in his account up to 1650 he had corrected 'the uncertain, mistaken, false and contradictory accounts…of the Irish rebellion by writers influenced by selfish views and party animosities, or unfurnished with proper and authentic materials and memoirs'.[75] For the remainder of his study he divided the life of Ormond into two segments. The first, treating of the years 1649–60, described how Ormond and his wife and children attended upon King Charles II and his mother in various Continental locations, during which, according to Carte, Ormond was continuously active, even to the extent of putting his life in danger in seeking to secure the restoration of the monarchy. The second segment dealt with the career of Ormond from the Restoration of 1660 to his death in 1688. In this, Carte celebrated how, after his years in exile, Ormond had again 'found himself in his native country, happy in the favour of his Prince, and in the esteem of the world, and dignified with various honours and employments'.[76]

By 'native country' Carte meant England, but Carte believed that Ormond 's rightful place of employment was in Ireland where he had been appointed by King Charles I as Lord Lieutenant, and which Carte, and presumably Ormond, considered a life-time appointment. This expectation, as it transpired, fell little short of becoming a reality since Ormond served as Lord Lieutenant from 1662 to 1669 and again from 1677 to 1685, and much of the narrative queried why Ormond had been dismissed in 1669 and discussed various conspiracies that had been designed to humiliate him further. Here, Carte's essential proposition was that Ormond's enemies were the same or the successors to the same Protestant zealots and parvenus who had been Ormond's opponents in Ireland before 1650, now allied with those who had acquired their land and positions in Ireland during the Cromwellian era. This amalgam of foes, according to Carte, was intent on frustrating Ormond's efforts to reinstate some of those Irish people (Catholic as well as Protestant) who had proven themselves loyal subjects of the Crown previous to 1650, and who had been forced to concede land and office to Cromwellians. Carte represented these opponents of Ormond as venomous people who, as he described it, plotted to seize power, made several attempts on Ormond's life, and fabricated supposed Catholic plots to overthrow the monarchy in which they implicated Ormond. The greatest conspiracy, according to Carte, was that of 1669, hatched between Ormond's enemies at court and those in Ireland, linked by Roger Boyle, earl of Orrery, that had effected his dismissal as Lord Lieutenant.[77]

---

[75] Carte, *Life…of Ormond*, vol. 3, Preface.   [76] Carte, *Life…of Ormond*, vol. 2, 200.
[77] For a re-appraisal of this episode see James I. McGuire, 'Why was Ormond dismissed in 1669?', *Irish Historical Studies*, vol. 17 (1972–3), 295–312.

146 IMAGINING IRELAND'S PASTS

Carte acknowledged that 'the interval between governments', 1669–77, proved 'a very disagreeable time' for Ormond, but that on April 1677 he forgot 'the inconvenience of court coldness' when he was 'summoned to sup with the king' who, before he reinstated him as Lord Lieutenant, pronounced publicly that Ormond was 'the fittest person to govern Ireland'.[78] This second segment of Carte's treatment of Ormond's life, 1650–88, was largely celebratory as Carte saluted Ormond's social elevation to the rank of duke in the Irish peerage in 1660, his appointment then also as Stewart of the Household, and—the ultimate honour—his elevation in 1683 to becoming 'duke of Ormonde' in the English peerage, the same 'title which had been so many hundred years in his family'.[79] This combination of achievements, claimed Carte, demonstrated how 'happy was it to the English that Ireland was then under one who was not only inclined, but knew how, to preserve it in peace, and prevent the miseries of an intestine war, which, had it begun there, would, in all probability, have spread into England, and involved the three kingdoms, as it had done in 1641'.[80]

By thus emphasizing how his hero had influenced the course of events, Carte—like the authors of the two Clanricard Memoirs—was illustrating that true nobles, acting in consort with legitimate monarchs, could effect improvement in the human condition. However, by his repeated use of counterfactuals, Carte also demonstrated how human affairs could enter upon a downward spiral either when monarchs did not follow good counsel, or when they took advice from those who were not truly noble. Carte thus distanced himself from providential historians and explained how through his study of the past he was hoping to identify 'the real motives and secret springs of action, which inspired and influenced the conduct of persons and parties'.[81]

This investigation led him to conclude that rank alone was no guarantee of worthy behaviour. As proof of this, Carte looked to England in the months leading up to the execution of Strafford, where 'there was scarce a nobleman about the king who was not either a bitter enemy of [Strafford], or a secret favourer of the Scots and ready to sacrifice the English honour and the king's service to their private resentments and their factious and selfish views'.[82] Such deviant behaviour satisfied Carte that people holding noble titles could act dishonourably whenever they put private interest above the public good, and he believed that the Civil War in England was the product of such a conjuncture. However, he also believed that what was exceptional in England had become the norm in Ireland where most holders of office and even of noble title were English people of low standing and inadequate education who had risen to wealth and position through fraud. The inadequacy of those who had governed Ireland was

[78] Carte, *Life...of Ormond*, vol. 2, 436, 441, 445.   [79] Carte, *Life...of Ormond*, vol. 2, 524.
[80] Carte, *Life...of Ormond*, vol. 1, 2.   [81] Carte, *Life...of Ormond*, vol. 3, Preface.
[82] Carte, *Life...of Ormond*, vol. 1, 105.

EIGHTEENTH-CENTURY ARISTOCRATIC HISTORIES OF IRELAND 147

proven for Carte by the failure of the reformation to win converts there, by the dilapidated condition of the church, and by the alienation of potentially loyal Irish subjects from the Crown. In so criticizing those who had actually exercised power in Ireland, Carte imagined that the outcome could and would have been different had successive monarchs chosen to govern the country through the agency of nobles of ancient lineage with a record of loyalty to the Crown. If this had occurred, he suggested, those at the upper reaches of society, whether of Old English or Gaelic origin, would have conformed in religion, after which they would have cultivated a cohort of loyal subjects by extending patronage to them since 'next to the insecurity of their estates there was no grievance which before the troubles so much affected the Roman Catholics of Ireland as their utter incapacity for preferment'.[83]

What Carte and the two historians of the Clanricard family had to say was not far distant from what was being said by the Old English authors such as those who had penned the Remonstrance of 1642, and those who wrote histories in that mode into the eighteenth century. However, the aristocratic historians parted company with the Old English authors over several fundamental issues. First, they appeared willing to embrace reformed elite members of Gaelic society as their social equals where Old English authors, particularly in their discussion of the 1641 rebellion, implied that their Gaelic co-religionists were, in contrast to themselves, spendthrift and incompetent. Aristocratic historians differed more sharply with Old English authors over the issue of religious reform, which they identified as laudable and achievable. However, they argued that the opportunity to secure a shift in religious allegiance from a compliant elite had been lost once power was shifted from the ancient aristocrats to recently arrived officials whose avariciousness alienated potentially loyal subjects from church as well as state. Given these circumstances, these elite historians, like the Old English authors, believed that religious tolerance should be extended to Catholics who were politically loyal but they differed from Old English authors in recommending that Catholic clerics who fostered extreme political views, or hindered the work of evangelization, should feel the full rigour of the law.

Historians representing the interests of the older aristocratic families differed even more fundamentally from Protestant authors, providential or otherwise, when they lamented the opportunities for reforming Ireland that had been lost due to the corruption and ineptitude of those officials who had wormed their way to the top in government and in the social order. They were exceptional also among historians—Protestant and Catholic—in holding out no prospect of Ireland returning to a lost golden age, and no hope that reform measures were on the brink of producing results. They wrote rather to negotiate a readmission to

---

[83] Carte, *Life... of Ormond*, vol. 2, 483.

148   IMAGINING IRELAND'S PASTS

the ranks of the service nobility of those families whose histories they wrote in the hope that their current members might have the opportunity to guide the policies of the Crown to positive ends as earlier generations of the same families had done. As they pleaded this case, they imagined a past where the Crown and the church had been defrauded by their supposed servants with the result that the opportunity to reform Ireland had been frittered away by a ruling group bent on their own self-advancement. This was deeply resented by those being attacked, and gave rise to a new stream of historical writing designed to legitimize the actions of the ancestors of the country's new ruling elite.

5.4 New Histories for New Nobles

The one who responded most emphatically to the challenge was Arthur Collins, an English antiquarian and authority on England's peerage, who in 1756 published a two-volume compilation under the title of *Letters and Memorials of State*.[84] The purpose of the publication, according to its editor, was 'to do homage to the memory' of 'the lives and actions of the Sidneys and their noble ancestors' whose reputations had been tarnished by the political actions of some family members during the sixteenth and the seventeenth centuries. The progenitors whose careers were detailed in the Collins compilation included Edmund Dudley, the author of 'The Tree of Commonwealth' who had been executed by King Henry VIII, his son John Dudley, viscount Lisle and later duke of Northumberland, who had been executed early in the reign of Queen Mary for attempting to have his daughter-in-law, Lady Jane Grey, rather than Mary Tudor, succeed King Edward VI on the English throne, and John Dudley's son Robert, later earl of Leicester, 'the great favourite of Queen Elizabeth'. Leicester died without a male heir, which meant that his lands and title fell to Robert Sidney, the second and sole surviving son of Leicester's sister Lady Mary Dudley by her husband Sir Henry Sidney, she being 'the only child of John, duke of Northumberland, that left issue'.[85]

This sequence justified Collins in culling documents from the Sidney family archive at Penshurst in Kent and also from official state papers, which together provided 'just and authentic accounts' of how a succession of Sidney family members had rendered service to the state during the sixteenth and seventeenth centuries. Those whose careers were considered in detail included Sir Henry Sidney who had served Queen Elizabeth on two occasions as governor of Ireland while being simultaneously Lord President of Wales; his son Sir Philip Sidney

---

[84] *Letters and Memorials of State in the reigns of Queen Mary, Queen Elizabeth, King James, King Charles I, part of the reigns of Charles II and Oliver's usurpation* by Arthur Collins Esq., author of *The Peerage of England* (London, 1756).

[85] *Letters and Memorials of State*, vol. 1, preface, and 17, 19, 21, 31.

who, before his soldier's death in the Netherlands in 1586, was considered by Queen Elizabeth to be 'the jewel of her time'; Philip's younger brother Robert, who, as mentioned, became 2nd earl of Leicester; his son Robert, 3rd earl of Leicester, who, following the execution of Strafford, was nominated by King Charles I to be Lord Lieutenant of Ireland and who, after 1660, became a courtier of King Charles II; and this Robert's two sons Philip, Viscount Lisle, and Algernon Sidney who each became members of 'the parliament faction' during the English Civil War and served for that cause in Ireland. This service included Lisle being appointed by Parliament in 1645 to be 'General Governor of Ireland' and then, after 'the cruel murder of the king', his becoming a member of the Commonwealth's Council of State. Later, in 1658, Lisle supported the bid of Richard Cromwell to succeed his father as Lord Protector. After this, according to Collins, Lisle withdrew from public affairs even though he secured a 'general pardon' from King Charles II, but his brother Algernon who was a principled republican, remained in exile on the Continent until 1677, after which he was executed in 1683 allegedly for attempting to overthrow the government of King Charles II.[86]

Collins's narration of the life stories of individual members of the Sidney family offered him an opportunity to discourse on such matters as fighting in the Low Countries in the sixteenth century; on the patronage that had been extended to men of letters by female as well as male members of the Sidney family; on several diplomatic missions in which different Sidney family members had been involved on behalf both of Crown and Commonwealth; on British domestic policies during the decades of Civil War; and on how various members of the Sidney family had influenced, or been affected by, the Restoration. Over and above all these was the involvement of a succession of Sidney family members with Ireland. Collins seems to have believed that his account of how so many of the Sidney family had, at great cost to themselves, upheld British interests in Ireland in turbulent times, redeemed the reputation of the entire family from any taint associated with the rash actions by some family members in supporting parliament and the Commonwealth against the king. As he thus rehabilitated the reputation of one of Britain's leading noble houses, Collins also provided an alternative elite interpretation of Ireland's history during the sixteenth and seventeenth centuries to what had been advanced by Carte and the Clanricard memorialists.

The largest bulk of documents in Collins's collection concerned the service of Sir Henry Sidney in Ireland because, as Collins pronounced, 'our historians agree, that he first civilized the Irish by bringing them under obedience to the laws of England'.[87] This appraisal by Collins drew upon the narration that Sidney himself had written towards the end of his career of his time spent in Ireland. There, he

---

[86] *Letters and Memorials of State*, vol. 1, preface, and 85–96, 98–104, 114–20, 121–45, 146–52.
[87] *Letters and Memorials of State*, vol. 1, preface.

150 IMAGINING IRELAND'S PASTS

represented himself as a man who had proposed policies that would have led to a certain reform of the country, only to find himself discredited by representatives from the Pale and by Thomas Butler, 10th earl of Ormond, who through 'misreport, slander and calumniation' had convinced Queen Elizabeth that Sidney should be recalled on the grounds that he was 'a chargeous and wasteful servant'.[88] Sidney's disappointment, according to Collins, was all the more acute because 'from his infancy' he had been 'bred and brought up with King Edward the sixth who treated him with great familiarity, even as a companion, and was many times his bedfellow' and 'drew his last breath in his arms'. Sidney, averred Collins, became, through his education and association, 'the most complete young gentleman in the court', and Collins believed that, had King Edward lived, Sidney's 'eminent abilities could not have failed to have advanced him to the highest posts and honours'.[89]

By thus associating Henry Sidney with Edward VI, Collins was implying that, from the outset of his tenure in Ireland, he was committed to the rigid Protestant policies with which he, his son Philip, and his brother-ion-law Leicester later came to be identified. This means that Collins, like some recent historians, disregarded how, during his early service in Ireland, Henry Sidney was well respected within the Pale community and kept his religious preferences concealed from a population that he knew to be still attached to Catholicism.[90]

Sidney also initially enjoyed support within the Pale community in Ireland because of his avowed hostility to the great noble houses and the military influence they wielded within their lordships. By his actions Sidney was rejecting the notion, articulated at the court of Queen Elizabeth by the earl of Ormond who, like Sidney, had been a boy companion of King Edward VI. This alternative view, which Carte had detailed, held that the Crown should, as was the case with England, govern the country through the medium of existing loyal elites. Where Carte had represented this as the only policy that might have reformed Ireland, Collins looked positively on the efforts of Sidney to curtail the military, legal, and fiscal powers of all lords, and to have them subjected to the supervision of provincial presidents who would be nominated from the top by the governor and supported from below by provincial council that would include bishops, lesser landowners, and tenants-in-chief from the relevant province.[91] This stratagem, as

---

[88] 'Notes to be imparted to Philip Sidney', *Letters and Memorials of State*, vol. 1, 295; Brady, ed., *A Viceroy's Vindication?*

[89] *Letters and Memorials of State*, vol. 1, preface, and 76–8; Brady, ed., *A Viceroy's Vindication?*

[90] For a recent representation of Sidney as a rigid Protestant see Hutchison, *Calvinism, Reform and the Absolutist State*; on Sidney's earlier tolerance of Catholicism within the Pale see Chapter 1.

[91] On this policy in general and for the difference in the character of provincial presidencies as envisaged by Sidney and as recommended by previous reformers see Nicholas Canny, *The Elizabethan Conquest of Ireland: A Pattern Established, 1565–1576* (Hassocks, nr. Brighton, 1976), 93–116, esp. 98; for a recent narration of an older view, David Heffernan, *Debating Tudor Policy in Sixteenth Century Ireland* (Woodbridge, 2018).

EIGHTEENTH-CENTURY ARISTOCRATIC HISTORIES OF IRELAND   151

Collins made clear, had provoked the brothers of Ormond to rebel, and while Collins acknowledged that Ormond had eventually persuaded them to surrender to Sidney as governor, as Carte had made clear, Collins reiterated that Ormond himself was as much opposed, as were his brothers, to having central government interfere in the affairs of his lordship. Moreover, Collins explained how their philosophical difference became known at court when the young Philip Sidney, on his return to England from his continental tour, provoked 'some dispute [at court] with Thomas earl of Ormond, on behalf of his father... and though he was the queen's kinsman, and high in her favour, Sir Philip could not restrain showing his resentment to that noble peer'.[92]

Collins celebrated, just as Carte had disparaged, the fact that Henry Sidney and his son Philip became clients of Leicester, when Ormond was becoming more attached to the cautious William Cecil, Lord Burghley, who remained unconvinced of the merits of Sidney's ambition to reform society in Ireland by curtailing the influence of the great lords.[93] Where Carte had shown sympathy for the moderate policies of Ormond that for a time were supported by Burghley and the parsimonious queen, Collins looked positively on Sidney's introduction into Ireland of English-born functionaries with a previous record of service to Sidney himself or to Leicester, or to Leicester's brother Ambrose, earl of Warwick. This meant that Collins held a negative view of Ormond being put in charge of the military operation in Munster when the earl of Desmond entered into open insurrection against the Crown, and this meant also that he lauded Ormond's dismissal and his replacement by Arthur, Lord Grey de Wilton.[94] Collins also took the opposite view to Carte when he welcomed the fact that the form of settlement proceeded with in Munster following the suppression of the Desmond revolt was a plantation in which the vast bulk of confiscated land was assigned to English proprietors rather than to the earl of Ormond and the other Irish-born lords who had fought with Ormond against the Munster rebels. Collins did not agree with Carte that most of the grantees in the Munster plantation had been nominees of Sidney and Leicester. However, he did point to continuity in policy by asserting that Sidney's 'knowledge of affairs in Ireland was far greater than any one of his time' and that he had transmitted this knowledge to 'his successors' so they could 'build on his foundations and frame their designs after his desires and policy'.[95]

In support of this, Collins cited the advice that Sidney had offered to Lord Grey when he took up duty as governor. Here, he showed that Sidney had suggested to Grey which of the officers that Sidney had introduced to Ireland should be

[92] *Letters and Memorials of State*, vol. 1, 100.
[93] See also Christopher Maginn, *William Cecil, Ireland and the Tudor State* (Oxford, 2012).
[94] On the politics of this see Canny, *Making Ireland British*, 65.
[95] *Letters and Memorials of State*, vol. 1, 92.

152 IMAGINING IRELAND'S PASTS

retained, and how he should 'go about the extirping of those cannibals' who had lived 'offensively to English men and Irish government above 400 years' in those parts of Wicklow that were proximate to Dublin.[96] Such evidence satisfied Collins that it was Sidney's policy of plantation, rather than Ormond's stratagem to build Crown influence in Ireland upon existing loyal nobles, that was eventually adopted by the government of Queen Elizabeth and that was persisted with by successive governments into the seventeenth century. Collins was also of the view that the Sidney influence in Ireland persisted long after his service there. In support of this he contended that Robert Devereux, 2nd earl of Essex, was a close friend of Robert Sidney with whom he had served in the Low Countries, and that many from the new cohort of officers introduced to Ireland by Essex remained in the country after that earl's brief term as governor. This connection between the Devereux and Sidney families was 'cemented', according to Collins, by the marriage of Leicester to the mother of Essex and the marriage of Essex himself to the widow of Philip Sidney.[97]

What Collins was saying essentially was that the policy favoured by Henry Sidney for reforming Ireland not only became official government policy but that many of the English officers and officials brought to Ireland, initially by Sidney and his associates and then by Essex, remained in the country after the disgraced Essex had given way to Lord Mountjoy. The essential difference between Collins and Carte on this point was that what had been excoriated by the Clanricard historians and by Carte as the beginning of official corruption was regarded positively by Collins. He essentially welcomed the establishment in Ireland during the later decades of Elizabeth's reign of a cohort of Crown servitors who would rule the country in the seventeenth century and become the progenitors of a new elite who would dominate Ireland into the foreseeable future. Later, when Collins discussed the services rendered in Ireland by members of a later generation of the Sidney family, that is Philip, Lord Lisle, and Colonel Algernon Sidney, he was implying that those who promoted reform as part of the Cromwellian settlement of the country were, in effect, continuing the policy of reforming the country from the top downwards, which had been devised by Sir Henry Sidney in the sixteenth century. Collins was therefore saluting as heroes the adventurers, and presumably their descendants, who had set Ireland on the path of reform, and was conceding that those who had lost their lands or influence to make way for them were those who, in succeeding generations, had been opposed to the civil as well as the spiritual reform of the country.

---

[96] Sidney to Lord Gray, 'How to proceed in his government of Ireland', *Letters and Memorials of State*, vol. 1, 279–83; quotation 281.

[97] *Letters and Memorials of State*, vol. 1, 115; Collins seemed unaware that Walsingham's daughter, who was made a widow for a second time by the execution of Essex, later became the wife of Richard, 4th earl of Clanricard.

5.5 Charles Smith's Critique of the New Nobles

Where the Collins compilation made the case that a continuity in policy for Ireland was enabled by the involvement of Sidney family members with the country over several generations, Charles Smith (1715?–62), an apothecary and antiquarian associated with Lismore and Dungarvan in County Waterford, had some years previously expounded on the reform achievements of those English people and their descendants who had been attracted to Ireland when these reform policies and stratagems were first unfurled towards the end of Elizabeth's reign. He did this in a sequence of Irish county histories published in Dublin, some under the patronage of the short-lived Physico-Historical Society.[98] The most comprehensive of these histories was that of the County and City of Cork, published in 1750, but the model that Smith would follow sequentially in his county histories of Waterford, Cork, and Kerry had been set out in *The Ancient and Present State of the County of Down*, written by Smith in association with Walter Harris (the same man we encountered in Chapter 4 as editor/translator of James Ware) and published in 1744.[99] This initial volume of what was intended to be a comprehensive sequence of Irish county histories was dedicated to Sir Hans Sloane, a 'native of the county' who had proven himself a 'patron and encourager of natural knowledge in all countries'.[100]

This, and all subsequent histories in the county series, was organized topographically, which allowed authors to guide their readers from barony to barony pointing out places of interest and identifying the proprietors, most of them of English and Scottish origin, who owned the more profitable land and had promoted 'improvements' on their estates. The authors, sometimes aided by the responses provided in previously circulated questionnaires, and sometimes primed by landed proprietors, identified the impressive residences, deer parks, Protestant churches, church monuments, and charter schools that had been established by these proprietors. Readers were reminded also of the existence in County Down of an indigenous Catholic population by the occasional mention of holy wells frequented by the 'credulous vulgar', and also of the sites, and 'the histories of that calamitous time', that called to mind 'the rebellion of 1641' when 'the Protestants in and about Down suffered grievously'.[101]

---

[98] Michael Brown, *The Irish Enlightenment* (Cambridge, Mass., 2016), 287–9; for a biographical note on Charles Smith see that by Rosemary Richey and Sinéad Sturgeon, *Dictionary of Irish Biography*, vol. 8, 1014.

[99] On improvement in general see Toby Barnard, *Improving Ireland? Projectors, Prophets and Profiteers, 1641–1786* (Dublin, 2008), esp. 115–19.

[100] *The Ancient and Present State of the County of Down, containing a chorographical description* (Dublin, 1744), Dedication to Hans Sloane.

[101] *The Ancient and Present State of the County of Down*, 35.

154   IMAGINING IRELAND'S PASTS

The question of the responsibility of Protestant proprietors to promote religious reform was discussed in considerable detail in the Down volume in a 'discourse' on the 'charter scheme' which the authors were satisfied had produced such 'good effects...in several counties of the kingdom' that they expected 'soon' 'to see it universally received'. The authors claimed that 'charter working schools promoted by Gentlemen' for the education of 'Popish children' were being established because 'all Protestant Gentlemen condemn the superstitious and idolatrous worship of the church of Rome' and abhorred and detested 'her bloody and destructive doctrines and principles'. They were also being supported, it was pronounced, for the practical reason that proprietors were eager 'to see their lands tenanted, planted and improved by a race of honest and industrious Protestants, that they and their posterity may continue to live in peace and quiet, free from the danger of any future insurrections or rebellions'. Penal laws, they lamented, had proven of little benefit in effecting conversions because they did not act as a deterrent from practising Catholicism 'especially [for] the lower sort who [had] nothing to lose'. Therefore it seemed to the authors that 'the wit of man could not suggest a more effectual or rational scheme for making [Ireland] a Protestant nation' than the fostering of charter schools that would '[secure] the rising generation of Papists to the interest of that Protestant state which their Popish forefathers [had] more than once brought into very great danger'.[102]

When Charles Smith, this time working alone, published his history for County Cork in 1750, he identified the various charter schools that had been established by several proprietors there, and he, like their founders, saluted their foundation as works of charity.[103] However, he conceded that the English and Protestant character of County Cork was due more to plantations than to charter schools. By plantations he meant first the formal Munster plantation of Elizabeth's reign; second the informal plantation promoted there by Richard Boyle, later 1st earl of Cork, after he had acquired, expanded upon, and re-peopled several of the plantation estates that had been devastated during the wars of the 1580s and 1590s; and third the establishment in the county of some 'new names' following the defeat of the Irish during the 'civil wars' fought between 1641 and 1652. This more recent wave of proprietors, claimed Smith, 'contributed to strengthen the English in those parts and [to] weaken...the Irish' many of whom, he remarked, had been transplanted into Connacht.[104]

---

[102] *The Ancient and Present State of the County of Down*, 17–19; on the subject generally David Hayton, 'Did Protestantism fail in early eighteenth-century Ireland? Charity Schools and the enterprise of religious and social reformation, c.1690–1730', in A. Ford, J. McGuire, and K. Milne, eds., 'As by Law Established', 166–85.

[103] Charles Smith, *The Ancient and Present State of the County and City of Cork* (Dublin, 1750); the page references to that work in this chapter are to the two-volume edition published in Cork in 1815.

[104] Smith, *The Ancient and Present State of...Cork*, vol. 1, 50, 55, 57, 58.

EIGHTEENTH-CENTURY ARISTOCRATIC HISTORIES OF IRELAND 155

Smith looked positively on the multi-layered character of English settlement of County Cork, and praised the improvements introduced by the planters of all generations. By improvements he meant the mansions, castles, churches, church memorials, gardens, canals, deer parks, manufacturing towns, and charter schools they had established. The individuals named ranged from Walter Raleigh to the Percevals, to the earls of Inchiquin (strictly speaking of Gaelic ancestry but connected through marriage with the St Legers), to Alan Brodrick, viscount Midleton, and to John Perry who had been able to establish himself in Cork, according to Smith, because he had 'acquired a very considerable fortune in the island of Antigua and other foreign plantations'.[105] Collectively these had, he suggested, eroded the potency that Catholics had once enjoyed throughout the county, and his occasional reference to the presence there of Catholics in 1750 was usually in the context of referring to docile 'superstitious Irish devotees' frequenting holy wells 'on certain days of the year'.[106] It was only at Macroom, where much land still remained in Catholic possession, that 'the Romanists [had] a splendid mass house erected on an eminence at the entrance into the town, with a handsome altar, a pulpit and confessional chair'.[107]

As Smith detailed the general transformation that had been promoted throughout the county, he reserved principal praise for members of the Boyle family, beginning with Richard, 1st earl of Cork, whom he described as 'the greatest advancer of every improvement... that ever the kingdom knew'. He also credited the same individual (mistakenly as it happens) with having 'built the town of Bandon, and so stocked and planted the country [surrounding countryside] with English' that there was not in Bandon 'a Popish inhabitant, nor will the townsmen suffer one to dwell in it, nor a piper to play in the place, this being the music formerly used by the Irish in their wars'. This success of Cork had been achieved, according to Smith, despite the attempt by Thomas Wentworth, earl of Strafford, to destroy the earl's reputation and wealth by imposing on him a fine of £15,000 'in an arbitrary, unjust and illegal manner'.[108] Such was Smith's admiration for the achievements of Richard Boyle that he twice cited the alleged observation of Oliver Cromwell that 'if there had been an earl of Cork in every county, the Irish could never have rebelled'.[109]

Smith lavished almost equal praise upon Richard Boyle's second son Roger, Baron Broghill (1st earl of Orrery in 1660), who had been identified by Carte as Ormond's principal adversary. Smith saluted him because Roger Boyle had preserved and enabled the expansion of the English interest in the county when it had been threatened by the 'horrid Irish rebellion' of the mid-seventeenth

---

[105] Smith, *The Ancient and Present State of... Cork*, vol. 1, 117, 120, 141, 147.
[106] Smith, *The Ancient and Present State of... Cork*, vol. 1, 142; see also 139.
[107] Smith, *The Ancient and Present State of... Cork*, vol. 1, 181.
[108] Smith, *The Ancient and Present State of... Cork*, vol. 1, dedication and 55, 92, 236–7, 239.
[109] Smith, *The Ancient and Present State of... Cork*, vol. 1, dedication; vol. 2, 171.

century. Then, to clarify his admiration for Roger Boyle, Smith dedicated this county history to John, 5th earl of Orrery, to whose 'ancestors', pronounced Smith, County Cork owed 'many great advantages'.[110] These included the town and magnificent house of Charleville, which the 1st earl of Orrery had built in the 1660s. Smith also credited Roger Boyle, then baron Broghill, with the recovery from rebel hands of the house built by his father at Castlemartyr that had, at the time of writing, been further 'improved' by the honourable Henry Boyle, speaker of the Irish House of Commons. Broghill also, according to Smith, recovered much land from rebel hands after 1641, and also a sequence of houses including at Blarney 'a very strong castle, and noble seat of the earls of Clancarty, who forfeited a great estate in this county for their adhering to King James'.[111]

Roger Boyle featured even more prominently in the 'civil history' section of Smith's county study. In this, Smith explained how the first news of the 1641 rebellion was brought to Richard Boyle, 1st earl of Cork, when he was dining with an assembly of county gentry, Catholic as well as Protestant, at the house of his son-in-law, Lord Barrymore. There, at the announcement of the startling news, claimed Smith, all expressed themselves ready to act collectively to maintain order, only to find that the Catholic Lord Muskerry had no sooner parted their company than he was 'up in arms' and joined with the rebels from County Tipperary who had invaded County Cork.[112] The only military experience that Roger Boyle, Baron Broghill, had had up to this point, claimed Smith, was when he had attended with his oldest brother Richard, Viscount Dungarvan (later to become 2nd earl of Cork and 1st earl of Burlington in the English peerage) upon the king at York at the outset of the wars of the three kingdoms. This experience, claimed Smith, gave Broghill confidence to join with Morrogh O'Brien, baron of Inchiquin, in defending the Protestant interest in the county after 1641. His principal exploit at this stage was at the Battle of Liscarroll where another Boyle brother, Lewis, Viscount Kinalmeaky, was killed.[113] While Smith gave credit to Inchiquin for the ultimate destruction of the Munster Confederate army at the Battle of Knocknanuss in 1647, he praised Broghill because he, more than Inchiquin, won the confidence of Viscount Lisle and the English parliament when their support was vital to the survival of Protestants in Cork. He also suggested that Lisle's judgement was commendable since Inchiquin later entered into negotiations with Ormond and switched his allegiance to the king. Broghill, on the other hand, had remained a steadfast supporter of the English parliament,

---

[110] Smith, *The Ancient and Present State of ... Cork*, vol. 1, dedication, vol. 2, 116–17.

[111] Smith, *The Ancient and Present State of ... Cork*, vol. 1, 116, 125, 131, 141, 166.

[112] Smith, *The Ancient and Present State of ... Cork,* vol. 2, 117; Smith may have acquired much of the detail from the biographical sketch of the 1st earl of Orrery composed by his chaplain Thomas Morrice and published in *A Collection of the State Letters of ... Roger Boyle 1st earl of Orrery* (Dublin, 1743).

[113] Smith, *The Ancient and Present State of ... Cork*, vol. 2, 115, 135.

EIGHTEENTH-CENTURY ARISTOCRATIC HISTORIES OF IRELAND 157

and later of Cromwell and his closest associates, as long, claimed Smith, as this served the interest of Protestants in Cork.[114] Then Smith explained how, at the appropriate time, Broghill, working in conjunction with a younger brother Francis, Lord Shannon (who had been in exile with the king), helped facilitate the Restoration of King Charles II. Broghill, said Smith, was rewarded for this service to the new king by being created earl of Orrery and appointed as Lord President of Munster. In this office, according to Smith, he proved 'very active in diverting any designs prejudicial to his county'.[115]

Smith also showed how Orrery's rehabilitation as a royalist ran in parallel with that of Sir Charles Coote who 'secured a strong party for the king in Ulster' for which he was created earl of Mountrath in 1660 and appointed president of Connacht. Smith pointed out that Orrery and Mountrath, together with Sir Maurice Eustace, were appointed as joint Lords Justices pending the return of Ormond to Ireland, this time as duke and Lord Lieutenant.[116] During his interlude as Lord Justice, Orrery, according to Smith, exerted such influence over the re-settlement of land in Ireland in the aftermath of the Restoration that he felt justified in saying that the Act of Settlement was 'drawn up chiefly by the earl of Orrery'. This service, according to Smith, brought Orrery into disfavour not only with disappointed Catholics but also (and here he was challenging Carte) with some Cromwellians who resented being deprived of power and some of the property they had recently acquired. Smith therefore complimented Orrery both for his vigilance against potential Catholic intrusion into Cork from the Continent and against 'plots' by 'fanatics' to seize control of government in Dublin, which, according to Smith, he 'discovered to the lord lieutenant'.[117]

This account ran counter to that given by Carte, who had represented Orrery as an implacable opponent of Ormond. Smith did not deny that tension developed between the two nobles, but he blamed Ormond rather than Orrery for this. Thus where Carte had suggested that Orrery was the person most responsible for the dismissal of Ormond as Lord Lieutenant in 1669, Smith implied that a small-minded Ormond had been conspiring to destroy Orrery. As evidence, Smith detailed how, when Ormond as Lord Lieutenant conducted a tour of County Cork, he was entertained lavishly by Orrery, which aroused jealously rather than gratitude in Ormond who, 'having...observed the great interest and influence lord Orrery possessed in this county, he could not help listening to malicious insinuations, lord Orrery being then talked of to succeed as lord lieutenant; nor

---

[114] Smith, *The Ancient and Present State of... Cork*, vol. 2, 159–62, 169.
[115] Smith, *The Ancient and Present State of... Cork*, vol. 2, 177, 178.
[116] Smith, *The Ancient and Present State of... Cork*, vol. 2, 177–8; it should be noted that Mountrath was the son of the Sir Charles Coote, killed in action in 1642, whose memory had been reviled by Catholic commentators; for biographical sketches of the two Charles Cootes see those by Robert Armstrong and Aidan Clarke, *Dictionary of Irish Biography*, vol. 2, 827–8 and 828–30.
[117] Smith, *The Ancient and Present State of... Cork*, vol. 2, 181, 182, 184.

was the duke easy till the presidency court was suppressed and till lord Orrery was divested of all means to vie with the lord lieutenant either in grandeur or power.'[118] Here, Smith was alluding to the abolition of the presidencies of Munster and Connacht in 1672, ostensibly in the interest of administrative efficiency, but really because Ormond wished to abolish Orrery's power base. Carte suggested that Ormond had gone further because Orrery was not only passed over when the Lord Lieutenancy fell vacant in 1669 but was summoned to England (Smith assumed at the instigation of Ormond) to defend himself from charges that could have led to his impeachment by the English parliament. Smith recorded with apparent satisfaction how Orrery cleared himself of all charges. He therefore described how Orrery won his way back into the king's confidence and, despite being out of office, preserved County Cork safe both from foreign invasion and papist rebellion when the international political climate was uncertain and the Dublin government, to which Ormond had been reappointed as Lord Lieutenant, indolent.[119]

Praising Orrery for his vigilance in keeping possible foreign invasion at bay during the 1670s would have seemed relevant to Smith's Protestant readers of 1750 who believed that the Jacobites had intended to stage an incursion in Munster to coincide with the futile effort of the Jacobite 'Pretender' in 1745–46 to recover the British throne from the Hanoverians. This recent happening gave Charles Smith further reason to emphasize the parts played by the 1st earl of Orrery, and his father, the 1st earl of Cork, in civilizing, improving, and making county Cork secure for the Protestant interest. Therefore he dedicated his history to the 5th earl of Orrery, who, he remarked, resembled the first holder of that title in being a man of 'public spirit...generosity and love of liberty [and with] the same taste for the polite arts...celebrated throughout Europe'.[120] However, Smith's ultimate intention was to give credit for the ordered and prosperous condition of County Cork to all Protestant proprietors in the county and to the Protestant settlers who had chosen to make their homes there. These, he believed, would have a fresh opportunity to enrich the county when they exploited the untapped natural resources that he itemized in the concluding section.[121]

In this, and in the handful of other county histories with which Charles Smith was associated, he was complementing what Arthur Collins would have to say in the *Letters and Memorials of State*. There, as we saw, Collins reached three principal conclusions concerning Ireland's history in the sixteenth and

---

[118] Smith, *The Ancient and Present State of... Cork*, vol. 2, 186–7.

[119] Smith, *The Ancient and Present State of... Cork*, vol. 2, 189–90; for a biographical note on Orrery see that by Toby Barnard, *Dictionary of Irish Biography*, vol. 1, 741–5.

[120] Smith, *The Ancient and Present State of... Cork*, vol. 1, dedication; for an excellent appraisal of the literary achievements of the 1st earl of Orrery see John Kerrigan, *Archipelagic English: Literature, History and Politics, 1603-1707* (Oxford, 2008), 244–67; and for a biographical sketch of John, the 5th earl, see that by Linde Lunney, *Dictionary of Irish Biography*, vol. 1, 722.

[121] Smith, *The Ancient and Present State of... Cork*, vol. 2, 234 ff.

seventeenth centuries which endorsed the arguments of the county historians. The first held that Ireland had been in greater need of reform in the mid-sixteenth century than had been the case in the twelfth century. The second maintained that Sir Henry Sidney and succeeding governors who had followed his advice laid the groundwork for its comprehensive reform. Collins's third conclusion, and that to which the county historians attached greatest importance, held that the responsibility for implementing reform on a countrywide basis had been left to the officials and planters (and their descendants) who had been introduced to the country over the course of the sixteenth and seventeenth centuries. Thus, as Smith explained in his history of Kerry, 'the English undertakers, particularly the citizens of London, began at this time [the early seventeenth century] to plant, build and improve the province of Ulster, as the first earl of Cork and other adventurers did that of Munster'.[122]

These county histories of the mid-eighteenth century were thus in a sense exercises in self-congratulation as the authors set out to demonstrate that those who had been entrusted with implementing these reforms had taken their responsibility seriously. Thus, for example, they showed how county Cork, which was endowed with good quality land and commercial potential, had been developed by its relatively new cohort of proprietors to the point where, at least in external appearance, it could have been mistaken for an English county. The measure of their achievement was provided first by backward glances both to the sixteenth century, when the grand experiment had been launched, and to 1641 and the years immediately thereafter, when all progress had been set at naught, and finally by sideward glances to counties where progress had been less marked. The principal historical dimension, as noted, detailed how the ancestors of the current Protestant proprietors had acquired, improved, and then recovered their properties to the point where it was unthinkable that they would ever again be disturbed.

The accounts of the trials that Protestants had suffered and overcome in the mid-seventeenth century may have been designed, as had been the case with the providential histories, to put readers on their guard against complacency and future challenge. However, the authors of the county histories seem to have been even more concerned to demonstrate that what had happened then was no longer conceivable in a radically changed environment. Smith's most telling illustration of the depth to which the Protestant interest had fallen in the seventeenth century came from his own native county of Waterford where he alleged that, following the disturbances of 1641, 'the rebels had a printing press at Waterford where one Thomas Borke, an Irish printer, published a scandalous remonstrance of the confederate papists at Trim, with his Majesty's arms affixed thereon, which was

---

[122] Smith, *The Ancient and Present State of . . . Kerry* (Dublin, 1756), xiv.

160   IMAGINING IRELAND'S PASTS

with insolence and ostentation, published at Oxford.'[123] This brought Smith back to considering the Catholic *Remonstrance*, the arguments of which, as mentioned in Chapter 4, were still being touted in the eighteenth century by Catholic apologists such as John Curry. Smith was making the point that the impertinence of printing such a document addressed to the king was inconceivable in the middle of the eighteenth century. This was the case because those who had been the beneficiaries of the confiscations of the sixteenth and seventeenth centuries had proven themselves to be true nobles by improving the country to the point where it was possible to conceive that the indigenous population, or at least their children who would be raised in charter schools, would be reformed in religion as well as in civil comportment. In taking this stance, Smith conceded that 'improvement' had not been universally applied. Thus for County Kerry, Smith lamented how that county had been 'unsettled' by the 'wars of 1641' because the Protestant presence there had been thin on the ground. Even as he conceded this, Smith rejoiced that Sir William Petty had become the owner of extensive property in county Kerry from which base his descendants were 'enriching, beautifying and rending this county happy.'[124]

The Physico-Historical Society, a body that represented Protestant commercial and professional as well as landed interests, sponsored most of these eighteenth-century county histories. Moreover, given his close associations with both Lismore and Dungarvan (each a power base for the earls of Cork), we can take it that Charles Smith was beholden to the Boyle family on which he lavished such fulsome praise. The county histories with which Smith and Walter Harris were associated complemented from a local perspective what Arthur Collins would publish but a few years later on more general developments in Ireland from Elizabethan times to the middle of the eighteenth century. Smith was at one with all authors of what we have described as aristocratic historians in that he proceeded from the assumption that historical events were determined principally by human agency and that the prime movers were those who held elite positions in society. He was also in agreement with Collins that the true test of nobility was what individuals had contributed to the improvement of their society in the relative recent past rather than what ancestors had accomplished in the mists of antiquity. He therefore, as Collins would do a few years later, distanced himself from what had been written about Ireland's past by those who wrote on behalf of ancient noble houses who, as he saw it, attached excessive importance to antiquity as a test of nobility. Another factor that separated Smith from the purists was in expressing confidence that the present generation of elite leaders in Ireland were

---

[123] Smith, *The Ancient and Present State of... Waterford* (Dublin, 1746; 2nd edition, 1774), 142–3 (this reference is to the second edition).

[124] Smith, *The Ancient and Present State of... Kerry*, xiv; for a recent discussion of the history to the alleged backwardness of Kerry see Marc Caball, *Kerry, 1600–1730: The Emergence of a British Atlantic County* (Dublin, 2017).

EIGHTEENTH-CENTURY ARISTOCRATIC HISTORIES OF IRELAND   161

every bit as committed to upholding and advancing the material and spiritual improvement of the country as nobles of ancient lineage had ever been. This meant that as he brought each of his county studies to an end, he concluded that Ireland was on the brink of becoming more harmonious, more prosperous, more Protestant, and more committed to the Crown than ever before.

5.6 Conclusion

This chapter, based on histories and documentary compilations published in 1722, 1735–36, 1744, 1750, 1756, and 1757, to which we may add the edition of the letters of Thomas Wentworth, earl of Strafford, published in 1739, and a biographical sketch, with some letters, of Roger Boyle, 1st earl of Orrery, published in 1743, draws attention to an ongoing polemic about the past that was pursued or sponsored by Irish nobles during the early eighteenth century.[125] Reading through this selection of aristocratic histories—there were other such, both published and contemplated—leaves no doubt that, as a group, Ireland's peers were far from united by the 'common ideals of nobleness' that Jane Ohlmeyer has suggested bonded what was a peerage 'of mixed race and religion and of old and new families who promoted the royal "civilizing" and Anglicizing agenda'.[126] It strikes me that the principal factor that created friction within an otherwise seemingly united nobility was that opposing groups of aristocrats chose to imagine different pasts as a means of establishing that their families were honourable as well as noble.

The authors/editors whose work we have considered, all apparently Protestants, seemed more urbane than the providential historians in that all wished to appear scientific by supporting their arguments with evidence, usually drawn from family archives.[127] They also seemed to agree that, in secular matters, people shaped their own destinies, and that the protagonists in human affairs came usually from the upper reaches of society and were, as Jane Ohlmeyer has indicated, guided by some moral purpose to reform or improve society. They were also satisfied that Ireland's populations were amenable to civil and religious reform and that the process of reform had been under way since the sixteenth, if not since the twelfth, century. Authors were also united in thinking that the entitlement of families and individuals to be considered honourable, after which

---

[125] *The earl of Strafford's Letters and Dispatches, with an essay towards his life by Sir George* Radcliffe, ed., William Knowler (London, 1739); *A Collection of the State Letters of…Roger Boyle 1st earl of Orrery*.

[126] Jane Ohlmeyer, *Making Ireland English: The Irish Aristocracy in the Seventeenth Century* (New Haven, Ct., 2012), 18, 471, 481–2.

[127] That even Thomas O'Sullevane was Protestant, or at least an attender at Protestant service, is suggested by his familiarity with the style and content of populist sermons given on the anniversary of the 1641 rebellion.

162 IMAGINING IRELAND'S PASTS

they might properly be received into the ranks of nobility, should be determined by the contribution they had made to Ireland's reform. Therefore our authors studied history particularly to find evidence of how the families with which they were associated had promoted reform, and to defend any actions of family members that had been questioned by critics.

A prime example of such defensive writing comes from the selection of the letters of the earl of Strafford edited by William Knowler. In introducing his text, Knowler pronounced that he had undertaken the task 'to vindicate [Strafford's] memory from those aspersions which it is grown too fashionable to cast upon him, of acting upon arbitrary principles, and being a friend to the Roman Catholics.'[128] Knowler—and Carte had anticipated him in this—seemed to think that vindication could best be achieved by vilifying opponents. Thus he cleared Strafford's reputation for being an arbitrary ruler by producing documents to show how an innocent man had been brought to the scaffold by a conspiracy between officials in Ireland, whose corruption he had exposed, and incendiaries in the English parliament who were seeking evidence to justify the execution of their most formidable opponent. Then, in defending Strafford from the charge of being lenient towards Catholics, Knowler presented evidence that Strafford, or Wentworth as he then was, had no choice but to appear tolerant of Catholicism. This was so, according to Knowler, because the material resources that properly belonged to the church had been so pilfered by the Protestant officials and planters who had dominated the country before his arrival that there were not sufficient educated clergy available to instruct any would-be converts in true religion, or sufficient churches in adequate repair to accommodate them. Thus Knowler used his publication to expose the moral failure of the English-born officials who had dominated government in Ireland prior to 1633 when Wentworth first arrived there. The evidence cited by Knowler complemented what Carte had had to say of the amoral character of individuals within this same official group, especially Parsons, Borlase, and Coote, who had risen to particular prominence after Strafford had left the country and who had been implicated in his execution.

The two collections also questioned the honour of the Boyle planter family in Ireland both before 1633 and after 1660. Knowler published a seam of documents concerning the legal test case that Wentworth had brought against Richard Boyle, 1st earl of Cork (acknowledged to be the most successful planter of his generation in Ireland), to sustain his case that members of this planter/official group had been unscrupulous in their disregard for the property and independence of the church. For his part Carte questioned the integrity of the second generation of the same family by exposing how the 1st earl of Cork's second surviving son Roger

---

[128] *Strafford's Letters*, ed., Knowler, Dedication, sig. A1 v.

EIGHTEENTH-CENTURY ARISTOCRATIC HISTORIES OF IRELAND   163

Boyle, baron Broghill (created 1st earl of Orrery in 1660), had been an unprincipled supporter of Cromwell before he became the most malign opponent of the 1st duke of Ormond during his first period of service as Lord Lieutenant.

It is likely that this dual attack upon the role of the Boyle family in the history of Munster and of Ireland prompted the publication both of Smith's series of county histories and of the short biography of Orrery, written by Orrery's former chaplain, and embellished with letters written by Orrery in the 1660s. The county histories, as noted, drew particular attention to the works of 'charity'—a word that was given such elasticity that it extended even to plantation itself—that had been promoted in Munster by several members of the Boyle family over several generations. These endeavours, it was suggested, had rendered that province more prosperous and more English-like than any of the other three provinces of Ireland, and was thus the ultimate proof that the Boyles were an honourable as well as a deservedly ennobled family. At the same time, the volume on Orrery produced evidence that he was a selfless, and unappreciated, supporter of Ormond when he had first come into office as Lord Lieutenant. These publications that dealt with the particular were, I have suggested, rounded off by the appearance in 1756 of Collins's *Letters and Memorials of State*, that made the case that a reform agenda for Ireland which had been adumbrated by Sir Henry Sidney in the sixteenth century had been advanced further by several members of that same family over several generations, and by those, and the successors of those, who Sidney and his successors had placed in the country either as officers of state or as planters. Taken collectively, these publications combined to make the case that the grand project of reform that had been unfolded in the sixteenth century had been proceeded with systematically, and, as was being argued in Smith's county histories, had brought it to the point where it was on the brink of being fulfilled in all its aspects. More generally, this group of authors seemed of the view that the reform agenda would have been fulfilled long since, had it not been obstructed by the older nobility and their Catholic associations, especially at the time of, and immediately following, the 1641 rebellion, and again in 1688–89 after King James had been ousted from the throne.

Those who represented the views of the older nobility were adamant that the opportunity to reform the country lay in the past rather than the future, and had been lost because the new arrivals, when seizing control of the government and of the better resources of the country, had alienated a would-be loyal population from state and church and driven them to rebel in 1641 and again in 1689. Things would have been different, they claimed, if the Crown had sought to rule through, and in co-operation with, the established nobles who were familiar with the country and its complexities and who enjoyed the respect of its diverse popula- tions. Again Knowler put the case of the traditionalists better than any of them- selves had done by citing from a letter written by Wentworth in 1636, where he predicted that James Butler, who had been raised as a Protestant under careful

164 IMAGINING IRELAND'S PASTS

'superintendency' in England, would prove 'a great assist, as well in inviting others to be of his religion, as in the Civil Government, it being most certain that no people under the sun are more apt to be of the same religion with their great lords, as the Irish be'.[129]

This chapter has shown that what we have described as aristocratic history was certainly more urbane than what had preceded it, and also added to the store of knowledge by publishing some of the documentary evidence left by those actors who, they contended, had sought, on behalf of the government in London, to make Ireland a more peaceful and prosperous place. The problem remained that each body of fresh evidence could be superseded by another, and historians failed to agree on how to interpret the ever-growing body of information. While succeeding authors extended the range of discussion concerning the significance of what had happened in Ireland during the sixteenth and seventeenth centuries and considered some of the more contentious issues in broader contexts, their fundamental difference remained that which had divided the providential authors: what had been the nature of the rebellion of 1641 and who had been most responsible for it?

---

[129] Lord Deputy to Wandesford, Master of the Rolls, 25 July 1636, *Strafford's Letters*, ed., Knowler, vol. 2, 13–23; quotation 18–19.

6
Enlightenment Historians of Ireland and their Critics

6.1 Introduction

The aristocratic historians whose publications we have discussed in the Chapter 5 considered themselves attuned to the most advanced social and political thinking of their generation not least because each believed that historical enquiry belonged within the secular domain. They therefore distanced themselves from the providential interpretations of Ireland's history that still enjoyed currency at the time they were writing. All also seemed convinced that their use of primary sources to which they enjoyed privileged access was in itself proof of their independence of mind and would confound their opponents.

The histories written by our aristocratic authors may have thus appeared 'scientific' but they were certainly not 'philosophical' as this term was understood by Voltaire, the best-known author of the French Enlightenment in Ireland, and by David Hume who was probably read by more people in Ireland than Voltaire.[1] The first shortcoming of the aristocratic historians by the standards of these two *philosophes* was that their arguments tended to be submerged in documentary compilations or in turgid narratives that were swamped in citation from contemporary documents. The aristocratic authors would also have fallen short of what the *philosophes* would have expected because they could not agree on what it was to be a proper noble in Ireland, and were clearly incapable of imagining how the descendants of the many invaders who had established footholds in the country might have constituted themselves into a single Irish people or nation. The ability to so conceptualize would have been considered essential for anybody contemplating a philosophical history for Ireland once David Hume, a Scotsman, explained that, in undertaking to write a *History of England*, he was setting out to explain how the descendants of an equally diverse succession of invaders of England had, by 1688, become members of a single nation bound by agreement on a shared set of political principles.[2]

---

[1] On the popularity of Voltaire in Ireland see chapters by Máire Kennedy, Geraldine Sheridan, and Graham Gargett, Graham Gargett and Geraldine Sheridan, eds., *Ireland and the French Enlightenment, 1700–1800* (Basingstoke, 1999).

[2] David Hume, *The History of England from the Invasion of Julius Caesar to the Revolution in 1688* (London, 1762); different segments of the work had been published—some with the title *History of*

Imagining Ireland's Pasts: Early Modern Ireland through the Centuries. Nicholas Canny, Oxford University Press (2021).
© Nicholas Canny. DOI: 10.1093/oso/9780198808961.003.0006

166   IMAGING IRELAND'S PASTS

The most formidable challenge facing any would-be philosophical historian of Ireland was that all previous mention of a nation by historians had been defined in exclusivist terms. There were some who believed the nation to be composed of those who had retained the religion and culture of those who had inhabited the island previous to the twelfth century. Another group believed that the descendants of these original inhabitants and of their twelfth-century conquerors had become bonded into an Irish nation by a shared Catholicism and an evolving mutual respect for each other's culture. Then a third school defined the political nation as Protestant, out of the belief that only those who understood how the Protestant Reformation had released people from the tyrannies of the past could appreciate the benefits of individual liberty without which no political nation could exist.

The task facing those in Ireland wishing to be philosophical historians was rendered more difficult for purely cultural reasons because some commentators, usually of English descent but not necessarily Protestant, believed that any civility that existed in Ireland was a product of English conquest. Given that this conquest was incomplete, this definition left significant elements of the country's populations incapable of becoming members of a civil community such as had developed in England and in other European nations. Matters were further complicated because educated Catholics who considered themselves enlightened and who enjoyed a modicum of wealth had established The Catholic Association in 1756, which morphed into The Catholic Committee of 1760, with the purpose of negotiating the political rehabilitation of Catholics on the grounds that the operation of the so-called Penal Laws was anomalous in an enlightened age.[3]

Such arguments introduced an edge to existing Protestant/Catholic tensions, as did the heightening of the ever-present sectarian fissures in Irish rural society associated with growing pressure on land resources that was a consequence of demographic increase. One manifestation of this was the formation of such communal protest groups as the Catholic Whiteboys and Rightboys and the Protestant Oakboys and Peep O'Day boys whose activities led to disquiet, atrocity, and uncertainty.[4]

Great Britain—between 1754 and 1761, but the composite 6 vol. *History of England* was published in 1762 and went into one hundred editions. On the sequencing of Hume's publications see James A. Harris, *Hume: An Intellectual Biography* (Cambridge, 2015). Quotations from Hume in this chapter are taken from a reprint of the first edition published in 6 vols. (London, 1841).

[3] Protestant resentment over Catholic challenges to what Luke Gibbons refers to as 'the Whig consensus' is discussed in several essays, Luke Gibbons and Kieran O'Conor, eds., *Charles O'Conor of Ballinagar, 1710–91: Life and Works* (Dublin, 2015); see especially the introduction and chapters by John Wrynn, Hilary Larkin, and Luke Gibbons. The survival of Catholics has been treated in James Livesey, *Civil Society and Empire; Ireland and Scotland in the Eighteenth-Century Atlantic World* (New Haven, Ct., 2009), esp. 95–108.

[4] Samuel Clark and James S. Donnelly, eds., *Irish Peasants: Violence and Political Unrest, 1780–1914* (Madison, Wi., 1983).

ENLIGHTENMENT HISTORIANS OF IRELAND AND THEIR CRITICS 167

Under these circumstances, it became difficult to imagine an Ireland not wracked by cultural and religious differences, but some, nonetheless, had attempted to do so in previous centuries.[5] Some authors at the elite level would have focused any such history on those fleeting moments when it had seemed possible that those Catholics who were prepared to swear allegiance to the Crown would be recognized as subjects equal with Protestants. At the same time, doctrinaire Protestants could not countenance any such professions being valid, and looked forward to the culmination of a historical process that would result in the creation of an Irish nation when Catholics would finally abandon their attachment to 'popery' as a prerequisite to their being accepted as Crown subjects. The challenge therefore remained to construct a record of the past that would make it possible for people of diverse ethnic and denominational ancestries to imagine themselves as members of one Irish nation under the British monarchy.

6.2 David Hume's Concern with Early Modern Ireland

We have already noted that an obvious template of how such a history might be assembled was provided by David Hume's six-volume *History of England* that was published in composite form in 1762.[6] This at first seemed attractive for aspirant historians of Ireland because it was a history of England alone rather than the history of Britain that Hume had originally contemplated. Its appearance therefore seemed to invite somebody to write a companion history of Ireland, especially since a *History of Scotland, 1542–1603* by William Robertson had been published in 1759.[7] An added attraction of Hume's exemplification of philosophical history was that methodologically all that seemed to be required of would-be authors, besides possessing what Hume termed 'a philosophical mind', was to consult the most authoritative existing histories on the subject in question with a view to composing a readable and balanced adjudication between conflicting interpretations.[8]

Nonetheless, Hume's *History of England*, and the volumes that preceded it, presented challenges to anybody contemplating a parallel history of Ireland. One was that Hume, in the course of referring to the jurisdiction that English rulers had claimed over Ireland since the twelfth century, and the extent to which events in Ireland had shaped English identity, had almost prescribed what should be the

---

[5] For the difficulties encountered in seeking a resolution for this conundrum see Jacqueline R. Hill, 'Popery and Protestantism, Civil and Religious Liberty: The Disputed Lessons of Irish History, 1690–1812', *Past and Present*, no. 118 (1988), 96–129.

[6] Hume's progress with this work and what preceded it may be followed in Harris, *Hume: An Intellectual Biography*, 305–407.

[7] William Robertson, *History of Scotland, 1542–1603* (3 vols., London, 1759).

[8] Hume, *The History of England*, vol. 5, 195; Harris, *Hume*.

168 IMAGINING IRELAND'S PASTS

themes of any such a history of Ireland. Despite such dogmatism, many educated people in Ireland looked forward to what this 'unbiased, dispassionate and independent thinker' would have to say of Ireland from the moment he announced he was engaged upon a general history of England.[9] However, even as they awaited its publication, Charles O'Conor and John Curry, who put themselves forward as enlightened upholders of the Catholic interest in Ireland, were taken aback by what Hume had had to say of the 1641 rebellion in Ireland in a preliminary publication that treated of the English Civil War of the seventeenth century. Hume's comments brought it home to them that the 'balanced' view, at which any historian, however philosophical, might arrive concerning any controversial subject, would rely upon the authorities the author chose to consult. In this context, O'Conor and Curry were alarmed that what Hume seemed to know of events in Ireland in 1641 was based almost entirely on John Temple's *History of the Irish Rebellion*. This should not have surprised them since Temple had written fluently, and his son, Sir William Temple, a patron and associate of Jonathan Swift, had been a thoughtful essayist and a skilful diplomat and would have been considered an early representative of enlightened thinking.[10]

Having taken note of the influence that John Temple's account was having on Hume's understanding of the 1641 rebellion, O'Conor and Curry made overtures to Hume through influential contacts, requesting that before he would commit himself to a definitive judgement on that subject in his *History of England* he should weigh Temple's opinion against alternative views presented by such as Roderic O'Flaherty or by Curry himself. However, as David Berman has demonstrated, while Hume entertained these overtures, he allowed his original thinking on the subject to stand in the first composite edition of his *History of England*, published in 1762. Then, in the first revised edition of the work that appeared in print in 1770, Hume did tone down what his Irish Catholic critics referred to as his 'declamatory virulence', by reducing his original assessment that insurgents had killed something between 200,000 and 250,000 British Protestants in 1641 to the more modest figure of 40,000 deaths. As a further concession, Hume added the cautionary note 'if this estimate itself be not, as is usual in such cases, very much exaggerated'.[11]

While Hume's Irish Catholic critics may have been pleased that he had conceded some ground, albeit belatedly, they did not seem to appreciate that numbers were not the crucial issue for Hume. It was rather, as had been the case with Voltaire in 1756 when he had written his *Essai sur les mœurs*, that these

---

[9] David Berman, 'David Hume on the 1641 Rebellion in Ireland', *Studies*, vol. 65, no. 258 (1976), 101–12, quotation 101; Hilary Larkin, 'Writing in an Enlightened Age? Charles O'Conor and the Philosophes', Gibbons and O'Conor, eds., *Charles O'Conor of Ballinagar*, 97–115.

[10] On William Temple (1628–1699) see the biographical note by John Gibney, *Dictionary of Irish Biography*, vol. 9, 301–2.

[11] Berman, 'David Hume on the 1641 Rebellion', 105–7.

ENLIGHTENMENT HISTORIANS OF IRELAND AND THEIR CRITICS   169

authors had accepted Temple's proposition that the Irish rebellion of 1641 was analogous to the St Bartholomew's Day massacre of 1572 in France. That Hume believed this analogy to be valid is apparent from his denunciation of the 1641 rebellion when, as he put it, 'the sacred name of religion resounded on every side' while the 'enormities' were being enacted. Therefore, when Hume in his 1770 edition revised his estimate of the numbers killed in 1641, he did not recant his depiction of the Irish rebellion of 1641, as 'an event memorable in the annals of human kind and worthy to be held in perpetual detestation and abhorrence'.[12]

Commentators on what Hume had to say on this subject have sometimes considered that he, as a Scotsman, was being crudely anti-Irish, and do not seem to appreciate that the ultimate targets of Hume's venom were the Scottish Covenanters who, he argued, had unleashed a cycle of violence in 1638 when they had gone to war against their king by 'communicating their barbarous zeal and theological fervour to the neighbouring nations'. Their example, as Hume represented it, had been followed by the English mob at the instigation of Puritans in the English parliament who wanted to see Strafford, Laud, and King Charles executed. It was only then, according to Hume that 'the people' in Ulster, and in Ireland generally, had been prompted by what was happening in Scotland and England to engage in their bloody actions to which they had been encouraged 'by their leaders and their priests'.[13] Hume contended that the horrors that were enacted in 1641, which he depicted graphically, provoked further violence, this time in England, when what 'enthusiastic Protestants' had pronounced to be 'the peculiar guilt of the Irish Catholics' was 'extended in English minds to all Catholics', including English Catholics, as well as 'to the prelitical party'. Consequently, said Hume, England itself became engulfed by bloody violence 'during that zealous period'.[14] At the same time, he claimed, an independent variant of religious zeal was promoted in Ireland by a papal nuncio 'full of arrogance, levity and ambition', who, according to Hume, exerted great influence in the country until English control was re-established by Oliver Cromwell. As Hume identified Cromwell's intervention in Ireland as the factor that brought the cycle of conflict that had begun in 1638 to a final bloody conclusion, he represented Cromwell as a cynical pragmatist rather than a zealot. His cynicism, he averred, was made manifest when Cromwell resorted to slaughter at the siege of Drogheda in 1649 with a view to discouraging resistance elsewhere in Ireland. In doing so, pronounced Hume, he 'pretended' that this 'severe execution' was in

[12] Graham Gargett, 'Voltaire's View of the Irish', in Gargett and Sheridan, eds., *Ireland and the French Enlightenment*, 152–70, esp. 160; Voltaire, *Essai sur les mœurs et l'esprit des nations*, ed., René Pomeau (Paris, 2 vols., 1961), vol. 1, 514; Hume, *The History of England*, vol. 5, 67.

[13] Hume, *The History of England*, vol. 5, 55; Hill, 'Popery and Protestantism', 111–12.

[14] Hume, *The History of England*, vol. 5, 73, 193; by the 'prelitical' party Hume meant Archbishop Laud and those prelates who supported him who, Hume suggested, were regarded by the extremists as little different from Catholics.

170   IMAGINING IRELAND'S PASTS

retaliation for 'the cruelty of the Irish massacre, but he well knew that almost the whole garrison was English'.[15]

Hume therefore always dwelt on events in Ireland in the context of developments in the three kingdoms because he, like Voltaire, had been led to believe (presumably by Temple) that what had happened in Ireland in 1641 provided a classical example of the evil that was invariably let loose upon the world whenever religious enthusiasm gained control over the minds of any population. Even then, Hume's representation of the Irish as a barbaric people was something he could hardly have avoided because he and most Enlightenment authors, like humanist historians in previous centuries, proceeded from the assumption that civility had derived ultimately from the ancient world when Romans had extended civil order from its Roman heartland by conquering barbaric peoples. Once he accepted this idea, Hume could hardly represent Irish people as other than barbaric because 'as they were never conquered or even invaded by the Romans from whom all the western world derived its civility, they continued still in the most rude state of society'. To sustain this proposition Hume, like the earlier humanist historians and those Protestant authors who had followed their lead, invoked the writings of Gerald of Wales.[16]

Once Hume had accepted as valid the appraisal given by Gerald of Wales of the condition of the Irish in the twelfth century, he pronounced that responsibility for bringing the benefits of ancient civilization to the Irish had passed from the Romans to the English, once King Henry II had undertaken to conquer Ireland in the twelfth century. Then, taking his cue from Sir John Davies (discussed in Chapter 3), Hume asserted that the English had failed to meet this responsibility by leaving the Irish for four centuries living 'like wild beasts' growing 'every day more intractable and more dangerous'.[17] Thus, proclaimed Hume, the Irish lived even into the sixteenth century 'in that abject condition' in which all other people in northern and western Europe had been 'before they received civility and slavery from the refined policy and irresistible bravery of Rome'. The consequence for the Irish, claimed Hume, in a passage that he had possibly borrowed from Spenser's *View*, was that 'when [in the sixteenth century] every Christian nation was cultivating with ardour every civil art of life, that island, lying in a temperate climate, enjoying a fertile soil, accessible in its situation, possessed of innumerable harbours, was still, notwithstanding these advantages,...inhabited by a people whose customs and manners approached nearer those of savages than of barbarians'.[18] Hume did not blame the Irish for this because, having been denied by the English the benefits of the civilization of ancient Rome, they lacked 'that curiosity and love of novelty by which every other people in Europe had been

---

[15] Hume, *The History of England*, vol. 5, 300.
[17] Hume, *The History of England*, vol. 4, 143.

[16] Hume, *The History of England*, vol. 1, 363.
[18] Hume, *The History of England*, vol. 4, 144.

ENLIGHTENMENT HISTORIANS OF IRELAND AND THEIR CRITICS 171

seized'. Their woeful condition, he stated, was due entirely to the neglect of the English who, in Hume's opinion, were, by the sixteenth century, less suited to fulfilling their civilizing role because they themselves were becoming 'violently agitated' by religious disputation, with the result that 'the old opposition' of the Irish to 'the manners, laws and interest of the English' became 'now inflamed by religious antipathy, and the subduing and civilizing of that country seemed to become every day more difficult and more impracticable'.[19]

In offering this overall appraisal of the condition of Ireland in the sixteenth and seventeenth centuries and in his mention of specific events from those centuries, Hume, as already mentioned, drew upon what had been written by Temple and Davies, but he also made specific reference to the writings of Camden and Cox, as well as to Collins, *Letters and Memorials of State*, and Knowler, *The Earl of Strafford's Letters* (both considered in Chapter 5). These authorities enabled him to pronounce that, with few exceptions, successive English rulers and officials had grossly mismanaged Ireland in the sixteenth and seventeenth centuries. Among the exceptions was 'Sir Henry Sidney' whose counsel was ignored but whom Hume adjudged to have been 'one of the wisest, and most active governors that Ireland had enjoyed for several reigns'. For the seventeenth century, Hume admired Thomas Wentworth, earl of Strafford, especially for his use of 'discretionary authority'. Such, declared Hume with apparent approval, had been 'exercised even in England...during that age', but 'in Ireland...was still more requisite, among a rude people, not yet thoroughly subdued, averse to the religion and manners of their conquerors, [and] ready on all occasions to relapse into rebellion and disorder'. Therefore, for Hume, Strafford was the 'magnanimous statesman' who had 'the capacity, genius [and] presence of mind' to have the English monarchy belatedly fulfil its obligation to redeem the people of Ireland from barbarism. Moreover, according to Hume, Strafford was proceeding towards 'an undisputed victory' as long as 'argument and reason and law had any place'. However, according to Hume, his best efforts had been subverted by 'the open violence of his fierce and malevolent antagonists' in Scotland, England, and Ireland, which gave rise to the cycle of violence, with its climax in the 1641 rebellion in Ireland, which Hume was citing as an exemplar of what happened in human affairs whenever reason gave way to emotion.[20]

It will be clear that in his narrative Hume was concerned to isolate religious and political zealots in all three kingdoms for condemnation. He reprimanded the English repeatedly throughout his *History of England* for having neglected their mentoring responsibility towards the Irish after they had conquered them, which left him free to consider the Irish to be the innocent victims of this neglect. Such philosophical points were lost on Curry and O'Conor, who would have been

---

[19] Hume, *The History of England*, vol. 4, 144.
[20] Harris, *Hume*, 368–87; Hume, *The History of England*, vol. 5, 32–4.

172 IMAGINING IRELAND'S PASTS

appalled at how Hume had limited his reading on Ireland's history to Gerald of Wales and the long succession of authors who had written in that tradition. These included Temple who had interpreted the rebellion of 1641 as a predictable consequence of the barbaric condition of the Irish as Gerald of Wales had described it. They would have derived little satisfaction from the use that Hume had made of what Roderic O'Flaherty had written on the 1641 rebellion, because the resulting correction in detail was left to the second edition of the *History of England* and did not influence Hume's overall interpretation. They regretted especially that Hume had chosen to ignore both what O'Flaherty, and O'Conor himself, had written on Ireland's history before the conquest of the twelfth century, and had neglected also the Old English perspective on more recent events as this had been presented by the Lords of the Pale in their Remonstrance of 1642 and by Curry in his own more recent publications. Therefore, as O'Conor and Curry would have seen it, Hume's narration, despite its philosophical appearance, had made no allowance for the existence of an ancient Irish civilization that had existed independently of that of ancient Rome. An even greater transgression in their eyes was that Hume had ignored the pleas of Curry that the Penal Laws against Catholics should be rescinded on the grounds that they contravened basic civil liberties. Instead, as they and other exponents of civil rights for Catholics perceived it, Hume had lent his reputation to make credible a biased rendition of Ireland's past that had frequently been challenged and discredited. Moreover, Hume made the rendition an essential element of his *History of England* that was destined to go into one hundred editions and remain one of the most extensively read histories in the English-speaking world in the half-century that followed. Hume's refusal to fully retract what he had originally published on Ireland therefore convinced Curry that he had 'laid down the arms of philosophy to wield those of spiritual hatred'.[21]

6.3 An Irish Contribution to Philosophical History?

Some of Ireland's more urbane Catholics, such as Curry and O'Conor, and those liberal Protestants who sympathized with them, had believed for some time that philosophical history presented them with a fresh possibility to argue from history that all loyal subjects in Ireland should be treated as equals under the law. To take advantage of this they had been contemplating a philosophical history of Ireland with the intention of giving Ireland a place in 'the moral histories of human progress', as Luke Gibbons and Kieran O'Conor have phrased it.[22] The promoters of this enterprise believed that any such account would give particular

---

[21] Hume, *The History of England*, vol. 4, 146; Berman, 'David Hume on the 1641 Rebellion', 103.
[22] Gibbons and O'Conor, eds., *Charles O'Conor of Ballinagar*, Introduction, 21.

ENLIGHTENMENT HISTORIANS OF IRELAND AND THEIR CRITICS   173

attention to Ireland's earliest history, following the example set by the Catholics Rothe and Keating and the Protestants Ussher and Ware when they had been writing their confessional histories in the previous century. The priority of those who saw merit in promoting a philosophical history for Ireland was that they hoped it would advance two propositions: first, that a highly developed civilization had flourished in Ireland independently of, and previous to, that of ancient Rome, and second, that Irish scholars had rekindled Christian civilization on the European Continent, and even in Britain, following the barbaric invasion of those societies that had occurred after the collapse of the Roman Empire. The eighteenth-century promoters of a philosophical history hoped therefore to prove 'scientifically' what had been argued in the seventeenth century to a different purpose and from a relatively small evidential base.[23]

Roderic O'Flaherty in his *Ogygia* had already published the preliminary work for such a narrative in 1685, and Charles O'Conor had expanded upon his ideas in the eighteenth century.[24] The latter, and a small number of other scholars, Protestant as well as Catholic and including one woman, Charlotte Brooke, believed that the case they were making for an ordered and cultured Irish society in ancient times would make an impression on sceptical readers only if it could be shown that the survivors of that ancient civilization had sustained a continuing literary output into modern times. Given that the sceptics they most wanted to impress were Protestants in Ireland and policy makers in Britain, it seemed necessary to have examples of this literature translated into English and published. This ambition, as it transpired, was not to be realized until 1789 when Charlotte Brooke published her *Reliques of Irish Poetry*, modelled on Thomas Percy, *Reliques of English Poetry*, which had been in print since 1765.[25]

As scholars within this coterie proceeded with their work and debated how the reputation of the Irish might be redeemed, they reached a consensus on the shape that a philosophical history for Ireland might assume. The bulk of the volume would treat of Ireland's political, religious, and cultural achievements previous to the twelfth-century conquest. Attention would then be given to the extent to

---

[23] Wrynn, 'Charles O'Conor as a philosophical historian', Gibbons and O'Conor, eds., *Charles O'Conor of Ballinagar*, 72–80; Hill, 'Popery and Protestantism', 98–9, 102–3, 106.
[24] Roderic O'Flaherty, *Ogygia: seu Rerum Hibernicarum Chronologia & etc* (London, 1685); interest in and debate over *Ogygia* persisted through the eighteenth century but a full English translation by James Hely, a Church of Ireland clergyman, was not published in Dublin until 1793; Clare O'Halloran, *Golden Ages and Barbarous Nations: Antiquarian Politics and Cultural Politics in Ireland, c. 1750–1800* (Cork, 2004), 18–19, 26, 38, 76, 161; Charles O'Conor, *Dissertation on the Antient History of Ireland* (Dublin, 1753).
[25] *Charlotte Brooke's, Reliques of Irish Poetry* [1789], ed., Lesa Ní Mhunghaile (Dublin, 2009); Clare O'Halloran, '"A Revolution in our moral and civil affairs": Charles O'Conor and the Creation of a Community of scholars in late eighteenth-century Ireland', Gibbons and O'Conor, eds., *Charles O'Conor of Ballinagar*, 81–96; Micheal Brown and Lesa Ní Mhunghaile, 'Future Past: Enlightenment and Antiquarianism in the Eighteenth Century', Kelly, ed., *The Cambridge History of Ireland*, vol. 3, 380–405.

174   IMAGINING IRELAND'S PASTS

which the positive aspects of this indigenous culture had been fused with that of their conquerors. The sixteenth and seventeenth centuries would get lesser attention in such a history other than to explain, as had been done already by both Carte and Curry, how potentially loyal Irish subjects of the British monarchy had been provoked into rebellion by avaricious government officials seeking to seize their positions and estates. It seemed appropriate also that any such philosophical history should, following the example of Roderic O'Flaherty, question the credibility of the extracts from the 1641 depositions that had sustained the argument of John Temple, and other like-minded Protestants of his and future generations, concerning the causes and character of the 1641 rebellion. The inclusion of such a polemical section came to be considered all the more necessary once Voltaire, and then Hume, had successively endorsed the proposition of Temple that the Irish rebellion in its intent and ferocity was analogous to the much-maligned St Bartholomew's day massacre.

While it was relatively easy to agree on what shape a philosophical history of Ireland might take, it was more difficult to decide on who was best equipped to write it, most particularly after 1762 when it had become clear that any such a history would now have to respond to what Hume had had to say of Ireland in his *History of England*. We know from Walter Love's investigation of the discussion that took place concerning a choice of author that Charles O'Conor favoured somebody who was a member of the Church of Ireland. He may have expected that such an author would build upon what Ussher and James Ware had written of Irish culture in early medieval times and beyond, and would thus earn respect among Protestant and English audiences for Ireland's much-maligned Catholic population. On the other hand, as Love discovered, John Curry, who probably wanted the commission for himself, was not satisfied that any Protestant, and most especially not any Protestant clergyman, was capable of writing the empathetic account that the occasion required. However, as was explained by Love, an intervention of Edmund Burke, a known moral supporter of Irish Catholics, resulted in the choice of author for a philosophical history of Ireland falling to Thomas Leland, a Church of Ireland clergyman, and a fellow of Trinity College, Dublin, with whom O'Conor had previously co-operated in scholarly pursuits.[26]

As it transpired, Curry's misgivings were proven correct since the three-volume *History of Ireland* published by Thomas Leland in 1773 was almost a parody of what had been adumbrated by those who believed that the purpose of any philosophical history should be to redeem the reputation of Irish people in the past so that their descendants who expressed loyalty to the Crown could become

---

[26] Walter D. Love, 'Charles O'Conor of Belanagare and Thomas Leland's "philosophical" history of Ireland', *Irish Historical Studies*, vol. 13 (1962), 1–25.

ENLIGHTENMENT HISTORIANS OF IRELAND AND THEIR CRITICS   175

members of the political nation regardless of their lineage or religious profession.[27] Leland indicated in a sequence of preliminary 'discourses' to the history proper that he was conscious that *his* history would disappoint his sponsors, and declared himself 'armed against censure only by an integrity' that had confined 'him to the truth' in an account that he considered free of the 'prejudices and animosities' that had characterized previous history writing on Ireland. He had proceeded, he claimed, with a 'diligent and attentive inspection of different evidence with a careful use of his private judgement', and was 'exhibiting the authorities he chose to follow, without generally engaging in critical and controversial discussion'.[28]

Leland's stated concern to avoid controversy was belied by his condescending dismissal of recent publications on the history of Ireland previous to the introduction there of Christianity. In doing so he acknowledged that he was 'totally unacquainted with the Irish language', and was therefore reliant on the 'zealous friendship and assistance of Charles O'Connor [sic], Esq' and on 'the antiquarians... to establish the authenticity' of the conclusions that had recently been drawn from the evidence that had survived from the ancient past. Notwithstanding his acknowledged insufficiency and reliance on others to guide his judgement, Leland asserted that the claims being made for the accomplishments of the Irish in ancient times were explicable only when one recognized that they were being put forward by scholars representing a population that had been 'depressed for many ages and reduced to a mortifying state of inferiority'. He pronounced that *Ogygia* by O'Flaherty, and the works of Keating, 'the Irish historian', were marred by 'enthusiastic zeal' in their search for a founding legend for Ireland that would justify considering the Irish people as a nation equal to any other in Europe.[29]

Next, when discussing how Christianity had first been established in Ireland and what consequences had flowed from it, Leland found himself reliant upon, while dissenting from, what had been said of the subject by Ussher. He accepted Ussher's findings that Christianity had established a foothold in Ireland and had even inspired some holy men to engage in missions throughout Europe, on which latter subject he cited Charles O'Conor as an authority. Then, having taken account of the arguments advanced in this secondary literature, Leland concluded that Christianity had 'at least restrained the natural vices' of the people of Ireland even when it 'could not eradicate them'. Then—to make clear his disagreement with Ussher and Ware—Leland pronounced that Christianity had not been

---

[27] Thomas Leland, *The History of Ireland from the Invasion of Henry II with a preliminary discourse on the ancient state of that Kingdom* (3 vols., Dublin, 1773).

[28] Leland, *The History of Ireland*, vol. 1, 'Preliminary Discourse', iii, iv.

[29] Leland, *The History of Ireland*, vol. 1, 'Preliminary Discourse', v; 'Preliminary of the History of Ireland, previous to the Introduction of Christianity', vi, viii, xvii.

176   IMAGINING IRELAND'S PASTS

'so deeply imbibed, or blended so thoroughly with the natural principles of the people, as to produce any extraordinary reformation.'[30]

When it came to discussing 'the ancient manners' of the Irish, Leland laid claim to patriotic Irish credentials by denouncing the 'odious and disgusting' 'representations' that had been made of them by some English authors. He considered, however, that such debasement did not justify the inclination of Irish authors to 'break out into the most animated encomiums of their own ancestors'. Then he pronounced that, having studied translations of some ancient Irish texts that had been made available to him by the antiquary Charles Vallancey, 'a native of England' who had given 'laborious attention to the ancient language of Ireland', he had arrived at what he considered the balanced opinion that the Irish had, at best, developed 'an imperfect civilization'. Even this, Leland believed, had become diminished over time since Fynes Moryson had found, at the outset of the seventeenth century, that 'the old natives had degenerated... to a state inferior to that in which the English found them in the days of Henry the second'. After this, and now taking Sir John Davies rather than Moryson as his mentor, Leland attributed the degeneration, to which Moryson had made reference, to the failure of the English government to extend English justice to the Irish who, because of this neglect, had become coarsened by 'the wars of several centuries'.[31]

The final of Leland's preliminary discourses concerned the invasions of Ireland previous to that of Henry II. By comparison with these, the conquest launched by Henry II had been 'easy and successful'. This success meant that for Leland in 1773, as for Borlase in 1680, and for Hume in 1762, the subject matter for any philosophical history of Ireland should concern 'the progress of English power in Ireland... through the conflict of many ages, short intervals of peace, the sudden revival of hostilities, the suppression of civil war, the attempts to compose all national disorders, and the final contest in the cause of James the Second'. He expressed himself confident that this 'general and connected history' would lead to the happy outcome when, during the joint reign of William III and Queen Mary II, 'the authority of the crown of England' was finally established 'in a country' that was then acknowledged as 'a respectable member of the British Empire'.[32]

This summation of what Leland had to say in his preliminary discourses will make it clear why those who had commissioned him to write a philosophical history felt betrayed even before they had begun to read the history proper. They had even more reason to be disappointed when they took note of the episodes of

---

[30] Leland, *The History of Ireland*, vol. 1, 'Preliminary of the Establishment of Christianity in Ireland and the Consequences of this event', xviii–xxix, esp. xix, xx, xxii.

[31] Leland, *The History of Ireland*, vol. 1, 'Preliminary of the Ancient Manner of the Irish', xxvii, xxx, xxvii; Leland was here relating the trope of degeneration, which had traditionally been associated with Irish people of English descent, to those of Gaelic origin.

[32] Leland, *The History of Ireland*, vol. 1, 'Preliminary Discourse', i–ii.

ENLIGHTENMENT HISTORIANS OF IRELAND AND THEIR CRITICS   177

Ireland's history that Leland had decided to concentrate upon. He chose to ignore the history of Ireland prior to the twelfth-century conquest of the country after his cursory and, as we saw, dismissive remarks on the subject offered in his sequence of preliminary 'discourses'. Then, from the conquest forward, the history of the country was structured around the regnal years of British monarchs, other than the Interregnum to which Leland dedicated forty pages.[33] The reigns to which Leland devoted most attention were that of Henry II, to which he assigned 154 pages,[34] that of Henry VIII, which he discussed in 64 pages,[35] that of Elizabeth I, which was covered in 191 pages,[36] that of James VI and I, considered in 67 pages,[37] that of Charles I, to which he dedicated a mammoth 346 pages,[38] the reign of Charles II, which he treated in 79 pages,[39] the reign of James II, to which he allocated 82 pages,[40] and the joint reigns of William and Mary, with which he concluded his history with 47 pages of text.[41] These figures show that Leland's *History of Ireland* was overwhelmingly a history of early modern Ireland within which special attention was given to events in Ireland during the reign of Charles I.

This concentration was obviously the inverse of what the advocates of a philosophical history of Ireland had hoped for, and Catholics among them would have been equally unhappy with Leland's identification of the authorities on which he principally relied. Proceeding from Gerald of Wales, Leland made regular reference to Ware, Ussher, Camden, Bale, Hooker, Moryson, Davies, Harris, Cox, Carte, Temple, Borlase, Ludlow, Orrery, Nalson, Thurloe, as well as some manuscript sources from the holdings in Marsh's Library and in the library of Trinity College, Dublin. Among these latter were the manuscripts of Bishop Sterne, which included both the 'Aphorismical Discovery' and the 1641 depositions. In so far as Leland drew upon sources of Catholic provenance other than the 'Aphorismical Discovery', it was from the writings of Philip O'Sullivan Beare, which established to his satisfaction that Catholic conspiracies to overthrow the British monarchy with the aid of Continental powers had been a reality during the late sixteenth and the early seventeenth centuries. Then, for the Restoration period, as we shall detail later, Leland referred to what had been written on that subject by Hugh Reily, a Jacobite author whose

---

[33] Leland, *The History of Ireland*, vol. 3, 336–407.
[34] Leland, *The History of Ireland*, vol. 1, 1–154.
[35] Leland, *The History of Ireland*, vol. 2, 122–86.
[36] Leland, *The History of Ireland*, vol. 2, 219–410.
[37] Leland, *The History of Ireland*, vol. 2, 411–78.
[38] Leland, *The History of Ireland*, vol. 2, 478–88, vol. 3, 1–336.
[39] Leland, *The History of Ireland*, vol. 3, 408–87.
[40] Leland, *The History of Ireland*, vol. 3, 488–570.
[41] Leland, *The History of Ireland*, vol. 3, 571–618.

178 IMAGINING IRELAND'S PASTS

publications, like those of O'Sullivan Beare, had been studiously ignored by the Catholic sponsors of philosophical history.[42]

Drawing, as Hume had done, on the opinions of John Davies, Leland faulted successive English monarchs for their failure in bring Ireland's indigenous population under the rule of English law. This neglect, he contended, led to the situation that in Ireland, unlike in England, 'the people' were not 'prepared' for 'the Reformation' that had been 'favoured' by 'the first reformers in other parts of Europe' as also in England where Henry VIII 'became an instrument of providence to introduce the first beginnings of Reformation into his kingdom.'[43] He cited from the experience of John Bale in Ossory (discussed in Chapter 1) to prove the unpreparedness of the Irish for reform, and he concluded that during the reigns of Edward VI and Queen Elizabeth 'the business of religious reformation in Ireland' became 'nothing more than the impositions of English government on a prejudiced and bigoted people, not sufficiently obedient to this government, not sufficiently impressed with fear, or reconciled by kindness.'[44] Leland attributed the Irish rebellions that occurred during the reign of Queen Elizabeth principally to the lust for power of recalcitrant lords, but he suggested that the obstreperousness of these lords became ever more threatening as their pride was 'inflamed by a few bigoted ecclesiastics.'[45] Then, having detailed how each rebellion had been suppressed, he concluded that the one positive Irish achievement of Queen Elizabeth's reign, besides victory in the field, had been the foundation of Trinity College, Dublin, on which he furnished considerable detail.[46]

Then, as he described first the Catholic insurrections in the Munster towns at the outset of the reign of King James I and how they had been 'vigorously opposed and suppressed', and then the repeated 'futile efforts' of the 'native Irish', culminating in the O'Doherty revolt of 1608 to 'harass and distress the government', he concluded that cumulatively these 'only served to confirm their subjection.'[47] He believed that it was the dominance the government had established that had made it possible for it to proceed with a plantation in Ulster, which, unlike the Elizabethan plantation in Munster, promised to treat the Irish 'with particular indulgence.'[48]

Leland considered that 'the passion for planting which King James indulged was actuated by the fairest and most captivating motives'. These included his wish to 'entice [the Irish] from their barbarism' by intermixing them with planters,

---

[42] For a biographical note on Hugh Reily see that by John Cronin, *Dictionary of Irish Biography*, vol. 8, 439.

[43] Leland, *The History of Ireland*, vol. 1, 157–8; it is unusual to find this reference to providential intervention in a history that represented itself as philosophical.

[44] Leland, *The History of Ireland*, vol. 1, 200–1.

[45] Leland, *The History of Ireland*, vol. 2, 288, 306–7.

[46] Leland, *The History of Ireland*, vol. 2, 319–26.

[47] Leland, *The History of Ireland*, vol. 2, 416, 429.

[48] Leland, *The History of Ireland*, vol. 2, 431.

ENLIGHTENMENT HISTORIANS OF IRELAND AND THEIR CRITICS   179

which ambition, averred Leland, led James to consider himself 'the destined reformer and civilizer of a rude people; and was impatient for the glory of teaching a whole people the valuable arts of life, or improving their lands, extending their commerce, and refining their manners'.[49] These admirable ambitions were disappointed, according to Leland, because of 'fraud' and the 'avarice and rapine' of 'hungry adventurers' who did not always meet their contractual obligations. Then, in a passage that he obviously borrowed from Carte, Leland declared the early seventeenth century in England to have been 'an age of project and adventure' and 'they who were too poor, or too spiritless to engage in distant adventures, courted fortune in Ireland'. Again, following Carte and Davies, Leland considered that the 'more discerning' of 'the old Irish lords and chieftains' who had suffered 'the miseries of Tyrone's rebellion... were grateful to government' for the benefits of English law that promised to liberate them 'from slavish submission' to superiors. However, he believed that the defects he had identified in the Ulster plantation scheme as it unfolded, and the government's declared intention to have an equally 'extensive plantation in the province of Connacht', had alienated those Irish lords who had been prepared to co-operate with official plans. This did not surprise him since Ireland remained 'a country accustomed to violence [with] a people irritated and insulted, enflamed by superstition, pressed by necessity, and stimulated by the suggestions of the turbulent and factious'. Under those circumstances, he considered it 'extraordinary' that the king had been 'enabled to execute his schemes of innovation' given the weakness of the government and the poverty of the army at that time.[50]

The pessimism of Leland concerning the condition of Ireland in the first half of the seventeenth century contrasted sharply with Hume's opinion that this had been the moment when a peaceful future for Ireland could have been secured. As he distanced himself from Hume while remaining loyal to Whiggish principles, Leland pronounced that whatever possibility there had been of melding the diverse populations in Ireland into a single polity had been lost once 'the subjects of Ireland', whom he sometimes referred to as 'the Popish party', commenced 'assembling and deliberating among themselves on all national matters, as their right and privilege'. Here, he had in mind the proceedings in the Irish parliament of 1613–14 and the subsequent efforts by the Old English Catholic 'faction' to negotiate the 'Graces' from King Charles I without consultation either with the Irish parliament or the Dublin administration. The resulting cleavage between Protestant and Catholic groups in Ireland, he argued, became all the wider because (and here his opinion accorded with that of Hume and Carte) most of those from England who had settled in Ireland were 'fraught with the puritanical

---

[49] Leland, *The History of Ireland*, vol. 2, 465.
[50] Leland, *The History of Ireland*, vol. 2, 472, 473, 479.

180 IMAGINING IRELAND'S PASTS

spirit' and their clergy had been 'provoked' by the 'insolence' of the Old English in negotiating the Graces.[51]

Then, in his discussion of the interlude when Ireland was ruled by 'Lord Wentworth, better known by his superior title of Strafford', Leland, in sharp contrast to Hume and also Carte, believed that Strafford's governance hindered rather than furthered conciliation between the opposing groups. He believed that Strafford's administration had been considered 'odious and arbitrary' by all parties since that 'imperious nobleman...regarded [Ireland] as a conquered kingdom in the strictest sense' and considered himself entitled, with an 'air of careless insolence', to tread roughshod over opponents, thus further alienating all parties from the government. Leland noted, with approval, how Strafford attempted to curb the 'insolence of the Romish party', but he expressed dismay at how Lord Mountnorris had been made to suffer from Strafford's 'utter intoxication of power and greatness'. Leland deplored Strafford's choice of John Bramhall—the man that Oliver Cromwell afterwards called...the Canterbury of Ireland—to act as an enforcer of discipline in the Church of Ireland, and he showed sympathy for Richard Boyle, the 1st earl of Cork, when he discussed the repeated humiliation that Cork had endured at the hands of Strafford.[52] In detailing Cork's sufferings, Leland implied that Cork, rather than Strafford, should have been selected as governor, because he 'was possessed with a spirit suited to his exalted rank; not with a despicable pride of family that reposes fastidiously on its advantages with a contemptuous disregard of all inferiors, but with a liberal and generous solicitude for the welfare of those he governed'.[53] Cork was also well equipped to become governor of Ireland, according to Leland, because of his proven record as a planter in Munster and because 'the errors of Popery were offensive to his religious principles and [because] that barbarism which generally attended it in Ireland was equally repugnant to his schemes of political improvement'.[54]

This particular outburst showed Thomas Leland to be in tune with the arguments of Charles Smith (considered in Chapter 5), whom Leland possibly considered a fellow enlightened Whig. Thus, like Smith, he could not conceive of all the inhabitants of Ireland being bonded into a single nation unless Catholics renounced their allegiance to the Pope. The remainder of his book was therefore largely devoted to reconstituting what had happened in Ireland in 1641 and to discussing the rejection by the papacy of the various attempts made by more conciliatory Catholics in later decades to reconcile their allegiance to their faith with loyalty to a Protestant monarch. Leland's investigations into such matters combined to demonstrate that the suppression of Catholicism, or at least winning the agreement of Catholics to sever their allegiance to the papacy, was the essential prerequisite to forging a single Irish nation. And when Leland pronounced that

[51] Leland, *The History of Ireland*, vol. 2, 479, 481, 507, 509.
[52] Leland, *The History of Ireland*, vol. 3, 10, 11, 12, 13, 34, 35.
[53] Leland, *The History of Ireland*, vol. 3, 6.   [54] Leland, *The History of Ireland*, vol. 3, 7.

'the design' behind the 1641 rebellion was 'nothing less...than the utter subversion of all the late establishment of property' and 'an establishment for the Romish religion, with all the splendour and affluence of its hierarchy', he was further revealing his belief that final unity between the different populations in Ireland could be achieved only when one side became dominant over the other.

While those who had sponsored Leland to write a philosophical history of Ireland were agreed that his work betrayed what had been expected of him, they did not give him credit for having added to what was previously known about the outbreak of the 1641 rebellion. He, like the more liberal historians who preceded him, acknowledged that factors besides the inveterate perversity of Irish papists had been responsible for the outbreak of rebellion in 1641. Among the factors he identified were Irish grievance over the unjust way in which they had been treated by British authorities and planters, and Strafford's curt dismissal of Irish Catholic expectations that what the king had promised them in the Graces (of which Leland did not approve) would become statute law. Then, having engaged on a close reading of the 1641 depositions that were readily available to him in the library of Trinity College, Dublin, where he held a chair and fellowship, Leland broke with Temple, Jones, and their associates, and more pertinently with Hume, by pronouncing that, in the early stages of the rebellion, 'no indiscriminate massacre was as yet committed'. Then, following a careful investigation of the relevant depositions, Leland also dismissed the contention of Roderic O'Flaherty and John Curry, which had been endorsed by Carte, that British soldiers had been the first to engage in indiscriminate slaughter in November 1641 in a supposed attack upon the Catholic population of Islandmagee. Leland did not deny that a massacre of Catholics had occurred at Islandmagee, but he cited several depositions to show first that this incident had taken place in January 1642 rather than in November 1641 as O'Flaherty and then Curry had contended, and that the slaughter of defenceless people had been on a much smaller scale than had been alleged by the Catholic authors and by Carte.

This emendation to what Catholics had assumed to be received wisdom was, as we learn from Walter Love, brought to Curry's attention by a Catholic compositor who had been working on Leland's history at proof stage. This advance notice gave Curry the opportunity to have an outraged retort ready to go to press from the moment that Leland's volumes appeared in print. However, in this, Curry could do little to refute Leland's case that the military reverse suffered by Phelim O'Neill and his supporters at Lisburn in November 1641 had 'provoked this savage [Phelim O'Neill] and his barbarous followers to a degree of rage truly diabolical' that culminated in the massacre of Protestants at the bridge at Portadown, which incident Leland, like many previous Protestant authors, depicted in graphic language.[55]

---

[55] Walter D. Love, 'Charles O'Conor of Belanagare and Thomas Leland's "philosophical" history of Ireland', 13–16; Curry, *An Historical and Critical Review*; Leland, *The History of Ireland*, vol. 3, 118, 127, 128.

182   IMAGINING IRELAND'S PASTS

Leland was less condemnatory of the 'more refined' Old English than of the Gaelic Irish when he discussed how 'the contagion of rebellion' had spread quickly throughout the country. This did not amount to him becoming sympathetic to the Old English who, he believed, were aggrieved only because of 'their prejudices and discontents'. Nonetheless, he endorsed Carte's opinion, which was also that of the authors of the Catholic *Remonstrance* in 1642 and of Curry in 1758 (discussed in Chapter 4), that it was ill-advised actions by the lords justices that had driven the Old English to take up arms. He also, like Carte, conceded that once the Old English had taken to arms it became 'the favourite object both of the Irish governors and the English parliament [to seek] the utter extirpation of all the Catholic inhabitants of Ireland'.[56] Leland lamented such extremism, which, he contended, was reciprocated by Catholics once the nuncio became involved there, and was persisted with during the Interregnum, when positions became so polarized 'that Ireland, at this period, [did not] afford any materials for the Historian'.[57]

Leland's cursory treatment of the Interregnum left him free to give considerable attention to the years after the Restoration. Here, following Carte, he wrote admiringly of the endeavours of Ormond to steer a middle course between the extremes favoured by Protestant zealots, whose various plots Leland condemned, and the ambitions of the 'presumptuous Papists', whose repeated rejection of compromise he found puzzling. The only explanation he could offer for the refusal of Catholics to be more accommodating when Ormond was prepared to be conciliatory to those willing to swear allegiance to the Crown was that Catholic leaders knew that 'the royal brothers'—Charles II and the future James II—had entered into a 'private agreement with France' with the 'purpose of establishing a Popish interest in Ireland'. It thus became a fixed opinion of Leland that only Irish Catholic knowledge of the Secret Treaty of Dover could explain why they had conspired incessantly to overthrow the Act of Settlement, which he himself considered an equitable redistribution of Irish property between Royalists and Parliamentarians and between Catholics and Protestants.[58] Leland complained particularly of 'the insolence of the presuming prelate' Peter Talbot, who had served as Catholic Archbishop of Dublin during the 1670s, for exhorting Catholics against swearing allegiance to the British monarchy.[59]

Such inflexibility further convinced Leland that the restored Stuarts had intended from the moment of their return in 1660 to reinstate Catholicism in Ireland. Leland was satisfied that what he had suspected was proven by King

---

[56] Leland, *The History of Ireland*, vol. 3, 147, 154, 166.
[57] Leland, *The History of Ireland*, vol. 3, 400.
[58] Leland, *The History of Ireland*, vol. 3, 442, 434, 454, 462, 465, 473, 474, 489; R. Hutton, 'The Making of the Secret Treaty of Dover, 1668–70', *The Historical Journal*, vol. 29 (1986), 297–318.
[59] Leland, *The History of Ireland*, vol. 3, 462, 465; for a biographical note on Peter Talbot see that by Aidan Clarke, *Dictionary of Irish Biography*, vol. 9, 245–6.

ENLIGHTENMENT HISTORIANS OF IRELAND AND THEIR CRITICS   183

James II who, in Leland's words, had 'a bigoted and passionate affection for Popery', when he elevated Richard Talbot, brother to the archbishop, to become earl and then duke of Tyrconnell before appointing him to be governor of Ireland. Leland conceded that Tyrconnell was in some respects a victim of circumstances because 'in his youth' he had been 'witness' to 'the carnage' inflicted by Cromwell upon 'Drogheda, and, on his escape from this infernal scene, naturally retained a violent abhorrence of fanatics, in which denomination he included all of the Protestant party'.[60] However, he believed that such prejudice should have disqualified Tyrconnell from office, and he found it unsurprising that Protestants had been overcome by 'panic', believing that 'the Irish' intended another 'general massacre', once the king had appointed Tyrconnell as governor. Tyrconnell's unsuitability for the position, according to Leland, was further proven when, encouraged by 'the insolence of popish clergy' and the 'bigotry of James', he brought forward legislation in the Irish parliament of 1689 to reverse the Act of Settlement in favour of Catholics, and to the detriment of Protestants. This, as Leland put it, was only prevented by another 'contest for power' that was eventually won by William of Orange, husband to Mary, one of King James's Protestant daughters. After the succession of William and Mary, pronounced Leland, 'the authority of the crown of England [was] unalterably established' in Ireland.[61]

This narrative, which proceeded from the moment that the Irish were depicted as a barbaric people by Gerald of Wales to the completion of what Leland considered the final conquest of Ireland by William of Orange, was clearly not what the promoters of a philosophical history for Ireland had expected. As the criticism poured forth, culminating in John Curry's *An Historical and Critical Review* that appeared in 1775, Leland remained satisfied that what he had published complied in every respect with the standards required of a philosophical historian, and that it was Curry who was failing to recognize boundaries.

Leland, as noted, was concerned to dismiss the notion of an ancient Irish civilization that had cherished individual freedom because, as Hilary Larkin has phrased it, this was challenging 'the hegemonic narrative about English liberty' that was vital to Protestant Whig identity.[62] Having discredited what was being said by antiquarians of Ireland's ancient past as a myth, Leland believed himself justified in commencing his narrative with the invasion of King Henry II because this was consistent with the view of the *philosophes* that all civilization had been

---

[60] Leland, *The History of Ireland*, vol. 3, 489, 501; for a biographical note on Richard Talbot, earl, later duke, of Tyrconnell see that by James McGuire, *Dictionary of Irish Biography*, vol. 9, 248–56; Pádraig Lenihan, *The Last Cavalier: Richard Talbot (1631–91)* (Dublin, 2014).

[61] Leland, *The History of Ireland*, vol. 3, 511, 512–13, 532, 618; a scholarly edition of the acts has been pieced together in *The Acts of James II's Irish parliament of 1689*, ed., John Bergin and Andrew Lyall (Dublin, 2016).

[62] Hilary Larkin, 'Writing in an Enlightened Age?', 99; Livesey, *Civil Society and Empire*, 91.

184 IMAGINING IRELAND'S PASTS

promoted through conquests that could be traced ultimately to Ancient Rome. Then, as he proceeded with his narrative into the early modern period and paused to consider what he considered to have been the barbaric behaviour of the Irish in 1641 and again in 1689, Leland, like a true *philosophe*, condemned all, regardless of denomination, who had permitted zeal to have command over reason. Among those he condemned were Puritans who, as he saw it, had fomented the disorder in England that had led to the killing of the king, and who during the Interregnum, had given free rein to the zeal that, he contended, had wreaked as much havoc in England as in Ireland. At the same time, Leland, as a man of the Enlightenment and as a Protestant, associated Catholicism with bigotry and extremism, even as he expressed sympathy for Catholics of moderate political views who in the past, as in the present, seemed anxious to rehabilitate themselves politically by swearing allegiance to the British monarchy. As he saluted such people—and here he would have had in mind Charles O'Conor and Sylvester O'Halloran as well as his adversary John Curry—Leland made it clear that he believed them to be deceiving themselves.[63] He did this by demonstrating that those Catholics who, at various times in the seventeenth and eighteenth centuries, had expressed a willingness to take an oath of allegiance to the British monarchy as proof of their political loyalty had been condemned by the papacy and had bowed to that superior authority. Thus even as he sought to avoid 'offending some or all of those' who were accustomed to view their past 'through the medium of their passions and prepossessions', he considered that the proven subservience of all Catholics to the papacy showed that all of that denomination would remain unfit to enjoy, and benefit from, civil liberty until such time as they renounced papal authority.[64] Leland was clearly in line with Hume and Voltaire and other figures of the Enlightenment in this hostility to the papacy and in his suspicion of Catholicism in general. He differed from the mainstream Enlightenment figures only in that, where they considered most organized religions to be irrational, he implied that the mainstream Protestantism of the established Church of Ireland could be an effective instrument in keeping enthusiasm at bay. It was thus, as Leland saw it, making subjects more amenable to government.

The general propositions that Leland advanced were, as noted, supported in some instances by close attention to detail and he proved himself an innovative historian when he looked critically at the 1641 depositions both to refute Temple's argument that the insurgents had engaged upon a premeditated massacre of Protestants, and to explode the contention, made initially by O'Flaherty and repeated by Curry, that it was a Protestant massacre of Catholics at Islandmagee

---

[63] On Sylvester O'Halloran see Clare O'Halloran, *Golden Ages and Barbarous Nations*, 107–9; Claire E. Lyons, 'An imperial harbinger: Sylvester O'Halloran's *General History* (1778)', *Irish Historical Studies*, vol. 39 (2015), 357–77.

[64] Leland, *The History of Ireland*, vol. 3, 86.

ENLIGHTENMENT HISTORIANS OF IRELAND AND THEIR CRITICS 185

that had commenced the bloodshed that had rendered the 1641 rebellion infamous. The other issues over which he paused in the later section of his work concerned the Act of Settlement which Leland considered an equitable arrangement.

As he advanced his arguments, Leland made it clear that he was meeting the essential requirement of a philosophical historian by attempting to arrive at a balanced appraisal of the controversial subjects under discussion based on a close reading of what had been written on those subjects regardless of the different perspectives and prejudices of the various authors. In this respect, on 1641, as we saw, he had consulted both the depositions where Protestants had represented themselves as victims of the assault, and the anonymous 'Aphorismical Discovery', which viewed the conflict of the mid-seventeenth century in Ireland from the perspective of Owen Roe O'Neill and of the papal nuncio, who had together pursued a Catholic political agenda. Then, when it came to his discussion of the Restoration Settlement, Leland made it clear that he had consulted Carte who had credited the duke of Ormond with fashioning a scheme that sought to treat all interested parties fairly, after which he had taken account of what had been written on the subject by Hugh Reily. This latter had decried how the Act had led to 'the settlement indeed of rebels and traitors, but the ruin of royal subjects' as a result of which it could be stated that 'no king, since the creation of the universe [had] proven so bountiful to the worst of rebels at the cost of his faithful subjects'.[65]

Therefore, as well as presenting what might have been considered orthodox accounts of the controversial episodes in Ireland's history of the early modern centuries, Leland summarized, and explained why he dissented from, what O'Sullivan Beare had written of conflict in Ireland between 1579 and 1603, what the author of the 'Aphorismic Discovery' had had to say of conflict in Ireland in the mid-seventeenth century, and what Hugh Reily had written of the Act of Settlement. One of his purposes in doing so, as I have suggested, was to comply with the requirement of philosophical history that authors take all perspectives into account before arriving at a final appraisal of any episode. However, another purpose would have been to expose how these strident Catholic interpretations of historical events in Ireland during the early modern centuries had been disregarded by the Catholic promoters of philosophical history who would have their readers imagine a past where their ancestors had behaved as cautiously and reasonably as they themselves were doing in the present. Leland was not denying that there were some within the Irish Catholic community in the past who had behaved reasonably, just as there were some Catholics in the present with whom he was prepared to engage in scholarly and even social exchanges. However, he believed that the weight of evidence showed that at moments of crisis the moderates had always been forced to give way to extremists who took their

---

[65] Hugh Reily, *The Impartial History of Ireland* (London 1742), 43, 65–6.

186   IMAGINING IRELAND'S PASTS

directions from the Pope. Leland was effectively saying that no matter how much he, as a man of the Enlightenment, might have personally favoured a relaxation of the Penal Laws so that those educated Catholics with whom he interacted might become his political equals, he was demonstrating from the historical record that any such relaxation was certain to give free rein to the papacy, and to the extremists whom he believed to be invariably controlled by the papacy. Thus he was able to argue from history that it was reasonable as well as pragmatic to uphold the political arrangements that had been decided upon after William and Mary had ascended the throne. To do otherwise, he argued, would not only have placed in jeopardy the liberties that had been then guaranteed but would—as had been made clear by the writings of Hugh Reily—invite challenges to the Act of Settlement that was the bedrock of Protestant interest in Ireland.

This rendition of Leland's three-volume history may convey the impression that the discussion about a possible philosophical history for Ireland was, like so much else, a debate between Catholics and Protestants or even more narrowly one between Leland and a small group of educated Catholics that included O'Conor, Curry, and Sylvester O'Halloran. The discussion as it developed did come down to that. However, at the outset it had included some Protestant scholars whose patriotic feelings had been offended by the Irish being portrayed as barbarians by Enlightenment figures, and who had dabbled in antiquarianism both to find evidence of an ancient Irish civilization and to trace a distinguished lineage for Ireland's first inhabitants and the language they used. The more effusive, as exemplified by Charles Vallancey, a Flemish-born, English-raised, engineer, army officer and *savant* of Huguenot ancestry, went so far as to claim the Irish language to be 'the oldest and purest in the world'.[66] However, few of these, including the enthusiastic Vallancey, as Clare O'Halloran has explained, ever contemplated connecting their musings about Ireland's ancient past to present politics.[67] Others, usually Protestant, as we again learn from Clare O'Halloran, considered such speculation about a glorious ancient Irish past to be politically dangerous and began to ridicule that which they lacked the competence to refute.[68] Leland, as noted, remained respectful of the endeavours of the anti-quarians but he bowed to the views of the traditionalists and distanced himself from what was being written of Ireland's ancient past. The consequence was that his history became essentially one of early modern Ireland and may be read as a contribution by Leland from history to the political debate of his generation relat-

---

[66] Cited in Clare O'Halloran '"A Revolution in our moral and civil affairs"', 88; on Vallancey more generally see Clare O'Halloran, 'An English Orientalist in Ireland: Charles Vallancey (1726–1812)', in Joep Leerseen, A.H.van der Weel, and Bart Westerweel, eds., *Forging in the Smithy: National Identity and Representation in Anglo-Irish Literary History* (Amsterdam, 1995), 161–74; for a biographical note on Vallancey (1725?–1812) see that by Monica Nevin, *Dictionary of Irish Biography*, vol. 9, 635–6.

[67] O'Halloran, 'An English Orientalist in Ireland', 167.

[68] O'Halloran, *Golden Ages and Barbarous Nations*, 59–62.

ing to the possible relaxation of the Penal Laws that would make it possible to admit the more prosperous and docile members of the Catholic community as members of the political nation. Leland's Catholic sponsors, who would soon become his adversaries, were hopeful that philosophical history would justify such a relaxation whereas Leland argued from history that any piecemeal interference with the social, political, and religious settlement that had been agreed for Ireland during the reigns of William and Mary would undermine the entire edifice on which the liberty and security of enlightened people, by which he meant the Protestant population, rested.

6.4 Popular Challenges to Philosophical History

It will be evident from the foregoing that Thomas Leland's *History* advanced historical enquiry into Ireland's past during the early modern centuries in several respects, not least by introducing civility into his debate with educated Catholics while using history to sustain a rigid Protestant position on the political issues of the day. Leland's endeavours, and those of his opponents, brought some disputed historical questions to a conclusion and pointed the way to the resolution of others, most notably by inviting a historical interrogation of the 1641 depositions. However, neither party to the philosophical history debate captured the imagination of Ireland's English-speaking Catholic community either at home or in exile. Instead, Hugh Reily had portrayed a very different image of Ireland's early modern past, and Mathew Carey did likewise much later. Carey, in fact, wrote dismissively of all philosophical history while representing himself as a man of the Enlightenment.

We have noted that Hugh Reily's historical arguments had been in circulation long before Leland and his adversaries had commenced their debate. Leland made reference to Reily's condemnation of the Act of Settlement to embarrass those who contended that the political rehabilitation of those Catholics who enjoyed relatively secure positions in the country would be sufficient to placate Catholic discontent. While Reily's text may have served Leland's purposes in this way it continued to offer a counter view to the opinions both of Leland himself and of the moderate Catholics with whom Leland debated, because the original text, as well as updates and expansions upon it, continued to be published regularly throughout the eighteenth century and into the early decades of the nineteenth century.

Reily had first offered his opinions in print in *Ireland's Case Briefly Stated*, which was published either in France or Belgium shortly before his death in 1695. This was republished soon thereafter under the title *The Genuine History of Ireland*, which title was retained on inside pages when it was republished as *The Impartial History of Ireland*. It was published under this title perhaps one hundred

188 IMAGINING IRELAND'S PASTS

times over the course of the eighteenth century and into the early years of nineteenth century, sometimes in expanded and updated versions.[69] The editors and authors of the expansions of the various versions did not identify themselves, but Niall Ó Ciosáin suggests that it was retitled *The Impartial History* so it could be read as a Catholic response to the stridently Protestant account of the Jacobite Williamite conflict that had been presented in George Story, *The Impartial History of the Affairs of Ireland* (Dublin, 1691).[70]

Therefore, although he himself had been dead since 1695, Reily's voice persisted on behalf of the dispossessed, or at least the Jacobite dispossessed, for more than a century thereafter. The image of Ireland's early modern past that he portrayed was very different from that fostered by those on either side to the philosophical debate, and his radical views obviously reached an altogether more extensive audience. He, as noted, had put forward the view that Catholics in Ireland could never become reconciled to their lot until the Restoration Settlement was reversed, but this is just one sample of the radical opinions advanced by Reily in a history that might best be described as a denunciation of English rule in Ireland from the onset of the Reformation to the end of the reign of King Charles II.[71]

While Reily presented himself as a voice of the dispossessed, his narrative is very different from equivalent seventeenth-century verse narratives written in Irish (discussed in Chapter 3). The fundamental difference is that Reily believed that outcomes that had had negative consequences for Ireland's Catholic population were the products of human design rather that divine intervention. For the reign of Queen Elizabeth, Reily attributed Ireland's woes to the queen herself, whom he deemed a bastard. He accused her of having secured Irish agreement for her Reformation legislation for Ireland by 'tricks and sinister ways'. She had, he contended, brought the legislation before 'a packed convention...under the notion of a parliament' in the knowledge that it would never have been sanctioned 'by the free and legal consent of the representative body of the nation' given that 'not one in 500 of the natives was then Protestant or became so during Queen Elizabeth's reign'. Even then, claimed Reily, the queen left in abeyance the powers that had been given to her to enforce the Reformation until after the Armada year of 1588. Then her government had seized upon the

---

[69] For a biographical note on Hugh Reily see that by John Cronin, *Dictionary of Irish Biography*, vol. 8, 439; I personally have tracked down editions of *The Impartial History of Ireland* (London, 1720, 1742, 1754, 1762, 1768, 1787); besides these a Dublin edition of 1833 with 'the whole revised and brought down from 1676 to the present time by a gentleman of this city'. All quotations in the present book are from the London edition of 1742.

[70] Niall Ó Ciosáin, *Print and Popular Culture in Ireland, 1750–1850* (Basingstoke, 1997), 106.

[71] Jacqueline Hill, '1641 and the Quest for Catholic Emancipation, 1691–1829', Brian Mac Cuarta, ed., *Ulster 1641: Aspects of the Rising*, 159–72; Patrick Kelly, '"A Light to the blind": the voice of the dispossessed élite in the generation after the defeat at Limerick', *Irish Historical Studies*, vol. 24 (1985), 431–62.

ENLIGHTENMENT HISTORIANS OF IRELAND AND THEIR CRITICS   189

attempted invasion of England by Spain as a pretext 'to force her pretended reformation' on the country's population.[72]

Reily, as a committed Jacobite, was more circumspect about apportioning blame for the mistreatment accorded to Irish Catholics during the reigns of the Stuart monarchs. Thus he represented King James VI and I as a monarch who had never forgotten the 'barbarous murder' of his mother in which Queen Elizabeth had connived. This, according to Reily, had made the king well disposed to giving recompense to those Irish lords who had lost their estates as a consequence of defeat in the Elizabethan wars. However, said Reily, that king had been diverted from his good intentions by 'crook-backed Cecil', who contrived a sequence of conspiracies to justify the persecution of Catholics in both England and Ireland.[73] Then, during the reign of King Charles I, Irish lords were driven to the point where they 'saw no security but in arms', first, because Wentworth set 'to enrich himself and his creatures' at the expense of Catholic landowners, and then because Sir William Parsons and Sir John Borlase, as joint governors, were 'not only rank Presbyterians but openly for the Parliament against the King'.[74] Subsequently, according to Reily, when the rebellion that had been provoked by these officials began to spill outside the confines of Ulster, the Lords Justices 'made no effort to suppress it', hoping rather to profit at the expense of Catholic landowners once the country would be again brought 'under the lash of the law'.[75] Finally, when it came to King Charles II, Reily accepted that that monarch had thought well of Irish Catholic gentlemen because of their proven loyalty to his father, and because he had become acquainted with many of them during their shared years in exile. However, he, like his grandfather before him, had, according to Reily, been diverted from his intended benevolence towards them by 'the craft and corruption of some grandees'. The result, according to Reily, was that the dispossessed Irish Catholic proprietors were abandoned and King Charles was instead 'strangely imposed upon, to reward his inveterate enemies'.[76] Then, claimed Reily, notwithstanding the favour that Charles had thus extended to 'the Cromwellians of Ireland', these had engaged upon a series of conspiracies against their king, the most serious of which was the alleged Irish Popish Plot of 1678–79 that had led on 1 July 1681 to the execution of Archbishop Oliver Plunkett in London on which Reily provided considerable detail.[77]

Reily also differed from the providential historians who had spoken for the dispossessed in the seventeenth century, by claiming that he, through his own

---

[72] Reily, *Impartial History*, 3.
[73] Reily, *Impartial History*, 5; Reily was making reference to the fact that Sir Robert Cecil, later first earl of Salisbury, had been a hunchback.
[74] Reily, *Impartial History*, 10, 14.   [75] Reily, *Impartial History*, 16.
[76] Reily, *Impartial History*, 37, 50.
[77] Reily, *Impartial History*, 74; on the context to the execution see John Gibney, *Ireland and the Popish Plot*.

190 IMAGINING IRELAND'S PASTS

endeavours, sought to arrive at 'the truth' of what had happened over two turbulent centuries through the combined study of 'authentic records and the most impartial memoirs of the time'. Of these two he considered the most reliable to be oral testimony from 'living witnesses of quality and undoubted probity', which he contrasted with the 1641 depositions that he denounced as 'the malicious, incoherent and, in some cases, morally impossible relation of others' that had been used by Temple and Archbishop King to sustain 'the many calumnies thrown' on the Irish.[78]

Having thus laid claim to scientific credentials, Reily proceeded with his narrative proper. In this, he repeated several traditional Catholic arguments including that—later shown by Leland to be untrue—which held that it was the supposed Protestant massacre of Catholics at Islandmagee in November 1641 that had set the 1641 rebellion on its bloody course. However, Reily also introduced fresh arguments concerning the conflict of the mid-seventeenth century that became fixed in the Catholic repertoire of grievances at a popular level. Among these was his contention that any murder of Protestants by Catholics that had taken place had been 'in the very beginning of the confusion' and 'committed by the unruly mob...contrary to the orders of their leaders'. This, Reily contended, contrasted with the revenge killing of Catholics that had been put into effect 'by public orders' by Protestant commanders such as Sir Charles Coote, Lord Broghill, and later by Oliver Cromwell. Then, following the example of Petty, who Reily considered 'an ingenious inquisitive person', Reily thought it 'manifest there were six times more of the Catholics massacred than of the Protestants upon that revolution'. He sustained this by suggesting that, after the initial turmoil, Protestants had either fled to England and Scotland or enjoyed the security of defensible buildings in Ireland, whereas Catholics were, for twelve years, left 'exposed in the open country to the fury of their merciless enemies' where they were 'butchered upon all occasions'.[79]

Reily's text, as John Gibney has shown, is usually referred to today because of what he had to say of the 1641 rebellion and its consequences.[80] At the time of its publication, and for the following century, it had a special importance because of the fresh reasons it gave Irish Catholics to feel aggrieved over the events in Ireland from the commencement of the reign of Queen Elizabeth to the close of that of King Charles II. During that time, according to Reily, the country had been subjected to not one but 'several revolutions', the most pernicious being that associated with the Act of Settlement, promoted during the reign of Charles II. More importantly, Reily had insisted that these revolutions lacked any moral purpose

[78] Reily, *Impartial History*, title page; preface, viii–x.
[79] Reily, *Impartial History*, 21–2; what Reily had to say of the slaughter of largely defenseless Irish by English parliamentary forces, and their Irish Protestant allies, has been shown by James Scott Wheeler to have happened at the closing stages of the conflict, James Scott Wheeler, *Cromwell in Ireland*.
[80] Gibney, *The Shadow of a Year*, 79–81.

ENLIGHTENMENT HISTORIANS OF IRELAND AND THEIR CRITICS   191

because 'religion was made a stalking horse to violence and rapine' and Irish leaders from the sixteenth century onward were left with no option but to engage in 'a necessary self defence' that exposed them to yet further confiscation.[81] His overall appraisal of England's involvement with Ireland during the entire period was that the English had never seriously contemplated converting the Irish to the Protestant faith but that their 'zealous reformers...took more care to make the land turn Protestant than the people'.[82]

Reily clearly envisioned his history as a call to action to reverse the injustices that he believed Irish Catholics had suffered over the course of the sixteenth and seventeenth centuries. As he structured it as such he would have realized that, in the aftermath of military defeat, there was no possibility of reversing the revolutions that had been perpetrated, short of James II or his heirs recovering the British Crown. Those who continued to edit and expand upon his work, and, in 1772, to translate it into the Irish language (presumably to provide material for sermons to Irish speaking congregations), must have been similarly motivated to see 'truth and justice' achieved.[83] They, for much of the time, could conceive of no means to meet this objective. However, the continuous republication of Reily's exhortations rekindled a deep sense of grievance about the past among a broad spread of Ireland's Catholic population. This meant that, for the bulk of Ireland's Catholic population, the interpretations being advanced by philosophical historians, regardless of the religion of the authors, would have had little meaning for their lives.

One who shared this view and who cited Hugh Reily's history with critical respect was Mathew Carey (1760–1839), who had come to prominence in Dublin during the late 1770s as a radical journalist who admired the American Revolutionary cause.[84] Carey would have considered himself no less enlightened than any of the philosophical historians but he alienated them, Protestant and Catholic alike, because he pursued what they had to say concerning the injustices of the past to what Carey considered their logical conclusion. This held that there could be no remedy for these injustices until the political connection linking Ireland with Britain was severed. The hostility shown by the Catholic elite to his printed advertisement in 1781 for a pamphlet he was about to publish, entitled *The Urgent Necessity of an Immediate Repeal of the Whole Penal Code against the Roman Catholics, candidly considered*, persuaded Carey that he had best seek refuge in France rather than face arrest at the behest of his co-religionists.

---

[81] Reily, *Impartial History*, 32.   [82] Reily, *Impartial History*, preface, v.

[83] Details on the translation in the biographical note by Cronin.

[84] For a biographical note on Mathew Carey see that by Johanna Archbold and Sylvie Kleinman, *Dictionary of Irish Biography*, vol. 2, 339–42; for an excellent appraisal of Carey as an Irish Catholic radical who remained loyal to his principles as a republican government was being established in the United States, Maurice Bric, 'Mathew Carey, and the "Empire of Liberty" in America', *Early American Studies*, vol. 11 (2013), 403–30.

These wished to see Carey arrested because they feared that their own case for a modest relaxation to the penal code that would benefit elite Catholics was being placed in jeopardy by Carey's brazenness.[85] After an interlude in France where he made the acquaintance of some French radicals, including the marquis de la Fayette, as well as Benjamin Franklin who was representing the American Revolutionary cause in Paris, Carey returned to Dublin where he resumed his radical journalism, this time addressing the question of parliamentary reform. His intemperate views, published this time in *The Volunteers Journal: or Irish Herald*, resulted in him spending an interval in prison as a preliminary to him facing libel charges.[86] Rather than await the outcome of a case that would have ruined him, Carey fled to Philadelphia in 1784 where, thanks to introductions from Franklin and financial support from la Fayette, he soon became a successful journalist, now writing principally about American issues.

Carey with one of his brothers became successful publishers and pamphleteers in Philadelphia, treating of such diverse matters as medical information, American literature and politics, and a Catholic version of the Bible. Ireland did not much feature in what Carey wrote during those years but, as Maurice Bric has explained, the two issues that had most exercised him in Ireland—hostility to oligarchy and freedom of the press—continued to influence his contribution to debates concerning the evolving character of society and politics in the new American republic.[87] Carey was also acquainted with the revolutionary and then counter-revolutionary turn that politics in Ireland had taken during the closing decades of the eighteenth century, because Philadelphia and its environs was already home to a sizeable Irish emigrant community (Protestant, usually Ulster Presbyterian, and Catholic) when he settled there in 1784.[88] This immigrant presence was soon augmented by a continuing flow from Ireland that included many members of the Society of United Irishmen evading arrest and, later again, some survivors of the brutal government suppression of the 1798 rebellion. These political refugees became a radicalizing force in the politics of Pennsylvania, and of the early American republic more generally, almost from the moment of their arrival.[89]

---

[85] Michael S. Carter, 'Mathew Carey; the Mind of an Enlightened Catholic (Carey in Ireland, 1760–1784)' (unpublished paper given at the McNeill Center, University of Pennsylvania, 2011), 12; Carter, to whom I owe thanks for permission to cite from this paper, here corrects the previously held view that the 'offensive' pamphlet had been advertised in 1779; the pamphlet itself is analysed in the early section of Bric, 'Mathew Carey, and the "Empire of Liberty" in America'.

[86] Bric, 'Mathew Carey, and the "Empire of Liberty" in America'.

[87] Bric, 'Mathew Carey, and the "Empire of Liberty" in America'.

[88] On the general background see Maurice Bric, *Ireland, Philadelphia and the Re-Invention of America, 1760–1800* (Dublin, 2008), esp. 120–1, 157–8, 249, 283, 294, 313.

[89] Bric, *Ireland, Philadelphia and the Re-Invention of America*; Alan Taylor, *The Civil War of 1812: American Citizens, British Subjects, Irish Rebels and Indian Allies* (New York, 2010); Martin J. Burke, 'The Poetics and Politics of Nationalist Historiography: Mathew Carey and the *Vindicae Hibernicae*', Leerssen, Van Der Weel and Westerweel, eds., *Forging in the Smithy*, 183–94.

ENLIGHTENMENT HISTORIANS OF IRELAND AND THEIR CRITICS   193

Mathew Carey was active within this community in exile, and discovered that many of the 'prejudices' against Irish Catholics that had been fostered by Protestant historians in Ireland had been 'translated from their native soil by emigrants'.[90] In order to prevent such prejudices from provoking sectarian division in the multi-denominational community that he wished to see unified around republican principles in Pennsylvania, Carey took it upon himself 'to expose a few of the multifarious errors and falsehoods' that had been perpetuated by the authors he had identified.[91] To this end he had been assembling material that would inform such a corrective, and, according to himself, in 1819 he rushed to complete a book that he entitled *Vindicae Hibernicae* because an English picaresque novel that had opened its narrative with a Protestant-inspired rendition of the 1641 rebellion in Ireland had been circulating widely in the United States. To counter what he regarded as gross misrepresentation, he concentrated his vindication of Ireland on its history during the sixteenth and seventeenth centuries.[92]

In this history Carey drew upon the work of Hugh Reily in listing the injustices that Ireland's Catholics had suffered during those centuries, and he also acknowledged his indebtedness to the publications of John Curry, 'an indefatigable writer'.[93] However, Carey was totally at odds with Reily in being opposed to all monarchies and oligarchies whether Jacobite or Hanovarian, which left him free, unlike the Jacobite Reily, to denounce the Stuart monarchs. Thus, for Carey, King James VI and I was devoured by 'the cravings of the passion for spoliation and plantations', and his son was no better. This led to chapters on subjects such as the 'wholesale spoliation in Ulster' effected by James I, and the 'projected spoliation of Connaught' envisaged by Strafford.[94] Then, following both Curry and Reily, the author detailed how 'the pretences of plots and conspiracies were constantly employed throughout the centuries' as a pretext for depriving Irish people of their lands and lives.[95]

Carey was also at one with previous Catholic authors in Ireland in challenging the depositions as a source of information on the events of 1641, and he thus denied 'the pretended bloody massacre' of defenceless Protestants by Catholics in 1641 that had been cultivated by Temple. In acknowledging that some killing of Protestants had taken place, Carey, like Reily, considered these incidents were inconsequential when compared with the number of Catholics killed by Protestants in cold blood over the entire eleven years of disturbance. On this, he pronounced, in a passage that would have resonated with his American audience, 'that the

---

[90] Mathew Carey, *Vindicae Hibernicae or Ireland Vindicated* (Philadelphia, 1819), Preface, x–xi.
[91] The phrase comes from the subtitle to Carey, *Vindicae Hibernicae*.
[92] Burke, 'The Poetics and Politics of Nationalist Historiography'; Gibney, *The Shadow of a Year*, 96–7.
[93] Carey, *Vindicae Hibernicae*, preface, xxv.
[94] Carey, *Vindicae Hibernicae*, 188; and titles of Chapters 7 and 9 respectively.
[95] Carey, *Vindicae Hibernicae*, 302.

massacres perpetrated on the Irish by St Leger, Monro, Tichborne, Hamilton, Greville, Ireton and Cromwell were as savage, as ferocious, as brutal, and as bloody as the horrible feats of Cortes or Pizarro, Atilla or Ghengis Khan'.[96]

Carey thus, like Temple, Voltaire, and Hume, universalized what had occurred in Ireland in 1641 but his point of comparison was completely different from theirs. Where they had expounded on the atrocities supposedly committed by Catholics in Ulster, he elaborated on the killing of Catholics by Protestants, especially during the Cromwellian years. On 1641 itself, Carey broke new ground by concentrating on what allegedly had happened in Dublin rather than on events in Ulster, and in representing the revelation by Owen O'Connolly of a Catholic plot to seize Dublin Castle as 'a legend'.[97] Carey's first contention was that any testimony provided by O'Connolly should have been considered dubious because he was a servant of, and owed his primary allegiance to, Sir John Clotworthy, 'one of the most envenomed enemies of the Roman Catholics'. On this basis, Carey charged that O'Connolly had been used by Clotworthy and the Dublin officials to conjure up 'a sham plot' that would justify the further expropriation of lands held by Irish lords.[98] Then, to substantiate this claim, Carey interrogated the account given by O'Connolly under oath of his journey from Ulster to Dublin, and he exposed it as implausible if not impossible.[99] Therefore, for Carey, the arrest, examination, and supposed confessions made by those Ulster lords whom O'Connolly had chosen to be his drinking partners in Dublin on the night of 22 October 1641 had all been contrived by Clotworthy and the Dublin authorities to advance their objectives.[100] This, Carey proclaimed, meant that 'O'Connolly's pretended discovery of a conspiracy was one unvaried strain of perjury'.[101]

Mathew Carey followed this by arguing that the history of Ireland for the entire early modern period concerned the relentless humiliation, expropriation, and slaughter of Irish Catholics by Protestant officials and settlers with the connivance of, or active support from, authorities in England. This account, as noted, was designed primarily to redeem the reputation of Irish Catholics from the slurs that had been cast upon them by their Protestant adversaries in Ireland and that were being relayed to Protestants in the United States. This was being done not only in the offending picaresque novel but also in the expanded editions of Foxe's *Book of Martyrs* being circulated in Protestant communities in the United States that

---

[96] Carey, *Vindicae Hibernicae*, preface, xiv.
[97] Carey, *Vindicae Hibernicae*, 324.   [98] Carey, *Vindicae Hibernicae*, 333.
[99] Carey, *Vindicae Hibernicae*, 324–33.
[100] Carey, *Vindicae Hibernicae*, 324; the family background of O'Connolly and his previous associations with his foster brother Hugh Oge MacMahon, as well as with Clotworthy, have been discussed in Andrew Robinson, 'Owen Connolly, Hugh Og Mac Mahon and the 1641 rebellion in Clogher', Eamon Darcy, Annaleigh Margey, and Elaine Murphy, eds., *The 1641 Depositions and the Irish Rebellion* (London, 2012), 7–20.
[101] Carey, *Vindicae Hibernicae*, preface, xiv.

ENLIGHTENMENT HISTORIANS OF IRELAND AND THEIR CRITICS 195

identified the alleged victims of the 1641 rebellion in Ireland as Protestant martyrs and detailed their alleged sufferings.[102]

Carey may have written his *Vindicae Hibernicae* primarily with an American audience in mind, but he also wanted to see it circulate in Ireland. However, as John Gibney has explained, the book failed to win any significant sponsorship in Ireland, since it was shunned by Ireland's Catholic leaders because it had been published by a radical who had already caused them problems in their dealings with the government before he had fled the country in 1784, and who had since become known in the United States as a Francophile and an extreme opponent of Britain. Thus, while Catholic leaders in Ireland, who now included bishops, still complained of the injustices from which their ancestors had suffered, they did so in the context of detailing the persistent loyalty of these ancestors to the British monarchy other than when they had been forced to defend themselves from government agents who later proved themselves unfaithful to the Crown. Such pleading had earned Catholics relief from the more onerous of Penal Laws of which authors such as John Curry, Sylvester O'Halloran, and Charles O'Conor had complained. The outstanding grievance of Ireland's Catholic leaders was that they had been denied the full emancipation of Catholics—by which they meant the right to contest elections to parliament—that they had expected would be conceded to them once the Act of Union came into force in 1801. However, even in the face of such disappointment, Catholic leaders remained hopeful that emancipation would still be achieved through negotiations. This meant that the leaders of Ireland's Catholic elite could not countenance the idea of Mathew Carey that Catholics would become fully emancipated only when they cast aside their deference to oligarchy—including oligarchy within the Catholic Church— and proved that they, and the church to which they belonged, could become fit members of a republic.[103]

In so far as Catholic elite leaders of the time welcomed any history of Ireland that voiced opinions that were more demanding than what Curry and O'Halloran had written in the previous century, it was the revised and updated rendition of Reily's *Impartial History* that was published by a 'gentleman of Dublin' in 1833. This was published to celebrate the winning by 'Mr O'Connell' in 1829 of the Catholic emancipation they had so long pursued, and to offer assurance that with this new freedom Catholics would continue as loyal subjects of the British monarchy.[104]

Mathew Carey would obviously have considered the shunning of his book by the Catholic oligarchy in Ireland not only as a confirmation of their previous

---

[102] I owe this point to conversations with Martin J. Burke.
[103] For a discussion of Carey's understanding of how Catholics might be 'emancipated' into a republican polity, Bric, 'Mathew Carey, and the "Empire of Liberty" in America'.
[104] Hugh Reily, *The Impartial History of Ireland* (Dublin, 1833), 137.

196 IMAGINING IRELAND'S PASTS

rejection of him but also a rejection by them of the enlightened principles that he had long upheld. However, according to Carey, it was not only those historians who wrote on behalf of Ireland's Catholic elite but also those who had written what they had described as philosophical history who, in Carey's opinion, had failed to proclaim the fundamental truth that true reform could be achieved in Ireland, as it had been in the former British colonies in North America, only by severing the political connection with Britain. Reason had led him to this conclusion as early as 1781, and his subsequent experience in the early American republic, including his association with Franklin, Jefferson, and Washington confirmed him in his view. Therefore, when it came to writing Ireland's history in his *Vindicae Hibernicae* of 1819, he saw no need to conjure up images of an antique past in which Irish people might take pride. For him there was ample evidence from the early modern centuries that Irish Catholics had always comported themselves as reasonable people until they had been denied justice and exposed to ruthless exploitation by Protestant and British oppressors. Therefore, in the light of what he had read by those who represented themselves as authorities on Ireland's history, Carey added the names of Hume and Leland to those of Temple, Borlase, Carte, Warner, and others who had rendered 'The History of Ireland...almost one solid mass of falsehood and imposture, erected particularly during the seventeenth century, on the basis of fraud and perjury'.[105]

6.5 Conclusion

It is unsurprising that Catholics in Ireland who had endured the worst of the cataclysm that had beset their ancestors over the course of the seventeenth century should have looked to history to bolster their claims for a relaxation of the legislation that had excluded them from political life and hindered them in economic and professional affairs. They were able to make a plausible case for fairer treatment by pointing to those critical occasions in the past when their ancestors had professed allegiance to the Crown and had acted in accordance with their words. Having thus, as they saw it, put the record straight and proven in a scientific manner that their progenitors had been punished rather that rewarded for their loyalty, they became confident that philosophical historians would be able to support their case by showing that the discrimination which Catholics had been forced to endure on grounds of religion was unreasonable as well as unjust, and was therefore contrary to the spirit of the Enlightenment.

This chapter has shown how the hopes and expectations of such people were frustrated by two principal factors. The first was that many Enlightenment figures,

---

[105] Carey, *Vindicae Hibernicae*, preface, xiii.

ENLIGHTENMENT HISTORIANS OF IRELAND AND THEIR CRITICS 197

both in France and within the jurisdictions of British monarchy, were not convinced by the arguments being put forward by Ireland's Catholics, especially since many of their ancestors, in the sixteenth and seventeenth centuries, were known to have been closely linked to the papacy, an institution that, in most enlightened circles, was considered an opponent of reason and a source of tyranny. We noted how these misgivings were stated most graphically by David Hume in his *History of England*, especially where Hume, inspired by what John Temple had written of the 1641 rebellion in Ireland, represented that episode as a re-enactment of what had occurred in France on St Bartholomew's Day in 1572. It was explained how Hume's intervention placed Catholic exponents of a philosophical history for Ireland on the defensive.

It was further noted that the arguments being advanced from history to justify a relaxation of the Penal Laws was not helped by the fact that those who wrote on behalf of the dispossessed Catholics who had been forced into exile continued to circulate a version of Ireland's history in English that represented the sixteenth and seventeenth century as an era of unremitting persecution and argued that the injustices perpetrated by the state would be remedied only when the descendants of those who had been treated unjustly were restored to their estates at the expense of those who had been rewarded undeservedly. The fact that these propositions, published initially from the Continent by a Jacobite exile, were republished regularly, and expanded upon by anonymous editors for more than a century, undermined the arguments of the Catholic leaders within Ireland, and the liberal Protestants who sympathized with them, that a modest relaxation of the Penal Laws was all that was required to produce communal harmony.

It was shown in the chapter how the persisted articulation of such views not only compromised the case being made by elite Catholics for the redress of grievance through gradual reform but also alarmed those liberal Protestants who had been ready to assist them in advancing their claim through history for reform in the present. The result of this, as we saw, was that the one sponsored philosophical history written by Thomas Leland actually reached a conclusion from history that there was no case for relaxing any Penal Laws. Finally, it was shown that the credibility of those Catholics who favoured a gradualist approach to reform was further discredited when Mathew Carey, another exile, but one who had made his home in revolutionary America rather than in Catholic Europe, endorsed, and added to, the popularly held view of the persecutions and injustices that Catholics in Ireland had suffered in the sixteenth and seventeenth centuries. Carey had argued even before he left Ireland in 1784 that a severance of the political connection with Britain was a prerequisite for reform in Ireland. His case became more compelling in 1819 when he argued from reason that a remedy for Ireland's grievances could be found only by following the example of the republic of the United States by severing its connection with Britain. Only such, he believed, would enable people of talent to displace those with inherited wealth and position as leaders of society just as had happened in the United States after they had achieved independence. Carey believed that if this course were followed in Ireland, as some revolutionary leaders had attempted in 1798, those who supported it would reconstitute themselves as a new nation that would include people of all denominations and of all social backgrounds. Carey was able to speak with confidence in 1819 because he had witnessed such becoming a reality among the settler population of Pennsylvania that included many Irish, both Protestants and Catholics. Moreover, Carey took pride in the role he had played in creating this new polity where he had achieved wealth and social position of which he could only have dreamt had he remained at home.

7
The Vernacular Alternatives Composed during the Age of Revolutions

7.1 Introduction

Those authors, with the exception of Mathew Carey, whose histories we have been considering in Chapters 5 and 6, were primarily concerned with the fortunes of social elites in Ireland over the course of two turbulent centuries. These seemed unaware of, or indifferent to, more popular historical narratives of Ireland's past that were circulating within both Protestant and Catholic communities. The reality was that vernacular interpretations of Ireland's history for the early modern centuries were proving resilient. In effect, competing popular narratives were being continuously composed by authors for the benefit of the Protestant and Catholic communities to which their respective authors belonged. This chapter will show that such vernacular histories gained fresh vigour towards the close of the eighteenth century when the possibility of extending the political and social rights of some Catholics gave rise to controversy. Popular interest and commentary was aroused further when what seemed an ongoing process of gradually restoring political rights to Catholics of social consequence was brought to a sudden halt in 1795. Public interest was intensified once the United Irishmen began to contemplate a rebellion that actually erupted 1798.[1] This insurrection was suppressed brutally by the state, supported by the overwhelmingly Protestant yeomanry, and the largely Catholic militia. This and the subsequent enactment of an Act of Union that came into force in 1801 lent a new urgency to the composition of vernacular versions of the past. These were designed to assure the respective Catholic and Protestant audiences to whom they were addressed that the aspirations of their progenitors were not being abandoned. Authors also encouraged their popular audiences to strengthen the resolve of their social betters to live up to the standards of their antecedents and uphold the interest of their communities.

A study of some of these compositions will show that many authors repeated the messages that had been conveyed by those who had preceded them in their

---

[1] For a summary of the political background, Thomas Bartlett, 'Ireland during the Revolutionary and Napoleonic Wars, 1791–1815', James Kelly, ed., *The Cambridge History of Ireland*, vol. 3, *1730–1880* (Cambridge, 2018), 74–101.

Imagining Ireland's Pasts: Early Modern Ireland through the Centuries. Nicholas Canny, Oxford University Press (2021).
© Nicholas Canny. DOI: 10.1093/oso/9780198808961.003.0007

200   IMAGINING IRELAND'S PASTS

respective vernacular traditions. It will also be shown that they displayed some knowledge of, and occasionally borrowed from, printed histories. An examination of the relevant texts will reveal also that interaction between vernacular and elite history was not all one way, and that language difference was not necessarily a barrier to mutual comprehension, if it ever had been.

7.2 Catholic Vernacular Histories of Ireland

The most frequently cited Irish language poetry of the eighteenth century is that known popularly as *Aisling*, or vision, poetry where frequently a personified Ireland, usually in the guise of a beautiful if bedraggled woman, visited the poet in a dream. In this, she bewailed her present pitiful condition before leaving the author with the assurance that both their difficulties would be resolved once the exiled Catholic nobility returned, usually with military aid, from France or Spain.[2]

Such prophetic verse, with its obvious Jacobite intonations, continued to be composed into the nineteenth century, even if their messages were never as universally optimistic as suggested. Even when they led to no hopeful conclusion, such compositions were not as providential as the Gaelic verse of the seventeenth century, but they helped raise the political consciousness of Ireland's Catholics at the lower social levels by reminding them both of how downtrodden they had become, and that redemption was nigh even if this was to involve no more than a change of proprietors.[3] However, some authors of Irish political verse in the eighteenth century also took account of present realities and assessed what fresh possibilities to improve their circumstances were being presented by the changing course of events. Thus, as Vincent Morley has shown, some Irish-language poets were quick to take notice of the outbreak of the Revolutionary War in Colonial British America in 1776. These were aware that some leading Irish Protestants were taking advantage of that distant conflict to secure political progress for themselves by employing the Protestant Volunteer force they had mobilized, ostensibly to defend the country in the event of French invasion, to extract constitutional concessions from the government concerning the independence of the Irish parliament. However, while all authors of the vernacular verse that has been examined by Morley recognized that the Protestant Volunteers were pursuing greater constitutional independence for Ireland, he shows how some authors calculated that this would bring no benefit to the bulk of the population since the Irish Volunteers, like the American Revolutionaries, were committed

---

[2] This generalization derives from individual poems such as *Cáit Ní Dhuibhir* which school children of my generation in Ireland learned to sing as well as to recite; for one version of this particular poem, *Nua-Dhunaire*, vol. 3, ed., Tomás Ó Concheanainn (Dublin, 1978), 4–5.

[3] The complexity and diversity of the genre is discussed in Breandán Ó Buachalla, *Aisling Ghéar*, 449–662; on seventeenth-century providential verse see Chapter 4.

Protestants, and a reformed Irish parliament would remain an exclusively Protestant body. Thus, as Morley has phrased it, some concluded that the struggle being pursued in America was 'a civil war among the traditional enemies of Ireland'.[4] On the other hand, Irish-language poets of the following decade showed themselves ready to recognize revolutionaries in France (including Napoleon Bonaparte) as potential allies in their quest for liberation. This occurred even though Catholic bishops, who would have considered themselves the spiritual guides for such poets, denounced the French Revolution with loathing, especially because of its assault on the church in France, including on the Irish colleges in which many of Ireland's church leaders had been trained. The tension between poets and their church was resolved once the poets saluted Daniel O'Connell as the person who would lead Irish Catholics from thraldom in its several dimensions.[5]

While almost all Irish-language scholars were concerned about future redemption, their expectations were based on past experience. Thus Vincent Morley has shown how eighteenth-century copyists of seventeenth-century manuscripts kept their audiences acquainted with the verse narratives of Ireland's history, especially *Tuireamh na hÉireann* (discussed in Chapter 4) that had been circulated continuously in manuscript copy from the moment of its initial composition.[6] Morley has also explained how some eighteenth-century scholars, notably Aodh Buí Mac Cruitín (*c.*1680–1755), augmented and updated the narrative in that text to take account of the fresh humiliations and continuing threats that Catholics were experiencing.[7] Authors persisted into the early years of the nineteenth century with their efforts to heighten the sense of grievance that they believed their audience should feel over the injustices suffered by earlier generations of Catholics.

This sense of injustice that was felt by those at the bottom tiers of Irish rural society was articulated memorably in the surviving verses of Antaine Raifteraí (1799–1835), a fiddler, versifier, and singer, who eked out an itinerant existence in his native County Mayo and in County Galway during the early decades of the nineteenth century. These give us some sense of how the narrative of Ireland's history expounded by the verse histories of the seventeenth century had become part of popular memory within the community of the Catholic poor and offered them some explanations for their current miserable plight. The most historical of Raifteraí's surviving verse compositions is *Seanchas na Sceithe* [the Narrative of the Bush] where his rendition of Irish history, and indeed world history, was so

---

[4] Vincent Morley, *Irish Opinion and the American Revolution, 1760–1783* (Cambridge, 2002), esp. 183–6; on the politics of the Volunteer movement see James Kelly, 'The Politics of the Protestant Ascendancy, 1730–1790', James Kelly, ed., *The Cambridge History of Ireland*, vol. 3, *1730–1880*, 48–73.

[5] Breandán Ó Buachalla, *Aisling Ghéar*, esp. 648; Vincent Morley, *The Popular Mind in Eighteenth-Century Ireland*, 265–9.

[6] Morley, *Ó Chéitinn go Raiftearaí*; for *Tuireamh na hÉireann* see O'Rahilly, ed., *Five Seventeenth-Century Political Poems*, 50–82.

[7] Morley, *An Crann os Coil*.

202 IMAGINING IRELAND'S PASTS

obviously derived from the verse narratives of the seventeenth century that some themes, vocabulary, and even phrases used in the seventeenth-century poems, notably in *Tuireamh na hÉireann*, reappear in his compositions.[8] Given that Raifteraí had been blind from the age of five he could have appropriated these verse histories only when hearing them recited by others, but this did not prevent him from donning a scholarly pose and citing Geoffrey Keating (Dochtúir Céitinn) as his authority on Ireland's early history.

The core element of Raifteraí's narrative was that Ireland's tribulations could be traced back to the moment when Luther had turned his back on the Pope and the Blessed Sacrament. Raifteraí identified King Henry VIII and Queen Elizabeth as the instruments in Ireland of this apostate, and he accused Elizabeth of having brought an end to what he called an *Eaglais Ghaelach* [the Irish/Gaelic church]. He associated King James, and later Strafford, with the measurement of land, including even mountains and bogs, by chain, and he considered their endeavours as a preliminary to the comprehensive plantation promoted by Cromwell and the hordes that accompanied him to Ireland. His followers, according to Raifteraí, assigned broad acres to 'Cromwellians' and banished the illustrious Irish nobility [*lucht cóistí agus eachtraí*, people of coaches and deeds] to the bogs and mountains. The only person, according to Raifteraí, who might have halted this calamity was Owen Roe O'Neill, and he lamented that his premature death cancelled the possibility of preserving anything that Raifteraí held dear. The poet also looked favourably on the military accomplishments of Patrick Sarsfield, but he cursed King James II [*Séamas an chaca*, James the turd] who, by marrying his daughter to William of Orange, had not only brought destruction on himself but had unleashed a sequence of events that had resulted in the Irish being left with no choice but to become foreign, and foreigners being made Irish [*Gaelach Gallda agus Gallda Gaelach*]. This outcome left Raifteraí with the sole consolation that the power of God was greater than that of the Cromwellians and that redemption had been assured by St John in the Book of Revelation.[9]

Raifteraí's rendition of the past can be regarded as classic vernacular history since it was communicated primarily to a popular audience through recitation and singing, and because it conveyed some impression of how authors perceived that the population at large, and not just elites, had been affected by the turn of events in the preceding centuries. Raifteraí, like the Catholic authors who had written of Ireland's history in English prose, expressed regret that Catholic proprietors had been forced to give way to Cromwellians, but his reference to the deprived as *lucht cóistí agus eachtraí* [people of coaches and deeds] conveys some

---

[8] Nollaig Ó Muraíle, 'Mise Raiftearaí an Stairí?', John Cunningham and Niall Ó Ciosáin, eds., *Culture and Society in Ireland since 1750; Essays in honour of Gearóid Ó Tuathaigh* (Dublin, 2015), 97–110, esp. 99.

[9] *Raifteraí: Amhráin agus Dánta*, ed., Ciarán Ó Coigligh (Dublin, 1987), 137–48.

THE VERNACULAR ALTERNATIVES   203

sense of Raifteraí's appreciation of the social gulf that separated him from any conceivable landowner, Protestant or Catholic. This implies that he, unlike Hugh Reily and his editors, was not convinced that a simple re-transfer of property from planter to native would do anything to improve his condition or that of the rural poor he addressed.[10] And, unlike the Catholic authors of prose histories, Raifteraí evinced no respect for any British monarch or ruler, Stuart, Cromwellian, or Hanoverian. Moreover, the concern expressed by Raifteraí, like that articulated by the seventeenth-century Irish-language poets, was that all aspects of life in Ireland, and not just land ownership, had been polluted by people of British Protestant descent whom he considered alien to the country. Thus in one memorable passage, which probably reflected his own encounters with Protestant proselytizers who were an active presence in the west of Ireland at the time he was writing, Raifteraí mocked how, from the outset of the Reformation, different groups had picked individual meanings from the core of the Irish-language Bible [as lár an Bhíobla Ghaelaigh]. The consequence, according to Raifteraí, was that what had started as a coherent reform movement had splintered into a prolif-eration of sects, among which he named Anabaptists, Seekers, Quakers, Protestants, Swadlers, and Presbyterians. All of these subdivisions, according to Raifteraí, had been in existence before the word Cromwellian [san am sin ní raibh caint ar Chromwellians] had been coined as a generic description for all who belonged to the contrary faith. This splintering had occurred also, he claimed, before Cromwell—an fear a thóg Éire [the man who took Ireland]—had arrived in the country.[11] Even when we allow for anachronism and the liberties that Raifteraí took with historical sequence, the sectarian animosity to which he gave voice was consistent with that of the seventeenth-century poems from which he drew his inspiration. So also was his concluding prayer to the Virgin seeking to have the world that he knew turned upside down.[12]

While Raifteraí's Seanchas na Sceithe is an excellent example of Catholic vernacular history, it was not solely the product of a remembered past that had been transmitted orally from generation to generation. Essentially, those who continued to make copies of seventeenth-century verse that had been stored in manuscript form always assisted memory. Then also, as previously noted, eighteenth-century poets sometimes augmented and revised the seventeenth-century renditions of Ireland's past which, in turn, were preserved in manuscript.[13]

---

[10] On Reily see Chapter 6.

[11] Raifteraí, ed., Ó Coigligh, 146 lines 325–8; Irish language Bibles were being used by Protestant missionaries in the west of Ireland at the time Raifteraí was writing; such had not been available in the sixteenth century.

[12] In his prayer to Mary, Raifteraí, like many vernacular poets of the seventeenth century, drew analogies with card games. However, his request to the Virgin that she permit the diamond to trump the spade strikes me as incongruously profane; Ó Raifteraí, ed., Coigligh, ed., 146, lines 401–2.

[13] On the manuscript transmission and translation into English of Tuireamh na hÉireann, O'Rahilly, ed., Five Seventeenth-Century Political Poems, 50–9.

204 IMAGINING IRELAND'S PASTS

The storage, occasional adaptation, and transmission of this body of knowledge owed something also to print culture because it is likely that the seventeenth-century priests who were authors of some of the better-known Irish-language verse histories of Ireland drew upon the prose histories of Ireland that had been published in Latin in Catholic Europe, including that of Philip O'Sullivan Beare.[14] Thus the radical edge to the Irish-language vernacular histories of Ireland of each succeeding century can be attributed in part to seventeenth-century Continental influence. The edge had in one sense become more radical than that in any seventeenth-century composition because authors now attributed their sufferings more to human agency, and were less resigned to conceding that their existing lowly position was the consequence of providential punishment for the past transgressions of their ancestors.

The radicalization of Catholic vernacular history through Continental association took a new turn in the eighteenth century when a history of Ireland by the Abbé James Mac Geoghegan was published in French between 1758 and 1763. Mac Geoghegan was himself an émigré who had served for a time as chaplain to the Irish regiments in the royal army of France and his three-volume compilation, as its title suggests, dealt with the history of Ireland from prehistoric times to the author's own generation.[15] One of Mac Geoghegan's principal concerns (as with his seventeenth-century predecessors) was to refute the depiction that had been given by Gerald of Wales of the social condition of the Irish in the twelfth century because this, in his experience, continued to blacken the reputation of Irish people on the Continent. Readers there, he claimed, were still acquainted with the denigration of the Irish by Gerald of Wales through a 1602 Frankfurt edition of his work that William Camden had sponsored.

After he had challenged everything negative that Gerald of Wales had had to say of Irish culture, Mac Geoghegan looked closely at what had transpired in Ireland during the sixteenth and seventeenth centuries as a means of explaining why so many Irish nobles and soldiers had been forced to abandon their country and make careers in Continental armies. This made it possible for him to conclude his history with a boastful account of the achievements of the more prominent of these soldier-exiles, especially those who had served the French monarch. These priorities explain why Mac Geoghegan's history was primarily a history of Ireland during the early modern centuries, as he devoted five hundred of the eight hundred pages of printed text to Ireland's history between 1535 and 1691, followed by a glorification of the service of Irish soldiers in Continental warfare, especially in the French royal army, after they had fled Ireland following the defeat of the Jacobite cause in 1691.

[14] On O'Sullivan Beare see Chapter 2.
[15] Abbé [James] Mac Geoghegan, *Histoire d'Irlande Ancienne et Moderne* (3 vols., vol. 1, Paris, 1758, vol. 2, Paris, 1762, vol. 3, Amsterdam, 1763).

THE VERNACULAR ALTERNATIVES   205

Given his military interest, Mac Geoghegan was particularly concerned to identify Irish Catholic leaders who had distinguished themselves in war, whether at home or abroad. This, for the sixteenth century, meant rehabilitating the reputation of Hugh O'Neill, earl of Tyrone, who had always been depicted as a formidable opponent in narratives by English or Protestant authors. He was considered militarily capable by such authors because they could show that he was a person of their own creation who had served his military apprenticeship with English troops before he perversely turned against his queen. Such renditions had given Irish language authors all the more reason to downplay O'Neill's role in the Nine Years War, and, as Mícheál Mac Craith has explained, to give principal credit to O'Neill's associate and brother-in-law, Red Hugh O'Donnell, for mobilizing opposition to the government of Queen Elizabeth.[16] Mac Geoghegan corrected this narrative and restored the reputation of Hugh O'Neill by linking the details on his military endeavours that had been provided both by the sympathetic O'Sullivan Beare and the hostile Thomas Gainsford, with the testimonial to O'Neill's religious motivation that had been offered in 1598 to Pope Clement VIII by Peter Lombard, in a letter entitled *De Regno Hiberniae*. Mac Geoghegan had got to know of this letter from a surviving copy of a corrupt printed edition that had been published by the Franciscans in Louvain in 1632. This copy was rare because most of the print run had been destroyed by British agents as they rolled off the press because of the concern in 1632 that a previously unpublished letter, written as long ago as 1598, should disturb the existing political order.[17] On the authority of this rare surviving copy of the printed text, Mac Geoghegan concluded that Ireland's population, and particularly the population of Ulster, were *gens flecti nescia* [a people that will not bend] and, among Ulster leaders, Mac Geoghegan isolated Hugh O'Neill in language that one would associate more with Revolutionary France than the *ancien régime*, as *'un bon citoyen'* who had promoted *'la nation'*.[18]

This rehabilitation in print of the reputation of one Irish hero is significant for our discussion of the connections between historical narratives communicated in print and those expressed in Irish verse because Mac Geoghegan had no sooner praised the military achievements of Hugh O'Neill than this theme was taken up in praise poems in Irish. Then, as Vincent Morley has demonstrated, the interconnection between manuscript and print cultures assumed a new aspect when these Irish language poems depicting Hugh O'Neill as a hero for Ireland

---

[16] Mícheál Mac Craith, 'Creideamh agus Athartha', in Máirín Ní Dhonnachdha, ed., *Nua Léamha* (Dublin, 1996), 7–19.

[17] Peter Lombard, *De Regno Hiberniae, sanctorum insula, commentarius* (Louvain, 1632); on the confiscation of the Louvain imprint see the introduction by P.F. Moran to Peter Lombard, *De Regno Hiberniae, insulsa sanctorum, commentaries*, ed., P.F. Moran (Dublin, 1868).

[18] Mac Geoghegan, *Histoire d'Irlande*, vol. 3, 474–5.

and for Catholicism were translated into English and printed in that form in the *Irish Magazine* for the benefit of Ireland's English-reading Catholic public.[19]

The work of Morley and others has not only explained how oral culture, manuscript culture, and print culture interacted with each other in Ireland but also how messages that were conveyed in different languages—Latin, Irish, French, and English—fed off each other in the making of both vernacular histories and printed histories. However, Niall Ó Ciosáin has demonstrated that the simple act of translation did not necessarily result in a text making the leap from one culture to another, as he points out that a manuscript translation into Irish of Hugh Reily's *Impartial History*, which had been available since 1772, made no apparent impact on Catholic oral culture. It fell on deaf ears, or blind eyes, presumably because Reily's text had been concerned almost exclusively with the fate of Catholic landowners when the audiences being addressed in vernacular verse of the late eighteenth century, as we saw with Raifteraí, was concerned with the welfare of the wider Catholic community.[20]

In this respect even the anonymous Dublin editor of the expanded 1833 edition of Reily's text seems to have recognized that the original text appealed to too narrow an audience since, in summarizing its contents, he made the *Impartial History* seem more radical than the original had been by stating that Reily had detailed 'the tyranny of Henry, the cruelty of Elizabeth, the infamy of Edward's deputies, the supineness of Charles I, the ingratitude of Charles II [and] the butcheries of the ruffian Cromwell'. This summation made Reily's narrative appear disrespectful of all English rulers whereas in fact, Reily, as a Jacobite, had proceeded cautiously in his discussion of the three Stuart kings who had reigned in Ireland 1603–76. However, the 'gentleman of Dublin' who edited and augmented the 1833 edition of the *Impartial History* and brought the story forward to 1829, upheld the caution of Reily when he asserted that 'the Catholics of Ireland during this period were not only loyal, but as Plowden and other English historians say, were too subservient to their tyrannical oppressors', by whom he meant Cromwell and his associates and those, of later generations, who were guided by the views and actions of Cromwell. Here, our Dublin gentleman of 1833, like Reily himself in 1691, considered the execution of Archbishop Oliver Plunket in 1681, to which Reily had devoted considerable attention, including a woodcut, as the most reprehensible of the many misdeeds committed of the entire early modern period. This enabled our anonymous editor of 1833 to return to Reily's Jacobite refrain, and to praise King James II from whom 'the people of Ireland had more substantial justice in his short reign than during that of his successors for one hundred years afterwards'. This justified this editor of Reily in maligning 'some men who call themselves friends to popular liberty' but who had

---

[19] Morley, *Ó Chéitinn go Raiftearaí*, 223–68.
[20] Ó Ciosáin, *Print and Popular Culture*, 104–5.

cast aspersions on 'the character of James, in order exalt the reputation of the usurper William' [of Orange].[21]

The 1833 author of the extension to Reily's *Impartial History* not only lamented the 'cruelties that had been perpetrated in Ireland' during the seventeenth century but also the recent British historians and their Irish Protestant counterparts who had tried to gloss over them. Here, he listed Clarendon, Bishop Burnett, and Archbishop King, all of whom he described as recent transmitters of the denigrations of the Irish that had been communicated by Gerald of Wales, Hanmer, Campion, Spenser, and Camden. The concern of all these, he proclaimed, had been to 'misrepresent Ireland and the character of her people'.[22] At the same time he made much of the loyalty of Catholics to the Crown even in the face of provocation. Thus, while our author regretted 'the slow decay of everything Irish' during the era of the Penal Laws, he suggested that Ireland's miseries had come to an end when 'Mr O'Connell arose', and attempted to 'unite all classes' over the issue of Catholic Emancipation.[23]

The 'gentleman of Dublin', who edited what Reily had written and added his own addendum that brought the narrative forward from the end of the reign of Charles II, where Reily had left off, to Catholic Emancipation in 1829, was probably correct in thinking that 'all classes' of the Catholic population rejoiced at the success of O'Connell in winning a right for Catholics to sit in the Westminster parliament. However, our author made no reference to any material benefit that had accrued to the majority of Ireland's Catholic population from O'Connell's achievement, and the history that he wrote made it clear than the issue of social amelioration had never been on the agenda. The first half of his publication, still called the *Impartial History*, reproduced Reily's original publication in which the overarching message had been that a reversal of the Cromwellian and Williamite settlements was a prerequisite to rectifying the many injustices from which Irish people had suffered during the early modern centuries. Then, having communicated this message faithfully, our author identified the exclusion of Catholics from parliament after 1691 as the ultimate injustice that Catholics had suffered over the entire time because this had given 'ascendancy' to the followers of King William, who had then enacted the Penal Laws, thus reducing 'Ireland to a state of vassalage'.[24] This author's views accorded with those of Charles O'Conor, John Curry, and Thomas Wyse,[25] all members of the Catholic Association (later the Catholic Committee), to whom he made admiring reference. He, like these,

---

[21] Hugh Reily, *The Impartial History of Ireland* (Dublin, 1833), 77, 81, 91; on the execution of Archbishop Plunket see Chapter 6.

[22] Reily, *The Impartial History*, 1833 edition, 93–4.

[23] Reily, *The Impartial History*, 1833 edition, 136–7.

[24] Reily, *The Impartial History*, 1833 edition, 99.

[25] For a biographical note on Thomas Wyse (1701?–70) see that by C.J. Woods, *Dictionary of Irish Biography*, vol. 9, 1070–1.

rehearsed grievances from the past only to the extent that this was necessary to persuade the government of the day to concede to Catholics the civil rights to which their ownership of property entitled them. To this end, the 1833 editor of the *Impartial History* alluded to the consistent loyalty of Catholics during the entire period 1676–1829. Then, pronouncing that the insurrection of 1798 was 'far from being a Catholic Rebellion', he expressed himself satisfied that what had been designed as 'the healing measure of the Union' might have produced the harmony that had been intended by its initial proposers had it not been subverted by 'the Union plot' to ensure that the Orange interest would remain dominant in the country.[26] Given his conviction that Ireland's inherited problems could be remedied by constitutional adjustment, this 'gentleman' of Dublin, in sharp contrast to the authors of Irish-language verse, wrote approvingly of the Volunteers and agreed with their proposition that 'the dispute with America...tended much to invigorate the drooping spirits of Irishmen, and the situation of Ireland was so analogous to that of America at the time, that it created mutual feeling and sympathy.'[27]

What has been said suggests that different shades of opinion are discernible in what Catholic authors of the late eighteenth century and the early nineteenth century had to say about Ireland's early modern past depending on which Irish Catholic audience they were addressing and who, besides this audience, they wanted to impress. They were agreed that British rulers, supported by their agents in Ireland, had, in the name of religion, acted tyrannically towards the Irish people, by which designation all authors meant Irish Catholics. Proceeding from that common assumption, the authors of Catholic vernacular histories provided details on the sufferings of their ancestors in graphic detail, even to the extent of using their narrations to encourage their audiences to seek vengeance for past persecutions and to achieve some improvement in their material and social circumstances. On the other hand, those authors who hoped to secure some incremental improvement in the condition of those Catholics who had retained a moderately secure position in society, and on whose behalf they were writing, tended to be measured in their citation of grievances from the past. Instead they used them judiciously to remind the authorities in Britain of their moral obligation to restore civil rights to members of the Catholic elite who had survived the cataclysm of the sixteenth and seventeenth centuries and had always been loyal to the Crown.

These differing views on Ireland's history in the early modern centuries and the use to which grievances from the past might be put to alleviate the position of some Catholics in the present were sufficiently reconciled by Daniel O'Connell to justify the claim of the 'gentleman' of Dublin that O'Connell had united all classes

---

[26] Reily, *The Impartial History*, 1833 edition, 125, 126, 134–5.
[27] Reily, *The Impartial History*, 1833 edition, 129.

THE VERNACULAR ALTERNATIVES   209

of Catholics. O'Connell was able to achieve this reconciliation because in his political speeches he gave no consideration to constraint when he reminded his audiences of the injustices that their ancestors had experienced, particularly during the sixteenth and the seventeenth centuries, and he led his auditors to believe that he was on the brink of rectifying these injustices in a way that would benefit the condition of everybody.

We get some insight into the repertoire of grievances from which O'Connell drew his speeches from his book, *A Memoir on Ireland Native and Saxon*, published in 1843. The seventeenth-century episodes on which he furnished details included the atrocities committed by Cromwell at Drogheda and Wexford, the transplantation by Cromwell of supposedly 80,000 Irish to the West Indies of whom but twenty were alive six years later, the depredations of Ireton at Limerick and of Morrogh O'Brien, Baron of Inchiquin, at the Cathedral at Cashel, and the multiple harsh actions of Sir Charles Coote in 1642. Then, for the sixteenth century, he detailed, among the many massacres he identified, the execution of the foreign soldiers who had surrendered at Smerwick in 1579, the slaughter of Brian O'Neill and his company by Walter, earl of Essex, at a feast to which they had invited them, the atrocity of 1578 at Mullaghmast where many of the unsuspecting Irish lords of Leinster had been killed by their English hosts, and the 'deliberately created Famine' that had caused the depopulation of Munster in the 1580s.

Since O'Connell had been reared in his early years in an Irish-language environment it is likely that he first got to know of this litany of atrocities from renditions of the vernacular verse narrations first composed in the seventeenth century, or from remembered renditions of what O'Sullivan Beare had written on the subject in Latin, or perhaps even from reading O'Sullivan Beare.[28] We know that in his political speeches he pronounced on the injustices suffered by the Irish, by which he meant Irish Catholics, by making bold assertion without any reference to evidence. However, in this printed text, which he addressed to Queen Victoria without any confidence that it would be read by the young monarch, O'Connell repeated the charges so that his queen might become 'intimately acquainted with the confiscations, the plunder, the robbery, the domestic treachery, the violation of all public faith, and of the sanctity of treaties, the ordinary wholesale slaughters, the planned murders, the concerted massacres,

---

[28] The Gaelic background from which O'Connell emerged in mentioned in Oliver MacDonagh, *The Hereditary Bondsman: Daniel O'Connell, 1775–1829* (London, 1988), 7–29; see also Gearóid Ó Tuathaigh, 'Gaelic Ireland, popular politics and Daniel O'Connell', *Journal of the Galway Archaeological and Historical Society*, vol. 34 (1974–5), 21–34. It is worth noting that O'Connell grew up in the same region of County Kerry as the author of *Tuireamh na hÉireann*, who, incidentally, is thought to have been an O'Connell. Daniel O'Connell also sometimes addressed his audiences in Irish from political platforms, on which see Niall Ó Ciosáin, 'Beart pobail agus Délitearthacht san Athrú Teanga in Éirinn', Cunningham and Ó Ciosáin, eds., *Culture and Society in Ireland since 1750*, 86–96, esp. 88.

210 IMAGINING IRELAND'S PASTS

which have been inflicted upon the Irish people by the English governments'.[29] Cumulatively, he contended, these demonstrated that 'no people on the face of the earth were ever treated with such cruelty as the Irish'. However, in his published work, unlike in his speeches, O'Connell cited from English or Irish Protestant authors to bear witness to each allegation he made concerning the atrocities suffered by Ireland's Catholics.[30] Thus O'Connell claimed that in isolating episodes where the Irish had suffered grave injustice, he had confined himself to those where the 'facts' had been recorded 'not by Catholic, or inimical writers; but by Protestant historians and Protestant officers, high in command and authority under the Protestant Crown of England; such documents being addressed in general to the Sovereign; and being, as to the statement of facts, of the most unimpeachable authenticity'.[31] Even worse than the sufferings inflicted on the Irish, proclaimed O'Connell, was that they had been 'atrociously refused historical justice, and accused of being the authors and perpetrators of assassinations and massacres of which they were only the victims'.[32] Here, he was referring to the use that had been made of the 1641 depositions by Temple and other contemporary officials, and also by subsequent Protestant historians, to blacken the reputation of all Irish Catholics. On this subject O'Connell was satisfied that the reliability of the depositions as a historical source had been discredited by critical historians, and his only concern was that Temple's allegation that Ireland's Catholic leaders in 1641 had planned the massacre of all Protestants in the country had been 'taken up by that infidel falsifier of history, Hume'.[33]

As O'Connell enumerated the past sufferings of the Irish, and as he compiled lists of Catholics and of Gaelic chieftains who had been 'slaughtered by the Protestants', he was being no less a vernacular historian that the Irish-language poets of the seventeenth century or authors in the eighteenth and early nineteenth centuries who had followed their example, especially when he peppered his political speeches with unsubstantiated descriptions of real or imagined atrocities from the past.[34] However, in *A Memoir on Ireland Native and Saxon*, he parted company with vernacular history in several respects. First, he was addressing an English audience to inform them of 'the wrongs which Ireland has suffered, and

---

[29] Daniel O'Connell, *A Memoir on Ireland Native and Saxon* (first published 1843; reprinted Port Washington, N.Y., 1970), Preface, vii–viii; O'Connell, as he mentioned on his title page, adapted the title of his book from lines by Thomas Moore where the poet had pronounced that 'On *our* side is Virtue and Erin-/On *theirs* is the Saxon and Guilt'.

[30] O'Connell, *A Memoir*, 8.   [31] O'Connell, *A Memoir*, 81–2.

[32] O'Connell, *A Memoir*, 8.

[33] O'Connell, *A Memoir*, 325; O'Connell's concern with Hume would have been, as pointed out in Chapter 6, that Hume's *History of England* had continued to enjoy a staggeringly wide circulation.

[34] O'Connell's most recent biographer refers to 'the aggression and vulgarity' of his speeches; Patrick Geoghegan, *King Dan: The Rise of Daniel O'Connell, 1775–1829* (Dublin, 2008), viii; the vulgarity was certainly exemplified in the Maguire/McGarrahan legal case discussed by Geoghegan, 246–7.

which Ireland is suffering from British misrule'.[35] Second, he sustained the arguments he put forward in his short narrative with a body of 'Observations, Proofs and Illustrations' that made up the larger section of his book.[36] The third fundamental difference between what O'Connell wrote and what the vernacular historians asserted was that where they identified iniquities from the past to justify some possible overthrow of the social order, O'Connell, the lawyer and political leader, used his narrative to make the British authorities feel guilty about government misrule in the past. His purpose in doing so was to encourage officials to the point where they might remove the disabilities that still made life difficult for those Irish Catholics that he considered qualified to become members of the political nation. The minimum he expected was that the government would either broaden the franchise so that Irish Catholics would enjoy the same rights as Scots and English under the Act of Union, or repeal the Act of Union and restore an Irish Parliament to Dublin. Significantly, in neither instance, did he display any hostility to monarchy or to Ireland being governed from England, as Mathew Carey had done, nor did he make any promises concerning the material improvement in the condition of the country's poor.

A prime example of how O'Connell exploited the past in print, as he would have done from an election platform, is his rhetorical outburst where he enquired: 'Did Stanley show none of the temper of Ireton in his Coercion Bill? Is none of the spirit of Coote and of Parsons to be found (in a mitigated form) in those who refuse to the Catholic people of Ireland their just share of elective or municipal franchises; and who insist that the Irish shall remain an inferior and a degraded caste, deprived of that perfect equality of civil and religious liberty, of franchises and privileges—which equality could alone constitute a Union, or render a Union tolerable?'[37] Thus in the constitutional targets he set himself and in the use he made of carefully documented evidence from history to sustain his arguments, O'Connell was perpetuating the work of the Catholic Committee in an effort to negotiate an improvement in the legal standing of those Catholics whose economic and social circumstances were secure. Like the members of the Catholic Committee, he used grievances from the past to support his case from history but he broke with them in his unwillingness to settle for incremental reform in his flamboyant, as opposed to discreet, citation of atrocities from the past to bolster his case, and in his abrasive use of language in print and even more so on public platforms. These latter were the attributes of O'Connell that won him wide appeal within the broader Catholic community and convinced them that O'Connell was their champion as much as he was the hero of those Catholics who were their

---

[35] O'Connell, *A Memoir*, 8.   [36] O'Connell, *A Memoir*, 49–406.

[37] O'Connell, *A Memoir*, Preface, ix; Stanley was Lord Edward Stanley who was to become prime minister in 1852 but who, as Secretary of State for Ireland, had introduced a Coercion Bill in 1833 that was suspended and revived intermittently thereafter as the government required.

212   IMAGINING IRELAND'S PASTS

social superiors and whose constitutional rights was his primary concern. Thus by his careful deployment of remembered grievances, O'Connell possibly did more than anybody else of his generation to fix in the minds of his Catholic audience that the narrative of Ireland's history during the early modern centuries that had been sketched out by Irish vernacular authors of the seventeenth century was valid and immutable.

7.3   Protestant Vernacular Histories of Ireland

Employing the adjective vernacular to describe some of the history cultivated by Irish Protestants may seem incongruous since Protestants in Ireland in the seventeenth and eighteenth centuries were more literate in the English language than were Catholics in any language, and were also more attuned than Catholics to using print as a medium for communication.[38] Also, from the moment of its first publication in 1646, Temple's *The Irish Rebellion* became more influential than any other text in shaping Protestant understanding of Ireland's history. The publication history of Temple's work that has been tracked by several historians also shows that fresh editions of the work were produced whenever Protestant control of the country seemed in jeopardy, and authors also regurgitated and elaborated upon Temple's arguments, thus disseminating them further. However, while Protestants in Ireland in later decades may have had their understanding of Ireland's history shaped by printed texts such as that by Temple, what they read was regularly reinforced, and perhaps re-interpreted, by sermons, particularly those preached on 23 October. This date had been set aside by an Irish act of state in 1642, and again by an act of the Irish Restoration Parliament in the 1660s, as one on which to thank God for having delivered Protestants from the general massacre intended by the Pope and his agents in Ireland. Thus, as noted in Chapter 5, Thomas O'Sullevane, writing in 1722 on behalf of the Protestant 10th earl of Clanricard, expressed alarm at the impact that the 'hideous relations' being preached from the pulpit each year concerning the events of 1641 were having on the minds of the 'vulgar'.[39]

We get some sense of what such 'hideous relations' involved in the analysis made by Richard Ansell of some of the 23 October sermons that were subsequently printed. Printed sermons were obviously but a fraction of all that had been preached in every Protestant church (Presbyterian as well as Church of Ireland) on each commemoration day. However, Ansell's samples, taken from statutory

---

[38] Raymond Gillespie and Andrew Hadfield, eds., *The Oxford History of the Irish Book*, vol. 3, *The Irish Book in English, 1550–1800* (Oxford, 2006), see, for example, 6, 26, 149–50.

[39] Toby Barnard, 'The Uses of 23 October 1641 and Irish Protestant Celebrations', *English Historical Review*, vol. 106 (1991), 889–920; Chapter 5, p. 128.

THE VERNACULAR ALTERNATIVES 213

sermons preached during the years 1689–92, are sufficient to show that Temple's message was not only relayed but was reinforced and re-interpreted by the clergy who delivered sermons to suit more immediate purposes. Thus the sermons dealt not only with what the preachers believed had happened in 1641 in renditions that were frequently garnered from Temple but also with what would likely have been the fate of Protestants in Ireland after 1688 had God not chosen William of Orange to be their deliverer. The preachers' interpretation of the rebellion of 1641, and their assertions that a further massacre of Protestants had been in prospect for 1689, led to the conclusions that the Irish, because they were Catholics, would never accept the existing political and social order as a permanent arrangement. Therefore, as they looked to the future, the various clerics predicted that Protestants in Ireland were destined to experience a similar onslaught once every half-century unless they mended their ways and remained constantly alert against Catholic plots. Ansell shows that, as these preachers, and the pamphleteers who followed in their wake, narrated what had occurred in Ireland between 1641 and 1689, they gave scant attention to the Cromwellian interlude given that the behaviour then of the ancestors of many within their community did not reflect well on their loyalty. Instead, they traced Protestant title to land in Ireland to the Restoration Act of Settlement, thus obviating reference to the Cromwellian confiscation. By making reference to the Act of Settlement, preachers were providing themselves with an opportunity to allude to the persistence of Catholics in seeking to have it reversed, especially in the Jacobite parliament of 1689.[40]

This mingling in the printed sermons of 1689–92 of what had become a well-rehearsed Protestant vernacular version of the past with fresh information about more recent events featured again during the 1760s and the two following decades when the Protestant interest, particularly in Munster, was threatened by Whiteboy disturbances. In his discussion of the reaction to these attacks, Ultán Gillen has shown that the exhortations of the clergy of the Church of Ireland, initially in sermons and then in print, became ever more shrill, and followed what were by now recognizable Protestant renditions of Ireland's early modern history. Gillen shows that the concern of this group of clergy was to convince their auditors that the Whiteboys were exploiting agrarian grievances to justify an assault on Protestant clergy who benefited from the tithes that Catholic farmers, among others, were required to pay to an established church they did not attend.[41]

Since Temple's *The Irish Rebellion* became the source from which more militant Protestant preachers drew their inspiration when relating recent threats to past experience, it seems that Temple's text had become a Protestant counterpart to

---

[40] Richard Ansell, 'The 1688 Revolution in Ireland and the Memory of 1641', Mark Williams and Stephen Paul Forrest, eds., *Constructing the Past: Writing Irish History, 1600–1800* (Woodbridge, 2010), 73–93.

[41] Ultán Gillen, 'Constructing Counter-Revolutionary History in Late Eighteenth-Century Ireland', Williams and Forrest, ed., *Constructing the Past*, 136–54.

214 IMAGINING IRELAND'S PASTS

Tuireamh na hÉireann, which, as we saw, included a trove of information on which Catholic authors drew and elaborated upon whenever they were confronted by fresh challenges. The difference was that Temple's narration had first been circulated in print and afterwards popularized in sermons and reprinted editions, whereas *Tuireamh na hÉireann* was first communicated orally and transmitted to later generations both in manuscript form and by word of mouth. However, the post-composition experience of the texts was similar in that each was appropriated by later authors and adapted to supply a historical context and structure for interpreting more recent events. We noted how this was done effectively by Aodh Buí Mc Cruitín, who, when drawing upon *Tuireamh na hÉireann*, was able to make the case that the humiliations being experienced by Catholics in the eighteenth century were consistent with those endured by their ancestors in the sixteenth and seventeenth centuries. Several Protestant authors adapted Temple's *The Irish Rebellion* in the same fashion to fit with current experiences and none more blatantly than Sir Richard Musgrave (1746?–1818) in a sequence of publications of the late eighteenth century that preceded his mammoth composite work, *Memoirs of the Different Rebellions in Ireland*, first published in 1801.[42]

Musgrave, who had been M.P. for the borough of Lismore in County Waterford before the Act of Union brought an end to the Irish parliament, came from a minor gentry background and had served as High Sheriff for County Waterford. In that capacity he had been responsible for confronting the potential threat of Whiteboy outrages that had been afflicting the neighbouring counties of Tipperary and Kilkenny from 1759 into the 1780s.[43] By taking a hard stand against this subversive agrarian movement that threatened, but did not unduly disturb, his own county, Musgrave came to be recognized by alarmed clergy in the Church of Ireland as a prime defender of rural ministers and their families who had become the target of Whiteboy attacks once members of this oath-bound society isolated the mandatory payment of tithes by Catholic farmers to the established church as a major grievance. As he detailed and deplored their activities, Musgrave represented the Whiteboys, and similar Catholic agrarian groups—notably the Defenders who operated principally in Ulster—as part of a wider Catholic conspiracy intent on 'subverting the constitution, and separating

---

[42] Richard Musgrave, *Memoirs of the Different Rebellions in Ireland* (Dublin and London, 1801); all references here are to the reprint of the third edition of 1802, prepared and edited by Steven Myers and Delores McKnight (Fort Wayne, Ia., 1995).

[43] Musgrave, *Memoirs*, 'Origin of the White Boys', 27–44; see also 'Origin of the Defenders', 45–59; 'Origin of the Catholic Committee', 66–81, and 'Origin of the United Irishmen', 82–112; on Musgrave and his association with more conservative Protestant interests see James Kelly, ' "We were all to have been massacred": Irish Protestants and the experience of rebellion', Thomas Bartlett, David Dickson, Dáire Keogh, and Kevin Whelan, eds., *1798: A Bicentenary Perspective* (Dublin, 2003), 312–30, esp. 325–30; and David Dickson, 'Foreword' to Musgrave, *Memoirs*, ii–xiii; for a biographical note on Musgrave see that by C.J. Woods, *Dictionary of Irish Biography*, vol. 6, 840–1.

Ireland from England, with the assistance of France'.[44] For him, these popular agrarian movements were linked to the political lobbying conducted by the Catholic Committee on behalf of Catholics who enjoyed a more secure position in society. His overall contention was that the combination of these forces had prepared the way for the formidable countrywide conspiracy mobilized by the United Irishmen that, as he saw it, had culminated in the Irish rebellion of 1798. To support his case, Musgrave asserted that the Whiteboys had been 'headed, marshalled, and disciplined...by officers who had served in the Irish brigades, in the French service', working in tandem 'with the French who meditated an invasion of Ireland'. As he deplored French plotting against British and Protestant interests in Ireland, Musgrave saw nothing incongruous about linking the aid, which, he contended, the French royal government had been intending to provide to Irish insurgents in the middle of the eighteenth century, with the aid that the stridently anti-Catholic revolutionary government that had overthrown the French monarchy actually supplied to the United Irishmen in 1798.[45] Musgrave also glossed over the inconvenient truth that most of the early leaders of the United Irishmen were Protestant, and he succeeded in depicting the rebellion instigated by the United Irishmen as the outcome of Catholic plotting because some of its leaders, including Wolfe Tone, were 'Protestant barristers of abilities, but desperate circumstances, and totally destitute of all religious principles' who had been previously employed as pamphleteers for the Catholic Committee 'for the purpose of lulling the suspicion of Protestants in general' by 'varnishing over' the claims of 'the Catholic cause...with the semblance of general and abstract liberty'. By such 'decoying', he claimed, the Catholics had succeeded in winning support from 'such...[Protestants] as had revolutionary designs, particularly the Presbyterians'.[46]

Musgrave thus traced all late eighteenth-century conspiratorial activity in Ireland previous to 1798 back to the Catholic Committee. He asserted that after its first meeting in 1757, the Committee had quickly 'assimilated to the Confederate Catholics, assembled at Kilkenny in the year 1641 [sic]'.[47] Having thus conjured up a connection between the Catholic Committee and the Catholic Confederation it became easy for Musgrave to represent the 1798 rebellion as a re-enactment of that of 1641 which, following Temple, he alleged, had been hatched by the papacy with support from Britain's Continental enemies with the purpose of ridding Ireland of Protestants and Protestantism. For Musgrave, therefore, the actions of the Catholic rebels of 1798, together with those Protestants who had been duped into supporting them, was a re-enactment of what had

---

[44] Musgrave, *Memoirs*, 28.   [45] Musgrave, *Memoirs*, 29.   [46] Musgrave, *Memoirs*, 82.

[47] Musgrave, *Memoirs*, 66; the Catholic Confederation was in fact established in 1642 and Musgrave probably dated its origin to the previous year in order to suggest a connection between it and the rebellion of 1641.

216   IMAGINING IRELAND'S PASTS

failed to meet its objective in 1641. Thus he could argue 'that the Irish Roman Catholics in general [had] for two hundred years, manifested a marked hostility against the Protestant empire, which all the rebellions kindled on the score of religion, or in which its influence chiefly predominated, unquestionably prove'.[48]

Musgrave rendered this representation of the 1798 rebellion plausible by focusing attention on the rebellion in County Wexford to which, as Tom Dunne has established, there had been a decided sectarian edge, and by largely ignoring the rebellion in Ulster where most of the insurgents had been disgruntled Protestants (principally Presbyterians).[49] Musgrave made his very detailed rendition of what had occurred in Wexford and south Leinster even more similar to Temple's account of what had occurred in 1641 by bolstering it with narratives, many of them sworn, that had been provided by 'eye witnesses' who were 'still living'. These, for him, were an equivalent of the 1641 depositions.[50] This meant that for Musgrave and his readers the tribulations experienced by the Irish Protestants of his generation were, like those suffered by their counterparts in 1641, caused by the determination of Catholics, inspired by the papacy through their priests to reverse the spiritual, civil, and material benefits of the Protestant Reformation, first in Ireland and then further afield, and to restore tyrannical government everywhere.

Where Temple had argued that Catholics had been able to go about their nefarious task in 1641 because Protestants had been lulled into believing that Catholics had become reconciled to the established order, Musgrave contended that it had become possible for Catholics to renew their effort to get rid of Protestants in 1798 because the Catholic Committee had convinced the government to relax the laws that had been designed to keep Catholics in check. Temple had concluded his text in 1646 by prescribing the measures he considered necessary to uphold the positive outcomes that had resulted from repeated English conquests and re-conquests of Ireland. Now, Musgrave concluded his *Memoirs of the Irish Rebellion* by appealing to conservative opinion in Britain as well as in Ireland to ensure that the fruits of the most recent victory achieved in 1798 by British forces and their Irish supporters over Irish insurgents would not be frittered away under the recent Act of Union.[51] This would inevitably happen, according to Musgrave, if the government conceded the demand being made by

---

[48] Musgrave, *Memoirs*, 'Author's Preface to the Third edition', xx.

[49] Tom Dunne, *Rebellions: Memoir, Memory and 1798* (2005; 2nd revised ed. Dublin, 2010); for a brief summary of the Ulster dimension, Guy Beiner, *Forgetful Remembrance: Social Forgetting and Vernacular Historiography of a Rebellion in Ulster* (Oxford, 2018), 34–9.

[50] Musgrave, *Memoirs*, 875; Beiner in *Forgetful Remembrance*, 90–103, makes the case that few in Ulster were ready to come forward with information on the Ulster dimension to the 1798 rebellion which may partly explain the geographical bias to Musgrave's collection of eyewitness accounts. However, Beiner also acknowledges, 91, that Musgrave distorted the evidence concerning Ulster.

[51] On the influence of Musgrave on Conservative opinion in Britain see James Sack, *From Jacobite to Conservative* (Cambridge, 1993), esp. 96.

Irish Catholics, and being supported by British politicians of liberal inclination and some liberal Irish Protestants. This demand was that they should grant to Catholics the right to be returned as members of the parliament at Westminster that had been expanded under the Act of Union to include members representing Irish constituencies. To do so, Musgrave thundered, would cancel the most fundamental of the laws that had been enacted at Westminster, as well as in the Dublin parliament, in the aftermath of the Glorious Revolution, and that had been designed to uphold the constitutional and religious liberties of Protestants.

Musgrave's *Memoir* of 1801 therefore drew many of its arguments from the memories of Ireland's early modern past that were cherished by the particular Irish community he was addressing. The store of memories that Musgrave drew upon were those that had been detailed in Temple's *The Irish Rebellion* and had been regularly refreshed in the minds of members of the Irish Protestant community in the many sermons on the 1641 rebellion they would have heard preached on the anniversary of that rebellion. To this extent it was an outgrowth of Protestant vernacular history that Musgrave strove to make appear more 'scientific' and more broadly focused in three ways. First, he bolstered his argument with an extensive, if selective, collection of witness statements that extended to twenty-seven appendices.[52] Second, he addressed his history to an English Protestant audience as well as to his co-religionists in Ireland. And the third innovation is that he used his narrative of events in Ireland during the early modern centuries to expound on imperial matters. In this, Musgrave used history not only to put his co religionists in Ireland on their guard against future onslaughts but to argue, for the benefit of his English readers, that since Ireland had become 'a matter of Imperial concern', following the passage of the Act of Union, the authorities in Britain should recognize their special responsibility to keep Ireland under firm control because the security of the entire empire required this.[53]

As he elaborated upon this broader theme, Musgrave demonstrated his skills as a vernacular historian by drawing upon the reservoir of anti-Catholic sentiment that he knew to be deeply embedded in the minds of English, no less than Irish, Protestants since the time of the Reformation. He opened the subject about what provision should be made for the future security of the empire by stating that the rebellion of 1798 in Ireland had exposed as erroneous and simple-minded the previous proposition, espoused by liberal opinion in Britain as well as in Ireland, 'that the concessions made to the Roman Catholics, for above twenty years, would have attached them to the State, and would have united them with their Protestant fellow subjects, in the bonds of brotherly love and Christian charity'.[54] Such specious arguments, he

---

[52] Musgrave, *Memoirs*, 595–911.
[53] Musgrave, *Memoirs*, 'Author's Preface to the Third Edition', xxi.
[54] Musgrave, *Memoirs*, 'Author's Preface to the Third Edition', xvii.

218 IMAGINING IRELAND'S PASTS

pronounced, had not only been shown to be 'impracticable' but would 'always' be so, even if contemplated for application in an imperial context. This, he pronounced, would inevitably be the case because 'the tenets of their religion, and the conduct of their priests' rendered Catholics always 'hostile to a Protestant state, and to their Protestant fellow subjects, and...a fruitful source of discord and rebellion, ever since the introduction of the Reformation'.[55] Thus, as the publication of his book coincided with the Act of Union coming into force in 1801, Musgrave alerted his British audience to the likelihood that, 'popish priests' would behave in an 'imperial' context as they had done previously in Ireland, this time 'perverting the populace of England' by persuading them to support a foreign invasion guided by 'Buonoparte' in whose hands 'the sovereign pontiff' had become 'a mere engine' ready, as always, to disturb 'the peace of society in Protestant states'.[56]

Musgrave's principal concern in 1801 was to warn Protestants in Britain of the dangers they faced due to the new political configuration that was coming into force. He wished to alert them also to the even greater responsibility that fell upon them to maintain order in Ireland lest disturbance there should disrupt the entire United Kingdom. However, he also took time to consider what Protestants in Ireland could do to secure a better future for themselves. In doing so, he cast his mind over the scheme that had been proposed in 1744 by Walter Harris and Charles Smith, discussed in Chapter 5, to use charter schools to secure the conversion to Protestantism of the children of the Catholic tenants of Irish Protestant landowners. This scheme had been put forward in 1744 when, after a half-century of peace, Protestants were beginning to feel themselves at home in Ireland since they owned the vast bulk of the land in the country, were firmly in control of the country's commerce, and constituted perhaps one third of the country's population. This sense of well-being no longer obtained a half-century later because, in the intervening period, the country had experienced a rapid demographic increase and a consequent pressure on limited resources that had resulted in Protestants becoming vastly outnumbered in all provinces of the country except Ulster, and in landowners and rural clergy experiencing intermittent threats from a proliferation of oath-bound agrarian societies. Worse still, the authority of the state itself had been challenged briefly in 1798 by a French invasion linked to local rebellion.

Such factors explain why Musgrave cast his mind back to the Harris/Smith proposal of 1744 with which he would certainly have been familiar because Smith, like Musgrave himself, had been linked to the town of Lismore and the associated patronage dispensed from Lismore Castle.[57] Now, in 1801, when

---

[55] Musgrave, *Memoirs*, 'Author's Preface to the Third Edition', xviii.

[56] Musgrave, *Memoirs*, 'Author's Preface to the Third Edition', xxv.

[57] The patronage in 1801 already belonged to the Dukes of Devonshire who, through marriage, had come to inherit the vast estate of the earls of Cork, established in the seventeenth century by Richard Boyle whose 'charitable' work had been isolated for particular praise by Charles Smith.

Musgrave looked to the 1744 proposal, he saw the need to modify it because, in his view, the Harris/Smith project had failed to meet its objective because the youths who had been converted to Protestantism had no sooner left the confines of the charter schools than they were 'unremittingly teased and persecuted till they conform[ed] to the popish superstition'. Their 'relapse', he concluded, was as a consequence of 'the fanatical spirit of proselytism' that was 'inseparable from popery'. Under Musgrave's revised scheme, the charter schools would continue as before but the moment the pupils completed their training and religious conversion, they would be settled in towns to be established by the government in which 'English manufacturers with large capitals' would establish 'manufactories' where employment would 'be exclusively, and rigidly, apportioned to Protestants'. Each such town would, every year, employ as 'apprentices' 1,000 or 1,200 'children of eleven years' taken from charter schools and foundling hospitals where they would have been bred 'in useful industry', and where, in these Protestant enclaves, they would be protected from attempts to draw them back to Catholicism. Thus, according to Musgrave, history would be repeating itself because these new towns would correspond to 'Derry and Bandon, two Protestant towns established in the reign of James I', each of which had remained free of 'the rebellions kindled by popish fanaticism', and whose inhabitants had always fought 'in defence of the constitution in church and state'.[58]

Musgrave, in his *Memoirs of the Different Rebellions in Ireland* added significantly to what had previously been known of Whiteboy activity in Munster, and of events in Wexford in 1798. However he, as O'Connell would do some forty years later in *A Memoir on Ireland Native and Saxon*, also shaped recent events to fit a well-established template. In Musgrave's case this meant lending fresh authority to a pre-existing narrative that represented Protestants as the promoters in Ireland of enterprise and freedom who, when circumstances permitted, became victims, through no fault of their own, of merciless attacks from their Catholic subordinates. These, he contended, were being spurred on by their priests and supported by England's Continental enemies in an effort to bring Ireland, and Britain also, back under the sway of papal tyranny from which they had escaped at the time of the Reformation.

7.4 Conclusion

We have noted in previous chapters how authors who wrote Ireland's history from the vantage point of elites believed themselves to be imagining Ireland's early modern past in a novel and verifiable fashion. What has been detailed in this chapter shows that, under the pressure of rapidly changing events that culminated

---

[58] Musgrave, *Memoirs*, 'Author's Preface to the Third Edition', xx.

in the rebellion of 1798 followed by the passing of the Act of Union, another group of historians looked to the past, not with a view to comprehending complexities and influences that had been overlooked by previous authors, but to confirm and reinforce what their communities had always understood had been the experience of their recent forbears. In an environment where political and denominational positions became ever more polarized these authors were therefore using history to enhance group solidarity and to vindicate both the recent actions of the groups they were addressing, and the actions they hoped these groups would pursue in the near future. They also wished to demonstrate that these actions were as their ancestors would have wished them to be.

This atavistic dimension to history writing meant that the distinction was less clear between history that had originally appeared in print and that which had derived from narratives designed for oral communication. Thus, while some of the works that appeared in print, such as the memoirs published respectively by Richard Musgrave and Daniel O'Connell, were lengthy and furnished with formidable bodies of supporting material, the narratives they presented were hardly more sophisticated than the more popular versions of the past that had been in circulation within their respective communities since the seventeenth century. If this justifies describing these versions of the past as vernacular history this does not mean that they were no more than extensions on the vernacular histories that had been composed in the seventeenth century. They were essentially different from these because, while authors still expressed gratitude to providence for past deliverances, they were less inclined stoically to accept any setbacks their respective communities had experienced as a providential punishment for past transgressions. To this extent authors attached greater importance to human agency than had the providential historians, even if the actors they identified were more frequently villains than heroes. Moreover, their exhortations to their respective audiences to guard themselves against further assaults and to shape their worlds, as their ancestors would have wished, were more frequently addressed to the community at large rather than to individuals. It was this reticence about identifying heroes, as we shall see in Chapter 8, that Ireland's next generation of historians set themselves to overcome.

8

Re-Imagining Ireland's Early Modern Past

The Young Ireland Agenda, Dissident Views, and the Catholic Alternative

8.1 Introduction

One striking outcome of the efforts that had been made to rewrite Ireland's history between the optimistic 1760s and the gloomy 1830s was that philosophical historians had failed to agree on a narrative to which all educated Irish people, regardless of religious or political affiliation, could subscribe. At the same time well-established popular renditions of developments in Ireland during the sixteenth and seventeenth centuries had gained fresh vigour. This latter development occurred because authors on opposing sides in bitter political debates enlisted history to sustain their conflicting arguments during this era of revolution and counter-revolution.

The group of intellectuals from both Protestant and Catholic backgrounds who associated themselves with *The Nation* newspaper, established in 1842 by Thomas Davis, John Blake Dillon, and Charles Gavan Duffy, wanted, among other things, to succeed where others had failed by imagining a past for Ireland with which people of all classes as well as creeds might identify. Their ambition was to employ history to sustain their efforts to surmount communal and denominational divisions, thus countering the efforts of those who, they realized, were using history to achieve group advantage. This chapter will detail how this objective was pursued, especially during the 1840s. It will also explain how the project ran into difficulties because the group failed to agree among themselves on a definition of Irish nationality or on which memories from the past should be cherished and which jettisoned. A second problem arose when those engaged upon imagining a new past for Ireland encountered representatives of a re-invigorated Catholic Church who had clear ideas about what purpose history should serve and on why memories of past suffering should be cultivated.

8.2 The Historians of Young Ireland and the Early Modern Past

The group of Protestant and Catholic intellectuals associated with *The Nation* newspaper are most often represented, as they have been most recently by Roy

Imagining Ireland's Pasts: Early Modern Ireland through the Centuries. Nicholas Canny, Oxford University Press (2021).
© Nicholas Canny. DOI: 10.1093/oso/9780198808961.003.0008

222   IMAGINING IRELAND'S PASTS

Foster, as the creators, or re-creators, of a Romantic vision of Ireland's past.[1] It will be shown in this chapter that one of the lasting achievements of the *Nation* group was indeed the invention of a vernacular history that was romantic, heroic, and teleological. This, however, was but one of their historiographical ambitions, since, as will be shown, they saw themselves also to be taking up where the philosophical historians of the eighteenth century had left off. Before they undertook the task of re-imagining Ireland's past, they had begun to cultivate a sense of nationality to which all elements of the population might subscribe. The leaders of the movement had discussed such matters as members of the College Historical Society at Trinity College, Dublin with which several were associated, or through their involvement with O'Connell's Repeal Association, or by activity in both organizations. When it came to politics, all members of the group favoured the repeal of the Act of Union, and because they were members of the Repeal Association they were at liberty to use its reading rooms to circulate their newspaper and other publications and to promote discussion.[2] Some of the group later broke with O'Connell on a variety of issues. These included the use of physical force to further political objective, of which O'Connell and the Catholic bishops disapproved, and supporting non-denominational university education, to which the Catholic bishops and O'Connell were vehemently opposed. Those who voiced their dissent over such matters at meetings of the Repeal Association came to be known collectively, if at first mockingly, as representatives of Young Ireland. Some Young Irelanders considered themselves to be keeping alive the principles of 1798 in opposition both to the conservative strictures of people such as Richard Musgrave, whom they dismissed as Orange bigots, and to those they identified as self-serving representatives of 'Old Ireland', by which they meant O'Connell with his closest supporters, and the Catholic bishops.[3]

The charismatic Thomas Davis (1814–45), the leading Young Ireland exponent of a new history for Ireland, was a Protestant barrister and graduate of Trinity College, Dublin, who was anxious to have somebody trace the development over time of an Irish nation composed of people of Irish birth regardless of denomination, social position, or ethnic origin.[4] One source of inspiration for Davis was the writings of the French historian Augustine Thierry (1795–1856)

---

[1] R.F. Foster, 'The First Romantics; Young Irelanders between Catholic Emancipation and the Famine', Foster, *Words Alone: Yeats and his Inheritances* (Oxford, 2011), 45–90.

[2] Thomas Davis, 'Reading Rooms', Thomas Davis, *Essays and Poems with a Centenary Memoir, 1845-1945* (Dublin, 1945), 81–3.

[3] James Quinn, *Young Ireland and the Writing of Irish History* (Dublin, 2015). O'Connell himself sometimes rejoiced in being considered a representative of Old Ireland; see Richard Davis, *The Young Ireland Movement* (Dublin, 1987), 71.

[4] For a biographical note on Davis see that by John Neylon Molony, *Dictionary of Irish Biography*, vol. 3, 82–6; Thomas Davis, 'The History of Ireland', Thomas Davis *Literary and Historical Essays*, ed., C[harles] G[avan] D[uffy] (Dublin, 1846), 28–38; these essays, published originally by Davis in *The Nation*, were brought together in book form by Gavan Duffy following Davis's death in 1845.

RE-IMAGINING IRELAND'S EARLY MODERN PAST   223

who had written of the evolution in France of a community that included peasants, townsmen, and middle classes no less than nobles and clergy. Davis was equally impressed by the plans of another French author, Jules Michelet (1798–1874), to write a grand narrative for France from the earliest times to the present. That Davis had his colleague John Mitchel in mind to undertake an equivalent project for Ireland is suggested by one playful reference made by Davis to Mitchel as Mitchelet.[5] Davis would have been equally inspired by Thomas Carlyle who, in the words Ann Rigney, believed that history was an 'essence' to be distilled from 'innumerable' biographies, which meant that he, no less than Michelet, was as much concerned with the 'nameless peasant' as with 'the king'.[6]

This Young Ireland group were not working in isolation since histories of other European nations and proto-nations were being undertaken along similar lines by authors in several jurisdictions in mid-nineteenth-century Europe. Their promoters, like the Irish group, seemed of the opinion that the publication of a multitude of parallel national histories would serve as a first step towards the creation of a new politics of Europe, or indeed of the world. This would be based on interactions within a community of nation states rather than on negotiations between what they considered the corrupt interlocking empires that dominated the world of their time.[7]

Any such new history for Ireland, pronounced Davis—and here he seemed to be echoing what Thomas Carlyle had had to say of heroes and hero worship— would 'seize a character' whose actions had exemplified the 'pressure of a great mind on his time, and on after times'.[8] Davis believed that what was required in the short term for Ireland—or at least for those people with but limited schooling- was the identification of some heroes in whom the population might take pride. He considered that no previous historian of Ireland had attempted anything of this kind other than the Abbé Mac Geoghegan who, according to Davis, had been able to do so because 'writing in France [he] was free from English censorship, writing from "the Brigade" he avoided the impudence of Huguenot historians'. It was now possible for Davis to refer freely to Mac Geoghegan's work in the knowledge that his audience would know of what he was speaking because it had

---

[5] Davis, 'The History of Ireland', 37; Michelet's project was not completed until 1867 by which time it extended to nineteen volumes.

[6] Ann Rigney, *Imperfect Histories: The Elusive Past and the Legacy of Romantic Historicism* (Ithaca, N.Y., 2001), 99–120; quotations 104, 107.

[7] On the European picture, Stefan Berger with Christoph Conrad, *The Past as History: National Identity and Historical Consciousness in Modern Europe* (London, 2015); and on the Irish dimensions James Quinn, *Young Ireland.*

[8] Davis, 'The History of Ireland', 37; while this emphasis on the influence of 'the great man' shows that Davis, like others in Young Ireland, were impressed with this dimension of the writings of Thomas Carlyle, James Quinn points to some ambivalence in this admiration; Quinn, *Young Ireland*, 39–40. On the ambiguous relationship that developed between several of the Young Ireland figures (especially Gavan Duffy) and both Jane and Thomas Carlyle see Foster, *Words Alone* 18, 24, 45, 46–7, 48–50, 56, 62, 77, 80–2.

been recently translated into English and published in Dublin. He could proceed therefore to praise Mac Geoghegan for having countered the 'sneers of the Deist Voltaire, and the lies of the Catholic Cambrensis'. He praised him even more because, as a writer, he was elegant, 'graphic, easy and Irish...not a bigot, but apparently a genuine Catholic'.[9] The particular virtue of Mac Geoghegan's work, in the eyes of Davis and also of Mitchel, was that it had detailed what Irish soldiers had achieved in foreign service and thus helped 'to rescue Ireland from the reproach that she was a wailing and ignorant slave'. For Davis the past should be studied not (and here he was obliquely contrasting his views on what purpose history should serve with those of O'Connell) 'to acquire a beggar's eloquence in petition but a hero's wreath in strife'.[10]

Davis first attempted to advance his ambition through 'A Ballad History of Ireland'. His English-language ballads, some of which were anthologized after his death in 1845, were directed towards the increasing element of the population that was conversant (or even literate) in English, and were intended especially to augment the instruction of pupils attending the English-language national schools that had been established by the state, but that deliberately excluded instruction in history from the curriculum. Davis expected his 'Ballad History' to become a new vernacular history that would 'make Irish History familiar to the minds, pleasant to the ears, dear to the passions and powerful over the taste and conduct of the Irish people in times to come'. Such history, as Davis acknowledged, would have little to say of 'events' but would instead promote an awareness of and pride in 'nationality' by bringing knowledge of the achievements of Ireland's past heroes 'to every cabin and shop in the land' by means of 'books, pictures, statuary and music'.[11]

Roy Foster has recognized how Davis and his colleagues promoted pride in nationality among all levels of Irish society in this Romantic fashion. In doing so he has underestimated the extent to which Davis in particular considered it necessary to cultivate an understanding of Ireland's history more conventionally in closely-argued prose histories that would both document the achievements of Ireland's heroes and 'make up a record of English crime and Irish suffering in order to explain the past, to justify the present, and caution the future'.[12] These volumes amounted to much more than what Foster has described dismissively as

---

[9] Davis, 'The History of Ireland', 31; by 'The Brigade' Davis meant the Irish Brigade in the French army, and the Huguenot historians would have been those serving the cause of William of Orange; Cambrensis was Gerald of Wales; on Mac Geoghegan see Chapter 7; Mac Geoghegan's History was translated as follows, Abbé Mac Geoghegan, *History of Ireland Ancient and Modern* (English trans. P. O'Kelly, 3 vols., Dublin, 1832); another Dublin edition appeared in 1844 and a New York edition was published by D & J Sadlier in 1848.

[10] Davis, 'The History of Ireland', 31.

[11] Davis, *Literary and Historical Essays*, 231–40, and 29.

[12] Davis, 'The History of Ireland', 28.

RE-IMAGINING IRELAND'S EARLY MODERN PAST 225

'a series of influential primers on Irish history'.[13] They were more consequential than that since they required their designated authors to reconsider key episodes in the history of the early modern centuries when most such 'crimes' and 'sufferings' had occurred, and when hope for future reconciliation could also be discerned. To set examples of how this might be achieved, Davis himself engaged in a study of what he called the Patriot Parliament of 1689, and he commissioned his colleague John Mitchel (1815–75) to write an equally prescriptive text that took the form of a biography of Hugh O'Neill, earl of Tyrone.[14]

Davis's own exemplary work on the 1689 parliament appeared in 1843 as a sequence of lengthy articles in a Whig journal called *The Citizen,* which ran in parallel with publications in the *Dublin Magazine* where, in a 'conscientious and scholarly' manner, Davis had reconstituted from fragmentary sources the records of the Irish parliament of 1689 that had been destroyed by government decree in 1695.[15] Given the outlets he chose, Davis was obviously targeting Protestant readers in the first instance, although it is probable that he also intended to publish his work as a book and thus reach a wider public. He had not done so before his death in 1845, and the work did not become available in book form until 1893 when Charles Gavan Duffy brought the articles together and published them under the title *The Patriot Parliament of 1689.*[16]

Davis's research enabled him to identify most members who had attended in either house of the 1689 parliament, and to reconstitute the principal enactments that that parliament had contemplated. On the basis of this evidence, Davis argued that the parliament of 1689 was more entitled than that of 1782 to be considered a patriot assembly. By doing so he was challenging his readers, particularly his Protestant readers, to take into account the possibility that the Catholic members of the 1689 parliament had been justified in their wish to revise, if not to reverse, the Restoration Act of Settlement. He would have been considered provocative by the readers of both *The Citizen* and the *Dublin Magazine* because members of the Protestant community in Ireland were accustomed to consider the Act of Settlement as the bedrock on which the estate titles of most Protestant proprietors were based. Davis's second objective in writing the history of the 1689 parliament was to demonstrate that, by virtue of its more representative membership and of the more ambitious legislative

---

[13] Foster, *Words Alone,* 68.

[14] John Mitchel, *The Life and Times of Aodh O'Neill, Prince of Ulster, called by the English, Hugh, Earl of Tyrone*...(Dublin, 1845); for a biographical note on Mitchel see that by James Quinn, the *Dictionary of Irish Biography,* vol. 6, 523–7; also James Quinn, *John Mitchel* (Dublin, 2008).

[15] The words come from the 'Introduction' to *The Acts of James II's Irish Parliament of 1689,* eds., John Bergin and Andrew Lyall (Dublin, 2016), xxi–xxii; see also James Quinn, 'Thomas Davis and the Patriot Parliament of 1689', James Kelly, John Mc Cafferty, and Charles Ivar McGrath, eds., *People, Politics and Power: Essays on Irish History, 1660–1850 in honour of James I. McGuire* (Dublin, 2009), 190–202.

[16] Thomas Davis, *The Patriot Parliament of 1689,* ed., Charles Gavan Duffy (London, 1893).

226 IMAGINING IRELAND'S PASTS

programmes it had considered, the parliament of 1689 was more entitled to the appellation 'Patriot parliament' than was the Parliament of 1782. At the same time, Davis made the case that the opposition politics of the eighteenth century associated with such liberal, or even radical, Protestant figures as William Molyneux, Jonathan Swift, and Charles Lucas, and the 'patriot' ideology that underpinned that politics, had had its origin in the 1689 assembly.

To meet the first of his objectives, Davies supplied a brief historical background to the events leading up to 1689. He might well have culled his narrative from Hugh Reily or his imitators because he commenced with a condemnation of the 'appetite for conquest…inflamed by bigotry on the English side' that had characterized Elizabethan rule in Ireland, and that had driven 'the native who had been left unaided to defend his home, [to seek] foreign counsels…to guard his altar and his conscience too'. Then, as he proceeded to the Stuart monarchs, Davis pronounced that King James VI and I had 'completed…by treachery' the work of plantation commenced by Elizabeth, which left the Irish of Ulster reduced to serfhood under rapacious 'conquerors'. Those who had thus lost their lands, according to Davis, were left desirous of 'restitution and vengeance', the opportunity for which was 'hastened' by the 'ferocity of Parsons and Borlase'. Then, when discussing the 1641 rebellion, Davis, like Reily or even Mathew Carey, argued that Protestant officials and subsequent authors, in order to justify the suppression and dispossession of Catholics during the Cromwellian era, had invented the fiction that the Catholic 'rebels' of 1641 had intended to massacre all Protestants in the country. Since, according to this rendition of the past, the Cromwellian plantation had been legitimized by fallacious arguments, Davis decreed it to be the most sordid of all of Ireland's plantations. On these grounds, Davis condemned as shameful the Restoration Act of Settlement because it had given 'reality to a revolution which transferred the lands of the natives to military colonists'.[17] Given this, said Davis, it was 'monstrous to suppose the parliament [of 1689] ought to have respected the thirty-eight years usurpation of savage invaders', including some 'sordid capitalists of London', who had collectively 'plundered' the 'ancient gentry' and effected a 'revolution…which transferred the lands of the natives to military colonists'.[18] The action of the parliamentarians of 1689 in seeking to annul this travesty was entirely logical, said Davis, since it would have been the 'ambition' of 'most men' who had been subjected to anything resembling the 'Cromwellian robbery' 'to take the first opportunity of regaining their property, their natural independence, and religious freedom'.[19] The Parliamentarians

---

[17] Davis, *The Patriot Parliament of 1689*, 69; on Hugh Reily and his imitators see Chapters 6 and 7; on Mathew Carey see Chapter 7.

[18] Davis, *The Patriot Parliament of 1689*, xci, 5, 69, 141.

[19] Davis, *The Patriot Parliament*, 4–7.

of 1689 had therefore done no more, according to Davis, than 'to secure the rights, the property and honour of the nation'.[20]

Davis was aware that the audience he was addressing in 1843 had been convinced by authors such as Archbishop William King and Walter Harris that the Irish parliament of 1689 had been notoriously anti-Protestant, and that its action in repealing the Act of Settlement had 'furnished the enactors of the Penal Laws with excuses' to justify the debasement of the majority of the country's population.[21] By presenting a contrary view, Davis hoped to win over liberal Protestants to his way of thinking. Therefore, to substantiate his arguments, he provided detail on the membership of the 1689 parliament and its legislative programme to show that, in both these respects, it compared favourably with the parliament of 1782. The outstanding feature of the 1689 parliament, said Davis, was that it was 'the first and last which ever sat in Ireland since the English invasion, possessed of national authority, and complete in all its parts'. By stating that it had been uniquely complete, Davis meant that, as well as having members of both houses of parliament, the assembly of 1689 had enjoyed the presence of a ruling British monarch—in the person of King James II.[22] The parliament was exceptional, and 'patriotic' also according to Davis, because its members included some of Ireland's 'greatest soldiers, Mc Carthy, Tyrconnell and indeed most of the Colonels of the Irish Regiment' who, both at home, and subsequently on foreign fields, proved themselves 'fearless patriots, who were ready to fight, as well as to plan, for Ireland'.[23] The 1689 parliament was also a more representative assembly than that of 1782 because Catholics had been specifically excluded from the latter. As Davis drew attention to the presence of some Protestants, including some Protestant bishops, in the 1689 parliament, he pronounced that 'the mistake' it had made for which he 'heartily censure[d]' it, was that, by declaring forfeit the property of those who had fled Ireland to join King William in England, it had exposed itself to the erroneous charge that it had excluded Protestants and thereby gave substance to the argument that it was not a truly national assembly.[24]

When it came to assessing the relative merits of the legislative programmes of the two parliaments, Davis looked as much to the address given by King James to the 1689 assembly and to the legislation suggested for possible enactment as he did to the laws that were actually debated and passed. On this basis he concluded that the 1689 assembly had proceeded with more of the agenda of what he termed Protestant colonial nationalism than the 1782 parliament had done. The programme of the 1689 assembly, he declared, had included such remedy to the Act of Settlement 'as may be consistent with Reason, Justice and the Public Good

---

[20] Davis, *The Patriot Parliament*, 137 and 3.   [21] Davis, *The Patriot Parliament*, 141.
[22] Davis, *The Patriot Parliament of 1689*, 39–40.
[23] Davis, *The Patriot Parliament of 1689*, Preface, xciv; Davis was here showing how much he had been impressed by Mac Geoghegan's history.
[24] Davis, *The Patriot Parliament of 1689*, 64–7, 141.

of [the king's] people'.[25] Then also, said Davis, the assembly of 1689 had denied the English parliament the right to legislate for Ireland, and had thus established Ireland as 'a distinct kingdom' more comprehensively than had the 1782 parliament.[26] Furthermore, according to Davis, the assembly of 1689 had 'anticipated more than 1782' by granting freedom of conscience and 'religious equality' to all, and symbolized this by admitting Protestant as well as Catholic prelates as members of the upper house. The 1689 parliament, he claimed, was even more far-sighted in this respect because it had stipulated that the money to be collected from tithes should be shared between the churches for the maintenance of their respective clergies in proportion to the numbers of their adherents within the country's population.[27]

On the basis of these findings, Davis pronounced that 'the idea' that had motivated the patriotic members of the 1782 parliament was 'to be found full-grown in 1689'. This, for Davis, meant that 'the pedigree of [Ireland's] freedom [was] a century older than we thought, and Ireland had another Parliament to be proud of' besides that of 1782. More to the point, Davis identified William Molyneux as the link between the two assemblies because 'in 1698 just nine years [later], while the acts of this great Senate were fresh, Molyneux published his *Case of Ireland*'.[28] Thus, proceeding from the assumption that *post hoc* always means *propter hoc*, Davis drew a conclusion that the proceedings of the 1689 parliament had inspired Molyneux to write his *Case*, which in turn had provided 'the achievers of the revolution of 1782 with principles and a precedent'.[29]

From the evidence he cited, Davis was convinced that the members of the 'Patriot' parliament of 1689 had acted with justification and restraint, but he accepted that the 'descendant of the Williamite' would not be immediately persuaded of this. However, he remained hopeful that his account of the assembly would give reason to this person of Williamite ancestry 'to sympathise with the urgent patriotism and loyalty of the parliament, rather than dwell on its errors, or on the sufferings which civil war had inflicted on his forefathers'.[30] Whenever this representative of the planter interest was brought about to this way of thinking, Davis was confident that he would enter an accord with the 'heir of the Jacobite' after which 'both' would be 'brought to deplore the falsehoods, corruption and

---

[25] Davis, *The Patriot Parliament of 1689*, 40–42, the quoted words concerning the Act of Settlement came from the king's speech as Davis masked the fact that the intention of the majority to repeal both Poynings's Act of 1494 and the Act of Settlement in its entirety was abandoned on the insistence of the king, eds., *The Acts*, eds., Bergin and Lyall, xxxv.

[26] Davis, *The Patriot Parliament of 1689*, 138.

[27] Davis, *The Patriot Parliament of 1689*, Preface, xciv; *The Acts*, eds., Bergin and Lyall, xxxiv–xxxv.

[28] Davis, *The Patriot Parliament of 1689*, preface, xciii; for the best edition of the *Case* by William Molyneux with comments on the uses to which it was put in the eighteenth century, Patrick Hyde Kelly, ed., *The Case of Ireland's Being bound by Acts of Parliament in England, Stated*, Dublin, 1698 (Dublin, 2018).

[29] Davis, *The Patriot Parliament of 1689*, 1–2.

[30] Davis, *The Patriot Parliament of 1689*, 38–9.

RE-IMAGINING IRELAND'S EARLY MODERN PAST 229

forgeries of English aristocrats, the imprudence of an English king, and the fickleness of the English people'.[31] Such a reconciliation, pronounced Davis, would exemplify the beneficial influence of philosophy on people's thinking and would demonstrate how history 'which [had] been the armoury of faction, may become the temple of reconciliation'.[32]

Davis's plea, based on history, for reconciliation between traditional adversaries was directed primarily at Protestants. Mitchel, on the other hand, in his biography of Hugh O'Neill, appealed to Catholics to disregard the unquestioned wrongs that their ancestors had suffered, particularly at the time of plantation in Ulster, in the interest of the greater good of creating a new Irish nation. He undertook this biography as one of the 'Library of Ireland' series of books that Davis commissioned and that would be 'devoted to the history, poetry, antiquities and literature of Ireland'. In this series, according to P.S. O'Hegarty, Davis 'decided what was to be written and who was to write it...and...they wrote what he dictated'. An 'Advertiser' used to launch the series announced that every book published would be 'National in aim, in heart, in principle' intending 'that Ireland may take her just position among intellectual nations'. This would be achieved, according to the 'Advertiser', once 'Irish History' was revived 'in its truth and purity cleared of the falsehood and prejudice so long and so strenuously heaped upon it'.[33] By this was meant a history that would be purged of the denominational and cultural polemics that had marred previous histories of Ireland. Instead, as Davis would have it, history should be written only by those who were to be 'searchers for truth' and who would 'not approach the subject unless it be in a spirit enlightened by philosophy and warmed by charity'.[34]

As he set about advancing Davis's agenda in his biography of Hugh O'Neill, Mitchel began by giving his readers reason to take pride in the achievements of 'Aodh O'Neill, Prince of Ulster', as Mitchel described the hero of his narrative. O'Neill's principal accomplishment, according to Mitchel, was that he had brought together in Ulster, and throughout Ireland, those who had been traditional rivals and who had united under his leadership to oppose the Crown forces that threatened their independence during the closing decade of the sixteenth century.[35] The disunity among Irish lords previous to this merger

---

[31] Davis, *The Patriot Parliament*, 38–9.   [32] Davis, *The Patriot Parliament*, 38–9.

[33] 'Library of Ireland Advertiser', single sheet filed in RIA, under Haliday Pamphlets for the year 1846, no. 1979. As the book series proceeded, updated versions of the 'Advertiser' were sometimes bound within the covers of other publications in the series. One such updated advertisement was bound inside the back cover of the copy held in the library of the RIA of Thomas Mac Nevin, *The Confiscation of Ulster* (Dublin, 1846); P.S. O'Hegarty, 'The Library of Ireland, 1845–7', M.J. Mc Manus, *Thomas Davis and Young Ireland, 1845–1945* (Dublin, 1945), 110–12, quotation 112. See also James Quinn, *Young Ireland*, esp. 11–15, 24–41, 42–59.

[34] Davis, *The Patriot Parliament of 1689*, 38–9.

[35] Quinn, *Young Ireland and the Writing of Irish History*, 4–5 and *passim*; Mitchel, *The Life and Times of Aodh O'Neill*.

230 IMAGINING IRELAND'S PASTS

satisfied Mitchel that 'there was still no Irish nation' when O'Neill had begun his work. This gave him reason to marvel how 'the grandson of the Dundalk blacksmith' and an autodidact grew up to be equally 'at home in the halls of Greenwich as Dungannon', and had succeeded in healing 'the feuds of rival chiefs, and out of these discordant elements to create and bind together an Irish nation'.[36]

This narrative was in keeping with what Mac Geoghegan had said of O'Neill when he had rehabilitated his reputation in the 1760s. However, Mitchel seems to have been more reliant on Gainsford or Stafford (considered in Chapter 3) than on Mac Geoghegan, when he pronounced that religion had contributed little to his hero's success since 'O'Neill was apparently no strict Catholic, and whenever he visited Dublin scrupled not to accompany the Lord Deputy to the church'.[37] O'Neill's religious laxity, that Mitchel considered a virtue, made his achievement in blending 'national feeling and religious zeal' all the more remarkable. Mitchel therefore saluted O'Neill as 'the deliverer of his country and most gracious champion of the Catholic religion' who almost brought an end to a corrupt government and presented a formidable challenge to 'the detested spirit of English imperialism'.[38]

Having deemed opposition to empire—which Mitchel loathed—to have been O'Neill's principal objective, Mitchel showed no hesitation about praising his every military achievement and giving credit to him for all accomplishments rather than to the dashing Red Hugh O'Donnell, whom he represented as a romantic figure whose vision was no more expansive than that of his progenitors. However, in praising O'Neill, Mitchel had to concede that he had been ultimately defeated, and in doing so he looked more critically at what O'Neill had accomplished. On the positive side, Mitchel credited O'Neill with having fashioned a 'distinct nation'. This included the 'Milesian Irish', of which O'Neill himself was a member, together with some of the Catholic descendants of the English conquerors of the twelfth century who had been persuaded by O'Neill to lay aside their customary animosity towards all things Gaelic and to accept him as their leader. However, the harsher reality for Mitchel was that the outcome of the Battle of Kinsale meant that the 'nation' that O'Neill had forged had been 'defeated and finally subdued', after which, following the death of Queen Elizabeth, her successor King James VI and I was given the opportunity to introduce a plantation to Ulster.

As he described the process of plantation in Ulster, Mitchel, like Davis in his discussion of the Cromwellian confiscation, expressed his revulsion at the injustices inflicted on the Irish who had remained in Ulster after their defeated leaders had fled to the Continent. It was then, he said, that 'marauding adventurers' had been given the opportunity to seize lands formerly held by the

---

[36] Mitchel, *Aodh O'Neill*, 73, 74, 77.   [37] Mitchel, *Aodh O'Neill*, 76-7.
[38] Mitchel, *Aodh O'Neill*, 142, 218.

RE-IMAGINING IRELAND'S EARLY MODERN PAST   231

Gaelic Irish, and to introduce 'the church of the stranger' that then persecuted those unwilling to accept its doctrines.[39] However, after this moving condemnation, Mitchel, unlike Davis in relation to the Cromwellian plantation, argued that the experience of dispossession and colonization was not unique to Ireland since civility had always been advanced by means of conquest. Thus, as he saw it, the behaviour of British settlers in Ireland, however deplorable, was no more reprehensible than the actions of those who had founded the Roman Empire. Thus Mitchel, unlike Davis in relation to the Cromwellians, encouraged forgiveness towards the planters in Ulster for their depredations because, as with the establishment of the Roman Empire, there had been some positive consequences from their scheme of expropriation and colonization in Ulster. The positive outcome was that with the plantation 'new blood was infused into old Ireland, [and] the very undertakers that planted Ireland grew racy of the soil and their descendant's children became, thank God, not only Irish but united Irish'.[40] Here, Mitchel was referring to the involvement of many of Ulster Presbyterian descent—the stock to which he himself belonged—in the rebellion of the United Irishmen in 1798. This, as he saw it, legitimized the presence in Ireland of the descendants of the Ulster planters and made them members of a new Irish nation that, unlike the nation forged by Hugh O'Neill and defeated on the field of Kinsale, embraced Protestants as well as Catholics. Therefore, in relation to the descendants of the Ulster planters, Mitchel decreed that after more than two centuries on their estates, theirs was 'far too old a title to be questioned... [and] it would now be ill striving to unplant them'.[41] Mitchel was thus calling on people of Gaelic origin to abandon any expectations they may have fostered of recovering what their ancestors had lost in the Ulster plantation. Then he pleaded also with Catholics more generally to cast aside any bitter memories they had because of religious persecution in previous centuries since these episodes were 'all past and over', and 'the very penal laws, last relics of that bloody business, [were] with the days before the flood'.[42] In this, Mitchel was adhering to Davis's prescription for the formation of a new nation within which all people of Irish birth would cast aside 'bigotry' and 'feel a love of all sects, a philosophical eye to the merits and demerits of all, and a solemn and haughty impartiality in speaking of all'.[43]

Since Mitchel's text on Hugh O'Neill, like that of Davis on the 1689 parliament, was prescriptive, it remains to consider how each influenced the behaviour and attitudes of their associates in the Young Ireland movement and also the audiences in Ireland to which each was directed. The Davis text on the 1689 parliament was, as I have suggested, aimed primarily at Protestant readers, and there is no evidence to suggest that many, or any, within this wider community were persuaded

[39] Mitchel, *Aodh O'Neill*, 73–7.   [40] Mitchel, *Aodh O'Neill*, vii.
[41] Mitchel, *Aodh O'Neill*, vii–viii.   [42] Mitchel, *Aodh O'Neill*, xi.
[43] These words come from Thomas Davis, *Literary and Historical Essays*, ed., C.G.D., 37–8.

232   IMAGINING IRELAND'S PASTS

by his arguments. Within the Young Ireland group, Mitchel showed some twenty years later, when he next wrote on Ireland's history, that he accepted without question what had been argued by Davis. In this narrative Mitchel, by now an exile in the United States, bewailed how Catholics who had remained in Ireland had suffered from the Penal Laws, but his dejection over this was offset because a 'thoroughly Irish spirit' had been kept alive by the Irish regiments of the French army who, after they had fallen foul of 'the dark record of the English atrocity in Ireland', had been motivated by a burning desire 'to encounter and overthrow the British power upon any field', on which he cited the Abbé Mac Geoghegan. Then he pronounced that this manifestation of Irish patriotism had run in parallel to 'a Colonial Nationality' that he associated with Swift, Lucas, and the Volunteers, and that, he believed, had flourished 'among the English in Ireland'.[44] Mitchel did not identify any specific connection between the two, nor did he seem to consider it important to establish such a link. However, Thomas D'Arcy McGee, who had also been assigned by Davis to write one of the Library of Ireland volumes, acknowledged that it was far from easy 'to connect former ages of Catholic nationalism with our hereditary modern league for parliamentary independence'.[45] However, D'Arcy McGee had no sooner identified the problem than he declared a solution and pronounced, presumably on the strength of what Davis had written, that 'the life of William Molyneux...was a link between the old and new phases of nationality'. This, for D'Arcy McGee, meant that Irish nationality had never died because when 'the Celtic spirit had emigrated-the Catholic spirit was paralyzed-the "spirit of Molyneux" substituted them both'.[46] Even if this assertion made little impression on Protestants of unionist inclination it became a trope in all future nationalist history writing on Ireland that traced a seamless development in Irish national sentiment over time.

If the arguments put forward by Davis concerning the historical significance of the 1689 parliament failed to register with the Protestant hard core, the controversial pleas that Mitchel had addressed to Catholics in the course of writing his biography of Hugh O'Neill won an early endorsement from one Catholic author. This was Thomas Mac Nevin, (1814–48), a journalist, historian and lawyer, and also a close associate of Davis, who had commissioned him to write two volumes

---

[44] John Mitchel, *The History of Ireland, from the Treaty of Limerick to the Present Time* (Preface to the New York edition, 1868).

[45] Thomas D'Arcy McGee, *The Irish Writers of the Seventeenth Century* (Dublin, 1846), 228.

[46] D'Arcy McGee, *The Irish Writers*, 238–9. Patrick Kelly has made it clear that reference to the 'spirit of Molyneux' supposedly made by Grattan in the Irish parliament on 16 April 1782 came from an interpolation to that speech made four decades after the event, *The Case*, ed., Kelly, 250. Patrick Kelly shows further that D'Arcy McGee's argument was even more implausible because Molyneux had always held that one solution to what he saw was the anomaly of having an English parliament legislate for Ireland when the country had a parliament of its own was to have Ireland ruled directly from England with representation at Westminster from the Protestant Nation; *The Case*, ed., Kelly, 37.

for the Library of Ireland series.[47] In the first, entitled *The History of the Volunteers of 1782*, Mac Nevin explained how this exclusively Protestant body, formed at the behest of Irish Protestant landowners to seek 'the recovery of Irish independence' had been inspired by Molyneux, Swift, and Lucas, and thus also, following the logic of Davis, by the parliament of 1689. They had made progress, he claimed, by collaborating with Flood, Grattan, and other 'Patriots' in the Irish Parliament of 1782 to use their position as the only significant armed force in the country to persuade the Rockingham Ministry to revoke the 1720 Declaratory Act that had reiterated the claims of the English parliament to legislate for Ireland. As well as looking backwards in time, Mac Nevin also looked forward. In so doing, he identified 'strong analogies between the case of America and Ireland'. For him, as also for Michael Doheny (1805–62) in a volume in Library of Ireland series on the American Revolution, 'the example of America' in challenging the authority of Britain proved 'contagious', especially 'in Ireland [which] was not long without showing some of the symptoms of revolution'.[48]

'Volunteering' was therefore, according to Mac Nevin 'a new spirit' inspired by the 1776 American 'declaration of war against old and obsolete opinions, systems and dispositions'. Mac Nevin, at this point, had reached the same position as Mitchel as is apparent from his remark that 'the spirit of volunteering' was nowhere more conspicuous than in the Ulster counties that had been subjected to plantation. In these counties in 1782, he pronounced, 'armed liberty walked most boldly amongst the scenes of former confiscation'.[49] He also saluted this 'army of the people [as]...a democratic army', because the Volunteers 'elected their own commanders' from among those of their social betters who, like their 'general', James Caulfeild, Lord Charlemont (1728–99), had a previous record of 'active patriotism'.[50] For Mac Nevin, the Volunteers could also be described as 'the National Army of [17]82' because, while this force represented only the 'Protestant Nation', Catholics had 'looked with pride upon the glorious pageant of their armed countrymen'.[51]

What had happened in 1782 was in Mac Nevin's words 'the great revolution' that bore witness to the manifestation of an Irish national sentiment among the country's Protestant population. This sentiment, he contended, was expressed

---

[47] Thomas Mac Nevin, *The History of the Volunteers of 1782* (Dublin, 1845); for a biographical note on Mac Nevin see that by James Quinn, *Dictionary of Irish Biography*, vol. 6, 157–8.

[48] Mac Nevin, *The History of the Volunteers*, 54–6; Michael Doheny, *The History of the American Revolution* (Dublin, 1846); for a biographical note on Doheny see that by Desmond McCabe and James Quinn, the *Dictionary of Irish Biography*, vol. 3, 355–6. The background to this episode is summarized, Kelly, 'The Politics of Protestant Ascendancy, 1730–1790', Kelly, ed., *The Cambridge History of Ireland*, vol. 3, *1730–1880*, 48–73.

[49] Mac Nevin, *The History of the Volunteers*, 80, 152.

[50] Mac Nevin, *The History of the Volunteers*, 81, 82, 108; for a biographical note on Charlemont see that by James Kelly, *Dictionary of Irish Biography*, vol. 2, 428–31.

[51] Mac Nevin, *The History of the Volunteers*, 24, 35, 83.

234   IMAGINING IRELAND'S PASTS

even more strongly with the formation of the Society of United Irishmen, which Mac Nevin considered a natural extension of the Volunteers.[52] Mac Nevin identified this evolving nationalism particularly with Molyneux, whose 'Case of Ireland', he pronounced, had been 'burned by the common hangman at the bidding of the English House of Commons'. However, he contended that Irish nationality had been boosted, in the generation of Flood and Grattan, by 'the American Revolution, the giant birth of a new world of liberty', and carried even further by the United Irishmen.[53] What most amazed Mac Nevin was the strength of the Volunteering movement in those parts of Ulster that had been subjected to plantation, and that Lord Charlemont, the leader of the Irish Volunteers, was a direct descendant of Sir Toby Caulfeild who had been one of the principal beneficiaries of plantation in Ulster. Mac Nevin, like Mitchel, considered plantation to be no more than 'national robbery', legitimized by 'the usual slanders of English avarice'. However, notwithstanding his personal opinion of the morality of plantations, Mac Nevin reached the same conclusion as had Mitchel that the sufferings and injustices endured by the native population of Ulster had been justified because 'in the scene of plunder and oppression, a new race [would] rise, which [would] compensate the miseries of the Ulster plantation'.[54]

Given Mac Nevin's ready willingness as a historian to comply with the prescriptions laid down by both Mitchel and Davis for a revised history of Ireland, it is unsurprising that Davis assigned Mac Nevin the further task of writing on the plantation of Ulster: a topic that most Catholic authors regarded with revulsion. It seemed at the outset that Davis had chosen well because, as with his book of the previous year on the Volunteers, Mac Nevin proved himself a master at sustaining his arguments with vivid word pictures. In this respect he commenced *The Confiscation of Ulster* with the pronouncement that 'nothing [could] surpass the agreeable picture given' in the Montgomery manuscript of 'the settlement' of Scots in the Ards peninsula in County Down. There, he proclaimed, 'every body...minded his own business at the plough and spade, and building, and the nursing of orchards, and the planting of fruit trees and the making of ditches. The old wives spun...young girls plied their nimble fingers and nimbler tongues, and every one was innocently busy'.[55] Mac Nevin accepted that this bucolic scene could easily seduce those prepared to overlook that 'the greatness of the Montgomeries and Hamiltons' had been established 'in the land

[52] Mac Nevin, *The History of the Volunteers*, Preface.
[53] Mac Nevin, *The History of the Volunteers*, 35, 37, 55; when he asserted that Molyneux's *Case* had been publicly burned on the instruction of the English parliament Mac Nevin was repeating two nationalist fictions that Patrick Kelly has traced to the Irish radical Charles Lucas, to the 1749 and 1770 editions of the text, and to remarks made by Wolfe Tone in 1792, *The Case*, ed., Kelly, 47–8.
[54] Mac Nevin, *The History of the Volunteers*, 28–30.
[55] Mac Nevin, *The Confiscation of Ulster*, 85.

of the O'Neills'.[56] At this point Mac Nevin was reflecting how the Clandeboye O'Neills had become displaced through fraud and commercial devices, but he contended that his ability to turn a blind eye to injustice was strained beyond endurance when he witnessed how the fertile land of the province had fallen into 'the barbarian hand of English rapine' when the official plantation policy was implemented in the heartland of Ulster. In stating his revised position he returned to one of the rationalizations for plantation that had been offered by Mitchel, and registered his dissent from it by likening what had happened in Ulster to the Roman colonization of Britain, to the expulsion of the Moors from Spain, to the actions in the New World of 'bloody Cortes and the insatiable Pizarro', and to the colonial actions of 'perfidious Frenchmen' in North Africa at the moment he was writing. In doing so he respectfully reverted to Mitchel's argument that 'human enlightenment demands its victims', but then, having given due consideration to this aphorism, he concluded that 'the march of civilization [had] been too often upon the crushed hearts, and plundered rights of man'. This, he contended, had been never truer than with the Ulster plantation, which he now described as 'the most abandoned scheme of national ruin and confiscation that ever was devised by avarice, incivility and perpetrated by triumphant fraud'.[57] Its most reprehensible aspect, he contended, was that it had been decreed as one of the conditions for plantation that the 'mere Irish' could never become equal with the planters. This realization forced Mac Nevin to rethink the praise he had lavished on the Volunteers only the year before. Now, on reflection and confronted with new evidence, Mac Nevin conceded that 'for one short period, brilliant, futile and delusive, a new spirit seemed to arise in the principalities of the O'Neills and the O'Donnells', but he concluded with a heavy heart that, having taken account of the grave injustice associated with the plantation in Ulster, 'the reasons of Molyneux' and 'the inspired eloquence of Grattan' had achieved nothing because 'alas! even in that great movement the "mere Irish" were to be again excluded' and what might have been 'a great army' of Volunteers was made 'a mere gew gaw and a pageant and what might have been a National Revolution little more than a military pantomime'.[58]

Mac Nevin offered no explanation, apart from the evidence of injustice that had come to his attention when he had looked closely in the plantation process in Ulster, why, within a year, he had reversed his opinion not only on the plantation in Ulster but also on the Volunteers. In the course of doing so, he left no doubt that he was consciously parting company with Mitchel, because he could not reconcile Mitchel's argument that all of Ireland's sufferings in the past could be

---

[56] Mac Nevin, *The Confiscation of Ulster*, 97; on the actual acquisitions in Ulster of the Montgomerys and Hamiltons, Raymond Gillespie, *Colonial Ulster: The Settlement of East Ulster, 1600–1641* (Cork, 1985).

[57] Mac Nevin, *The Confiscation of Ulster*, 249, 264.

[58] Mac Nevin, *The Confiscation of Ulster*, 147–8.

236 IMAGINING IRELAND'S PASTS

blamed on a remote English state with the reality that the descendants of some of the agents of that state, starting with the heirs of Sir Arthur Chichester, still enjoyed the benefits of what Mac Nevin now characterized as seventeenth-century pillage. Neither could the 'patriotism' of Charlemont blind Mac Nevin to the fact that the wealth and expansive cultural interests of that nobleman had been enabled by the ill-gotten gains of his ancestor. Mac Nevin's acknowledgement of such evidence may go some way to explain his sudden abandonment of the new history. However, the death of Davis in September 1845 was possibly of equal importance in explaining his volte-face. He and Davis had always been close, and Mac Nevin was devastated by the death of a man who, he declared, had been 'more than a brother [who he had] loved better than all the brothers' he had.[59] However, while the death of Davis may have left Mac Nevin bereft, it also freed him from the obligation to use his talents to sustain an argument with which he, as a Catholic, found it difficult to identify.

As Mac Nevin ceased to cleave to the orthodoxy that had been proclaimed by Davis and then by Mitchel, he was falling into line with the other Catholics who were involved with the Library of Ireland series. One such was Charles Gavan Duffy (1816–1903) who had agreed with Davis's request that he write of the 1641 rebellion under the title *The Rising of the North*, only to plead lack of time to bring it to completion. Instead, he published *The Ballad Poetry of Ireland* within the series, and there, as we shall note later, he did encourage reconciliation between the two traditions in Ireland but not, as he would have seen it, by presenting a version of the past with which he would have felt uncomfortable.[60] Moreover, we can see from the précis provided by Fr. C.P. Meehan of what Gavan Duffy had intended to write in *The Rising of the North* that Gavan Duffy had no intention of suggesting to his co-religionists that Irish Catholics should overlook or forgive the many injustices associated with the plantation in Ulster and the enforcement of the Protestant reformation.[61] Then in 1893, by which time Gavan Duffy had become a venerable statesman, he explained that he had come to believe, and perhaps had always believed, that Davis's ambition to fashion a new Irish nation based on a shared past had never been more than a chimera. Instead, Gavan Duffy spoke of 'two nations'—one Catholic, whose members had become bonded together by shared ancestral persecution, and the other Protestant, whose members had been inspired by the words and example of Swift, Grattan, and the Volunteers—and his hope of 1893 was that the members of each 'nation' had

---

[59] Cited in Quinn. 'Biographical note', 168.

[60] For a biographical note on Charles Gavan Duffy by Patrick Maume, *Dictionary of Irish Biography*, vol. 3, 505–8; Charles Gavan Duffy, *The Ballad Poetry of Ireland* (Dublin, 1845).

[61] For Meehan on what Duffy might have written, C.P. Meehan, *The Confederation of Kilkenny* (Dublin 1846), 'Introduction' addressed 'To the readers of The Library of Ireland', v–xii; Duffy himself returned to the subject of the 1641 rebellion in 1893 when he indicated that what Meehan had said of his intentions had been correct; Davis, *The Patriot Parliament of 1689*, 'Introduction' by Duffy, xxxv–lvi.

RE-IMAGINING IRELAND'S EARLY MODERN PAST   237

learnt from history how 'the wicked past should be understood and deplored', thus bringing them to 'understand each other and live at peace hereafter'.[62]

This suggests that Gavan Duffy, no less than Mac Nevin, had always felt uneasy by the strictures of Davis and Mitchel that Irish people (Protestant and Catholic alike) should learn to forget what they had been led to believe had been the injustices and the threats experienced by their ancestors in the interest of bringing the two together within a composite nation. This had never made sense to Fr. Charles P. Meehan (1812–90), a committed member of the Repeal movement who became linked to Young Ireland, presumably through his friendship with Gavan Duffy to whom he was not only a friend but also a father confessor.[63] Davis had commissioned Meehan to write two volumes for the Library of Ireland series but since these did not appear until 1846 and 1847, he was under no pressure to conform to the orthodoxies being promoted by the deceased Davis. One of the two volumes, and the second to be published, entitled *The Geraldines*, discussed conflict in Munster in the sixteenth century as this had been reflected upon in exile during the early years of the seventeenth century by Dominic (or Daniel) O'Daly, an Irish Dominican priest.[64] As a Catholic priest, Meehan remained convinced that the persecutions inflicted on Irish people by English and Scottish intruders in past centuries had been religiously motivated, but that these had also hoped to deprive the Irish of their estates by provoking them to rebel. At the same time, as a translator of Dominic O'Daly, Meehan, like O'Sullivan Beare in the seventeenth century, was convinced that when James Fitzmaurice Fitzgerald, and then the earl of Desmond, had opposed the forces of the Crown in the sixteenth century they were fighting primarily to defend their faith and only incidentally to preserve their inheritances. This interpretation of events in the sixteenth century did not necessarily contradict what Mitchel had had to say of an emerging Irish nationalism that had culminated in the achievements of Hugh O'Neill. However, as we may recall, Mitchel had argued that the nation that had then emerged had been brought to an abrupt end on the field of Kinsale.

Meehan's dissent from this view became clear from his second contribution to the series published under the title of *The Confederation of Kilkenny*.[65] Here, as Meehan filled in the early seventeenth-century background to the establishment of the Confederation in 1642, he detailed how government officials had persisted

---

[62] Davis, *The Patriot Parliament of 1689*, 'Introduction' by Duffy, vii–viii.

[63] On Meehan see the entry by Linda Lunney and James Quinn, *Dictionary of Irish Biography*, vol. 6, 467–8.

[64] Fr. C.P. Meehan, *The Geraldines, earls of Desmond, and the persecution of the Irish Catholics* (Dublin, 1847), this essentially was a translation of Dominic O'Daly, *Initium, incrementum, et exitus familiae Geraldinorum, Desmoniae comitum, palatinorum Kyerriae in Hibernia, ac persecutionis haeriticorum description* (Lisbon, 1655); more generally on O'Daly see Margaret Mac Curtain, *Ambassador Extraordinaire: Daniel O'Daly, 1595-1662* (Dublin, 2017); for Dr Mac Curtain's appraisal of the Meehan text, 246–64.

[65] Meehan, *The Confederation of Kilkenny*.

238   IMAGINING IRELAND'S PASTS

with the practices of the sixteenth century by their use of the 'rack and the thumbscrew' and of the proselytizing 'School of Wards'—as he mockingly described the Court of Wards—to 'subvert the religion of Irish Catholics and divest them of their patrimonial inheritance'. As a consequence, Meehan found it unsurprising that the 'people' had entered upon rebellion in 1641 because they had been 'goaded to desperation', and he considered this a further manifestation of the Irish nationalism that, according to Mitchel, had died on the field of Kinsale. This belief gave Meehan reason to rejoice that what had commenced as a rebellion became a 'revolution' on 23 October 1642—precisely a year after the Protestant date of commemoration for the 1641 rebellion—when Catholics of Gaelic and Old English ancestry entered into a 'coalition' with each other and established a 'Confederation, the avowed object of which was to assert by force of arms the free and independent exercise of the Catholic religion and the restoration of the churches to their rightful inheritors'.[66]

In *The Confederation of Kilkenny*, Fr. Meehan showed himself as adept as any other writer in the Library of Ireland series at advancing his argument through word pictures. The most moving of his many constructs was that of the 'spirit-stirring scene' when 'the Catholic deputies' were assembling in Kilkenny to establish 'the federative government', guided by 'a congregation of bishops' who had declared the war on which they were about to engage to be 'lawful and pious'.[67] He was impressed also by the 'rapid transition [of the Irish] from heart-breaking thraldom to [the] bold and armed independence' that had been enabled by the return of Owen Roe O'Neill and Thomas Preston from the exile to which 'religious persecution had driven them... from their homes'. The efforts of these 'men [who] drew their swords' for the 'independence' of 'the Faith' had, claimed Meehan, been further supported by the Pope, since Ireland was 'fully devoted to the Chair of St Peter'. Philip IV of Spain and 'chivalrous France' had, he claimed, also supported these endeavours.[68] Meehan was certain 'that the men who were engaged' with this bid for religious freedom 'must have prevailed had they been true to themselves and firmly banded together'. Tragically, according to Meehan's narrative, their common purpose was lost because 'mutual jealousies, distinctions, temporizing expediency and wily diplomacy broke their compact awry and left them victims to the horrors which subsequently desolated the land'.[69]

When it came to the question of nationality, Meehan, in his history of the Catholic Confederation, was writing to explain how the emergence of a fully fledged Irish nation had been frustrated by a variety of factors. Prime among these, he claimed, was the duplicity and incompetence of such as Lords Clanricard, Inchiquin, and Antrim as well as General Thomas Preston. However, his principal wrath was reserved for James Butler, marquis, and future duke of

[66] Meehan, *The Confederation*, vi, vii, viii, ix.   [67] Meehan, *The Confederation*, ix, 14, 41.
[68] Meehan, *The Confederation*, 14.   [69] Meehan, *The Confederation*, ix.

Ormond, whose 'fortunes and those of his adherents were created out of the ruin of the Catholics'.[70] On the other hand, he lavished praise on Owen Roe O'Neill whose 'name and reputation changed [the] design' of those who had led the initial rebellion 'and determined them to strike another blow for their native land'.[71] There was no doubt in Meehan's mind that O'Neill, and therefore the Irish Catholic nation, would have achieved total victory if only the leaders of the Confederation had supported him at critical junctures. This was particularly true, according to Meehan, since O'Neill enjoyed the full confidence of Rinuccini, the papal nuncio, who, he claimed 'loved Ireland and would have died for her independence'.[72] As Meehan rounded on those who had branded the nuncio a bigot, he borrowed the language of liberals when asserting that Rinuccini had pursued an 'enlightened policy in insisting on freedom of conscience and the untrammelled exercise of [Catholicism]'. Moreover, Meehan believed that Rinuccini would have succeeded in this endeavour had he not had 'to contend with men who were the avowed and unrelenting enemies of the Irish Catholics'.[73] For Meehan therefore the failure of Rinuccini meant that the Confederation had failed in its purpose and that Irish nationalism had suffered a major reverse, primarily because of the sectional and ideological divisions within its ranks that had emerged during the course of the conflict. Therefore, where Meehan had opened his narrative with a pen picture of the initial assembly of the Confederation, he concluded it with a moving description of the scene of bitter disappointment that was enacted in Galway from whence Rinuccini finally abandoned his 'luckless nunciature' and 'hastened to retire from that fated land, where to use his own sentiment "he had never seen the sun"'.[74]

Meehan's consolation, as he brought *The Confederation of Kilkenny* to a conclusion, was that while the Irish nation had suffered a major blow from the overthrow of the Confederacy and the rise of Cromwell, it had not proven fatal. That Ireland would 'soon rise from thraldom and provincialism, to take her place amid the nations' was clear to Meehan because 'a Confederation of another sort...a great unarmed Confederacy... [had] sprung up and done more for the "dear old land" than all that the sword of Owen Roe was able to accomplish'.[75] Some, but not all, in the Young Ireland movement would have looked favourably on Meehan's obvious salute to O'Connell. However, the stance he took both as a historian and as commentator on contemporary events is likely to have encouraged dissent within the Young Ireland movement. Meehan's insistence that the Irish nation was the product of an amalgamation between Catholics of Gaelic and Old English descent who had become bonded by religious persecution would have convinced some of his Young Ireland colleagues that nothing had changed

---

[70] Meehan, *The Confederation*, 227.   [71] Meehan, *The Confederation*, 38.
[72] Meehan, *The Confederation*, 227.   [73] Meehan, *The Confederation*, 225.
[74] Meehan, *The Confederation*, 224.   [75] Meehan, *The Confederation*, 228, xi–xii.

from the previous century. However, Meehan's blatant disregard for the orthodoxy preached by Davis and Mitchel must have encouraged other Catholic contributors to the Library of Ireland series to similarly break the code since he enjoyed the moral authority of a priest and continued to be a member in good standing of Young Ireland.

Gavan Duffy seems to have detected a rise of ideological dissent within the ranks even before the death of Davis, and it may have been in the interest of avoiding division that he opted as his contribution to the Library of Ireland series to publish *The Ballad Poetry of Ireland* rather than his projected *Rising of the North*. It seems from the ballad poems he chose for publication that, already in 1845, he was moving away from the notion of the existence of a singly unified nation that Davis and Mitchel hoped to prove through history, and towards the 'two nation theory' that he would articulate clearly in 1893. This is suggested by his inclusion within the collection not only of emigration laments and 'native ballads'—some of them English renditions of Irish-language originals—but also of some 'Anglo Irish ballads—the production of educated men, with English tongues but Irish hearts' who had grown 'to be national gradually, but instructively and half consciously'.[76] Gavan Duffy was clearly intent on striking a balance between the two by juxtaposing Catholic ballads such as James Clarence Mangan's 'Lament for the Tironian and Tirconnellian Princes, buried in Rome', with William Drennan's 'The Wake of William Orr', which saluted this Protestant 'proto-martyr' for the Republican cause who had been executed in 1797 as part of the official effort to discourage the rebellion that officials knew to be brewing in Ulster, and that broke out anyhow the following year. In that collection also Gavan Duffy included 'Oliver's Advice: an Orange Ballad' by Colonel Blacker together with 'The Orange and the Green' by Gerald Griffin that celebrated a meeting of minds between individuals from opposing denominational camps that had come in contact with each other, initially in the town of Bandon—an Orange outpost—and later in Wexford during the course of the 1798 rebellion.[77]

It is clear that, with his *Ballad Poetry of Ireland*, Gavan Duffy was contributing an instalment to 'A Ballad History of Ireland' that Davis wanted to see in print as well as committed to memory. However, in the course of doing so Gavan Duffy was concerned in 1845 to use his poetic selection from two remembered pasts to demonstrate that Protestants and Catholics in Ireland of polar opposite views could learn to co-operate with each other in the interest of creating a more harmonious community. His success in demonstrating how this could be achieved through verse may explain why the Library of Ireland series, which had been

[76] Charles Gavan Duffy, *The Ballad Poetry of Ireland*, citation is from the 40th edition (Dublin, 1874).

[77] Duffy, *The Ballad Poetry*, 102–9; 80–2; 83–6; 96–100; the term protomartyr is that used by Guy Beiner, who has detailed the case of William Orr, *Forgetful Remembrance*, esp. 59–84.

principally dedicated to publishing the prose histories that Davis had commissioned, began after his death to publish more literary and dramatic material rather than histories. This switch seemed all the more reasonable because it had become clear that would-be authors of the commissioned histories were experiencing difficulties over disregarding inherited memories from the past that were proving inconvenient when they tried to imagine an early modern past that fitted with the prescription of Davis.

Thus, apart from the reconsideration about the past that was stimulated by some of the prose histories we have been discussing, the enduring contribution of Young Ireland to re-imagining Ireland's past was effected through historical ballads published in *The Nation* and other newspapers both before and after the death of Davis. Many of these were subsequently anthologized, and later again republished in school textbooks, and they proved extraordinarily popular. Thus, Gavan Duffy's *Ballad Poetry of Ireland*, originally published in 1845, had gone into a sixth edition by 1846, by which time it had already achieved 'a larger circulation than any book published in Ireland since the Union'.[78] Many poems, as Davis had intended, expounded on England's wrongs and Ireland's sufferings, and several of them, such as Davis's own 'Celts and Saxons' and 'Orange and Green will Carry the Day', made the case that it was place of birth rather than creed that determined what it was to be Irish. This was as a preliminary to arguing that when people in Ireland learned to cast aside their differences that England was exploiting to its advantage, nothing would stand in the way of the country achieving its full potential.[79]

Some ballads were set to music that was composed specifically for the purpose, but more were set to well-known airs, which meant that they could enter into the repertoire of vernacular history almost from the moment of composition. This vernacular version of Ireland's past departed consciously from the fatalistic accounts presented in Gaelic verse of previous centuries where Ireland had been portrayed as a forlorn figure bereft of defenders in the aftermath of humiliating defeat. Instead, authors conjured images of a past in which, in each succeeding generation, some Irish leaders had come forward to defend the country from oppression. It was then suggested that these heroes had kept a national spirit alive even when their victories had been more moral than martial. Aubrey de Vere (1814–1902) proved especially inventive when in writing of the Battle of Kinsale, December 1601, he converted what had been an ignominious defeat into a glorious victory by focusing on the winter march of Ulster's leaders to the field of battle rather than on the conflict itself. For the mid-seventeenth century, several authors, including Davis, stated confidently that their hero, Owen Roe O'Neill,

---

[78] P.S. O'Hegarty, 'The Library of Ireland, 1845–7'; Gavan Duffy, *The Ballad Poetry*, Preface to the 6th edition (Dublin, 1846).
[79] Davis: *Essays and Poems*, 191–4.

would have been more than a match for Cromwell had 'they' not poisoned him as he marched southwards to confront Cromwell's invading army. Patrick Sarsfield was similarly lauded for his achievements on the field of battle, first fighting for the Jacobite cause in Ireland and then on the Continent in the service of France. Fighting for France meant fighting against the 'Saxon foe', and Sarsfield was pictured by Davis dying from his wounds 'on Landen's plain' and wishing that his blood had been spilt 'for father-land'.[80] This attention to the military endeavours of Irish exiles in Continental warfare shows how the Abbé Mac Geoghegan influenced the poetic histories no less than he had done the prose histories written by Young Ireland authors. Thus the exploits of the so-called Wild Geese and of Clare's Dragoons became known and sung about by nationally minded communities in Ireland, and battles and sieges in far distant places, ranging from Ramillies to Cremona to Neerwinden and Fontenoy, became as familiar to Irish audiences as the Yellow Ford, Benburb, and Aughrim. All, as James Quinn has stated, 'attached a special importance to proving that the Irish were as brave (if not braver) than other nations'. It is possible that they may have seen a particular need to emphasize this because, as Padraig Lenihan has established, the authors would have known that the English authorities were aware that the military reputation of the Irish in Continental warfare was as often associated with cowardice, treachery, and indiscipline as with valour.[81]

These romantic verses were the product of amalgamations of superficial gleanings from historical sources with fanciful flights of imagination. Collectively they resulted in the creation of a pantheon of heroes who, whether victors or vanquished, were deemed to have upheld the spirit of an Irish nation. These heroes were set in opposition to a gallery of villains who were accused of having become corrupt pawns of Britain's imperial interests by engaging in nefarious acts such as the alleged poisoning of Owen Roe O'Neill, or disregarding the terms of Treaty of Limerick, or having the Act of Union passed by 'perjury and fraud'. This imagining of a glorious past for Ireland not only fulfilled the dream of Thomas Davis to have 'A Ballad History of Ireland' that would make Irish people proud of their past but it also prevented the historians associated with Young Ireland from splitting openly along denominational lines as seemed about to occur when they were engaged upon conventional histories sustained by documentary evidence. They were able to avoid such a possibility by attributing Ireland's past sufferings, and current woes, to the iniquities of evil Albion and its base agents in Ireland rather than to wider divisions between the Catholic and Protestant populations of Ireland. The persistent inference, no longer subjected to scrutiny,

---

[80] Davis, 'The Death of Sarsfield', *Essays and Poems*, 210–11; Sarsfield had been wounded at Neerwinden, near Landen, in present-day Belgium.

[81] James Quinn, *Young Ireland*, 4–5; Padraig Lenihan, 'The Irish Brigade, 1690–1715', *Eighteenth-Century Ireland/Iris an dá chultúr*, vol. 31 (2016), 47–74.

RE-IMAGINING IRELAND'S EARLY MODERN PAST   243

was that were it not for 'English oppression, and falsehood and guile' the vast bulk of Ireland's Protestant population would have followed the lead of 'the men of patriot pen/Swift, Molyneux and Lucas' to join the majority of Catholics as members of a common nation.[82] Even John Mitchel in 1868, who once had been encouraging Catholics to forget about grievances from the past, had come to appreciate during his years in exile in the United States that memories of 'the long agony of the Penal Laws... [and how] the pride of the ancient Irish race was stung by daily hourly humiliations' had been important in keeping alive an Irish animus against Britain.[83]

8.3 Revived Catholicism and the Early Modern Past

The ambitions of the Young Ireland movement in all its dimensions were regarded with suspicion by the leaders of the Catholic Church in Ireland, which seemed even jealous of its communications outreach. For its part the Catholic Church had become an increasingly self-assured body from the moment that the Penal Laws had been relaxed. One measure of the Catholic Church's revival was the increase in the number of priests, brothers, and nuns it was able to assign to pastoral and charitable work and to the schooling of children at home and in exile. In Ireland this work was conducted principally in the many new churches, schools, hospitals, and seminaries that the church had been able to construct with the support of voluntary subscription from a generous laity. The ultimate proof of the newfound confidence of this re-energized church was that many priests became conspicuous supporters of the various political campaigns of Daniel O'Connell (1775–1847) who had secured Catholic Emancipation in 1829.[84]

Catholic church concerns about the Young Ireland movement derived from several factors. Some church leaders were troubled that Protestants who were known upholders of the liberal principles of the Enlightenment were prominent among its leaders. This was made manifest to the church when several Young Irelanders spoke in favour of non-denominational university education knowing that the bishops, and O'Connell, were seeking to have the government support a Catholic university. Another concern was that some members of the movement espoused military action to further their nationalist ambitions and thus parted company with O'Connell who eschewed violence to advance his objectives.

---

[82] These sentiments were expressed by Davis in 'The Dungannon Convention, 1782' and in 'Song of the Volunteers of 1782', the latter to be sung to the air of 'The Boyne Water', *Thomas Davis: Essays and Poems with a Centenary Memoir*, 220–2.

[83] John Mitchel, *The History of Ireland, from the Treaty of Limerick to the Present Time* (preface to the New York edition, 1868).

[84] On the political background Patrick M.Geoghegan, 'The Impact of O'Connell, 1815–1850', and Maura Cronin, 'Popular Politics, 1815–1845', James Kelly, *The Cambridge History of Ireland*, vol. 3, *1730–1880*, 102–27, and 128–49.

244 IMAGINING IRELAND'S PASTS

This provided some Young Irelands with further reason to make the charge that O'Connell and his closest associates had become corrupted by their political associations with Whig politicians in Britain. Criticism of O'Connell incurred the wrath of some Catholic clerics, starting with John McHale (1791–1881), Archbishop of Tuam, and the first Maynooth-trained priest to have been made an archbishop. McHale and his associates identified Daniel O'Connell as an exemplary lay leader for Catholic Ireland, and his standing with the bishops was further enhanced when O'Connell died in Genoa in 1847 as he was travelling for an audience with Pope Pius IX.[85]

To these Irish objections to Young Ireland were added others that related to developments in Continental Europe, and more particularly in the Italian peninsula, during the first half of the nineteenth century. We have already taken note of the loathing of the senior clergy in the Catholic Church in Ireland for the French Revolution and its underlying principles, which led to the view that revolutionary action and Catholicism were mutually exclusive.[86] This outlook did not change as the nineteenth century proceeded when those from Ireland who could afford seminary training on the Continent rather than in Maynooth looked to Rome rather than to France or Spain. In Rome they found that the same liberal principles that had been invoked to justify revolution in France were being cited in Italy to promote the unification of the multiple states in the Italian peninsula into a single polity to be organized on liberal principles. These ambitions were especially threatening for the church because Cavour and Mazzini, the two senior promoters of the unification of Italy, identified the Pope, who ruled over the Papal States in central Italy, and the Bourbon monarchy, that dominated southern Italy, as the two principal obstacles in the way of the creation of a new Italian nation state that they considered to have been defined as much by geography as by culture. This hostility to what were being depicted as antiquated survivals from a feudal past led, in 1848, to an invasion of the Papal States by revolutionary troops that forced Pope Pius IX and his court to flee from Rome and seek temporary refuge in the Bourbon monarchy to the south. Then, when the Pope later returned to Rome, he became reliant on military support provided by Louis Napoleon of France to uphold his position.

These developments in Italy made a profound impression on the Roman-educated Paul Cullen (1803–78) who was head of the Irish College in Rome before he was appointed by the Pope to serve first as Archbishop of Armagh, 1849–52, and then, 1852–78, as Archbishop in Dublin. There, in 1866, he was designated Ireland's first Cardinal. Cullen, who many credit with renovating Irish Catholicism to become the dynamic, dogmatic, authoritarian, and evangelical

---

[85] For a biographical note on O'Connell see that by Gearóid Ó Tuathaigh, *Dictionary of Irish Biography*, vol. 7, 181–200.

[86] See Chapter 7, 201.

RE-IMAGINING IRELAND'S EARLY MODERN PAST 245

religion it was to remain from his time until the 1960s, returned to Ireland with the conviction that liberal nationalist movements were invariably hostile to papal authority. This, for him, meant that Young Ireland was no different from Young Italy.[87] These experiences and attitudes do much to explain the persistent hostility shown by Cullen (and several of Ireland's Catholic bishops) towards all liberal and subversive movements in Ireland. However, it was left to Cullen's nephew, Patrick Francis Moran (1830–1911), to address the issue of writing Ireland's history, and to explain how an alternative history for Ireland to that proposed by the more liberal historians of Young Ireland might be imagined, especially for the early modern centuries.[88]

Moran in 1861 acknowledged Cullen as 'the first patron and encourager of his studies'. By this he meant that it was Cullen who had brought him to Rome in 1841 to complete his schooling after the death of Moran's widowed mother, who was Cullen's half-sister.[89] When he had graduated from school, Moran enrolled in a seminary in Rome to become a priest and after his ordination proceeded to doctoral studies. He proved a gifted student and made a favourable impression on some of the senior ecclesiastics in Rome, including the future Pope Leo XIII. This meant that on the completion of his doctorate he was appointed almost immediately as Professor of Hebrew at *Propaganda Fide* and served also as Vice Rector of the Irish College in Rome. It is clear from his first historical publications, which appeared while he was still in Rome, that, for Moran, all human institutions were by definition imperfect, and that the interlude spent by people (or at least godly people) on earth would be times of 'trials and persecutions', as had been foretold by the Redeemer, and as had been proven by the martyrs of the early church who 'the more they were cut down, the more did Christians increase'.[90] This, he pronounced, had been further proven 'in every age of the church', and he was especially admiring of Pope Pius IX who had 'himself suffered so much from the enemies of religion', for having, even in 'times of irreligion and indifference', ignored the scoffs and sneers 'of a wicked and unbelieving press' and canonized those who had died for the faith in Japan during the sixteenth century even though these had been considered 'traitors and rebels to the government under which they lived'.[91]

---

[87] For a biographical note on Cardinal Paul Cullen see that by Colin Barr, *Dictionary of Irish Biography*, vol. 2, 1071–6, see also Barr, 'The re-energising of Catholicism, 1790–1880', James Kelly, *The Cambridge History of Ireland*, vol. 3, *1730–1880*, 280–304.

[88] For a biographical note on Patrick Francis Moran, see that by John Molony, *Dictionary of Irish Biography*, vol. 6, 673–4.

[89] Dedication page to P.F. Moran, *Memoirs of the Most Rev Oliver Plunket* (Dublin, 1861).

[90] Patrick Francis Moran, *Historical Sketch of the Persecutions suffered by the Catholics of Ireland, under the rule of Cromwell and the Puritans* (Dublin, 1862, 2nd edition Dublin, 1884, and 3rd edition Callan, Co. Kilkenny, 1903); references here are to the 1903 reprint, preface, ix–xi.

[91] Moran, *Historical Sketch*, xii–xiv.

246   IMAGINING IRELAND'S PASTS

Given such examples, Moran thought it 'strange' that Catholics in Ireland had been 'careless' of those of their forefathers who 'like true soldiers of Christ' had died for their faith and whose lives, if they were documented, could have been a source of 'great edification' to future generations. This neglect, he believed, could be partly explained by the lack of 'written records' because many who had suffered for the faith, as had been the case with Archbishop Oliver Plunket in the seventeenth century, had destroyed their papers lest they be used as evidence against them. This, he contended, meant that knowledge of what they had suffered existed 'only in the memory of the faithful', which was insufficient to have the Pope declare as martyrs those who, in the face of persecution, had preserved the 'faith of St Patrick, pure and uncontaminated'. However, he did not consider the case hopeless because even when it was 'vain to seek for a complete and consecutive history of the persecutions' that Irish people had suffered, it was possible to glean information on 'the sufferings of individuals' from 'private letters and documents'. Therefore, with a view to enabling 'a history of the martyrs of the Irish church', Moran devoted much time during his years in Rome, 1841–66, to delving into various archives for evidence of Irish people who had suffered (or even died) for their faith, particularly during the sixteenth, seventeenth, and eighteenth centuries. Moran's efforts, as we know from the biography of Paul Cullen being written by Colin Barr, were facilitated by Cullen who used his contacts in Rome to make sure than all relevant documents would be released to Moran from archives that, up to this point, had been inaccessible to researchers.[92]

As he undertook this research, Moran recognized that, in garnering 'unpleasant recollections', he, as had been the case with Pope Pius IX when he had canonized the Japanese martyrs, was putting himself 'in opposition' to 'the tendency of the present age to repair the wrongs of past times and to heal the wounds then inflicted' by allowing 'past grievances be forgotten'. Here, he was countering the Young Ireland argument for historical reconciliation as this had been articulated by Mitchel and Davis, and for a time by Mac Nevin. In doing so, he pondered if 'the present age [was] so liberal as it pretends; or whether the Catholic religion, and the Catholic people in general—and the poor especially—[had] been treated in Ireland with such generosity as to make them forget all past grievances'. Then, by way of rhetorical response, he 'asked whether the spirit of former times [was] not still active, and still tending by occult means, the same ends, which were so long sought for by open persecution' which, as he never doubted, was to have Irish Catholics abandon their faith.[93]

Since he considered this conspiracy to be an ongoing process, Moran thought it necessary to remind Irish people how those of their seventeenth-century

---

[92] Moran, *Historical Sketch*, xiv–xvi; I am grateful to Colin Barr for offering me the opportunity to read two draft chapters of his forthcoming biography of Cardinal Paul Cullen.

[93] Moran, *Historical Sketch*, xvii–xviii.

ancestors who had fought 'to defend their country, their king, and their religion', under the banner of the Confederacy (and here he was clearly taking Fr. Meehan's *Confederation of Kilkenny* as his guide), had been 'sacrificed in thousands by sanguinary hordes of fanatical Puritans, and other furious enemies of the Catholic religion pretending to be lovers of liberty, but, in reality, enemies of all rights, human and divine'.[94] Moran further insisted that reviving 'the memory of past grievances', would not, as was being suggested by liberal critics, necessarily excite 'feelings of hatred and rancour'. Rather, he contended, the revival of such memories would encourage 'charity and forbearance' among the readers of such history because it would supply them with 'new illustrations of the power of Christian faith' in making persecuted people 'submissive and obedient in the time of trial and affliction'.[95] The study of such episodes would also, he insisted, make readers more aware of 'who were the real friends, and who the enemies of progress and knowledge' during that era of persecution in Ireland which had 'scarcely a parallel in the history of the church'. Then, to illustrate this point, Moran devoted the third appendix of his *Historical Sketch* to detailing the consistent support provided by the Holy See to Ireland during the sixteenth, seventeenth, and eighteenth centuries. In this he gave greatest attention to the support provided by Archbishop Rinuccini to the Catholic Confederacy, but rather than treat this as a unique event, he represented Rinuccini's appointment as consistent with what he considered to be previous practice since, he contended, the papacy had appointed 'pro-nuncios' to Ireland in Elizabethan times.[96]

P.F. Moran intended in his *Historical Sketch* to explain how 'a history of the martyrs of the Irish church might be written', and he considered that historians should be devoting themselves to reconstituting the lives of such real heroes rather than, as was being recommended by Young Ireland, the lives of those who had supposedly devoted their lives to the pursuit of some fanciful and ill-defined Irish nation. In doing so, Moran showed himself conversant with the writings of those Young Ireland historians who, he believed, lacked sympathy with Catholicism. His fundamental criticism was that the archives they had consulted provided no understanding of the motivations, actions, and sufferings of Catholics, and he insisted that historians could arrive at a rounded appreciation of Ireland's history only when the material that shed light on the trials endured by Catholics had been 'better examined and published'.[97]

To exemplify what might be done to remedy this deficit, Moran, in 1874—by this time Bishop of Ossory—published a collection of documents entitled *Spicilegium Ossoriense*. These documents illustrated both the concern of successive Popes over the plight of Catholics in Ireland from the onset of the

---

[94] Moran, *Historical Sketch*, xvii.   [95] Moran, *Historical Sketch*, xix–xx, xxxiv.
[96] Moran, *Historical Sketch*, xxi, 1, appendix 3.   [97] Moran, *Historical Sketch*, xvi.

248   IMAGINING IRELAND'S PASTS

Reformation to 1800, and how various Popes had come to the assistance of Ireland's Catholics in different ways. These documents, most of them in Latin, came from a range of archives in Rome and from that of the Irish College in Salamanca. His selection also shed light on the condition of the Catholic Church in Ireland at various junctures, and gave details on the ministries of various Irish bishops, ranging from Dermot O'Hurley in the sixteenth century to Oliver Plunket in the late seventeenth, and the trials they had endured for the faith. The subject of martyrdom was never far from Moran's mind and his compilation included two surviving lists of people who had died for the faith in Ireland. One, composed by a Jesuit named John Holing, concerned the reign of Queen Elizabeth and identified, under the categories of bishops, priests, laymen and laywomen, those who had been put to death for their faith in Elizabethan times. The second was a list, submitted to Rome in 1662, of 'the Irish martyrs of the Franciscan Order, under the Puritans'.[98]

Moran was himself concerned more specifically with the subject of episcopal martyrdom and had already, in 1861—while he was still in Rome—written on the execution of Archbishop Oliver Plunket in 1681.[99] Then, in 1884, he proceeded further to provide details on the deaths of Dermot O'Hurley (1584), Richard Creagh (1588), and Cornelius O'Devany (1611), in the course of introducing an edition he had prepared of the *Analecta Sacra* by David Rothe, one of his predecessors as Bishop of Ossory, and the predecessor with whom Moran felt most affinity. The original of this text, already discussed in Chapter 2, had been published serially by Rothe between 1617 and 1619, and Moran now made it available, still in the original Latin, in a published composite form.[100] It held special appeal for Moran because it provided evidence that Penal Laws against Catholics had been in force since the Reformation and were not just an eighteenth-century phenomenon. Moran was also attracted by Rothe's contention that an Irish Nation (*Nationis Hibernorum*) had been forged on this anvil of persecution, and that Irish nationalism was, therefore, essentially Catholic and included Irish Catholics who lived in exile as well as those who had remained at home. Rothe's text was also important to Moran because it traced the history of Irish Catholicism backwards in time to St Patrick, and then demonstrated how religious and political matters had become inextricably interlinked as the different strands of Catholic people in Ireland were melded into a single composite nation as they underwent a succession of trials of their faith during the sixteenth and seventeenth centuries.

---

[98] Patrick Francis Moran, *Spicilegium Ossoriense, being a collection of original letters and papers illustrative of the History of the Irish Church from the Reformation to the year 1800* (Dublin, 1874); for the lists of martyrs see 82–108 and 437.

[99] Moran, *Memoirs of ... Oliver Plunket.*

[100] Rothe, *Analecta Sacra*, ed., Moran; on Rothe and his *Analecta* see Chapter 2.

RE-IMAGINING IRELAND'S EARLY MODERN PAST   249

What Rothe had argued in the *Analecta Sacra* in the seventeenth century confirmed what Moran himself had had to say in 1868 of the formation of an Irish nation when he had published an edition of the letter that Peter Lombard had addressed to Pope Clement VIII in 1599 to solicit support for the war then being waged by Hugh O'Neill against the forces of Queen Elizabeth. We have previously noted in Chapter 7 how a corrupt edition of this letter had been published in 1632, and how the Abbé Mac Geoghegan had made use of a rare surviving copy of this corrupt text in his reconstruction of the career of Hugh O'Neill.[101] Moran had secured the original manuscript copy of the letter from the Roman archives and he edited and published it in 1868 because it provided what he took to be definitive proof that Hugh O'Neill had been an exemplary Catholic who had gone to war primarily for the defence of his beliefs and for those of the Irish nation, whether of Gaelic or Old English ancestry, who had joined his Confederacy. The Hugh O'Neill, as he had been depicted by Lombard in 1599, rediscovered by Mac Geoghegan in the 1760s, and rehabilitated by Moran in 1868, thus contrasted sharply with the heroic, but calculating, figure portrayed in 1845 by John Mitchel as a person who had made a cynical use of Catholicism to further his nation-building ambitions.

In this, Moran provided a practical demonstration of how evidence from the Catholic archive could be used to counter what he took to be the opinions of liberals who drew on sources that were hostile to Catholicism. Also, through his various publications and editions Moran furnished the material that he considered necessary for writing a composite history of Ireland's Catholic peoples that would integrate religious with secular history. Any such history would, as David Rothe had done in his *Analecta*, commence with an account of how Christianity had been introduced to Ireland by St Patrick and later disseminated by Irish missionaries to a European continent that had become benighted because of barbaric invasions. It would also explain how Christianity in Ireland had withstood the onslaught of Scandinavian invaders, after which it had become more diverse and brought into closer communion with Rome in the centuries following a further invasion of Ireland—this time from England and Wales, led by King Henry II. The history would acknowledge the long-term political and cultural divisions that had resulted from this English conquest, but would show also how the two distinct populations of Gaelic and English ancestry had been brought closer together from the time of the Reformation by the merciless onslaught of Protestant invaders from England and Scotland who used religion as a cloak to cover their acquisitiveness. The core of such a history would demonstrate therefore how a single Irish Catholic nation had been fashioned from this experience, after which its members began to defend their faith and inheritance.

---

[101] Lombard, *De Regno Hiberniae, sanctorum insula, commentaries*, ed., Moran; for a previous discussion of this text and the 1632 edition see Chapter 7, 205.

250 IMAGINING IRELAND'S PASTS

The history would also show how this resistance was encouraged and supported by the papacy through the medium of Ireland's Catholic bishops, who in turn had persuaded a sequence of Ireland's secular leaders—James Fitzmaurice Fitzgerald, the earl of Desmond, Hugh O'Neill, Owen Roe O'Neill, Patrick Sarsfield, and, ultimately, Daniel O'Connell—to deploy their talents and resources for the defence of their faith and their patrimonies. Another instalment would explain how those Irish who had suffered defeat and been forced into exile had received shelter in the Catholic countries of Europe at the behest of the papacy. This would provide the ultimate proof that 'the Roman pontiffs [were] at every period, the fathers of our country, the guardians of our persecuted people [and] the support of our exiled clergy'.[102]

The narrative that Moran adumbrated in his various publications was superficially not unlike that favoured by the Young Ireland historians that it set out to oppose. The similarity was that, like the Young Irelanders, Moran would have the history of the early modern centuries structured around the actions of heroes who had presented stern resistance to 'barbaric intruders'. However, what Moran had in mind differed in several fundamental respects from what Davis and Mitchel had prescribed. First, it insisted that the papacy and the Irish bishops, rather than Irish lords, had been the protagonists who had encouraged resistance to the Protestant onslaught of the sixteenth and seventeenth centuries. This meant that the leaders from Ireland's laity chosen for special praise by Moran were those who, as he represented it, had engaged in military or political conflict at the behest of their spiritual superiors, and with continuous guidance from them. Again, like Mitchel and Davis, Moran contended that an Irish nation had emerged from a fusion between persecuted Catholics of Gaelic and of English ancestries who were of Irish birth. Moran considered this outcome remarkable because he believed that previous to this development residents within the English Pale had had 'nothing Irish-like in them but the Catholic religion'.[103]

As Moran, like Rothe, included these two groups within his Irish nation, he conceded no place within it either for the descendants of 'the fanatic Covenanters' who he associated with the Cromwellian and other Protestant conquests of the country, or the successors of Irish-born Protestant lords such as Ormond and Inchiquin who, as he perceived it, had behaved 'treacherously' during the wars of the seventeenth century. Neither did his nation embrace the heirs of Catholic lords who, during the course of that same conflict, had refused to be guided by their bishops and the papal nuncio.[104] Finally, where Davis and Mitchel had cherished the memory of those they identified as Ireland's lay heroes of the past in the hope that this would kindle a spirit of inclusive nationalism among succeeding generations of Irish people, Moran solicited veneration for those, mostly clergy,

---

[102] Moran, *Historical Sketch*, 312.   [103] Moran, *Historical Sketch*, 17.
[104] Moran, *Historical Sketch*, 19, 23, 29, 35.

'whose courage and constancy in dying' for their faith was likely to prove a source of edification for Irish people of his and future generations and thus help 'preserve the sacred tradition of the country'.[105]

It is clear that Moran had given close attention to the publications of the historians of Young Ireland during his years in Rome and took lessons from what Fr. Meehan had had to say of the Confederation of Kilkenny as he reflected on how he might counter the assumptions and prescriptions of Davis and Mitchel. While some of his challenges stemmed from his use of an alternate archive, he differed from the more secular of the Young Ireland authors over the nature and character of an Irish nation, and he remained unconvinced that any Irish nation had a natural entitlement to statehood any more than had the putative Italian nation being promoted by revolutionary forces in the Italian peninsula. Then, when it came to writing history, Moran believed that the object of scholarly attention should always be people rather than places, and the people whose history he would have written were Catholics who had retained their positions in Ireland or had been forced to seek refuge abroad either because of religious persecution or economic deprivation.

If Moran seemed anxious during the closing years of his sojourn in Rome to write such a history of Ireland's Catholic peoples, particularly one that treated of their sufferings during the early modern centuries, he did not have the opportunity to proceed with it because his time there came to an abrupt end in 1866 when his uncle Paul Cullen, who had just been made Ireland's first Cardinal Archbishop, summoned him to Dublin to become his secretary. In Dublin, Moran combined his work as secretary to the Cardinal with being Professor of Biblical Studies at the College of the Holy Cross at Clonliffe, which had been established as a seminary for the training of priests for the Dublin Archdiocese and for missions overseas. Moran also became joint editor of the *Irish Ecclesiastical Record*: a magazine that had been established by Cullen in 1864 to rival and dispute with the Protestant *Irish Ecclesiastical Gazette*. In all of these capacities, and later as Bishop of Ossory (1872–84) Moran strove to enhance the intellectual horizons of the parish clergy in Ireland, most of them products of the national seminary at Maynooth. Moran, like Cullen, believed that the priestly formation provided to seminarians in Maynooth fell short of that provided in the seminaries and universities of Rome. To help remedy this Moran introduced a pedagogic dimension to his publications, many of which were directed at priests to remedy what he considered deficits in their education. He was particularly concerned to make priests better acquainted with the history of the universal church and of the Irish Church, and better able to counter the arguments of both Protestants and liberals.

---

[105] Moran, *Historical Sketch*, Dedication.

252 IMAGINING IRELAND'S PASTS

The exhortations of Moran, no less than the source material he had himself garnered from the Roman archives and made available in print, explains why bishops in several Catholic dioceses released some of their priests from normal pastoral duties, and gave them the opportunity to illustrate how Catholics from the dioceses and parishes in which they served had suffered persecution, and even death, in defence of their faith and communities. The resulting outpouring in print, usually in hefty tomes, of Catholic interpretations of the histories of parishes, dioceses, and people, provided priests more generally with material to counter the well-honed interpretations that Protestant divines had been publishing for decades to defend the privileged position that the Church of Ireland enjoyed. At the same time, the emphasis that such Catholic writing placed on religious difference as a source of conflict, and its insistence that Irish nationalism was by definition Catholic, meant that it countered the notion fostered by liberals that Irish nationality was available to all Irish-born people, regardless of religious affiliation, and that Ireland's heroes were those who had striven to create a state to accommodate this nation.

In dissenting from the belief that history should be used to serve such a political end, Moran and like-minded authors were not disregarding past politics. On the contrary they admired those, notably Owen Roe O'Neill and Daniel O'Connell, who had taken political action to achieve greater freedom for the practice of Catholicism, and who, as they represented it, had taken advice from their spiritual superiors. What they objected to was the glorification of the nation state as an end in itself, and this was consistent with their view that all forms of secular government were transitory, and were worthy of support only to the extent that they did not hinder godly pursuits. This did not mean that Moran and those clerics who agreed with him were necessarily admirers of British rule in Ireland but they do seem to have considered the government of the day to be as acceptable as one could expect in an imperfect world, and better than many governments in Continental Europe that were stridently anti-Catholic. Their particular solace was that the government remained open to negotiation, particularly concerning the role of the Catholic Church in education and in the care of the infirm and poor, even when it did not always bend to their wishes in such matters. It was logical therefore that they should think better of the existing government in nineteenth-century Ireland than of any conceivable republic that might result from revolutionary action.

Moran and most of his fellow bishops would therefore have been at odds also with Mitchel and other hard-line nationalists over their strident anti-imperial stance. He, and several Irish bishops, looked benignly on imperial governments, and in the case of the British Empire were appreciative that it offered employment and places of settlement for large numbers of Irish Catholic emigrants. In this light it is unsurprising that Moran agreed with the papacy in 1884 to resign his position as Bishop of Ossory and accept an appointment as Archbishop of Sydney

RE-IMAGINING IRELAND'S EARLY MODERN PAST   253

where, within a year, he was elevated to become the first Cardinal Archbishop in Australasia. There, the Catholic community, which was overwhelmingly Irish in composition, was befuddled by the pro-imperial stance of their Cardinal Archbishop that was evident from the moment he became their spiritual leader.[106] The logic to the frequently controversial political positions that Moran adopted stemmed from his belief that the British Empire, like the Roman Empire before it, could become a vehicle that might be used to help spread the Gospel. Moran therefore believed himself responsible not only for preserving and consolidating the faith among the pre-existing Catholic community in Australia but also for using Australia as a base from which to evangelize the populations of Polynesia and Melanesia, to which end he worked until his death in 1911.[107]

Thus, while Moran, like most of the Catholic bishops with whom he had worked in Ireland, remained unimpressed by Mitchel's persistent hostility to British imperialism, they were also unconvinced by Mitchel's further contention that conflict in Ireland in the past, like communal differences in the present, were the product of British machinations to divide and rule. The contrary view, which Moran had gone to considerable length to document, held that the turbulence of Ireland's history, especially in the sixteenth and seventeenth centuries, was the consequence of the attempts made by fanatical Protestants to impose their religion on an Irish Catholic population who remained determined to uphold their faith. Then, as he approached more recent times, Moran contended that continuing communal conflict in Ireland was no longer the fault of British rule in Ireland, but a residue rather of these earlier sectarian differences that were being kept alive by Freemasons and the Orange Order. Then, more pointedly, Moran believed that these differences were being exploited and inflamed by the Fenians and other extreme nationalist groups that drew their inspiration from secular revolutionary organizations in Continental Europe who, like them, were pursuing godless ephemeral ends without consideration of the spiritual consequences that would result from their actions.

8.4 Conclusion

This chapter has revealed the enthusiasm with which the more prominent historians of Young Ireland set about re-imagining Ireland's history for the sixteenth, seventeenth, and the eighteenth centuries. They proceeded from the conviction that here, if anywhere, they would be able to identify a sequence of

---

[106] Nicholas Canny, 'How the Local can be Global and the Global Local: Ireland, Irish Catholics, and European Overseas Empires, 1500–1900', Patrick Griffin and Francis D. Cogliano, eds., *Ireland and America: Empire, Revolution and Sovereignty* (Charlottesville, Va., 2021), 23–52, esp. 41–8.

[107] Elizabeth Malcolm and Dianne Hall, *A New History of the Irish in Australia* (Cork, 2018), 143, 213.

leaders, Protestant as well as Catholic, who might be considered framers of Irish nationality. Identifying heroes who had opposed British interference in Irish affairs did not present much difficulty, nor did isolating anti-heroes who could be declared guilty of inhumane actions. However, they did experience problems over reaching a consensus on what had motivated Ireland's heroes to take action, and on which memories from the past should be cherished and which discarded.

As it transpired, all of the historians associated with Young Ireland could agree on a future for Ireland that would enjoy an independent, or at least semi-independent, political status, but they found it more difficult to agree on a historical narrative that would be compatible with this autonomous future to which they aspired. Essentially, Thomas Davis, with John Mitchel in agreement with him, wanted to project backwards in time the harmonious future they imagined for Ireland, and each demonstrated by exemplary histories how this might be achieved. However, it was also explained in this chapter that the manipulation of evidence that was required to imagine a heroic past that would link seamlessly with the present and a possible future raised difficulties for those Young Ireland historians who were Catholic. Their essential problem was that they were being required to disregard, or forgive, the degradations that their ancestors had suffered on grounds of religion, frequently at the hands of the progenitors of Protestant families of their acquaintance that still derived benefit from those injustices of the past. It was explained in this chapter that their difficulties became more pronounced when the unexpected death of Thomas Davis in September 1845 deprived the group of the moral leader who had aroused interest in writing a revised history for Ireland in the first instance. This was compounded by the fact that, when C.P. Meehan, a Young Ireland priest-historian, published *The Confederation of Kilkenny* in 1846, he openly defied the prescription that had been recommended by Davis. He argued instead that Catholicism was the defining characteristic of Irish nationhood. This seemed to defeat the purpose of the historical project since it made it difficult to imagine how Protestants might become fully fledged members of such a nation.

This led to a discussion of how Charles Gavan Duffy intervened to prevent the Young Ireland project of imagining a new past for Ireland from sundering along denominational lines. He did so by demonstrating in an edited collection of ballad poetry that it was possible to use verse to extol the virtues of national heroes, and to revile those who opposed them, without necessarily engaging in the painful, and potentially divisive, issue of authentication that was required when writing evidence-based history. Thus verse history, which Davis had originally intended to complement rather than displace prose narratives, became the enduring Young Ireland contribution to the creation of a new vernacular history for Ireland in which, in each succeeding generation, a sequence of Irish heroes, some Catholic and some Protestant, fostered and upheld the spirit of the nation against the guile and might of British imperialists.

Since we have identified C.P. Meehan as the prime dissident within the ranks of the Young Ireland group we must recognize that what attracted Fr. Meehan to Young Ireland in the first instance, besides his friendship with Gavan Duffy, was a deep hatred of British rule in Ireland and a readiness to countenance those in the Young Ireland movement who would use physical force to advance their objectives. These positions placed Meehan at odds with the Catholic Church authorities of his generation, but Meehan nonetheless remained very much a Catholic priest in his outlook. He had, after all, been trained in Rome where he had been ordained in 1835. Meehan seems to have been homesick during his years in Rome, as is suggested by his reminiscence published in 1868 in his most enduring book, *The Fate and Fortunes of Hugh O'Neill... and Rory O'Donnell*, that, as a seminarian, he had paid regular visits to the grave of his two heroes and remained convinced (as he documented in this book) that these two lords had willingly sacrificed their power and position in Ireland, and died as exiles in Rome, for love of their faith no less than their country.[108] Given this conviction it is likely that Meehan was disturbed to see O'Neill portrayed by Mitchel as a proto-nationalist who had used Catholicism to promote a secular agenda. There can be no doubt that in 1846, when he published *The Confederation of Kilkenny*, he set out to correct this view by arguing that Ireland's true Irish heroes were those who had fought for Catholicism, and who, in the course of doing so, had also pursued greater independence for Ireland.[109]

We noted how this dissident view struck a chord with other Young Ireland authors, most memorably Thomas Mac Nevin. We saw also how this discord within the movement came to the attention of P.F. Moran, a key figure within the institutional Catholic Church, who exploited it to his advantage when he set out to challenge the Young Ireland project on re-writing Ireland's history. One of Moran's concerns was that the traditional modes of communication employed by the church—exhortation through books, pamphlets, sermons, and hymns—was not proving as effective as the Young Ireland method of disseminating highly emotive messages in verse and song concerning a sequence of heroes who had supposedly upheld and furthered the national cause in successive generations. This would have been problematic for Moran, and for others at the upper reaches of the Catholic Church, because that church, like its Protestant counterparts, had specialized in cultivating memories of past sufferings of their co-religionists as a means of encouraging loyalty to the faith. It was probably to rival the Young Ireland project of identifying secular heroes that P.F. Moran drew upon what Meehan had said of the *Confederation of Kilkenny* when he registered his

---

[108] C.P. Meehan, *The Fate and Fortunes of Hugh O'Neill... and Rory O'Donnell* (Dublin, 1868); Elizabeth Fitzpatrick, 'The Exilic Burial Place of a Gaelic Irish Community at San Pietro in Montorio, Rome', *Papers of the British School at Rome*, vol. 85 (2017), 205–39; I am grateful to Professor Fitzpatrick for discussions of her archaeological investigation and for sending me a copy of her paper.
[109] The biographical note on Meehan by Linde Lunney and James Quinn.

disagreement with Mitchel's exhortation to Catholics to discount religious persecutions in the past in the interest of cultivating inter-communal harmony in the present and into the future. This intervention by Moran was as a preliminary to his drawing attention to evidence concerning 'some few' Irish people, all of them bishops, who were known to have died for the faith in the hope that this evidence would convince the papacy that their names should be 'enrolled among the privileged Martyrs of Holy Church'. However, Moran proved himself more expansive in his views when he declared that 'our whole people might justly be regarded as a nation of martyrs'. In the light of this, he considered it appropriate that some should be recognized as national heroes whenever it could be established that they had taken guidance from their spiritual superiors and had fought for religious liberty, by which he meant freedom to practise Catholicism.[110] Moran was thus asserting that the Catholic Church, more than Young Ireland, was committed to the liberties that were most important to people's lives. This, for him, meant that those in Ireland, like their counterparts in Italy, who presented their message in the language of the Enlightenment, were really intent on subverting religion that Moran considered to be the ultimate guarantor of humane values.

The challenge that Moran presented to the historians of Young Ireland meant that two different images of an Irish past during the early modern centuries were formulated at the mid-point of the nineteenth century. They were in agreement in that each alluded to the bitter persecutions that Irish people had suffered during a turbulent era and each also represented the sixteenth and seventeenth centuries as a heroic phase of Ireland's history. The difference was that in one instance the heroes had fought to keep alive the dream of an Irish nation based on the island of Ireland that would be inclusive in character, whereas heroes for the other were those who had fought to achieve religious liberty for Irish Catholics whether they lived at home or in exile. Each, as it transpired, was to prove potent in influencing future history writing of Ireland. Together, they marked a sharp departure from how Ireland's history had been approached in previous generations where prime attention had been given to sufferings that had been endured in the past rather than to policies that might be pursued in the future.

---

[110] *Analecta Sacra*, ed., Moran, xii.

9

Re-Imagining Ireland's Early Modern Past during the Later Nineteenth Century

9.1 Introduction

Chapter 8 investigated how authors within the Young Ireland movement sought to reach agreement on a version of Ireland's past that would trace a seamless progression of Irish national consciousness over time with which people of all traditions in their own generation might identify. One of their purposes was to imagine a past for Ireland that could be seen to have run in parallel with the Whig interpretation of English or British history that was being harnessed to promote pride of past achievement, and thus unity, among the diverse subjects of the British monarchy. It was explained why the nearest the Young Ireland authors came to realizing their ambition was in the realm of ballad history rather than in evidence-based discourse. However, it was also explained that a resurgent Catholic Church considered that even this partial success presented a challenge to the pastoral message it wished to communicate to much the same public. The chapter therefore proceeded to discuss how P.F. Moran took it upon himself on behalf of the Catholic Church to prescribe how an alternative Irish past might be imagined that would sustain rather than detract from the evangelization effort of the church both at home and in those parts of the world where Irish Catholic emigrant communities flourished. However, P.F. Moran, no less than the Young Ireland authors, limited himself to a purely intellectual exercise, as he, like them, interpreted the events of the three previous centuries without reference to the harsh realities of the present, including the Great Famine and the political challenges that followed in its wake.

The present chapter will show how a fresh cohort of authors began to take account of current realities while they still debated about the past. We shall see how these authors, whether they took their inspiration from the Young Ireland authors or from Moran's alternative view of the past, or whether they rejected both, were quick to relate their interpretations of Ireland's history both to the convulsions caused by the Great Famine, and to the great Irish political issues of the later nineteenth century, particularly the Land War and the demands for Home Rule for Ireland.

Imagining Ireland's Pasts: Early Modern Ireland through the Centuries. Nicholas Canny, Oxford University Press (2021).
© Nicholas Canny. DOI: 10.1093/oso/9780198808961.003.0009

9.2 Refining Catholic Interpretations in a Time of Uncertainty: The Writings of Margaret Anna Cusack

The reticence about connecting historical discourse to current events was, as we shall see, abandoned progressively as the nineteenth century proceeded, and competing interpretations of the history of early modern Ireland became ever more present-minded. In tracing this trend we shall look first at how the Catholic nationalist interpretation of the past that had been defined by P.F. Moran developed over time. We saw in Chapter 8 how, when Moran addressed historical questions, he tended to refrain from offering explicit comment on contemporary events, other than when these impinged upon the pastoral role of the church or on education. This reticence of Moran may be attributed in part to his inherent conservatism that became more pronounced because of his presence in Rome when the short-lived Roman Republic, 1848–49, was established and the papal court was forced to flee for refuge to the Bourbon monarchy in southern Italy. As a consequence, and until he left Ireland for Australia in 1884, Moran limited his historical commentary to carefully chosen subjects that had a bearing on religious issues. However, as noted, he did offer occasional guidance on how a Catholic interpretation of Ireland's history aimed at a popular audience might be structured.

Moran, during the years he spent in Ireland (1866–84) addressed most of his publications to priests, nuns, and brothers, and left it to them to reach out to the wider literate public. His enduring influence on history writing related to his critique of what Young Ireland authors were attempting, and to his prescription on how an orthodox Catholic interpretation of Ireland's past might be structured. Several priests followed his advice but their works tended to be either locally focused or ponderously dull, or both. Neither charge could be brought against the work of Margaret Anna Cusack (1829–99) who, in 1868, writing under her name in religion of M[ary] F[rancis] C[lare], published *An Illustrated History of Ireland, from the earliest period*, that she described on an inner fly-leaf as *A Popular History of Ireland*. This reached such a wide public that, after the sale of its first printing of 2,000 copies, it went in 1869 into a second edition, and then, in that same year, into a third edition of 11,000 copies. After this, Cusack published a sequence of historical publications on local as well as national history that reinforced what she had had to say in her *Illustrated History*. And then in 1877 she published a mammoth volume entitled *A History of the Irish Nation*.[1]

---

[1] M.F. Cusack, *An Illustrated History of Ireland, from the earliest period* (London, 1868, 1869); citation here is from the third 1869 edition that reprinted the Prefaces to the first and second editions. She also published M.F. Cusack, *The Student's Manual of Irish History* (London, 1870); *A History of the Irish Nation: Social, Ecclesiastical, Biographical, Industrial and Antiquarian* (London, 1877).

THE LATER NINETEENTH CENTURY   259

Cusack had been born into a dysfunctional, professional Protestant family in Dublin, and after her parents had separated, her mother took her to England where, after some years spent in an upper-class girls' boarding school, she became an Anglican nun. Disillusioned by this experience, Cusack later converted to Catholicism and joined a Catholic convent in England. Then in 1860 she returned to Ireland and was professed in Newry, County Down, as a member of the Poor Clare order of Catholic nuns. Her mentor in the convent was Mary O'Hagan, sister to Thomas O'Hagan, the Lord Chancellor of Ireland.[2] Cusack—always conscious of rank—accepted Mary O'Hagan as her social equal, and as Sister Mary Francis Clare accompanied O'Hagan to Kenmare in County Kerry in 1861 when O'Hagan became abbess of the St. Clare's convent she had founded in that town. Soon thereafter Cusack took to describing herself as The Nun of Kenmare, and, although belonging to an enclosed order dedicated to the welfare of the poor, the abbess exempted Cusack from many of the order's restrictions. This gave her freedom to pursue her scholarly interests and to correspond with many lay male scholars and publishers in England and Ireland. Through these contacts, Cusack maintained an extensive correspondence and had books, newspapers, and even manuscript collections sent on loan to her in the convent. By such means she kept abreast of, and offered opinions on, current as well as historical issues.[3]

After she had settled in Kenmare, Cusack claims she was 'approached' to write a general history of Ireland to explain the unique contribution that Irish people had made to 'the history of the different races that form an integral portion of the British Empire'. She was, she remarked, reluctant to accept this invitation and was even discouraged by some people on the grounds that 'Irishmen did not support Irish literature; above all, that the Irish clergy were indifferent to it, and to literature in general'. Despite such hesitation and discouragement she decided to proceed and was pleasantly surprised to find that the charges concerning the general ignorance of Irish priests were 'unfounded'. Instead, she concluded that while priests were not necessarily well versed in literature, they were 'unquestionably' dedicated to 'the spread of education amongst their people'.[4] Cusack was also pleased that her work received the 'approbation' of 'many distinguished prelates' in Ireland, and also of some English Catholic bishops. Such plaudits, as she reported in the second edition to the *Illustrated History*, gave her reason to refute the 'imputation' that a 'deficiency in cultivated tastes' obtained among the 'ecclesiastics of Ireland'. Cusack was especially appreciative of those Catholic clergy who

---

[2] For a biographical note on Mary O'Hagan (Sister Mary Michael) see that by Georgina Clinton and Sinéad Sturgeon, *Dictionary of Irish Biography*, vol. 7, 814–15; for a note on her brother Thomas O'Hagan by Patrick Geoghegan, *Dictionary of Irish Biography*, vol. 7, 815–16.

[3] For a biographical note on Cusack see that by Patrick Maume, *Dictionary of Irish Biography*, vol. 2, 1131–6; for a full biography see Irene Ffrench Eagar, *The Nun of Kenmare* (Cork, 1970). See also Sr. M. Francis Clare Cusack, *The Nun of Kenmare: An Autobiography* (London, 1889). This, her first autobiography, was reprinted by Routledge (London, 1998) with a valuable introduction by Maria Luddy.

[4] Cusack, *Illustrated History*, Preface to the first edition, 15, 16.

had 'been most earnest and generous in their efforts to promote the circulation of the work' in their schools and colleges.[5] These, she said, agreed with her that it was a 'disgrace' that Irishmen had no opportunity in their schooling to get 'to know their history perfectly'. Moreover, those priests who encouraged her, feared, as did Cusack herself, that 'an Irish youth' learning only of Britain's history and being exposed to the 'taunt of belonging to a despised nation', would become 'ashamed of his country' and, worse still, 'ashamed of his faith'.[6] Cusack also acknowledged the assistance she had received from the heads of the Mercy and Presentation orders of nuns in Ireland who, by introducing her history to their schools, had furthered her own 'desire...to raise her countrywomen to higher mental efforts than [were] required by the almost exclusive perusal of works of fiction'. Then, to further promote this liberation, together with her own ambition to be taken seriously as an author, Cusack enquired rhetorically 'if women may excel as painters and sculptors why may not a woman attempt to excel as an historian?'.[7]

The interpretation of Ireland's past that Cusack outlined was largely as Moran would have wished, as she detailed how Ireland had 'been deluged with blood again and again [and had] been defeated in a temporal point of view again and again; but spiritually never'. Then, in line with the arguments of Young Ireland authors, she pronounced that 'far from being a history of failures', Ireland provided 'a history of the most triumphant success—of the most brilliant victories'. However, she reverted to being a Catholic historian when she announced that the principal of these victories had been in the spiritual domain since 'the Irish' had proven themselves 'the only nation on earth of whom it [could] be truly said that they were never apostatized nationally'.[8]

The two factors, according to Cusack, that had spurred Ireland's leaders to unparalleled feats of bravery during their centuries of trial were their deep sense of grievance both over the land question and the church question. The first, she stated, could be traced back to the reign of Henry II, while 'the difficulties of the Church question commenced in the reign of Henry VIII'. As she isolated grievances over land as an issue to be considered, Cusack was going further than P.F. Moran would have done, particularly by making what she wrote appear relevant to contemporary discussion of the Irish land question in Britain as well as in Ireland. She pronounced that Irish grievances over land could be related ultimately to the 'selfishness of colonists' in succeeding generations whose behaviour explained why the Irish had come to consider 'English adventurers as

---

[5] Cusack, *Illustrated History*, Preface to the second edition, 2–3.

[6] Cusack, *Illustrated History*, Preface to the second edition, 4, 6; for the concern of more prosperous Catholics in securing education for their children that would equip them for imperial service see Ciaran O'Neill, *Catholics of Consequence: Transnational Education, Social Mobility and the Irish Catholic Elite, 1850–1900* (Oxford, 2014).

[7] Cusack, *Illustrated History*, Preface to the second edition, 11–12.

[8] Cusack, *Illustrated History*, Preface to the second edition, 5.

THE LATER NINETEENTH CENTURY   261

little better than robbers, and treated them as such'. Cusack's narrative described how 'the Anglo Normans dispossessed the native Irish, the followers of the Tudors dispossessed the Anglo-Normans, and the men of the Commonwealth dispossessed them all'. The associated persistent struggle over land, she insisted, became especially bitter in the sixteenth and seventeenth centuries when 'the object of the Englishman was to obtain a home and fortune...the object of the Irishman to keep out the intruder'.[9]

The resulting tension, according to Cusack, was intensified by religious difference, with Irish leaders, notably Hugh O'Neill, becoming ever more committed to defending their faith as well as their lands. Then, also as their adversaries became more inclined to kill and even massacre their opponents, they cited religion as the justification for their actions. On this subject, Cusack treated specifically of the 'martyrdom' of Dermot O'Hurley who had been 'tempted' to betray his religion 'with the offer of earthly honours', that of Terence O'Brien, Bishop of Emly, who, in 1651, had been put to death at the direction of Ireton, and finally the martyrdom of Oliver Plunket during the reign of Charles II. The death of Plunket, according to Cusack, was contrived principally by Henry Jones, the Protestant Bishop of Meath, who was greatly 'influenced by fanaticism' having 'served in Cromwell's army, and had all that rancorous hatred of the Catholic Church so characteristic of the low class from whom the Puritan soldiery were drawn'.[10] Cusack was equally condemnatory of Irish-born Protestants who had been guilty of atrocities, and here she instanced Morogh O'Brien, baron of Inchiquin, to whom she attributed the massacre of 3,000 Catholics at Cashel, and James Butler, marquis of Ormond who, notwithstanding the 'partiality' of Carte's biography, had, in her view, led 'a career of duplicity' that had been 'crowned with success' but only 'in the temporal sense'.[11]

Cusack provided much detail on actual or alleged atrocities inflicted by Protestants upon Catholics and again, like Moran, she countered the opinion that such 'a painful subject' should be overlooked lest it excite 'violent feelings'. Instead, she, like Moran, thought the sufferings of Catholics should be highlighted because they provided proof of the steadfastness of the Irish in their faith and enlivened 'a history over which the angels in heaven rejoice, and of which the best, the holiest and the noblest of the human race may justly be proud'. Moreover, she pronounced that another purpose of studying history, especially at school level, was to make pupils aware of 'the duty of forgiveness of enemies [and] of patient endurance of the mighty power of moral force'.[12] She reinforced this message in her second book, *The Student's Manual*, specially designed for use in schools.[13]

---

[9] Cusack, *Illustrated History*, 431, 519.   [10] Cusack, *Illustrated History*, 446, 453, 507, 525–7.
[11] Cusack, *Illustrated History*, 491, 520.
[12] Cusack, *Illustrated History*, Preface to the second edition, 5–6.
[13] Cusack, *The Student's Manual*.

However, Cusack's main achievement was her *Illustrated History* where she consciously reached out to a mass audience in Ireland, England, and the United States. Her key arguments were sustained by carefully chosen illustrations prepared for print by Henry Doyle, who would become Director of the National Gallery of Ireland in 1869. With this work, Cusack succeeded, in a way that none of the many priest historians of her generation did, in popularizing the Catholic interpretation of Ireland's history, largely as P.F. Moran had prescribed it.[14] She placated the many priest-historians of her generation who had written parish, diocesan, and even national histories by describing them as 'admirable' even as Cusack herself must have realized that they lacked the appeal of her *Illustrated History*.[15] On the other hand, Cusack seemed flattered by John Mitchel's comment in *The Irish Citizen* that, by writing her history, 'a woman [had] accomplished what men [had] failed to do'. It may have been as a concession to Mitchel and the inclusive national history he had espoused in the 1840s, that she, as Moran would never have done, adjudged 'Irish Protestants [to have] been quite as national as Irish Catholics', leading to her hope, which was not unlike that cherished by Charles Gavan Duffy, that the two populations would 'work together harmoniously for the good of their common country' once the 'bane of religious difference [came to be] removed'. The removal to which Cusack was referring was the anticipated passage of the Irish Church Act that was duly enacted by the Westminster parliament in 1869 and came into force on 1 January 1871. This Act, devised by Gladstone largely at the behest of Irish nationalist parliamentarians, separated the Church of Ireland from the state church in England and then decreed that the Church of Ireland would no longer be the official religion in Ireland because it commanded the spiritual allegiance of but a fraction of the country's population that was becoming relatively smaller due to demographic change. Cusack, expecting that this legislation would be steered successfully through parliament, considered herself free to salute the Volunteers as 'patriots' and to admire the Protestant 'celebrated writers' of the eighteenth century.[16] However, she made this apparent enthusiasm appear condescending when she pronounced that 'in Ireland there were few learned men in the Established Church, and [that] even Ussher', whom she compared unfavourably with Roderic O'Flaherty and Dualtach Mac Fhirbishigh, 'seems to have been painfully indifferent to the necessity of superior education'.[17]

Cusack broke new ground by including a politically charged discourse on the 'serfdom of the Irish tenant' in the preface to the first edition of the *Illustrated History* that was reproduced in subsequent editions. This 'discourse', she said, had

[14] For a biographical note on Henry Doyle see that by Rebecca Minch, *Dictionary of Irish Biography*, vol. 3, 442–3.

[15] Cusack, *Illustrated History*, 427. [16] Cusack, *Illustrated History*, 12, 591–2.

[17] Cusack, *Illustrated History*, 586.

THE LATER NINETEENTH CENTURY   263

been criticized as an unwarranted trespass by a historian into contemporary politics. This is not surprising since it had brought her to conclude that she saw little future for Irish landlords, most of whom were Protestant in religion, in a rapidly changing Irish political environment. Her argument, based on what she had witnessed and heard in Kerry, was that landlords in Ireland, unlike their counterparts in England whose solicitude she had witnessed, 'generally neglected' what she considered their responsibility to offer 'relief' to the poor. She was able to sustain this by showing that, from their meagre resources, her convent in Kenmare gave more to sustain the poor in times of need than did some landowners. Then she, like many contemporaries, isolated for particular criticism those landlords who were absent in England from their estates, and therefore, as she saw it, delinquent in meeting their moral obligations.[18]

After this digression into present politics with which she introduced her *Illustrated History*, Cusack reverted in the history proper to what Moran would have expected of her. There, she used evidence from the past to endorse Moran's conclusion that the Irish nation was a Catholic nation, and pronounced that its 'future' rested 'in the hands of the Irish hierarchy' and that the responsibility of its members was to 'follow as they lead'.[19] She appeared to modify this conclusion slightly in *A History of the Irish Nation* when she stated that she had no wish 'to slight, or to give pain to members of the Protestant Church of Ireland, some of whom are our nearest relatives, some of whom have given us the most hearty co-operation in long years of literary labour. But we would ask them to read the simple, authentic, indisputable details of the attempts made by England to compel this nation to follow her in her change of creed'.[20] However, Cusack was not satisfied with chastising the current generation of Protestants, including her brother, because their ancestors had tried to compel, rather than persuade, Ireland's Catholics to conform in religion. Instead, in *A History of the Irish Nation*, Cusack made clear her commitment to what was becoming the orthodox Catholic interpretation, as she announced, that she would be writing of 'the grandeur and dignity of centuries of steadfast resistance to oppression, and of the heroic character of men like Sarsfield, O'Neill and O'Donnell'. These names showed that Cusack, like P.F. Moran, would isolate from the litany of national heroes proclaimed by the Young Ireland idealists, only those that she believed had fought for their faith. This was because, for Cusack, as also for Moran and the other Catholic clerical authors she cited, the Irish nation was by definition a Catholic nation.[21] It was relatively easy for Cusack to popularize this exclusive definition because, for her, as for Moran, defining any collectivity as a nation did not entitle its members to constitute themselves into a distinct political entity. On the contrary, Cusack,

[18] Cusack, *Illustrated History*, Preface to the first edition, 23–33.
[19] Cusack, *Illustrated History*, Preface to the second edition, 9.
[20] Cusack, *History of the Irish Nation*, 6.   [21] Cusack, *History of the Irish Nation*, 1.

no less than Moran, was an admirer of empire. Therefore, as noted, she had declared one of her purposes in writing Ireland's history to be that of making her readers, and especially readers who were pupils in Ireland's Catholic schools, proud of the achievements of their ancestors so they could consider themselves the equals of English, Scots, and Welsh people within a shared British monarchy and empire.

At the same time, Cusack had brought history more emphatically into the political arena than P.F. Moran had ever done. The enthusiasm she expressed for the imminent disestablishment of the Church of Ireland, and her denunciation of those landowners who were absentees from their estates and those who had been niggardly in providing for the poor during times of hardship and famine, meant that Cusack was, in effect, decreeing that neither belonged properly within an Irish community. Political activists of her generation would obviously have read such criticism as an endorsement of their frequently illegal actions and ambitions. Moreover, in making such criticism, Cusack was clouding the distinction that Moran had been careful to preserve between a history that pointed to the need for the elimination of all legal and social disabilities from which Catholics suffered, and a history that was being used to justify a political agenda. Therefore the nationalism that Cusack was advocating would have been considered threatening by many Protestants in Ireland because, by arguing from history that the Church of Ireland deserved to be disestablished, and that some landowners should be disempowered or even dispossessed, she was threatening the two principal supports that were available to isolated Protestant communities in many parts of rural Ireland.

Cusack never relented on the position she had adopted in 1868 even after she had left Ireland, as she did in 1884, and after she had abandoned her life in a succession of Catholic convents, had embraced Methodism, and, in her later publications, had engaged in a vitriolic attack upon Jesuits and the Catholic Church establishment in Ireland, the United States, and England. This controversial conclusion to a colourful life did nothing to detract from the popularity of Cusack's histories, which continued to be used extensively in Catholic secondary schools in Ireland. However, her histories also served to give legitimacy to the view, already widely held in nineteenth-century Ireland, that the struggle over the ownership of land and the struggle for the attainment by Catholics of full religious equality were inextricably linked.

9.3 Rethinking Inclusivity in an Era of Conflict: The Trajectory of John Mitchel

The radical turn taken by Cusack in her histories was probably influenced by what she had heard in Kerry of the response of some landlords to the trauma of

THE LATER NINETEENTH CENTURY 265

the Great Famine, and by her own witness, in subsequent years, to the indifference of some local landowners towards the plight of the poor. John Mitchel, who, as noted in Chapter 8, had been identified by Thomas Davis as the person best suited to write a full-scale history of Ireland, also became increasingly intolerant of landlords, and was horrified at the plight of the poor in Ireland, and began to conclude that their debased condition had revolutionary potential. Mitchel did eventually, in 1867, publish a *History of Ireland*, but on a scale and of a tone very different from what either Davis, or Mitchel himself in the 1840s, would have considered appropriate. Essentially Mitchel's previous expectation that the different segments of Ireland's population would prove ready to forget and forgive remembered grievances in the interest of enjoying a harmonious future had been dimmed by the tragedy of the Great Famine and by more recent political events.

Circumstances, including Mitchel's arrest and conviction on a charge of treason in May 1848, his transportation overseas as a convicted prisoner, his escape to the United States from Van Diemen's Land, and his subsequent narration of these events in his *Jail Journal*, all combined to make Mitchel an even more bitter opponent of British rule in Ireland than he had been in the 1840s.[22] Moreover, he had also become convinced that he could assist Irish people in escaping from the 'helot' status to which they had been subdued only by fomenting 'disaffection' between the people, the landowners, and the government. Mitchel would have been encouraged in this view by politicized members of the large Irish Catholic emigration community in the United States, many of them refugee survivors from the Great Famine. However, surprisingly, he had little time for the various secret societies that these emigrants had established, including the Fenians. Despite his reservation concerning such revolutionary groups in the United States during the 1860s, his knowledge of them gave Mitchel hope that Ireland's Catholics would become agents of revolution because the members of such groups seemed more independent of the authority of bishops than their counterparts at home. On this subject Mitchel, like his fellow exile Mathew Carey of an earlier generation, deplored the influence in Ireland of the Catholic bishops and of those he described disparagingly as Castle Catholics whose only concern, as he saw it, was to secure position and favour from the government.[23]

Mitchel's preoccupation with sustaining himself and his family as a journalist in New York, and then as a small-scale planter in Tennessee, and later again as an apologist for the Confederate cause during the American Civil War, did not allow him to undertake, much less complete, the multi-volume *History of Ireland* that Davis had thought him capable of delivering. However, the idea remained with

---

[22] Mitchel published his 'Jail Journal' serially in his first New York newspaper, *The Citizen*, between January and August 1854.

[23] Mitchel had already been giving frequent vent to these views in his *Jail Journal of 1854*; see the book edition Dublin, 1913; on Mathew Carey see Chapter 6.

him until he did publish a two-volume *History of Ireland* in 1867. This was different from what was in prospect in the 1840s, first, in that it gave no attention to the early medieval past that was previously considered necessary to prove and laud the civility of Ireland's inhabitants before the twelfth-century invasion. More surprisingly, it gave scant attention to the early modern centuries that Mitchel had previously considered essential to understanding the present. Instead, he left it to readers to consult the Abbé Mac Geoghegan on both subjects, thus suggesting that he was more prepared than in the 1840s to endorse a Catholic interpretation of Ireland's history in earlier centuries. This freed him to begin his two-volume *History of Ireland* with the Treaty of Limerick from which he proceeded with subjects of which Mac Geoghegan would have approved: 'the deliberate breach of the Treaty of Limerick', the enactment of the Penal Laws, the exile from Ireland of Irish soldiers and officers after they had been denied the promised benefits of their surrender at Limerick, and the 'achievements' of these soldiers 'in French and other services'.[24]

The past on which Mitchel dwelt was therefore a military one associated with the Irish who had been forced into exile. He represented their careers as glorious compared with the drab existence of those who had remained at home to suffer 'the long agony of the Penal laws when the pride of the ancient Irish race was stung by daily, by hourly humiliations, and their passions goaded to madness by brutal oppression'.[25] 'The inhabitants of Ireland' were then, he now acknowledged, 'definitely divided into two castes': those he described as 'the depressed Catholics' and 'the Protestants of Ireland [who] had lately grown numerous, wealthy and strong'. He believed that, in the decades following their subjugation, the Catholics in Ireland were 'done with national sentiment and aspiration for a time'. However, he still mentioned that among Protestants 'there arose immediately, strange to say, a strong sentiment of Irish nationality' of which he found evidence as early as 1692 in the parliament of that year where, through his arrogance, Lord Lieutenant Sydney made himself 'exceedingly unpopular with the people of the English colony in Ireland'.[26]

Here Mitchel was repeating what he, Davis, D'Arcy McGee, and the other idealists of the 1840s, had had to say of what he now described as 'the Colonial Nationality among the English of Ireland'. However, where Mitchel would previously have linked this expression of Irish nationality with what had preceded it and with what was to follow, he now drew attention to how English rulers had deliberately disrupted all expressions of Irish nationality because these presented a threat to Britain's imperial might. Moreover in 1867 he seemed to accept, as he

---

[24] John Mitchel, *The History of Ireland, from the Treaty of Limerick to the present time in two volumes* (New York and Dublin, 1867); quotations in this chapter are from the 3rd edition (Dublin, James Duffy, n.d); quotation here from the Introduction.
[25] Mitchel, *History of Ireland*, Introduction, vi.   [26] Mitchel, *History of Ireland*, vol. 1, 13, 20.

had not done in the 1840s, that Irish nationalism had also failed to reach its potential because of the lack of commitment of many in Ireland who should have supported it. Where a younger optimistic Mitchel had implied that all Protestants and their descendants in Ireland were potential colonial nationalists, or even potential United Irishmen, he now acknowledged that many Protestant settlers and their descendants had been, and still were, intransigent unionists. Moreover he now also admitted that some Protestants who had once espoused nationalist positions had since recanted, and he was convinced that some of Ireland's Catholic leaders, and especially Catholic bishops, had acquiesced in their community being suppressed by a hostile government. Thus in 1867 Mitchel spoke indignantly, as he had not done in the 1840s, of 'the Protestant party' who he considered even more responsible than the British government for the enactment of the Penal Laws. This party included 'the Cromwellian squires' who, he declared, had persistently opposed any expressions of Irish nationality.[27] Then, as he discussed the descendants of settlers who had arrived in Ireland in the plantations previous to that of Cromwell and who had enlisted in the Volunteers of 1782, Mitchel now reflected, after the manner of Mac Nevin in 1846, that they had not been as forthright in their support of inclusive nationalism as they might have been. Thus, on Lord Charlemont, he praised him for 'being great in reviews' and for having done 'his official duties well', but otherwise he dismissed him as 'a man of limited capacity but of much cultivation' who 'never could expand his mind wide enough to grasp the idea of associating in the new nation the two millions of Catholics'. He had not done so, said Mitchel—in complete contradiction of his 1840s verdict on the Ulster Plantation—because Charlemont was 'the descendant of one of the adventurers who had come over in Queen Elizabeth's reign and had been rewarded for his exertions in helping to crush O'Neill with large grants of confiscated estates'.[28]

Mitchel was therefore no longer interested, as he had been in the 1840s, in having people forget about the wrongs inflicted on the Irish in the past. On the contrary, he now seemed of the opinion that the rehearsal of past grievances would increase the people's 'disaffection', which he now wanted to encourage because he considered it necessary if Irish people were ever to make a bid for freedom. While Mitchel still expressed admiration for 'Colonial Nationality', he was less confident of its potential because so many Protestant leaders had been corrupted by the grants of plantation land that their ancestors had received at the outset of the seventeenth century. In so far as Mitchel still believed that there had been an opportunity to bring Catholics and Protestants together as one nation in the late eighteenth century, he credited an Englishman, Lord Fitzwilliam, with providing it during his 'short administration' in 1795, when he had proposed to

[27] Mitchel, *History of Ireland*, vol. 1, 10, 232.   [28] Mitchel, *History of Ireland*, vol. 1, 224–5.

place legislation before the Irish parliament that would have given Catholics the right to vote and take seats in that assembly. 'Every patriotic Irishman', declared Mitchel, 'must look back with unavailing regret to the lost opportunity' when 'the two nations which make up the Irish population' were 'well disposed to amalgamate and unite' and when 'there was really at that moment a disposition to bury the hatchet of strife'. Mitchel did not need to explain to his readers that this opportunity had been lost because Pitt had chosen to recall Fitzwilliam who, in the view both of the English government and of conservative Protestants in Ireland, had exceeded his brief. The construction that Mitchel chose to place upon the dismissal of Fitzwilliam was that it 'did not suit the exigencies of British policy' to have Irish nationalism flourish. Instead, he claimed, officials in England and their supporters in Ireland had deliberately provoked an 'insurrection in order that there be a Legislative Union'. Thus, claimed Mitchel, 'the chief object of the Government and its agents' between 1795 and 1797 had been 'to invent and disseminate fearful rumours of intended massacres of all the Protestant people by the Catholics'. This objective, he asserted, had been furthered by the Orange order which, he contended, had been established in 1795 to draw away Protestant support for Irish nationalism under the 'specious appearance of zeal for Church and King'.[29]

It is clear that as Mitchel proceeded to detail the rise of the United Irishmen and their conduct of the insurrection of 1798, he accepted that their hope of success had been limited from the outset both because of the determination of the British authorities to suppress the movement, and because of the divisions within the Protestant ranks that, he claimed, had been fomented by the government and its Irish agents. Another problem, he believed, was that the Catholic bishops were suspicious of the links between the United Irishmen and revolutionaries in France and preferred Catholic 'submissiveness under oppression' over allowing a revolution to proceed. Thus, in discussing the Catholic clergy of the time, Mitchel could speak positively only of Fr. John Murphy whose action in mobilizing Catholics to engage with the 1798 insurrection in Wexford led Mitchel to pronounce that 'if the other thirty-two counties had done as well as Wexford, there would have been that year an end to British domination'.[30]

Following this narration of how a genuine Irish effort at national self-assertion had been frustrated, Mitchel's account of Ireland's history in the nineteenth century was a gloomy depiction of the plight under the Union of 'the unfortunate Irish nation, bound hand and foot, muzzled, disarmed and half-starved [that] could but writhe helplessly under the lash of its greedy tyrant'.[31] This metaphor

---

[29] Mitchel, *History of Ireland*, vol. 1, 391–2; for a recent appraisal of these events, Thomas Bartlett, 'Ireland during the Revolutionary and Napoleonic Wars, 1791–1815'.

[30] Mitchel, *History of Ireland*, vol. 1, 379, 516.   [31] Mitchel, *History of Ireland*, vol. 2, 341.

THE LATER NINETEENTH CENTURY 269

from slavery came readily to mind because Mitchel had first-hand knowledge of how oppressive that system could be when a master proved tyrannical rather than paternalistic. Then his choice of the adjective greedy was to reinforce his emotive argument that the Great Famine in Ireland was 'artificial' since '1,500,000 men, women and children were carefully, prudently and peacefully slain by the English government in the midst of abundance which their own hands had created'.[32] As he proceeded, Mitchel gave some begrudging praise to O'Connell's success in achieving the Emancipation Act of 1829, however 'imperfect, and stunted and guarded' it had been. His success, claimed Mitchel with a hint of jealously, had elevated O'Connell 'to the highest pinnacle of popular favour' so that he became 'almost worshipped' by 'the Catholics' as 'their Heaven-sent deliverer'. However, he then mentioned that O'Connell himself, 'and the more thoughtful amongst his friends and supporters', had appreciated from the outset that 'there was no salvation for Ireland but in a repeal of the odious, fraudulent union', most especially once 'the people...found that emancipation did not save them from starvation'.[33] As Mitchel traced the course of the campaign for Repeal, he returned to the Young Ireland charge of the 1840s that O'Connell and his associates had become corrupted through association with the Whig party at Westminster. To this he added the accusation that O'Connell had been a 'despotic disciplinarian' who had been unwilling to contemplate the use of physical force even when it was clear 'that the majority of the Irish nation desired to undo the Union with England'. O'Connell's ultimate weakness in the eyes of Mitchel in 1867 was that he 'chose to identify himself with the higher class of Catholics, who thought enough had been done and called it freedom when themselves were free'.[34] However, Mitchel attributed greatest responsibility for the complacency of Irish leaders in the face of oppression to 'the Irish Catholic bishops' who had 'been so useful to the British government ever since the Union'.[35]

The only light that Mitchel could see shining out of the unremitting gloom of Ireland's history during the reign of Queen Victoria concerned the creation of a 'smaller association composed of very different men' from those close to O'Connell. This was the association linked to Thomas Davis who with his 'friend' John Dillon had established the Nation newspaper in 1842 which 'for several years was, next to O'Connell, the strongest power on the national side'. This 'gifted circle of educated young men both Protestant and Catholic' who 'soon received the nickname of Young Ireland, which designation they never themselves assumed nor accepted', were, claimed Mitchel, determined 'to lift up the Irish case high above both Catholic claims and Protestant pretensions and unite all sects in the one character of "Irishmen" to put an end to English domination. Their idea

[32] Mitchel, *History of Ireland*, vol. 2, 459.
[33] Mitchel, *History of Ireland*, vol. 2, 320–3.
[34] Mitchel, *History of Ireland*, vol. 2, 342–8.
[35] Mitchel, *History of Ireland*, vol. 2, 469.

270 IMAGINING IRELAND'S PASTS

was precisely that of the United Irishmen even if they hoped to achieve the desired end in a very different manner'.[36]

Mitchel did not spell out the differences but he consistently suggested that an Irish insurrection, which he had been working towards prior to his arrest in May 1848, and which he was again encouraging in the 1860s, should, unlike the rebellion of the United Irishmen in 1798, rely principally on the resources of Ireland's own population and that of its own exiles (now, like Mitchel himself, mostly in the United States) rather than on assistance from any foreign power. Mitchel also believed that any such insurrection, if it was to prove successful, would necessarily be preceded by an educational drive to counter that associated with the so-called National Schools that had been promoted by the British government seeking after 'the formation of the minds of young Irishmen and the moulding of their first impressions in such a way that they might forget they were Irish, and feel and think as like English children as possible'. Therefore, as he saw it (and here he was belittling the objections to the National Schools that had been raised by Catholic bishops), 'the intention [was] not so much to convert Catholic children as to denationalise them' by keeping them 'as much as possible ignorant of the history of their own country—a very prudent and politic design if it could only have been accomplished'.[37]

This suggests that Mitchel had in 1867 come to believe that the purpose of familiarizing Irish people with their history was to promote disaffection rather than to achieve the inter-communal reconciliation that he had espoused in the 1840s. He still obviously identified with the heroic history of Ireland's past, particularly during the early modern centuries, that had been cultivated both in the verse history of Young Ireland and in the prose text of the Abbé Mac Geoghegan, and he still encouraged people to venerate as heroes those who had sacrificed their lives in challenging the might of the British Empire at home and on foreign fields. However, in 1867 as Mitchel looked from this imagined past to a possible future, he asserted that Ireland's only hope of redemption rested in physical force as he, who had direct experience of blood sacrifice after the loss of two sons fighting for the defeated Confederate cause in the American Civil War, pronounced that 'no country is hopelessly vanquished whose sons love her better than their lives'.[38] Mitchel was obviously encouraged in this belief by those Irish exiles in the United States with whom he associated and who belonged to various secret societies that were dedicated to achieving the liberation of Ireland from British rule by any means.

In advocating this course, which the Fenians actually attempted to little effect in 1867, Mitchel knew that he (or those who followed his advice) would necessarily

---

[36] Mitchel, *History of Ireland*, vol. 2, 348–9; Mitchel significantly omitted the name of Gavan Duffy from among the founders of *The Nation*. They had parted politically long before this.

[37] Mitchel, *History of Ireland*, vol. 2, 328.   [38] Mitchel, *History of Ireland*, vol. 2, 470.

THE LATER NINETEENTH CENTURY 271

proceed against the wishes of Ireland's Catholic bishops and in opposition to the majority of Ireland's Protestant population on whose support a younger Mitchel had assumed he could rely. On the first of these issues Mitchel was confident that he could appeal over the heads of Ireland's Catholic bishops to those he identified as 'the people' in the expectation that they would support him given what they had suffered in the recent past, and given also what they had learnt from Young Ireland verse history of what their ancestors had suffered in previous centuries. When it came to Protestants, Mitchel, as mentioned, believed that there were still some idealists within the Irish Protestant community who would support his cause. And it would have seemed to him in 1867 that one of these was John P. Prendergast who, just two years before the appearance of Mitchel's *History*, had published a book entitled *The Cromwellian Settlement of Ireland* that Mitchel, and most nationalists, came to consider the most authoritative indictment of landlordism in Ireland.[39]

9.4 Landowners in Ireland's History: The Musings of John P. Prendergast

John P. Prendergast (1808–94), like Mitchel and Thomas Davis, attended Trinity College, Dublin, but had already graduated and was undertaking his training as a barrister before the other two matriculated. After his call to the bar in 1830 Prendergast took over from his father in 1836 as land agent to Lord Clifden. In that capacity he became acquainted with, and sympathetic towards, the demands of tenants for greater security of tenure. This made him an authority on the contentious question of tenant rights and on the need for land reform in Ireland. This in turn brought him to study the history of land ownership in Ireland, which drew his attention to the possibility that his remote antecedents, who, he fancied, had been significant landowners in County Tipperary, had lost their property and social position to Cromwellians. It may have been curiosity about their fate that persuaded Prendergast to investigate the surviving sources appertaining to the Cromwellian settlement of Ireland. As a lawyer with experience in estate management, Prendergast gave a scientific appearance to his study by including among his appendices two coloured maps—one describing the Transplantation to Connacht and the other the division of lands between Adventurers and Soldiers in County Tipperary where his Prendergast ancestors had supposedly originated.[40]

---

[39] John P. Prendergast, *The Cromwellian Settlement of Ireland* (London, 1865).
[40] For a biographical note on Prendergast see that by Christopher Woods in *Dictionary of Irish Biography*, vol. 8, 280–1; greater detail is available in Ciaran Brady, 'John P. Prendergast (1808–1893) and the Anglo-Irish Writing of Irish History', Győző Ferencz and Janina Vesztergom, eds., *Presence Is*

Prendergast's scrutiny of the relevant sources established to his satisfaction that the Prendergast family, of Anglo Norman descent, had occupied an estate in the vicinity of Carrick on Suir in County Tipperary, where he believed their position as subjects of the English Crown had remained uncontested until, during the reigns of Edward VI, Mary I, and Elizabeth I, the government decided upon 'the new conquest of Ireland'. This meant that 'the conquest of the lands of the Irish for the purpose of new colonizing or planting them with English was resumed', after a cessation of three hundred years.[41] Prendergast credited Edmund Spenser with having written the most comprehensive statement on how such a plantation might be proceeded with, and he considered that Lord Mountjoy, who had reduced the country 'to a howling wilderness' during the later stages of the Nine Years War (1594–1603), had provided a practical example on how the country might be prepared for the implementation of a comprehensive plantation, this time in Ulster.[42]

As Prendergast provided a brief summary of Ireland's history during the first half of the seventeenth century, he pronounced that 'the peace of despair' had prevailed until the Irish entered upon 'The Great Rebellion of 23 October 1641' with the purpose of recovering the lands of which they had been deprived through the previous plantation. In addressing this controversial subject, Prendergast deemed there had been 'no massacre' of Protestants in 1641 and that, in the struggle that followed upon the insurrection, 'the English were to the full as bloody as the Irish', especially since they made 'the English law... nothing but the will of the strongest [which] made killing no murder'. Prendergast contended that the harsh actions of the Dublin administration against those suspected of being sympathetic towards the revolt had enjoyed the fulsome support of the English parliament. There, he contended, it had been pronounced that 'the work of Queen Elizabeth and James I, would now be perfected. The Irish would be rooted out by a new and overwhelming plantation of English, another England would speedily be formed in Ireland'.[43]

Before Prendergast proceeded with his task of detailing the mechanics of the settlement, he explained that while the 'new English settlers', who were granted land in Ireland following the Cromwellian military victory, were 'filled with the intensest national and religious hatred of the Irish... their object was rather to extinguish a nation than to suppress a religion'. This, for him, meant that the enactment of Penal Laws against Catholics a half-century later was 'nothing but the complement' to the previous Cromwellian settlement, and were designed to demean the population rather than convert them to Protestantism.[44]

No Island, Writings in Honour of William John McCormack (Budapest, 2020), 31–68. I am grateful to Professor Brady for letting me see an advance copy of this paper.

[41] Prendergast, Cromwellian Settlement, v, vii, xiv.
[42] Prendergast, Cromwellian Settlement, 12–15, lix.
[43] Prendergast, Cromwellian Settlement, 1, 2, 4, 7, 10–11.
[44] Prendergast, Cromwellian Settlement, Preface, v.

THE LATER NINETEENTH CENTURY 273

Prendergast considered that there were two unique and pernicious features to the Cromwellian settlement. The first was that, as well as taking possession of land by force, the Cromwellians had sought to transplant the former owners and their dependants far from the vicinity of their former residence and to re-settle them in distant parts of the country since—and here he related his narrative to nineteenth-century experience—'America was not then accessible for the habitation of the Irish nation'.[45] The second unique feature was that this plantation was directed against people of English descent, including Prendergast's own ancestors, as well as against the native Irish. Thus, in his shrill introduction to *The Cromwellian Settlement*, Prendergast pronounced that those who went from England to settle in Ireland in 1652 were worse than the Vandals who had invaded Spain 'for the Vandals came as strangers and conquerors in an age of force and barbarism, nor did they banish the people though they seized and divided their lands by lot. However the English in 1652 were of the same nation as half of the chief families in Ireland, and had at that time had the island under their sway for five hundred years'.[46]

The mechanics of the Cromwellian confiscation, as Prendergast described it, showed how the army prepared the entire country for plantation, and how all surviving Irish Catholic landowners were reduced to the status of tenants on what previously had been their own estates.[47] This, he argued, had opened a way for the settlement on Irish lands of the 'Adventurers': that is some English people who, in 1642, had given money on loan to the government to enable the re-conquest of Ireland. The officers and soldiers in the Cromwellian armies who had achieved the re-conquest of the country, and who were compensated for arrears in pay with debentures on Irish land then joined these 'Adventurers' as settlers. The scheme, as Prendergast described it, was designed to render 'as purely English, the entire area from the river Boyne to the river Barrow'.[48]

Prendergast's next contention was that officers in the army came to dominate the settlement because, once they had been appointed to clear the ground for plantation and to manage the scheme, they had the opportunity to lay claim to the choice parcels of land 'near six years before the Adventurers began to come over in any number to take possession of their lots'. The officers had also 'obtained their desires', according to Prendergast, because they were in charge of the lotteries which assigned the parcels of land in each county and barony. They were, moreover, in a position, he contended, to buy out at a low price the debentures that had been allocated to 'the common soldiers [who] had no voice in the

---

[45] Prendergast, *Cromwellian Settlement*, 27.   [46] Prendergast, *Cromwellian Settlement* IV, v, xi.
[47] Prendergast, *Cromwellian Settlement*, 26.
[48] Prendergast, *Cromwellian Settlement*, 133; on the 'Adventurers' see Karl S. Bottigheimer, *English Money and Irish Land: The 'Adventurers' in the Cromwellian Settlement of Ireland* (Oxford, 1971); David Brown, *Empire and Enterprise: Money, Power and the Adventurers for Irish Land during the British Civil Wars* (Manchester, 2020).

274   IMAGINING IRELAND'S PASTS

matter'.[49] To add substance to his arguments, Prendergast described how the distribution of lands to the Adventurers was managed from Grocers' Hall in London.[50] Theoretically, he said, Ireland was 'being divided between the Adventurers, the English army and the government' all of whom were 'considered as new purchasers of their several portions'. The idea, he said, was that these collectively would have 'the great opportunity so long looked for... for improving the country and rendering it fruitful, prosperous and flourishing as the mother country of England'.[51] The idealism behind the scheme was further underlined, according to Prendergast, by the letter sent to one Mr Harrison in New England and other 'English planters [who were] invited back by the government from America'.[52]

The establishment of an English-style settlement, claimed Prendergast, was to be enabled by the clearance of all native inhabitants from the areas that were to become purely English. These, where they could not prove themselves innocent of any crimes against the government during the entire period, 1641–52, were to be given the opportunity to 'transplant'. This required them to leave their patrimonies accompanied by their dependants 'wives, daughters and children' by 1 May 1654 to the Province of Connacht and County Clare, which area 'Parliament had assigned... for the habitation of the Irish nation'. At the same time, according to Prendergast, those Protestants who held land in Connacht or Clare were to be granted land in one of the other three provinces. This, he contended, would have left Connacht with County Clare for the 'imprisonment of the nation' because of 'its peculiar suitableness for the purpose of imprisonment'.[53]

The longest and most emotive section of Prendergast's book was that concerning the proposed transplantation and the efforts of some individuals who had been ordered to transplant to appeal against their removal. For this purpose he made use of the relevant documents in Dublin Castle where he 'found the records of a nation's woes'.[54] Most of the appeals, he said, came from 'the noble and the wealthy, men of ancient English blood, descendants of the [twelfth-century] invaders' with relatively few from the 'native Irish [who were] too poor to pay

[49] Prendergast, *Cromwellian Settlement*, 95, 127–8, 81.
[50] Prendergast's overall thesis has been recently challenged in David Brown, *Empire and Enterprise*, where that author makes the case that it was the Adventurers, operating out of Grocer's Hall, who had been driving the process to gain possession of Irish land since 1642, who were jealous of all suggestions that the army should be paid off with confiscated Irish and who were most influential in having the Cromwellian settlement upheld after the Restoration of Charles II.
[51] Prendergast, *Cromwellian Settlement*, 116; for a twentieth-century appraisal of the progressive ambitions of the scheme, T.C. Barnard, *Cromwellian Ireland: English Government and Reform in Ireland, 1649–1660* (Oxford, 1975).
[52] Prendergast, *Cromwellian Settlement*, 120.
[53] Prendergast, *Cromwellian Settlement*, 25, 27, 117; while this was the theory that held true for a time it has been made clear in recent scholarship, most effectively in John Cunningham, *Conquest and Land in Ireland: The Transplantation to Connacht, 1649–1680* (Woodbridge, 2011), that the impracticality of the transplantation became quickly apparent and was diluted.
[54] Prendergast, *Cromwellian Settlement*, Preface, xx.

THE LATER NINETEENTH CENTURY   275

scriveners'. Prendergast was fascinated to find among the appeals one from William Spenser, grandson of Edmund Spenser, whose views were being cited by the Cromwellians to justify the entire scheme. This William Spenser had, under the terms of the Cromwellian settlement, forfeited the estate that had been assigned to his grandfather in the Munster plantation because he had lapsed to Catholicism. Given this, and given that William Spenser knew of Cromwell's admiration for what his grandfather had written of Ireland, he appealed the decision directly to Cromwell who had 'endeavoured but, in vain, to save his lands for him'.[55] Prendergast chose to cite this particular experience not only because of its piquancy but also because it upheld his contention that the army officers who managed the Cromwellian settlement would brook no appeal that threatened their enrichment.

Prendergast also cited from the experience of his own supposed ancestor and namesake. This was a John Prendergast who had similarly appealed to the Lord Protector against the confiscation of his ancestral property in County Tipperary. This appeal had also proven futile, but Prendergast contended that, rather than transplant to the desolation of Connacht, his ancestor had chosen to become a swordsman in Spain where he served until King Charles II was restored to the Crown. Restoration, however, brought no satisfaction to the original John Prendergast who, the author now argued, had to reconcile himself to becoming a tenant to the Adventurer who had become owner of his ancestral estate. We are left to assume that it was at this juncture that his family had conformed to Protestantism.[56]

Even more touching in Prendergast's account of the transplantation process was his extensive quotation from the certificates that the designated grantees were required to present to commissioners at Loughrea as they travelled to take up occupancy of the lands assigned to them in Connacht and Clare—an area that Prendergast persistently described as derelict. These certificates contained the names and a physical description of each assignee and of each accompanying family member and servant. Therefore, as Prendergast stated graphically, 'from the grey-haired sire to the blue-eyed daughter of four years old, the family portraiture [of each assignee was] given in the transplanters' certificates'. Again, Prendergast referred to appeals that some individuals lodged against their removal, and he conceded that some modifications had been introduced to make transplantation less harsh. However, Prendergast insisted that such overtures and actions only gave fresh opportunity to the officers to enrich themselves.[57] To illustrate this he discussed the refusal of the authorities to give William Cheevers of Monkstown in Dublin a dispensation from having to transplant to Connacht.

[55] Prendergast, *Cromwellian Settlement*, 44.
[56] Prendergast, *Cromwellian Settlement*, Preface, xiv, xv.
[57] Prendergast, *Cromwellian Settlement*, 32, 67.

276 IMAGINING IRELAND'S PASTS

Cheevers, he pointed out, was one of those unfortunates who had never been a rebel but was unable to prove that he had been 'in constant good affection' towards the government and was therefore technically not eligible for an exemption. His real 'crime', said Prendergast, was that 'he had a fine house and estate' that General Ludlow coveted and received as a grant.[58] By such means, pronounced Prendergast, the Cromwellian settlement had brought about the exile to Connacht of those who, until the reign of King Henry VIII, had been 'so full of schemes for confiscating the lands of the Irish and transplanting or extirping them'.[59] The consequence, he claimed, was that 'some went mad, others killed themselves, others lived on and founded families in their Final Settlements which subsist to the present day, like some of the Talbots and Cheevers, and some laid their bones in Connacht whose heirs got restoration of the monarchy'.[60]

Prendergast cited examples of each such outcome, but the overall thrust of his argument was that the high idealism, or zeal, that had offered some moral legitimacy to the project quickly gave way to the cupidity of Cromwellian officers. The theory that extensive areas were to become entirely English in habitation was disregarded, he contended, principally because grantees in such places saw merit in retaining the existing Irish tenants and support staff, and/or because some grantees and their subordinates married Irish wives. Those who hankered after the original purity of the scheme, claimed Prendergast, sometimes gave voice to 'calumnies' against Irish doctors and midwives, or issued occasional orders 'for the arrest of all transplantables untransplanted'.[61] However, Prendergast considered such outbursts and actions to be exceptional, and even as he acknowledged that some leniency was later permitted, he concluded that it came too late to mitigate the havoc, impoverishment, and starvation that the Cromwellian settlement had brought upon Ireland and its inhabitants. Some towns, he asserted, had experienced the ultimate affliction by being cleared of all inhabitants, which brought them to utter ruin. Such language would have reminded his readers of the more recent calamity of the Great Famine, and nobody would have missed the irony of Prendergast's overall appraisal that the 'desolation', which the Cromwellian settlement had brought on the country, 'was, as usual, only preparatory to the improvement of Ireland'.[62]

Prendergast was not only an Irish Protestant but also one who accepted Ireland's Union with Britain as valid, and a person who was professionally associated with the landlord system. However, in the course of his work as a lawyer, he

---

[58] Prendergast, *Cromwellian Settlement*, 68–9. [59] Prendergast, *Cromwellian Settlement*, 43.
[60] Prendergast, *Cromwellian Settlement*, 76.
[61] Prendergast, *Cromwellian Settlement*, 127–8, 131, 138–9, 141.
[62] Prendergast, *Cromwellian Settlement*, 143–4; my reading of this comment is at odds with the contention of Ciaran Brady that in his private correspondence, as also in his practice as a land agent, Prendergast seemed indifferent to the tragedy of the Great Famine, Brady, 'John P. Prendergast and the problem of history writing'.

THE LATER NINETEENTH CENTURY   277

had become aware of deficiencies in landholding in Ireland and sympathetic to the plight of tenants. Since his ambition was to promote reform and since he was hoping to do so through history, it is unsurprising that he looked to the writing of the Young Ireland authors and was considerably influenced by their ideas. This would explain his depicting those, whether of Gaelic or Anglo-Norman descent, who had been stripped of their lands to make way for Cromwellian settlers as members of an Irish nation, and those who benefited from Cromwellian settlement as members of an English garrison whose descendants were opposed to any manifestation of Irish nationality.

Prendergast seems to have remained convinced of the correctness of his conclusions, based on historical investigation, to the end of his career. Therefore, in his second book, *Ireland from the Restoration to the Revolution*, published in 1887, he endorsed the Young Ireland view that the Restoration land settlement had, for the most part, perpetuated the injustice visited upon Irish Catholic proprietors in the Cromwellian settlement. However, as he saw it, the monarchy could not have acted differently for the pragmatic reason that it was only by placating the Cromwellians in this way, and by accommodating Irish-born Protestants such as Roger Boyle and Charles Coote who had become agents of Cromwell in Ireland, 'could the King and the Royalists be restored'.[63] However, he could see that what was pragmatic for the Crown proved disastrous for Ireland's Catholics. This justified his assertion that the Restoration settlement, which he described as a 'Tragedy in Three Acts' was 'responsible to a great degree' for the subsequent instability of Ireland. It had provoked instability, he claimed, because those of the Irish (including Prendergast's own ancestors) who had been deprived of their estates by the Cromwellians due to the support they had provided both to Charles I and Charles II during the Wars of the Three Kingdoms, had never forgotten their disappointment when they had not been compensated for their losses at the time of the Restoration. The result, said Prendergast, was that ever since the 1660s Ireland was 'always settling but never settled'.[64]

Because Prendergast was a reformer, he hoped in 1865 that by publishing *The Cromwellian Settlement* he would hasten the demands coming from many sources to rectify some of the anomalies that existed in the management of land in Ireland. His hope, like that of many reformers of the time, was that amelioration could be achieved most readily by consolidating the position of tenants relative to that of landowners, and to raise awareness among landowners of the need to manage their estates more efficiently and more equitably. He seemed to believe in 1865 that if these reforms were put into effect that settled conditions would ensue because it would be in the interest of tenants as well as landowners to maintain

---

[63] John P. Prendergast, *Ireland from the Restoration to the Revolution, 1660–1690* (London, 1887), Preface, iii, and 4–5, 35, 59–60.

[64] Prendergast, *Ireland from the Restoration to the Revolution*, Preface, vi, viii.

278 IMAGINING IRELAND'S PASTS

order. Because reform was his intention, Prendergast welcomed the publicity that his book received in *The Nation* and he wrote in the pages of that newspaper to defend, and further elaborate upon, his arguments. These left no doubt that, in his opinion, the Catholic population had reason to feel aggrieved because of the injustices of previous centuries, and his work seemed to give scientific proof to the idea that the tenants of his generation were the descendants of the proprietors who had been dispossessed by Cromwell.

By the time Prendergast published *Ireland from the Restoration to the Revolution*, he had reason to regret that he had ever published *The Cromwellian Settlement*. By then he had come to see that the book had been used not so much to put the government on the path of reforming the landholding system in Ireland as to justify its overthrow. This did not result in Prendergast changing his opinion of what he had said of *The Cromwellian Settlement* nor did he raise any objection to its being kept in print. Moreover, he opened *Ireland from the Restoration to the Revolution* with a rehearsal of how Irish people remembered the injustices of the seventeenth century, and what these were.[65] The views Prendergast held about the past in 1887 were different from those he had expressed in 1865 to the extent that he argued that no matter how grave were the injustices that people had suffered in the past, they did not justify the endeavours of the 'headstrong men' of his own generation to promote a fresh 'social revolution' that would further unsettle the country. Here, Prendergast was making obvious reference to Michael Davitt and Charles Stuart Parnell and their associates in the Land League, and also to the British politicians, particularly William Gladstone. The latter, who Prendergast had previously admired as a promoter of land reform, had now, he believed, pandered to the wishes of the revolutionaries by bringing forward the Land Act of 1881, which had made it possible for tenants, with state assistance, to become owners of the land they had previously leased from their landlords. This was anathema to Prendergast whose idea of an ordered rural society was one dominated by landowners who would rent out their lands to tenants at a fair rent and monitor the use they made of their farms.

In line with this, Prendergast insisted in 1887 that while *The Cromwellian Settlement* had exposed the unjust means by which one cohort of proprietors had come to acquire property in the past, this revelation did not invalidate landownership or justify the expropriation of existing landlords. In making this case, Prendergast borrowed an argument that Mitchel had used in the 1840s to explain why the Ulster Plantation should remain undisturbed. Now, in discussing the Restoration Settlement, Prendergast reminded his readers that this was 'an event of over two hundred years antiquity' which was so firmly anchored in law that 'Englishmen have given their daughters to Irishmen in reliance on that

---

[65] Prendergast, *Ireland from the Restoration to the Revolution*, 145.

THE LATER NINETEENTH CENTURY   279

settlement of property...and millions of money have been lent on it'. Given that marriage and mortgage transactions had been conducted on the assumption that title to land in Ireland was secure, Prendergast now pronounced that any effort 'to undo' what had been accepted as final in the 1660s and again in the 1690s 'would be a gross breach of faith, and cause Ireland to remain unsettled, perhaps for ages'. Moreover, while he expressed no regrets for having exposed the injustices that Irish people had suffered in the past, Prendergast now pleaded 'that the present landlords of Ireland had [had] no part in the Cromwellian Conquest' and that dispossessing them would involve 'driving out of the island the only class accustomed to government'.[66]

In so far as Prendergast could contemplate change to land ownership in 1887 it would have to be gradual and determined by market forces and would go no further than replacing one group of landowners with another, as had happened when encumbered estates had been put on the market after the Great Famine. On that occasion, insolvent proprietors had been obliged to sell out their estates to cash-rich individuals, usually from England and Scotland, who, as Prendergast saw it, had added a cohort of people with entrepreneurial flair as substitutes for some of Ireland's most profligate proprietors. Even as Prendergast encouraged further reform of this kind in 1865, he contemplated what a 'strange irony' it would be if the estates of some of Ireland's insolvent landlords would be purchased, not by 'English Capitalists' as had happened after the famine but by some of the many 'sons of Ireland' who had been forced into exile to escape poverty but who would now return 'armed with American and Australian gold'.[67]

Prendergast clung more rigidly to conservative positions to the end of his life in 1894 even though his arguments became increasingly futile as Tory politicians no less than Liberals in Britain were won over to the idea that the promotion of peasant proprietorship in Ireland was the best means of restoring stability to the country. This was seen clearly by Michel Davitt, who Prendergast would have considered the most pernicious of Ireland's revolutionaries. As Davitt reflected in 1904 on the achievements of his lifetime, he too, like Prendergast, who had now been dead for ten years, recognized that the breakthrough for the Land League had come with the Land Act of 1881. However, Davitt looked positively at that which had alarmed Prendergast as he exulted at how peasant proprietorship had 'completely revolutionized the system of land tenure upheld in Ireland for over two centuries by English rule'. As he savoured that victory, Davitt revealed that what he knew of the history of land ownership in Ireland, and certainly the language he used to summarize that history, had come largely from Prendergast's

---

[66] Prendergast, *Ireland from the Restoration to the Revolution*, Preface, viii–ix.
[67] Prendergast, *Cromwellian Settlement*, 120; he would have meant gold literally since many nineteenth-century Irish emigrants had been attracted to take their chances in gold fields in Australia, New Zealand, and California.

280 IMAGINING IRELAND'S PASTS

The Cromwellian Settlement. Thus Davitt expressed pride in having defeated 'the feudal garrison' and 'English invaders' who had used every pretext—'the interests of "true religion" in one reign, of "law" and loyalty in the next, of the blessings and enlightenment of English domination always'—to promote a sequence of 'confiscations, settlements, plantations and forfeitures' the purpose of which was 'to seize and own the land of Ireland'.[68]

9.5 One Unionist's Re-Interpretation of Ireland's Early Modern Past: The Contribution of J.A. Froude

What has become evident in this chapter so far is the extent to which the views of three historians of Ireland—Cusack, who presented a Catholic interpretation of events, Mitchel who put himself forward as a nationalist revolutionary, and Prendergast who was a Unionist voice—had reached some degree of consensus concerning events in Ireland in the sixteenth and seventeenth centuries following the shock of the Great Famine and the social trauma that followed. They were of one mind that Ireland's history during the early modern centuries had also been horrific, and had brought the two principal segments of the country's population (those of Gaelic and those of Anglo-Norman descent) closer together even to the point, as some liked to believe, that they had become members of an Irish nation defined by shared suffering and a shared Catholicism. They were also agreed that the rebellion of 1641 was unsurprising when account was taken of the injustices associated with the plantations, and they all conceded that the Irish had been no more bloody than the settlers during the struggle that followed. This meant that all of our authors were also convinced that most British settlers and their descendants, and most emphatically those who were products of the Cromwellian conquest, had never been, and had no desire to become, part of any Irish nation. Despite their negative view of those who had come to Ireland with Cromwell, our authors still liked to believe there would be a place for Protestants within an Irish society, or even an Irish nation, of the future, and they conceded, or even rejoiced, that some Protestants of the eighteenth century had contributed to the development of an Irish sense of nationality.

We noted how this positive view was counterbalanced by their questioning the position of landowners whose estates had been acquired fraudulently or who had failed to meet their social obligations at moments of stress. Mitchel went further to query if there should be a future in Ireland for any landowners, and he linked a craving for a break-up of the landlord system to his desire forcefully to sever

---

[68] Micheal Davitt, *The Fall of Feudalism in Ireland: The Story of the Land League Revolution* (London, 1904), Preface, xviii, and 10.

Ireland's political connection with Britain and its Empire. Prendergast, a committed Unionist and a defender of the social status quo, regarded such opinions with alarm, as he began to despair that what he had written about Ireland's past to encourage reform was being used to justify subversion. Cusack also remained attached to Union and to Empire, and one of her purposes in writing history was to ensure that Irish Catholics would no longer have reason to apologize for the actions of their ancestors and would be prepared to participate as equals with Crown subjects from Scotland and England within the various services of the British Empire.

This summation of what was written by our three authors will be sufficient to show that agreement between them never went beyond the essentials, and that none of them was a coherent thinker. However, their agreement that Irish Catholics had been treated unfairly during the early modern centuries when added to the trauma of the famine, contributed to the idea that some reparation was due to them. Nobody was yet clear on what this would involve, but the build-up of historical evidence and argument tended to erode the credibility of Irish landowners whose position was under continuous scrutiny during the nineteenth century. Some of these narratives lent support to the idea that political reform in the present—including the possible granting of Home Rule—would be required to compensate for past injustices, while others looked forward to Irish people, regardless of denomination, being able to compete as equals with English and Scots people for positions within the British Empire.

Such contemplation about the past, even when it was incoherent, was clearly having an influence on the formulation of British policies for Ireland in the nineteenth century. This challenged those who were opposed to such policies to present a version of the past that could be used both to defend the existing social order and to justify firm, rather than conciliatory, policies. John Prendergast was an obvious candidate to write such a history but he disqualified himself because he had consistently refused to recant the opinions he had expounded in 1865 in *The Cromwellian Settlement*. Moreover, the qualifications he advanced in 1887 in *Ireland from the Restoration to the Revolution* were largely ignored and Prendergast continued to be associated in the popular mind as the author of *The Cromwellian Settlement*.

When nobody resident in Ireland seemed prepared to formulate a counter view to the emerging consensus on Ireland's past and its future prospects, the deficit was made good by James Anthony Froude (1818–94), a self-conscious Englishman who knew Ireland well, having visited the country in 1840–41, 1844, 1845, and 1848. He considered himself qualified to write a counter-narrative because he had long held the view that the greatest failure of English government through the centuries had been that of not taking its responsibilities in Ireland seriously. Froude had expressed such opinions in occasional journalistic pieces and in his history of Tudor England, but his considered position on the history of

282 IMAGINING IRELAND'S PASTS

Ireland and the relationship of that history to present policy took the form of a book published in 1872, entitled *The English in Ireland in the Eighteenth Century*.[69]

Froude, as we know from an intellectual biography by Ciaran Brady, was already a recognized English public intellectual who greatly admired Thomas Carlyle, who, as we learn from Ciaran Brady, reciprocated Froude's admiration for him both by admitting him to his inner family circle and by nominating him to be his official biographer.[70] By the 1870s, Froude was a polymath who had dabbled in the writing of fiction, philosophy, and political economy, while also being an editor of consequence, and an apologist for the British Empire. His major publication was a multi-volume *History of England from the Death of Wolsey to the Death of Elizabeth* that had been published sequentially between 1856 and 1870. Tudor history had attracted him because the reigns of the Tudor monarchs had witnessed the triumph of the Protestant Reformation that, in his view, had liberated English people from the intellectual tyranny of Rome and thus enabled their future imperial and cultural greatness.[71] However, and here he took his inspiration from the writings of Edmund Spenser, Froude considered Tudor rulers to have been negligent in not bringing Ireland under effective English control when they had the opportunity to do so. Furthermore, again following Spenser, he believed that the difficulties experienced by subsequent English governments in managing Ireland, were a manifestation of the providential punishment that had befallen England because of the failure of the government of Queen Elizabeth to live up to its responsibility towards Ireland. Froude's pontification concerning the past was confirmed by his personal observation when he first visited Ireland in 1840–41 as tutor to the family of an evangelical Church of Ireland clergyman. There, Froude became convinced that little had changed since Spenser's day with, as Brady has described it, Protestants being as 'a people under siege, abandoned by their government and by a corrupt and ineffectual Established Church while all around them lurked bitter seditious Catholics, eager, at the first spark of rebellion...to cut their throats'.[72]

While Froude resorted occasionally to providential explanation for the course of events, he more frequently drew on the concepts and vocabulary of Victorian science, including social science, in which to formulate his arguments. Thus he contended that England had a responsibility to govern Ireland, in the present as in the past, because countries, like individuals, were 'infinitely unequal in ability and worthiness' and that, as with people, 'the superior part [had] a natural right to govern [and] the inferior part [had] a natural right to be governed'. This principle, according to Froude, was all the more valid 'when two countries, or

---

[69] J.A Froude, *The English in Ireland in the Eighteenth Century*, 3 vols., (London, 1872).

[70] Ciaran Brady, *James Anthony Froude: An Intellectual Biography of a Victorian Prophet* (Oxford, 2013), 353.

[71] Brady, *Froude*, 198–232.   [72] Brady, *Froude*, 74–6, quotation 76.

sections of countries, [stood] geographically so related to one another that their union under a common government will conduce to the advantage to one of them'. Where such contiguity obtained, he insisted, the apparent weaker of the two 'could continue separate as long only as there is equality of force between them'. Then, lest it be thought that he was asserting that, as in the animal world, 'might constitutes right', Froude explained that 'among reasonable beings right is for ever tending to create might'.[73]

Then as he descended from theory, Froude conceded that some groups in Ireland had, at various times, challenged England's claim to rule over the country. The fact that all such efforts had failed, satisfied Froude that this confirmed England's entitlement to rule, given that relations between countries were analogous to interaction between humans whereby 'the better sort of men submit willingly to be governed by those who are nobler and wiser than themselves; organization creates superiority of force: and the ignorant and selfish may be, and are, justly compelled for their own advantage to obey a rule which rescues them from their natural weakness'.[74] This for him proved the falsity of the 'assumption' of several Irish authors that considerations such 'as race and language' justified 'the independence of nations...as if each separate race and community had a divine title deed to dispose of its own fortunes, and develop its tendencies in such direction as seems good in itself'. Such an assumption, claimed Froude, could be exposed as erroneous when one enquired 'what constitutes a nation?'. For Froude the answer to this question was that 'the right of a people to self government consists and can consist in nothing but their power to defend themselves'.[75]

At this point, Froude proceeded much as Spenser had done three centuries earlier, or as Gerald of Wales had done in the twelfth century, to condemn the Irish for their deficiencies in establishing state institutions. 'The incompleteness of character' in the Irish, he proclaimed, was 'conspicuous in all that they do and have done; in their history, in their practical habits, in their arts and in their literature...they have no secular history, for as a nation they have done nothing which posterity will not be anxious to forget'. Because of the shortcomings of the Irish, Froude believed it would prove beneficial for all—particularly the Irish—if the English fulfilled their obligation to over-rule them because 'the Irish [had] shown themselves at all times, and in all places, capable of the most loyal devotion to anyone who will lead and command them'. As evidence for this Froude—in what might have been an updating of what Abbé Mac Geoghegan had written— cited their service as 'soldiers in the French or English armies' as also in 'the modern police'.[76]

Having thus revealed his presumptions and prejudices, Froude presented his history of Ireland where, for the sixteenth century, he identified 'the central faults

---

[73] Froude, *English in Ireland*, vol. 1, 1–2.
[74] Froude, *English in Ireland*, vol. 1, 2.
[75] Froude, *English in Ireland*, vol. 1, 2–3.
[76] Froude, *English in Ireland*, vol. 1, 22–3.

284   IMAGINING IRELAND'S PASTS

of Elizabeth's Irish administration' to have been its failure to introduce 'Protestant colonies' who might 'have maintained themselves with ease in the Pale' at a time when the Irish chiefs were so 'feeble' and divided among themselves that 'a mere handful of English soldiers' would have been able to 'shatter' any 'rebellion' that the actions of the soldiers might have provoked. Then, when discussing the government's eventual introduction of colonies to the provinces, he complained that it had not made sufficient resources available to support them. Consequently, the soldiers who had been 'placed in a country to repress *banditti*' became, for lack of pay, 'little better than *banditti* themselves'. This, for Froude, meant that it was 'the negligence of Queen Elizabeth' that had enabled the occurrence of the rebellion of the 1590s that had almost brought an end to England's control over the country. This rebellion had proven challenging, claimed Froude, because the queen had rescued Hugh O'Neill from his father's fate of being murdered by kinsmen, and had him 'brought up at the court as a Protestant in the midst of the most brilliant circle which any capital in Europe could show'. There, according to Froude, O'Neill developed 'high qualities both as a commander and a politician', and thus, when he forsook his loyalty, became 'the most formidable Irish antagonist'.[77] Apart from O'Neill, who was ultimately defeated, the government, according to Froude, had had nothing to fear in Ireland because for most Irish people 'to rise against England was a game in which success was always possible, and defeat had no peril, for the conquerors either could not, or dared not, inflict effectual punishment'.[78]

Froude considered that English policy towards Ireland had taken a more promising course in the seventeenth century when the government undertook the 'systematic colonization of Ulster, long understood to be the only remedy for the chronic disorder'. Moreover, it appeared to him that England was then in a position to meet the challenge because, in a passage he probably borrowed from Carte, he argued that after prolonged peace at home, 'hundreds of thousands of active enterprising men, ... were looking for openings to push their fortunes. They had been turning their thoughts to America but here in Ireland was an America at their own doors with the soil ready for the plough'. Consequently, he stated, farmers, merchants, weavers, mechanics, and labourers had travelled 'over to earn a living by labour' in Ulster with the result that, 'for the first time, the natural wealth of Ireland began to reveal itself'. These also, unlike the colonists of the twelfth century, 'were saved from degeneration into the native type by their religion'.[79]

If Froude looked positively on the Ulster Plantation, he believed that progress had been hindered by various factors. First, he complained of how through

[77] Froude, *English in Ireland*, vol. 1, 50–1, 58–9.   [78] Froude, *English in Ireland*, vol. 1, 66.
[79] Froude, *English in Ireland*, vol. 1, 68–72; for the possible passage from Carte that Froude may have drawn upon see Chapter 5, 138.

THE LATER NINETEENTH CENTURY 285

'mistaken tenderness' all crimes committed against Queen Elizabeth had been forgiven; then, for the same reason, he claimed that the Catholic Church had been permitted to flourish; and the worst shortcoming was that when Catholics had remained as 'one body' the Protestants had become divided doctrinally, which divisions were, he believed, exacerbated by Wentworth. On the other hand, Froude credited Wentworth with recognizing that Ireland 'was a conquered country possessing no rights but such as he was inclined to allow', and had therefore designed 'to carry the principles of colonization a step further, and settle Connacht as Ulster had been settled'. Faced by these threats, claimed Froude, 'religious indulgence' seemed to 'satisfy the Anglo Norman Catholics' but not 'the true Irishman' whose 'passions...were for the land, and he saw the land in large slices passing away from him to the stranger'.[80]

Another difficulty, according to Froude, was that when 'England offered them [the native Irish] material prosperity; they did not care for prosperity. England talked of order; the order of England was to them tyranny and spoliation'. This incompatibility of views explained for Froude how the Irish came to 'the edge of the greatest event in Irish history, the turning point on which all later controversies between England and Ireland hinge'. This turning point, he identified as the rebellion of 1641, on which, he stated, the volumes of depositions stored in the library of Trinity College, Dublin, told 'the tale with perfect directness', leaving no doubt that what had happened in Ulster 'rivalled in carnage the horrors of St. Bartholomew'.[81] Here, Froude was repeating the verdict of Temple whose 'language in describing [what had happened, rose] into a tone of profound and tragic solemnity'. Given such clarity, Froude considered as perverse those 'Catholic historians' who chose 'to think that the massacre of 1641 was a dream'. Froude was aware of the objections they had raised to the various estimates of the numbers killed in the rebellion that had been offered by authors such as Temple, Clarendon, Petty, and Carte. However, instead of reopening the dispute on which he did not consider himself qualified to speak with authority because he had not consulted the depositions in the original, he concluded diplomatically that 'the evidence proves no more than that atrocities had been committed on a scale too vast to be exactly comprehended'.[82]

Following a brief narration of the ensuing war, and on the various efforts made by Ormond to arrive at a conciliation with the former insurgents, Froude entered upon a discourse on justice, which 'in all times and places [meant] protection and encouragement to the industrious, the honest, and the worthy; repression and punishment of the idle and mutinous, who prefer to live at their own wills on the spoil of other men's labours'. Notwithstanding his previous negative comment on Ireland and its people, Froude now contended that it was 'in the Irishman's nature'

---

[80] Froude, *English in Ireland*, vol. 1, 77–81.   [81] Froude, *English in Ireland*, vol. 1, 83–4.
[82] Froude, *English in Ireland*, vol. 1, 83, 99, 109, 111, 112.

to have 'a special appreciation of just dealing', and that despite it being frequently 'said' that 'the Celtic peasant' preferred 'the tyranny of his own chiefs to the orderly rule of the stranger' this theory had 'scarcely had a fair trial' until the forces of Oliver Cromwell had achieved total victory over all opponents in Ireland. Following this, pronounced Froude, 'for the first and last time, a government was...established in Ireland which, for the ten years that it endured, was to administer the country in the sole interest of honest labour—where the toiler was to reap the fruit of his toil, the idle and the vicious to reap the fruit of their devices'. This appraisal, which would have offended all Irish Catholic readers and liberal Protestants, should not have come as a surprise to them given both Froude's strict Protestant upbringing and the admiration he had for Thomas Carlyle and his edition of *The Letters and Speeches of Oliver Cromwell*. In offering it, Froude recognized that 'the perverseness of tradition [had] made these years a byword of tyranny', because 'the victims of the Cromwellian settlement [had] had the making of history', and their views had gone unchallenged because of 'English carelessness and prejudice'.[83]

As Froude set out to rectify this imbalance by defending the Cromwellian conquest of Ireland with its alleged atrocities, he again found that 'history, ever eloquent in favour of the losing cause—history which [had] permitted the massacre of 1641 to be forgotten, or palliated or denied, [had] held up the storming of Drogheda to eternal execration, had not given fair coverage to Cromwell'. Therefore, after a rehearsal of what had happened at Drogheda, Froude absolved Cromwell from what, he contended, were false accusations.[84] This absolution was as a preliminary to his praising Cromwell's period of rule in Ireland when 'no wrong doing—no tyrannous oppression of the poor' was permitted as Cromwell set out 'to rule Ireland for Ireland's good'. Again, by Froude's reckoning, other positive features of Cromwellian government were that no distinction was made then between England and Ireland since both were administered from Westminster, 'Romanism [which was], steadily repressed, must have died out, as Protestantism died in Spain and Italy', and 'Cromwell, alone of all Irish governors, understood [the] central principle of Irish management'. This principle held that when 'authority [was] just as well as strong' and when an Irishman was given 'a just master he [would] follow him to the world's end'.[85]

Having thus summarized what he considered positive about Cromwell's plans for Ireland, Froude regretted how these benefits had been frittered away after the Restoration when a conciliatory mode of government was resumed. He argued that the British government had been given a second opportunity at the time of the Glorious Revolution to revert to where Cromwell had left off, but he

---

[83] Brady, *James Anthony Froude*, 376; Froude, *English in Ireland*, vol. 1, 120.
[84] Froude, *English in Ireland*, vol. 1, 123–5.   [85] Froude, *English in Ireland*, vol. 1, 137, 140.

THE LATER NINETEENTH CENTURY   287

concluded that this had been squandered because two centres of power had been re-established. Rather than this, claimed Froude, Ireland's 'separate constitution should have been abolished, the two countries re-united as Cromwell had designed, and thus, far better than by any separate detailed condition, the Irish admitted to the full participation of every British privilege. So long as there were two centres of political life, and two legislatures, the idea of a separate nationality and of a separate interest persistently survived, and absenteeism of the most mischievous kind could not be prevented'.[86]

This narrative of events in Ireland during the sixteenth and seventeenth centuries served as an introduction to Froude's main concern, which was to narrate what had transpired in Ireland in the eighteenth century. This, for him, was again an unhappy story because, despite challenges from such peasant dissidents as Houghers and Whiteboys, whose activities were detailed by Froude, many of the landed Protestant elite whose dominance in the country had been re-established by the Williamite conquest and further entrenched by the Penal laws had chosen to indulge in pathetic 'Patriot' challenges to British authority rather than become firm supporters of government.[87] Some of their number, according to Froude, had placed their community in even further jeopardy by becoming absentees in England, thus abandoning their responsibility towards their dependents and towards the country of their adoption. Froude hoped, by exposing such delinquency, to resolve the issue of absenteeism, and he rejoiced that the Act of Union in 1801, which had conceded representation to Ireland in the Westminster parliament, had restored the unitary state that had been first established by Cromwell. The failure of this to immediately produce the orderly society that should have resulted was due not to any deficiency in the formula itself but because 'England' had lacked firmness in 'her efforts to harmonize her relations with her wayward dependency'. Instead, she had 'taken those who [had] made the loudest noise at their own estimation' and had 'thought alternately, and with equal unsuccess, how she can coerce or conciliate those who gave her trouble', and had 'rarely troubled herself to consider...how to encourage industry and honest labour; how to prevent oppression and save the working peasant from being pillaged by violence or unjust law'.[88]

It is clear from this summation both of Froude's interpretation of Ireland's history during the sixteenth and seventeenth centuries and of his commentary on the variation between schemes of coercion and conciliation to which recent British authorities had resorted for managing Ireland that he was drawing lessons from that history to guide present policy. Given this, it is hardly surprising that

---

[86] Froude, *English in Ireland*, vol. 1, 217.

[87] Houghing involved the mutilation of animals by cutting the Achilles tendon; for Froude's description of the activities of the Houghers see Froude, *English in Ireland*, vol. 1, 416 forward, and for his discussion both of Whiteboys and 'Patriots' see vol. 2.

[88] Froude, *English in Ireland*, vol. 1, 120.

288   IMAGINING IRELAND'S PASTS

Froude's use of history to deny people of Irish 'race' any entitlement to consider themselves a nation, and to establish that the Irish were incapable of governing themselves, provoked outrage among all who fostered national aspirations for Ireland and united them, whether they lived in exile or at home, against Froude's interpretation of Ireland's past.[89] However, while he knowingly offended Irish nationalists, Froude did not endear himself either to successive British governments or to landowners in Ireland. On the contrary, he pilloried both for grave dereliction of duty in failing to bring good order to Ireland when they had been presented with repeated opportunities to do so. By 1719, he thundered, 'the majority of Irish noblemen were already absentees', while, by 1782, 'the Protestant colonists were once more dreaming of separation and a revival of Irish nationality [when] the question [of] what that nationality was to be in their present heat they scarcely cared to consider'.[90] He further insisted that it was 'the insanity of the English colony' in dabbling with liberal principles that had again brought it to the point of destruction in 1798, which rebellion he detailed after the manner of Sir Richard Musgrave, whose history of that episode Froude cited with approval.[91] If anything could explain the failure of Protestants in Ireland to fulfil their obligation to reform the country, it was, claimed Froude, that their hands had been tied by ill-advised government interference. Thus, he insisted, government should never have created division among Protestants in Ireland by conceding to 'the Anglican Establishment...a power of persecuting those who had carried out more thoroughly the principles of the Reformation' than they themselves had done. Furthermore, he claimed, government should have withheld any clemency towards Catholics after 1691 because 'the loyal colonists were dismayed to perceive that the Catholics were handled as tenderly as ever'.[92] Ultimately, as Froude interpreted it, the steps taken to reform Ireland had been defeated as 'the Penal Laws had failed to coerce the Catholics into conformity. The Charter Schools had failed to convert them because the English government had interposed to protect the Catholic clergy'.[93]

Such criticism of the Protestant interest in Ireland and of England's errors in governing the country did nothing to assuage the fury voiced by Irish nationalists of all stripes against Froude's *The English in Ireland*. On the other hand, notwithstanding his vilification of Irish Protestants for their repeated dereliction of duty, Froude's contribution was welcomed as a lifeline by Irish upholders of the Union. These, as we shall see, soon took to culling arguments and evidence from Froude's *The English in Ireland* to sustain their own interpretations of Ireland's past that they composed to assist them in averting the cataclysm that seemed

---

[89] I am grateful to Sarah Covington for information on the hostility that Froude encountered from audiences composed largely, but not exclusively, of Irish emigrants, in Boston, New York, and Philadelphia when he engaged in a lecture tour of those cities, September to December 1872. Professor Covington proposes to detail this subject in her forthcoming book, *Remembering Oliver Cromwell in Ireland.*
[90] Froude, *English in Ireland*, vol. 1, 390, vol. 2, 277.   [91] Froude, *English in Ireland*, vol. 3, 494.
[92] Froude, *English in Ireland*, vol. 1, 214, 220.   [93] Froude, *English in Ireland*, vol. 2, 11.

THE LATER NINETEENTH CENTURY   289

about to engulf them. Where Irish nationalists had taken to identifying heroes whose actions in the past inspired pride in the present and confidence for the future, upholders of the Union were now encouraged to take inspiration from Oliver Cromwell. His example, claimed Froude, had shown that 'a government, strong, just and impartial with honest men to administer it, was Ireland's sovereign necessity. It was the one remedy which, except during the nine years of the Commonwealth, had never been applied'.[94] Nor was this summation of Ireland's past entirely of Froude's own construction since he acknowledged that it had been drawn largely from a speech in support of the Act of Union delivered in the Irish House of Lords on 10 February 1800 by John Fitzgibbon, earl of Clare. This, in Froude's words, offered in 'substance...a summary of Irish History from the Reformation to the present'.[95]

9.6 Conclusion

It will have become clear from this chapter that the various groups who had been taking an interest in the writing of Ireland's past were forced by circumstances to reconsider the interpretations they had previously considered appropriate. The first of these circumstances was the Great Famine, and with it the perceived ineptitude of the government in alleviating the distress it had caused, and the perceived indifference of most of Ireland's landed elite towards the famine's victims. The second, not unrelated, factor was the development of a more radical politics in Ireland that advanced claims for the reform, and ultimately the abolition, of the landlord system, and also the achievement of Home Rule. Others, including Mitchel, favoured the use of revolutionary action to achieve the total independence of Ireland from Britain, and many who promoted ameliorative action were consciously seeking to stave off this possibility. Under these circumstances, both government and landed elite were exposed to a barrage of criticism, as authors who approached the history of Ireland more critically than had their predecessors questioned the origins of the political, religious, and social systems that appeared to have produced such inequity, injustice, and calamity. We noted that as both government and elite became the subjects of unremitting criticism because of past and present policies, defenders of the Union seemed, for a time, incapable of imagining a counter-narrative. Essentially, they found it increasingly difficult to defend what was coming to be represented as indefensible.

The task, as we saw, was taken up by an Englishman, James Anthony Froude. That author proceeded from the assumptions held by Thomas Carlyle, as these have been summarized by Roy Foster, that 'misrule, oppression, and the hopeless economics of absentee landlordism and potato dependency' were the ultimate

---

[94] Froude, *English in Ireland*, vol. 3, 472.   [95] Froude, *English in Ireland*, vol. 3, 494.

'causes of Irish degradation'.[96] However, still taking his inspiration from Carlyle, Froude accorded Oliver Cromwell the status of a hero not only because he had defeated all foes but had also integrated Ireland with Britain in a unitary state and had introduced a cohort of enterprising landlords to displace the indigenous ones who, as Froude portrayed them, had been guilty of oppressing the poor while being disobedient to successive monarchs. Cromwell, he insisted, was also fully justified in seeking to suppress Catholicism in Ireland because 'at the bottom of every rebellion in that country' since the Reformation were to be found Catholic bishops and clergy'.[97] However, where Carlyle had by 1849 come to despair of Ireland, following his second visit to the country, Froude remained optimistic that Ireland might yet be improved if governments adhered to the formula offered by Cromwell. Had this been done in the past, according to Froude, Ireland's past would likely have been less fractious and might even have been saved the cataclysm of the Great Famine.

The intervention of Froude, as we shall see in Chapter 10, inspired a new generation of Unionist historians to defend their own actions and those of their ancestors, particularly as they took to composing histories that looked at developments at a local rather than a national level. As they did so they displayed a familiarity with the interpretations they were seeking to discredit, while among their nationalist opponents the arguments in Froude's *The English in Ireland* became the subject of such contention that they became almost better known than those being advanced by the authors who were seeking to refute them. This tendency to give exposure to the views of opponents was not new to Irish discourse, and while Froude gave principal credit in his text to authors such as Temple, Musgrave, and Fitzgibbon, whose opinions he was corroborating, he let it be known that he had also reflected upon the writings of those whose arguments he was opposing. Thus he made regular reference to Prendergast, and of the eighteenth century authors to whom he referred, he pronounced that 'the story' of John Curry concerning what Froude insisted on calling the 'massacre' of 1641 would 'not bear examination'. Even as he did so, especially as he looked to the politics of his own time, Froude conceded that Curry's argument had been 'well contrived' both because it had represented Catholics as 'victims' and because it complied with 'the growing sentiment that the past had better be forgotten'.[98] In opposing the idea that any memory of the past should be jettisoned, this Unionist critic of liberal sentiment found himself in agreement with P.F. Moran, a conservative of a different stripe and the leading Catholic interpreter of Ireland's past. Froude, and no doubt his admirers, seemed aware that the interpretations favoured by nationalist authors did not necessarily correspond with those of Catholics, as he mentioned almost mockingly 'the boast of a cardinal', who can only have been Paul Cullen, 'that Irish nationality is the Catholic religion'.[99]

---

[96] R.F. Foster, 'The First Romantics', *Words Alone*, 83.
[97] Froude, *English in Ireland*, vol. 1, 210.   [98] Froude, *English in Ireland*, vol. 2, 13.
[99] Froude, *English in Ireland*, vol. 2, 279.

10
Fresh Unionist Re-Appraisals of the History of Early Modern Ireland

10.1 Introduction

Many within Ireland's Unionist community considered themselves to be under siege throughout much of the nineteenth century and for a variety of reasons. What they had always taken to be their entitlement to represent their communities in parliament had been weakened considerably by the enactment of Catholic Emancipation in 1829; their control over municipal government was also being steadily eroded; and they lost one of their principal bulwarks when the legislation disestablishing the Church of Ireland came into force in 1871.

The Great Famine of 1845–49 further undermined the Unionist community in Ireland: economically, because the alleviation of distress among the famine-stricken population necessitated an increase in rates that brought many landed families into bankruptcy, and morally, because many social commentators, in Britain no less than in Ireland, attributed the human tragedy that had occurred either to the profligacy or the incompetence of Irish landowners. The predicament of landowners was exacerbated when a series of crop failures between 1876 and 1879 aroused widespread fear in Ireland that another famine was imminent. This was the background to the Land War of 1879–81 where the Land League led by Michael Davitt mobilized opposition to landlords. The position of landowners and the Unionist population more generally became even more threatened when Charles Stewart Parnell, himself a Protestant landowner from County Wicklow, established a link between agrarian grievance and demands for Irish Home Rule. This boded ill for Unionists after the Westminster election of 1880, when William Gladstone, the new Liberal Prime Minister, took a personal interest in alleviating Irish grievances and improving the lot of Irish tenants.

History writing played its part in eroding the confidence of most Irish Unionists, because, as noted, almost all historians of Ireland who labelled themselves as nationalists, or Catholics, or liberals tended to trace the problems of the present to the injustices of the past, particularly the early modern past. As they did so, several suggested that harmony would never be restored to Ireland until some reparation was offered to the current generation of Catholics for the sufferings of their ancestors. This implied that consideration had to be given to remedying the negative impact of the plantations of the sixteenth and seventeenth

Imagining Ireland's Pasts: Early Modern Ireland through the Centuries. Nicholas Canny, Oxford University Press (2021).
© Nicholas Canny. DOI: 10.1093/oso/9780198808961.003.0010

centuries. The Cromwellian Plantation was that most frequently criticized, to the point where it became a commonplace to denounce all landlords as either Cromwellians or absentees. Such tagging meant that landlords were being frequently defined as aliens within the communities in which they held their estates, or even as parasites when they were known to be absentees. Such charges continued to be pressed even when they conflicted with evidence that many nineteenth-century proprietors belonged to families whose presence in Ireland long predated Cromwell. Scant attention was also given to the fact that a significant proportion of landowners, and particularly of lesser landowners, was of indigenous ancestry and Catholic in religion.

John Prendergast's *The Cromwellian Settlement* was, as we saw, the work that did most to lend authority to the view that most Irish estates had been acquired unjustly under the Cromwellian scheme. The author, ironically, owned some land and managed more, and was a Protestant who was also committed to Ireland's Union with Britain.

Prendergast's later attempt to persuade his readers that his findings did not justify precipitate action to reverse past injustices offered scant solace to proprietors since his suasions fell on deaf ears. Landowners and their advisors were appreciative of James Anthony Froude for espousing their cause even when they were reluctant publicly to follow his advice that they should salute Oliver Cromwell as their hero and take pride in how Cromwell, and those in Ireland who had supported him, had defeated all opponents. Upholders of the status quo did, however, see merit in Froude's further advice that not all proprietors in Ireland were of Cromwellian descent, and that those of their ancestors who had supported Cromwell had been morally justified in doing so because of the perfidy of Ireland's Catholics who, it was alleged, had intended in 1641 to massacre all Protestants in the country. Rather than openly proclaim such arguments that were likely both to offend Catholics and elicit negative comment from opinion formers in Britain and Ireland, it was left to a new generation of authors to advance them subtly in fresh versions of Ireland's history for the sixteenth and seventeenth centuries that were designed to serve the needs of the Protestant and Unionist communities of the late nineteenth century.

10.2 County History or Country History

Some authors, notably Froude, favoured the construction of a Unionist grand narrative of Ireland's history that would explain why no Irish nation had ever existed, or had a right to exist, and why Ireland should therefore be ruled by Britain. Some Irish Unionist authors, more conscious than Froude of their own traditions and of the precariousness of their present circumstances, were attracted rather to a history that would bear witness to the long and positive association that their families had had with Ireland, and recognized that this could best be done through the medium of county or local history rather than through the history of the country as a whole. The writing of county histories also held appeal for people of this disposition both because the Irish county was an institution of English creation with which their ancestors had been associated in the sixteenth and early seventeenth centuries, or even in medieval times. They also had a fondness for the county as a unit of study because most of Ireland's landed proprietors who had held seats in parliament, initially in Dublin and then at Westminster, had been chosen by their peers to represent their counties. It was also within the county, or its principal subunit the barony, that property owners had traditionally assisted the government in upholding good order and administering English justice.

Historians in Ireland of Unionist disposition would also have been aware of, and comfortable with, those county histories that had been composed in the mid-eighteenth century by Charles Smith, or by Smith in association with Walter Harris, under the auspices of Dublin's Physico-Historical Society. This series, discussed in Chapter 5, was never completed to cover all of Ireland's thirty-two counties but it was clearly the model that guided the Reverend P. Fitzgerald, a vicar of the Church of Ireland, and his co-author J.J. McGregor, in writing *The History, Topography and Antiquities of the County and City of Limerick*, published in 1826–27. There, the authors had exulted on 'the utility of local history and topography' because it had the potential to provide detailed knowledge of the resource potential of each county. They also presumed that access to such knowledge at a micro level had 'contributed not a little to the prosperity' of England 'that mighty favoured country'.[1] Other would-be authors of Irish county histories were also impressed by the county histories of England being published intermittently over the course of the nineteenth century, until they became institutionalized in 1903 as the Victoria County Histories of England. Fitzgerald and Mc Gregor marvelled that 'in the sister island, not only every county and city, but every village and hamlet [had] its history'. In similar fashion, when F. Elrington Ball brought a multi-volume *History of the County of Dublin* to completion in 1902, he explained that he had taken the parish as the most logical 'geographic unit' around which to organize his succeeding chapters, 'because in England it has been found the most convenient division for local history'.[2]

All such examples would have been attractive to those in Ireland wishing to challenge what were becoming nationalist and Catholic orthodoxies of Ireland's

---

[1] On Charles Smith and Harris see Chapter 5; Reverend P. Fitzgerald and J.J. Mc Gregor, *The History, Topography and Antiquities of the County and City of Limerick*, 2 vols. (Dublin, 1826, 1827), preface to vol. 2, i.

[2] Fitzgerald and Mc Gregor, *Limerick*, vol. 2, preface, i; F. Elrington Ball, *A History of the County of Dublin, The People, Parishes and Antiquities from the earliest times to the close of the eighteenth century* (3 vols., Dublin, 1902) preface.

294   IMAGINING IRELAND'S PASTS

history. They were especially attractive because the authors of county histories, whether in England or Ireland, had always enjoyed elite patronage, had been deferential in tone, and had proceeded from the assumption that the prosperity and well-being of their respective county communities, in the past as in the present, relied upon the benevolent oversight of patriarchal proprietors who, regardless of political or religious affiliation, best understood the needs and the problems of their respective counties. Authors also usually acknowledged that it was the progenitors of the existing proprietors who, in the past, had provided for the defence of county communities, and because two of their number had usually served as county representatives in parliament, initially in Dublin and later at Westminster.

10.3 County Kerry as a Test Case: The Early Writings of Mary Agnes Hickson

It seems appropriate that we should begin our consideration of the county histories written in Ireland in the later nineteenth century with Mary Agnes Hickson (1825–99) because she serves as a link between the past and the future in the writing of county histories in Ireland. Hickson can be linked to the past because she was inspired by her father, a Protestant solicitor in Tralee, and some of his scholarly friends and relatives, notably Arthur Blennerhassett Rowan (1800–61), Church of Ireland Archdeacon of Ardfert. One of Hickson's ambitions was to become, like these mentors, an investigator into the antiquities and history of Kerry with a view, as Marc Caball has phrased it, to creating 'a non-partisan sense of local identity, which transcended political and religious allegiances, to foster pride and appreciation of the county's heritage'.[3] Hickson can also be linked to the future because she was closely associated with Froude, during his early visits to Ireland, who had acknowledged having learned much of Ireland from 'Miss Hickson'.[4]

Hickson, as it transpired, never actually wrote the county history of Kerry that she, her father, and his associates had hoped would provide a moral boost to the isolated Protestant community in Kerry which then constituted less than 4 per cent of the county's population.[5] She hesitated from doing so because she had

---

[3] For a biographical note on Hickson see that by Frances Clarke, *Dictionary of Irish Biography*, vol. 4, 679, and for further details Gerald O'Carroll, 'Mary Agnes Hickson and Writing the History of Kerry', Maurice J. Bric, ed., *Kerry: History and Society* (Dublin, 2020), 221–42; Russell McMorran, 'Mary Agnes Hickson: "Forgotten Kerry Historian"', *Kerry Magazine*, no. 11 (2000), 34–7; on the Protestant milieu in Tralee, Marc Caball, 'Past Romance and Living Interest. A.B. Rowan and the *Kerry Magazine* (1854–6)', *North Munster Antiquarian Journal*, vol. 54 (2014), 113–24, quotation 124.

[4] Mary Hickson, *Ireland in the Seventeenth Century, or the Irish Massacres of 1641–2, their causes and results* (2 vols., London, 1884).

[5] Caball, 'Past Romance and Living Interest', 112, 119.

been pre-empted by M.F. Cusack, the 'Nun of Kenmare'—author of the *Illustrated History of Ireland* discussed in Chapter 9—who had, in 1871, with benefit from local subscriptions, published a history of Kerry.[6] Hickson found this publication especially vexatious both because Cusack's work was no more than her Catholic-nationalist interpretation of Ireland's history writ small, and because, as Hickson saw it, Cusack had behaved unprofessionally by negotiating with Captain Rowan—probably without Hickson's knowledge—to secure a loan into her convent of the papers of his father 'the late Archdeacon Rowan' so she could use them for her county history. This privileged access had given Cusack knowledge of the various propositions that Archdeacon Rowan and Hickson had intended to prove through history, and thus enabled Cusack to counter these arguments before Hickson had committed them to print. One of Hickson's cherished propositions was that intercommunal relations in Kerry were more relaxed than in other counties of Ireland because many planter families had intermarried with those of existing proprietors. On this, Cusack conceded that some intermarriage between natives and newcomers had happened in Kerry, and she made specific reference to the marriage between Ann Petty with the head of the Fitzmaurice family. The groom, as Cusack put it, represented 'the oldest Anglo-Norman settlers in the county', whereas Ann Petty was heiress to the estates that had been accumulated in Kerry and Limerick by Sir William Petty, the Cromwellian cartographer, and by the regicide Sir Hardress Waller whose daughter had become Petty's wife. This alliance that gave rise to the Petty–Fitzmaurice dynasty (subsequently earls of Kerry and of Shelbourne and Marquesses of Lansdowne) was, according to Cusack, an entirely mercenary arrangement. Thus, as Cusack would have it, if there was any explanation for how Kerry was 'saved' from the 'worst of the miseries…which distinguished and disgraced the seventeenth century' in Ireland, it was because of 'its remoteness and its poverty' rather than because of matrimonial alliances between elite families of different ancestries.[7] Hickson would have considered this explanation perverse, and the resulting tension that developed between these two women historians of Kerry was exacerbated by the tirade that Cusack launched against Froude in the preface to her county history. Here, Cusack took Froude to task because, after he had 'spent several summers in Kerry', he had, in his journalistic work, mocked the Catholic gentry in the county and cast aspersions on the Catholic clergy there for their 'barbarism and superstition'.[8]

---

[6] M.F. Cusack, *A History of the Kingdom of Kerry* (London, Dublin, and Boston, 1871), Preface, vii, and viii–xii, and for Cusack's subscription list see appendices, lxix–lxxxiii.

[7] Cusack, *History…of Kerry*, 269–74.

[8] Cusack, *History…of Kerry*, Preface, viii–xii; the offending piece 'A Fortnight in Kerry' had originally appeared in *Fraser's Magazine* of which Froude was editor; on this phase of Froude's career see Brady, *Froude*, 233–61.

Frustrated and enraged by what Hickson considered Cusack's trespass upon a subject on which she had intended to write, Hickson produced evidence to sustain her preferred interpretation of the history of County Kerry in an edited two-volume compilation of documents entitled *Selections from Old Kerry Records* that she had published in 1872 and 1874 at her own expense. The miscellany was not entirely new since it drew upon research conducted by Rowan, who had died in 1861, and on journalistic pieces that both Rowan and Hickson had published in local newspapers. However, by publishing in book form a compilation of documents together with the interpretation she drew from them, Hickson obviously aimed to reach a wider audience since she had the two volumes published in London. Her investment proved worthwhile since, as we shall see, the template set by Hickson influenced Unionist authors writing the histories of other counties.[9]

One purpose of the miscellany was to prove that Protestant proprietors in Kerry, as in Ireland generally, were not universally of Cromwellian origin and from menial backgrounds as had been pronounced consistently in vernacular Irish verse, and reiterated in some recent national histories that seemed bent on denigrating the country's landowners. To refute such claims, Hickson published documents, some garnered from the archives by A.B. Rowan, to which she appended long introductions that traced the transmission from generation to generation of the title to the 'seignories' that had been assigned in County Kerry to English grantees under the terms of the Munster Plantation that had followed upon the defeat of the Desmond Rebellion of the 1580s. Hickson's commentaries also drew attention to the distinguished lineages of the Protestant families from England who had been introduced to Munster, and more especially to County Kerry, during that plantation process. In doing so she gave prime attention to the Conway, Blennerhassett, Crosbie, and Denny families—the last being the family that 'for near three hundred years' had dominated the town of Tralee and its surrounds. She had further reason to give particular, and favourable, attention to the Dennys because they controlled the church benefices that had been held by several members of her mother's family, the Days. Hickon's collaborator, A.B. Rowan, who had prepared the document entitled 'Tralee of the Dennys', also, as a clergyman, owed much to Denny patronage.

The genealogical document prepared by Rowan illustrated the English ancestry and connections of Sir Edward Denny, Kt. Bt., who was 'the founder of the Irish line'. It showed that Denny had first served in Ireland under the command of Lord Grey de Wilton and that he, together with other distinguished English officers, accompanied Grey at the overthrow and slaughter of the foreign intruders who had come ashore at Smerwick to help dissidents in Munster. Denny's pedigree

---

[9] Mary Agnes Hickson, *Selections from Old Kerry Records*, 2 vols. (London, 1872, 1874).

UNIONIST RE-APPRAISALS OF IRELAND'S HISTORY   297

showed him to be the younger son of Joan Champernoun and her husband Sir Anthony Denny who had been a member of the privy chamber of King Henry VIII. The document then suggested that, through his own merits, Edward Denny had come to enjoy the civil and then the military patronage of William Cecil, Lord Burghley, and that he himself, or his siblings, were linked with the families of Burghley, Sir Francis Walsingham, and Sir Walter Raleigh either through blood or marriage. The document also explained that Denny had died in 1599 when war in Munster was at its height and when Tralee Castle was in ruins, but that, during the reign of James I, what remained of the castle had been refurbished. Hickson gave credit to Denny's grandson, also Edward, for the renovation, in the course of which she mentioned that his wife, Margaret Edgecombe from Cornwall, had been maid of honour to Queen Elizabeth.[10]

An accompanying document entitled 'Memoir to the Blennerhassett pedigree, A.D. 1580–1736' showed that the Blennerhassett family and that of Jenkin Conway, a Welsh officer who had acquired the seignory in the vicinity of Killorglan, on which he had built Castle Conway which later devolved to the Blennerhassets, came from equally distinguished backgrounds.[11] Then, a document in the second volume pleaded that Patrick Crosbie who 'was the first of the Crosbie family who had obtained estates in Ireland'—his grant being in Tarbert—was of English rather than of Irish lineage as some had suggested. His principal credential, according to Hickson, was that he was 'a highly trusted agent' of Burghley and Sir George Carew who designated him 'the Queen's Messenger'.[12] Collectively, these case studies sustained Hickson's argument that the leading Protestant families in Kerry, or at least those she chose to dwell upon, had been well established in the county before Cromwell arrived in Ireland, and that none of them was of mean or mechanical background. Later, when Hickson worked with A.B. Grosart in editing the *Lismore Papers*, which were, in effect, the papers of Richard Boyle, the first earl of Cork, she encountered evidence that not all English settlers in Ireland had come from such distinguished service lineages.[13] However, while Hickson had to disregard the modest origins of Boyle himself, whom she described diplomatically as an 'able and astute man', her work on the *Lismore Papers* proved beneficial to her Kerry interests. What was most useful was evidence that many of the Protestant families of her generation in Kerry, and throughout much of Munster, were descended from settlers who had been introduced to Ireland by Boyle, and therefore predated Cromwell by several

[10] Hickson, *Old Kerry Records*, vol. 1, 135–43.
[11] Hickson, *Old Kerry Records*, vol. 1, xx–xxi; 'Introductory Memoir to the Blennerhasett Pedigree, A.D. 1580–1736', 1–32, and the text itself, 33–108.
[12] Hickson, *Old Kerry Records*, vol. 2, 1–26; quotation 1.
[13] On Boyle and his background see Canny, *The Upstart Earl*.

298   IMAGINING IRELAND'S PASTS

decades.[14] Among such settlers, as Hickson had already pointed out in her *Old Kerry Records*, were the ancestors of her own father's family, the first of whom had arrived from England as an ordained clergyman in 1594 and was 'appointed rector of certain Kerry parishes' after which 'a great number' of her ancestors had become 'clergymen of the established church'.[15]

Another contention that Hickson was able to sustain with the evidence she published in her miscellany was that individuals from this new wave of distinguished settler families who had arrived in Munster and in Kerry in the sixteenth and seventeenth centuries had found spouses among the pre-existing landed families. Thus, for example, she detailed how Conway Blennerhassett had married Elizabeth, daughter of Major Thomas Lacy, 'one of the most ancient Anglo-Norman families' whose estates were in County Limerick.[16] Furthermore, she showed how the recent settlers, like those who had preceded them in the twelfth century, had forged marriage alliances also with families of Gaelic stock, including with descendants of MacGillycuddy of the Reeks and of O'Sullivan Mór. It was convenient for Hickson that the editor of *The MacGillycuddy Papers* had recently documented this point.[17] Such hybridity, Hickson suggested, had produced some unexpected outcomes such as Mrs Fitzsimons, 'the accomplished daughter of the late Daniel O'Connell, M.P.', being 'herself a descendant through both parents of Conways and Blennerhassetts'.[18]

Most of the documents selected by Hickson showed how the Munster, and more particularly the Kerry Protestant families to whom she gave most attention, had remained loyal to the interests of Britain at the times of political disruption in the seventeenth century. She detailed also how these Protestant families had suffered greatly from these disruptions, even if they had benefited from them once the government had recovered its authority. As Hickson did so, she took notice also of the fate of Catholic landed families whose every loss proved a gain, in the long term, for their erstwhile Protestant neighbours. Thus her second volume included, among other matters, an edition of the certificates of the persons from Kerry transplanted to the province of Connacht and County Clare in 1653.[19] Even as she identified those individuals and their dependants who had been named in the certificates for removal either to the distant barony of Boyle in County Roscommon, or the inhospitable baronies of Inchiquin and Burren in

---

[14] Alexander B. Grosart, ed., *The Lismore Papers* (1st series, 4 vols., London, 1886, 2nd series, 4 vols., London, 1887), 2nd series, vol. 1, 291. Grosart explained (1st series, vol. 1, Introduction, xxvi, 2nd series, vol. 1, Introduction, xxvi) that he had employed 'Miss Rowan—daughter of the lamented Archdeacon Rowan—as his 'copyist' and Miss Hickson both as a transcriber and as author of 'a number of the most masterful Notes and Illustrations'.

[15] Hickson, *Old Kerry Records*, vol. 2, Preface, viii and 'Church Records; Diocese of Ardfert', 27–31.

[16] Hickson, *Old Kerry Records*, vol. 1, 20.

[17] W. Maziere Brady, ed., *The MacGillycuddy Papers: A Selection from the family archives of 'The MacGillycuddy of the Reeks'* (London, 1867).

[18] Hickson, *Old Kerry Records*, vol. 1, 26.   [19] Hickson, *Old Kerry Records*, vol. 2, 31–6.

County Clare, Hickson speculated that 'not all listed were actually transplanted'. Rather, she 'suspect[ed that] Colonel David Crosbie's influence, even with the Lord Protector himself, saved not a few', and that Lord Broghill (Roger Boyle) and the Knight of Kerry 'may have obtained grace for others'.[20] Notwithstanding this, Hickson acknowledged that many Catholics in the 1650s, and again in the 1690s, who had lost their lands, became soldiers of fortune in Continental service. However, even as she identified 'The Kerrymen of the Brigade, A.D. 1692', she insisted that some of the exiles had later returned to recover portions of their property. She also contended that 'all those who went into Connacht' in the 1650s had 'returned at the Restoration, and many obtained portions of their old estates and leaseholds'.[21] Even as she suggested that discontinuity in landownership in Kerry was not especially sharp, she acknowledged that scope had been provided for some 'Cromwellians' to secure property in the county. However, she then pointed out that some, and here she mentioned the Godfreys, the Sandes, and the Batemans, had accepted the dispossessed Irish as tenants on their properties. Thus from the documents she had included in her two volumes, Hickson satisfied herself that the Irish Catholics who had lost land and status had become reconciled to their lot as 'old feuds and strifes healed quickly in our clannish little county'. Moreover, she suggested that the diverse, but increasingly interconnected, elite families in Kerry would have continued to live in harmony and that more Catholics might have become assimilated into Protestant society, had it not been for occasional external interference into county affairs that had led invariably to the destruction of property and the impoverishment of all.[22]

The Rev W. Maziere Brady, the editor of *The MacGillycuddy Papers*, probably encouraged Hickson to imagine that the history of Kerry since the sixteenth century had been characterized more by continuity than by disruption. These papers, as Brady had put it, provided 'a valuable and entirely trustworthy illustration of the mode in which the estates of an Irish chieftain were, in part, preserved to his descendants, notwithstanding their confiscation under the reign of Queen Elizabeth, and in despite of the Act of Settlement and other legal dangers and difficulties to which Irish properties were exposed during subsequent reigns'. This was all the more remarkable, according to Brady, because, through most of the eighteenth century, the 'heads of the family were Roman Catholic'. The key to the family's survival, according to Brady, was that these heads had taken their lesson from the fate of the ruling MacGillycuddy, who had been 'drawn into' rebellion by the O'Sullivan Mór in Elizabeth's reign, because, thereafter, the family had remained 'loyal subjects of the English crown' for two centuries and a half.[23]

---

[20] Hickson, *Old Kerry Records*, vol. 2, 32. [21] Hickson, *Old Kerry Records*, vol. 2, 32, 230–49.

[22] Hickson, *Old Kerry Records*, vol. 2, 32.

[23] W. Maziere Brady, ed., *The MacGillycuddy Papers*, Preface, iii–iv.

300   IMAGINING IRELAND'S PASTS

Even as Hickson, like Brady, minimized what Catholics had lost, she pointed out that the descendants of many who had recovered their property had conformed in religion over the course of time and intermarried with Protestant landed families. This convinced Hickson that the blood of some of the many Kerrymen who had served in Lord Clare's dragoons and whose deeds Thomas Davis had lauded in verse, flowed in the veins of many Kerry families who traced their origins in Ireland to the plantations. Furthermore, she pointed out that the Petty–Fitzmaurice alliance that had been treated disparagingly by Cusack had established a link between Cromwellians and 'the illustrious house of Fitzmaurice, a branch of the old Geraldine race'.[24] Her genealogical investigations exposed connections even between settler families and Irish Republicans with the Blennerhassetts being related to Thomas Addis Emmet.[25]

Following the example of Charles Smith, Hickson mentioned 'A Tour of Ireland in 1775' by P. Luscombe where that author had described the mansions and improvements introduced by planter families to Kerry, including the construction of Ballyscripin 'the seat of the Spring family, ancestor of the Rt. Hon. Lord Monteagle'.[26] Hickson commented also on the surprise of Luscome 'to meet with traces of an education, taste and culture one did not expect to find existing at that time in a county so remote from the metropolis'. It all meant, said Hickson, that 'the home circle at Castle Conway in olden times was evidently a refined and educated as well as a pleasant one'.[27]

Hickson believed that one reason why Kerry's landed Protestants had appeared refined was because they had been religiously tolerant. To sustain this she explained how, during the eighteenth century, some Protestant families had enabled Catholic neighbours to subvert the Penal Laws by becoming trustees of estates that would otherwise have been forfeited to the Crown. On the other hand, she conceded that not all landowning families in Kerry had lived up to their social responsibilities and here she isolated the earl of Powis then 'the owner-in-chief' of the seignory in Castleisland, assigned to the Herbert family in the 1580s, 'whose only connection with the place is in the rent of £1,900 a year'. However, she consoled herself that the negligence of the absent Herberts was being compensated for by the 'resident gentlemen who had lately built handsome mansions' in the vicinity of Castleisland. She therefore did not allow this irresponsibility of the Herbert family to disturb her overall argument that the Protestant families in Kerry had, for centuries, been an integral part of the county community who had taken an interest in the history and antiquities of the county and interacted easily with their peers even when these were Catholic. She

---

[24] Hickson, *Old Kerry Records*, vol. 2, 296–300.   [25] Hickson, *Old Kerry Records*, vol. 1, 31.
[26] Hickson, *Old Kerry Records*, vol. 1, 25–6; here, she was referring to Thomas Spring-Rice second baron Monteagle of Brandon.
[27] Hickson, *Old Kerry Records*, vol. 1, 27.

suggested that the Crosbies were more typical than the Herberts with the present 'owner of Ardfert Abbey [being] much respected in Kerry as a good and "improving" resident landlord'.[28]

Those who threatened communal tranquillity in Kerry, according to Hickson, were not the Protestant landowners but the minority of unreconciled Catholics who, through the centuries, had been lacking in tolerance and generosity, and receptive to external agents wishing to disturb the harmony of the county. The most extreme example was the discord that had broken out in Ireland on 23 October 1641, which Hickson designated St Ignatius's Day. Soon thereafter, she claimed, the discontented elements in Kerry proved themselves to be 'unchanged Ethiopians since the bygone times' who had 'swooped down from their penal settlements around the Causeway [and] set fire to Lord Kerry's new castle and St. Brendan's old Cathedral'.[29] As she recalled this in 1874, Hickson brought the 'sad winter time of 1641' into the present by expressing her hope that what had happened then was not about to be repeated and that the generally peace-loving people of her 'native county' would not 'in the reign of Victoria' be again 'misled by ambitious demagogues into the old well-worn paths of blood and tears and confiscation which our forefathers trod from century to century'.[30]

Hickson's compilation were obviously designed to defy those nationalist and Catholic historians whose recent published work had done much to marginalize and stigmatize landowners and Protestants throughout Ireland. It may have been the assurance with which Hickson pleaded her case that attracted other Unionist authors to write histories of their counties in the knowledge that, by so doing, they were offering an assurance to landed proprietors that they still had an important role to play as leaders of their communities similar to that exercised in the past by their ancestors.

10.4 A Unionist Historian of County Sligo: W.G. Wood-Martin

What Hickson proposed for Kerry, no less than the county histories being published in England, must have inspired W.G. Wood-Martin (1847–1917) to devote several years to compiling material for his *History of Sligo: County and Town* that was published sequentially in three volumes in 1882, 1889, and 1892.[31]

---

[28] Hickson, *Old Kerry Records*, vol. 2, 10; vol. 1, 190; the Herbert in question at the time of writing was George, 4th earl of Powis.

[29] Hickson, *Old Kerry Records*, vol. 2, 3; I am assured by Dr Brian Mac Cuarta, S.J. that the feast of St Ignatius of Loyola is actually on 31 July, the anniversary of that saint's death. Hickson was obviously distorting the truth by deliberately confusing the feast day of the founder of the Jesuit order with that of the medieval St Ignatius of Antioch thus reinforcing her contention that 1641 would never have occurred had it not been for the external interference by the papacy and Jesuits into the affairs of a harmonious world.

[30] Hickson, *Old Kerry Records*, vol. 2, 33.

[31] W.G. Wood-Martin, *History of Sligo: County and Town* (3 vols., Dublin, 1882, 1889, 1892); on Wood-Martin see Mary O'Dowd, *Power, Politics and Land; Early Modern Sligo, 1568–1688* (Belfast,

302   IMAGINING IRELAND'S PASTS

The author, who came from a Church of Ireland minor gentry family in Sligo, was a British officer who, at this point in his career, was associated with the Sligo Artillery. As his three volumes were appearing in print, he was moving upwards in the ranks from being major to becoming lieutenant colonel and finally colonel of his regiment. His military service and his membership of the Orange Order, of which he later became Grand Master, indicated his political and religious allegiance, as did his previous historical work on the contribution made by Sligo recruits to the defence of Enniskillen during the Jacobite–Williamite conflict.[32] The prejudices that one would expect from a person with such credentials feature in his writing, but this did not deter him from attempting 'a thoroughly faithful and vivid picture of the whole life of the county of Sligo from its cradle upwards... to historic and comparatively modern days'. When he finally came to his third volume, with 1892 as its terminal date, he expressed the hope that his endeavour might have aroused in his readers 'a feeling and more lively interest and more earnest love for the County and Town of Sligo'.[33]

While these objectives were similar to those articulated by Hickson, she had not actually written a coherent county history and for models Wood-Martin would have had to look to English examples. These would have shown the need to give consideration to the topography, etymology, and legendary lore of the county, and in attempting this Wood-Martin was able to draw upon a tradition of antiquarian scholarship in Ireland with which landowners and Protestants had long associations. He could also exploit the records of the Ordnance Survey that seemed to enjoy a respect in Ireland that traversed denominational and political boundaries. This aspect of the undertaking proved relatively easy for Wood-Martin because he was already respected as an antiquarian. He appeared less interested in the history of Sligo during the medieval centuries and, as he coursed through these, he paused only to record the imprint made by more forceful rulers on the county such as, for example, Richard de Burgo, the Red Earl, 'the most powerful subject in Ireland', who had 'made war, raising and deposing at his pleasure the native chiefs of Connacht and Ulster, but also founded numerous monasteries and castles in various parts of Ireland' including 'the castles of Ballymote, Corran and Sligo, in the present County Sligo'.[34] While he mentioned cultural achievements during ancient and medieval times, and particularly the cultural contributions of institutions and people with Sligo associations, Wood-Martin concluded, condescendingly, that the totality marked 'no remarkable

---

1991), 146–7; O'Dowd's volume provides a reliable narrative of Sligo's history during the early modern centuries.

[32] W.G. Wood-Martin, *Sligo and the Enniskilleners from 1689–1691* (Dublin, 1880); in this respect Wood-Martin fits the pattern of what David Fitzpatrick has had to say of Orangeism and Irish military history, Fitzpatrick, *Descendancy: Irish Protestant Histories, since 1795* (Cambridge, 2014), 21–40.

[33] Wood-Martin, *History of Sligo*, preface to vol. 1, and preface to vol. 3.

[34] Wood-Martin, *History of Sligo*, vol. 1, 213.

UNIONIST RE-APPRAISALS OF IRELAND'S HISTORY   303

advance in civilization or education...except in the case of those who were destined for the priesthood'. On the political front, Wood-Martin asserted that the history of what later became the county of Sligo had, in previous centuries, been modulated by 'feuds among petty rival chiefs', occasioned principally by 'the absence of a fixed law of succession', which he, following in the tradition set by such as Stanihurst and Sir John Davies, considered a recipe for chaos.[35] The first serious attempt to bring this inherent disorder to an end was made, according to Wood-Martin, at the time of the Composition of Connacht of 1585 when 'O'Connor Sligo [the principal lord] voluntarily renounced his Irish style and title, agreed to abolish Irish gavelkind and tanistry, and to hold his land by English tenure'. An even more positive outcome, according to Wood-Martin, was that this placed all other 'chiefs in Sligo under his authority' when they 'agreed to follow his example'. 'Thus', proclaimed Wood-Martin, 'Sligo theoretically was brought to the status of an ordinary English county'. He then bemoaned that whatever was then achieved had been cancelled in 1588 when Spain, and thus also the papacy, interfered in the affairs of the county following the wreck off the Sligo coast of some the ships belonging to the defeated Spanish Armada. Thereafter, he pronounced, Sligo became embroiled in the Nine Years War when 'every ones hand [was] uplifted against his neighbour'.[36]

This conspectus of what happened in Sligo, previous to its establishment as a county in 1585, and what had transpired before it could enjoy the fruits of peace, prepared the way for his second volume that dealt with developments in Sligo 'from the accession of King James 1 to the Revolution of 1688'. This, in the words of Wood-Martin, was a period during which 'Sligo, in common with many other parts of Ireland...frequently—we might say almost continuously—felt the cruel scourge of war'.[37]

Here, Wood-Martin paused to investigate the ownership of land in Sligo during the earlier part of the seventeenth century, and he, like Hickson in the case of Kerry, came away satisfied that the amount of land 'forfeited to the crown, and given or sold to Protestant settlers' was 'surprisingly small'. Again, like Hickson, he contended that stability and harmony would likely have prevailed were it not for external intervention, this time that by Lord Deputy Wentworth in the 1630s who, treating 'Saxon and Celt alike' with his 'iron rule', set himself a task that was 'nothing less than the establishment of British settlers in the entire western province', including in Sligo.[38] Wood-Martin considered that this meddling in what he portrayed as a harmonious society resulted in the introduction of some Protestant families to Sligo but at the cost of embroiling the county in the 'popular

[35] Wood-Martin, vol. 1, *History of Sligo*, ix, xii.
[36] Wood-Martin, vol. 1, *History of Sligo*, 300, 312, 317.
[37] Wood-Martin, vol. 2, *History of Sligo*, 4.
[38] Wood-Martin, *History of Sligo*, vol. 2; Chapter 11 treats of the Wentworth episode.

304 IMAGINING IRELAND'S PASTS

uprising' of 1641, which he likened to the eruption of a volcano, and which he described graphically by citing from the 1641 'depositions' for that county. He believed that the disturbance in Sligo was precipitated by 'the lords of the Irish' whose 'original intentions' he could not fathom, but who, after they had broken the mould, became powerless 'to restrain their subordinates' once their 'passions had been aroused', this being 'but the natural result of stimulating the passions of an ignorant people'.[39]

The long-term consequence of the popular outburst and assault upon the Protestant population of Sligo, in which Catholic lords had participated, was, according to Wood-Martin, the confiscation of much of the land of the county held by Catholics, the enlargement of the estates held by those Protestants who already had a foothold there, and the addition of some new proprietors to the Protestant ranks. Unlike Hickson, he did not suggest that Catholics had become reconciled to their loss, but argued rather that this re-distribution gave rise to what Wood-Martin described as 'internecine strife' between the Protestant and Catholic landed interests in the county that spilled over into the military conflict that beset the entire country from 1688 to 1691. Wood-Martin recognized that the consequence for Catholic proprietors of this war was a further confiscation of property once William and Mary were secure on the British throne. In expressing sympathy for those who had lost their estates, he insisted that they were not the only ones to suffer because 'at the close of the struggle many Protestants found themselves ruined', and he insisted that those who had lost most in this, as in all military conflict, were 'the unfortunate inhabitants who had joined neither of the rival parties under arms'.[40] The outcome was all the more regrettable, he claimed, because it should have been clear to the Catholic proprietors, whom he was depicting as the aggressors, that the outcome to any communal conflict was a foregone conclusion since, long before 1688, the Protestant landowners had formed themselves into 'local military organizations'. These Protestants, he claimed, were 'in great part' descendants of those who had upheld the Protestant interest in the county following the insurrection of 1641, and they included 'members of Colonel Richard Coote's regiment of horse, [and of] Colonel Charles Coote's regiment of horse and his regiment of foot'.[41]

Wood-Martin must have known that isolating members of the Coote family for praise would have raised the ire of Catholic readers given the criticism voiced both in vernacular verse history and in more recent nationalist and Catholic grand narratives of the part played by earlier generations of Cootes in Irish warfare between 1641 and 1653. Wood-Martin took the risk of offending Catholic sensibilities because he wished to illustrate, as Hickson had done for Kerry, how many of the Protestant landed families in Sligo, including the Cootes, had been

---

[39] Wood-Martin, *History of Sligo*, vol. 2, 59.   [40] Wood-Martin, *History of Sligo*, vol. 3, 1–2.
[41] Wood-Martin, *History of Sligo*, vol. 3, 4.

present in the county before the Cromwellian conquest. He made this same point graphically in his second volume when, in the course of discussing how Mr Parke had been 'shut up' in Newtown Castle by the insurgents of 1641, he published, on the facing page, a nineteenth-century drawing of Newtown Castle on Lough Gill, 'the property of Major Roger Parke, 3rd dragoon guards'.[42]

Having thus explained selectively how the Protestant gentry of Sligo had come into being, Wood-Martin detailed how, through the eighteenth and into the nineteenth centuries, they had lived up to their responsibility to defend and contribute to the good governance of the county. He mentioned also that some had served the British Crown in foreign assignments. When it came to local service and representation, he gave credit to the Gore, Wingfield, Morgan, Coote, Ormsby, Wynne, O'Hara, and Cooper families. Then, in the matter of international distinction, he isolated for special mention Richard Coote, son of the 1st Baron Collooney who had fought for King William III, was rewarded with the title of earl of Bellamont, served as Treasurer and Receiver General to Queen Mary, and was then, in 1690, appointed as Governor of New England and New York and 'Admiral of those seas'. Wood-Martin also explained how, when the Volunteers had been raised in Ireland to protect the country from possible French invasion during the American Revolutionary War, the Sligo gentry, commanded by Mr Wynne, had contributed generously to these Volunteers—'a body of 100,000 men, self clothed, self disciplined and without pay'—who, as he put it, performed commendably in discharging 'the duties of the army' until 'unfortunately they afterwards turned their attention to politics upon which rocks they made shipwreck'.[43] In thus dismissing the role of the Volunteers in securing greater autonomy for the Irish parliament, Wood-Martin was doing as Froude would have wished by disregarding that aspect of the activity of the Volunteers which, as we saw in Chapter 8, explained why most nationalist authors looked benignly on them.

As he reflected on developments in Sligo over the seventeenth and more especially the eighteenth century, Wood-Martin expressed himself satisfied that 'prior to the year 1790, Protestants and Roman Catholics lived on very good terms' in Sligo, and continued to do so until 1794 when the 'Defenders' began to commit 'outrages' and to take 'unlawful oaths'. Even then, he was satisfied that 'the peasantry would not have risen' against Crown authority had not a French invading party come ashore at Killala in 1798.[44] Then, as in 1588, 1641, and 1688, he showed how external interference had precipitated disturbances in Sligo, which led to the flight of the Protestant clergy from the county, the destruction of

[42] Wood-Martin, *History of Sligo*, vol. 2, 60; the property had been originally acquired in 1628 by another Roger Parke.
[43] Wood-Martin, *History of Sligo*, vol. 3, 4–5, 8.
[44] Wood-Martin, *History of Sligo*, vol. 3, 11, 17.

their churches, the plundering of the houses of the gentry, and the impoverishment of the ordinary people who, again, he pointed out, were the principal victims of the disturbance. Wood-Martin emphasized how, after 1798, order was quickly restored to the county, and how Sligo fighting men contributed significantly both at the battle of Vinegar Hill that helped bring the 1798 conflict in Wexford to a conclusion, and to the British war effort against France that persisted until 1814. Wood-Martin explained that this latter effort had included Catholics as well as Protestants.[45]

The normal communal harmony that characterized life in County Sligo was then resumed, according to Wood-Martin, but only until 1822 when 'the titular bishop of Killala' intervened to impose a 'religious effect' upon the elections of that year in Sligo with the result that 'religious feeling was greatly excited' in the county. Tension mounted further, he claimed, when Daniel O'Connell visited the county in 1828 with a view to 'hunting' a sitting Member of Parliament to make way for a nominee of his choosing. Wood-Martin cited with disapproval 'a specimen of O'Connell's style of oratory' designed to mock and belittle his rival candidate named Martin (Wood-Martin's ancestor) and 'to inflame passions'. The consequence was that in 1829 'the mob broke the windows of almost every Protestant household in Sligo' and chaos persisted until 'in short liberty had degenerated into licence [and] votes were almost openly sold'.[46]

Wood-Martin's narrative of political events tapered off at this point even though his terminal date was 1892. This suggests that he had found the politics of nineteenth-century Ireland distasteful as the role previously played by Protestants was steadily eclipsed following the rise of O'Connell, and as the Catholic clergy became ever more active in elections. This elision meant that Wood-Martin never once mentioned the name of Parnell in his narrative, and his only reference to the activities of the Land League was his complaint that the 'popular element' in the courts of the Land Commission had been 'too strong and the legal element too weak' with the result that rents had been 'worked down' because 'a too willing ear' had been 'given to the extravagant claims made by the tenants for alleged improvements'. In the course of this discussion, Wood-Martin admitted that 'rack-renting' had been practised by some proprietors in the county, but he insisted that it was not 'general, nor as a rule, common', and was, to some degree, offset by land improvements implemented by some landlords at their personal expense.[47]

Wood-Martin seemed resigned to the loss by landowners (and particularly Protestant landowners) of their political power in the county even as he considered it ironic that this had occurred at the very moment when, within the

[45] Wood-Martin, *History of Sligo*, vol. 3, 22–5.
[46] Wood-Martin, *History of Sligo*, vol. 3, 39–40, 51, 53, 62.
[47] Wood-Martin, *History of Sligo*, vol. 3, 293–4, 296–7.

town of Sligo, Protestants had become more numerous and more denominationally diverse than ever before. Rather than dwell on this, his continuing narrative detailed how members of the Protestant community continued to play a role in promoting improvements in both the county and the town of Sligo that was consistent with their earlier record. Their contribution previous to the 1820s included the creation of 'plantings' at Markree, Annaghmore, Hazlewood, and Templehouse, the 1756 investment by Lord Shelbourne in promoting Ballymote as a linen town, experiments in the hatching of salmon fry and the production of kelp, and the development of Sligo town in 1750 to become a provisioning port for British fleets which served as a stepping stone towards Sligo becoming a steam shipping port to Liverpool in the nineteenth century.[48] Wood-Martin also gave attention to the role the gentry had played in reducing, and even staving off, the sufferings of the 'population' in times of pestilence, and also whenever the potato or flax crops fell short of expectations or failed outright. He dated such calamities to 1765, 1802, 1812, 1816, 1817, 1821, 1832, and 1845–48. This sequence persisted, he insisted, even to 1879 when 'the potato crop was again almost an entire failure'. He acknowledged ruefully that the efforts of landowners, combined with those of the government and philanthropic bodies, to prevent the calamity of the Great Famine had not been sufficient to meet that challenge, but he suggested that landowners were not the only ones whose endeavours had fallen short when he mentioned that, 'even so late as the year 1861', it still rankled in the minds of the merchants how the food intended to relieve hunger in Sligo had been disposed of.[49]

If Wood-Martin acknowledged that the landed elite had been incapable of averting the Great Famine, he credited them with lessening the effect of a catastrophe that he considered inescapable because of the excessive 'dependence' of the population upon the potato crop. In doing so, he mentioned particularly the emigration schemes that landowners had promoted as early as 1832, and he chronicled their contribution to combating disease. This led Wood-Martin to a detailed consideration of the major contribution made by the gentry, and by the Victorian state, to the spectacular improvement of the county and of the town of Sligo through the construction of roads, bridges, canals, ports, workhouses, artisan dwellings, a gaol, a fever hospital, a lunatic asylum, police barracks, a waterworks, cemeteries, and eventually the railway. As he described the physical improvement to Sligo town that had been achieved by official bodies in a relatively short time, Wood-Martin detailed also the vital contribution that had been made by businesses, philanthropic bodies, and churches of all denominations to the physical appearance of the town through the construction of banks, churches, a Catholic cathedral, schools, and accommodation for clubs and voluntary

[48] Wood-Martin, *History of Sligo*, vol. 3, 241, 248, 259, 284.
[49] Wood-Martin, *History of Sligo*, vol. 3, 83.

308 IMAGINING IRELAND'S PASTS

societies. Several of these developments, such as the consecration of the Catholic Cathedral in 1874 'in the presence of Cardinal Cullen and most of the Roman Catholic bishops of Ireland, and also some from England and America', must have symbolized for Wood-Martin the eclipse of the once dominant Protestant community. However, while he voiced concern over occasional popular attacks upon the property of Protestants, he attributed these to incendiary priests or illegal societies, and he remained satisfied that the Catholic population continued to be well disposed towards their Protestant neighbours. Thus he exuded confidence that, in a political environment that was changing rapidly, the Protestants of the town and county of Sligo would continue to play an important role in the improvement of a community to which all belonged. Wood-Martin's optimism was possible because he, like Mary Hickson, was able to imagine an early modern past in which landed families had lived up to their responsibilities and in which the population at large had responded by recognizing them as natural leaders of their communities.

10.5 James Frost: An Elite Historian of County Clare

The success of Wood-Martin and of Mary Hickson is using history to identify a role for the landed elite of their respective counties in the present as well as in the past must have served as an inspiration for James Frost when he undertook a history of County Clare, which appeared in print in 1893, the year after Wood-Martin's third and final volume had been published.[50] The late arrival of Wood-Martin's final volume devoted to the nineteenth century would have been of little concern to Frost since his history proceeded from the 'earliest times to the beginning of the eighteenth century'.[51] He began, as had Wood-Martin on Sligo, with a topography of the Gaelic lordship of Thomond 'before the English settlement of the county', and, as with Wood-Martin, he relied considerably on the information on the topography and antiquities of the county compiled by the authors of the Ordnance Survey.[52] It was Frost's belief, as it had been that of Wood-Martin concerning the 'lordship of O'Connor Sligo', that 'before the territory of Thomond was formed into a county by the English it [had been] divided into distinct districts by the native inhabitants', and that the baronies into

[50] Cian O'Carroll, 'A Thomond Scholar—James Frost, MRIA., 1827–1907', *The Other Clare*, vol. 3 (1979), 26; I am grateful to Dr. Ciarán Ó Murchadha for this reference.

[51] James Frost, *The History and Topography of the County of Clare: from the earliest times to the beginning of the eighteenth century* (Dublin, 1893).

[52] Frost, *History of Clare*, 1; Gillian M. Doherty, *The Irish Ordnance Survey: History Culture and Memory* (Cork, 2004) shows how the survey had something to satisfy people of disparate views as, for example, by lauding the 'improvements' that had come with plantation while also giving close attention to what Doherty calls 'the long past' that treated of archaeological and historical sources relating to Ireland's ancient past.

UNIONIST RE-APPRAISALS OF IRELAND'S HISTORY   309

which the English had segmented the county in the 1580s corresponded to units
managed by lesser lords who had been subservient to the O'Brien dynasty. Each
such area, according to Frost, had been 'owned by its separate clan and presided
over by its particular chieftain' all of which had 'Brian Boroimhe and his
successors, kings of Thomond, as their lord paramount'.[53] Frost initially thought
more positively than Wood-Martin of Ireland's ancient past when he represented
it as close to idyllic with 'the natives, being masters of the land of their birth' and
with 'each sept, and each individual of the sept' having the opportunity to enjoy
his 'property absolutely free from any control of a man calling himself his
landlord'.[54] On reflection, he retracted this appraisal (without appearing to realize
he was contradicting himself) and pronounced (and here again he was in tune
with Wood-Martin) that 'of all the political institutions ever devised by human
ingenuity the system of clanship, as it had prevailed in Ireland, was the best
contrived for retarding the progress of civilization and preventing the material
prosperity of a people'.[55] Its defect, according to Frost, was that the 'clanship'
system encouraged each lord to transgress upon the territory of his neighbours.
Frost therefore, like Wood-Martin in the case of Sligo, welcomed the incorporation
in 1580 of the various segments of Thomond into the single county of Clare
because it brought an end to such internecine conflict. This appraisal was not
disturbed by his belief that the first step towards 'the establishment of the rule of
England', and the 'endeavour to subdue the people and bring them under the
British system of land tenure' had proceeded in 1542 only when the government
'brought over' the ruling O'Brien 'to their intentions' 'by the offer to him of
enormous bribes'. The 'bribery' involved, according to Frost, concerned the grant
by the Crown to the ruling O'Brien of the entire lordship of Thomond 'in fee
simple' together with a grant to him of 'the abbey lands within the lordship'.[56]

Thus, notwithstanding his backward glance to prehistoric times and the
intervening centuries, Frost, like Wood-Martin, believed that his essential story
began only with 'the formation of Thomond into an English County in 1580'.[57]
The commonality of the approaches of the two authors and the favourable
response of each to the introduction of English rule into their respective counties
may be attributed to the fact that Frost, like Wood-Martin, came from minor
gentry background and would, therefore, have been a strict upholder of the law,
as it was administered in the late nineteenth century, and would have been
opposed to the attempts then under way to subvert the existing social hierarchy
based on the ownership of land.

If we can assume that the social position of Frost and Wood-Martin accounts
for the cautious conservatism of each, Frost experienced difficulty in always

---

[53] Frost, *History of Clare*, 4.   [54] Frost, *History of Clare*, 235.
[55] Frost, *History of Clare*, 256.   [56] Frost, *History of Clare*, 235.
[57] Frost, title to chapter 13, *History of Clare*, 226.

310   IMAGINING IRELAND'S PASTS

seeming to support official policy in previous centuries because, while he was a landowner, he was also a Catholic and would have been keenly aware of the disabilities under which Catholic landowners had been forced to operate due to their continued loyalty to their faith. Moreover, he cannot have been ignorant of the religious sufferings of Catholics of all ranks in Ireland, and in County Clare, in past centuries, because memory of such sufferings since the time of the Reformation had been regularly revisited in vernacular Gaelic verse history, some composed by poets from County Clare.[58] The author's religious attachment would explain why, when detailing the positive attributes of Gaelic society in Thomond before it was fashioned into a county, he made special mention of how 'the church of the people...had [had] its rights clearly defined, and enjoyed the lands bestowed upon it by the munificence of pious benefactors'.[59]

Given this, it is unsurprising that Frost found fault with the extension of English rule into the former lordship only because 'the monasteries of Clare were [then] suppressed...[and] the brethren were expelled'. He instanced the experience of Quin Abbey that lay close to his own estate. This, in earlier centuries, had been endowed and patronized by the McNamara sept, only to be 'converted into a barrack by the English garrison' at the time of the Reformation. The abbey, he stated, was later recovered and restored to its original purpose by the McNamaras, but was again destroyed by the forces of Cromwell. On this occasion Rory McNamara, a friar, was 'taken and shot by Cromwell's officers near Clare Castle in 1651'. Mention of this remembered atrocity opened the way for Frost to list others in Clare who had died for their faith at the time of the Cromwellian conquest when the 'inhabitants' of the county 'for the greater part' 'were either slain or driven into exile; its priests proscribed and forced to flee into the mountains and woods to perform the divine offices; its pastures were denuded of cattle; and poverty and sorrow reigned throughout the land'.[60]

The ultimate 'policy of the English party' at this time, said Frost, was 'to extirpate the Catholic clergy' rather than to convert the population to Protestantism, as was evident, he believed, because 'the Puritans under Cromwell and Ireton...thought three Protestant ministers sufficient for the want of the whole county'.[61] Prior to that time, he contended, 'it was part of the plan devised for the subjugation of Ireland, that the Protestant religion should supersede the old faith of the inhabitants'. In support of this, Frost cited from the report of the Commission of 1622 that identified the Protestant clergy, most of them from England, who had been listed by the bishops of Killaloe and Kilfenora as holding appointments in the parishes of County Clare associated with their respective diocese.[62]

Frost believed that Catholicism had survived the Cromwellian era in Clare only because the people successfully hid some priests from the authorities. Then,

---

[58] Morley, *An Crann os Coill: Aodh Buí Mac Cruitín*.   [59] Frost, *History of Clare*, 235.
[60] Frost, *History of Clare*, 52–3, 527.   [61] Frost, *History of Clare*, 551–3.
[62] Frost, *History of Clare*, 550–1.

as he traced religious developments in the county from the Restoration of 1660 to the accession of William and Mary, Frost found but occasional breaks in 'English persecution' of the Catholic clergy, which gave him all the more reason to celebrate the tenacity of many Catholic priests in the county. He brought this subject to a close by citing the names of those priests 'listed' in 1704 as the Catholic clergy authorized by the authorities to remain in the county under the terms of the Penal Laws.[63]

Having thus given attention to the sufferings endured by Catholics in Clare because of their religion, Frost furnished a political narrative of the 'sanguinary struggle between the rival races that did not come to an end till the time of Cromwell and William III'. This, he believed, had been provoked by the efforts of the authorities to establish 'the rule of England' and 'to subdue the people, and bring them under the British system of land tenure'. We already noted his belief that the co-operation of the O'Brien dynasty with the wishes of the state in these matters had been for the better even if it had involved 'bribery'. Therefore, Frost expressed no sympathy for the 'invasion' of the county by Red Hugh O'Donnell in 1599 with the intention of using his army to reverse the settlement that had been agreed between the ruling O'Briens and the state.[64] Apart from what he had to say of its religious policy, Frost's principal criticism of the state during those years concerned the efforts of successive rulers to raise excessive rents from the property owners of the county. It was discontent over these levies, he believed, that had persuaded many Catholic landowners in Clare to join the 'rising of the Catholics that was general throughout the country' after the initial outbreak in Ulster in 1641. The more dramatic actions in Clare that Frost mentioned concerned attacks made by Catholics upon the Protestants who had settled in the County, principally as tenants on the Thomond estates. As with Wood-Martin for Sligo and Hickson for Kerry, Frost proved that atrocities had occurred in the county by citing from the depositions that had been collected from Protestant survivors of the onslaught. Frost was able to do so because Philip Dwyer, a Protestant clergyman, had extracted copies of depositions with relevance to the county from the originals and published them as an appendix to a history of the diocese of Killaloe.[65]

The uprising itself and the subsequent effort of the Protestants in Clare to retain and recover their positions led to what Frost described as 'the disastrous period of the Civil War of 1641' after which the 'Catholic people of Clare... like all other Catholic Irishmen of the time' took an 'active interest' 'in the proceedings of the Confederation of Kilkenny'.[66] As he skimmed over what happened in 'these disastrous times', he thought it was 'to be lamented that the heads of the great

---

[63] Frost, *History of Clare*, 552.   [64] Frost, *History of Clare*, 256–7.
[65] Philip Dwyer, *The Diocese of Killaloe. from the Reformation to the Close of the Eighteenth Century* (Dublin, 1878).
[66] Frost, *History of Clare*, 338.

312 IMAGINING IRELAND'S PASTS

family of O'Brien had lent their support to the cause of the English invader'.[67] Here, he made particular mention of Morrogh O'Brien, baron, and later earl, of Inchiquin who 'at one moment was a Confederate Catholic, at another a Protestant and Parliamentarian. After changing his political and religious creed no less than four times, Inchiquin at last died a Catholic'. However, while Frost cast doubts on the integrity of Inchiquin—popularly remembered by Catholics in Clare as *Murchadh na dTóiteán*; Morrogh of the Burnings—Frost refrained from dwelling on 'his exploits' outside the county, including Inchiquin's well-remembered sacking of Cashel with its cathedral.[68] His justification for exclusion was that these belonged 'to the general history of the country' and were relevant to the history of the county only in so far that 'it may be assumed that, amongst his followers and soldiers, were many of his kinsmen and tenants from Clare'. And while Frost considered that the 'conduct' of Inchiquin during 'the Civil War in Ireland...proved him to be an unscrupulous politician', he still saluted him as 'an able general'.[69]

This apologia for Inchiquin led Frost to a consideration of the Cromwellian settlement in Clare where existing Catholic proprietors were dispossessed to make way both for Protestant grantees and for 'innocent Papists', from within Clare itself and from other counties of Ireland, who had been assigned land in Clare as part of the transplantation of Catholics to the province of Connacht and to County Clare. One is left to assume that Frost's own ancestors were among those who were settled in the county under the transplantation scheme. This would explain his discussion of the usually futile efforts of dispossessed Irish Catholic proprietors to secure a return of their property under the Act of Settlement during the reign of King Charles II. As he lamented the failure of most Catholics to recover their estates, Frost mentioned the success of Donogh O'Brien, son of Conor O'Brien of Lemenagh and Dromoland, who 'had been slain in the king's service' and of his wife, Máire Rua MacMahon, in securing a recovery as 'an innocent Protestant' of the estates of which the family had been deprived 'by the usurped powers'. While mentioning that the children of Donogh O'Brien and Máire Rua had been brought up as Protestants, Frost remained silent on the stratagem supposedly used by Máire Rua to recover the family estates for her son despite the fact that these had long been considered infamous in the folkloric memory of Catholics in Clare.[70]

---

[67] Frost, *History of Clare*, 388.

[68] P.F. Moran, *Memoirs of...Oliver Plunket*, part the first, xv. There, Moran printed details of the atrocity at Cashel perpetrated by Inchiquin after he had first 'administered the covenant to his apostate followers'.

[69] Frost, *History of Clare*, 371, 388; for a biographical note on Inchiquin see that by John A. Murphy, *Dictionary of Irish Biography*, vol. 7, 67–9.

[70] Frost, *History of Clare*, 394; we see in Chapter 11 that Canon Patrick White exulted in narrating what was popularly remembered of Máire Rua; for a biographical note on Máire Rua see that by Maureen Murphy, *Dictionary of Irish Biography*, vol. 7, 61–2.

UNIONIST RE-APPRAISALS OF IRELAND'S HISTORY 313

Frost's account of further forfeitures and land re-allocations in subsequent decades was in effect a chronicle of the decline of Catholic proprietorship in County Clare as 'the inhabitants continued to be driven out to make way for the new settlers'. He also explained how those who escaped confiscation were impoverished by the poll tax imposed by 'Ireton's Lieutenants' that continued to be levied under the guise of subsidies during the reign of Charles II.[71] This, as he saw it, explained why those Catholics who continued to hold land in the county mobilized under the command of Daniel O'Brien, 3rd Viscount Clare, to support King James II when William of Orange challenged that king's authority.[72] The members of 'Clare's dragoons' who supported James (and who had been memorialized in a Young Ireland ballad by Thomas Davis and respected by Mary Hickson because of the many men from Kerry who had served in their ranks) were, according to Frost, but 'raw recruits' who performed badly at the Battle of the Boyne but who were nonetheless penalized by confiscation and exile after the final victory of William had been achieved. Frost, following Davis, considered that the later reputation of Clare's dragoons as brave fighting men was justified by their commendable performance in the wars of Continental Europe. Even when he conceded that most of the dragoons had died in poverty and exile, Frost represented their lot as preferable to that of the small number of Catholics (including Frost's own family) who remained in possession of some land in the county and suffered 'slavery and degradation at home under Penal laws'.[73]

This appraisal suggests that Frost seemed to think that it was Catholic landowners, rather than priests or peasants, who bore the brunt of the Penal Laws in Clare. However, unlike Hickson, he cited no evidence of intermarriage between these surviving Catholic landed families either with Protestant incomers or those indigenous families who had converted to Protestantism. While Frost regretted the loss of power, influence, and land by Catholic proprietors in his county, he seemed as ready, as was Wood-Martin in the case of Sligo and Mary Hickson in the case of Kerry, to accept what had occurred in the past as an accomplished fact. Thus, as already mentioned, while Frost expressed disappointment that the principal branches of the O'Brien family had sided with the government at critical junctures, this did not dilute his respect for that dynasty. Therefore in an appendix he published a 'pedigree of the family of O'Brien from Brian Boroimhe to 1717'. Similarly, while he recorded the slippage of land away from indigenous Catholic proprietors into the hands of Protestants, Frost showed nothing but respect for the descendants of these relatively recent English arrivals in the county, many of whom had only acquired land there when much of the estate of the earls of

[71] Frost, *History of Clare*, 527, 531–2.
[72] For a biographical note on Viscount Clare see that by Elaine Murphy, *Dictionary of Irish Biography*, vol. 7, 23–5.
[73] Frost, *History of Clare*, 567, 603.

314   IMAGINING IRELAND'S PASTS

Thomond had been auctioned in the early eighteenth century. Frost also illustrated his text with depictions of the nineteenth-century residences of some of these Protestant families who were relatively new to the county. Even when he frowned on the questionable manner by which one Thomas Spaight had first came into the possession of land in County Clare, he mentioned in a footnote that 'this Thomas Spaight [was] the ancestor of the highly respectable families of that name in Clare, Limerick and Tipperary...[and was] also represented in Clare in the female line by Robert Carey Reeves, D.L. of Besborough, Killinena and by Francis Morice, Esq of Springfield, Sixmilebridge'.[74] Also, as had been done both by Hickson and Wood-Martin in relation to their respective counties, Frost emphasized that relatively few of the Protestant landed families of his generation in Clare were of Cromwellian ancestry. And while he, like Hickson, had paused to celebrate the achievements of Clare's dragoons in the service of France, Frost also, like Hickson and Wood-Martin, occasionally saluted service by landed Protestant families from County Clare in British forces. Thus, when describing Coney Island on the River Shannon, he noted that there was a hill on the island 'on the summit of which stands a monument to the memory of one of the children of the late Field-Marshal Sir John Fitzgerald, K.C.B'.[75] Then, when listing in his appendices the names of those who had served as Members of Parliament for Ennis 1613–1880, and for County Clare 1583–1886, and those from the county who, during the era of the Penal Laws, had converted 'from Popery to Protestant religion', Frost showed nothing but respect for the actions and decisions of these individuals.

By choosing to write county history rather than country history, Frost, like Wood-Martin, had found a vehicle through which to encourage his readers to take pride in their county community by learning something of its past. Writing as a Catholic, the early modern past that Frost depicted appeared more tumultuous and more marred by injustice than what either Hickson or Wood-Martin was prepared to admit in respect to Kerry or Sligo during the same interlude. However, Frost associated the high point of injustice with the time when supporters of Cromwell and Ireton had ruled Clare. Even then, by invoking the 1641 Depositions as a source of information on what had transpired in County Clare in 1641 and 1642, he was conceding that Catholics, by their actions at that time, had brought upon themselves much of the punishments they had subsequently endured. Then, for the eighteenth century, he asserted that Catholic landed families such as his own, acting in consort with their Protestant counterparts, had fulfilled a paternalistic role in saving priests from the penalties they would otherwise have suffered had they been exposed to the full rigour of the law. Thus, although written by a Catholic, Frost's county history of Clare was no less a

[74] Frost, *History of Clare*, 537.   [75] Frost, *History of Clare*, 542.

celebration than were the county histories of Kerry and Sligo, written respectively by Mary Hickson and W.G. Wood-Martin, of how the landed families of the county had promoted improvement and communal welfare, Therefore, as he imagined a past for his county, Frost was joining Hickson and Wood-Martin in appealing, presumably to moderate nationalist opinion, for a continuance of what all Unionist authors were depicting as a benevolent social order.

10.6 An Ulster Perspective on Ireland's Past: The Writings of the Reverend George Hill

Given that Ulster was the Irish province most comprehensively planted in the seventeenth century, it comes as no surprise that in the nineteenth century it was the province with the highest percentage of Protestants among its population, and the province that stood most firmly against the various Irish political campaigns conducted in the first half of that century by O'Connell, and in the second part by Parnell. In the light of this it seems reasonable to expect that Protestant authors from Ulster would have been trenchant upholders of a rigid Protestant interpretation of Ireland's history for the early modern centuries. The writings of the Reverend George Hill, the most distinguished Ulster historian of his generation, come therefore as a surprise since they show him to have been a tolerant person ready at all times to blame the challenges that Protestant landed families were facing in the present to the harsh treatment that had been meted out by their progenitors to Catholics in the past. He was in a better position to be less defensive than the Unionist authors from Connacht and Munster whose works we have been considering because the primary audience to which he directed his writings were people of Ulster plantation stock rather than those of Cromwellian descent. This made his task easier because people of Ulster planter origin had not generally been demonized in the anti-establishment historical narratives that Unionist authors from other provinces were striving to counter. However, members of Hill's audience, whether they were of English or Scottish ancestry or whether they subscribed to the tenets of the Church of Ireland or those of Scottish Calvinism, were keenly aware that their ancestors had been forced in 1641, and again in 1688–89, to defend their position in the province from hostile assault by Catholics. Hill did nothing to minimize the significance of these onslaughts. However, he seemed to believe that popular resentment over them had been somewhat diluted by an awareness on the part of those who belonged to the Scottish Calvinist tradition, of which he was one, that their ancestors had been treated as second-class subjects relative to members of the Church of Ireland whose religion had been that established by law until 1871. Hill also seemed conscious that some within this community also remembered, even if discreetly, how

316   IMAGINING IRELAND'S PASTS

some of their ancestors had also become rebels as United Irishmen in 1798 when they had sought to rectify this position of inferiority.[76]

Another factor that may have contributed to the relative moderation of the views of Hill was that the lives of Unionists in Ulster—and particularly in rural Ulster—seemed less precarious in the nineteenth century than those of their counterparts in the other three provinces. Landowners and the Protestant rural farming population in Ulster, other than in particular areas of County Armagh, had been less troubled by agrarian violence than their counterparts in the other Irish provinces, and relations between tenant farmers and their landlords in Ulster were such that one of the early objectives of both reformers and agrarian agitators in nineteenth-century Ireland was to have the 'Ulster custom', which governed relations between tenants and landowners in that province, extended throughout the country. Also, at this juncture, Protestants in Ulster considered themselves less threatened than their co-religionists elsewhere in Ireland by the great political issues of the Victorian era, notably the Repeal of the Act of Union and the possible introduction of Home Rule to Ireland, because most parliamentary representatives for Ulster constituencies stood firmly against any such threats to the Union between Britain and Ireland.

It was against this background that the Reverend George Hill (1810–1900), a non-subscribing Presbyterian Minister and the first librarian at Queen's College, Belfast, wrote a sequence of histories, published between 1869 and 1889.[77] Two of these dealt with developments in the two counties in east Ulster (Antrim and Down) that had been subjected to unofficial plantation in the early seventeenth century. His other publications related more to the formal plantation that was promoted by the government in the six counties of Ulster that lay in the central and western part of the province.

Hill's first book was an edition of the so-called *Montgomery Manuscripts*, a compilation, we may recall, that had been cited from the original by Thomas Mac Nevin in his *Confiscation of Ulster*.[78] The manuscript in question was an eighteenth-century text detailing the experiences in Ulster from 1603 to 1706 of the Montgomerys, a Scottish settler family, who had flourished in County Down.[79] Hill's second volume explained how the Scottish MacDonnells who, during the sixteenth century, were considered a menace to English interests in Ireland, succeeded in the seventeenth century in becoming accepted by the Crown as one of the leading noble families in Ireland, also playing a political role

[76] On remembering 1798 see Beiner, *Forgetful Remembrance*.
[77] For a biographical note on Hill see that by Ian Montgomery, *Dictionary of Irish Biography*, vol. 4, 698–9.
[78] On Mac Nevin's citation see Chapter 8, 234.
[79] George Hill, ed., *The Montgomery Manuscripts* (Belfast, 1869).

UNIONIST RE-APPRAISALS OF IRELAND'S HISTORY   317

in Scottish and English affairs.[80] These books were followed by Hill's most frequently cited work, *An Historical Account of the Plantation in Ulster*, which he described as 'a connected narrative' explaining how an official plantation came to be launched and implemented in six of the nine counties of Ulster during the first two decades of the seventeenth century.[81] His final contribution was a two-volume collection of essays that treated of different aspects of plantation and British settlement in eight of the nine counties of Ulster.[82]

All of Hill's books, like Hickson's two volumes on Kerry, attached importance to the presentation and appraisal of documentary evidence. Thus *The Plantation in Ulster* was, in Hill's words, 'a compilation from state papers', including those he extracted from the Carew manuscripts. He complemented these documents with evidence drawn from patent rolls, inquisitions, the barony maps made in 1609 of six Ulster counties designated for plantation, the survey of that plantation conducted by Josias Bodley in 1613, and the Pynnar Survey completed by Captain Nicholas Pynnar in 1618–19. Hill published his edition of this last document within the volume.[83]

In order to contextualize the plantation in Ulster, Hill explained how, ever since the twelfth century, Ireland had been subjected to 'sundry plantations...whereof the first plantation of the English Pale was the best and the last plantation of the undertakers in Munster was the worst'.[84] What commenced in the twelfth century was the first of 'a long series of English invasions [and] but the adventure of a few private persons of freebooting proclivities'. One of these was John de Courcy who, with others, had brought 'plantations in Ulster on the sea coast'. This endeavour, according to Hill, was similar to how the de Burgos had established a plantation in Connacht, how Sir Thomas de Clare had established one in Thomond, and how the Fitzgeralds, Butlers, Barrys, Roches, and other English families had planted Munster.[85] While conceding that all of these medieval settler populations had 'degenerated' culturally over time, Hill's summation drew three conclusions. The first was that what was attempted in Ulster during the sixteenth and seventeenth centuries was not new, the second was that the native Irish population were the invariable losers from all such incursions, and the third was that it was speculators from England (and in the case of the Ulster Plantation also from Scotland) who were invariably the protagonists.

---

[80] George Hill, *An Historical Account of the MacDonnells of Antrim* (Belfast, 1873); for a modern appraisal of this transformation, Jane Ohlmeyer, *Civil War and Restoration in the Three Stuart Kingdoms: The Career of Randal Mac Donnell, marquis of Antrim, 1609-1683* (Cambridge, 1993).

[81] George Hill, *An Historical Account of the Plantation in Ulster at the Commencement of the Seventeenth Century, 1608-1620* (Belfast, 1877).

[82] George Hill, *Plantation Papers: or Historical Sketches in the Counties of Down and Antrim* (Belfast, 1888); Hill, *Plantation Papers, containing a summary sketch of the Great Ulster Plantation in the Year 1610* (Belfast, 1889).

[83] Hill, *Plantation in Ulster*, Preface, i, and 445–590.   [84] Hill, *Plantation in Ulster*, 70.

[85] Hill, *Plantation in Ulster*, 20, 70.

318 IMAGINING IRELAND'S PASTS

Then, in discussing the proximate background to the plantation in Ulster, Hill pronounced it to be 'well known that during many years before 1588 the English rule became rather popular than otherwise in the North', which he sustained by stating that the downfall of Shane O'Neill had been brought about by the O'Donnells 'rather than by the government'.[86] This brought Hill to the Attainder of Shane O'Neill, passed by the Dublin parliament of 1569–71, which vested in the Crown all territories in Ulster over which Shane O'Neill had claimed jurisdiction. This act acquired a belated importance, according to Hill, when Sir John Davies invoked it in the seventeenth century to establish Crown title to the lands that had remained in the hands of Irish lords in the intervening period. Hill also contended, this time on the authority of Sir Thomas Lee, an English author-adventurer of the sixteenth century, that a succession of Crown servitors had, by their unprincipled actions, driven a succession of Ulster lords to rebel who had been previously disposed to being loyal subjects. This ambition of servitors to enrich themselves at the expense of Irish lords appeared to have been frustrated in 1603, according to Hill, when King James had pardoned Hugh O'Neill and Rory O'Donnell for their rebellion against the government of Queen Elizabeth. Hill explained how this arrangement was resented by several 'English and Scottish speculators [who had been] wilfully indulging plantation'. Their leader, according to Hill, was Sir Arthur Chichester who became governor in 1605, after which he conspired to make those Irish lords who had been received to mercy by King James fearful for their safety. The result, according to Hill, was that in 1607 O'Neill and O'Donnell, accompanied by their families and principal supporters, 'fled simply for fear of arrest'.[87] With their departure, he continued, their lands were 'quietly abandoned to the planters', and Chichester became 'an able and unscrupulous advocate for the rooting out of the Irish population of Ulster by the introduction of English and Scottish'.[88]

Hill then explained how a scheme for plantation in Ulster, which he described variously as Chichester's 'revolutionary policy' and a 'fascinating business', was arrived at. In doing so, he detailed how, 'through one pretext or another', all Irish lords who had taken the side of the government during the course of the recent war were denied what they had been promised. This, he contended, opened up the scope of the plantation beyond what Chichester 'had at first even ventured to imagine'.[89] Hill thus credited Chichester with having conceived and managed the scheme, and he described Sir John Davies, the Attorney General, and Sir James Ley, the Chief Justice, as the 'civilisers' who had clothed Chichester's crude land grab in the language of reform. Sir Francis Bacon in London had, Hill conceded, also helped rationalize the scheme, but

[86] Hill, *Plantation in Ulster*, Preface, i.
[88] Hill, *Plantation in Ulster*, 57, 59.
[87] Hill, *Plantation in Ulster*, 22–59; quotation 57.
[89] Hill, *Plantation in Ulster*, 58, 64–5.

UNIONIST RE-APPRAISALS OF IRELAND'S HISTORY   319

he considered 'his performance...tawdry and commonplace when compared with the graphic sketches of Chichester and Davies'.[90]

The obstacle in the way of Chichester's scheme devised to benefit servitors alone was, according to Hill, the continued existence of native occupier-owners of land, whose number Chichester sought to minimize by sending some 'to Sweden to assist in fighting the battles of Gustavus Adolphus, the Protestant champion of the north'. At this point, according to Hill, Chichester would have preferred 'to have given nothing to the natives at all' but their numbers brought him to recognize 'the impolicy' of so doing.[91] It was only this, claimed Hill, that explained why some natives were allocated grants within the plantation scheme, but only for one life and not in their 'traditional places' of habitation. Instead, said Hill, they were allocated grants in specially designated 'native districts' where 'servitors' were assigned land in close proximity 'to watch and overawe' them. Moreover, said Hill, these allocations were in baronies that remained in 'comparative sterility even to the present day'. Even then, claimed Hill, greedy servitors 'soon became the owners' of these estates allocated to natives by negotiating terms with these one-life grantees.[92]

Chichester's desire for a servitor-only scheme received a further setback, claimed Hill, when King James 'became quite interested in the project' and insisted that it be made open to Scottish and English proprietors and settlers, even though Chichester had 'no special affection for Scotchmen high of low, gentle or simple'.[93] Another complication, claimed Hill, was that 'the philosophers in London...were of opinion that the population of Great Britain, north and south, had begun then somewhat to overflow its legitimate bounds, and that Ulster would prove such a timely outlet for many who might be induced "to leave their country for their country's good"'.[94] It was this, in Hill's opinion, that led to the requirement that grantees from England and Scotland, to be designated 'undertakers', be invited to take parcels of land on which they would retain only British Protestants as tenants. Servitors, including bishops, according to Hill, were also 'encouraged...to plant their lands with British tenants', but they generally ignored the injunction because they 'preferred Irish tenants' who were prepared to pay 'higher rent [and were] less trouble'. This preference, according to Hill, also made sense because the Irish excelled at animal husbandry and 'all agricultural pursuits', and, 'compared with their neighbours, whether English or Scotch,...only wanted peace to enable them to excel both as agriculturalists'.[95]

By emphasizing the competence of would-be Irish tenants, Hill was challenging 'a cherished faith' of Ulster Protestants that their own ancestors had been the

---

[90] Hill, *Plantation in Ulster*, 65, 69, 71.   [91] Hill, *Plantation in Ulster*, 64, 69.

[92] Hill, *Plantation in Ulster*, Preface, ii–iii; for a recent appraisal, Gerard Farrell, *The 'Mere Irish' and the Colonisation of Ulster, 1570–1641*.

[93] Hill, *Plantation in Ulster*, 71–3.   [94] Hill, *Plantation in Ulster*, 132.

[95] Hill, *Plantation in Ulster*, Preface, iv, viii.

introducers of advanced farming methods to Ulster. Another belief, he claimed, was that 'our worthy ancestors' had arrived in Ulster to establish themselves 'in a howling wilderness or, rather perhaps, in a dreary and terrible region of muirland and morass'. Instead, according to Hill, those 'shrewd and needy people whom we call our forefathers, and who dwelt north and south of the Tweed' were well informed by correspondents who were acquainted with the province that the land to be settled was 'fertile and productive', and that the official allocations being assigned were more generous than appeared on paper because they took no account of the 'waste land' being included within the assignments.[96]

These considerations satisfied Hill that when the process got under way for recruiting prospective planters in England and Scotland to settle in Ulster the supply exceeded the numbers required and necessitated a 'process of weeding out superfluous and suspected applicants'. Even then, Hill found that some who were granted estates were 'sorry planters' while others were 'rather chivalrous in their offers as compared with their means'. However, Hill remained satisfied that sufficient competent planters and tenants had been attracted to render the experiment viable. Therefore, in Hill's opinion, the scheme was placed in jeopardy only because of the disdain shown by its promoters towards the native population both in assigning grants to them and in clearing native tenants off the undertakers' estates. Chichester, in Hill's opinion, was the worst offender, and when referring to a letter he had written to Salisbury, Hill expressed outrage at how, in the course of writing to Salisbury on the subject of native clearance, 'the deputy could decant in the same breath about the transplanting of natives and the transporting of dogs and hawks'.[97]

This critique by Hill of the plantation process served as an introduction to his edition of the survey, completed by Captain Nicholas Pynnar in 1619, of how the planters had progressed up to that date. Pynnar's survey drew more attention to the delinquency than to the achievements of the planters. Therefore, at the end of his edition of the text, Hill remarked on the 'small number of British settlers' who had been introduced by the planters to 'the very best land in the province' whose 'natural fertility' was beyond question. Hill contended that what he described as the 'sadly halting progress towards the attainment' of the plantation's purpose would have been even worse had the planters been 'left to themselves [instead of being] compelled by government'. Overall, Hill concluded that Pynnar's survey presented 'a humiliating picture...after so much effort on the part of the government and such an appalling amount of suffering as had been thereby inflicted on the native population'. Then, as Hill looked beyond the particular to consider 'the general interests of Ireland as a nation', he pronounced that 'this settlement in Ulster, and in a minor degree...similar settlements or plantations in the other

---

[96] Hill, *Plantation in Ulster*, Preface, v–vii.   [97] Hill, *Plantation in Ulster*, 222.

provinces at the same period' were responsible for 'the awful scenes and events of the ten years of civil war commencing with [the rebellion of] 1641, the horrors of the revolutionary struggle in 1690, and the re-awakening of these horrors in 1798'. Thus, as Hill put it, from 'the dragons' teeth so plentifully and... so deliberately sown in this Ulster plantation [had] sprung up ghastly harvests of blood and death on almost every plain, and by almost every riverside, and in almost every glen of our northern province'.[98]

This negative verdict on how plantation was promoted in Ulster might suggest that an author of nationalist rather than of Unionist conviction had written it. However, there is no doubting that Hill was a committed Unionist, and one who had a strong attachment to, and admiration for the Protestant community of Ulster where, in his earlier career, he had officiated as a Calvinist minister. He differed in tone from authors such as Hickson and Wood-Martin not only because he was liberal rather than a conservative in his politics but also because he lived in a part of Ireland where, as yet, he had no reason to fear a future for a Protestant community that was strong on the ground. His liberalism left him in general agreement with John Prendergast with whom he corresponded and whose work he quoted with approval. Their contention was that the future of the Union, or at least a future in Ireland for Unionists, would be secure only if people in power were prepared to learn from history, and display some appreciation that British officials and adventurers of the past had inflicted grave injustices upon a potentially loyal native population, and that memory of these injustices still festered in the minds of the descendants of those who had been wronged. The ultimate injustice where Prendergast was concerned had been the transplantation of peace-loving proprietors with their dependents to Connacht and Clare as part of the Cromwellian settlement, while the ultimate injustices for Hill were the chicanery associated with the dispossession of native proprietors, and the enforced clearance of compliant Irish tenants from the estates of undertakers in the Ulster Plantation. Both Hill and Prendergast mustered substantial evidence in support of their arguments, and each imagined how the subsequent behaviour of the vanquished had been influenced by the injustices they had suffered. The two were thus united in attributing Ireland's turbulent history and disturbed present to memories of past injustices that had excited people to take revenge on those who had profited from their disinheritance. Thus, while Hill referred to the bloody episodes associated with the 1641 rebellion and to the depositions that bore witness to them, he represented this outburst as no more than what the settler community in Ulster could have expected given their earlier blatant robbery of natives of all social gradations. Just as Prendergast had done in 1865 when discussing the Cromwellian Plantation, Hill contended that the English and

---

[98] Hill, *Plantation in Ulster*, 590.

322 IMAGINING IRELAND'S PASTS

Scottish adventurers and planters who had been involved with the various efforts to plant Ulster in the sixteenth and seventeenth centuries had been driven by the desire to achieve social and economic advancement. Thus for Hill, as for Prendergast, what was said by the different waves of adventurers and settlers of their concern to civilize and/or to evangelize the native population was no more than a polite veneer to cover their acquisitiveness. Hill could therefore argue, as Prendergast had done, that confessional difference merely sharpened the edge of conflicts that stemmed ultimately from the way in which the native population had been marginalized, but not entirely eliminated, by adventurers and planters.

If George Hill's two major studies, the *MacDonnells of Antrim*, and *Plantation in Ulster*, can be considered contributions to provincial, national, or even transnational history, he like the other Unionist historians of his generation whose works we have been considering, seemed of the opinion that the best means of communicating to a targeted local audience was through the writing of county history. To this end, he published a series of studies in *The Northern Whig* (a liberal Unionist publication), each devoted to explaining how British settlement had first been established in eight of the nine counties of Ulster. Then in 1888 and again in 1889 he brought these county studies together in two volumes, entitled *Plantation Papers*. The first of these treated of English and Scots penetration into each of Counties Down and Antrim since 'the earliest recorded attempt at the plantation of English colonists in County Down... [by] Sir John de Courcy'.[99] The second described, chapter by chapter, how by 1610, British proprietors had established title to estates in each of Counties Armagh, Tyrone, Londonderry, Donegal, Fermanagh, and Cavan. To this, Hill added a brief addendum explaining why County Monaghan, the sole remaining county in Ulster, was not included within 'The Great Ulster Plantation'.[100]

In these county studies, Hill, like the authors of the other county histories to which we have given attention, identified the moment when British proprietors first established title to estates in the counties in question. Then, in several cases, he traced how ownership of estates had changed over time, thus giving him occasion, after the manner of Charles Smith, to identify those individuals who had constructed castles and ornate mansions that still adorned the countryside in the various counties he discussed. Such references would have assured Hill's readers that the inheritors of the great properties acquired by adventurers and speculators of the sixteenth and seventeenth centuries, such as Nicholas Bagenal, Arthur Chichester, and Moses Hill, had lived up to their responsibility to be improving landowners. Evidence that the leaders of their county communities had acted responsibly would have been welcomed by Hill's various audiences which we can take to have been largely Protestant. By drawing attention to such

---

[99] Hill, *Plantation Papers... Counties of Down and Antrim* (Belfast, 1888).
[100] Hill, Plantation *Papers... the Great Ulster Plantation... 1610* (Belfast, 1889).

UNIONIST RE-APPRAISALS OF IRELAND'S HISTORY   323

evidence, Hill was doing as the authors of the other county studies had done. However, he differed from the others on one essential point. We noted how Hickson, Wood-Martin, and even Frost, had cited evidence on how through the centuries landlords had been improvers because this justified their fundamental contention that Protestant landowners, and the relatively small Protestant communities that relied upon their support and patronage, had a further vital contribution to make to the continuing welfare of their county communities. By way of contrast, Hill recognized that the era of landlord dominance in Ireland was at an end. Therefore the lesson he was drawing from history was that the best assurance for the continued flourishing existence of the Protestant farming communities in the eight counties of Ulster to which he gave consideration was by learning to respect and co-operate with their Catholic neighbours who, as we saw, Hill considered no less proficient as farmers than the Protestants themselves.

In order to make his case, Hill discredited what he described as 'our folklore' by exposing startling evidence of the frequently fraudulent and aggressive means by which several of the prime parcels of land that were in Protestant ownership in every county of Ulster had been wrested from the native population several centuries before.[101] Thus, in one of his county studies, as Hill enumerated several fraudulent schemes that were operated in the seventeenth century by what he described as 'the planting department', he alluded to the criticism made by Lord Deputy Oliver St John of the duplicity of Edward Conway, Arthur Chichester, and Moses Hill. St John, as lord deputy, claimed Hill, was not only 'politically opposed to the whole ruthless scheme or game [but also]...wisely saw that the system must sooner or later be reversed, and that landlordism, as introduced by the plantation, would eventually be abolished'. This prescient seventeenth-century observation, claimed Hill, had been finally borne out because 'our government, now, Whig and Tory alike, and even our landlords now, Whig and Tory alike, are calling out lustily for the abolition of the dual ownership of land'.[102] Hill was therefore at one with the leaders of the Land League in looking forward to peasant proprietorship that was to become the normal system of landownership for Ireland with the passage of the Wyndham Land Purchase Act of 1903. Hill, writing from an Ulster perspective, saw nothing to fear from the social transformation he anticipated, provided members of the Protestant farming community were prepared to treat their Catholic counterparts as equals. This, he was suggesting, was no more than they deserved as he, like Prendergast, demonstrated from history that these Catholic tenants were, in many instances, the descendants of native proprietors who had been defrauded by the ancestors of

---

[101] Hill used the term 'our folklore' when explaining how the Cromwell landed family in Lecale in County Down were descended from Edward Cromwell, a great-grandson of Thomas Cromwell who had served Henry VIII, rather than, as was popularly believed, from his 'kinsman, Oliver Cromwell, Old Noll'; Hill, *Plantation Papers*, 1, 5.

[102] Hill, *Plantation Papers*, 1, 19.

324 IMAGINING IRELAND'S PASTS

the landlords who were now being incentivized by the state to make good for these past transgressions by conceding ownership of their farms to their-former tenants.

10.7 Conclusion

This appraisal of a sequence of county histories written by Unionist authors in the later part of the nineteenth century shows how all considered county history to be an effective vehicle for conveying their response to what they perceived as recurring threats to the serenity of the world they inhabited. Hickson, Wood-Martin, and Frost all recognized that landowners were those most threatened by the socio-political pressures of the time, and they all made use of history to show that, even during the sixteenth, seventeenth, and eighteenth centuries, the proprietors in their particular counties had been paternalistic upholders of their communities rather than the rapacious exploiters of the weak and defenceless as all landowners were being depicted by nationalist and by Catholic critics. Wood-Martin and Frost might be said to have had an interest in the subject because they were both landowners. However, Hickson, who came from modest circumstances, spoke highly of most landowners in Kerry not only because they patronized her but also because she recognized that the tiny Protestant community in the county, of which she was a stalwart supporter, could not endure without landlord support. Wood-Martin seems to have thought that the Protestant population in rural Sligo was in a similar precarious position, but he seemed confident that the flourishing and more denominationally diverse Protestant community in Sligo town rendered the continued presence of Protestants in town and county indispensible to the welfare of both.

The outlook of George Hill was strikingly different because he never contemplated that the future of a Protestant community was in doubt in any of the eight counties he had studied given their strong presence everywhere as tenant farmers. Because of this confidence, he considered himself at liberty to cast a cold eye over the history of eight of the nine counties in the province of Ulster, and to investigate critically how many of the principal landowning families had come to possess their properties and what use their descendants had made of it. As Hill took account of the improvements that had been introduced by landowning families, he concluded that these were far outweighed by evidence of the injustices inflicted by these same families on the native population as they seized control of the lands that had been in their possession for centuries. Given this record of repeated injustice, and given also the pace of the socio-political change that he and his readers were experiencing, Hill could contemplate an Ulster society without landlords. Due to this likelihood, Hill wrote primarily to disabuse his Protestant readers of any myths concerning the past history of their community they might have inherited and that were unlikely to be helpful to them in the future, and to alert them of the need to be conciliatory to those who would continue to be their Catholic neighbours. He had no doubt that these still fostered bitter and to his mind justified memories of how their ancestors had been mistreated. Hill's works shows that not all Unionist historians spoke with the same voice about Ireland's past even at a moment of tension. Rather, he, like Prendergast, seems to have believed that the best means of employing the past to guide future policy was by being guided by the evidence in the archives.

11

The Birth and Early Demise of a Liberal Interpretation of Ireland's Early Modern Past

11.1 Introduction

Our analysis of the sequence of county histories written by authors with Unionist sympathies during the second half of the nineteenth century indicates that every author expressed sympathy for the trials and losses experienced by the ancestors of their Catholic neighbours during the sixteenth, seventeenth, and eighteenth centuries, even when their chief concern was to highlight the sufferings of their own predecessors at several junctures over that same time. All authors made reference to the 1641 rebellion as proof of what Protestants had occasionally endured, but they saw the need to balance this with some acknowledgement of the traumas that Catholics, particularly those of lower social rank, had experienced at various junctures. This concern to appear balanced may have been influenced by the evidence concerning the sufferings of Catholics detailed in Prendergast's *Cromwellian Settlement of Ireland* even when this was tempered by the alternate view of Cromwell's intervention put forward by J.A. Froude. However, Unionist authors originally steered clear from the views of Froude out of the belief that by associating with them they would isolate themselves within their own county communities when their purpose was to show from history that the cultivation of intercommunal harmony was as beneficial to Catholics as to Protestants and to nationalists as to Unionists.

Our Unionist authors, all but one of them Protestant, were initially attracted by more liberal interpretations of Ireland's history because these offered an attractive alternative to the historical narratives being promoted by doctrinaire Catholics. These, as we shall see, had begun increasingly to brand Irish nationalism in exclusivist terms that would have left no place for Protestants within most county communities. The new 'impartial' appraisal of Ireland's history was best exemplified in the historical writings of W.E.H. Lecky (1838–1903) that had been in general circulation since 1871. Unionists had another reason to embrace Lecky's methods and arguments because he, an Irish-born historian resident in London, had come to be recognized as an arbiter on disputes concerning Ireland, whether historical or political, during the last quarter of the nineteenth century.

Imagining Ireland's Pasts: Early Modern Ireland through the Centuries. Nicholas Canny, Oxford University Press (2021).
© Nicholas Canny. DOI: 10.1093/oso/9780198808961.003.0011

THE BIRTH AND EARLY DEMISE OF A LIBERAL VIEW 327

However, as we shall see, once it became evident that Lecky's appeals for balance and impartiality were failing to win any positive response from Catholic-nationalist historians, and once politicians of all stripes in Britain adopted policies that were perceived to run contrary to the interest of Irish Unionists, there seemed every reason why Unionist authors should revert to a more militant view of Ireland's past. This, they hoped, would encourage members of their community to stake a claim to a place for themselves in Ireland into the foreseeable future.

11.2 W.E.H. Lecky: The Doyen of Liberal History

Donal McCartney, in his biography of Lecky, has shown that, after an undistinguished academic passage through Trinity College, Dublin, 1856–60, and extensive travel throughout Europe where he had read and reflected on the progress of civilization, Lecky took up residence in London where he lived comfortably from the rents collected on his Irish estates, located principally in County Carlow and Queen's County. In London, following the publication in 1865 of his two-volume study entitled a *History of the Rise and Influence of Rationalism in Europe* and a further two-volume publication in 1869 entitled a *History of European Morals from Augustus to Charlemagne*, Lecky came to be accepted as a scholar of consequence.[1] His reputation was further enhanced because, as Lecky acknowledged towards the end of his career, 'the Irish question [had just then] forced itself prominently on English opinion'. Under these circumstances, and given his strong convictions on what had become a publicly debated topic, Lecky decided to revisit and expand upon a scarcely noticed volume entitled *Leaders of Public Opinion in Ireland* that he had published anonymously in 1861. This, both in its original format and in the revised and expanded version that he published under his name in 1871, shows that Lecky identified with the liberal opinions of the moderate members of the Young Ireland movement. Lecky espoused these ideas because, during his student days at Trinity College, Dublin, he had been an active member of the College Historical Society, the student debating society that had been the principal forum for those Young Irelanders who had attended the college in the decade previous to Lecky's attendance there.[2]

In *Leaders of Public Opinion*, Lecky reflected on the critiques of Irish society that had been made over the centuries by figures such as Jonathan Swift, Henry Flood, Henry Grattan, and Daniel O'Connell. From this he concluded that the

---

[1] For a biographical note on Lecky see that by Donal McCartney, *Dictionary of Irish Biography*, vol. 5, 390–1, and for a full-scale biography, McCartney, *W.E.H. Lecky: Historian and Politician, 1838–1903* (Dublin, 1994), on his early career, 1–25.
[2] McCartney, *Lecky*, 7–10.

328   IMAGINING IRELAND'S PASTS

relative poverty and disorder of Ireland was due to the 'disaffection' rather than to the perverseness of the Catholic population. He conceded that they had good grounds to be disaffected because of the unjust means by which their ancestors had been deprived of their lands during the early modern centuries, and because of the fraudulent methods that the government had used to secure the passage through the Irish parliament of the Act of Union of 1800.

Lecky explained that the revised 1871 edition of *Leaders* acquired 'a sudden and most unexpected popularity' because it appeared 'when the conversion of Mr Gladstone to Home Rule took place', and because that Prime Minister had cited it 'as a justification for his policy' even though, as Lecky pointed out in 1903, he himself had 'emphatically repudiated' Home Rule for Ireland even in the moderate form in which it had been first proposed by Isaac Butt and contemplated by Gladstone. However, the fact that Gladstone 'and three or four members of his government' were taking advice from Lecky's 1871 edition of *Leaders of Public Opinion*, and that, as Lecky put it, his book 'was often cited...in political pamphlets and newspapers, on platforms and even in parliament', meant that his reputation in England as an authority on Irish affairs was assured.[3] At the same time, Lecky had come to be well regarded by liberals and nationalists in Ireland because of the detailed critical reviews of Froude's *The English in Ireland in the Eighteenth Century*, published in 1872, that had featured in *Macmillan's Magazine* in 1873 and 1874. These came to be widely known in Ireland because extracts from them had been reprinted in the Irish public press. The result, as McCartney has explained, was that, although a man of quiet Unionist convictions, Lecky came to be considered 'one of the intellectual leaders of Irish nationalism'. He acquired this reputation because his criticism of Froude was carefully argued, unlike the wild denunciations that were broadcast in the United States and in Ireland by such disparate authors as Fr. Tom Burke, John Mitchel, and John Prendergast.[4]

An older Lecky, who had become frightened by the turn that Irish politics had taken, had become embarrassed that his writings of the 1860s and 1870s continued to be cited in support of nationalist causes that he now considered dangerous. Under these changed circumstances, Lecky denounced them because they contained some of 'the worst specimens of...boyish rhetoric'.[5] However, despite Lecky's belated effort to distance himself from his earlier views, he stood consistently throughout his lifetime with the general outline of Ireland's history for the early modern centuries that he had first adumbrated in 1861 and 1871.

---

[3] W.E.H. Lecky, *Leaders of Public Opinion in Ireland*, 2 vols. (London, 1912), vol. 1, Preface, viii, xiii, xiv. In the preface to this 1912 edition that Lecky had written for the 1903 edition that had appeared shortly before his death, Lecky traced the publication history of the text.

[4] McCartney, *Lecky*, 77; Anne Wyatt, 'Froude, Lecky and the "humblest Irishman"', *Irish Historical Studies*, vol. 19 (1975), 261–85.

[5] Lecky, *Leaders*, vol. 1, Preface, xiv.

THE BIRTH AND EARLY DEMISE OF A LIBERAL VIEW   329

An updated version of this narrative did duty as his chapters on Ireland in his eight-volume *History of England in the Eighteenth Century*, which appeared sequentially between 1878 and 1890. Then Lecky published an embellished compilation of these chapters in 1892 as a separate five-volume *History of Ireland in the Eighteenth Century*. Lecky had originally intended these various contributions as a scholarly riposte to Froude's *The English in Ireland in the Eighteenth Century*. Knowledge of this provided further reason why they served as a beacon for all authors concerned with developments in Ireland in the sixteenth, seventeenth, and eighteenth centuries who wished to conform to liberal best practice.

Lecky considered that his special talent as a historian was his ability to adjudicate between the 'violently contradictory statements' of previous authorities by drawing upon an 'array of original evidence...from the opposite camps' to trace 'the true causes' of the major disjunctions that had occurred in Ireland during the early modern centuries, and to measure 'with accuracy and impartiality the different degrees of provocation, aggravation, palliation and comparative guilt' that attached to those episodes.[6] The principal disjunctions he identified were the rebellions of 1641 and of 1798. However, where Lecky is usually praised for bringing fresh evidence to bear on the origins and nature of the uprising of 1798, he relied almost entirely on common sense, and on the evidence cited in the eighteenth century by Thomas Carte, to explain the origin and nature of the Irish uprising of 1641. As he did so, he challenged the opinions and sources of contemporary Protestant authors, especially John Temple and Henry Jones, without examining the sources they had used. Therefore the historical exchanges that developed between Lecky and Froude on this issue were a perpetuation of the disputes concerning the origin and nature of the 1641 rebellion that had been debated ever since that event had taken place.

Lecky opened with an assertion that there were some 'peculiar tendencies, affinities and repulsions of the national intellect and character' of Irish people, and that doubt existed concerning 'how far the measure of civilization [in medieval times] extended beyond the walls of monasteries'. However, he, like Carte, but unlike Froude, did not attribute 'backwardness' to any innate and irremediable defect in the character of Irish people but rather to the 'calamity' of the Norman Conquest. When England itself had been conquered in 1066, claimed Lecky, order was quickly imposed upon the pre-existing indigenous population, but, in the case of Ireland, the twelfth-century conquest was 'protracted over no less than 400 years' with the result that 'two nations remained in Ireland for centuries in hostility'. It was only in the reign of Henry VIII, he claimed, that 'royal authority became in any degree a reality', and he asserted that from this foundation the government of Queen Elizabeth 'crushed the native population to

---

[6] W.E.H. Lecky, *History of Ireland in the Eighteenth Century*, 5 vols. (London, 1892), vol. 1, Preface, v.

330   IMAGINING IRELAND'S PASTS

the dust'. As he traced the course of the Elizabethan conquest, Lecky asserted that 'isolated episodes…as terrible as anything in human history' had then occurred. These, he argued, had suggested to the native population of the time that the English were engaged upon a 'war of extermination', which, he insisted, was untrue. Rather, he said, it was an English appetite for the 'confiscation of Irish land', rather than any desire to exterminate the people or to convert them to Protestantism, that had driven the conquest forward. Then, in a passage reminiscent of what each of Carte and Leland had written, he attributed the 'ferocity' associated with the Elizabethan wars in Ireland to 'the great impulse which the discovery of the New World and the religious changes of the sixteenth century had imparted to the intellect and character of Europe'. This spirit, according to Lecky, manifested itself in England, 'in an exuberance of many-sided activity equalled in no previous century' that led to an 'extraordinary growth of the spirit of adventure, a distaste for routine, [and] an extreme desire to discover new and rapid paths to wealth'. One dimension of this, said Lecky, was the growth of 'piracy' and the explosion of 'maritime enterprises'. This, he argued, made the English 'a race of discoverers', which, in the case of the English who ventured to Ireland, was manifested by their use of 'frivolous pretexts' to acquire 'great tracts of fertile territory, and to amass in a few years gigantic fortunes'. Here, he likened what happened in Ireland in the sixteenth and seventeenth centuries to the accomplishments of Clive and Hastings in India that had given rise to the debate at Westminster with which his readers would still have been familiar.[7]

Lecky could 'imagine what feelings [the wars in Ireland] must have planted in the minds of the survivors' who suffered both from the loss of their lands and 'apprehension of the extirpation of their religion'.[8] Then he argued that since conflicts in Ireland during the sixteenth-century were 'not wars of races [and] not to any considerable degree wars of religion', and that since Irish defeat was followed invariably by confiscation of property, it was not surprising that the Irish had concluded 'that they were to be driven from the soil'. Even then, he contended, if 'justice [had been] administered with impartial firmness', the Irish might have become reconciled to their loss. However, Lecky found that formal plantation had quickly given way to 'the trade of the Discoverer' that the Irish had hoped to bring to an end by securing the Graces from King Charles I. However, claimed Lecky, when that king, through his representative in Ireland, reneged on the Graces, the Irish became convinced that 'no promises or engagements on the part of the Government' would be honoured.[9] Matters became even more difficult for the Irish, according to Lecky, when the country's population experienced a natural 'rebound' after the restoration of peace following decades of conflict. This, said Lecky, had put a squeeze on resources which, when added to existing anxieties,

---

[7] Lecky, *History of Ireland*, vol. 1, 1–14.   [8] Lecky, *History of Ireland*, vol. 1, 10, 12.
[9] Lecky, *History of Ireland*, vol. 1, 26, 27, 30, 31.

THE BIRTH AND EARLY DEMISE OF A LIBERAL VIEW   331

explained why 'it needed little knowledge of human nature to perceive that the country was in imminent danger of drifting steadily to a fearful catastrophe'.[10]

Thus, from an early stage in his narrative, Lecky, like Carte, conceded that a rebellion in Ireland had become inevitable because of English injustice. He pronounced that 'the air' having become 'hot feverish [and] charged with rumours' became even more oppressive when the government of the country was entrusted to Sir William Parsons 'one of the most unprincipled and rapacious of the land-jobbers'. The Irish, said Lecky, had reason to consider themselves further circumscribed because 'the Puritanical party' in the English parliament, inspired by fierce anti-popery, 'were rising rapidly to power'. Then he further contended that rebellion against the king in Scotland had the 'double effect' in Ireland of providing an example for the Irish to follow, and occasioning 'panic' that Ireland would be attacked by the Scottish Covenanters. Thus, for Lecky, 'the great Irish rebellion', which eventually broke out on 23 October 1641, was not 'due to any single cause but represented accumulated wrongs and animosities of two generations'.[11] In this, he was at one with Carte with whose interpretation Lecky differed only in considering Wentworth as rapacious as any other English adventurer in Ireland, and in disregarding Carte's contention that Ormond, if he had been given Crown support, could have diverted the on-rushing calamity.[12]

Where he endorsed Carte, Lecky was obviously distancing himself from Froude, but he agreed with Froude that, by the late 1630s, an uprising in Ireland seemed unavoidable. However, where Froude had attributed the rebellion to a perverse desire of the Gaelic Irish to overthrow a civil and Protestant order, Lecky, following Carte, argued that it was the determination of English settlers and officials to find pretexts under the law to gain possession of the lands held by both Gaelic and Old English proprietors which explained both the initial outbreak of rebellion in Ulster and its spread throughout the country. When it came to considering the religious dimension to the revolt, Froude had attributed this to the progress made by militant Catholicism in Ireland, whereas Lecky contended that it was the articulation of anti-Catholic sentiment by radicals in the English parliament that introduced a religious aspect to an insurrection that was essentially about land.[13] Thus, for Lecky, 'in general the rebellion out of Ulster was a defensive religious war entered into for the purpose of securing a toleration and ultimately an establishment of the religion of the Irish people', whereas within Ulster 'the rebellion assumed a wholly distinct character and was speedily disgraced by crimes'. This, he contended in a patrician tone, was no less than what one would expect when an 'undisciplined rising of men in a very low stage of

---

[10] Lecky, *History of Ireland*, vol. 1, 23, 26.   [11] Lecky, *History of Ireland*, vol. 1, 39, 41, 42.
[12] On Carte's interpretation of this same episode see Chapter 5.
[13] On Froude's interpretation of this same episode see Chapter 9.

332 IMAGINING IRELAND'S PASTS

civilization' indulged in acts of 'private vengeance [and] atrocious murders' because of pent-up grievances over land.[14]

These atrocities were, Lecky acknowledged, 'both numerous and horrible', but had been 'grossly, absurdly and mendaciously exaggerated' by contemporary Protestant actors, especially John Temple and Henry Jones, to sustain their case that the Irish in 1641 had engaged in a 'pre-mediated massacre' of the Protestant population of the country. Lecky adjudged this proposition to be 'entirely untrue' since it relied on citation from the 1641 depositions which, without examining any besides those cited by Temple and Jones, he declared unreliable as evidence because 'hearsay evidence of the loosest kind [had been] freely admitted' at the time of their compilation. Therefore, while Lecky considered Temple's *History of the Rebellion* to be the most persuasive contemporary Protestant report of what had happened in 1641, he condemned it as 'a party pamphlet by an exceedingly unscrupulous man, who had the strongest interest in exaggerating to the utmost the crimes that were committed', and 'magnified' what had occurred 'to the dimensions of St. Bartholomew'.[15]

Once he had reached the conclusion that it was 'absolutely untrue that the rebellion of 1641 broke out with an attempted general massacre' of the Protestant population, Lecky proceeded to argue that the ensuing war was one of 'a desperate agrarian character' where the cruelties of the English contrasted sharply with the occasionally restrained, and even humane, behaviour of the Irish, until the Parliamentary forces led by Oliver Cromwell imposed a peace through tyranny. In his account of this campaign, Lecky described the Cromwellian slaughter at Drogheda, but, even more emotionally, the release of 'slave dealers...upon the land' which had resulted, he claimed, in 'many hundreds of boys and marriageable girls, guilty of no offence whatever, [being] torn away from their country, shipped to Barbados and sold as slaves' where they became victims of the 'planters' lusts'. The horror of these events, said Lecky, meant that even to his own time 'the name of Cromwell acts as a spell upon the Irish mind, and [had] a powerful and living influence in sustaining the hatred both of England and Protestantism'.[16] This, he believed, was because Cromwell's military victory was followed by the Cromwellian settlement, which in turn was largely endorsed by the Restoration settlement. The dispossessed Irish, according to Lecky, were thereafter left 'poor, broken, miserable and friendless...aliens in nationality and Papists in religion'. Lecky, taking his cue from Carte, believed that at the time of the Restoration the

---

[14] Lecky, *History of Ireland*, vol. 1, 45, 46, 60; Wyatt, in 'Froude, Lecky, and the "humblest Irishman"', alludes to the similarity between the arguments of Lecky and Froude. I concede her point that each looked on Irish people and their behaviour with disdain, but I am drawing attention here to fundamental differences in the historical interpretations of the two authors.

[15] Lecky, *History of Ireland*, vol. 1, 45–6, 60–1, 72, 75, 77. For an analysis of Temple's *History* see Chapter 4.

[16] Lecky, *History of Ireland*, vol. 1, 81, 82, 89, 102–5.

THE BIRTH AND EARLY DEMISE OF A LIBERAL VIEW   333

defeated Irish had 'managed their cause with little skill' because they had alienated the duke of Ormond who might have assisted them. However, Lecky believed that even an intervention by Ormond would have been no more than ameliorative. Therefore he stood by his conclusion, which accorded with that of Prendergast, that 'the Cromwellian settlement [was] the foundation of that deep and lasting division between the proprietary and the tenants which [he considered to be] the chief cause of the political and social evils of Ireland'.[17]

For Lecky therefore, the key to understanding the Ireland of his own generation lay in the history of that country during the sixteenth and the seventeenth centuries. It is clear, given the respect that was accorded to Lecky's opinions in both England and Ireland, that all historians who wished to be considered balanced and impartial should shape their narratives to comply with the interpretation he had put forward. Thus, as we noted in the sequence of county histories discussed in Chapter 10, authors who were Unionist and/or socially conservative by conviction were careful when writing the histories of their particular counties to cling to the template for the writing of Ireland's history that Lecky had provided. However, as we shall see Catholic-nationalist historians seemed indifferent to what he had written and seemed more concerned to win popular endorsement for their point of view at the local level than to appear balanced and impartial. Thus, as we shall see in our discussion of the alternative histories for Counties Sligo and Clare that were published in rapid response to the Unionist histories of those two counties discussed in Chapter 10, their authors seemed almost to derive pleasure from defying the methods and constraints encouraged by Lecky. This may have been because the texts they were determined to discredit had been presented in the cautious liberal mode favoured by Lecky, and because, as Catholic priests, they wanted publicly to show disrespect for Lecky whose opinions were known to be anti-clerical as well as liberal.

11.3 Archdeacon Terence O'Rorke and a Catholic History for County Sligo

We noted in the case of County Sligo that W.G. Wood-Martin had composed a narrative that represented the landowners of the county as benevolent, paternalistic people dedicated to advancing the welfare of the entire community. He further suggested that the county's population usually recognized the commitment of these proprietors to place and community, other than when the people were pressurized by external agents, usually Catholic clergy, to withhold the allegiance due to their social betters.

---

[17] Lecky, *History of Ireland*, vol. 1, 112, 107–9, 106.

334   IMAGINING IRELAND'S PASTS

This interpretation of Sligo's history was challenged emphatically by Archdeacon Terence O'Rorke (1819–1907), parish priest of the united parishes of Ballisodare and Kilvarnet, in an alternative two-volume *History of Sligo: Town and County*.[18] This priest was so irate at what he read in Wood-Martin's first two volumes that he rushed his book into print in 1890, two years before Wood-Martin was able to publish the third of his contemplated three-volume history.[19] O'Rorke's family ran a bakery in the town of Collooney in the parish of Ballisodare, and they could afford to support his seminary study in Maynooth, after which he became a Professor in the Irish College in Paris, 1847–54. After his return to pastoral duties in Ireland, O'Rorke followed the injunction of P.F. Moran that he should adopt history as a medium through which he might promote a deeper attachment to Catholicism among the population. This deference to Moran did not, as it transpired, serve O'Rorke's career advancement because, in 1870, O'Rorke's name had no sooner been put forward by the priests of his diocese to become the next bishop of the diocese of Achonry than P.F. Moran articulated his opposition to his elevation. Moran, as was usually the case also with Cullen, is likely to have wanted the position for somebody trained in Rome, but he may have been influenced also by a rumour that O'Rorke had once fathered a child. The resulting disappointment did not diminish O'Rorke's scholarly commitment, and his parish history of Ballysadare and Kilvarnet, published in 1878, earned him election the following year as a Member of the Royal Irish Academy.[20]

In his preface to this parish history, O'Rorke contrasted his accomplishment with the simpler task of writing a county history which, he believed, involved no more than 'extracting' from the 'published histories of Ireland and other books' those 'numerous passages' that appertained to the county in question, and 'recasting them, and arranging them in chronological sequence, adding here and there a little local colouring and description'. What emerged from such an exercise would not, he pronounced, be 'original and profound, but far from being, for all that, devoid of interest for the run of readers'.[21]

These remarks suggest that O'Rorke, in 1878, looked with disdain on such derivative work, whereas with his parish history he believed himself to be adding to existing knowledge by drawing on fresh sources concerning the parish that was 'at once his native place and his ecclesiastical charge'. He considered himself eminently equipped for the task since he was 'perfectly free from party and sectarian bias' and was therefore capable of showing 'the same impartiality

---

[18] For a biographical note on O'Rorke see that by Martin Timoney, *Dictionary of Irish Biography*, vol. 7, 884–5.

[19] T. O'Rorke, D.D., M.R.I.A., *The History of Sligo: Town and County*, 2 vols. (Dublin, 1890).

[20] Timoney, biographical note; Archdeacon Terence O'Rorke, *History, Antiquities and Present State of the Parishes of Ballysadare and Kilvarnet in the County of Sligo with notices of the O'Haras, the Coopers, the Percevals and other local families* (Dublin, 1878).

[21] O'Rorke, *History, Antiquities and Present State*, Preface.

THE BIRTH AND EARLY DEMISE OF A LIBERAL VIEW   335

towards Catholics and Protestants, towards high and low'. He was satisfied that others shared this view of him both because those sections of his parish history that had previously appeared in local newspapers had been well received, and because he had been welcomed into their houses at Annaghmore and Markree by their respective proprietors, Mr O'Hara and Colonel Cooper. More significantly, he boasted, these two principal Protestant landowners in the parish had given him 'access to family papers'.[22]

O'Rorke abandoned his professed disregard for county history once Wood-Martin's volumes began to appear and he rushed to prepare a counter view since Wood-Martin's work 'altogether fail[ed] to justify its title'. He also objected to Wood-Martin's history on a personal level because, in contravention to 'the usages of literary courtesy', it had failed to make any acknowledgement of O'Rorke's parish history.[23] As his county history proceeded, it became clear that O'Rorke's unstated objection to what Wood-Martin had written was that he had adapted his history of the county to fit a modified Protestant grand narrative of Ireland's history. O'Rorke, therefore, believed himself to be setting the record straight, possibly to prevent Catholic souls being led astray by Wood-Martin's deception.

Because his principal concern was to refute what Wood-Martin had had to say of Sligo's history, O'Rorke followed the same chronology as his adversary. Here, he conceded that Wood-Martin, who was acknowledged to be an accomplished archaeologist, had actually added to what was known of the antiquities of the county. When it came to history, however, O'Rorke offered an altogether more benign view of Gaelic institutional life than Wood-Martin had done, and he was effusive in his praise of the Christian life that had flourished in the county throughout the medieval centuries, notwithstanding the disturbances occasioned by the Viking invasions and the Anglo-Norman conquest. For him these glorious days ended dramatically with the Reformation and the associated Tudor Conquest of Ireland in the course of which the native proprietors were either defrauded of their lands or, as was the case with the O'Haras, complied with the wishes of the state in all matters, including in religion. O'Rorke had already accounted for this defection in his parish history where he had pronounced that 'no royal favour was beyond the reach of one of the old Irish gentry who had renounced the faith of his forefathers'.[24] For O'Rorke, unlike Wood-Martin, the establishment of Sligo as a county marked nothing worthy of note besides the arrival there of rapacious English Protestant landowners who introduced a cohort of Protestant clergy who were 'hypocrites, drunkards, know-nothings, mammonites, simonians' who

---

[22] O'Rorke, *History, Antiquities and Present State*, Preface.
[23] O'Rorke, *History of Sligo*, xx–xxi.
[24] O'Rorke, *History, Antiquities and Present State*, 237. For a more recent appraisal of this conversion see Thomas Bartlett, 'The O'Haras of Annaghmore c1600– c1800: Survival and Revival', *Irish Economic and Social History*, vol. 9 (1982), 34–52.

336 IMAGINING IRELAND'S PASTS

became 'the curse of religion while pretending to be its ministers'.[25] O'Rorke challenged Wood-Martin's contention that several of the Protestant landed families of Sligo predated the arrival of Cromwell, and cited John Prendergast's calculations that there were no more than 100 Protestants in County Sligo previous to 1641, after which 481 former soldiers and adventurers secured land there.[26] These, as he had already explained in his parish history, included the Cootes, the Coopers, the Wynnes, and the Joneses for whom 'the sword of Cromwell had cleared the way'.[27]

This appraisal of the transfer of land from Protestant to Catholic and from native to newcomer allowed O'Rorke to speak consistently throughout his volumes of 'the oligarchy of Cromwellian landlords' who had remained 'the virtual rulers of the county for more than two hundred years'.[28] In direct opposition to Wood-Martin, he represented these as having been 'particularly hostile to the people and to the people's religion'. Among the enemies of Catholicism he included several who had been identified as heroes in Wood-Martin's narrative, including Lord Collooney and Richard Coote. O'Rorke was particularly venomous against 'the Jones of Tireragh, so numerous once in the barony that you met them at every turn of the road; so powerful that they could do in the district just as they liked'. This particular animus may be attributed to O'Rorke's belief that a Mr Jones was the unacknowledged author of much of Wood-Martin's history.[29]

One of the few points on which our two historians of Sligo agreed was that, as O'Rorke phrased it, 'if left alone and unprovoked the people of Sligo, without distinction of creed, [were] inclined to live on friendly terms with one another'.[30] However, where Wood-Martin had identified meddling priests as the ones who inflamed passions and introduced disharmony, O'Rorke judged that 'sectarian and party feelings [had] run perhaps higher in [Sligo] than in any other county in Ireland' because of Protestant greed and zeal.[31] Thus, for O'Rorke, the most calamitous moment in the county's history, besides the introduction of the Protestant Reformation, had been the rising of 1641 that, he contended, had been forced upon the Catholic landowners of the county in a vain effort to defend what land they still retained. These defensive actions, he stated, had provided their Protestant enemies with the pretext to defraud them of whatever estates they still possessed, and to persecute their followers because of their religion. In his parish history, O'Rorke had already identified one Sir Frederick Hamilton as the most pernicious of those opponents who, as he represented it, had invaded Sligo from County Leitrim on the pretext that he wished to avenge the supposed murder of

[25] O'Rorke, *History of Sligo*, 309.   [26] O'Rorke, *History of Sligo*, 183.
[27] O'Rorke, *History, Antiquities and Present State*, 323; some of these families had some Irish ancestry as, for example, the Coopers who were descended from the Cornet Cooper who had married Máire Rua MacMahon O'Brien on whom see below 344, and note 60.
[28] O'Rorke, *History of Sligo*, vol. 2, 588.   [29] O'Rorke, *History of Sligo*, 187.
[30] O'Rorke, *History of Sligo*, 583.   [31] O'Rorke, *History of Sligo*, xxiii.

THE BIRTH AND EARLY DEMISE OF A LIBERAL VIEW 337

Protestants in Sligo town by the insurgents of 1641. Hamilton's 'memory' in Sligo, averred O'Rorke, was as 'odious' as 'that of Cromwell in Drogheda and Wexford', and he further claimed that in an era that was 'prolific in men of blood and iron such as Cromwell, the two Cootes, Sir William Cole, Lord Inchiquin etc', there was none with 'a heart more corrupt and sanguinary than that of this Sir Frederick'.[32]

O'Rorke returned to such episodes in his county history because the actions of Hamilton and his associates that had led to the dispossession of the traditional landowners of County Sligo, had been justified by Wood-Martin on the grounds that Catholics had been the aggressors in Sligo in 1641—a proposition that Wood-Martin had sustained by citation from the 1641 depositions. O'Rorke hardly needed to counter this suggestion because in his parish history he had already rejected the depositions as a source of evidence claiming they contained 'more falsehoods and perjuries than can be found in the records of any other proceedings that ever took place on this earth'.[33] While conceding that Catholics had committed some atrocities in Sligo in 1641, O'Rorke—the urbane pastor who had spent seven years in Paris—paraded his knowledge of the world by insisting that any such transgressions were 'slight when compared with atrocities more recent Franco-Prussian, Anglo-Indian, Carlist, Turco-Serbian etc'.[34] Thus, for O'Rorke, the principal reason for condemning Wood-Martin's *History of Sligo* was that he had transposed the traditional Protestant interpretation of the rebellion of 1641 upon the Sligo experience, and used it to justify both the dispossession of Catholic proprietors in the county as part of the Cromwellian confiscation, and the subsequent persecution and degradation of 'the people' of County Sligo on grounds of religion.

It is unsurprising in the light of this interpretation that those in the seventeenth and eighteenth centuries who had been heroes for Wood-Martin became villains for O'Rorke, and the reverse was the case when it came to the nineteenth century. Thus where Wood-Martin had identified the election of 1822, in which the Catholic bishop of Killala had encouraged priests to intervene, as the election that had brought an end to political civility, O'Rorke celebrated it as 'the first County Sligo election in which priests took an active part for 40 shilling freeholders'.[35] Then, as he praised Catholic priests for becoming politically engaged, O'Rorke, with a hint of irony, congratulated the 'rectors of the late Established Church' for having achieved 'a great religious advance' by their 'devotion to clerical duty' as compared with their predecessors of even 'eighty or ninety years' previously who, 'like Martha in the Gospel', had been 'troubled about many things' of a secular

---

[32] O'Rorke, *History, Antiquities and Present State*, 31.
[33] O'Rorke, *History, Antiquities and Present State*, 63.
[34] O'Rorke, *History, Antiquities and Present State*, 331.   [35] O'Rorke, *History of Sligo*, 370.

338   IMAGINING IRELAND'S PASTS

nature.[36] O'Rorke also looked to the future with confidence because at the time he was writing 'most of the Cromwellian families [had] disappeared from the county'.[37] This enabled him to describe with benign condescension how the 'young ladies of the first families' that had remained in the county now occupied themselves with charitable work, and who, together with the young men, were active in promoting concerts, lectures, debates, and bazaars. Even then, he cautioned that 'sectarian feeling' might be aroused through such seemingly innocuous pursuits since 'the subjects which are more commonly chosen [for debate were] St Patrick, the Armada, the Inquisition, Cromwell, Luther [and] the Reformation'.[38]

This brief summary indicates that O'Rorke was concerned not so much to add to existing knowledge about Sligo's history as to counter the interpretation that had been put forward by Wood-Martin. As he did so, O'Rorke pursued his narrative from the moment when 'the people of Sligo', by which he meant the Catholic population, had been unjustly deprived of their land and persecuted for their beliefs, until these travesties had begun to be reversed in relatively recent times. The shape and pace of his narrative was, as I have suggested, determined by Wood-Martin's history to which O'Rorke's account became a deliberate counter narrative. While O'Rorke loudly condemned some sources that Wood-Martin had used (most vociferously the 1641 depositions) he himself deployed few new sources besides 'memory', by which he meant Catholic popular memory, which he seemed to consider infallible. That his work fell short of the standards that would have been expected in England of a county history, especially in its failure to use administrative records compiled at a county level, was a matter of indifference to O'Rorke, since his purpose was to remind the Catholic community in Sligo of what their ancestors had suffered for their faith, and to prove that the Protestants there had, from the outset, been a foreign, malign, and persecuting presence whose era of dominance had come to an end. As such, it ran in direct opposition to the agenda of liberals who wished to acknowledge that all elements of the community had contributed to shaping a shared society.

11.4 Canon Patrick White: A Catholic-Nationalist Historian of County Clare

If we consider Terence O'Rorke's *History of Sligo* to be reactive and defiant, the book by Canon Patrick White (1836–1906) entitled The *History of Clare and the Dalcassian Clans of Tipperary, Limerick and Galway*, published in 1893 (the same year that James Frost launched his *History of Clare*), falls into the same category.

---

[36] O'Rorke, *History of Sligo*, 309.   [37] O'Rorke, *History of Sligo*, 187.
[38] O'Rorke, *History of Sligo*, 522.

THE BIRTH AND EARLY DEMISE OF A LIBERAL VIEW 339

However, it was much more than a mere rejoinder to what Frost had written because White proceeded beyond the criticism of the work of others to promote an interpretation based on evidence of his own choosing and that brought the story down to his own time.[39] White's criticism of the work of James Frost was oblique rather than confrontational and then principally because Frost, a landowner but also a Catholic, had drawn uncritically upon sources that had been printed as appendices to the *History of the Diocese of Killaloe*, published in 1878 by Canon Philip Dwyer.[40] If Dwyer bore the same ecclesiastical title as White the two did not belong to the same church, with Philip Dwyer being a Canon of the Church of Ireland Diocese of Killaloe and Vicar of the Parish of Drumcliffe (which included the county town of Ennis), whereas Patrick White was a Canon of the Catholic diocese of Killaloe and Parish Priest of Kilrush when he was writing his county history. White came from a prosperous farming family in Tulla in east Clare, had attended seminary in Maynooth, and had done most of his parish duty in Ennis and then in west Clare. There, he had been an active supporter of the Land League, especially while he served as Parish Priest of Miltown Malbay.[41] That Dwyer rather than Frost was White's principal target of attack is suggested by the cumbersome subtitle White chose for what was essentially a history of County Clare. The only logical explanation for his subtitle is that the Church of Ireland Diocese of Killaloe, of which Dwyer had written, incorporated the dioceses of Kilfenora and Kilmacduagh, and therefore included part of south County Galway and north County Clare as well as those areas of Counties Clare, Tipperary, Offaly, and Limerick that were included within the diocesan boundaries set by both churches.[42] In practice, the subtitle proved irrelevant because both Canons Dwyer and White were concerned essentially with tracing the course of events in County Clare. Therefore, in so far as White's reference to 'the Dalcassian clans' retained any significance, it was to suggest that the people of whom he wrote were descended from the ruling families of the Dál gCais who had dominated the lordship of Thomond before the greater part of that former lordship was designated as County Clare in 1580.[43] White used his

[39] Canon Patrick White, P.P., V.G., *The History of Clare and the Dalcassian Clans of Tipperary, Limerick and Galway* (Dublin, 1893).

[40] Dwyer, *The Diocese of Killaloe, from the Reformation to the Close of the Eighteenth Century*; despite its title Dwyer's narrative extended only to the early eighteenth century as was the case also with Frost's history of Clare.

[41] The career progression and political activities of Patrick White may be traced in Ignatius Murphy, *The Diocese of Killaloe, 1850–1904* (Dublin, 1995); esp. 205, 232, 251, 285, 289–300, 327, 340, 387, 389. White was Parish Priest of Kilrush with the ecclesiastical title of Canon when he was writing his history, but was already Parish Priest of Nenagh in County Tipperary when it was published in 1893. There, he was elevated to becoming Dean of the Catholic Diocese of Killaloe, which explains why the late Monsignor Murphy refers to him as Dean White.

[42] In Catholic Church reorganization of the nineteenth century the dioceses of Kilfenora and Kilmacduagh had been incorporated within a new Galway diocese.

[43] White, *History of Clare*, 20.

340   IMAGINING IRELAND'S PASTS

subtitle also to indicate that, following the example of P.F. Moran, he was more concerned with people than with place and that the objects of his attention were those both 'at home and abroad' descended from the original inhabitants of Thomond who constituted a 'people [who were] literally one family, bonded together by the well-defined ties of ancient blood and historic descent'.[44] As his narrative proceeded, it became clear that White considered a commonly shared Catholicism to be an even more potent bonding agent for his 'people'. He also made it apparent that he had no tolerance of the deferential social attitude encouraged by James Frost, Mary Hickson, and Wood-Martin and for which even Archdeacon O'Rorke in his history of Sligo had shown some lingering respect.

White's account was therefore an unapologetically Catholic-nationalist interpretation of the history of Clare that he intended as a replacement for what he obviously regarded as the Protestant apologia promulgated by Canon Dwyer that had been partly adopted by Frost. However, he intended that this vigorous history of his county would also spur the Catholic population of County Clare to improve their present condition after they had reflected on how their ancestors had overcome the vicissitudes that had beset them.

White began, as did all authors of county histories, with a description of the geography of County Clare, based both on his own observations, as well as the work published by O'Donovan and O'Curry under the auspices of the Ordnance Survey of the county. The archaeological evidence assured him that 'for many centuries before the introduction of Christianity' to the area that would later become County Clare, the Milesians and their descendants had fashioned 'a civilized government and a homogenous free people' superior to any other 'in Northern and Central Europe' because they 'had learned to substitute law for mere force'.[45] The 'one great blot' on this civilization, according to White, was that human sacrifice was practised in religious ceremonies, which, White believed, only came to an end when St Patrick brought Christianity to Ireland, and St Senan, his disciple, had preached the Christian message in the area that would later become County Clare.[46] The Christian society that flourished thereafter persisted until it was disturbed by the 'sacrilege' and 'unholy work' perpetrated by Viking invaders whose 'desecration' of the religious foundation of St Senan on Scattery Island, in the river Shannon, was later avenged by Brian Boroimhe at the battle of Clontarf (1014) in which 'some will see the hand of Providence'.[47] White then described the arrival in Ireland of King Henry II and 'the English enemy' who extracted 'mock submissions' from several Irish chieftains in Ireland including the O'Briens of Thomond.[48]

---

[44] White, *History of Clare*, Title page and Dedication.   [45] White, *History of Clare*, 15.
[46] White, *History of Clare*, 25–6.   [47] White, *History of Clare*, 7, 43–7.
[48] White, *History of Clare*, 130, 153.

THE BIRTH AND EARLY DEMISE OF A LIBERAL VIEW   341

White considered that such submissions lacked moral authority, but, for him, worse followed in 1537 when an Irish parliament 'consisting merely of the creatures of King Henry VIII' adopted that monarch's religious agenda for Ireland. The consequence for Clare was that, in 1543, the ruling O'Brien surrendered his 'ancient dignity of Prince of Thomond' in favour of an English title. This, according to White, was part of a more general government 'policy' of extending Crown authority in the country by 'bribing the chiefs with the plunder of the clans'.[49]

What was happening in Ireland and in Clare was, as White saw it, but one dimension of 'a complete revolution in the religious and political life of Europe' that began to impact upon Clare in 1569 when the first Protestants settled in the county. This, he said, had persuaded the papacy in 1571 to appoint Malachy O'Moloney as bishop of Killaloe to counter the activity of Protestants. O'Moloney's work, according to White, was hindered by 'the notorious Miler McGrath, a member of the Fermanagh family, [who] appeared in Thomond as Elizabeth's Archbishop of Cashel', with supervisory authority over the diocese of Killaloe.[50] However, the ultimate tragedy in the eyes of White, was that 'the degenerate O'Brien of that day' betrayed his clan because, after but 'a fitful opposition' to 'the English invaders', he 'surrendered his strong places' in the county, and 'sent his son Donogh to the English court as a hostage for his future good behaviour and to receive an English and Protestant education'.[51]

This defection of the ruling O'Brien, who had been installed as earl of Thomond, and the defection also of others of their kin, explained for White why when some ships of the Spanish Armada were wrecked off the coast of County Clare in 1588, Sir Turlough O'Brien of Ennistymon tracked down and killed the survivors. The general switch of allegiance by the O'Briens meant also that when 'the lords of Ulster', aided by Spain, challenged the authority of Queen Elizabeth, the earl of Thomond joined 'the English in the attack on the Northern Princes', leaving Tadhg Caoch Mac Mahon as 'the only one of note from Clare' who fought 'on the Irish side' at 'the disastrous defeat at Kinsale'.[52]

The success of English arms and the refusal of King James VI and I to countenance a restoration of Catholicism to Ireland's towns, left the country (and the county), White claimed, open to exploitation by Protestant clergy and by adventurers 'taken from the lowest class in English and Scottish towns and cities'.[53] White contended that the exploitation and injustices that followed meant that 'if ever a revolt was justified in any country it was that of 1641 in Ireland'.[54] He was aware that the Catholic onslaught upon Protestant settlers associated with that insurrection had extended to County Clare, and that the Protestant residents in Clare, who had survived the attack, had given testimony of their experiences

---

[49] White, *History of Clare*, 174–6.   [50] White, *History of Clare*, 187–8.
[51] White, *History of Clare*, 186–7, 191, 193.   [52] White, *History of Clare*, 220–1.
[53] White, *History of Clare*, 243.   [54] White, *History of Clare*, 244.

342   IMAGINING IRELAND'S PASTS

that had been recorded within the 1641 depositions. Those depositions relating to County Clare had been printed in Canon Dwyer's work and cited respectfully by James Frost. For White, however, as had been the case of O'Rorke in relation to the depositions for County Sligo, these did not constitute credible evidence because 'a little careful enquiry' had disclosed 'the fact that they were, for the most part, bold efforts of the imagination'.[55]

White's dismissal of the principal source cited to sustain the Protestant contention that they had been attacked by their Catholic neighbours provided him with the latitude to salute those from Clare who, he could now say, had joined the Confederate army for the positive purpose of defending their faith and their inheritances from those he represented as opportunistic Protestant zealots from England who would have deprived them of both. This gave him the opportunity also to admire how Archbishop Rinuccini, the papal nuncio, had supported those from Clare who had laid siege to Bunratty Castle, where 'he went into the trenches', to 'encourage on the men' by 'sharing their danger'. White claimed that the early success of the Confederate troops from the county meant that by 'the summer of 1646 Clare had not so much as an openly hostile foot on her soil'. This proved but a brief respite, according to White, because Ormond, Cromwell, and Ireton succeeded in reversing all that had been achieved. More degrading, in White's eyes, was that the 'exploits' on the English side of 'a Clareman', Morogh O'Brien, baron and later earl of Inchiquin, 'secured him the unenviable title of Morrogh na Thothaine—Morogh of the burnings'.[56]

White detailed Inchiquin's lineage, his association through marriage with the St Leger family in County Cork, and his switching of sides during the course of the conflict until Cromwell finally 'pushed him out of public life in Ireland'. He then condemned this most 'savage' and 'bitter' 'anti-Irishman' for his action as President of Munster in taking Cahir by treachery and then Cashel by force. In Cashel, claimed White, repeating what P.F. Moran had described several decades previously, Inchiquin 'literally butchered without mercy by fire and sword in the sacred sanctuary... about three thousand men, women and children in and about the cathedral of Cashel', including 'twenty priests' whose 'blood bespattered the altars upon which they had offered the Holy Sacrifice'.[57] White so exhausted his vocabulary of denigration on Inchiquin that all he could say in denunciation of Cromwell was that even the 'cruel, and savage and sanguinary... exploits' of Inchiquin paled by comparison with 'the ruthless deeds' of that 'psalm singing apostle of the Reformation'.[58]

This brought White to discuss the promotion in the county of a 'second great confiscation' when many of the proprietors in the county were dispossessed, and when Catholic families were 'transplanted' from extensive estates in other

---

[55] White, *History of Clare*, 244–7, quotation 247.   [56] White, *History of Clare*, 255.
[57] White, *History of Clare*, 256.   [58] White, *History of Clare*, 258.

THE BIRTH AND EARLY DEMISE OF A LIBERAL VIEW   343

counties in Ireland, and in Clare itself, on to small holdings of poor quality land in County Clare. Such action, according to White, was accompanied by the expulsion from the county of those priests who still ministered there in an effort to 'starve out Catholicism for want of pastors in Clare and Connacht'. The success of Cromwell also caused Catholic fighting men to become exiles on the European Continent in what White termed the 'first flight of the Wild Geese from Clare'. Their departure, he claimed, triggered 'the rush for plunder' in which a great number of Protestants secured estates in the county that would remain in the hands of their descendants into the 1890s. The only significant native proprietors who escaped losing their property, according to White, were 'the chief families of the O'Briens—notably the earl of Thomond, the earl of Inchiquin and the Dromoland O'Briens', an achievement that he found unsurprising given 'their well known temporizing policy'.[59] To authenticate this general castigation of the O'Brien dynasty, White recounted the success of Máire Rua MacMahon, the widow of Conor O'Brien of Lemenagh and Dromoland, in securing for her son the property that should have fallen into state hands because of the death of her husband when fighting in Crown service as a Catholic Confederate. She recovered the land, claimed White, by marrying Cornet Cooper, a Cromwellian officer, after she had ridden to Limerick to seek out General Ludlow with the offer that she would become the wife of any officer of Ludlow's choosing provided he would exempt the O'Brien property from confiscation.[60]

White considered that the Cromwellian disruption marked the ultimate break with the past in County Clare since, in his view, the wealth and influence of Catholics continued to be eroded during the reign of Charles II, and the persecution of Catholic clergy persisted. Therefore, for White, 'all the elements for strife' already existed in the 1680s, which explained why those few Catholic proprietors who had survived in Clare supported the Catholic King James II when William of Orange ousted him from his throne. It was then that Daniel O'Brien, Viscount Clare, whom White considered 'the only honourable man among the old aristocracy', formed his regiment of dragoons (memorialized, as we may recall, by Thomas Davis as Clare's dragoons, and mentioned respectfully by Mary Hickson) to support King James. The ultimate defeat of the Jacobite cause meant that those proprietors who had enlisted in Lord Clare's regiment were deprived of their estates when the Williamite government proceeded with what White described as the third confiscation of Clare property. Defeat led also to the departure from the county of 'Clare's dragoons' together with 'their wives,

[59] White, *History of Clare*, 293; the Wild Geese in Irish nationalist memory were those officers and soldiers who became exiles in the 1690s after the defeat of the Jacobite cause; White was here translating that backwards in time to the 1650s.

[60] White, *History of Clare*, 262; the O'Brien lands in question passed on to the son of Máire Rua by Conor O'Brien, who established his principal residence at Dromoland. Then the children of Máire Rua by Cornet Cooper established their principal estate at Markree in County Sligo.

344 IMAGINING IRELAND'S PASTS

their children, their families', the flouting by the government of the terms of surrender agreed upon at Limerick, and to the enactment of the Penal Laws which led to the 'ferocious, savage religious and civil persecution of the defeated Irish Catholics'. This enactment, in White's opinion, left England with 'a black record on the face of its history' such as was borne by 'no other country claiming to be regarded as civilized—Russia alone hardly excepted'.[61]

Canon White had, by then, reached the point at which the respective narratives of James White and Canon Philip Dwyer had tapered off. This provided him with the opportunity to press home his argument that it was the priests of County Clare who had suffered most gravely under the Penal Laws, as they had also in Cromwellian times. This sustained his further argument that the survival of Catholicism in the county was due principally to the endeavours of priests during trying times, rather than to the patronage of Catholic landowners, as Frost had contended. In doing so he did not discount the hardships suffered by Catholic proprietors during that era, and he especially lamented that Catholics had been precluded by the Penal Laws from bidding in 1712 for some of the County Clare estates of the earl of Thomond, who had been forced by financial difficulties to put his lands in the county up for auction. Some of the purchasers were already minor proprietors in Clare, who now became landlords of consequence whose descendants would dominate political life in the county until what White referred to as 'the present day'. White thought it 'fair' to mention that not all of these new proprietors had dealt 'harshly with those who had to accept tenancies from them', but his listing of their names—Ivers, Burtons, Gores, Westbys, MacDonnells, Westrops, Stackpools, Henns, Scots, Gabbetts' etc.—revealed that they were not members of the Dalcassian clans whose history he was narrating.[62]

Another disagreeable aspect to the application of the Penal Laws in the secular sphere, according to White, was that they had enabled unscrupulous Catholics to attain worldly success by the simple device of publicly converting to the Church of Ireland. White considered one of the most egregious of such apostates to be the father of John Fitzgibbon, 'a man of obscure family', who, after he had renounced his faith, rose to prominence through the practice of the law. Then, in White's opinion, the son who rose to become Lord Chancellor of Ireland, 1789–1802, became guilty also of 'treason to his country' because of the role he had played in securing for the government the passage of the Act of Union through the Irish parliament and was 'made earl of Clare for his treachery'.[63]

If the passing of the Act of Union was considered by many Catholics in Clare, as in Ireland generally, to represent the low point in their history, White celebrated

---

[61] White, *History of Clare*, 301.   [62] White, *History of Clare*, 295, 20.

[63] White, *History of Clare*, 328; the Fitzgibbon family had, in fact, no connection with County Clare besides the title granted to John Fitzgibbon; the Lord Chancellor himself had been born in Dublin and his father, who had converted to the Church of Ireland, had been born in County Limerick.

THE BIRTH AND EARLY DEMISE OF A LIBERAL VIEW   345

the new dawn that followed when Daniel O'Connell, backed by 'the priests and the people', and 'in tones of thunder', commenced his campaign in County Clare to secure the political and religious emancipation of Ireland's Catholic people. By electing O'Connell to Westminster, pronounced White, 'Clare had killed with one blow Protestant Ascendancy and Catholic Association'.[64] White was also encouraged because a reasonable percentage of the Catholic people of Clare had survived the Great Famine, and he rejoiced because, 'after the famine years', and with support from priests 'preaching to them in their own Irish language', they had, resisted 'the vigorous and persevering attempt made to proselytize' them. Then, as he approached his own time, he enthused because 'the descendants of the Dalcassian clans' who had persisted in the county had already recovered much of the land that, in past centuries, had fallen into Protestant possession by what he considered unjust means.[65]

As White described the role played by priests in encouraging Catholic forty-shilling freeholders to cast their votes in favour of O'Connell and against the wishes of their landlords, he persistently represented the landowners of Clare, most of them Protestant, as a parasitic presence, whose inadequacy as supposed defenders of their communities had been exposed during the years of the Great Famine. On this he provided some searing insight, based on what older parish priests of his acquaintance had told him, of the way in which priests they had known had put their own lives at risk when ministering to those suffering from hunger and disease.[66]

Such memories substantiated White's case that priests, not landowners, were the natural trustworthy leaders of their communities, and we are left to imagine that it was the example of an earlier generation of priests in supporting O'Connell that had inspired White himself to encourage tenants of his parish to attack landlordism through the agency of the Land League.[67] As he did so, White propagated the trope of many Land Leaguers that the ancestors of the tenants who cultivated the land had been its owners before it had fallen into the possession of landlords. Thus, when commenting on the sufferings endured by those of his parishioners in Miltown Malbay during the near-famine year of 1879, White lamented how 'crowds of decent people' had been left 'clamouring for food on the land which their forefathers owned'. He celebrated, however, that following this humiliation 'the people braced themselves for a final struggle with landlordism'.[68]

---

[64] White, *History of Clare*, 328; White's mention of the Catholic Association reveals his disrespect for the readiness of wealthier Catholics (and he might have had James Frost in mind) to settle for some amelioration in the condition of landed Catholics rather than persist with a demand for full emancipation.

[65] White, *History of Clare*, 6, 333, 365, 375.

[66] Ciarán Ó Murchadha, *Figures in a Famine Landscape* (London, 2016), 125.

[67] Murphy, *The Diocese of Killaloe, 1850–1904*, 232.   [68] White, *History of Clare*, 373.

White made no mention in his history of how he personally had assisted this struggle through his involvement with the Land League, or of his association with Parnell, or of his zealous anti-Parnellite activity following the exposure of Parnell's relationship with the wife of Captain O'Shea. The only hint in his history of his concern over such recent events was his mention of 'the deplorable division caused in the national ranks by the unhappy fall of Mr. Parnell'. However, he expressed confidence that these difficulties would soon be overcome, and he concluded his history by asserting that the people of Clare, as of Ireland generally, were on the point of recovering their 'right to self-government' of which they had been deprived in the sixteenth century.[69] For White therefore there was no longer any distinction between national history and Catholic history since the two had been absorbed into one.

In writing his *History of Clare*, White was less concerned than O'Rorke to appear academic, and he claimed to be doing no more than presenting a 'kind of elementary history for general readers'.[70] This lack of pretension enabled White, more readily than O'Rorke, to transpose to the county level the same narrative that was being unfolded in Catholic grand narratives expounded by other authors in national, parochial, or diocesan contexts. But if White's preference was to write county history, and if his ambition was to reach out to general readers, he was ultimately an exponent of Catholic narrative history the purpose of which, as it was defined as recently as 1991 by Fr. Hugh Fennig, was 'to make priests and people aware of their faith, not only as a gift of God, but as a sacred trust handed down at no small cost from those who tilled the same fields or lived in the same towns...centuries ago'.[71]

White, no less that O'Rorke in writing on County Sligo, was determined to correct the errors expounded by his rival, in this case Canon Dwyer who he believed had been accorded excessive respect by James Frost. White was duty-bound as a priest to ensure that Catholics and Catholicism were never cast in a bad light, but he looked also to the future as he reflected on the past. He boosted morale by explaining to his target audience with enthusiasm and conviction how the commitment of their ancestors to their faith had sustained them through difficult times, and he authenticated this narrative by referring to incidents that he knew were embedded in the popular memory. White was confident that this would be meaningful for his readers because he presupposed that the people of Clare, by which he always meant the Catholic population of the county, consti-tuted a single community, and he prompted them to think of the county in which they lived as a cultural space and not just an administrative unit of British creation. His confidence that he would succeed in this stemmed obviously from

---

[69] White, *History of Clare*, 153, 375.   [70] White, *History of Clare*, Preface.
[71] Foreword by Fr. Hugh Fenning to Ignatius Murphy, *The Diocese of Killaloe in the Eighteenth Century* (Dublin, 1991).

THE BIRTH AND EARLY DEMISE OF A LIBERAL VIEW   347

personal observation as he had been able to travel extensively throughout the county thanks to recent road building and rail construction. He would have been aware also that local newspapers, which in recent decades had begun to address county rather than regional or sectional audiences, were fostering a communal sense of belonging.[72] The fact that he chose to publish a New York edition of his history simultaneously with that published in Dublin suggests that White was aware that emigrant groups in cities in the United States were beginning to organize themselves into county associations and to identify themselves by their county of origin in Ireland.[73] In choosing the county as his unit of study, White was also following the example of Gaelic Athletic Association, founded in 1884, that had made an early decision to establish itself on county as well as parochial foundations.

One advantage of choosing to write of the history of his county rather than the country as a whole was that White, like O'Rorke, could select as the villains and heroes of their narratives those whose misdeeds and acts of heroism he knew would be vivid in local memory. Then, when it came to the nineteenth century, White was able to augment the historical memory of his audience by detailing the endeavours of a new-found hero, Fr. Michael Meehan, who had ministered to the starving and diseased population of west Clare at the height of the Great Famine. Meehan was also a hero for White because he had countered, and ultimately defeated, the proselytizing endeavours of Protestant evangelists, who, with the backing of one Marcus Keane, an estate agent cum landlord, had lured a starving population to attend their churches with the promise of food, and induced them to send their children to mission schools where they could evangelize them.[74] Fr. Meehan, as we learn from Ciarán Ó Murchadha, had been a capable self-publicist. However, White saw merit in seeing to it that the various exploits of which Meehan had boasted would be remembered by posterity because White could authenticate them by reference to conversations that he himself had conducted with priests of an older generation. Here, as elsewhere, White chose to cite oral rather than written evidence possibly because he considered his readers would be more easily persuaded by narrations that were authenticated by trusted witnesses.

While White was adept at deploying memory to identify, and even add to, a modest list of county heroes, he used that skill even more effectively to identify

---

[72] Ó Murchadha, in *Figures in a Famine Landscape*, 9–27, has much to say of the issues and geographic areas covered during the 1840s by the *Clare Journal*, later to be absorbed by the *Clare Champion*. He also discusses the differences between this newspaper and its competitor the *Limerick and Clare Examiner*.

[73] Miriam Nyhan, *The Fifth Province; County Associations in Irish America: A Guide to an Exhibition by Gluckman Ireland House* (New York, 2010); Eileen Sullivan, 'Community in Print: Irish-American Publishers and Readers', *American Journal of Irish Studies*, vol. 8 (2011), 41–76; I am grateful to Dr Marion Casey for drawing my attention to these publications.

[74] Ó Murchadha, *Figures in a Famine Landscape*, 99–135; Murphy, *The Diocese of Killaloe, 1850–1904*, 38–40.

348 IMAGINING IRELAND'S PASTS

the greater numbers to 'whom an evil fame popularly attaches'.[75] As he did so, he offered solace to his readers that while the many villains in his narrative appeared to have prospered materially at the expense of others, they, or their descendants, had suffered humiliation in the longer term. Thus, for example when discussing the Reformation, White considered it 'curious' that the 'descendants' of the 'apostate' Miler McGrath, 'like those of Martin Luther', had reverted to Catholicism and that 'some of them were by Cromwell transplanted into Clare'.[76] In the case of the hated Morogh, earl of Inchiquin, White acknowledged that, notwithstanding his infamous massacre of Catholics at Cashel, he had converted to Catholicism after he had fallen foul of Cromwell in Ireland and was forced to spend an interlude in exile as a Royalist in Continental Europe. White mentioned that Inchiquin had persisted in that faith after he had returned to Ireland and recovered his estates following the Restoration of King Charles II, and that he had 'died a Catholic' in 1673. Speaking as a priest, White had to welcome this conversion and to refrain from speculating if it had proven sufficient to atone for the heinous crimes of Inchiquin's earlier career. However, as a historian, White recounted with relish 'the popular belief' that the relatives of those in Ireland who had suffered at his hands had neither forgotten nor forgiven Inchiquin's past transgressions. This belief, according to White, held that after Inchiquin had been buried 'by his own request' in the Protestant St Mary's Cathedral in Limerick, where his ancestors were interred, 'his body was taken by night and flung into the river by some of the citizens who regarded it as desecrating the holy place'. White considered this story credible, not only because he, like Archdeacon O'Rorke, placed great store on Catholic folk memory but also because an inspection of Inchiquin's tomb that had been conducted in White's own lifetime had found the coffin to be empty.[77] He then explained how further posthumous humiliation awaited Inchiquin because his title failed in the male line in 1741 and reverted to the earl of Thomond in 1800. Even then it 'did not last long', said White, because 'by the death without issue in 1846 of William, Marquis of Thomond, the house of Morogh the Burner was wiped off the face of the earth'.[78] White seemed pleased that a similar indignity had befallen the detested John Fitzgibbon, earl of Clare, because, having left 'no male representative' on his death in 1802, his title also lapsed.[79]

The verve with which Canon White narrated such incidents, his persistence in representing the landowners in the county as intruders who did not belong there, and his optimistic pronouncements that the Catholic tenant farmers would soon displace these landowners socially and politically, combine to show how Patrick White's, *History of Clare and the Dalcassian Clans* represents a new type of county history and a new type also of Catholic-nationalist history. When we evaluate it as

[75] White, *History of Clare*, 295.
[76] White, *History of Clare*, 188.
[77] White, *History of Clare*, 257.
[78] White, *History of Clare*, 257.
[79] White, *History of Clare*, 328.

THE BIRTH AND EARLY DEMISE OF A LIBERAL VIEW 349

Catholic history, we can see that White had followed the advice of P.F. Moran in seeking to demonstrate, this time from the experience of a particular county rather than the country as a whole, what earlier generations of Catholics in Ireland had suffered for their faith. He also followed Moran's prescription in identifying individuals (in this case priests rather than bishops, and from the nineteenth century rather than from the sixteenth and seventeenth centuries) who might be considered as possible candidates for being declared martyrs for the faith. However, unlike Moran who remained aloof from direct involvement in politics during his years in Ireland, White was an interventionist who, from his selective narrative of past events in County Clare, strove with Manichean determination to promote a political as well as a religious awakening both among the Catholic population of rural County Clare and their relatives in exile.[80] However, unlike Moran, White was little interested in issues that did not concern County Clare or Ireland, and he made no mention of the British Empire, which Moran had considered a possible source of employment for Irish Catholics, as well as a potential platform from which to spread the faith throughout the world. The exception for White were those cities in the United States that had offered homes to many exiles from County Clare who he considered to be an integral part of the county community he was defining and addressing. However, once he began to think of exiles in this way, White, unlike Moran, seemed not interested in how they might spread the faith through missionary activity, but to be interested in how they might further political change at home, provided the Catholic Church approved of such change. White was therefore more explicit than Moran, or than O'Rorke for that matter, in stating that his ideal community (in this instance a county rather than a national community) would be exclusively Catholic, which immediately raised the issue of what would become of the Christians of different denominations who still existed within the county at the time he was writing.

White, like O'Rorke, was therefore making no concessions to the acceptance of difference or balance that was being encouraged by Lecky and earlier historians of a more liberal outlook. This is hardly surprising since, as noted, the orthodox Catholic approach to the study of history as this was represented by P.F. Moran was suspicious of, when not openly hostile to, liberal opinion and also of the sources used by secular authors. Therefore, given that the writing of county history had, up to this point, been almost a Protestant preserve, these early Catholic contributors to that genre were depriving those who were Protestant, Unionist, and even liberal, of the only historical safe haven they had previously enjoyed. More importantly, they were demonstrating that history written at the county level could be even more effective vehicles than narratives focused on the

---

[80] White, *History of Clare*, 6.

350 IMAGINING IRELAND'S PASTS

country as a whole to convey the essential Catholic politico-religious message that the county community was coterminous with the Catholic community and that its members would be compensated for that of which their ancestors had been deprived by ensuring that the future would become theirs.

11.5 Hickson's Response to the Exclusivist Turn

Since Terence O'Rorke, in the county history of Sligo published in 1890, and Patrick White, in the county history of Clare published in 1893, each conveyed the unambiguous message that membership of the Catholic Church was a prerequisite to being admitted as a member to a county community, it seemed to follow logically that only Catholics could be considered members of an Irish nation. This message can have taken few people by surprise since authors of Catholic historical interpretations had been trending towards this exclusivist paradigm since the seventeenth century, and had been given renewed vigour when P.F. Moran had revived the writings of David Rothe. Indeed, as noted in Chapter 10, it was to counter what M.F. Cusack had had to say on this subject in 1871 in relation to County Kerry that Mary Agnes Hickson had rushed to get her two-volume *Selections from Old Kerry Records* into print. Hickson's purpose, as we recall, was to reclaim a central and positive role in Kerry's history for the relatively small number of Protestant families who had resided in the county for centuries. And we noted how her most effective weapon in pleading her case was to demonstrate from genealogical data how, over the centuries, many settler families had become intermingled with the longest established families in the county.

Hickson seems to have come to the realization that making her case on the basis of evidence from Kerry alone was not having much impact, especially since County Kerry was considered by many to be exceptional by virtue of its remoteness from Dublin. Therefore, when Hickson set about challenging the growing intolerance she had detected in nationalist, including Catholic-nationalist, historical writing, she decided in her next book, published in 1884, to write of the experience of the country as a whole during the seventeenth century.[81] In this book, *Ireland in the Seventeenth Century*, Hickson, and also Froude who furnished the book with a lengthy preface, developed some of the arguments that Hickson had first expounded in *Selections from Old Kerry Records*. Her purpose she said was to challenge what she described as the 'absurdly romantic and unreal way' in which 'modern writers of the Nationalist or "Home Rule" schools' of historians treated 'the facts of Irish history'.[82]

---

[81] Mary Hickson, *Ireland in the Seventeenth Century*; this two-volume work has a preface by J.A. Froude.

[82] Hickson, *Ireland in the Seventeenth Century*, vol. 1, 40.

One of these facts to which Hickson believed they were not giving sufficient attention was that elite families from different ethnic and denominational lineages had tended over the centuries to intermarry with each other. Hickson believed that what she had already shown in relation to Kerry and neighbouring counties was true for the entire country. One consequence of such interbreeding at the elite level, she asserted, was that 'the Ireland' of her generation was 'the Ireland of the mixed race, as British in blood...as Great Britain itself'.[83] This reality, proclaimed Hickson, meant that all assertions for 'national independence', whether advanced in the seventeenth or in the nineteenth centuries, were no more than 'absurd aspirations' since 'a country so divided by races and clans and creeds...could not be called a nation at all'.[84]

Hickson now contended that interbreeding had not been confined to the elite. In her own case she claimed that she was fully entitled to consider herself Irish because she, like many other Irish-born people who bore 'the most thoroughly Saxon names', were 'generally like [herself] in the first, second, or third degree, of O'Connells, O'Sullivans and other ancient Irish clans, and value that descent highly'.[85] Froude considered that Hickson had a further entitlement to consider herself Irish because, in her writing, she frequently divulged 'her love of native country' as well as 'her love of justice', and, unlike himself, possessed 'no English prejudices'. Moreover, endorsing what she herself had said, Froude pronounced that Hickson was 'the descendant of some of the exiled and transplanted Irish and Anglo-Irish of 1649'.[86]

Hickson, as a historian, thought it important that she be considered Irish because she hoped, or even expected, that such a designation would exempt her from the charge, persistently levelled against Froude, that she lacked empathy for her subject because of English prejudice. This was all the more important to Hickson when she criticized the tendency of her nationalist, and particularly her Catholic-nationalist, adversaries to construct their narratives around 'hero-martyrs' who had given their lives for their 'country' and 'creed'. For the seventeenth century she described as pathetic their efforts to cast Sir Phelim O'Neill in that role since all 'impartial students of Irish history' considered that particular member of the O'Neill family as 'a weak, vain, cruel braggart'. She suggested helpfully that those 'Roman Catholics who desire to make a hero of any of the leaders of the fatal rebellion of 1641, had better choose Owen O'Neill' who 'for all his bigotry' was at least a 'chivalrous and able soldier who made war in an honourable fashion'.[87]

---

[83] Hickson, *Ireland in the Seventeenth Century*, vol. 1, 165–6.
[84] Hickson, *Ireland in the Seventeenth Century*, vol. 1, 101.
[85] Hickson, *Ireland in the Seventeenth Century*, vol. 1, 166.
[86] Hickson, *Ireland in the Seventeenth Century*, Preface by Froude, ix–x.
[87] Hickson, *Ireland in the Seventeenth Century*, vol. 1, 104–5.

352 IMAGINING IRELAND'S PASTS

If Hickson was contemptuous of the proclivity of Catholic-nationalist historians to structure their narratives around heroes—and also anti-heroes—she, according to Froude, remained 'keenly alive to the wrongs which her country [had] suffered at English hands, and on some points [he claimed] she [was] in full sympathy with Irish Nationalism'. While Hickson indeed proved as proficient as any nationalist author at rehearsing such wrongs, she—and Froude also—saw the need to weigh this catalogue of injustice against a list, as Froude put it, of the 'frightful crimes' that 'she firmly believe[d]' were 'committed' by 'many of her countrymen in 1641'. In thus rehabilitating the contention of Protestants that their ancestors had been the principal victims of the disturbances of the mid-seventeenth century, Hickson, with Froude, were challenging nationalist and Catholic authors who now habitually denied that any such attacks had taken place. More significantly, Hickson and her mentor were parting company with Lecky and other liberal authors who had been increasingly inclined to endorse the Catholic-nationalist position.

The matter that was now of greatest concern to Hickson and Froude was that, because of the persuasions of such as Lecky, Prendergast, and Hill, people of liberal disposition in England did not welcome any further historical interrogation of the events of 1641. The problem, as they saw it, was that members of the English public increasingly acknowledged—particularly in the aftermath of the Great Famine—'that they had much to repent in regard to Ireland', and therefore no longer had any desire 'to keep alive painful memories when they trusted and hoped it was needless to do so because ancient enmities between classes and creeds and the two islands were fast dying out'.[88] A further concern of Froude and Hickson was that Catholic-nationalist historians in Ireland, taking advantage of such English pusillanimity, were being emboldened to assert that the Irish in the seventeenth century had not been guilty of any crimes, safe in the knowledge that people of liberal outlook in England would welcome this denial. Such opportunism, complained Hickson, had been carried to the extreme by Charles Gavan Duffy when he had asserted, 'that no massacres of Protestants took place [in 1641, and] that the soldiers in the Irish army "never massacred" one Protestant in cold blood'.[89] But worse, in the view of Froude, was that similar denials were being voiced 'not only' by 'irresponsible agitators', among whom he may have been including Duffy, but also by 'reverend and grave historians, some of whom go so far as to say that there could have been no massacre'.[90]

The 'reverend' historian that Froude had in mind was, almost certainly, George Hill, since Hickson, in the main body of her text, commented disapprovingly on what Hill had had to say in his book of 1877 both of the plantation of Ulster and

[88] Hickson, *Ireland in the Seventeenth Century*, Preface by Froude, vii.
[89] Hickson, *Ireland in the Seventeenth Century*, vol. 2, 240–1.
[90] Hickson, *Ireland in the Seventeenth Century*, Preface by Froude, vi.

of the 1641 rebellion. To counter his arguments Hickson had referred readers back to what James Seaton Reid had had to say on those subjects in his *History of the Presbyterian Church in Ireland*, published initially in 1833 and then republished and expanded upon by W.D. Killen in a fresh edition of 1867. Hickson was particularly offended that Hill had described as unprincipled mercenaries the founders in Ulster of the families of Chichester, Clotworthy, Conway, and Hill, and she countered what Hill had said by drawing attention to Reid's contention, published long before Hill had written, that all such founding figures had been 'worthy persons who afterwards increased and made noble and loyal families where formerly had been nothing but robbing, treason and rebellion'.[91] Hickson valued Reid's text also because it upheld the Protestant trope that what had 'rendered' the province of Ulster 'so remarkable a contrast in point of wealth, intelligence and tranquillity to the other parts of Ireland' was the settlement there in the seventeenth century of significant numbers of Scottish and English Protestants.[92] Reid's book was also admirable in Hickson's eyes because he, following the lead set by Temple in 1646, attributed the outbreak of rebellion in Ulster in 1641 to the actions of Catholic priests who, Reid had reiterated, had deliberately made much of the disruptions occasioned by the plantations to increase the sense of grievance felt by the Irish population of Ulster. Hickson also drew attention to Reid's further allegation that the priests in the seventeenth century had hoped that the outraged Irish would expel and slaughter their unsuspecting Protestant neighbours, and thus open the way for the Catholic Church to recover its lost greatness.

While Hickson, and also Froude, lavished praise on Reid, their ultimate purpose was to use what he had had to say of plantation in Ulster to discredit the work of Hill. Their problem with Hill was that as a Protestant minister (admittedly an unsubscribing Presbyterian divine rather than a clergyman of either the Presbyterian Church of Ireland or of the Church of Ireland) his opinions were being taken seriously even by people of conservative disposition in England. At the same time, as the first librarian of Queen's College, Belfast—one of Ireland's three 'Godless colleges'—Hill's opinions were held in high regard by liberal politicians in Britain who had promoted the colleges against both Catholic and Tory opposition. By setting out to discredit Hill, Hickson, and also Froude, were casting doubt also on the scholarship of Prendergast to whom Hill had deferred as the leading authority on the history of early modern Ireland. Then, by questioning what both authors had written, they hoped to win over Lecky to their way of thinking. This was with the purpose of having a single Protestant interpretation of Ireland's history to counter the exclusivist and simplistic view of

---

[91] John Seaton Reid, *History of the Presbyterian Church in Ireland, comprising the Civil History of the Province of Ulster, from the accession of James the First; a new edition with additional notes* by W.D. Killen, D.D. 3 vols. (Belfast, 1867), 85.

[92] Reid, *History of the Presbyterian Church*, Preface to the first edition, v.

354 IMAGINING IRELAND'S PASTS

Ireland's past and future being promulgated by Catholic-nationalist authors. Thus Lecky's recommendation that well-meaning people should embrace a liberal interpretation of Ireland's past as a means of achieving national reconciliation in the present was not only being ignored by Catholic-nationalist historians who had come to believe that the future would be theirs but was now being considered defeatist by some Protestant authors anxious to make one final thrust to redeem traditional Protestant understanding of Ireland's history during the early modern centuries.

11.6 Conclusion

This chapter commenced with an explanation of how Lecky, not unlike Young Irelanders in the early 1840s, aspired to promote national reconciliation in Ireland through history. In order to advance this objective, he himself composed what he considered to be a balanced view of the past and explained to other historians how they might do likewise. By balance he meant making allowance for the sufferings and injustices that Ireland's Catholic population had suffered at the hands of British intruders before condemning Irish people for the rebellious actions in which some of their number had engaged as they attempted to recover something of what had been taken from them. We had noted in Chapter 10 how the authors of some Unionist county histories had taken guidance from Lecky by presenting narratives of events in Ireland during the 1640s and the 1690s that were more conciliatory than was customarily expected from Unionist authors. This, as noted, was categorically rejected by Catholic authors of county histories whose dual concerns were to challenge the arguments of their Unionist rivals, and to put forward a counter-narrative to demonstrate how Catholics who had been victimized in the sixteenth, seventeenth, and eighteenth centuries were in the process of recovering that which was rightfully theirs.

When it came to treating of what had long since been identified as the contentious events of the seventeenth century, Catholic historians such as P.F. Moran, O'Rorke, and White showed no hesitation about suggesting that it was the cupidity and insensitivity of Protestant settlers that had been entirely responsible for the uprising of 1641, and the conflict that had followed upon it. This meant that, when their narratives shifted from events of the seventeenth and eighteenth centuries to those of their own time and of the future that was being unfolded, they remained at best vague concerning what place would be left to Protestants within a society that they expected would be defined in Catholic-nationalist terms. O'Rorke and White evaded the issue by writing as if their respective counties had been entirely rural, thus suggesting that the problems associated with catering for religious plurality within any given community would evaporate once the break-up of landed estates that was then being promoted by the state had been fully implemented. In so doing these authors turned a blind eye to the larger and more heterogeneous Protestant populations that were becoming a presence of consequence in most sizeable provincial towns in Ireland due both to new commercial activity with which new Protestant immigrants were particularly associated and the more expansive role of the Victorian state that brought some Protestants with particular skills into provincial urban settings. Archdeacon O'Rorke ignored this dimension to life in the case of County Sligo, even when Wood-Martin cited it as proof of the continuing positive contribution that Protestants were making to the county community whose history they both were writing. Similarly, Canon White, in his history of County Clare, ignored recent urban, commercial, and infrastructural developments in the county, even though he had been an active supporter of the West Clare railway that helped establish Ennis as the commercial capital of what previously had been a county that had been economically segmented. By eliding such issues from the historical record, it became easier to imagine how the Catholics in their respective counties might, as a risen people, recover the political influence and property of which, according to both O'Rorke and White, Catholics had been unjustly deprived in the sixteenth and seventeenth centuries.

Such denunciations and prognostications raised understandable anxieties in the minds of Protestants, and it was to encourage resistance to the perceived attempt to marginalize Protestants and Unionists that Hickson, this time assisted and presumably advised by Froude, again took to publishing. She wrote no longer to convince incorrigible Catholic-nationalist authors that their arguments were fallacious but to persuade liberals that their attempts to find some middle ground between two irreconcilable positions were futile. Instead, Hickson hoped through a display of empirical evidence to attract such waverers to join her in presenting one united front against Catholic and nationalist historians who seemed determined to use the past to effect the destruction of Protestants and Unionists.

12

The Failure of the Imagination Concerning Ireland's Pasts

12.1 Introduction

It will have become clear at this juncture that some scholars in each succeeding century became convinced that the historical arguments they were pursuing would prevail over those of their opponents. Such confidence stemmed either from the belief of the authors that their opinions were sustained by evidence that was accessible to all, or because they enjoyed privileged access to information that they considered superior to all other. Those in the late nineteenth century who upheld their arguments by reference to information that was in the public domain seemed more confident than any previous generation of historians that truth would prevail over myth. This was because in Ireland, as in Britain and in several countries in Continental Europe, qualified scholars were being given free access to public archives. Moreover, a summary of the contents of such archives was being made available to the educated public in printed calendars that governments were commissioning and making available in scholarly libraries. The most enduring outcome from this official effort to promote a better understanding of the history of early modern Ireland was the publication from 1860 onward of a series of printed *Calendars of State Papers, Ireland*, treating of the years from 1509 to the close of the reign of Queen Elizabeth.[1] Once this project was under way, the government in 1864 employed John Prendergast, in association with Dr Charles William Russell, a Catholic priest who was president of St Patrick's College, Maynooth, to appraise and edit official documents relating to seventeenth-century Ireland. This second effort resulted in a series of *Calendars of State Papers, Ireland* that offered more generous summaries of documents than had the calendars for the Tudor years.[2]

All scholars, regardless of denominational or political affiliation, welcomed this greater access to official records, although some scholars on the Catholic-nationalist side continued to insist that evidence emanating from British

---

[1] The series begun in 1860 resulted in *Calendar of State Papers relating to Ireland, Henry VIII to Elizabeth* (London, 11 vols., 1860–1912).
[2] C.W. Russell and J.P. Prendergast, eds., *A Report on the Carte Manuscripts in the Bodleian Library* (London, 8 vols., 1871); Russell and Prendergast, eds., *Calendar of State Papers relating to Ireland, 1603–1625* (London, 5 vols., 1872–1880).

Imagining Ireland's Pasts: Early Modern Ireland through the Centuries. Nicholas Canny, Oxford University Press (2021).
© Nicholas Canny. DOI: 10.1093/oso/9780198808961.003.0012

THE FAILURE OF THE IMAGINATION CONCERNING IRELAND'S PASTS   357

government sources should be counterbalanced by documents that represented the views of the vanquished. Catholic historians, as discussed in several chapters, had long been assembling an alternative archive based on salvaged sources from Continental repositories that provided details on the experiences of people in Ireland who had suffered for their faith. More recently, nationalist scholars, including those primarily interested in Irish culture, had taken to editing and even translating into English, surviving material in the Irish language.[3]

Nationalists also began to identify and edit any papers that had survived from the Irish leaders who had spearheaded challenges to the government during the great conflicts of the seventeenth century. The most consequential of such compilations was that made by John T. Gilbert, an esteemed Catholic-nationalist historian, and an acknowledged authority on the history of Dublin City, who in 1879 published a multi-volume collection of 'original and authentic contemporary materials' under the title *Contemporary History of Affairs in Ireland, 1641–52*.[4] In this, Gilbert gave prominence to the anonymous text entitled the 'Aphorismical Discovery of Treasonable Factions' that had been preserved in Protestant hands, and to which occasional reference had been made by previous scholars, including Carte and Leland.[5] Gilbert pronounced that this text had been written in the seventeenth century by 'an Irish Royalist fully in sympathy with his countrymen who, devoted to Charles I, had taken arms for the defence of his [the king's] prerogative, and for the protection, as they alleged, of their own lives, properties and rights against the oppressions and hostile designs of the dominant Puritan faction'. Gilbert did not purport to agree with all that the anonymous author had had to say of how Catholics had become innocent victims of Protestant greed and oppression. His argument rather was that he, after the spirit of Lecky, was making this text available in print to enable historians 'to arrive at historical truth' by comparing the arguments presented there concerning 'eleven years of great historical importance' with the 'views of contemporaries of opposite interests' that had been provided in 'statements issued under Governmental licence, or compiled by writers influenced by political and religious prejudices and personal interest'.[6]

Since scholars of Unionist and Protestant allegiance had always attached primary importance to official archival material, it seemed reasonable to expect

---

[3] Bernadette Cunningham, 'Transmission and Translation of Medieval Irish Sources in the Nineteenth and early Twentieth Centuries', R.J.W. Evans and Guy P. Marchal, eds., *The Uses of the Middle Ages in Modern European States; History, Nationhood and the Search for Origins* (London, 2011), 7–17.

[4] Gilbert, ed., *Contemporary History of Affairs in Ireland, 1641–52*; for an appraisal of the full range of Gilbert's activities see the essays in Mary Clarke, Yvonne Desmond, and Nodlaigh P. Hardiman, eds., *Sir John T. Gilbert, 1829–1898: Historian, Archivist and Librarian* (Dublin, 1999).

[5] For earlier reference to this text see Chapters 4 and 6.

[6] Gilbert, ed., *Contemporary History*, quotations from Preface to vol.1, part 1, vii, ix, xvi; Preface to vol. 3, part lvi.

358   IMAGINING IRELAND'S PASTS

that only Catholic-nationalist authors would have considered it necessary in the 1880s to augment the government view of past events with supplementary material. However, as Unionist historians took stock of what was becoming available in official sources, they became overwhelmed by evidence of the malfeasance of Crown officials and soldiers that seemed to vindicate the justifications that Irish leaders of the time, and more recent Catholic and nationalist historians, had put forward to explain why Irish Catholics had entered into rebellion regularly during the sixteenth and seventeenth centuries. Already, as discussed in Chapter 9, John Prendergast, who was Protestant in religion and Unionist in politics, had been shocked by the evidence he had unearthed in official sources concerning the self-interest of the soldiers and government officials who had benefited from the Cromwellian settlement of Ireland.[7] Another who was disgusted by evidence of the delinquency of the officers of the Crown was Richard Bagwell (1840–1918)—a Unionist, a Protestant, and a resident landowner in County Tipperary—who between 1885 and 1890 published a three-volume narrative, based primarily on official sources, entitled *Ireland under the Tudors*. Moreover, Bagwell conceded that there was no evidence that any serious effort had ever been made to convert the bulk of Ireland's population to the Protestant faith. Given this, Bagwell argued that the government had been ill advised when it had decreed Protestantism to be the official religion of the state since this had given rise to what he considered understandable resentment that had persisted to his own time.[8]

We noted in Chapter 11 that when Hickson published her *Ireland in the Seventeenth Century*, the year before the first volume of Bagwell's *Ireland under the Tudors* appeared in print, she too had taken account of the conclusion to which the official record was pointing. However, unlike most Unionist authors, she did not despair that the case she wished to make would fail for lack of evidence. Instead, advised by Froude, she thought that the time was opportune to make one final effort to rehabilitate the traditional Protestant narrative of Ireland's history during the early modern centuries. In so doing, she, like all previous authors in that tradition, believed that the 1641 depositions offered the principal support for such an interpretation. This explains her determination to have this source given equal status with the material from the official archive that was being summarized in the *Calendar of State Papers* series. This demand must have taken people by surprise because, besides Leland and some Unionist historians of counties, relatively few of the authors whose work we have been considering in this volume had consulted many of the depositions in the original.

---

[7] This was discussed in Chapter 9.

[8] Richard Bagwell, *Ireland under the Tudors* (London, 3 vols., 1885–90); Marc Caball, History and Politics; Interpretations of Early Modern Conquest and Reformation in Victorian Ireland', Stefan Berger and Chris Lorenz, eds., *Nationalizing the Past: Historians as Nation Builders in Modern Europe* (Basingstoke, 2010), 149–69.

THE FAILURE OF THE IMAGINATION CONCERNING IRELAND'S PASTS   359

Attention is given in this chapter to how Hickson set about her task before explaining how other historians, who like her were Protestant in religion and Unionist in politics and who sympathized with her efforts, concluded that Hickson's agenda was proving more divisive than helpful. It will be shown that they arrived at this view because they doubted Hickson's judgement more than her integrity, and because they believed that the sources she had chosen with which to sustain her arguments did not outweigh the larger body of official evidence that was considered more credible by historians from all sides.

However, as we shall see, some other Unionists lost interest in Hickson's campaign because they had become convinced by the rapidly changing circumstances of the nineteenth century that it was no longer possible to influence present policy through history. It will be suggested that yet another reason why some Unionist scholars lost faith in history was because nationalist and Catholic-nationalist historians seemed no longer interested in re-engaging in debate with adversaries over disputed happenings during what they regarded as centuries of degradation. Instead of entering into dialogue with Unionist opponents, nationalists and Catholic-nationalists, who considered that their interpretation of events had been vindicated by neutral observers, particularly Lecky, considered themselves free to write general narratives of Ireland's history with the purpose of encouraging their readers to take pride in the achievements of their ancestors both in ancient times and in more recent centuries. This meant that they passed quickly over the early modern centuries other than to allude to the stout resistance that particular leaders had presented to their oppressors.[9]

12.2 Hickson's Last Stand

Once Hickson had taken account of the conclusions to which the published material from the official archives were leading, she decided to spend the summer of 1881 in the library of Trinity College, Dublin, to examine in the original the surviving depositions concerning the 1641 rebellion. She was attracted to this source because extracts from the depositions had been cited by John Temple, Henry Jones, and others in the seventeenth century to sustain a Protestant interpretation for the entire early modern period. Moreover, as previously noted, Hickson had already made use of the small number of depositions that related to events in County Kerry when she had attempted to reconstruct the course of the rebellion of 1641–42 in that county. After her summer sojourn in the archives, Hickson was even more confident that the depositions would enable her to rehabilitate the Protestant narrative that was being overlooked or discounted.

---

[9] R.F. Foster, *The Irish Story: Telling Tales and Making It Up in Ireland* (London, 2001), 1–22.

360   IMAGINING IRELAND'S PASTS

She therefore proposed to the relevant government officials that 'some fair-minded Catholic layman' should be appointed to prepare a calendar of the material that they would then authorize for publication by the Historical Manuscripts Commission.[10]

On receipt of this overture, the government referred the matter to John Prendergast, who had been employed by the government since 1864, either alone or in association with Dr Russell, to appraise and edit official documents relating to seventeenth-century Ireland.[11] Hickson is likely to have been displeased that her overture had been brought to Prendergast's attention both because she had long considered Prendergast's work on Cromwellian Ireland erroneous and vexatious, and because he, in association with Russell, had, in 1872, ignored the 1641 depositions as a historical source when they had identified and evaluated a vast array of other documentary sources relating to Ireland's history for the entire seventeenth century.[12]

When the request from Hickson to have a calendar of the depositions published, 'with the rest of the State Papers', was referred to Prendergast he, rather than expose himself to the charge that he had prejudged the issue, recommended to the Commission that it solicit a report instead from John T. Gilbert. The outcome was that Gilbert declared that the depositions were 'utterly untrustworthy' and did not warrant the expenditure of public money in having them calendared. To add insult to injury, according to Froude, Gilbert had justified his opinion by citing 'extracts from Mr Prendergast's works and from violent Nationalist writers like Curry and Carey'.[13] Froude and Hickson considered Gilbert's verdict perverse because he had himself recently published the 'Aphorismical Discovery'. This, in their eyes, meant that Gilbert was treating this anonymous tirade as a more reliable source of evidence than the depositions which, they insisted, were sworn, authenticated, official documents that deserved to be recognized as state papers.

When Hickson's plans were thus frustrated by what she considered an act of censorship, she decided to include substantial extracts from the depositions as appendices to her *Ireland in the Seventeenth Century*, stating that 'the history of

---

[10] Hickson, *Ireland in the Seventeenth Century*, vol. 1, 164, 127; Toby Barnard, writing of this episode, suggested that an impecunious Hickson was resentful because Gilbert and Prendergast were being paid by the government to edit official documents. This may be true but she made it clear here that she wanted a Catholic rather than herself to prepare her proposed calendar of the depositions for publication. Barnard, 'Sir John Gilbert and Irish Historiography', Clarke, Desmond, and Hardiman, eds., *Sir John T. Gilbert, 1829–1898*, 92–110; esp. 96.

[11] *A Report on the Carte Manuscripts in the Bodleian Library*, eds., C.W. Russell and J.P. Prendergast, (London, 8 vols., 1871); *Calendar of State Papers relating to Ireland, 1603–1625*, Russell and Prendergast, eds. (London, 5 vols., 1872–1880).

[12] They did so in *Calendar of State Papers relating to Ireland, 1603–1606*, eds., C.W. Russell and J.P. Prendergast (London, 1872), Introduction, i–cxviii.

[13] Hickson, *Ireland in the Seventeenth Century*, Preface by Froude, viii; Curry was John Curry whose writings were considered in Chapter 4, and Carey was Mathew Carey whose contribution was considered in Chapter 6.

THE FAILURE OF THE IMAGINATION CONCERNING IRELAND'S PASTS   361

the two islands [could] never be fully understood by any one who had not studied the depositions in Trinity College'.[14] What Hickson was now making available in print, claimed Froude, would enable readers to establish 'their own independent, impartial judgement' on the evidence presented, and would lead them to the inescapable conclusion, as it had led Temple in the seventeenth century, and had led Froude himself after he had read the extracts that Hickson was now publishing, that 'the Irish massacre of 1641 became part of European history, and held a place of infamy by the side of the Sicilian Vespers and the Massacre of St. Bartholomew'.[15] It was this truth, according to both Hickson and Froude, that Prendergast and Gilbert had suppressed because they were 'in sympathy with popular '"Irish ideas"...that the entire story' concerning the 1641 rebellion 'was a fabrication invented by the Puritan English as an excuse for stripping the Irish of their lands, that there never was a massacre at all, that not a Protestant [was] killed save in fair fight and open war, and that the evidence collected by commissions and published to deceive Europe [was] so extravagant that a glance suffices to detect its worthlessness'. Froude fulminated that, instead of acknowledging what they knew to be true, Gilbert and Prendergast had conspired to have it 'universally received and believed by the Irish people, both at home and in America' that their ancestors had been 'robbed' and been 'victims of abominable cruelties'. Their promotion of this distorted view of the past was, he continued, one of 'the causes which have exasperated the Irish race into their present attitude' whereby they could conceive of no solution to their problems short of bringing an end to landlordism and having Home Rule enacted.[16]

Hickson and Froude believed that by halting the publication of her proposed calendar of depositions, Prendergast and Gilbert had created the situation whereby no 'clear rejoinder' to the Catholic-nationalist narrative of Ireland's early modern past could be proven. Hickson's private initiative in publishing *Ireland in the Seventeenth Century* had, according to Froude, rectified this deficit because, as well as advancing her own interpretation of what had occurred in Ireland during that turbulent century, she had printed a reasonable sampling from the depositions together with a selection of documents concerning Cromwellian rule in Ireland. Together, claimed Froude, these would lead neutral observers towards 'the clear ascertainment of the truth or untruth of a story which touches so deeply

---

[14] Hickson, *Ireland in the Seventeenth Century*, vol. 1, 164, 100.

[15] Hickson, *Ireland in the Seventeenth Century*, Preface by Froude, v, ix; the notorious Sicilian episode occurred in Palermo in 1282 when the local population slaughtered the unsuspecting garrison and administrators of the Angevin king who governed the city as the bells sounded for vespers; the likening of the 1641 rebellion to the massacre of St Bartholomew's Day of 1572 had been made by Temple and repeated by many subsequent authors.

[16] Hickson, *Ireland in the Seventeenth Century*, Preface by Froude, v, vi; Froude would have been especially sensitive to the prevalence of such views among the exiled Irish community in the United States due to the hostile reception he had received when he had lectured there. I am grateful to Professor Sarah Covington for this insight.

362   IMAGINING IRELAND'S PASTS

the honour of English action in Ireland, [and would] do more towards allaying hatreds between classes, creeds and nations, than the most absolute reversal of the Act of Settlement of 1660–70, which arose out of, and had its justifications in, the crimes charged on the Irish in the depositions.[17]

Hickson's two volumes lived up to Froude's billing in that they included her edition of some of the depositions that had been generated by official bodies in Ireland during the 1640s and 1650s.[18] To these she had added extracts from the Carte Manuscripts where Catholics had acknowledged that massacres of Protestants by Catholics had occurred during the 1640s.[19] Hickson also included documents from the Commonwealth Records that showed how Commonwealth officials, including Oliver Cromwell, had been temperate in their dealings with those Irish Catholics who had been able to prove themselves innocent of any wrongdoing during the eleven-year interlude, 1641–52. To these she had appended copies of documents that showed how some Irish Catholics—including Catholic lords—had acknowledged that they had been treated equitably by the Commonwealth court system.[20]

This documentary compilation was assembled by Hickson to substantiate her interpretation of Ireland's history during the seventeenth century. In this, she contended that the Irish under their 'clansmen' had been exploited far more than was being acknowledged by Irish antiquarians in their romantic depictions of Gaelic society.[21] Consequently, she was able to argue, in direct contradiction of what had been said on the subject by George Hill, that the plantations of the seventeenth century had liberated most Irish people from the debased condition to which they had been reduced under the Gaelic order. Then, in her discussion of the Graces, Hickson argued that these were concessions that had been wrested from King Charles I at a moment of dire need, thus proving that 'the Irish, even as early as 1628, had begun to understand the value of that policy, summarised in this century in Daniel O'Connell's maxim, England's difficulty is Ireland's opportunity'.[22] In the light of this, Hickson considered that Sir William Parsons— whose name, she said, had been 'blackened' by Ormond and Carte—had been correct to block legislation in the Irish parliament that would have put the Graces on a legal footing.[23] On the question of religion, Hickson conceded that,

---

[17] Hickson, *Ireland in the Seventeenth Century*, Preface by Froude, xii.

[18] For discussions of the deposition collection generally see Aidan Clarke, 'The 1641 Depositions', Fox, ed., *Treasures of the Library*, 111–22; Clarke, 'The Commission for the Despoiled Subject, 1641–7', Mac Cuarta, ed., *Reshaping Ireland, 1550–1700*, 241–60; Clarke, 'About the Deposition Series', Aidan Clarke, ed., *1641 Depositions*, vol. 1, *Armagh, Louth and Monaghan*, (Dublin, 2014), xxvii–xxxix.

[19] 'Catholic accounts of the massacres', Hickson, *Ireland in the Seventeenth Century*, vol. 2, 240–56.

[20] 'Miscellaneous; Commonwealth Book', Hickson, *Ireland in the Seventeenth Century*, vol. 2, 236–7; 'Records of the High Court of Justice, 1652–54', Hickson, *Ireland in the Seventeenth Century*, vol. 2, 171–235.

[21] Hickson, *Ireland in the Seventeenth Century*, vol. 1, 4–9.

[22] Hickson, *Ireland in the Seventeenth Century*, vol. 1, 47.

[23] Hickson, *Ireland in the Seventeenth Century*, vol. 1, 38, 100.

THE FAILURE OF THE IMAGINATION CONCERNING IRELAND'S PASTS   363

'as a missionary church', the Church of Ireland had proven 'an utter failure' and that it was this that had enabled Catholicism, spearheaded by 'the chief conspirators, the Jesuit fathers', to become the dominant religion in the country. Then, in a passage reminiscent of what John Temple had written in 1646, Hickson pronounced that 'the English Protestant colonists remained, for the most part, confident in the good will of their Roman Catholic neighbours whose religion was now virtually supreme, or at the very least openly tolerated'.[24] Proceeding from there to identify the causes of the 1641 rebellion, Hickson conceded that politics in Ireland had been complicated by the collapse of royal authority, first in Scotland and then in England, because this had aroused fear and uncertainty among Irish Catholics. However, she insisted that the prime cause of the rebellion in Ireland was 'the usual impatient turbulence of Roman Catholic politicians under the control of fanatical priests' who had made compromise impossible by raising 'the judicature question and other impractical demands which, if granted, would have deprived England of all control over Ireland'.[25]

Therefore, for Hickson, the rebellion of 1641, and what she believed was the intended massacre of Ireland's Protestant population, was the outcome of plotting and conspiracy encouraged by 'the disbanded soldier and the political priest'. This explained, for her, why 'from the first day of the rebellion the rebels declared that the war was a religious one'. This declaration, according to Hickson, accounted for the horrors that Catholics had inflicted upon Protestants during the course of the rebellion, and the equally horrendous punishments that Protestants had meted out to Catholics once the Cromwellian forces had re-established what she considered to be England's legitimate claim to rule over Ireland. Hickson detailed some of the atrocities committed by the Cromwellian army that had rendered their conquest infamous, but she credited the Parliamentary armies, unlike the rebels of 1641, with having been a disciplined force. As proof of this, she claimed that the 'Cromwellians had prosecuted the murderers of the Catholics at Islandmagee'—a fact, she asserted, that had been 'totally' ignored by Gilbert in his *Contemporary History* when discussing these same murders.[26]

Hickson never missed an opportunity to belittle Gilbert, but Prendergast was always the principal target of her attack both because his views on the Cromwellian and Restoration settlements ran counter to hers and because, as a Protestant and Unionist, his work had persuaded many, including politicians in England, that Catholics had been treated unjustly under both schemes. She therefore called attention to every factual error and oversight she could detect in

---

[24] Hickson, *Ireland in the Seventeenth Century*, vol. 1, 79, 85, 96, 107.
[25] Hickson, *Ireland in the Seventeenth Century*, vol. 1, 101.
[26] Hickson, *Ireland in the Seventeenth Century*, vol. 1, 127; Hickson evaded becoming involved in the controversy concerning the precise numbers of Protestants killed in 1641 by stating that 'no accurate estimate [was] possible'; *Ireland in the Seventeenth Century*, vol. 1, 163; on the murders at Islandmagee and how they became part of the 1641 controversy see Chapters 4 and 6.

364   IMAGINING IRELAND'S PASTS

Prendergast's publications, suggesting always that he would not allow any inconvenient truth to stand in the way of his argument. The material she published on the Cromwellian conquest and settlement of Ireland was chosen by her to prove that both conquest and settlement had been justified, and had been to the ultimate benefit of the country, including its Catholic population. For Hickson, the suggestion that either the Dublin government of the 1640s or the Cromwellian regime that succeeded it had pursued 'a policy of extermination' of Catholics was but part of the 'romance of history' being cultivated by Catholic and nationalist authors. She also deployed the documentary material she had salvaged from the archives to establish that Cromwell and his officers had 'protected the native Irish who were disposed to live in peace and good will with their Protestant neighbours'. More generally, she argued that the beneficial outcome of all plantations (including that promoted by Cromwell) had been that 'the garden of Ireland [was] filled with the sturdy, industrious, freedom-loving men of the mixed race'.[27]

Hickson's *coup de grâce*, and her ultimate proof of the clemency of the Cromwellians, was her citation from a letter of 22 March 1653 addressed by Oliver Cromwell to the Committee of the Commonwealth in Ireland. In this, Cromwell had indicated that he personally had examined 'the petitions and papers of one John Prendergast' relating to the appeal made by that John Prendergast against a decree of transplantation. The document showed how Cromwell had concluded that the case deserved 'some tender regard', and had directed that John Prendergast be permitted to remain in his 'present estate and habitations'.[28] By resurrecting this communication, Hickson was suggesting that the present John Prendergast had deliberately falsified evidence to sustain his case that his namesake and supposed progenitor had been deprived of his ancestral property and status at the time of the Cromwellian settlement, and had chosen exile on the Continent over transplantation to Connacht.[29]

Reference to this and other such incidents also corroborated one of the more controversial contentions that Hickson had previously aired in *Selections from Old Kerry Records*. This was that the transplantation dimension to the Cromwellian settlement had in practice been less draconian, less comprehensive, and less enduring than was being asserted by Prendergast, Gilbert, and their nationalist and liberal admirers. This conclusion has been recently shown by John Cunningham's study of the transplantation to be justified by the evidence.[30] However, recent research casts doubt on Hickson's further assertion that when matters settled down natives and newcomers, Catholics and Protestants, continued to live amicably in close proximity to each other. She used this assertion to support her

---

[27] Hickson, *Ireland in the Seventeenth Century*, vol. 1, 11, 14–15.
[28] Oliver P. to the Committee of the Commonwealth in Ireland, 22 March 1653, Hickson, *Ireland in the Seventeenth Century*, vol. 2, 237.
[29] John Prendergast's treatment of the behaviour of his supposed ancestor is discussed in Chapter 9.
[30] Cunningham, *Conquest and Land in Ireland: The Transplantation to Connacht, 1649–1680*.

THE FAILURE OF THE IMAGINATION CONCERNING IRELAND'S PASTS 365

argument that this ease in relationship produced such a degree of intermixing between the different elements of the population that it was entirely fanciful to make any claim for the existence of an Irish nation that was genetically different from the population of Britain. The Cromwellian conquest, she claimed, had given those Irish who had remained in the country the opportunity to become absorbed into a British polity in which, had they taken advantage of it, they would have enjoyed all of the liberties and economic benefits associated with being British. Had the Irish done so, she pronounced, they would have been given the opportunity to participate as equal participants in Britain's glorious history, but, having spurned the opportunity, they were left as a people without any achievements in which they could take pride.

Given Froude's close association with Mary Hickson and the fulsome endorsement he gave to *Ireland in the Seventeenth Century*, it is difficult to establish which opinions in that volume were the author's own and which were reiterations of the arguments that Froude had previously advanced in *The English in Ireland in the Eighteenth Century* that had been found wanting by critics such Lecky and Prendergast because they lacked documentary support. Hickson's assembly of documents certainly substantiated some of the propositions that Froude had then advanced, and her interpretation of what had transpired in Ireland in the seventeenth century accorded very closely with what Froude had published on that subject in 1872 and republished in 1881. Apart from the edited documents that she had included in her book, Hickson differed from what Froude had published only in insisting that her scholarly method conformed with what had been recommended by Lecky, who she now praised as a man possessed of 'an unprejudiced mind'.[31]

Hickson's claim of 1884 that Lecky as well as Froude had advised her in her preparation of *Ireland in the Seventeenth Century* suggests that she fostered hopes that Lecky would now be won over to her way of thinking about Ireland's early modern past. She had reason to be optimistic because the course of political events of the late nineteenth century had left several Unionists and Protestants, who had published liberal interpretations of Ireland's past, concerned that what they had written had served to justify the sequence of events that, as they saw it, threatened to make them strangers in their own country. The most alarming developments that made them fear for their future were the atrocities associated with Fenianism in its American, British, and Irish configurations, and the Land War of 1879–81 that seemed to link illegal practices with what previously had appeared the constitutional route to reform pursued by Parnell and his supporters within the Irish parliamentary party.[32] At the same time, some liberally-minded

[31] Hickson, *Ireland in the Seventeenth Century*, vol. 1, 4.
[32] To gain some sense of the circum Atlantic horrors that terrified liberals as well as conservatives such as Hickson and Froude see Gillian O'Brien, *Blood Runs Green: The Murder that Transfixed Gilded Age Chicago* (Chicago, 2015).

366   IMAGINING IRELAND'S PASTS

Protestant historians who had thought well of Catholic Emancipation in 1829, and of the act of 1869 that had disestablished the Church of Ireland, were less comfortable with the enactment by Liberal Governments, led by William Gladstone, of the Irish Land Acts in 1870 and 1881. They were troubled also by the enactment in 1884 of a Tory reform measure, known as the Representation of the People Act, that effected a tripling of the size of the Irish electorate. Most disconcerting of all was the adoption by William Gladstone in 1885 of 'Home Rule for Ireland' as official policy for the Liberal Party.

Hickson played upon the unease that she knew her fellow Unionist historians shared over such issues, by alluding to parallels between the turbulent events of the seventeenth century and those of her own time. Thus, as she attributed the challenges that had beset the Protestant community of the seventeenth century to politicized priests and disbanded soldiers, she argued that the trials experienced by Unionists and Protestants of her generation in Ireland were the consequence of interference by priests in the electoral process, and by the endeavours of political activists in the United States and in Ireland to employ extra-legal methods to dispossess Irish landowners of their estates and to facilitate the political separation of Ireland from Britain. Hickson argued consistently, and cited evidence to sustain her case, that the Irish population of the seventeenth century had brought disaster upon themselves when they had given attention to false guides who had encouraged them to challenge British rule in Ireland. As she pointed to the calamity that had resulted from this, Hickson was hinting at the hazards that would face the Irish population of her generation if they too took guidance from those who would have them challenge the existing social order, and the integrity of Britain's United Kingdom and Empire. Thus, where Hickson in her historical narrative blamed the government of King Charles I for its failure to maintain order in Ireland and avert greater calamity, she faulted the politicians of her generation in Britain for neglecting their responsibilities towards Ireland. Instead, she argued, they were being misled by the specious arguments of historians—and here she referred persistently to Prendergast and Gilbert—who, she contended, were distorting the truth about the past in order to enrage, and thus force into rebellion, the majority population in Ireland that she still considered fundamentally loyal.

12.3 Unionist Reactions to Hickson's Challenge

Hickson's compelling argument was addressed to the wider Unionist community in Britain and Ireland. However, supported by Froude, she was focusing particularly on historians of Unionist sympathies, hoping that she could persuade some of them to rescind their liberal interpretation of Ireland's past and fall into line with her contention, and that of Froude, that Ireland and its peoples had

THE FAILURE OF THE IMAGINATION CONCERNING IRELAND'S PASTS 367

prospered in the past only when it had been held firmly under British control. She seemed hopeful that if Lecky and Prendergast could be persuaded publicly to distance themselves from their published views, it might give some British politicians reason to re-consider the policies they had embarked upon on the grounds that they were no longer justified by history. Her purpose was not lost on Lecky, who, in 1892, described Hickson's as an 'important work' even when it upheld several of Froude's arguments that Lecky was still disputing. Moreover, by 1892, Lecky had come to accept Froude, his former adversary, as a friend, and a decade later, in 1903, he acknowledged that Froude, who had died in 1894, had 'led the way' in the serious study of early modern Ireland. Lecky justified what was an apparent re-appraisal of his own work as well as that of Froude by mentioning that Froude was the surer guide to developments of the sixteenth and the seventeenth centuries because what Lecky himself had written of those centuries had been 'without an examination of the great manuscript collections'.[33]

Despite any misgivings that Lecky may have had about his own work, he proceeded in 1892 to publish the book for which he is best remembered in Ireland, his *History of Ireland in the Eighteenth Century*. In this, which many contemporaries considered to be Lecky's most comprehensive refutation of Froude, he reiterated and expanded upon what he had previously published in different formats on Ireland's history. To have done otherwise would have required him to forget that he had once derived satisfaction from thinking that his writings had set Gladstone on the path of reform for Ireland, and to reject that which had brought him to prominence as a seer. It would also have required him to abandon his ambition to appeal through reason to educated members of the Nationalist and Catholic-nationalist communities in Ireland in the hope that his balanced account of Ireland's history would persuade them to distance themselves from the views of extremists. Lecky obviously still hoped that he would achieve this latter objective by arguing from history that what the ancestors of the Irish had suffered in the past was finally being acknowledged, and that the British government of the day, of whatever complexion, was prepared to compensate those living in the present for these injustices of bygone centuries.

However, in 1892, and again shortly before his death in 1903, as he reflected on his life's work, Lecky seemed ready to retract, or at least to qualify, his previous insistence that Ireland's Catholic population had always been inclined towards loyalty other than when they had been driven to rebellion by British injustice. The qualification he now introduced was that 'agrarian crime and conspiracy' had played a part in all past tumults in Ireland, including the 1641 rebellion, the Whiteboy disturbances of the eighteenth century, the rebellion of 1798, Defenderism, and the Tithe War. In making this judgement and in decrying

---

[33] Lecky, *History of Ireland in the Eighteenth Century*, vol. 1, 80; Lecky, *Leaders of Public Opinion*, vol. 1, Preface, xv.

368   IMAGINING IRELAND'S PASTS

violence as a means of securing political ends, Lecky expressed himself satisfied that agrarian disturbance alone had never threatened the authority of governments other than when 'agrarian crime had an organisation and a purpose...to isolate the landowning class, to deprive them of different forms of power, and to cut the ties of traditional influence and attachment by which they were once bound to their people'. He believed that such a configuration possibly occurred in 1641, which he now believed explained why this rebellion had presented such a formidable challenge to the government of the day. Even if this did not hold true for the 1641 rebellion, Lecky was convinced that he was witnessing this three-pronged assault in the agrarian disturbances of the late nineteenth century. The ideas behind the assault, according to Lecky, were those of James Fintan Lalor (1807–49), 'one of the least known, but certainly not one of the least important of the seditious writers of 1848'.[34] Lecky pronounced that Lalor, following the example of the better-known authors of Young Ireland, had distorted what people had previously understood of Ireland's history during the early modern centuries. They had done so, he claimed, by invoking 'the doctrine of nationalities'—a doctrine that he, like P.F. Moran long before him, pointed out had been condemned by the Catholic Church because of its association with revolution in Continental Europe. Lecky contended that none of the Young Ireland authors had deployed this doctrine more effectively than John Mitchel, 'a much abler man' than Lalor, who, if he had made proper use of his talents, might have been 'almost in the foremost rank of the writers of his time'. However, claimed Lecky, Mitchel had instead 'adopted' the 'doctrines' expounded by Lalor and used them 'to form the type of the modern Irish agitation' used by Fenian conspirators during the Land War to threaten the rights of property and with it the liberty of individuals, and therefore also Ireland's connection with Britain.[35]

Lecky's implicit condemnation of all Young Ireland authors—and not only Lalor—who had inspired him in his student days indicates the extent to which he had been forced by circumstances to abandon the liberal positions of his youth. Already, Lecky had become more sympathetic to Tory than to Liberal policies for Ireland, believing that Gladstone had abandoned his principles in exchange for the parliamentary support of the Home Rule Party whose members were, as Lecky now saw it, determined to undermine the position of landlords in Ireland and to break Ireland's union with Britain. As he retreated from his earlier political position, Lecky saw no reason why he should apologize for doing so, stating in 1903 that it was 'somewhat extravagant to argue that a writer who condemned the Union in 1800 was necessarily favourable to its repeal eighty years later'.[36]

---

[34] Lecky, *History of Ireland in the Eighteenth Century*, vol. 5, 483; on Lalor see a biographical sketch by Mary E. Daly, *Dictionary of Irish Biography*, vol. 5, 272–5.

[35] Lecky, *History of Ireland in the Eighteenth Century*, vol. 5, 483–90; Lecky, *Leaders of Public Opinion*, vol. 2, 290; McCartney, *Lecky*, 151–61.

[36] Lecky, *Leaders of Public Opinion*, vol. 1, Preface, xiii.

THE FAILURE OF THE IMAGINATION CONCERNING IRELAND'S PASTS   369

It seems that while Lecky continued to support the concept of an inclusive Irish nationalism that had been espoused by Young Ireland, he now became emphatic in rejecting the contention of the Young Irelanders that, once an Irish nation had been acknowledged to exist, it was entitled to enjoy some degree of political autonomy from Britain. He was concerned to clarify his thinking on this point not only because the concept of Home Rule for Ireland had won wide acceptance within the Catholic community, and from some liberal Protestants, in Ireland but also because it was being considered reasonable by an increasing number of people, including politicians, in Britain.

This change in sentiment left Lecky an isolated figure in Ireland since the concept of any political separation between Ireland and Britain had always been anathema to him, and he had been opposed from the outset to incursions by the state upon the rights of property that had been encouraged by the Land League and legitimized by government legislation. Of even greater concern to Lecky was what Donal McCartney has described as 'the headlong rush towards egalitarianism—the political and social levelling that he had seen so much of in Ireland', which was also being legislated for, this time by a Tory government, through a broadening of the adult male franchise.[37] As Lecky took stock of all such changes, he, like several other historians of Ireland who cherished Union with Britain, became concerned that what he considered his balanced, evidence-based narration of events in Ireland during the sixteenth, seventeenth, and eighteenth centuries had resulted not in the development of mutual respect between peoples of diverse religious and political convictions but had, instead, provided nationalist leaders with further justifications for demanding social and political change. Moreover, Lecky could now also see how his historical publications had persuaded educated opinion, including political opinion, in Britain, of the need to assuage Irish nationalists by proceeding with the interventionist measures that were proving to be transformative rather than reformative. Lecky's concern that more ill than good had resulted from his historical pursuits may explain why in his later years he abandoned history and took to composing essays on the aspects of political life, that had become distasteful to him. At the same time he gave vent to his increasingly conservative views at Westminster where he attended from 1895 to 1902 as a Member of Parliament representing his old college in the Dublin University constituency.

Richard Bagwell was another historian who was similarly perturbed by the political changes of the closing decades of the nineteenth century. He, like Lecky, abandoned the liberal principles of his youth to become a staunch Unionist and die-hard conservative. Unlike Lecky, however, Bagwell did not allow his concerns about the present to divert him from writing about the past. Instead, he followed

[37] McCartney, *Lecky*, 160.

370 IMAGINING IRELAND'S PASTS

his three-volume *Ireland under the Tudors*, which had done much to discredit the concept of benevolent Tudor rule in Ireland, with a three-volume sequel, *Ireland under the Stuarts*, in which, again guided by the relevant *Calendars of State Papers*, Bagwell demonstrated how Ireland's Catholics had again been frequently treated unfairly by the successors to the Tudors. Bagwell, like Lecky, may have expected that this exposure of injustice in the past would bring the wider public, including the nationalist and Catholic publics, to recognize that governments and landowners of more recent times would take their Irish responsibilities more seriously. Not satisfied to await passively for such a response, Bagwell engaged in a frenzy of political activity to uphold the rights of landowners and to oppose the enactment of Home Rule, insisting always that, if given the chance, landowners and governments would behave more equitably than their predecessors had done. His activities suggest that Bagwell, more than Lecky, still fostered hopes that something of the paternalistic world he cherished could be salvaged from its wreckage that he was witnessing even as he wrote.[38] Another who had reason to question his endeavours as a historian was John Prendergast who, even when he had embarked upon his caustic criticism of Cromwellian rule in Ireland, had been a committed Unionist. This meant that, when the issue of Home Rule arose, he was as much opposed to it as he had been earlier to the break-up of landed estates. As it became ever more likely that both compulsory estate purchase and Home Rule would become a reality, Prendergast, like Lecky, reflected ruefully on how his exposure of the injustices that had been inflicted upon Irish Catholics by the Cromwellian and Restoration settlements had been used by Irish nationalists to legitimize a political agenda that spelt doom for the world he cherished.[39]

Any of these authors could have attempted to resolve their personal difficulties by retracting what they had previously written concerning British misrule in Ireland. None of them could do so because this would have required them to admit that what they had previously written had been intellectually dishonest. These authors would have been aware also that any retraction of their earlier views would have required them logically to endorse the contention of Hickson and Froude that there was no such thing as an Irish nation, and that the only true champion of the rights and liberties of Irish people had been Oliver Cromwell. Prendergast and Lecky and Bagwell would also have recognized that any retraction by them of their original views would have meant losing the undoubted respect they enjoyed within Ireland's Catholic-nationalist community, especially because of their clinical dissection of Froude's work. Because of this they continued to hope in vain that their nationalist admirers would become less inclined to adopt 'extreme' positions when they took account of the 'balanced' narratives on Ireland's history during the early modern centuries that they had been put before them.

---

[38] Richard Bagwell, *Ireland under the Stuarts* (London, 1909–16).   [39] Bartlett, 'Prendergast'.

THE FAILURE OF THE IMAGINATION CONCERNING IRELAND'S PASTS 371

When he witnessed no tempering in the demands of Irish nationalists, Lecky, in his later years, came to see more merit than he had previously acknowledged in the work of Froude. However, Lecky could never see Froude, as that author saw himself, as an English prophet, analogous to John Hooker in the sixteenth century or to Arthur Collins in the eighteenth, who had composed an exemplary history for Ireland when nobody in Ireland was equipped to undertake such a task. On the contrary, Lecky remained convinced that Froude, and Hickson whom he had come to consider an acolyte of Froude, were re-fighting lost causes with dubious evidence, and with arguments that he knew would cause further offence to Ireland's Catholic and nationalist populations.

Many Unionist historians in Ireland, including Lecky, therefore came to consider Froude more a propagandist than a historian, and considered him to be making blatant use of evidence from the past to serve present political purposes. As these recoiled from doing so themselves, they clung to Lecky's principle that historians should be guided to whatever conclusion the evidence might lead even when they found these conclusions uncongenial. To do otherwise, as they believed Froude was doing, would, as they saw it, have made them guilty of the same offence with which they now charged nationalist authors writing in the Young Ireland tradition.[40] These, as Lecky stated in 1903, were engaging in fanciful flights of the imagination to promote 'disloyalty to the crown... hatred of empire, disregard for individual liberty and all security of property'.[41] Therefore, as Lecky and Prendergast witnessed the death of the paternalistic world they had cherished, they believed themselves to be witnessing also the death of the 'directional history' with which they had been previously involved in the interest of promoting reform and staving off the revolution that they now saw engulfing them from every side.[42]

The pessimism about Ireland's future that became so burdensome for Lecky and Prendergast towards the end of their days was likely shared by many within Ireland's Unionist community. However, not all within that community shared the opinion that there was no future for them in Ireland or that the course of history led logically to that conclusion. The most notable exceptions were historians associated with the Protestant community in the province of Ulster. As Lecky and Prendergast were giving way to despair and as Catholic-nationalist historians dedicated themselves uncritically to tracing the emergence of an Irish nation, these became linked with what Alvin Jackson has described as the 'Ulsterization' of Irish Unionism. The 'Ulsterization' process, as Jackson has shown, was promoted by a range of associations dedicated to preserving a Unionist and Protestant character for society in the province of Ulster regardless of what transpired elsewhere

---

[40] McCartney, *Lecky*, 137–50. [41] Lecky, *Leaders of Public Opinion*, vol. 1, Preface, xii.
[42] The term 'directional history' comes from Francis Fukuyama, *The End of History and the Last Man* (London, 1992), 245.

372 IMAGINING IRELAND'S PASTS

in Ireland.[43] 'Ulsterization' manifested itself in the realm of history writing in the increasing attention that authors gave to illustrating the uniqueness of the Ulster experience, and the particularity of society in that province. This contrasted sharply with histories of other regions or counties in Ireland where, as noted in Chapters 10 and 11, authors, whether nationalist or Unionist, had begun to treat the histories of the particular communities they studied as microcosms of the history of the country as a whole.

If the 'Ulsterization' process is usually associated with the later decades of the nineteenth century, history writing in the province had been trending in that direction for several decades. Thus John Seaton Reid's *History of the Presbyterian Church in Ireland*, first published in 1833, although concerned with the manifestation of Presbyterianism throughout the country at large, had emphasized the unique character of society in Ulster that Reid attributed to the strong Presbyterian presence there that had no equivalent in the other three provinces of Ireland. It was this aspect of Reid's text that made it attractive to W.D. Killen when he republished it in an expanded edition in 1867, almost as an exemplary textbook in 'Ulster' history. Several of the points raised by Reid that were now endorsed by Killen—most emphatically those concerning the causes and character of the 1641 rebellion—would be disputed by the Reverend George Hill, whose major work on the Ulster plantation, discussed in Chapter 10, would appear in 1877. In this, and also in his later brief histories of eight of the nine counties in Ulster presented in *Plantation Acres*, Hill seemed at odds with most Unionist authors of his generation in welcoming some of the Irish land reforms of the nineteenth century. However, on closer scrutiny, Hill emerges as no less an 'Ulster' historian than Reid in that he too celebrated the unique history and character of his native province.

The fact that Hill, unlike Protestant and Unionist historians from the other provinces of Ireland, welcomed the passage of the Irish Land Act of 1870 was because he believed that the act involved no more than the extension to tenant farmers throughout Ireland of the benefits of the 'Ulster Custom' that had governed relationships between landowners and tenants in that province since the eighteenth century. Then, when Hill applauded the second Land Act of 1881, it was because he expected that those in Ulster who would most profit from the eclipse of the great landowners of the province, of whose ancestors he had been sharply critical, would be the Protestant tenant farmers who he considered the backbone of society in his native province. This outlook was unsurprising since Hill himself was the son of a Presbyterian tenant farmer and because, after his retirement from thirty years' service as librarian at Queen's College, Belfast, he had returned to live among those people in County Antrim whom he most admired, and with whom he felt most at ease. Hill's belief that such people were

---

[43] Alvin Jackson, 'The Origin, Politics and Culture of Irish Unionism, c. 1880–1916', Thomas Bartlett, ed., *The Cambridge History of Ireland*, vol. 4 (Cambridge, 2018), 89–116.

THE FAILURE OF THE IMAGINATION CONCERNING IRELAND'S PASTS 373

ready to live in harmony with their Catholic counterparts may have been influenced by his personal experience in his native County Antrim. It may have been influenced also by the plea for interdenominational tolerance that he had derived from his reading of what had been written by Young Ireland authors even as he eschewed their nationalist presumptions and aspirations.

As Hill wrote of plantation in Ulster where he decried the short-sighted avarice of the first generation of planters in the province, he identified the settlement of a coherent community of Protestant farmers and artisans as a long-term positive outcome that had made Ulster more stable and prosperous than the other provinces of Ireland. Hill, unlike the other Unionist authors whose works we have considered, also welcomed the broadening of the franchise in Ireland, safe in the knowledge that Protestant tenant farmers, and he hoped also their Catholic counterparts, would use their votes to uphold the connection with Britain regardless of what might happen elsewhere in Ireland. The only threat to communal harmony that Hill envisaged came from the possibility of sectarian division, and he was convinced by the liberal principles he espoused that this could be avoided. Not all Unionist writers of Ulster history were as broad-minded as Hill but they, unlike their southern Unionist counterparts, remained optimistic about the future and proud of the achievements of those who had resided in the province in previous centuries. This gave them a strong incentive to persist with writing the history of their provincial community as the enthusiasm for writing the history of Ireland waned among Unionists elsewhere in Ireland.

As these latter abandoned the field that had for centuries been a disputatious one, they were leaving it to those who would write the history of an Irish nation that frequently left no place for Protestants, much less for those of Unionist conviction. These nationalists authors tended to assert more than they questioned, and in their narratives passed quickly over early modern times and dwelt instead on the ancient past and on more recent times when, as they saw it, more unambiguous manifestations of Irish nationalism could be identified and lauded. This left fresh writing on early modern history very much to the writers of 'Ulster history'. That they filled the void is unsurprising since the seventeenth century was the time when the ancestors of Ulster's Unionist population had made their homes in the province, and the sixteenth and seventeenth centuries were those that had witnessed the religious independence from Rome that was fundamental to the identity of this population.

12.4 Conclusion and Epilogue

This chapter opened at the moment in the late nineteenth century when historians seemed more confident than ever before that greater access to public documents, either in the original or in calendared form, would result in a history of Ireland

374 IMAGINING IRELAND'S PASTS

on which all communities might agree. We have seen how this optimism was short-lived both because disagreements arose over what should be contained within a comprehensive archive for Ireland's history, and because the rapid course of political change meant that ever more scholars experienced difficulty in fitting any past they could imagine to the present they were experiencing. For nationalists their present fell short of their expectations because the Irish nation, whose history they were determined to write, was not being conceded the degree of political autonomy from Britain to which they, and now also Liberal politicians in Britain, believed the nation was entitled. Then for Unionists the social and political changes that had been promoted or permitted in Ireland by successive British governments, and others that were in prospect, suggested to them that Unionists and Protestants in Ireland would soon become aliens in the land in which their ancestors had lived for three centuries.

In the course of this chapter we noted three discernible responses by historians to the changes that had been proceeding so rapidly. The first was that of Lecky, who had hoped in 1892, when he published his *History of Ireland in the Eighteenth Century*, that by refuting the arguments of Froude, which Catholics and nationalists had found offensive, he would earn the goodwill of the moderates within the Irish Catholic community and persuade them to seek to reform the existing social and political order in preference to pursuing what he considered to be revolutionary ambitions. When this effort at persuasion failed, several Unionist historians lost hope in history and sought instead to uphold the morale of the Irish Unionist community by word and deed, and to dissuade the British government from proceeding with further changes that they considered detrimental to the interests of the Unionist community in Ireland. The second discernible response came from historians within the nationalist, including the Catholic-nationalist, community. These had been greatly encouraged when those they represented as independent witnesses, the most consequential being Lecky and Prendergast, had endorsed what had traditionally been considered Catholic-nationalist interpretations of several of the more controversial episodes from Ireland's history of the early modern centuries, particularly the 1641 rebellion and the Cromwellian settlement. Once this independent endorsement had become widely known, they saw no need to engage in further research on that phase of the country's history, and concentrated instead on composing narratives of Ireland's past that asserted how, through the centuries, a succession of Irish heroes had overcome seemingly insurmountable difficulties to fashion an Irish nation that would, in the foreseeable future, achieve autonomy from Britain. Such printed narratives were sustained, and communicated to a wider audience, by the ballad histories that had been initiated by Young Ireland, and that had pursued the same teleological path. The third response came from Unionist historians with Ulster associations. These, unlike Unionist historians from the other three provinces, looked to the future with the confidence that stemmed from the prosperity of a province that had a more diverse and more urbanized economy

THE FAILURE OF THE IMAGINATION CONCERNING IRELAND'S PASTS 375

and society than any of the other three provinces of Ireland. Their pride in this provincial achievement gave them reason to write histories of the province that would identify and explain the unique characteristics of society there. As they proceeded, they isolated the greater Protestant presence that had resulted from the plantations in the province as the factor that explained its relative success in the present, and gave its population reason why it should look with confidence to the future.

It seems therefore that during this interlude, both the nationalist historians and the Unionist historians who followed Lecky abandoned the effort to add to what was known about the early modern past through historical enquiry. Three scholarly groups who still had an interest in conducting fresh investigations into Ireland's early modern history filled the resulting void. First, Ulster Unionists historians remained committed to enquiring into the origins and achievements of their forbears, most especially after the bulk of Ulster's Protestant community set its mind against any Home Rule arrangement for Ireland. Second, in the realm of ecclesiastical history, a sequence of Catholic authors supported by a re-invigorated church reopened the issues that their seventeenth-century predecessors had disputed with Ussher and Ware and which they now contested with their Protestant counterparts. The resulting disputation re-kindled issues that may seem arcane today. Of these the question that most concerned early modern Ireland was whether a line of spiritual succession going back to St Patrick could be established for some, or any, of the bishops who had been appointed by Queen Elizabeth to benefices in Ireland. The third group to develop an interest in early modern Ireland was that associated with the academic turn that history writing had taken in Britain in the late nineteenth century. There, historians such as Sir Charles Firth, Samuel Gardiner, and Robert Dunlop, who were concerned initially with the great events of seventeenth-century English history, took guidance from Hume's proposition (discussed in Chapter 6) that developments in seventeenth-century England could be fully comprehended only when they were related to contemporary happenings in Scotland and Ireland.

The activities of these three groups became intertwined with what Ciaran Brady has described as the 'arrested development' of history as an academic discipline in Irish universities. The first entanglement occurred once it came to be accepted in Irish university circles of the 1920s and 1930s that anybody wishing to pursue an academic career in history would be advised to seek postgraduate training in Britain. This resulted in a significant cluster of Irish scholars attending at the Institute of Historical Research in London during the early 1930s, some of whom were to play a significant role in the promotion of professional history in Ireland over the next several decades.[44] The research interests of two of their

---

[44] Ciaran Brady, 'Arrested Development: Competing Histories and the Formation of the Irish Historical Profession, 1801–1938', Tibor Frank and Frank Hadler, eds., *Disputed Territories and Shared Pasts: Overlapping National Histories in Modern Europe* (London, 2011), 275–302, see 276;

376 IMAGINING IRELAND'S PASTS

number, T.W Moody and D.B. Quinn, who had received their undergraduate training at Queen's University, Belfast, where no Irish history was taught, had been awakened by the 'Ulster history' that had become popular in civil society in Belfast. Moody's Ph.D. topic in London, which he later transformed into a book entitled *The Londonderry Plantation*, was obviously a direct outcome from that interest.[45] Quinn's Ph.D. subject on early Tudor administration in Ireland had been partly inspired by the attention that George Hill had drawn to a significant English settlement along the coastline of north-east Ulster that had long predated the English and Scottish re-settlement of that area in the seventeenth century. Quinn's description of the residue of this medieval English presence in Ulster that he included as part of his doctoral thesis became the subject of some of his first published articles that he addressed particularly to an 'Ulster' audience. Some years later, Quinn's first published pronouncement on the theory of English colonization—a subject on which he was to become a global expert—had been triggered by what Hill had written in *Plantation Acres* of the effort made in the 1570s by Secretary Sir Thomas Smith to establish a plantation of the Ards peninsula in County Down.[46]

At the very moment that Ulster history and British academic history were becoming interlinked by the work of Moody and Quinn, Robert Dudley Edwards, who had received his undergraduate education at University College, Dublin, was establishing a connection between what, up to then, had been bitterly contested Irish ecclesiastical history and British academic endeavour. This occurred because Edwards used the elements of his craft that he had mastered in London to adjudicate upon the arguments over the nature and course of the Reformation in Ireland that continued to be pursued in Ireland by G.V. Jourdan, a Protestant academic at Trinity College, Dublin, and Fr. Myles Ronan, a strident upholder of the Catholic position on the same subject. Edwards put himself forward as an

---

D.W. Hayton, 'The laboratory for "scientific history": T.W. Moody and R.D. Edwards at the Institute of Historical Research', *Irish Historical Studies*, vol. 41 (2017), 41–57. It should be noted that at this point Ireland was politically divided into Northern Ireland and the Irish Free State (later the Republic of Ireland) since the Anglo-Irish treaty of 1922.

[45] T.W. Moody, *The Londonderry Plantation, 1609-1641: The City of London and the Plantation in Ulster* (Belfast, 1939); on the academic training to which Quinn and Moody had been exposed in Belfast, L.A. Clarkson, 'James Eadie Todd and the school of History at Queen's University, Belfast', *Irish Historical Studies*, vol. 41 (2017), 22–40; there are some insights into the Belfast and London experiences as these were recalled by D.B. Quinn in Nicholas Canny and Karen Ordahl Kupperman, 'The Scholarship and Legacy of David Beers Quinn, 1909-2002', *William and Mary Quarterly*, vol. 60 (2003), 843–60.

[46] D.B. Quinn, 'Anglo-Irish Ulster in the early sixteenth century', *Proceedings...of the Belfast Natural History and Philosophical Society*, 1933-1934 (1935), 28–42; Quinn, 'Sir Thomas Smith (1513-1577) and the beginnings of English Colonial theory', *Proceedings of the American Philosophical Society*, vol. 39 (1945), 543–60; K.R. Andrews, Nicholas Canny, and P.E.H. Hair, 'Preface, David Beers Quinn', K.R. Andrews, Nicholas Canny, and P.E.H. Hair, eds., *The Westward Enterprise: English Activities in Ireland, the Atlantic and America, 1480-1650* (Liverpool, 1978), v–xi; Canny and Kupperman, 'The Scholarship and Legacy of David Beers Quinn'.

THE FAILURE OF THE IMAGINATION CONCERNING IRELAND'S PASTS   377

arbiter of this gladiatorial-like contest in his first book, *Church and State in Tudor Ireland*, based on the earlier section of his London Ph.D. thesis.

In his book, Edwards made it clear that he considered that both Ronan and Jourdan fell short of the professional standards that he had mastered in London. Ronan, he believed, was inadequate as a historian because of inaccuracies and turgid prose, and Jourdan because of his ill concealed anti-Catholic prejudice. Both also, in Edwards' opinion, fell short of professional standards because they did not have sufficient knowledge of the relevant primary sources and their provenance.[47] Edwards expressed himself hopeful that his own investigation of the subject, over which the two contestants squabbled so bitterly, would bring an end to further undignified denominational point scoring concerning the Reformation in Ireland. Nonetheless, notwithstanding his professed neutral stance, Edwards wrote essentially to state the Catholic-nationalist position more effectively than Ronan had done. Thus the book was replete with references to such matters as the 'persecution' of Catholics by state officials; the passage of reformation legislation in the Irish parliament of 1536 because members had been 'intimidated' by Henry VIII; the enactment of the Elizabethan statutes of 1560 by a 'trick'; and the 'packing' of all parliaments (other than that convened by Queen Mary) that had to do with doctrinal matters. The work assumed an even more Catholic appearance by the addition of an appendix listing 'A Chronological List of The Irish Martyrs, 1534–1603'. P.F. Moran who had been dead since 1911, would, if he had lived, have given his imprimatur to the entire book because Edwards had derived his list of martyrs from the *Irish Ecclesiastical Record* of which Moran had been joint editor during his years in Ireland.[48]

When, with the benefit of hindsight, we look critically at these first books of each of Moody and Edwards, it becomes clear that neither was a promoter of the value free history that is frequently attributed to them. As Moody presented the involvement of the London merchant companies with plantation in Ulster in a positive light, he was clearly making a conscious contribution to Ulster history for which the great plantation of the seventeenth century had long been considered the cornerstone. Edwards was similarly contributing consciously to Catholic Nationalist history when he assured his readers that the ability of Ireland's Catholics to survive the travails of the sixteenth and seventeenth century 'laid the foundation of a unity which was ultimately to develop into an Irish nation'.[49]

---

[47] R. Dudley Edwards, *Church and State in Tudor Ireland: A History of Penal Laws against Irish Catholics, 1534–1603* (Dublin, 1935); G.V. Jourdan, *Reformation in Ireland in the 16th century* (Dublin, 1932); Myles Ronan, *Reformation in Dublin, 1536–58* (Dublin, 1926); Ronan, *Reformation in Ireland under Elizabeth, 1558–80* (Dublin, 1930).

[48] Edwards, *Church and State*, 308–12.   [49] Edwards, *Church and State*, 303, note 2.

378 IMAGINING IRELAND'S PASTS

These early publications of Edwards and Moody deserve special consideration because, as Ciaran Brady has explained, these two historians set the pace from the 1930s onward in professionalizing the conduct of historical research in Ireland.[50] However, while each of these two historians employed the referencing methods that conformed with what was then best practice in London, each sought also to explain how the study of the particular subjects they had chosen to investigate related to the unfolding of a grand narrative that led to a fairly predictable outcome. The end to which Moody's *Londonderry Plantation* looked forward was a prosperous Ulster based on commercial principles; and Edwards's *Church and State* looked forward to the eventual emergence of an Irish Catholic nation. In this respect the innovations introduced by Edwards and Moody were no more than an incremental improvement on the methods employed by the more thoughtful historians among their predecessors whose work they believed themselves to be superseding.

This suggests that it was not until the next generation that a fundamental change in the study of the early modern period at an academic level in Ireland became discernible. This happened when some of the students of Edwards and Moody, again inspired by historical developments in Britain and further afield, focused their minds on the resolution of problems that were of universal interest, and seemed unconcerned about dovetailing the subjects of which they wrote to fit with any master narrative, whether of the history of Ireland or that of Ulster. This independent approach was first evident in the work of Hugh Kearney, whose Ph.D. work had been supervised by Edwards, and that of Aidan Clarke, who had been a student of Moody.

Kearney's first book, *Strafford in Ireland*, was based on a Ph.D. thesis completed at University College, Dublin, under Edwards's supervision. It was characterized, as Edwards's own work had been, by a rigorous scrutiny of evidence, in this case of Strafford's papers that had only recently been opened to researchers, and by an astute appraisal of what others had written of the subject in previous decades and centuries. However, Kearney broke new ground by relating Strafford's economic activities in Ireland to investigations then under way by historians in Britain, and in some other countries of Europe, into how officeholders used the positions they held under the Crown to achieve advancement for themselves or for those who belonged to the same social position. At the same time Kearney addressed the nature of absolute rule and questioned if Strafford's brief period of rule in Ireland 'was indeed an English copy of the best continental model'.[51]

If Kearney was interrogating the nature of power in the seventeenth century, Aidan Clarke, who had completed his Ph.D. thesis under the supervision of

---

[50] Brady, 'Arrested Development', 277–8.
[51] Hugh F. Kearney, *Strafford in Ireland, 1633–41: A Study in Absolutism* (Manchester, 1959), quotation viii.

THE FAILURE OF THE IMAGINATION CONCERNING IRELAND'S PASTS   379

Moody at Trinity College, Dublin, set out in his first book, *The Old English in Ireland, 1625–42*, to explain what induced the particular group he had studied, who historically had been loyal to English institutions and government, to suddenly take up arms to defend themselves. Clarke, after a careful sifting of a wide range of evidence, showed how those who had been frequently represented as rebels by their English opponents were in fact 'reactionaries' seeking to restore equilibrium between a monarch and his subjects. Clarke was thus able to see that the Old English in arms were acting, as did other 'country parties' in Western Europe at that time to confront what they perceived to be challenges to their customary autonomy being pursued by an innovating state. In the light of this, it is not surprising that, after this consideration of the nature of the Old English involvement with insurrection in 1641, Clarke, in one of his publications that followed quickly upon the book, related the particular problem of why the Old English had taken up arms, to what many historians of the time considered to be the general crisis of the mid-seventeenth century.[52] Independently of what was happening within Ireland, D.B. Quinn, who had made his career in Britain, had also been universalizing Irish history by investigating how developments in Ireland in the sixteenth and the seventeenth centuries could be considered fruitfully in a colonial context.[53]

When they are considered together the work of these three historians did much to enhance the reputation in academic circles of early modern Ireland as an area in which to conduct research, because they explained why what happened in Ireland during those centuries had some wider significance. Essentially, their example both in contextualizing their subject and in using fresh sources and novel methods to shed light on the questions they posed, made it clear to subsequent generations of researchers that early modern Ireland was an epoch worthy of investigation in its own right, and not just a staging post in the unfolding of some grand narrative.[54] Many who engaged on this process, and certainly Kearney, Clarke, and Quinn who we might consider mould breakers, acknowledged that they were building on the work of historians who had written on the subject, sometimes centuries earlier. However, they believed themselves to be liberated from the tunnel vision of their predecessors because, unlike them, they were not concerned with any grand narrative, and believed that history was

---

[52] Aidan Clarke, *The Old English in Ireland, 1625–42* (London, 1966), quotation 234; Clarke, 'Ireland and the General Crisis', *Past and Present*, 48 (1970), 79–99; on a recent explication of the global dimension to the crisis, Geoffrey Parker, *Global Crisis: War, Climate Change and Catastrophe in the Seventeenth Century* (New Haven, Ct., 2013).

[53] Besides the publications of Quinn with an Irish dimension already cited, D.B. Quinn, *Ralegh and the British Empire* (London, 1947); Quinn, *The Elizabethans and the Irish* (Ithaca, New York, 1966).

[54] For examples of the new historiography and discussions thereon, Jane Ohlmeyer, ed., *The Cambridge History of Ireland*, vol. 2, *1550–1730* (Cambridge, 2018); Sarah Covington, Vincent P. Carey, and Valerie McGowan-Doyle, eds., *Early Modern Ireland: New Sources, Methods and Perspectives* (Abingdon, 2019).

380 IMAGINING IRELAND'S PASTS

as good as the questions posed and the sources deployed by the historian to provide answers to those questions.

The success of these historians, and those who have followed in their tradition, in securing international academic recognition for the research they engaged upon, and in attracting ever more scholars from Ireland and many other countries to dedicate their lives to the study of the subject, should not lead us to conclude that the older paradigms have died or been discredited, even within the academic community. On the contrary, the single most popular publication of the twentieth century on early modern Ireland was a biography of Hugh O'Neill by Seán Ó Faoláin, a novelist and political biographer. Ó Faoláin's biography was, in a sense, an updating of what John Mitchel had written on the same subject in the mid-nineteenth century, which was discussed in Chapter 8. However, Ó Faoláin went further than Mitchel because, in assigning O'Neill a role in a national grand narrative that Mitchel would not have acknowledged, he described him as 'an able politician and an able general and the only big man in all Irish History from beginning to end'.[55] Then, as had happened when Mitchel had written his biography of O'Neill in the nineteenth century, this secular representation provoked a reaction from a Catholic-nationalist author who wished to claim O'Neill as a martyr for the Catholic faith rather than for an Irish nation. The reaction came this time from Micheline Kerney-Walsh in a sequence of short papers that she published over several decades, and later brought together in a documentary compilation—*Destruction by Peace: Hugh O'Neill after Kinsale*. Here, the O'Neill exposed to public view by Kerney-Walsh from his correspondence with the Spanish court was a modest, serene and above all pious figure who had been forced into exile because he and his associates had been in fear of their lives due to their attachment to their Catholic faith.[56]

This example illustrates how some authors working outside the academic fold continued to believe that historical contributions have value only in so far as they contribute to sustaining a grand narrative. This view continued to prevail also within sectors of the academic community in Ireland, especially in literature departments where some scholars began to use the sources of which they had expert knowledge to sustain a national grand narrative, thus compensating for what they considered a betrayal of the national trust by their historian colleagues. Other scholars, including some in the social sciences as well as in literature, took to using the sources at their command to compose fresh grand narratives that drew upon Marxist no less than nationalist presumptions. The efforts of all such scholars, and the occasional historians who have endorsed their opinions, have

---

[55] Seán Ó Faoláin, *The Great O'Neill: A biography of Hugh O'Neill, earl of Tyrone 1550–1616* (London, 1942), 170–1.

[56] Micheline Kerney-Walsh, ed., *Destruction by Peace: Hugh O'Neill after Kinsale* (Armagh, 1986), 143.

enlivened discourse within and without the walls of academe.[57] However, this present book will hopefully have made it clear that the fundamental problem that has confronted historians of Ireland in every century since the sixteenth has been the difficulty in defining what is, or might become, an Irish nation. This in turn explains why historians in successive centuries have failed to arrive at a consensus on what should be the theme of any grand narrative for Ireland's history. In so far as this book has done anything to resolve the problem it may have been by suggesting that our knowledge about the past may be enriched if we as historians become less judgemental and disregard what so many of our predecessors considered a teleological imperative.

---

[57] The most fulsome endorsement by a professional historian of the criticisms raised by national-ists and Marxists alike was provided by Brendan Bradshaw in the book he published shortly before his death, Brendan Bradshaw, 'And so began the Irish Nation': Nationality, National Consciousness and Nationalism in Pre-Modern Ireland (Farnham, 2015); on the debate as it had been pursued down to the early 1990s, Ciaran Brady, ed., Interpreting Irish History: The Debate on Historical Revisionism, 1938–1994 (Dublin, 1994).

References

A: Primary Printed Sources, Including Printed Editions

The Acts of James II's Irish parliament of 1689, eds., John Bergin and Andrew Lyall (Dublin, 2016).

A.F.M.; Annals of the Four Masters: Annála *Ríoghachta Éireann, Annals of the Kingdom of Ireland by the Four Masters....to the Year 1616*, ed. and trans., John O'Donovan (7 vols., Dublin, 1851).

'An Aphorismical Discovery of Treasonable Faction', see under Gilbert, *A Contemporary History*.

Annals of Ulster, Annála Uladh....431–1131, 1155–541, ed. and trans., W.M. Hennessy and B. MacCarthy (4 vols., Dublin, 1887–1901).

Cogadh Gaedhel re Gallaibh: The War of the Gaedhil with the Gaill, or The Invasions of Ireland by the Danes and Other Norsemen, ed. and trans., J.H Todd, (London, 1867).

A perfect relation of the beginning and continuation of the Irish rebellion from May last [May 1641] to this present 12 January 1641 [1641/2] (London, 1641/2).

A Report on the Carte Manuscripts in the Bodleian Library, eds., C.W. Russell and J.P. Prendergast (8 vols., London, 1871).

Bagwell, Richard, *Ireland under the Tudors* (3 vols., London, 1885–90).

Bagwell, Richard, *Ireland under the Stuarts* (London, 1909–16).

Bale, John: *The Vocaycon of John Bale* in *The Harleian Miscellany*, vol. 6 (London 1810), 437–64.

Ball, F[rancis]. Elrington, *A History of the County of Dublin, The People, Parishes and Antiquities from the earliest times to the close of the eighteenth century* (3 vols., Dublin, 1902).

Borlase, Edmund, *The Reduction of Ireland to the Crown of England* (London, 1675).

Brady, W. Maziere, ed., *The MacGillycuddy Papers: A Selection from the family archives of 'The MacGillycuddy of the Reeks'* (London, 1867).

Bradshaw, Brendan, 'And so began the Irish Nation': Nationality, National Consciousness and Nationalism in Pre-Modern Ireland (Farnham, 2015).

Brooke, Charlotte, *Charlotte Brooke's, Reliques of Irish Poetry* [1789], ed., Lesa Ní Mhunghaile (Dublin, 2009).

Calendar of the Carew Manuscripts...Lambeth, 1515–74 [etc.] (6 vols., London, 1867–73).

Calendar of State Papers Ireland: Tudor Period, 1509–1547, eds., Steven G. Ellis and James Murray (Dublin, 2017).

Calendar of State Papers relating to Ireland, Henry VIII to Elizabeth (11 vols., London 1860–1912).

Calendar of State Papers relating to Ireland, 1603–1625, eds., C.W. Russell and J.P. Prendergast (5 vols., London, 1872–1880).

Campion, Edmund: *Two Bokes of the Histories of Ireland compiled by Edmunde Campion*, ed., A.F. Vossen (Assen, the Netherlands, 1963). See also under Ware, James.

384 REFERENCES

Carey, Mathew, *Vindicae Hibernicae or Ireland Vindicated* (Philadelphia, 1819).

Carte, Thomas, *The Life of James, duke of Ormond* (3 vols., London, 1735, 1736).

Clarendon: Edward Hyde, Earl of Clarendon, *A Short View of the State and Condition of the Kingdom of Ireland*, ed., Jane Ohlmeyer (Oxford, 2020).

Clarke, Aidan, *The Old English in Ireland, 1625–42* (London, 1966).

Clarke, Aidan, 'Ireland and the General Crisis', Past and Present, 48 (1970), 79–99. See also under Depositions.

Clarke, Samuel, *A generall martyrologie* (London, 1651).

Colgan, John, *Acta sanctorum veteris et maiores Scotiae, seu, Hiberniae sanctorum insulae* (Louvain, 1645).

Collins, Arthur, see under *Letters and Memorials of State...*

Commentarius Rinuccianus, de sedis apostolicae legatione ad foederatos Hiberniae catholicos per annos 1645-9, ed., Stanilaus Kavanagh (6 vols., Dublin, 1932–49).

Cox, Richard, *Hibernia Anglicana, or, The History of Ireland, from the Conquest thereof by the English to this present time* (London, 1689–90).

Crespin, Jean, *Actes des martyrs deduits en sept livres...Hus* (Geneva, 1564).

Curry, John, *Historical Memoirs of the Irish Rebellion in the year 1641, Extracted from Parliamentary Journals, State Acts and the most eminent Protestant Historians* (London 1758).

Curry, John, *An Historical and Critical Review of the Civil Wars in Ireland from the reigns of Queen Elizabeth to the Settlement under King William* (Dublin, 1775).

Cusack, M.F., *An Illustrated History of Ireland, from the earliest period* (London, 1868, 1869); citation here is from the third 1869 edition that reprinted the Prefaces to the first and second editions.

Cusack, M.F., *The Student's Manual of Irish History* (London, 1870).

Cusack, M.F., *A History of the Kingdom of Kerry* (London, Dublin, and Boston, 1871).

Cusack, M.F., *A History of the Irish Nation: Social, Ecclesiastical, Biographical, Industrial and Antiquarian* (London, 1877).

Cusack, M.F., *The Nun of Kenmare: An Autobiography* (London, 1889). Citation here is from a reprinted edition (London, 1998) with a valuable introduction by Maria Luddy.

Davies, John, *A Discovery of the True Causes why Ireland was never entirely subdued, and brought under Obedience of the Crowne of England, until the beginning of his Majesties happy raigne* (London, 1612).

Davies, John, *Le Premier Report des Cases et Matters en Ley...John Davys* (Dublin, 1615).

Davies, John, *A Report of Cases and Matters in Law Resolved in the King's Courts in Ireland Collected and Digested by Sir John Davies* (Dublin, 1762).

Davis, Thomas, *Essays and Poems with a Centenary Memoir, 1845-1945* (Dublin, 1945).

Davis, Thomas, *Literary and Historical Essays*, ed., C[harles] G[avan] D[uffy] (Dublin, 1846).

Davis, Thomas, *The Patriot Parliament of 1689*, ed., Charles Gavan Duffy (London, 1893).

Davitt, Micheal, *The Fall of Feudalism in Ireland: or the Story of the Land League Revolution* (London, 1904).

de Mariana, Juan, *Historiae de rebus Hispaniae* (Madrid, 1592).

de Mariana, Juan, *Historia general de España* (Madrid 1601).

Depositions: *1641 Depositions*, vol. 1, *Armagh, Louth and Monaghan*, ed., Aidan Clarke (Dublin, 2014).

Derricke, John, *The Image of Ireland, with a Discoverie of Woodkarne* (London, 1581) facsimile edition, ed., D.B. Quinn (Belfast, 1985).

REFERENCES   385

'*Destruction by Peace*': *Hugh O'Neill after Kinsale*, ed., Micheline Kerney-Walsh (Armagh, 1986).

Doheny, Michael, *The History of the American Revolution* (Dublin, 1846).

Duffy, Charles Gavan, *The Ballad Poetry of Ireland* (Dublin, 1845; citations here from the 40th edition, Dublin, 1874).

Dwyer, Philip, *The Diocese of Killaloe, from the Reformation to the Close of the Eighteenth Century* (Dublin, 1878).

Edwards, R. Dudley, *Church and State in Tudor Ireland: A History of Penal Laws against Irish Catholics, 1534–1603* (Dublin, 1935).

Fitzgerald Reverend P., and J.J. McGregor, *The History, Topography and Antiquities of the County and City of Limerick* (2 vols., Dublin 1826, 1827).

Five Seventeenth-Century Political Poems, ed., Cecile O'Rahilly (Dublin, 1977).

Foxe, John, *Acts and Monuments of these latter and perilous days* (London, 1563); known popularly as *Foxe's Book of Martyrs*.

Frost, James, *The History and Topography of the County of Clare: From the earliest times to the beginning of the eighteenth century* (Dublin, 1893).

Froude J.A., *The English in Ireland in the Eighteenth Century* (3 vols., London, 1872).

Gainsford, Thomas, *The True, Exemplary and Remarkable History of the Earl of Tyrone* (London, 1619).

Gainsford, Thomas, *The Glory of England* (London, 1618).

Gerald of Wales, *Giraldus Cambrensis, Expugnatio Hibernica: The Conquest of Ireland by Giraldus Cambrensis*, ed. and trans., A.B. Scott and F.X. Martin (Dublin, 1978).

Gerald of Wales, *Giraldus Cambrensis, The History and Topography of Ireland* trans. and ed., John J. O'Meara (revised edition, Mountrath, 1982).

Gilbert, J.T., ed., *A Contemporary History of Affairs in Ireland, from 1641–1652, with an appendix of original letters and documents* (3 vols., Dublin, 1879).

Grosart Alexander B., ed, *The Lismore Papers* (1st series 4 vols., London, 1886, 2nd series 4 vols., London 1887).

Haicéad, Pádraigín, *Filíocht Phádraigín Haicéad*, ed., Máire Ní Cheallacháin (Dublin, 1962).

Hall, John, see under Waring.

Hanmer, Meredith, see under Ware, James.

Harris, Walter, *The Whole Works of Sir James Ware concerning Ireland revised and improved* (Dublin, 1764).

Hickson, Mary Agnes, *Selections from Old Kerry Records* (2 vols., London, 1872, 1874).

Hickson, Mary Agnes, *Ireland in the Seventeenth Century, or the Irish Massacres of 1641–2, their causes and results* (2 vols., London, 1884).

Hill, George, ed., *The Montgomery Manuscripts* (Belfast, 1869).

Hill, George, *An Historical Account of the MacDonnells of Antrim* (Belfast, 1873).

Hill, George, *An Historical Account of the Plantation in Ulster at the Commencement of the Seventeenth Century, 1608–1620,* (Belfast, 1877).

Hill, George, *Plantation Papers: or Historical Sketches in the Counties of Down and Antrim* (Belfast, 1888).

Hill, George, Plantation *Papers, containing a summary sketch of the Great Ulster Plantation in the Year 1610* (Belfast, 1889).

Holinshed, *Chronicles: The Historie of Ireland from the first inhabitation... 1509, collected by Raphaell Holinshed, and continued... 1547 by Richard Stanyhurst* (London, 1577).

Holinshed, *The Second Volume of Chronicles containing the Description, Conquest, Inhabitation and Troublesome Estate of Ireland first collected by Raphael Holinshed and... continued... until this present time of Sir John Perrot... by John Hooker, alias Vowell* (London, 1587).

386 REFERENCES

Hooker, John, alias Vowell: see under Holinshed, *The Second Volume of Chronicles...*

Hume, David, *The History of England from the Invasion of Julius Caesar to the Revolution in 1688* (6 vols., London 1762; the edition cited here is 6 vols., London, 1841).

Jones, Henry, *A Remonstrance of divers remarkable passages concerning the church and kingdom of Ireland* (London, 1642).

Jourdan, G.V., *Reformation in Ireland in the 16th century* (Dublin, 1932).

Keating, Geoffrey, *Foras Feasa ar Éirinn le Seathrún Céitinn D.D.: The History of Ireland by Geoffrey Keating D.D.*, ed. and trans., David Comyn and P.S. Dinneen (4 vols., London, 1902–14).

Kearney, Hugh F., *Strafford in Ireland, 1633–41: A Study in Absolutism* (Manchester, 1959).

King, William, *The State of the Protestants of Ireland under the Late King James's Government* (London, 1691).

Lecky, W.E.H., *Leaders of Public Opinion in Ireland* (2 vols., London, 1912, first edition under Lecky's name 1871).

Lecky, W.E.H., *History of Ireland in the Eighteenth Century* (5 vols., London, 1892).

Leland, Thomas, *The History of Ireland from the Invasion of Henry II with a preliminary discourse on the ancient state of that Kingdom* (3 vols., Dublin, 1773).

Letters and Memorials of State in the reigns of Queen Mary, Queen Elizabeth, King James, King Charles I, part of the reigns of Charles II and Oliver's usurpation by Arthur Collins Esq., author of *The Peerage of England* (London, 1756).

Lombard, Peter, *De Regno Hiberniae, sanctorum insula, commentarius* (Louvain, 1632).

Lombard, Peter, *De Regno Hiberniae, insulsa sanctorum, commentarius*, ed., P.F. Moran (Dublin, 1868).

McGee, Thomas D'Arcy, *The Irish Writers of the Seventeenth Century* (Dublin, 1846).

Mac Geoghegan, Abbé [James], *Histoire d'Irlande Ancienne et Moderne* (3 vols., vol. 1, Paris, 1758, vol. 2, Paris, 1762, vol. 3, Amsterdam, 1763).

Mac Geoghegan, Abbé [James], *History of Ireland Ancient and Modern*, English trans. P. O'Kelly (3 vols., Dublin, 1832).

Mac Nevin, Thomas, *The History of the Volunteers of 1782* (Dublin, 1845).

Mac Nevin, Thomas, *The Confiscation of Ulster* (Dublin, 1846).

Mariana, see under de Mariana.

Meehan, C. P., *The Confederation of Kilkenny* (Dublin 1846).

Meehan, C. P., *The Geraldines, earls of Desmond, and the persecution of the Irish Catholics* (Dublin, 1847).

Meehan, C. P., *The Fate and Fortunes of Hugh O'Neill... and Rory O'Donnell* (Dublin, 1868).

Memoirs of the Right Honourable Marquis of Clanricarde, Lord Deputy General of Ireland (London, 1722).

The Memoirs and Letters of Ulick, Marquis of Clanricarde and Earl of St Albans...Lord Lieutenant of Ireland...now first published by the present earl of Clanricarde (London, 1757).

Messingham, Thomas, *Florilegium insulae sanctorum* (Paris, 1624).

Mitchel, John, *The Life and Times of Aodh O'Neill, Prince of Ulster, called by the English, Hugh, Earl of Tyrone...* (Dublin, 1845).

Mitchel, John, *Jail Journal; or Five Years in British Prisons* (published serially in New York, 1854, Dublin book edition, 1913).

Mitchel, John, *The History of Ireland, from the Treaty of Limerick to the Present Time* (2 vols., New York and Dublin, 1868).

Molyneux, William, *The Case of Ireland's Being bound by Acts of Parliament in England, Stated*, Dublin, 1698, ed., Patrick Hyde Kelly (Dublin, 2018).

REFERENCES 387

Moody, T.W., *The Londonderry Plantation, 1609-1641: The City of London and the Plantation in Ulster* (Belfast, 1939).

Moran, P[atrick] F[rancis], *Historical Sketch of the Persecutions suffered by the Catholics of Ireland, under the rule of Cromwell and the Puritans* (Dublin, 1862, citation is from the third edition, Callan, Co. Kilkenny, 1903).

Moran, P[atrick] F[rancis], *Memoirs of the Most Rev Oliver Plunket* (Dublin, 1861).

Moran, P[atrick] F[rancis], *Spicilegium Ossoriense, being a collection of original letters and papers illustrative of the History of the Irish Church from the Reformation to the year 1800* (Dublin, 1874).

See also under Lombard.

Moryson, Fynes, *An Itinerary* .... (originally published London, 1617, 4 vols., Glasgow, 1907-8).

Moryson, Fynes, 'The Irish Sections of Fynes Moryson's Unpublished Itinerary', ed., Graham Kew, *Analecta Hibernica*, 37 (1998), 79-132.

Moryson, Fynes, 'Of the Commonwealth of Ireland', C. Litton Falkiner ed., *Illustrations of Irish history and Topography* (London, 1904).

Musgrave, Richard, *Memoirs of the Different Rebellions in Ireland* (Dublin and London, 1801; the edition used and cited here is the third edition of 1802 prepared and edited by Steven Myers and Delores McKnight, Fort Wayne, Ia., 1995).

Nua-Dhunaire, vol. 1, ed., Pádraig de Brún, Breandán Ó Buachalla and Tomás Ó Concheanainn (Dublin, 1971).

Nua-Dhunaire, vol. 3, ed., Tomás Ó Concheanainn (Dublin, 1978).

Ó Bruadair, Dáibhí, *Duanaire Dháibhidh Uí Bhruadair*, ed., J.C. Mac Erlean (3 vols., London, 1910, 1913, 1917).

Ó Cléirigh, Lughaidh, *Beatha Aodha Ruaidh Uí Dhomhnaill by Lughaidh Ó Cléirigh*, ed., Paul Walsh (London, 1948).

O'Conor, Charles, *Dissertation on the Antient History of Ireland* (Dublin, 1753).

O'Connell, Daniel, *A Memoir on Ireland Native and Saxon* (first published 1843; reprinted Port Washington, N.Y., 1970).

Ó Faoláin, Seán, *The Great O'Neill: A biography of Hugh O'Neill, earl of Tyrone 1550-1616* (London, 1942).

O'Flaherty Roderic, *Roderick O'Flaherty's Letters... 1696-1709*, ed., Richard Sharpe (Dublin, 2013).

O'Flaherty Roderic, *A Chorographical Description of West or Iar Connacht, 1684 by Roderic O'Flaherty*, ed., James Hardiman (Dublin, 1846).

O'Flaherty Roderic, *Ogygia: seu Rerum Hibernicarum Chronologia & etc* (London, 1685).

Ormonious, see under *The Tipperary hero*.

O'Rorke, Archdeacon Terence, *History, Antiquities and Present State of the Parishes of Ballysadare and Kilvarnet in the County of Sligo with notices of the O'Haras, the Coopers, the Percevals and other local families* (Dublin, 1878).

O'Rorke, Archdeacon Terence, *The History of Sligo: Town and County* (2 vols., Dublin, 1890).

Orrery, Roger Boyle, first earl of, *A Collection of the State Letters of... Roger Boyle 1st earl of Orrery* [ed., Thomas Morrice] (Dublin, 1743).

O'Sullivan Beare, Philip, *Historiae Catholicae Iberniae Compendium* (Lisbon, 1621).

O'Sullivan Beare, Philip, *Ireland under Elizabeth*, ed. and trans., Matthew J.Byrne (Dublin, 1903).

O'Sullivan Beare, Philip, *Selections from the Zoilomastix of Philip O'Sullivan Beare*, ed., Thomas J. O'Donnell (Dublin, 1960).

388 REFERENCES

Pairlement Chloinne Tomáis ed., N.J.A. Williams, (Dublin, 1981).

Poems of the Butlers, ed., James Carney (Dublin, 1945).

Prendergast, John P., *The Cromwellian Settlement of Ireland* (London, 1865).

Prendergast, John P., *Ireland from the Restoration to the Revolution, 1660-1690* (London, 1887).

Quinn, D.B., 'Anglo-Irish Ulster in the early sixteenth century', *Proceedings... of the Belfast Natural History and Philosophical Society*, 1933-1934 (1935), 28-42.

Quinn, D.B., 'Sir Thomas Smith (1513-1577) and the beginnings of English Colonial theory', *Proceedings of the American Philosophical Society*, vol. 39 (1945), 543-60.

Quinn, D.B., *Ralegh and the British Empire* (London, 1947).

Raifteraí: Amhráin agus Dánta, ed., Ciarán Ó Coigligh (Dublin, 1987).

Reform Treatises on Tudor Ireland, 1537-1599, ed., David Heffernan (Dublin, 2016).

Reid, John Seaton, *History of the Presbyterian Church in Ireland, comprising the Civil History of the Province of Ulster, from the accession of James the First; a new edition with additional notes* by W.D. Killen, D.D. 3 vols. (Belfast, 1867).

Reily, Hugh, *The Impartial History of Ireland* (London 1742).

Reily, Hugh., *The Impartial History of Ireland* (Dublin, 1833; this edition was brought down to 1829 by a 'gentleman of the city').

'The Remonstrance of The Catholics of Ireland, given at Trim, 17 March, 1642', printed, John Curry, *Historical Memoirs of the Irish Rebellion in the year 1641, Extracted from Parliamentary Journals, State Acts and the most eminent Protestant Historians* (London, 1758), 226-47.

Robertson, William, *History of Scotland, 1542-1603* (3 vols., London, 1759).

Ronan, Myles, *Reformation in Dublin, 1536-58* (Dublin, 1926).

Ronan, Myles, *Reformation in Ireland under Elizabeth, 1558-80* (Dublin, 1930).

Rothe, David, *Analecta Sacra Nova et Mira de Rebus Catholicorum in Hibernia Pro fide & Religione gestis, divisa in tres partes*, ed., P. F. Moran (Dublin, 1884).

Rothe, David, *Hibernia resurgens* (Paris, 1621).

R.S., *A Collection of some of the Murthers and Massacres committed on the Irish in Ireland since 23rd October 1641* (London, 1662).

Sander, Nicholas, *De Origine ac Progressu Schismatis Anglicani* [1586], ed. and trans., D. Lewis (London, 1877).

Sidney, Henry, ed., *A Viceroy's Vindication? Sir Henry Sidney's Memoir of Service in Ireland, 1556-78*, ed., Ciaran Brady (Cork, 2002).

Smith, Charles with [Walter Harris], *The Ancient and Present State of the County of Down, containing a chorographical description* (Dublin, 1744).

Smith, Charles, *The Ancient and Present State of the County and City of Waterford*, (Dublin, 1746, 2nd edition, 1774).

Smith, Charles, *The Ancient and Present State of the County and City of Cork* (Dublin, 1750, Cork, 1815).

Smith, Charles, *The Ancient and Present State of... Kerry* (Dublin, 1756).

Spenser, Edmund, *A View of the Present State of Ireland* [1596], ed., W.L. Renwick (Oxford, 1970).

Stafford, Thomas, *Pacata Hibernia, Ireland Appeased and Reduced: or A History of the Late Warres of Ireland, Especially within the Province of Mounster...* (London, 1633).

Stafford, Thomas, *Pacata Hibernia; or a History of the Wars in Ireland, during the Reign of Queen Elizabeth* (2 vols., Dublin, 1810); an edition of the 1633 text.

Stanihurst, Richard, *Great Deeds in Ireland: Richard Stanihurst's* De Rebus in Hibernia Gestis, ed. and trans., John Barry and Hiram Morgan (Cork, 2013).

See also under Holinshed.

State Papers during the reign of Henry VIII (11 vols., London, 1830–52).

The Statutes at Large passed in the parliaments held in Ireland...1310–1786 (20 vols., Dublin, 1786–1801).

Strafford, Thomas Wentworth, earl of: *The earl of Strafford's Letters and Dispatches, with an essay towards his life by Sir George* Radcliffe, ed., William Knowler (London, 1739).

'The Supplication of the Blood of the English...Cryeng out of the Yearth for Revenge', ed., Willy Maley, Analecta *Hibernica*, 36 (1995), 1–77.

Temple, John, *The Irish Rebellion: or an History of the Attempts of the Irish Papists to extirpate the Protestants in the Kingdom of Ireland; together with the Barbarous Cruelties and Bloody Massacres which ensued thereupon* (London, 1646); the edition cited here is London, 1746.

The Tipperary Hero: Dermot O'Meara's Ormonious (1615), ed. and trans., David Edwards and Keith Sidwell (Turnhout, Belgium, 2011).

'Tuireamh na hÉireann', see *Five Seventeenth Century Political Poems.*

Ussher, James, *The Correspondence of James Ussher, 1600–1656*, ed., Elizabethanne Boran (3 vols., Dublin, 2015).

Ussher, James, *An Epistle Concerning the Religion of the Ancient Irish* (Dublin, 1622).

Ussher, James, *Archiepiscoporum Casseliensium et Tuamensium vitae* (Dublin, 1626).

Ussher, James, *De praesulibus Lageniae sive provinciae Dubliniensis* (Dublin, 1628).

Ussher, James, *A Discourse of the Religion Anciently Professed by the Irish and British* (London, 1631).

Ussher, James, *De scriptoribus Hiberniae* (Dublin, 1639).

Ussher, James, *De praesulibus Hiberniae* (Dublin, 1665).

Verse in English from Tudor and Stuart Ireland, ed., Andrew Carpenter (Cork, 2003).

Wadding, Luke: *Father Luke Wadding: Commemorative Volume*, ed., 'The Franciscan Fathers' (Dublin, 1957).

Ware, James, *A Historie of Ireland, collected by three learned authors, viz., Meredith Hanmer...Edmund Campion...and Edmund Spenser* (Dublin, 1633).

see also under Ware, Robert and Harris, Walter.

Ware, Robert, *The Antiquities and History of Ireland by...Sir James Ware* (Dublin, 1705).

W[aring] T[homas] with J[ohn] H[all], *A brief narration of the plotting, beginning and carrying of that execrable rebellion and butchery in Ireland* (London 1650).

White, Canon Patrick, P.P., V.G., *The History of Clare and the Dalcassian Clans of Tipperary, Limerick and Galway* (Dublin, 1893).

Wood-Martin, W.G., *History of Sligo: County and Town* (3 vols, Dublin, 1882, 1889, 1892).

Wood-Martin, W.G., *Sligo and the Enniskilleners from 1689–1691* (Dublin, 1880).

B: Secondary sources

Andrews, K.R., Canny, N.P., and Hair, P.E.H., 'Preface, David Beers Quinn', K.R. Andrews, N.P. Canny, and P.E.H. Hair, eds., *The Westward Enterprise: English Activities in Ireland, the Atlantic and America, 1480–1650* (Liverpool, 1978), v–xi.

Ansell, Richard, 'The 1688 Revolution in Ireland and the Memory of 1641', Williams and Forrest, eds., *Constructing the Past*, 73–93.

Armitage, David, *The Ideological Origins of the British Empire* (Cambridge, 2000).

Barnard, Toby, *Cromwellian Ireland: English Government and Reform in Ireland, 1649–1660* (Oxford, 1975).

Barnard, Toby '1641; a bibliographic essay', Brian Mac Cuarta, ed., *Ulster 1641*, 173–86.

390 REFERENCES

Barnard, Toby, 'The Uses of 23 October 1641 and Irish Protestant Celebrations', *English Historical Review*, vol. 106 (1991), 889–920.

Barnard, Toby, *Improving Ireland? Projectors, Prophets and Profiteers, 1641–1786* (Dublin, 2008).

Barnard, Toby, 'Sir John Gilbert and Irish Historiography', Clarke, Desmond and Hardiman, eds., *Sir John T. Gilbert, 1829–1898*, 92–110.

Barnard, Toby, 'Sir Richard Bellings': a Catholic courtier and diplomat from seventeenth-century Ireland, Mac Cuarta, ed., *Reshaping Ireland, 1550–1700*, 326–47.

Barr, Colin, 'The re-energising of Catholicism, 1790-1880', Kelly, *The Cambridge History of Ireland*, vol. 3, *1730–1880*, 280–304.

Bartlett, Thomas, ed., *The Cambridge History of Ireland* vol. 4 (Cambridge, 2018).

Bartlett, Thomas, 'Ireland during the Revolutionary and Napoleonic Wars, 1791-1815', Kelly, ed., *The Cambridge History of Ireland*, vol. 3, *1730–1880*, 74–101.

Bartlett, Thomas, 'The O'Haras of Annaghmore c1600–c1800: Survival and Revival', *Irish Economic and Social History*, vol. 9 (1982), 34–52.

Bartlett, Thomas with Dickson, David, Keogh, Dáire, and Whelan, Kevin, eds., *1798: A Bicentenary Perspective* (Dublin, 2003).

Beiner, Guy, *Remembering the Year of the French: Irish Folk History and Social Memory* (Madison, Wi., 2007).

Beiner, Guy, *Forgetful Remembrance: Social Forgetting and Vernacular Historiography of a Rebellion in Ulster* (Oxford, 2018).

Benton, Lauren, *Law and Colonial Cultures: Legal Regimes in World History* (Cambridge, 2002).

Berger, Stefan with Conrad, Christoph, eds., *The Past as History: National Identity and Historical Consciousness in Modern Europe* (Basingstoke, 2015).

Berger, Stefan and Chris Lorenz, eds., *Nationalizing the Past: Historians as Nation Builders in Modern Europe* (Basingstoke, 2010).

Berman, David, 'David Hume on the 1641 Rebellion in Ireland', *Studies*, vol. 65, no. 258, (1976), 101–12.

Binasco, Matteo, ed., *Luke Wadding, the Irish Franciscans and Global Catholicism* (N.Y and Abington, 2020).

Booth, Stephen, *The Book Called Holinshed's Chronicles* (Book Club of California, Los Angeles, 1968).

Bottigheimer, Karl, *English Money and Irish Land: The 'Adventurers' in the Cromwellian Settlement of Ireland* (Oxford, 1971).

Bradshaw, Brendan, *The Irish Constitutional Revolution of the Sixteenth Century* (Cambridge, 1979).

Bradshaw, Brendan, *'And so began the Irish Nation': Nationality, National Consciousness and Nationalism in Pre-Modern Ireland* (Farnham, 2015).

Brady, Ciaran, *The Chief Governors: The Rise and Fall of Reform Government in Tudor Ireland, 1536–88* (Cambridge, 1964).

Brady, Ciaran, *James Anthony Froude: An Intellectual Biography of a Victorian Prophet* (Oxford, 2013).

Brady, Ciaran, ed., *Interpreting Irish History: The Debate on Historical Revisionism, 1938–1994* (Dublin, 1994).

Brady, Ciaran, with Jane Ohlmeyer, eds., *British Interventions in Early Modern Ireland* (Cambridge, 2005).

Brady, Ciaran, 'Tudor Reform Strategies in Sixteenth-Century Ireland', Mac Cuarta, ed., *Reshaping Ireland, 1550–1700*, 21–42.

Brady, Ciaran, 'John P. Prendergast (1808–1893) and the Anglo-Irish Writing of Irish History', Ferencz and Vesztergom, eds.: *Presence Is No Island*, 31–68.

REFERENCES   391

Brady, Ciaran, 'Arrested Development: Competing Histories and the Formation of the Irish Historical Profession, 1801–1938', Frank and Hadler, eds., *Disputed Territories and Shared Pasts*, 275–302.

Bric, Maurice J., *Ireland, Philadelphia and the Re-Invention of America, 1760–1800* (Dublin, 2008).

Bric, Maurice J., 'Mathew Carey, and the "Empire of Liberty" in America', *Early American Studies*, vol. 11 (2013), 403–30.

Bric, Maurice J., ed., *Kerry: History and Society* (Dublin, 2020).

Brown, David, *Empire and Enterprise: Money, Power and the Adventurers for Irish Land during the British Civil Wars* (Manchester, 2020).

Brown, Michael, *The Irish Enlightenment* (Cambridge, Mass., 2016).

Brown, Michael and Lesa Ní Mhunghaile, 'Future Past: Enlightenment and Antiquarianism in the Eighteenth Century', Kelly, ed., *The Cambridge History of Ireland*, vol. 3, 380–405.

Burke, Martin J., 'The Poetics and Politics of Nationalist Historiography: Mathew Carey and the *Vindicae Hibernicae*', Leerssen, Van Der Weel and Westerweel, eds., *Forging in the* Smithy, 183–94.

Butler, W.F., 'The Policy of Surrender and Re-grant', *Royal Society of Antiquaries of Ireland Jrl.*, 43 (1912/13), 47–65 and 99–127.

Caball, Marc, *Poets and Politics: Reaction and Continuity in Irish Poetry, 1558–1625* (Cork, 1998).

Caball, Marc, *Kerry, 1600–1730: The Emergence of a British Atlantic County* (Dublin, 2017).

Caball, Marc, 'Religion, culture and the bardic elite in early modern Ireland', Ford and McCafferty, eds., *The Origins of Sectarianism*, 158–82.

Caball, Marc, 'Past Romance and Living Interest. A.B. Rowan and the *Kerry Magazine* (1854–6)', *North Munster Antiquarian Journal*, vol. 54 (2014), 113–24.

Caball, Marc, 'History and Politics; Interpretations of Early Modern Conquest and Reformation in Victorian Ireland', Berger and Lorenz, eds., *Nationalizing the Past*, 149–69.

Campbell, Ian, *Renaissance Humanism and Ethnicity before Race: The Irish and the English in the Seventeenth Century* (Manchester, 2013).

Canning, Ruth, *The Old English in Early Modern Ireland: The Palesmen and the Nine Years' War, 1594–1603* (Woodbridge, 2019).

Canny, Nicholas, 'The Formation of the Old English Elite in Ireland' (Dublin, published O'Donnell lecture, 1975).

Canny, Nicholas, *The Elizabethan Conquest of Ireland: A Pattern Established, 1565–1576* (Hassocks, nr. Brighton, 1976).

Canny, Nicholas, *The Upstart Earl: A Study of the Social and Mental World of Richard Boyle, First Earl of Cork, 1566–1643* (Cambridge, 1982).

Canny, Nicholas, *Making Ireland British*, 1580–1650 (Oxford, 2001).

Canny, Nicholas, 'The Haliday Collection: a printed source for the seventeenth century', *Proceedings of the Royal Irish Academy*, vol. 113 (2013), 279–307.

Canny, Nicholas, 'Irish Sources for Spenser's View', *Spenser Studies*, 31, 32. (2017/2018), 495–510.

Canny, Nicholas, '1641 in a colonial context', Ó Siochrú and Ohlmeyer, eds., *Ireland 1641*, 52–70.

Canny, Nicholas, 'How the Local can be Global and the Global Local: Ireland, Irish Catholics, and European Overseas Empires, 1500–1900', Patrick Griffin and Francis D. Cogliano, eds., *Ireland and America: Empire, Revolution and Sovereignty* (Charlottesville, Va., 2021), 23–52.

Canny, Nicholas, with Karen Ordahl Kupperman, 'The Scholarship and Legacy of David Beers Quinn, 1909–2002', *William and Mary Quarterly*, vol. 60 (2003), 843–60.

Carey, Vincent P., *Surviving the Tudors: The 'Wizard' Earl of Kildare and English Rule in Ireland, 1537–1586* (Dublin, 2002).

Carey, Vincent, 'John Derricke's *Image of Ireland*, Sir Henry Sidney and the Massacre at Mullaghmast, 1578', *Irish Historical Studies*, 31 (1999), 305–27.

Carroll, Clare, *Circe's Cup; Cultural Transformations in Early Modern Ireland* (Cork, 2001).

Carroll, Clare, *Exiles in a Global City: The Irish in Early Modern Rome, 1609–1783* (Leiden, 2017).

Carroll, Clare, 'Irish and Spanish cultural and political relations in the work of O'Sullivan Beare', Hiram Morgan ed., *Political Ideology in Ireland*, 229–53.

Carroll, Clare, 'From Defeat to Defiance; O'Sullivan Beare's account of the battle of Kinsale, the campaign in west Cork, and the Great March', Morgan, ed., *The Battle of Kinsale*, 217–28.

Carter, Michael S., 'Mathew Carey; the Mind of an Enlightened Catholic (Carey in Ireland, 1760–1784)' (unpublished paper given at the Mc Neill Center, University of Pennsylvania, 2011).

Casway, Jerrold I., *Owen Roe O'Neill and the Struggle for Catholic Ireland* (Philadelphia, 1984).

Clark, Samuel and Donnelly, James S., eds., *Irish Peasants: Violence and Political Unrest, 1780–1914* (Madison, Wi., 1983).

Clarke, Aidan, *The Old English in Ireland, 1625–42* (London, 1966).

Clarke, Aidan, 'Ireland and the General Crisis', *Past and Present*, 48 (1970), 79–99.

Clarke, Aidan, *Prelude to Restoration in Ireland: The End of the Commonwealth, 1659–1660* (Cambridge, 1999).

Clarke, Aidan, 'The 1641 depositions', Fox, ed., *Treasures of the Library*, 111–22.

Clarke, Aidan, 'The 1641 rebellion and anti-popery in Ireland', Mac Cuarta, ed., *Ulster 1641*, 139–57.

Clarke, Aidan, 'The commission for the despoiled subject, 1641–7', Mac Cuarta, ed., *Reshaping Ireland*, 241–60.

Clarke, Mary, Desmond, Yvonne, and Hardiman, Nodlaigh P., eds., *Sir John T. Gilbert, 1829–1898: Historian, Archivist and Librarian* (Dublin, 1999).

Clarkson, L.A., 'James Eadie Todd and the school of History at Queen's University, Belfast', *Irish Historical Studies*, vol. 41 (2017), 22–40.

Connolly, S.J., *Contested Island: Ireland, 1460–1630* (Oxford, 2007).

Connolly, S.J., *Divided Kingdom, Ireland, 1630–1800* (Oxford, 2008).

Cosgrove, Art, ed., *A New History of Ireland*, vol. 2 *Medieval Ireland, 1169–1534* (Oxford, 1987).

Covington, Sarah, '"Those Savage Days of Memory": John Temple and his Narrative of the 1641 Rebellion', Dillane, McAreavey, and Pine, eds., *The Body in Pain*, 57–76.

Covington, Sarah with Carey, Vincent P., and McGowan-Doyle, Valerie, eds., *Early Modern Ireland: New Sources, Methods and Perspectives* (Abingdon, 2019).

Cregan, Donald, 'Catholic Admissions to the English Inns of Court', *Irish Jurist*, 5 (1970), 95–114.

Cregan, Donald, 'Irish Recusant Lawyers in Politics in the Reign of James 1', *Irish Jurist*, 5 (1970), 306–20.

Cronin, Maura, 'Popular Politics, 1815–1845', Kelly, ed., *The Cambridge History of Ireland*, vol. 3, *1730–1880*, 128–49.

Cunningham, Bernadette, *The World of Geoffrey Keating: History, Myth and Religion in Seventeenth-Century Ireland* (Dublin, 2000).

Cunningham, Bernadette, *The Annals of the Four Masters: Irish History, Kingship and Society in the Early Seventeenth Century* (Dublin, 2010).

Cunningham, Bernadette, 'Myths and Memoirs of Ulick Burke, Marquess of Clanricarde (1604–1658)', *Journal of Galway Archaeological and Historical Society*, vol. 71 (2019), 7–18.

REFERENCES   393

Cunningham, Bernadette, 'Transmission and Translation of Medieval Irish Sources in the Nineteenth and early Twentieth Centuries', Evans and Marchal, eds., *The Uses of the Middle Ages in Modern European States*, 7-17.

Cunningham, Bernadette, 'Loss and Gain: Attitudes towards the English Language in Early Modern Ireland', Mac Cuarta, ed., *Reshaping Ireland, 1550-1700*, 163-86.

Cunningham, John, *Conquest and Land in Ireland: The Transplantation to Connacht, 1649-1680* (Woodbridge, 2011).

Cunningham, John, 'Milton, John Hall and Thomas Waring's Brief Narration of the Rebellion in Ireland', *Milton Quarterly*, 53 (2019), 69-85.

Cunningham, John and Ó Ciosáin, Niall, eds., *Culture and Society in Ireland since 1750: Essays in honour of Gearóid Ó Tuathaigh* (Dublin, 2015).

Darcy, Eamon, *The Irish Rebellion of 1641 and the Wars of the Three Kingdoms* (Woodbridge, 2013).

Darcy, Eamon with Margey, Annaleigh and Murphy, Elaine, eds., *The 1641 Depositions and the Irish Rebellion* (London, 2012).

Davis, Richard, *The Young Ireland Movement* (Dublin, 1987).

Dickson, David, 'Foreword' to Richard Musgrave, *Memoirs*, ii-xiii.

Dictionary of Irish Biography, see under McGuire.

Dillane, Fionnuala, McAreavey, Naomi, and Pine, Emilie, eds., *The Body in Pain in Irish Literature and Culture* (London, 2016).

Doherty, Gillian M., *The Irish Ordnance Survey: History Culture and Memory* (Cork, 2004).

Downey, Declan, 'Purity of blood and purity of faith in early modern Ireland', Ford and McCafferty, eds., *The Origins of Sectarianism*, 216-28.

Dunne, Tom. J., 'The Gaelic Response to conquest and colonization: the evidence of the poetry', *Studia Hibernica*, vol. 20 (1980), 7-30.

Dunne, Tom. J., *Rebellions: Memoir, Memory and 1798* (2005; 2nd revised ed., Dublin, 2010).

Edwards, David, *The Ormond Lordship in County Kilkenny, 1515-1642: The Rise and Fall of Butler Feudal Power* (Dublin, 2003).

Edwards, David with Lenihan Pádraig and Tait, Clodagh, eds., *Age of Atrocity: Violence and Political Conflict in Early Modern Ireland* (Dublin, 2007).

Edwards, David and Rynne, Colin, eds., *The Colonial World of Richard Boyle, First Earl of Cork* (Dublin, 2018).

Ellis, Steven G., *Tudor Ireland: Crown, Community and Conflicts of Cultures, 1470-1603* (London, 1985).

Ellis, Steven G., 'John Bale, bishop of Ossory, 1552-3' *Journal of the Butler Society*, vol. 2, 1984, 283-293.

Ellis, Steven G., 'Historiographical Debate: Representations of the Past in Ireland: whose Past and whose Present?' *Irish Historical Studies*, 27 (1990-91), 289-308.

Empey, Mark, Ford, Alan, and Moffitt, Miriam, eds., *The Church of Ireland and its Past: History, Interpretation and Identity* (Dublin, 2017).

Empey, Mark, 'Creating a Usable Past: James and Robert Ware', Empey, Ford, and Moffitt, eds., *The Church of Ireland and its Past*, 36-56.

Evans, R.J.W. and Marchal, Guy P., eds., *The Uses of the Middle Ages in Modern European States: History, Nationhood and the Search for Origins* (Basingstoke, 2011).

Farrell, Gerard, *The 'Mere Irish' and the Colonisation of Ulster, 1570-1641* (Cham, Switzerland, 2017).

Ferencz, Győző and Vesztergom, Janina, eds., *Presence Is No Island. Writings in Honour of William John McCormack* [Publicationes Bibliothecae Academiae Scientiarum Hungaricae 44.] (Budapest, 2020).

394 REFERENCES

Ffrench Eagar, Irene, *The Nun of Kenmare* (Cork, 1970).

Finnegan, David, 'Old English views of Gaelic Irish History and the emergence of an Irish Catholic nation', Mac Cuarta, ed., *Reshaping Ireland, 1550–1700*, 187–213.

Fitzmaurice, Andrew, *Sovereignty, Property and Empire, 1500–2000* (Cambridge, 2014).

Fitzpatrick, Elizabeth, 'The Exilic Burial Place of a Gaelic Irish Community at San Pietro in Montorio, Rome', *Papers of the British School at Rome*, vol. 85 (2017), 205–39.

Fletcher Alan and Gillespie, Raymond, eds., *Irish Preaching, 700–1700* (Dublin, 2001).

Ford, Alan, The *Protestant Reformation in Ireland, 1590–1641* (Frankfurt am Main, 1985).

Ford, Alan, *James Ussher: Theology, History, and Politics in Early-Modern Ireland and England* (Oxford, 2007).

Ford, Alan with McGuire J. and Milne, K., eds., '*As by law established': The Church of Ireland since the Reformation* (Dublin, 1995).

Ford, Alan, and McCafferty, John, eds., *The Origins of Sectarianism in Early Modern Ireland* (Cambridge, 2005).

Ford, Alan, 'The Irish historical renaissance and the shaping of Protestant history', Ford and McCafferty, eds., *The Origins of* Sectarianism, 127–57.

Ford, Alan, 'Shaping History: James Ussher and the Church of Ireland', Empey, Ford, and Moffitt, eds., *The Church of Ireland and its Past*, 19–35.

Ford, Alan, 'Past but still Present: Edmund Borlase, Richard Parr and the Reshaping of Irish History for English Audiences in the 1680s', Mac Cuarta, ed., *Reshaping Ireland, 1550–1700*, 281–99.

Fitzpatrick, David, *Descendancy: Irish Protestant Histories, since 1795* (Cambridge, 2014).

Foster, R.F., *The Irish Story: Telling Tales and Making It Up in Ireland* (London, 2001).

Foster, R.F., *Words Alone: Yeats and his Inheritances* (Oxford, 2011).

Foster, R.F., *Vivid Faces: The Revolutionary Generation in Ireland, 1890–1923* (London, 2014).

Fox, Peter., ed., *Treasures of the Library, Trinity College, Dublin* (Dublin, 1984).

Frank, Tibor and Hadler, Frank, eds., *Disputed Territories and Shared Pasts: Overlapping National Histories in Modern Europe* (Basingstoke, 2011).

Fukuyama, Francis, *The End of History and the Last Man* (London, 1992).

Garcia Hernán, Enrique, de Bunes, Miguel Ángel, Recio Morales, Óscar, and García García, Bernardo J., eds., *Irlanda y la monarquía Hispánica, Kinsale, 1601–2001: Guerra, política, exilio y religion* (Madrid, 2002).

Gargett, Graham and Sheridan, Geraldine, eds. *Ireland and the French Enlightenment, 1700–1800* (Basingstoke, 1999).

Geoghegan, Patrick M., *King Dan: The Rise of Daniel O'Connell, 1775–1829* (Dublin, 2008).

Geoghegan, Patrick M., 'The Impact of O'Connell, 1815–1850', Kelly, *The Cambridge History of Ireland*, vol. 3, *1730–1880*, 102–27.

George, J.A., 'The vocaycon of Johan Bale, 1553: a retrospective sermon from Ireland', Fletcher and Gillespie, eds., *Irish Preaching*, 94–107.

Gibbons, Luke and O'Conor, Kieran, eds., *Charles O'Conor of Ballinagar, 1710–91: Life and Works* (Dublin, 2015).

Gibney, John, *Ireland and the Popish Plot* (Basingstoke, 2009).

Gibney, John, *The Shadow of a Year: The 1641 Rebellion in Irish History and Memory* (Madison Wi., 2013).

Gillen, Ultán, 'Constructing Counter-Revolutionary History in Late Eighteenth-Century Ireland', Williams and Forrest, ed., *Constructing the Past*, 136–54.

Gillespie, Raymond, *Colonial Ulster: The Settlement of East Ulster, 1600–1641* (Cork, 1985).

Gillespie, Raymond, 'Temple's Fate; reading *The Irish Rebellion* in late seventeenth-century Ireland', in Brady, Ciaran and Ohlmeyer, Jane, eds., *British Interventions*, 315–33.

Gillespie, Raymond and Hadfield Andrew, eds., *The Oxford History of the Irish Book*, vol. 3, *The Irish Book in English, 1550–1800* (Oxford, 2006).

Grafton. Anthony, *Forgers and Critics: Creativity and Duplicity in Western Scholarship* (Princeton, N.J., 1990).

Harris, James A., *Hume: An Intellectual Biography* (Cambridge, 2015).

Hayton, David, W., 'Did Protestantism fail in early eighteenth-century Ireland? Charity Schools and the enterprise of religious and social reformation, c.1690–1730', Ford, McGuire, and Milne, eds., '*As by Law Established*', 166–85.

Hayton, David, W., 'The laboratory for "scientific history": T.W. Moody and R.D. Edwards at the Institute of Historical Research', *Irish Historical Studies*, vol. 41 (2017), 41–57.

Hazard, Benjamin, *Faith and Patronage: The Political Career of Flaithrí Ó Maolchonaire, C.1560-1629* (Dublin, 2010).

Heal, Felicity, 'Appropriating History: Catholic and Protestant Polemics and the National Past', Kewes Paulina, ed., *The Uses of History in Early Modern England* (San Marino, Ca., 2006), 105–28.

Heffernan, David, *Debating Tudor Policy in Sixteenth Century Ireland* (Woodbridge, 2018).

Hill, Jacqueline R., 'Popery and Protestantism, Civil and Religious Liberty: The Disputed Lessons of Irish History, 1690–1812', *Past and Present*, 118 (1988), 96–129.

Hill, Jacqueline R., '1641 and the Quest for Catholic Emancipation, 1691–1829', Mac Cuarta, ed., *Ulster 1641: Aspects of the Rising*, 159–72.

Howe, Stephen, *Ireland and Empire: Colonial Legacies in Irish History and Culture* (Oxford, 2000).

Hutchison, Mark, A., *Calvinism, Reform and the Absolutist State in Elizabethan Ireland* (London, 2015).

Hutton, R., 'The Making of the Secret Treaty of Dover, 1668–70', *The Historical Journal*, vol. 29 (1986), 297–318.

Jackson, Alvin, 'The Origin, Politics and Culture of Irish Unionism, c. 1880–1916', Bartlett, ed., *The Cambridge History of Ireland* vol. 4, 89–116.

Jefferies, Henry, *The Irish Church and the Tudor Reformations* (Dublin, 2010).

Kane, Brendan, *The Politics and Culture of Honour in Britain and Ireland, 1541–1641* (Cambridge, 2010).

Kane, Brendan and McGowan-Doyle, Valerie, eds., *Elizabeth I and Ireland* (Cambridge, 2014).

Kearney, Hugh, *Strafford in Ireland, 1633–41* (Manchester, 1959).

Kelley, Donald R., *Foundations of Modern Historical Scholarship: Language, Law and History in the French Renaissance* (New York, 1970).

Kelly, James, ed., *The Cambridge History of Ireland*, vol. 3, *1730–1880* (Cambridge, 2018).

Kelly, James, 'The Politics of the Protestant Ascendancy, 1730–1790', Kelly, ed., *The Cambridge History of Ireland*, vol. 3, *1730–1880*, 48–73.

Kelly, James, '"We were all to have been massacred": Irish Protestants and the experience of rebellion', Bartlett, Dickson, Keogh, Whelan, eds., *1798: A Bicentenary Perspective* (Dublin, 2003), 312–30.

Kelly, James with McCafferty John, and McGrath, Charles Ivar, eds., *People, Politics and Power: Essays on Irish History, 1660–1850 in honour of James I. McGuire* (Dublin, 2009).

Kelly, Patrick, '"A Light to the blind": the voice of the dispossessed élite in the generation after the defeat at Limerick', *Irish Historical Studies*, vol. 24 (1985), 431–62.

Kerrigan, John, *Archipelagic English: Literature, History and Politics, 1603–1707* (Oxford, 2008).

Kewes, Paulina, ed., *The Uses of History in Early Modern England* (San Marino, Ca., 2006).

Kilroy, Gerard, *Edmund Campion: A Scholarly Life* (London, 2015).

Larkin, Hilary, 'Writing in an Enlightened Age? Charles O'Conor and the Philosophes', Gibbons and O'Conor, eds., *Charles O'Conor of Ballinagar*, 97–115.

Leerssen, Joep, *Mere Irish and Fíor-Ghael: Studies in the Ida of Irish Nationality, its Development and Literary Expression prior to the Nineteenth Century* (Cork, 1996).

396 REFERENCES

Leerssen, Joep with van der Weel A.H., and Westerweel, Bart, eds., *Forging in the Smithy: National Identity and Representation in Anglo-Irish Literary History* (Amsterdam, 1995).

Lenihan, Pádraig, *Confederate Catholics at War, 1641–49* (Cork, 2001).

Lenihan, Pádraig, *The Last Cavalier: Richard Talbot (1631–91)* (Dublin, 2014).

Lenihan, Pádraig, 'The Irish Brigade, 1690-1715', *Eighteenth-Century Ireland/Iris an dá chultúr*, vol. 31 (2016), 47–74.

Lennon, Colm, *Richard Stanihurst, the Dubliner, 1547–1618* (Dublin, 1981).

Lennon, Colm, 'Political thought of Irish Counter-Reformation churchmen; the testimony of the "*Analecta*" of Bishop David Rothe', Morgan, Hiram, ed., *Political Ideology in Ireland, 1541–1641*, 181–202.

Livesey, James, *Civil Society and Empire; Ireland and Scotland in the Eighteenth-Century Atlantic World* (New Haven, Ct., 2009).

Love, Walter D., 'Charles O'Conor of Belanagare and Thomas Leland's "philosophical" history of Ireland', *Irish Historical Studies*, vol. 13 (1962), 1–25.

Lyons, Claire E., 'An imperial harbinger: Sylvester O'Halloran's *General History* (1778)', *Irish Historical Studies*, vol. 39 (2015), 357–77.

McBride, Ian, *Eighteenth-Century Ireland: The Isle of Slaves* (Dublin, 2009).

McCafferty, John, *The Reconstruction of the Church of Ireland: Bishop Bramhall and the Laudian Reforms, 1633–1641* (Cambridge, 2007).

McCafferty, John, 'John Bramhall and the Church of Ireland in the 1630s', Ford, McGuire and Milne, eds., '*As by law established*'.

MacCarthy-Morrogh, Michael, *The Munster Plantation: English Migration to Southern Ireland, 1583–1641* (Oxford, 1986).

McCartney, Donal, *W.E.H. Lecky: Historian and Politician, 1838–1903* (Dublin, 1994).

McCormick, Ted, 'Restoration Politics, 1660–1691', Jane Ohlmeyer, ed., *The Cambridge History of Ireland*, vol. 2 (Cambridge, 2018), 96–119.

Mac Craith, Mícheál, 'The political and religious thought of Florence Conry and Hugh McCaughwell', Ford and McCafferty, eds., *The Origins of Sectarianism*, 183–202.

Mac Craith, Mícheál, 'Creideamh agus Athartha', Ní Dhonnachdha, ed., *Nua Léamha*, 7–19.

Mac Cuarta, Brian, S.J., ed., *Ulster 1641: Aspects of the Rising* (Belfast, 1993).

Mac Cuarta, Brian ed., *Reshaping Ireland, 1550–1700: Colonization and its Consequences; essays presented to Nicholas Canny* (Dublin, 2011).

Mc Culloch, D., 'Foxes, firebrands and forgery; Robert Ware's pollution of reformation history', *Historical Journal*, 54 (2011), 307–46.

Mac Curtain, Margaret, *Ambassador Extraordinaire: Daniel O'Daly, 1595–1662* (Dublin, 2017).

MacDonagh, Oliver, *The Hereditary Bondsman: Daniel O'Connell, 1775–1829* (London, 1988), 7–29.

MacDonagh, Oliver, *States of Mind: A Study of Anglo-Irish Conflict, 1780–1980* (London, 1983).

McGowan Doyle, Valerie, *The Book of Howth: The Elizabethan Re-conquest of Ireland and the Old English* (Cork, 2011).

See also under Kane.

McGuire, James I., 'Why was Ormond dismissed in 1669?', *Irish Historical Studies*, vol. 17 (1972–3), 295–312.

McGuire, James I. and James Quinn, eds., *Dictionary of Irish Biography* (9 vols., Cambridge, 2009).

McHugh, Jason, '"Soldier of Christ": the political and ecclesiastical career of Nicholas French, Catholic bishop of Ferns (1603–1678)' (Ph.D. thesis, NUI Galway, 2005).

McHugh, Jason, '"For our own defence": Catholic Insurrection in Wexford, 1641–2', Mac Cuarta, ed., *Reshaping Ireland, 1550–1700*, 214–40.

Mc Manus, M.J., *Thomas Davis and Young Ireland, 1845–1945* (Dublin, 1945).

REFERENCES 397

McMorran, Russell, 'Mary Agnes Hickson: "Forgotten Kerry Historian"', *Kerry Magazine*, 11 (2000), 34–7.

Mac Niocaill, Gearóid, *The Medieval Irish Annals* (Published O Donnell lecture, Dublin, 1975).

Macpherson, C.B., *The Political Theory of Possessive Individualism* (Oxford, 1962).

Maginn, Christopher, *William Cecil, Ireland and the Tudor State* (Oxford, 2012).

Maginn, Christopher, '"Surrender and Regrant" in the Historiography of Sixteenth-Century Ireland', *Sixteenth Century Journal*, 38 (2007), 955–74.

Malcolm, Elizabeth and Hall, Dianne, *A New History of the Irish in Australia* (Cork, 2018).

Maley, Willy, *Nation, State and Empire in English Renaissance Literature* (Basingstoke, 2003).

Morgan, Hiram, ed., *Political Ideology in Ireland, 1541–1641* (Dublin, 1999).

Morgan, Hiram ed., *The Battle of Kinsale* (Bray, 2004).

Morgan, Hiram, 'Un pueblo unido…: the politics of Philip O'Sullivan Beare', Garcia Hernán, Bunes, Recio Morales, and García García, eds., *Irlanda y la monarquía Hispánica, Kinsale, 1601–2001*, 265–82.

Morgan, Hiram, '"Tempt not God too long, O Queen": Elizabeth and the Irish Crisis of the 1590s', Kane and McGowan-Doyle, eds., *Elizabeth I and Ireland*, 209–38.

Morley, Vincent, *An Crann as Coill: Aodh Buí Mac Cruitín, c. 1680–1755* (Dublin, 1995).

Morley, Vincent, *Irish Opinion and the American Revolution, 1760–1783* (Cambridge, 2002).

Morley, Vincent, *Ó Chéitinn go Raiftearaí: Mar a cumadh stair na hÉireann* (Dublin, 2011).

Morley, Vincent, *The Popular Mind in Eighteenth-Century Ireland* (Cork, 2017).

Morley, Vincent, 'Irish Jacobitism, 1691–1790', Kelly, ed., *The Cambridge History of Ireland*, vol. 3, 23–47.

Murphy, Ignatius, *The Diocese of Killaloe in the Eighteenth Century* (Dublin, 1991).

Murphy, Ignatius, *The Diocese of Killaloe, 1850–1904* (Dublin, 1995).

Nicholls, Kenneth, 'The Other Massacre: English Killing of Irish, 1641–2', Edwards, Lenihan and Tait, eds., *Age of Atrocity*, 176–91.

Ní Dhonnachdha, Máirín, ed., *Nua Léamha* (Dublin, 1996).

Nyhan, Miriam, *The Fifth Province; County Associations in Irish America: A Guide to an Exhibition by Gluckman Ireland House* (New York, 2010).

O'Brien, Gillian, *Blood Runs Green: The Murder that Transfixed Gilded Age Chicago* (Chicago, 2015).

Ó Buachalla, Breandán, *Aisling Ghéar: na Stíobhartaigh agus an tAos Léinn, 1603–1788* (Dublin, 1996).

Ó Ciardha, Éamonn, *Ireland and the Jacobite Cause, 1685–1766: A Fatal Attraction* (Dublin, 2002).

Ó Ciosáin, Niall, *Print and Popular Culture in Ireland, 1750–1850* (Basingstoke, 1997).

Ó Ciosáin, Niall, 'Beart pobail agus Délitearthacht san Athrú Teanga in Éirinn', Cunningham and Ó Ciosáin, eds., *Culture and Society in Ireland since 1750*, 86–96.

O'Carroll, Cian, 'A Thomond Scholar- James Frost, MRIA., 1827–1907', *The Other Clare*, vol. 3 (1979), 26.

O'Carroll, Gerald, 'Mary Agnes Hickson and Writing the History of Kerry', Bric, ed., *Kerry; History and Society*, 221–42.

O'Connor, Thomas, 'The Catholic Church and Catholics in an Era of Sanctions and Restraints', Kelly, ed., *The Cambridge History of Ireland*, vol. 3, 257–79.

Ó Cróinín, Dáibhí, 'Archbishop James Ussher (1581–1656) and the history of the Easter', *Studia Traditionis Theologiae*, vol. 26 (2018), 309–51.

O'Dowd, Mary, *Power, Politics and Land: Early Modern Sligo, 1568–1688* (Belfast, 1991).

Ó Fiaich, Tomás, 'Republicanism and Separatism in the Seventeenth Century', *Léachtaí Cholm Cille*, 2 (1971), 74–87.

398 REFERENCES

O'Halloran, Clare, *Golden Ages and Barbarous Nations: Antiquarian Politics and Cultural Politics in Ireland, c. 1750–1800* (Cork, 2004).

O'Halloran, Clare, 'An English Orientalist in Ireland: Charles Vallancey (1726–1812)', Leerseen, van der Weel and and Westerweel, eds., *Forging in the* Smithy, 161–74.

O'Halloran, Clare, ' "A Revolution in our moral and civil affairs": Charles O'Conor and the Creation of a Community of scholars in late eighteenth-century Ireland', Gibbons and O'Conor, eds., *Charles O'Conor of Ballinagar*, 81–96.

Ó hAnnracháin, Tadhg, *Catholic Reformation in Ireland: The Mission of Rinuccini, 1645–1649* (Oxford, 2002).

O'Hegarty, P.S., 'The Library of Ireland, 1845–7', Mc Manus, *Thomas Davis and Young Ireland*.

Ohlmeyer, Jane, *Civil War and Restoration in the Three Stuart Kingdoms: The Career of Randal Mac Donnell, Marquis of Antrim, 1609–1683* (Cambridge, 1993).

Ohlmeyer, Jane, *Making Ireland English: The Irish Aristocracy in the Seventeenth Century* (New Haven, Ct., 2012).

Ohlmeyer, Jane, ed., *The Cambridge History of Ireland*, vol. 2, *1550–1730* (Cambridge, 2018).

O'Keefe, Mairéad, 'The Politics of Irish Protestants, 1641–1660' (M.A. thesis, NUI Galway, 1991).

O'Leary, Brendan, *A Treatise on Northern Ireland*, vol. 1, *Colonialism* (Oxford, 2019).

Ó Muraíle, Nollaig, *The Celebrated Antiquary Dubhaltach Mac Fhirbhisighh (c. 1600–71): His Lineage, Life and Learning* (Maynooth, 1996).

Ó Muraíle, Nollaig, 'Mise Raiftearaí an Stairí?', Cunningham, John and Ó Ciosáin, Niall, eds., *Culture and Society in Ireland since 1750: Essays in honour of Gearóid Ó Tuathaigh* (Dublin, 2015), 97–110.

Ó Murchadha, Ciarán, *Figures in a Famine Landscape* (London, 2016).

O'Neill, Ciaran, *Catholics of Consequence: Transnational Education, Social Mobility and the Irish Catholic Elite, 1850–1900* (Oxford, 2014).

Ó Riain, Pádraig, ed., *Geoffrey Keating's Foras Feasa ar Éirinn: Reassessments* (London, 2008).

O'Scea, Ciaran, *Surviving Kinsale: Irish Emigration and Identity Formation in Early Modern Spain, 1601–40* (Manchester, 2015).

Ó Siochrú, Micheál, *Confederate Ireland, 1642–49: A Constitutional and Political Analysis* (Dublin, 1999).

Ó Siochrú, Micheál and Ohlmeyer, Jane, eds., *Ireland 1641: Contexts and Reactions* (Manchester, 2013).

Ó Tuathaigh, Gearóid, 'Gaelic Ireland, popular politics and Daniel O'Connell', *Journal of the Galway Archaeological and Historical Society*, vol. 34 (1974–5), 21–34.

Pagden, Anthony, *The Fall of Natural Man: The American Indian and the Origins of Comparative Ethnology* (Cambridge, 1982).

Palmer, Patricia, *Language and Conquest in Early Modern Ireland: English Renaissance Literature and Elizabethan Imperial Expansion* (Cambridge, 2001).

Parker, Geoffrey, *Global Crisis: War, Climate Change and Catastrophe in the Seventeenth Century* (New Haven, Ct., 2013).

Pawlisch, Hans, *Sir John Davies and the Conquest of Ireland* (Cambridge, 1985).

Perceval-Maxwell, Michael, *The Outbreak of the Irish Rebellion of 1641* (Dublin, 1994).

Pérez Tostado, Igor, *Irish Influence at the Court of Spain in the Seventeenth Century* (Dublin, 2008).

Quinn, D.B., *The Elizabethans and the Irish* (Ithaca, N.Y., 1966).

Quinn, D.B. See also under Quinn, D.B. and under Derricke in Section A.

Quinn, James, *Young Ireland and the Writing of Irish History* (Dublin, 2015).

Quinn, James, *John Mitchel* (Dublin, 2008).

REFERENCES   399

Quinn, James, 'Thomas Davis and the Patriot Parliament of 1689', Kelly, McCafferty and McGrath, eds., *People, Politics and Power*, 190–202.

Rapple, Rory, *Martial Power and Elizabethan Political Culture: Military Men in England and Ireland, 1558–1594* (Cambridge, 2009).

Recio Morales, Óscar, *Ireland and the Spanish Empire, 1600–1825* (Dublin, 2010).

Redworth, Glyn, 'Perfidious Hispania? Ireland and the Spanish Match, 1603–23', Morgan, ed., *The Battle of Kinsale*, 255–64.

Rigney, Ann, *Imperfect Histories: The Elusive Past and the Legacy of Romantic Historicism* (Ithaca, N.Y., 2001).

Robinson, Andrew, 'Owen Connolly, Hugh Og Mac Mahon and the 1641 rebellion in Clogher', Darcy, Margey, and Murphy, eds., *The 1641 Depositions and the Irish Rebellion* (London, 2012).

Sack, James, *From Jacobite to Conservative* (Cambridge, 1993).

Salmon, Alexander, ed., *The Spanish Match: Prince Charles's Journey to Madrid, 1623* (Aldershot, 2006).

Silke, J.J., 'Later relations between Primate Peter Lombard and Hugh O'Neill', *Irish Theological Quarterly*, vol. 22 (1955), 15–30.

Silke, J.J., 'Primate Lombard and James I', *Irish Theological Quarterly*, vol. 22 (1955), 124–50.

Simms, J.G., *The Williamite Confiscation in Ireland, 1690–1703* (London, 1956).

Smyth, W. and Whelan, K., eds., *Common Ground: Essays on the Historical Geography of Ireland* (Cork, 1988).

Stollberg-Rilinger, Barbara, 'La communication symbolique à l'époque pré-moderne. Concepts, thèses, perspectives de recherche', *Trivium*, vol. 2 (2008), http://journals.openedition.org/trivium/1152.

Sullivan, Eileen, 'Community in Print: Irish-American Publishers and Readers', *American Journal of Irish Studies*, vol. 8 (2011), 41–76.

Taylor, Alan, *The Civil War of 1812: American Citizens, British Subjects, Irish Rebels and Indian Allies* (New York, 2010).

Thompson, I.A.A., 'Castile, Spain and the monarchy: the political community from *patria natural* to *patria nacional*', Kagan, Richard and Parker, Geoffrey, eds., *Spain, Europe and the Atlantic World: Essays in Honour of John H. Elliott* (Cambridge, 1995), 125–59.

Veach, Colin, 'Conquest and Conquerors', Brendan Smith, ed., *The Cambridge History of Ireland*, vol. 1, *600–1550* (Cambridge, 2018).

Wanegffelen, Thierry, *Une difficile Fidélité. Catholiques malgré le concile en France XVIe–XVIIe siècles* (Paris, 1999).

Wheeler, James Scott, *Cromwell in Ireland* (Dublin, 1999).

Whelan, Kevin, 'The regional impact of Irish Catholicism, 1700-1850', Smyth and Whelan, eds., *Common* Ground, 253–77.

Williams, Mark and Stephen Paul Forrest, eds., *Constructing the Past: Writing Irish History, 1600–1800* (Woodbridge, 2010).

Working, Lauren, 'Locating Colonization at the Jacobean Inns of Court', *Historical Journal*, vol. 61 (2018).

Wrynn, John, 'Charles O'Conor as a philosophical historian', Gibbons and O'Conor, eds., *Charles O'Conor of Ballinagar*, 72–80.

Wyatt, Anne, 'Froude, Lecky and the "humblest Irishman"', *Irish Historical Studies*, vol. 19 (1975), 261–85.

Index

For the benefit of digital users, indexed terms that span two pages (e.g., 52–53) may, on occasion, appear on only one of those pages.

Achonry 334
Actes and Monuments of the Church (Foxe, John) 17–18
Actes des martyrs (Crespin, Jean) 98
Acts of Parliament
   Act of Attainder 68–9
   Act of Settlement 157, 182–7, 190–1, 212–13, 225–6, 299, 312, 361–2
   Act of Union 195, 199, 210–11, 214–22, 242–3, 287–9, 316, 327–8, 344–5
   Adventurers' Act 143–4
   Declaratory Act 232–3
   Emancipation Act 268–9
   Irish Church Act 262
   Irish Land Acts 365–6, 372–3
   Land Purchase Act 323–4
   Representation of the People Act 365–6
   Restoration Act of Settlement 212–13, 225–8
Adrian IV, Pope 41, 54–5
Affane, Battle of 136
Aisling poetry 119–21, 200
America, United States of 193–5, 197–8, 231–2, 242–3, 262, 264–5, 270, 273–4, 284, 307–8, 328, 346–9, 360–1, 366
   Civil War 265–6, 270
   Irish emigrants to 192, 346–7
   Irish exiles in 270, 348–9
   Revolution 191–2, 200–1, 232–4, 305
Analecta Sacra (Rothe, David) 38–46, 76–7, 83–4, 248–50
ancestry
   Anglo-Norman 272, 276–7, 280, 294–5, 298
   British 98–9, 280, 303–4, 320–1
   Cromwellian 276–7, 313–14, 337–8
   Dalcassian 338–40, 344–5, 348–9
   English 2–4, 7, 10, 12–13, 18–23, 27, 29, 44, 48–50, 52–6, 86, 112–13, 115–16, 118, 166, 239–40, 273, 296–7, 315–16
   Gaelic 22–3, 34, 48–50, 52–3, 55–9, 79–80, 106, 118, 122–3, 155, 249–50
   Huguenot 186–7
   Milesian 31–2, 48–51, 230, 340
   Old English 45–6, 104–5, 121, 237–8, 249–50

Ancient and Present State of the County of Down (Smith, Charles) 153
Annaghmore 306–7, 334–5
Annals of the Four Masters 3, 30–1
Annals of Ulster 3–4
Anne, Queen of Denmark 62–3
Anne, Queen of Great Britain 131–3
Ansell, Richard 212–13
Antrim 106–7, 142–3, 238–9, 316, 322, 372–3
"Aphorismical Discovery of Treasonable Faction" 124, 134, 177–8, 185–6, 357, 360
apocalyptic historians 14–24, 62–3, 83–4, 93–4, 97, 100, 103–4, 115–16
Ardfert 294, 300–1
Armagh 6–7, 42, 75–7, 244–5, 316, 322
atrocities 30, 106–9, 166, 194, 209–12, 231–2, 261, 285–6, 310–11, 332, 337, 363, 365–6
Aughrim, Battle of 131–2, 241–2
Australia 252–3, 258, 279
authors
   Catholic 36–7, 106–8, 121–2, 181, 193–4, 202–3, 208, 213–14, 232–5, 352, 354, 375
   Irish 36–7, 57, 60, 101–2, 176, 283
   nationalist 290, 305, 352–5, 357–8, 363–4, 371, 380
   Old English 29–30, 36, 39, 44
   Protestant 23–4, 29–30, 32, 44, 79–80, 91, 93–4, 99, 103–4, 106–8, 121–4, 147–8, 170, 181, 205, 209–10, 213–14, 315–16, 329, 353–4
   Unionist 292–3, 296, 301–8, 314–16, 324, 326–7, 333, 354, 358, 371–3
   Young Ireland 241–2, 251, 255–8, 260, 276–7, 367–8, 372–3

Bacon, Sir Francis 80–1, 318–19
Bagenal, Nicholas 322–3
Bagwell, Richard 357–8, 369–70
Bale, John 14–20, 23, 44, 177–8
"Ballad History of Ireland" (Davis, Thomas) 224, 240–3
Ballad Poetry of Ireland (Gavan Duffy, Charles) 236–7, 240–1

402 INDEX

Bandon 218–19, 240
Barclay, John 52
Barr, Colin 246
Barrow, River 273
Barry family 55, 317
Beatha Aodha Ruaidh Uí Dhomhnaill
(Ó Cléirigh, Lughaidh) 34–5
Bedell, William 86–7
Belfast 316, 353–4, 372–3, 375–6
Benburb, Battle of 120–1, 241–2
Berman, David 168
Blennerhassett family 297–300
Bodley, Josias 317
Bonaparte, Napoleon 200–1, 217–18
Book of Common Prayer 15–16, 77–8
Book of Revelation 202
Borlase, Sir John 99, 141–4, 177–8, 189, 195–6
Bóroimhe, Brian 54, 313–14, 340
Bourbon monarchy 244, 258
Boyle family 155, 160–1, 163
Boyle, Lewis 156–7
Boyle, Richard 154–7, 162–3, 180, 297–8
Boyle, Roger 102, 108, 145, 155–7, 161,
277, 298–9
Boyne, Battle of 313
Boyne, River 273
Brady, Ciaran 12–13, 282, 300, 375–6, 378
Brady, Rev. W. Maziere 299
Bramhall, John 82–3, 180
Bric, Maurice 192
British Empire 176, 252–3, 259–60, 270,
280–2, 348–9
Brodrick, Alan 155
Brooke, Charlotte 173
Bunratty Castle 342
Burgh, John Smyth de 128–9, 132
Burgo, Richard de 302–3
Burke family 34–5, 55, 125–33, 137–8
Burke, John 64–5, 126
Burke, Michael 127–8
Burke, Richard 63–6
Burke, Sir Thomas 63–4
Burke, Fr. Tom 328
Burke, Ulick [na gceann] 126–30, 137–8
Butler Revolt, the 8, 22, 61
Butler, Charles 133
Butler, James 102, 114–16, 129–30, 133–48,
163–4, 238–9, 261
Butler, Margaret 130–1
Butler, Piers 130–1, 135
Butler, Thomas 14–15, 42, 130–1, 133–50
Butlers of Ormond 7–8, 14–17, 21–2, 42, 55, 58,
102, 114–16, 118–19, 126, 129–31, 133–52,
155–8, 162–3, 182, 238–9, 250–1, 261,
285–6, 317, 331–3, 342, 362–3

Byrne family 113–14
Byrne, Phelim 141–2

Caball, Marc 58, 294
Calendars of State Papers 356, 358, 369–70
Calvinist-s 140–2, 315–16, 321–2
Camden, William 52, 77–8, 80–1, 171, 177–8,
204, 207
Campbell, Ian 47–8
Campion, Edmund 4–14, 16–18, 21–4, 52,
80–1, 207
Carew, Sir George 61–5, 297–8, 317
Carew, Sir Peter 20–2, 61–3
Carey, Mathew 191–9, 210–11, 226–7, 265
Carlow 327
Carlyle, Thomas 223–4, 285–6, 289–90
Carrick on Suir 272
Carroll, Clare 47–8
Carte, Thomas 130–1, 133–52, 155–8, 162–3,
173–4, 177–82, 185, 195–6, 261, 284–5,
329–33, 357, 362–3
Cashel, massacre at 261, 342, 347–8
Castle Conway 297–8, 300
Castleisland 300–1
Catholic-s
  agrarian groups 214–15
  Association 166, 207–8, 344–5
  authors 36–7, 106–8, 121–2, 181, 193–4,
    202–3, 208, 213–14, 232–5, 352, 354, 375
  Church 38, 195, 221, 243–4, 247–8, 252, 255–7,
    261, 264, 284–5, 348–50, 352–3,
    367–8
  civil rights for 171–2, 207–8
  clergy 34–5, 37, 39–40, 45, 92–3, 102, 111–12,
    115–16, 259–60, 268, 287–8, 294–5, 306,
    310–11, 333, 343–4
  Committee 166, 207–8, 211–12, 215–17
  community 42–3, 51–6, 81, 90–1, 112–13,
    185–7, 206, 211–12, 252–3, 266–7, 338,
    349–50, 368–9, 374–5
  Confederacy 59, 90–1, 104–7, 110–12,
    114–16, 118, 123, 126–9, 156–7,
    215–16, 237–40, 246–7, 249, 251, 254–6,
    311–12, 342–3
  dispossessed 189, 197, 277–8, 312, 342–3
  elite 39–40, 45, 51, 73–4, 107–8, 191–2,
    195–8, 208
  emancipation 195–6, 207–8, 243, 268–9,
    291, 365–6
  exiles 57, 342–3
  gentry and landowners 89, 105–7, 109, 189,
    206, 273, 294–5, 309–11, 313–14, 336–7, 344
  historians 37, 110, 138, 260, 285, 294–5,
    326–7, 333, 338–59, 361–2, 371–2, 374–5,
    377, 380

INDEX 403

histories, vernacular 200–12
humiliation of 118–19
injustices against 40–1, 109–10, 191–3, 195,
 197–8, 201, 354, 369–70
intellectuals and scholars 100–2, 221–2
interpretations, refining 258–64
Jamaica, transportation to 118–19
landowners 105–7, 109, 111–12, 189, 206,
 309–11, 313–14, 336–7, 344
lords and nobility 66, 82, 90–1, 97, 115–16,
 156–7, 200, 250–1, 304, 362
martyrology 40–1
massacres of 181, 184–5, 190, 347–8
militia 199
monarchy, plots to overthrow 145
Munster, insurrections in 178
nationalist community 367, 370, 374–5
oral culture 206
Penal Laws against 103, 105–6, 120–1, 154,
 166, 171–2, 185–7, 195, 197–8, 207–8, 227,
 230–2, 242–3, 248, 265–7, 272, 287–8,
 300–1, 310–11, 313–14, 343–4
persecutions suffered by 42–4
property, confiscation of 103, 110, 120–1,
 159–60, 190–1, 209–10, 212–13, 230–5,
 273, 275, 279–80, 299, 301, 304, 313,
 329–31, 337, 342–4
Protestant narrative, responses to 104–11
rebels 108, 207–8, 215–16
re-considerations of Ireland's early modern
 past during Age of Revolutions 199
Remonstrance of 104–6, 108–9, 171–2, 182
Sligo, history for 333–8
tolerance for 38, 82
Whiteboys and Rightboys 166, 213–15, 219,
 287, 367–8
Caulfeild, James (Lord Charlemont) 233–6,
 266–7
Caulfeild, Toby 233–4
Cavan 322
Cavour, Camillo Benso 244
Cecil, William 42, 151, 296–7
Charlemagne 130–1, 327
Charles I 59, 81–4, 89, 91, 96, 99–100, 108–9,
 112–13, 116–17, 121, 126–8, 131, 139,
 144–5, 176–7, 179–80, 189, 206–7, 277,
 330–1, 357, 362–3, 366
Charles II 100–1, 105–7, 119, 126–9, 131, 144–5,
 148–9, 156–7, 176–7, 188–91, 206–7, 261,
 275, 277, 312, 343–4, 347–8
Cheevers, William 275–6
Chichester, Sir Arthur 42–3, 235–6, 319–20,
 322–4
"Chronological List of The Irish Martyrs,
 1534–1603" 377

Church and State in Tudor Ireland (Edwards,
 Robert Dudley) 376–7
Church of England 4–5, 78, 82–3
Church of Ireland 54–5, 81–3, 174, 183–4, 264,
 291, 294, 315–16, 365–6
Citizen (journal) 225–6
civil rights 171–2, 207–8
civil war in
 America 265–6, 270
 England 126, 131, 146–9, 167–8
 Ireland 108–9, 311–12
Clanricard Burkes; see Burke family.
Clare, County 274–6, 298–9, 308–15, 321–2,
 333, 338–50, 354–5
Clare, Richard de ("Strongbow") 54–5
Clare, Sir Thomas de 317
Clare's Dragoons 241–2, 300, 313–14, 343–4
Clarendon Papers 134
Clarendon, Edward Hyde 207, 285
Clarke, Aidan 378–80
Clement VIII, Pope 205, 249
Clifden, Lord 271
Clonliffe 251
Clontarf, Battle of 6–7, 54, 340
Clotworthy family 352–3
Clotworthy, Sir John 142–3, 194
Coercion Bill 211–12
Cole, Sir William 336–7
Colgan, John 76
Collins, Arthur 148–52, 158–61, 163, 171, 371
Collooney 334
Cologne 39
Comerford, Gerald 42
Committee of the Commonwealth 364
communal protest groups 166, 214–15,
 287, 305–6
 Houghers 287
 Oakboys 166
 Peep O'Day boys 166
 Rightboys 166
 Whiteboys 166, 213–15, 219, 287, 367–8
Compendium (O'Sullivan Beare, Philip) 47–8
Coney Island 313–14
Confederate Ireland; see Catholic Confederacy.
Confederation of Kilkenny (Meehan, Charles
 Patrick) 237–40, 246–7, 254–6
confiscation of Catholic property 103, 110,
 120–1, 159–60, 190–1, 209–10, 212–13,
 230–5, 273, 275, 279–80, 299, 301, 304, 313,
 329–31, 337, 342–4
Confiscation of Ulster (Mac Nevin,
 Thomas) 234–5, 316–17
Connacht 31, 33–4, 126–7, 130–1, 154, 271,
 274–6, 302–3, 315–16, 321–2, 342–3
Conry, Florence 46

404 INDEX

Conway, Edward 323–4
Conway, Jenkin 297–8
Cooper family 305, 335–6
Coote family 304–5, 335–7
Coote, Sir Charles 143, 157, 190, 211–12, 277, 304
Coote, Richard 305, 336
Cork 153–61, 180, 342
Cornwall 296–7
counter-narratives in the sixteenth and seventeenth centuries 29
county history 155–6, 292–315, 322, 324, 334–5, 337–40, 346, 348–50
Courcy, John de 54–5, 317
Cox, Richard 171, 177–8
Creagh, Archbishop Richard 42, 44–5, 248
Cremona, Battle of 241–2
Crespin, Jean 98
Cromwell, Oliver 89, 99–100, 113–21, 123, 155–7, 162–3, 169–70, 180, 182–3, 190, 202, 206–7, 209, 241–2, 277, 286–92, 311, 314–15, 326, 332–3, 337–8, 342–3, 347–8, 362, 364, 370
Cromwellian Settlement of Ireland (Prendergast, John Patrick) 270–1, 292, 326
Cromwellian
  confiscations of Catholic property 110, 120–1, 212–13, 230–1, 273, 275, 337
  conquest of Ireland 344, 360, 363–5, 369–70
  settlement 276–7, 312, 321–2, 332–3, 357–8, 364–5, 374–5
Crosbie, Colonel David 298–9
Crosbie, Patrick 297–8
Cullen, Paul 244–6, 251, 290, 307–8
Cunningham, Bernadette 52, 124, 129
Cunningham, John 93
Curry, John 107–11, 159–60, 167–8, 171–2, 174–5, 181–7, 195, 207–8, 290
Cusack, Margaret Anna 258–65, 280–1, 294–6, 300, 350
Cusack, Sir Thomas 15–17

Dalcassian clans 338–40, 344–5, 348–9
Daniel, William 86–7
Davells, Henry 31
Davies, Sir John 52, 60, 66–75, 85–8, 95–9, 170–1, 176–9, 226–7, 302–3, 318–19
Davis, Thomas 221–3, 225–31, 234–7, 240–3, 246, 250–1, 254, 264–7, 269–71, 300, 313, 343–4
Davitt, Michael 278–80, 291
Day, John 17–18
De rebus in Hibernia gestis (Stanihurst, Richard) 27
"De Regno Hiberniae" (Lombard, Peter) 205

De scriptoribus Hiberniae (Ware, James) 79–80
Defenderism 367–8
Defenders, the 214–15, 305–6
Denny, Sir Anthony 296–7
Denny, Sir Edward 296–7
Depositions of 1641 93, 96–7, 106–7, 173–4, 177–8, 181, 184–5, 187, 189–90, 193–4, 209–10, 216, 285, 303–4, 311, 314–15, 321–2, 332, 337–8, 341–2, 358–62
Derricke, John 17–23, 25–6, 122
Derry 82–3, 218–19, 322, 375–6
Desmond, Sir John of 21–2, 31
Desmond Rebellion 35, 136, 139–40, 151, 296
Devereux, Robert 151–2
Dieu, Louis le 77
Dillon, John Blake 221, 269–70
Discovery of the True Causes why Ireland was never entirely subdued, and brought under Obedience of the Crowne of England, until the beginning of his Majesties happy raigne (Davies, Sir John) 67, 72–5, 85–6
dispossessed, the
  Gaelic lords 141
  history for 38, 45–51, 58, 110–21, 123, 141, 188–90, 197, 261, 277–8, 298–9, 312, 332–3, 342–3
  Irish 38, 45–51, 58, 110–21, 123, 141, 188–90, 197, 260–1, 264, 277–8, 298–9, 312, 332–3, 342–3
  Jacobite 188
Do chuala scéal do chéas gach ló mé (Haicéad, Pádraigín) 115–16, 118
Donegal 114–15, 322
Douai 51–2
Dover, Secret Treaty of 182
Down, County 42, 153–4, 234–5, 259, 316–17, 322, 375–6
Doyle, Henry 262
Drogheda 4–5, 98–9, 169–70, 182–3, 209, 286, 332–3, 336–7
Dromoland 312, 342–3
Drumcliffe 338–40
Drury, Sir William 31
Dublin 4–7, 11–16, 19, 32, 35, 42, 75–8, 81, 86, 90–2, 94, 96–7, 103, 142–3, 153, 157–8, 191–2, 194, 206–9, 216–17, 224, 244–5, 251, 259, 271, 275–6, 285, 292–4, 327, 346–7, 359–60, 376–9
Dublin Castle 32–3, 89, 91, 96–7, 194, 274–5
Dublin Magazine 225–6
Dublin University 369
Dudley, John 148
Dudley, Lady Mary 148
Dudley, Robert 148

INDEX 405

Dudley, Robert 148
Duffy, Charles Gavan (*see also* Gavan Duffy,
  Charles) 298, 352–3
Dunboy Castle, Siege of 61, 64
Dunlop, Robert 375
Dunne, Tom 216
Dwyer, Canon Philip 311, 338–42, 344, 346–7

Edgecombe, Margaret 296–7
Edward II 41
Edward III 7, 25–6
Edward VI 8, 14–17, 26–7, 79, 83–4, 99–100,
  136, 148–51, 178, 206–7, 272
Edwards, David 135
Edwards, Robert Dudley 376–8
Éirigh mo dhúiche le Dia (Haicéad,
  Pádraigín) 115–16
Eleven Years War 105–6, 111–12
elite
  Catholic 39–40, 45, 51, 73–4, 107–8, 191–2,
    195–8, 208
  families 45, 86, 294–5, 298–9, 351
  landed 289, 307–9
  of the Pale 86
  Planter 123
  Protestant 86–7, 103–4, 287
Elizabeth I 8, 13–14, 24–6, 32–3, 35, 40–4, 63–6,
  79, 83–4, 89–100, 103–4, 107–9, 116–17,
  120–1, 130–1, 134, 139–40, 142, 148–54,
  178, 188–91, 202, 205–7, 226–7, 230, 247–9,
  266–7, 272, 282–5, 296–7, 299, 318, 341, 356
Elizabethan wars in Ireland 108–9, 143,
  189, 329–30
emigrants, Irish 46, 192, 252–3, 257, 265, 346–7
Emmet, Thomas Addis 300
Empey, Mark 79
English Civil War 126, 131, 146–9, 167–8
English community in Ireland 2–4, 7, 9–10, 12–14,
  16–17, 20–5, 27–30, 90–1; *see also* Pale.
"English in Ireland in the Eighteenth Century"
  (Froude, James Anthony) 288–90, 328–9
English Law 48, 70–2, 85, 112–13, 178–9
English-speaking community in Ireland 17, 29,
  77, 124, 187
Enlightenment historians of Ireland 165
Ennis 338–40
Ennistymon 341
Essai sur les moeurs (Voltaire) 168–9
Eustace, James 31–2, 35
exiles
  Catholic 45–6, 57, 342–3
  clergy 45–6
  Irish 45–51, 55–9, 110–11, 113–14, 241–2,
    255, 270, 298–9, 342–3, 348–9

Old English 38–9
  soldier-exiles 204, 342–3
Expugnatio Hibernica (Gerald of Wales)
  2–3, 20–1

families, elite 45, 86, 294–5, 298–9, 351
Famine, Great 265, 279–80, 289–91,
  307–8, 347
*Fate and Fortunes of Hugh O'Neill... and Rory
  O'Donnell* (Meehan, Charles Patrick) 255
Fenians 253, 265, 270–1, 365–8
Fennig, Fr. Hugh 346
Fermanagh 322, 341
Fifteen Years War 49–50
Firth, Sir Charles 375
Fitz Aldemel, William 54–5
Fitz Stephen, Robert 54–5
Fitzgerald family 10–11, 21–2, 55, 317
Fitzgerald, James Fitzmaurice 31–2, 237
Fitzgerald, Field-Marshal Sir John 313–14
Fitzgerald rebellion 8, 10–11, 31–2
Fitzgibbon, John 288–90, 344, 347–8
Fitzmaurice, Thomas 64
Fitzpatrick, Barnaby 14–16, 32
Flood, Henry 232–4, 327–8
Fontenoy, Battle of 241–2
Foras Feasa ar Éirinn (Keating,
  Geoffrey) 51–6, 124
Ford, Alan 86–7, 98–9
Foster, Roy 224–5, 289–90
Foxe, John 17–18, 23, 25–6, 98
Foxe's Book of Martyrs (Foxe, John) 17–18,
  98, 194–5
France 57, 106, 168–9, 187–8, 196–7, 200–1,
  205, 218, 244, 313–14
Franklin, Benjamin 191–2, 195–6
Freemasons 253
French, Bishop Nicholas 138
Frost, James 308–15, 322–4, 338–42,
  344, 346–7
Froude, James Anthony 280–90, 292–4, 305,
  326, 328–32, 350–5, 358, 360–2, 365–7,
  370–1, 374–5

Gaelic Athletic Association 346–7
Gaelic Ireland 3, 29–35, 51, 112–13
Gaelic lords and lordships 2–3, 8, 54–5, 68–9,
  71–2, 86, 141, 308–9
Gainsford, Thomas 60–9, 72–3, 84, 86–7, 108–9,
  205, 230
gall (term) 3–4
Galway 31–2, 34–5, 100–1, 106, 128–9, 201–2,
  238–9, 338–40
Gardiner, Samuel 375

406 INDEX

Gavan Duffy, Charles 221, 225, 237, 240, 254, 352
General Martyrologie (Clarke, Samuel) 100
Genuine History of Ireland (Reily, Hugh) 187–8
George I 133
George II 132
Gerald of Wales 2–3, 5–7, 10–12, 20–1, 25, 29,
    39–41, 43, 48–9, 52–5, 57–8, 79–81, 86–7,
    98, 100, 122–3, 170–2, 177–8, 183, 204,
    207, 283
Gibney, John 190–1, 195
Gilbert, Humphrey 22
Gilbert, John T. 357, 360–6
Gillen, Ultán 213
Gladstone, William 262, 278, 291, 328, 365–9
Glorious Revolution 216–17, 286–7
Godwin, Francis 80–1
Gore family 305, 344
Grattan, Henry 232–7, 327–8
Grey de Wilton, Arthur, Lord 32, 139–40,
    151, 296–7
Grey, Lady Jane 148
Griffin, Gerald 240
Grosart, Alexander B. 297–8
Gustavus Adolphus 319

Haicéad, Pádraigín 115–16, 118
Hall, John 93–4, 99–100
Hamilton, Sir Frederick 193–4, 336–7
Hanmer, Meredith 52–4, 80–1, 207
Harmonia (Stanihurst, Richard) 4
Harris, Walter 101–2, 177–8, 218–19, 227, 293
Henrietta Maria, Queen 62–4
Henry II 2, 6–7, 21, 25–6, 41, 45, 48, 54–5, 83–4,
    95, 97, 176–7, 183–4, 249–50, 260–1, 340
Henry IV of France 94–5
Henry VII 10–11
Henry VIII 3–6, 10–11, 16, 21–2, 25–6, 41, 44,
    48, 66–8, 71, 79–81, 83–4, 99–100, 116–17,
    120–1, 130–1, 148, 176–8, 260–1, 275–6,
    296–7, 341, 377
Hibernia Anglicana (Cox, Richard) 126–7
Hickson, Mary Agnes 294–305, 307–9, 311,
    313–15, 317, 321–4, 338–40, 343–4,
    350–4, 358–73
Hill, Reverend George 315–24, 352–4, 362–3,
    372–3, 375–6
Hill, Moses 322–4
Historia Catholicae Iberniae Compendium
    (Beare, Philip O'Sullivan) 45–51
Historia et Topographia (Gerald of
    Wales) 2–3, 20–1
historians
    apocalyptic 14–24, 62–3, 83–4, 93–4, 97, 100,
    103–4, 115–16

aristocratic 125, 147, 160–1, 165
Catholic 37, 110, 138, 260, 285, 294–5, 301,
    326–7, 333, 338–59, 361–2, 371–2, 374–5,
    377, 380
Enlightenment 165
Humanist 19–20, 25–7, 170
nationalist 294–5, 326–7, 333, 338–59, 361–2,
    371–2, 374–5, 377, 380
philosophical 166, 183, 185, 191–2,
    196, 221–2
Protestant 36, 99, 104–5, 122, 193, 209–10,
    365–6
Unionist 290, 301–8, 322, 324–5, 357–8,
    366, 371–5
Young Ireland 221–43, 256–7
Historical Account of the Plantation in Ulster
    (Hill, George) 316–17, 322
*Historical and Critical Review of the Civil Wars in
    Ireland from the reigns of Queen Elizabeth to
    the Settlement under King William* (Curry,
    John) 108–10, 183
Historical Manuscripts Commission 359–60
*Historical Sketch of the Persecutions suffered by
    the Catholics of Ireland, under the rule of
    Cromwell and the Puritans* (Moran, Patrick
    Francis) 246–7
Historie of Ireland (Ware, James) 80–1
historiography, humanist 4, 27–8
History of Clare (Frost, James) 314–15, 338–40
*History of Clare and the Dalcassian Clans of
    Tipperary, Limerick and Galway* (White,
    Canon Patrick) 338–40, 346, 348–50
History of England (Hume, David) 165, 167–8,
    171–2, 174, 196–7
*History of England from the Death of Wolsey to
    the Death of Elizabeth* (Froude, James
    Anthony) 282
History of England in the Eighteenth Century
    (Lecky, William Edward Hartpole) 328–9
*History of European Morals from Augustus to
    Charlemagne* (Lecky, William Edward
    Hartpole) 327
History of Great Britain (Clarendon, Edward
    Hyde) 126–7
History of Ireland (Leland, Thomas) 174–7
History of Ireland in the Eighteenth Century
    (Lecky, William Edward Hartpole) 328–9,
    367, 374–5
History of Scotland, 1542–1603 (Robertson,
    William) 167
History of Sligo (Wood-Martin, William
    Gregory) 301–2, 337
History of Sligo: Town and County (O'Rorke,
    Archdeacon Terence) 334, 338–40

INDEX 407

History of the County of Dublin (Elrington
  Ball, F.) 293
History of the Diocese of Killaloe (Dwyer, Canon
  Philip) 338–40
History of the Irish Nation (Cusack, Margaret
  Anna) 258, 263–4
History of the Irish Rebellion (Temple, John) 98,
  106–7, 167–8
History of the Presbyterian Church in Ireland
  (Reid, John Seaton) 352–3, 372
"History of the Reign of Henry VIII" (Stanihurst,
  Richard) 10–11
*History of the Rise and Influence of Rationalism in
  Europe* (Lecky, William Edward
  Hartpole) 327
*History, Topography and Antiquities of the County
  and City of Limerick* (Fitzgerald,
  Reverend P.) 293
history
  aristocratic 125–33
  county 155–6, 292–315, 322, 324, 334–5,
    337–40, 346, 348–50
  Dispossessed, for the 38, 45–51, 58, 110–21,
    123, 141, 188–90, 197, 261, 277–8, 298–9,
    312, 332–3, 342–3
  new 60, 148–53
  philosophical 165–8, 171–96
  Ulster 315–24
  vernacular 123–4, 199, 221–2, 224, 241–2,
    254, 304–5, 309–10
Holinshed, Raphael 5, 10–11, 20–1
Holinshed's Chronicles 5, 10–14, 20–2, 24, 29
Holy Cross, College of the 251
Home Rule, Irish 257, 281, 289, 291, 316, 328,
  350, 360–1, 365–6, 368–70, 375
Hooker, John 20–4, 27, 29–30, 43–4, 62–3, 79,
  177–8, 371
Houghers, the 287
Huguenots 98, 186–7
Humanist-s 1–2, 4, 16, 18–21, 23–9,
  43–4, 170
Hume, David 165, 167–74, 176, 178–81, 183–4,
  194–7, 209–10, 375

Illustrated History of Ireland (Cusack, Margaret
  Anna) 258, 261–4, 294–5
Image of Ireland, with a Discoverie of Woodkarne
  (Derricke, John) 17–21
Impartial History of Ireland (Reily, Hugh) 187–8,
  195, 206–8
Impartial History of the Affairs of Ireland (Story,
  George) 187–8
independence, Irish 200–1, 226–7, 231–3, 255,
  289, 351

injustices
  against Catholics 40–1, 109–10, 191–3, 195,
    197–8, 201, 354, 369–70
  against Irish people 33–4, 48, 108–9, 116–17,
    197, 207–10, 230–1, 233–4, 236–7, 278–9,
    321–2, 324–5, 341–2, 354, 369–70
  against Old English 110–11
  against Ulster, native population of 233–4,
    236–7
  associated with the plantations 280
  of the past 237, 254, 277–81,
    291–2, 367
Inquisition 337–8
Institute of Historical Research 375–6
Interregnum 100–1, 176–7, 182–4
Ireland from the Restoration to the Revolution
  (Prendergast, John Patrick) 277–8, 281
Ireland in the Seventeenth Century (Hickson,
  Mary Agnes) 358, 365–6
Ireland under the Tudors (Bagwell,
  Richard) 358, 369–70
Ireland
  early modern past 199, 221, 326
  Elizabethan wars in 108–9, 143, 189,
    329–30
  independence for 200–1, 226–7, 231–3, 255,
    289, 351
  liberation of 118–19, 200–1, 270
  "Ireland's English Reformation" 87–8
Ireton, Henry 193–4, 209, 211–12, 261, 310,
  313–15, 342
Irish authors 36–7, 57, 60, 101–2, 176, 283
Irish Citizen 262
Irish College
  in Paris 334
  in Rome 244–5
  in Salamanca 247–8
Irish dispossessed, the 38, 45–51, 58, 110–21,
  123, 141, 188–90, 197, 260–1, 264, 277–8,
  298–9, 312, 332–3, 342–3
Irish Ecclesiastical Gazette 251
Irish Ecclesiastical Record 251, 377
Irish emigrants 46, 192, 252–3, 257,
  265, 346–7
Irish exiles 45–51, 55–9, 110–11, 113–14, 241–2,
  255, 270, 298–9, 342–3, 348–9
Irish Home Rule 257, 281, 289, 291, 316, 328,
  350, 360–1, 365–6, 368–70, 375
Irish independence 200–1, 226–7, 231–3, 255,
  289, 351
Irish lords 35–6, 49–50, 63–6, 69–70, 72, 84, 97,
  178–9, 189, 318
Irish Magazine 205–6
Irish missionaries 48

408 INDEX

Irish national identity, nationalism, and nationality 221, 231–4, 237–9, 248, 252–4, 257, 262, 266–8, 276–7, 287–90, 326–8, 352, 368–71, 373
Irish parliament 68–9, 71, 73–4, 212
"Irish Rebellion: or an History of the Attempts of the Irish Papists to extirpate the Protestants in the Kingdom of Ireland" (Temple, Sir John) 94–5, 98, 103–4, 106–7, 167–8, 212–14
Islandmagee, massacre at 106–7, 181, 184–5, 190
Italy 244–5, 251, 255–6, 258, 286
Itinerary (Moryson, Fynes) 61–2

Jail Journal (Mitchel, John) 265
Jamaica, transportation to 118–19
James II 103, 119–20, 131–3, 163, 176–7, 182–3, 191, 202, 206–7, 227, 313, 343–4
James VI & I 39–44, 47, 62–3, 67–9, 73, 83–4, 99–100, 108–9, 112–13, 116–17, 133, 137–8, 178–9, 189, 193, 202, 218–19, 226–7, 230, 272, 296–7, 303, 318–19, 341–2
Jefferson, Thomas 195–6
Jesuits 45–6, 91, 264
Jews 57–8
Jones, Henry 92–3, 329, 332, 359–60
Jones, Colonel Michael 114–15, 144
Jourdan, G.V. 376–7

Kearney, Hugh 378–80
Keating, Geoffrey 51–6, 58–9, 73–4, 110, 117–19, 124, 172–3, 175, 201–2
Kenmare 259–60
Kent 126, 148–9, 153, 159–60
Kerry 64, 153, 158–60, 259, 262–5, 294–305, 311, 313–15, 317, 324, 350–1, 359–60, 364–5
Kildare
House of 8, 13, 21–2
rebellion 8, 10–11, 21–2
Kilfenora 310, 338–40
Kilkenny 11–12, 15–16, 39, 133–4, 214–16
Castle 133–4
Confederation of 59, 123, 126–7, 237–40, 246–7, 251, 254–6, 311–12; *see also* Catholic Confederacy.
Killala 305–6, 337–8
Killaloe 310–11, 338–41
Killen, William Dool 352–3, 372
Killinena 313–14
Killorglan 297–8
Kilmacduagh 338–40
Kilrush 338–40
Kilvarnet 334

King, Archbishop William 103, 227
Kinsale, Battle of 31–2, 34, 45–6, 61–6, 130–1, 230–1, 237, 241–2, 341, 380
Knowler, William 162–4

Lacy, Hugo de 54–5, 130–1
Lacy, Major Thomas 298
Lalor, James Fintan 367–8
Land Commission 306
Land League 291, 306, 345–6
Land War 257, 291, 365–8
landowners
Catholic 105–7, 109, 111–12, 189, 206, 309–11, 313–14, 336–7, 344
in Ireland's history 271–80
Old English 75, 104–5
Protestant 218, 232–3, 301–4, 306–7, 316, 322–3, 334–6, 345
Larkin, Hilary 183–4
Leaders of Public Opinion in Ireland (Lecky, William Edward Hartpole) 327–8
Lecky, William Edward Hartpole 326–33, 349–50, 352–4, 357, 365–72, 374–5
Lee, Sir Thomas 318
Leicester, Earl of 4, 13–14, 139–40
Leiden 27, 77
Leinster 3, 31, 35, 209, 216
Leland, Thomas 174–87, 195–8
Lemenagh 342–3
Lenihan, Padraig 241–2
Leo XIII, Pope 245
Letters and Memorials of State (Collins, Arthur) 148, 158–9, 163, 171
Letters and Speeches of Oliver Cromwell (Carlyle, Thomas) 285–6
liberal interpretation of Irish history 326
Liberal Party 365–6
Limerick 64–5, 298, 313–14, 338–40, 343–4, 347–8
Treaty of 242–3, 265–6
Lindsay, Mr Justice 129
Liscarroll, Battle of 156–7
Lismore Castle 218–19
Lismore Papers (Grosart, Alexander B.) 297–8
Livy 1, 6–7
Lixnaw, Baron 64
Lombard, Peter 35–6, 38
London 318–19, 327, 375–7
London, Treaty of (1604) 38–9, 42
Londonderry Plantation (Moody, T.W.) 375–6, 378
Lorraine, Duke of 126–7, 132, 144
Loughrea 275–6
Louis Napoleon 244
Louvain 205

INDEX 409

Love, Walter 174, 181
Low Countries 35, 57, 141–2, 149, 151–2
Lucas, Charles 225–6, 232–3, 242–3
Ludlow, General 275–6, 342–3
Luther, Martin 120–1, 202, 337–8, 347–8
Lynch, John 106

Mac a Bháird, Owen Roe 30–1
Mac Craith, Mícheál 205
Mac Cruitín, Aodh Buí 201, 213–14
Mac Fhirbishigh, Dualtach 262
Mac Geoghegan, Abbé James 204–6, 223–4,
    230–2, 241–2, 249, 265–6, 270
Mc Mahon, Máire Rua 312, 342–3
Mac Morrogh, Dermot 3
Mac Murrogh, Cahir 3
Mac Nevin, Thomas 232–7, 246, 255–6,
    266–7, 316–17
McCafferty, John 87–8
McCartney, Donal 327, 369
MacDonnell family 316–17, 322, 344
MacDonnells of Antrim (Hill, George) 322
McGee, Thomas D'Arcy 231–2, 266–7
MacGillycuddy of the Reeks 298
MacGillycuddy Papers (Brady, Rev.
    W. Maziere) 298–9
McGowan-Doyle, Valerie 27–8
Macmillan's Magazine 328
McNamara, Rory 310
Malby, Sir Nicholas 31
Mangan, James Clarence 240
Markree 306–7
martyrs 40–1, 43
Marxism 380–1
Mary I 8, 10–11, 14–17, 79, 136, 148, 272, 377
Mary II 103, 133, 176–7, 182–3, 185–7,
    304–5, 310–11
Mary, Queen of Scots 42–3, 112–13
massacres
    Cashel 261, 342, 347–8
    Drogheda 98–9
    Islandmagee 106–7, 181, 184–5, 190
    Mullaghmast 31, 209
    of Catholics 181, 184–5, 190, 347–8
    of Protestants 109–10, 181, 184–5,
        212–13, 272
    of the Irish 193–4
    Portadown 181
    1641 106–7, 109–10, 181, 184–5, 190, 193–4,
        209–10, 285–6, 290, 292, 360–1
    Smerwick 209
    St Bartholomew's Day 94–5, 168–9, 173–4,
        196–7, 332, 360–1
    Wexford 98–9
Maynooth 243–4, 334, 356

Mayo 34–5, 201–2
Mazzini, Giuseppe 244
Meath 31, 77, 261
Meehan, Charles Patrick 236–40, 243–4,
    251, 255
Meehan, Fr. Michael 347
Melanchton, Philip 23
Memoir on Ireland Native and Saxon (O'Connell,
    Daniel) 209–11, 219
Memoirs of the Different Rebellions in Ireland
    (Musgrave, Sir Richard) 219
Memoirs of the Irish Rebellion (Musgrave, Sir
    Richard) 216–17
Methodism 264
Milesians 31–2, 48–51, 230, 340
Miltown Malbay 345
Mitchel, John 222–5, 229–40, 242–3, 246,
    249–56, 262, 264–71, 278–81, 289, 328,
    367–8, 380
Molyneux, William 225–6, 228, 231–5, 242–3
Monaghan 322
monarchy
    Bourbon 244, 258
    British 25–6, 39, 47, 98–9, 110, 112–13,
        127–8, 130, 138, 167, 173–4, 177–8, 182–4,
        195–7, 257, 263–4
    Catholic plots to overthrow 145
    English 25–6, 29, 44–5, 87, 171–2
    French 214–15
    restoration of 145, 275–6
    Spanish 34–5, 38–9, 46, 49–50, 63
Monkstown 275–6
Monro, Robert 193–4
Monteagle, Lord 300
Montgomery family 316–17
Montgomery, Hugh 140
Montgomery Manuscripts (Hill, Reverend
    George) 316–17
Moody, T.W. 375–9
Moran, Patrick Francis 244–53, 255–8, 260–4,
    290, 334, 338–40, 342, 348–50, 354–5,
    367–8, 377
Morgan family 305
Morgan, Hiram 13–14, 47–8
Morice, Francis 313–14
Morley, Vincent 120–1, 200–1, 205–6
Morogh the Burner, House of 347–8
Moryson, Fynes 52, 85–6, 108–9, 130–1, 176–8
Mountgarret, Lord 15–16
Mountjoy, Lord 61–6, 152, 272
Mullaghmast 31, 209
Multifarnham 91
Munster 22–4, 30–2, 35, 45–6, 49–50, 61–2, 64–5,
    119–20, 126–7, 130–1, 142, 151, 154, 158–9,
    163, 178, 209, 219, 237, 296–9, 315–17

410 INDEX

Murphy, John 268
Músgail do mhisneach, a Banbha (Haicéad, Pádraigín) 115–16
Musgrave, Sir Richard 213–20, 287–8, 290

Napoleon 200–1, 217–18
Napoleon, Louis 244
Nation (newspaper) 221, 241
national grand narratives
    and the conduct of historical research in Ireland 378–81
    Catholic 304–5, 346
    France 222–3
    Protestant 335
    Unionist 292–3
nationalist authors 290, 305, 352–5, 357–8, 363–4, 371, 380
nationalist historians 294–5, 326–7, 333, 338–59, 361–2, 371–2, 374–5, 377, 380
Nationis Hibernorum (Rothe, David) 41, 50–1, 55–6, 248
Neerwinden, Battle of 241–2
New England 273–4, 305
New York 265–6, 305, 346–7
Newry 259
Newtown Castle 304–5
Nine Years War 38, 65–6, 112–13, 142–3, 205, 302–3
nobles, new 148–61
Normans and Conquest 6–7, 40, 48–51, 54–5, 74, 117, 335–6
Norse invaders 1–3, 6–7, 41, 54, 117, 335–6
Northern Whig 322

Ó Bruadair, Dáibhí 113–14, 119–20
Ó Buachalla, Breandán 120–1
Ó Ciardha, Éamonn 120–1
Ó Ciosáin, Niall 187–8, 206
Ó Cléirigh, Lughaidh 32–5, 115–16
Ó Cléirigh, Muiris 30–1
Ó Conchubhair, Toirdhealbach 114–15
Ó Domhnaill, Aodh Rua; *see* O'Donnell, Red Hugh.
O'Brien family 308–9, 311–14
O'Brien, Conor 30–1, 312, 342–3
O'Brien, Daniel 313, 343–4
O'Brien, Donogh 64, 68–9, 312
O'Brien, Morrogh 118–19, 156–7, 261, 311–12, 342
O'Brien, Sir Turlough 341
O'Brien, Teig 30–1
O'Connell, Daniel 200–1, 208–12, 220–2, 224, 243–4, 249–50, 252, 263–4, 268–70, 306, 315–16, 327–8, 344–5, 362–3

O'Connolly, Owen 96–7, 194
O'Conor, Charles 167–8, 171–5, 183–7, 195, 207–8
O'Daly, Dominic 237
O'Devany, Cornelius 42, 248
O'Doherty revolt 178
O'Donnell family 236–7, 318
O'Donnell, Red Hugh 31–5, 61, 205, 230, 311
O'Donnell, Rory 318
Ó Faoláin, Seán 380
O'Flaherty, Roderic 100–1, 106–8, 127–8, 168, 171–5, 181, 184–5, 262
O'Hagan, Mary 259
O'Hagan, Thomas 259
O'Halloran, Clare 186–7
O'Halloran, Sylvester 183–4, 186–7, 195
O'Hara family 305, 335–6
O'Hegarty, P.S. 229
O'Hurley, Dermot 35, 42, 247–8, 261
O'Moloney, Malachy 341
O'Moore, Rory Oge 18–19
O'Neill, Brian 209
O'Neill, Con 8, 65–6, 68–9
O'Neill family 68, 109, 234–5, 351
O'Neill, Hugh 31–5, 61–2, 65–9, 99–100, 205–6, 224–5, 229–33, 237, 249–50, 255, 261, 263–4, 266–7, 283–4, 318, 351, 380
O'Neill, Owen Roe 112, 115–16, 120–1, 185, 202, 238–9, 242–3, 249–50, 252
O'Neill, Sir Phelim 181, 351
O'Neill, Shane 8, 44–5, 68–9, 318
O'Neill, Turlough Luineach 18–20
O'Rorke, Archdeacon Terence 333–8, 340–2, 346–50, 354–5
O'Scea, Ciaran 57–8
O'Sullevane, Thomas 127–8, 212
O'Sullivan Beare, Donal 46
O'Sullivan Beare, Philip 36, 45–52, 55–6, 58–9, 61, 111–12, 115–16, 121, 177–8, 185–6, 203–5, 209–10, 237
O'Sullivan Mór 298–9
O'Toole, Lawrence 6–7
Oakboys, the 166
Offaly 139–40, 338–40
Ogygia (O'Flaherty, Roderic) 173, 175
Ohlmeyer, Jane 161–2
Old English authors 29–30, 36, 39, 44
Old English community in Ireland 12–13, 16–17, 20–5, 27–30, 32, 36–46, 59, 90–1, 104–6, 109–10, 112–16, 118–19, 121, 123–4, 143–4, 146–7, 171–2, 179–80, 182, 237–40, 249, 331–2, 378–9
Old English exiles 38–9

INDEX 411

Old English in Ireland, 1625–42 (Clarke,
   Aidan) 378–9
Old English landowners 75, 104–5
Orange Order 253, 267–8
Orange, William of; *see* William III.
Ormond; *see* Butlers of Ormond.
Ormsby family 305
Orrery, earls of 102, 108, 145, 155–8, 161–3,
   177–8
Ossory 14–17, 32, 39, 178, 247–8, 251–3
Ossory, Bishop of 14–17, 247–8, 251–3

Pacata Hibernia (Stafford, Thomas) 61–3, 130–1
Pairlement Chloinne Tomáis 113–14
Pale, the 5, 7, 9–14, 17–18, 22–3, 29–30, 48–9,
   54, 72, 75, 77, 86, 90–1, 104–5, 127–8,
   149–51, 171–2, 250, 283–4, 317
   Lords of 86, 127–8, 171–2
   Old English landowners of 75, 104–5
Palmer, Patricia 85–6
pamphleteers 65–6, 79–80, 91–3, 96–7,
   192, 212–15
Paris 39, 191–2, 337
Paris, Matthew 16
Parke, Major Roger 304–5
Parnell, Charles Stuart 278, 291, 315–16, 346
Parsons, Sir William 141–3, 189, 211–12, 331
Patriot Parliament 224–6, 228–9
Patriot Parliament of 1689 (Gavan Duffy,
   Charles) 225
Peep O'Day boys, the 166
Pelham, Edmund 85
Pelham, Sir William 32
Penal Laws 103, 105–6, 120–1, 154, 166, 171–2,
   185–7, 195, 197–8, 207–8, 227, 230–2,
   242–3, 248, 265–7, 272, 287–8, 300–1,
   310–11, 313–14, 343–4
Pennsylvania 192–3
Perrot, Sir John 30–1, 155
Petty, Ann 294–5
Petty, Sir William 127–8
Philadelphia 191–2
Philip III 31–3
Philip IV 47
philosophical historians 166, 183, 185, 191–2,
   196, 221–2
philosophical history 165–8, 171–96
Physico-Historical Society 160–1, 293
Pius IX, Pope 243–4, 246
Plantation Acres (Hill, Reverend
   George) 372, 375–6
Plunket, Archbishop Oliver 189, 206–7,
   246–8, 261
Poor Clare order of Catholic nuns 259

popes
   Adrian IV, Pope 41, 54–5
   Clement VIII, Pope 205, 249
   Leo XIII, Pope 245
   Pius IX, Pope 243–4, 246
   Urban II, Pope 54
Portadown 181
Prendergast, John Patrick 270–81, 290, 292,
   321–6, 328, 332–3, 335–6, 352–4, 356–8,
   360–7, 369–72, 374–5
Presbyterians 202–3
Preston, General Thomas 238–9
propagandists 18, 93, 371
Protestant-s
   apocalyptic tradition and views 23–5, 62–3, 100
   Ascendancy 344–5
   authors 23–4, 29–30, 32, 44, 79–80, 91, 93–4,
      99, 103–4, 106–8, 121–4, 147–8, 170, 181,
      205, 209–10, 213–14, 315–16, 329, 353–4
   community 90, 92, 97, 100, 103, 122, 124,
      217, 225–6, 270–1, 294–5, 306–8, 321–2,
      324–5, 366, 371–2, 375
   elite 86–7, 103–4, 287
   historians 36, 99, 104–5, 122, 193, 209–10,
      365–6
   landowners 218, 232–3, 301–4, 306–7, 316,
      322–3, 334–6, 345
   massacre of 109–10, 181, 184–5,
      212–13, 272
   narrative 57, 104–11, 358–60
   Oakboys and Peep O'Day boys 166
   re-considerations of Ireland's pasts
      90–104, 199
   Reformation 1, 44, 50–1, 92–3, 111–12, 166,
      178–80, 188–9, 202–3, 216–19, 236–7,
      247–50, 282, 287–90, 309–10, 335–8, 342,
      347–8, 376–7
   settlers 90, 96–7, 106–7, 158, 194–5, 297–8,
      303–4, 320–2, 341–2, 354–5
   vernacular histories of Ireland 212–19
   zealots 29–30
Pynnar, Captain Nicholas 317, 320–1

Quakers 202–3
Queen's College 316, 353–4, 372–3
Queen's County 327
Queen's University 375–6
Quin Abbey 310
Quinn, D.B. 375–80
Quinn, James 241–2

Raifteraí, Antaine 201–4, 206
Raleigh, Sir Walter 22, 155, 296–7 [Note: also
   appears as "Ralegh"]

412 INDEX

Ramillies, Battle of 241–2
Rathmines, Battle of 144
rebellion
  Butler 8, 22, 61
  Connacht 130–1
  Desmond 35, 136, 139–40, 151, 296
  Fitzgerald 8, 10–11, 31–2
  Kildare 8, 10–11, 21–2
  Leinster 35
  Munster 32, 35
  O'Doherty 178
  of 1641 89, 125–8, 146–7, 153–7, 159–60,
    163–4, 167–74, 180–1, 183–5, 190–1,
    193–7, 209–10, 212–13, 215–17, 226–7,
    236–8, 272, 280, 285, 301, 303–6, 311,
    320–2, 326, 329, 331–3, 336–7, 341–2,
    351–5, 359–63, 367–8, 372, 374–5, 378–9
  of 1798 192, 197–9, 207–8, 214–22, 230–1,
    240, 268, 270, 287–8, 305–6, 315–16,
    320–1, 329, 367–8
  Tyrone's 108–9, 136–7, 178–9; see also Nine
    Years War.
  Wyatt's 136
Reduction of Ireland to the Crown of England
    (Borlase, Edmund) 106–7
Reeves, Robert Carey 313–14
Reformation 1, 44, 50–1, 92–3, 111–12, 166,
    178–80, 188–9, 202–3, 216–19, 236–7,
    247–50, 282, 287–90, 309–10, 335–8, 342,
    347–8, 376–7
regicide 99–100
Reid, James Seaton 352–4
Reily, Hugh 177–8, 185–91, 193–4, 202–3, 206–8
Reliques of English Poetry (Percy, Thomas) 173
Reliques of Irish Poetry (Brooke, Charlotte) 173
"Remonstrance of the Catholics of Ireland"
    104–6, 108–9
revenge killings 107, 190
Revolutions, Age of 199
Rightboys, the 166
Rinuccini, Archbishop Gian Battista 59, 111–12,
    246–7, 342
Rising of the North (Duffy, Charles
    Gavan) 236–7, 240
Robertson, William 167
Roche family 113–14, 317
Rome 39, 244–6, 248, 255
  Ancient 230–1, 258
  Irish College in 244–5
Ronan, Fr. Myles 376–7
Roscommon 298–9
Rothe, David 38–45, 47–52, 54–6, 58–9,
    76–8, 83–4, 110, 118–19, 172–3,
    248–51, 350

Rowan, Arthur Blennerhassett 294–7
Royal Irish Academy 334
Russell, Dr Charles William 356, 360

Salamanca, Irish College in 247–8
Sander, Nicholas 22, 32
Sarsfield, Patrick 202, 249–50, 263–4
Scattery Island 340
Scotland 39, 91, 112–13, 279, 315–16, 375
Scottish settlers 316–17, 319
Seanchas na Sceithe (Raifteraí,
    Antaine) 201–4
secret societies 265, 270
Seekers 202–3
Selections from Old Kerry Records (Hickson,
    Mary Agnes) 296, 350, 364–5
settlers
  Anglo-Norman 294–5
  British 98–9, 230–1, 280, 303–4, 320–1
  Cromwellian 276–7
  English 73–4, 85–6, 114–15, 272–3, 297–8,
    319, 331–2
  Protestant 90, 96–7, 106–7, 158, 194–5,
    297–8, 303–4, 320–2, 341–2, 354–5
  Scottish 316–17, 319
  twelfth-century 26–7
Shannon, River 313–14, 340
Shelbourne, Lord 306–7
Sidney, Colonel Algernon 148–9, 152
Sidney, Sir Henry 4–5, 7–14, 16–21, 24–5, 31,
    148–52, 171
Sidney, Sir Philip 126, 148–53
Sidney, Robert 141, 143, 148–9, 151–2
Silke, John J. 38
Simancas 32–3
Sixmilebridge 313–14
sixteenth and seventeenth centuries, composing
    counter-narratives in 29
Skeffington, Sir William 7
Sligo 301–9, 311, 313–15, 324, 333–42, 346–7,
    350, 354–5
Sloane, Sir Hans 153
Smerwick 108–9, 209
Smith, Charles 153–61, 163, 180–1, 218–19,
    300, 322–3
Smith, Sir Thomas 375–6
societies, secret 265, 270
Spain 32–4, 38–9, 45–6, 57–8, 61, 64–5, 244,
    275, 286
  conflict with United Provinces 47
  expedition force at Kinsale 45–6
  Jews expelled from 57–8
  military support in Ireland 34–5, 45–7,
    49–51, 200

INDEX 413

Spanish Armada 65–6, 302–3, 337–8, 341
Spenser, Edmund 23–4, 52, 80–1, 97, 207,
    272, 282
Spenser, William 274–5
Springfield 313–14
St Bartholomew's Day Massacre 94–5, 168–9,
    173–4, 196–7, 332, 360–1
St Ignatius's Day 301
St John, Oliver 42–3, 202, 323–4
St Laurence O'Toole 41
St Leger family 135, 155, 342
St Leger, Sir Anthony 8, 16–17, 193–4
St Leger, Sir William 142–3
St Malachy 41
St Patrick 6–7, 11–12, 25, 39–41, 48, 76–81,
    83–4, 248, 337–8, 340
Stafford, Thomas 60–9, 72–3, 84, 86–7, 108–9,
    130–1, 230
Stanihurst, James 4–5, 9–10, 13
Stanihurst, Richard 4–5, 10–15, 18, 20–4, 27,
    29–30, 39–40, 43, 48, 52–8, 79–80, 302–3
Stearne, John 134
Stollberg-Riliger, Barbara 19
Strafford, 1st Earl of; see Wentworth, Sir Thomas.
Strafford in Ireland (Kearney, Hugh) 378
Swift, Jonathan 167–8, 225–6, 232–3, 236–7,
    242–3, 327–8

Talbot, Peter 182
Talbot, Richard 119–20
Temple, Sir John 94–100, 104–6, 141, 167–8,
    171, 173–4, 177–8, 189–90, 194–7, 209–10,
    216–17, 290, 329, 332, 352–3,
    359–60, 362–3
Temple, Sir William 167–8
Templehouse 306–7
Tennessee 265–6
Thierry, Augustine 222–3
Thirty Years War 47
Thornton, Sir George 64–5
Thurloe 177–8
Tichborne, Sir Henry 193–4
Tipperary 51–2, 115–16, 214–15, 271–2, 275,
    313–14, 338–40
Tithe War 367–8
Touchet, James 143
"Tour of Ireland in 1775" (Luscombe, P.) 300
Tralee Castle 296–7
"Treatise containing a Plain and Perfect
    Description of Ireland" (Stanihurst,
    Richard) 10–13, 20–1, 27
"Tree of Commonwealth" (Dudley,
    Edmund) 148
Tremayne, Edmund 22–3

Trim 104–5
Trinity College (Dublin) 75–8, 81, 177–8,
    221–2, 271, 285, 327, 359–61, 376–9
Tuam 106
Tuireamh na hÉireann 116–18, 201–2, 213–14
Two Bokes of the Histories of Ireland (Campion,
    Edmund) 5–6, 10–11
Tyrconnell, earls of 119–20, 182–3, 227
Tyrell, Captain Richard 64
Tyrone 322
    earls of 8, 31–5, 61–2, 65–9, 99–100, 108–9,
    205, 224–5
Tyrone's rebellion 108–9, 136–7, 178–9;
    see also Nine Years War.

Ulster 3–4, 32–6, 45, 61, 65–6, 72–4, 85–7,
    89–91, 96–7, 99–100, 104–7, 109–13,
    127–8, 141–3, 157–9, 169–70, 178–9, 189,
    192–4, 205, 214–16, 226–7, 229–37, 241–2,
    266–7, 272, 278–9, 284–5, 302–3, 315–25,
    331–2, 341, 352–4, 371–8
    Annals of Ulster 3–4
    colonization of 230–1, 234–5, 284
    Confiscation of Ulster (Mac Nevin,
        Thomas) 234–5, 316–17
    "Custom" 316, 372–3
    "Great Ulster Plantation" 322
    Historical Account of the Plantation in Ulster
        (Hill, Reverend George) 316–17,
        322, 372
    history 315–24
    "Irish" population of 109–11, 318, 352–3
    lords of 33–4, 90–1, 110–11, 194, 318, 341
    perspective on Ireland's past 315–24
    planters and plantation in 45, 73–4, 89,
        99–100, 112–13, 178–9, 226–7, 229–37,
        266–7, 272, 278–9, 284–5, 315–22, 352–4,
        373, 377
    population as *gens flecti nescia* 205
    Presbyterians 230–1
    "Prince of Ulster" 229–30
    Protestant demographic in 218, 315–16, 318,
        321–2, 371–2, 375
    Protestant settlers in 106–7, 320–2
    rebels and rebellion in 35–6, 90–1, 104–5,
        127–8, 141–3, 216, 240, 311, 331–2, 352–3
    "spoliation in Ulster" 193
    survivors of Spanish Armada in 65–6
    Ulster army 151–2
    "Ulsterization" of Irish Unionism 371–2
Unionist-s 280–9, 291
    authors 292–3, 296, 301–8, 314–16, 324,
        326–7, 333, 354, 358, 371–3
    community 366–7, 371–2, 374–5

414 INDEX

Unionist-s (*cont.*)
  historians 290, 301–8, 322, 324–5, 357–8, 366–7, 371–5
  histories 333, 354
  reactions to Hickson's challenge 366–73
  re-appraisals of Ireland's history during early modern centuries 291
  re-interpretation of Ireland's early modern past 280–9
  scholars 359
  trials experienced by 366
United Irishmen 199, 214–15, 270, 315–16
United States; *see* America, United States of.
University College (Oxford) 4, 11–12, 376–8
Urgent Necessity of an Immediate Repeal of the Whole Penal Code against the Roman Catholics (Carey, Mathew) 191–2
Ussher, Henry 75–6
Ussher, James 60, 74–84, 86–8, 90–1, 93–4, 97, 100–2, 140, 172–8, 262, 375
Ussher, Robert 77–8

Vallancey, Charles 176, 186–7
Van Diemen's Land 265
Vere, Aubrey de 241–2
vernacular history 123–4, 199, 221–2, 224, 241–2, 254, 304–5, 309–10
  Catholic vernacular histories of Ireland 200–12
  historiography 123–4
  Protestant vernacular histories of Ireland 212–19
Victoria County Histories of England 293
Victoria, Queen 269–70
View of the Present State of Ireland (Spenser, Edmund) 23–4, 26–7, 80–1, 170–1
Vikings; *see* Norse invaders.
Vindicae Hibernicae (Carey, Mathew) 193, 195–6
Vinegar Hill, Battle of 305–6
Vocacyon of John Bale (Bale, John) 14–15
Voltaire 165, 168–9, 173–4, 183–4, 194, 224
Volunteers Journal: or Irish Herald (Carey, Mathew) 191–2

Wadding, Luke 102
Waller, Sir Hardress 294–5
Walsh, Nicholas 42
Walsingham, Frances 130–1
Walsingham, Sir Francis 126, 130–1, 296–7
war, memorialists of 61–6
Ware, James 23–4, 60, 74–84, 86–8, 93–4, 97–104, 122–3, 153, 172–8, 375
Ware, Robert 101–2
Waring, Thomas 93, 98–100

Washington, George 195–6
Waterford 15–16, 35–6, 153, 159–60, 163–4, 214–15
Wentworth, Sir Thomas (1st Earl of Strafford) 63–4, 80–4, 87–9, 138, 140–1, 146–9, 155, 161–2, 169–71, 180–1, 193, 202, 284–5, 303–4, 331, 378
Westmeath 91, 103, 133, 142–3, 207–8, 216–17, 287, 291–4, 369
Wexford 98–9, 110–11, 209, 216, 219, 240, 268, 305–6, 336–7
Whelan, Kevin 110–11, 121
White, James 344
White, Patrick 338–50, 354–5
White, Peter 11–12
Whiteboys 166, 213–15, 219, 287, 367–8
Wicklow 141–2, 291
Wild Geese, the 241–2, 342–3
William I (the Conqueror) 6–7, 130–1
William III 103, 109, 119–20, 122–3, 131–3, 176–7, 182–3, 185–7, 206–8, 227, 304–5, 310–11, 313, 343–4
Williamite War 120–1
Wilton, Arthur Lord Grey de 32, 139–40
Wingfield family 305
Wolf, Reginald 10–11
Wolsey, Cardinal 8, 21–2, 282
Wood-Martin family 305
Wood-Martin, William Gregory 301–11, 313–15, 321–4, 333–40, 354–5
Working, Lauren 66–7
Wyatt's rebellion 136
Wycliffe, John 16
Wynne family 305, 335–6
Wyse, Thomas 207–8

Yellow Ford, Battle of 65–6, 241–2
Young Ireland 221, 257–60, 263–4, 268–71, 276–7, 313, 327, 354, 367–9, 371–5
  agenda 221
  and J.P. Prendergast 276–7
  and M.A. Cusack 260, 263–4
  and P.F. Moran 246–51, 255–8, 263–4
  authors 241–2, 251, 255–8, 260, 276–7, 367–8, 372–3
  ballad histories initiated by 374–5
  historians of 221–43, 256–7
  historical reconciliation, argument for 246, 257, 354
  Irish nationalism, concept of 368–9, 371
  liberal opinions and principles of members 243–4, 327, 354
  regarded with suspicion by Catholic Church in Ireland 243–5, 247
Young Italy 244–5